SALINGER ON FACTORING

AUSTRALIA
Law Book Co
Sydney

CANADA AND USA
Carswell
Toronto

HONG KONG
Sweet & Maxwell Asia

NEW ZEALAND
Brookers
Wellinaton

SINGAPORE AND MALAYSIA
Sweet & Maxwell Asia
Singapore and Kuala Lumpur

SALINGER ON FACTORING

FOURTH EDITION

BY

NOEL RUDDY LLB
SIMON MILLS MA (Cantab)
NIGEL DAVIDSON LLB

With a foreword by

PROFESSOR SIR ROY GOODE Q.C.

LONDON
SWEET & MAXWELL
2006

First edition 1991
Second edition 1995
Third edition 1999

Published in 2006 by
Sweet & Maxwell Limited
100 Avenue Road
London NW3 3PF
http://www.sweetandmaxwell.co.uk

Typeset by YHT Ltd.
Printed and bound in Great Britain by MPG Books,
Bodmin, Cornwall

No natural forests were destroyed to make this product,
only farmed timber was used and re-planted.

ISBN 04 21 8832 00

A C.I.P. catalogue record for this book
is available from the British Library

Foreword

It is now 14 years since Freddy Salinger's trail-blazing work on the law and practice of factoring first appeared. Written by one of the world's foremost experts in domestic and international factoring, its great merit has always been the combination of detailed practical insights with a deep knowledge of the relevant law exceeding that possessed by all but the more specialised lawyers.

The baton has now passed into younger hands, and it is significant that what was previously the work of a single man who was by profession an accountant (albeit a lawyer *manqué*!) now requires a team of three highly experienced legal practitioners. Together they have done an excellent job. Much has happened in the six years that have elapsed since the appearance of the last edition, not the least the major reforms of corporate insolvency law introduced by the Enterprise Act 2002 and the never-ending flow of case law relating to a floating charges, culminating in the decision of the House of Lords in *Re Spectrum Plus Ltd*, which still leaves a number of issues outstanding as to the characterisation of security interests. All these developments have been accurately captured by the editors of this fourth edition, which maintains the high standards of its predecessors. I have no doubt that it will be welcomed as warmly as its predecessors and have much pleasure in recommending it.

Roy Goode,
St. John's College,
Oxford
November 16, 2005

Preface to Fourth Edition

It is remarkable just how quickly time has passed since the Third Edition was published in 1999. In the intervening six years much has changed in the world of factoring in the UK, not least the number of companies and banks now providing factoring and invoice discounting services. Invoice discounting has become the facility of choice for many and has become widely available to both large and small enterprises. We are also seeing an ever increasing use of invoice finance in corporate transactions where "leveraging the sales ledger" is seen as an easy and convenient way to raise additional finance to assist fund a purchase of shares or assets. In addition, many more factoring companies are looking to broaden their services to clients with stock and equipment finance, loans and venture finance backed by warrants and other instruments.

Since the last edition, one judgment stands out above all as having huge importance to the invoice finance industry, that is the decision of the House of Lords in *National Westminster Bank plc v Spectrum Plus Ltd* [2005] 3 W.L.R. 58. The decision clarifies the law relating to fixed charges over debts so that it is now clear that a charge can only be characterised as a fixed charge if the proceeds of debts are paid into a blocked account for the benefit of the charge holder or into an entirely separate account also charged in favour of the charge holder. Currently, this level of control is rare. As as result it is expected that there will be a change in the lending culture as banks and other lenders reflect on the diminishing value of debts as security. For the independent factors the implications of *Spectrum Plus* may be the increased competition from bank-owned factors who have greater resources available to them and the ability to offer highly competitive rates.

We have dealt with *Spectrum Plus* and its implications in this new edition of the book and have also revisited those chapters requiring attention in light of the developments in the industry over the last six years. In particular, we have addressed the implications of the Enterprise Act 2002 and the general move towards the more collective regime of administration rather than administrative receivership; and the new FSA regime as it affects providers of credit insurance. We have not, however, expanded upon the other forms of asset finance now available as to do so would dilute the primary intention of the book, which is to examine and elucidate on legal issues as they affect the purchase of debts.

We have again asked our friend in the North, the eminent R Bruce Wood WS of Morton Fraser to assist us in reviewing and updating the passages on Scots law found in Ch.7. Otherwise the law in the book relates to English law and is stated on the basis of materials available to us at September 1, 2005.

Although in the foregoing we have referred to the developments in the

UK (principally in England and Wales) we have not overlooked the needs of those factors who wish to develop their international business. In particular an important Court of Appeal decision, *Raiffeisen Zentralbank Osterreich AG v An Feng Steel Co & Ors (The Mount I)* [2001] 2, which has gone some way to clarify the law relating to the priorities of assignments of international debts is discussed in Ch.11.

We could not end this Preface without paying tribute to the man whose name adorns the cover of this book. In view of his advancing years Freddy Salinger has asked us to take on the mantle of editorial responsibility for the book, which we agreed to undertake jointly. Despite having retired in 1988, after 25 years in the industry which included his stint as chairman of the Association of British Factors and his membership of several committees of the Factors Chain International, Freddy has since continued to be involved in the industry as a consultant and seen published three editions of this book. He also made substantial contributions to the discussions on the UNIDROIT Convention on International Factoring and the UNCITRAL Convention on the Assignment of Receivables in International Trade. He still sits on the Legal Committee of Factors Chain International. In the shadow of such achievements it is a privilege to be associated with this book and we hope that we have been able to bring to this new edition the same clarity of thought and expression as are to be found in the previous editions.

Noel Ruddy
Nigel Davidson

Paul Davidson Taylor
Chancery Court
Queen Street
Horsham
West Sussex RH13 5AD

Simon Mills

5 Paper Buildings
Temple
London
EC4Y 7HB

Acknowledgements

We are greatly indebted to a number of people for their assistance in the preparation of this new edition.

At Paul Davidson Taylor we are particularly grateful to Dinah Ritchie for her enormous assistance and patience and without whom we would never have made the deadline. To Louisa Aitkens, who acted as a research assistant for us in the summer of 2004, for gathering together over many volumes and from a variety of sources the case material and other reference materials which are referred to in the footnotes to the book.

We would also like to thank Nigel Cook who heads the insolvency unit at Paul Davidson Taylor for his contribution to Ch.11, and to R Bruce Wood WS of Morton Fraser in Edinburgh who reviewed and updated the contribution on Scots law in Ch.7.

From the industry Murray Chisolm of Fortis Commercial Finance Limited assisted us greatly in reviewing Chs 2, 3 and 5 and provided useful comments on modern factoring practice.

Roy Goode has kindly agreed to write a Foreword to this Third Edition and we are pleased to record our gratitude to him, as well as our admiration for his distinguished work in the law of commerce, credit and security.

We would also like to thank the following:

> Tim Corbett of Fortis Commercial Finance Limited who gave us his permission to publish their factoring agreement and specimens of their client accounting;
> Peter Ewen of Venture Finance PLC for allowing us to use an example of Venture's client accounting;
> Tony Murphy and his colleagues at Smith & Williamson for their input on FRS 5;
> Jeroen Kohnstamm of Factors Chain International for allowing us to publish a copy of the current Code of International Factoring Customs and some statistics;
> The Secretariat of UNIDROIT for a copy of the Ottawa Convention on Factoring;
> Tolley Publishing Co Limited for their permission for the reproduction of some of the passages contained in the first edition of the book;
> Brian Arculus of De Lage Landen International BV who created the diagrams in App.7.

Finally, we must acknowledge the patience and support of Jasmin Naim and Silvia Segatori of Sweet & Maxwell.

Table of Contents

Para.

CHAPTER 1
AN INTRODUCTION TO MODERN FACTORING OF
DEBTS—ITS ORIGINS AND NATURE

CHAPTER 2
THE APPLICATION OF FACTORING TO MODERN BUSINESS

CHAPTER 3
THE FACTOR'S RELATIONS WITH HIS CLIENT

CHAPTER 4
THE FACTOR'S RELATIONS WITH THE DEBTORS

CHAPTER 5
MUTUAL REVIEWS: THE FACTOR AND THE CLIENT

CHAPTER 6
INTERNATIONAL FACTORING

CHAPTER 7
THE LEGAL STRUCTURE OF FACTORING AND TRANSFER OF
OWNERSHIP OF THE DEBTS

CHAPTER 8
THE EFFECT OF NOTICE TO THE DEBTOR AND CONFLICTS
WITH THIRD PARTIES

CHAPTER 9
SET-OFF AND THE DEBTOR'S COUNTERVAILING RIGHTS

CHAPTER 10
THE FACTORING AGREEMENT—PAYMENT TO THE CLIENT BY
THE FACTOR AND OTHER TERMS

Table of Cases

Table of Statutes

Table of Statutory Instruments

Table of Civil Procedure Rules

CHAPTER 1

AN INTRODUCTION TO MODERN FACTORING OF DEBTS—ITS ORIGINS AND NATURE

To understand fully the modern practice of factoring of trade debts, it is **1–01** necessary to study its origins; to describe it briefly or define it is not an easy task. The reason for this difficulty is the absence of agreement among business and professional people (and not least among the practitioners of factoring themselves) as to what is and what is not factoring.

1. THE NATURE OF FACTORING

Definitions

The Concise Oxford Dictionary[1] has a definition of a factor as a company **1–02** that buys a manufacturer's invoices and takes the responsibility for collecting the payments due on them and of factoring as selling one's debts to a factor. This is a very wide definition; is the seller selling them to be provided with a service or with finance by being paid for before they are due to be paid? At the other extreme is a very restricted definition generally accepted in the United States:

> "...a continuing arrangement between a factoring concern and the seller of goods or services on open account, pursuant to which the factor performs the following services with respect to the accounts receivable arising from sales of such goods and services:
>
> (1) Purchases all accounts receivable for immediate cash.
> (2) Maintains the ledgers and performs other book-keeping duties relating to such accounts receivable.
> (3) Collects the accounts receivable.

---

[1] 10th ed. 1999.

(4) Assumes the losses which may arise from the customer's financial inability to pay (credit losses)."[2]

It should be noted that the author of this definition has been careful not to infer that the services are provided *for the seller* because, having purchased the accounts receivable (or debts), the factor is collecting and book-keeping for himself. The object of the arrangement for the seller is the complete relief from the need for the service. As a result the four items would be better described as functions.[3]

A Description for the United Kingdom

1–03   It is certain that few people concerned with factoring in the United Kingdom or Europe (whether as sellers of debts, buyers of them or advisers) would accept such a restrictive description. Few would even accept a definition by which, only if the factor were responsible for at least two of the functions mentioned in the last paragraph, would the arrangement be considered to be factoring.[4] There remain a few purists among the practitioners who would not regard as factoring an arrangement which provided finance by immediate cash payments but by which the factor carried out no other function; most would not consider it to be factoring unless the arrangement was disclosed to the debtors so that payments were to be made by them direct to the factor.

1–04   However, most practitioners would exclude from factoring debts incurred by individuals in their private capacity and debts payable by instalments or on long terms (*i.e.* usually considered to be more than six months from the delivery of the goods or performance of the services from which they arose). This restriction is not included in the narrow definition above but was probably implied. For simplicity in this book it has been accepted that the provision of finance alone by early payment by the factor for the debts (even if it remains confidential as regards the debtors) is included in the term. Accordingly, in this book, factoring is:

> The purchase of debts (other than debts incurred for goods or services purchased by a debtor for his personal, family or domestic use and debts payable on long terms or by instalments) for the purpose of providing finance, or relieving the seller from administrative tasks or from bad debts or for any or all of such purposes.

---

[2] See Carroll G. Moore, "Factoring A Unique and Important Form of Financing and Service" *The Business Lawyer* (1959) Vol.XIV, No.3.
[3] See also Ch.12, n.44.
[4] As contained in the 1988 UNIDROIT Convention on International Factoring (see paras 12–24 *et seq.*).

Factoring otherwise than by sale and purchase of debts

Factoring as described in this book has been limited to the carrying out of **1–05** these functions only by way of the sale and purchase of debts. Other means have been found to provide the same commercial effect but, after some excursions into other legal forms, in general, practitioners have followed the well trodden path. In particular, arrangements have sometimes been made for the factor to purchase the goods themselves from his client, the supplier, to pay immediate cash for them and to effect a sub-sale of the goods to the consumer through the agency of his client. In this way the client receives immediate funds for the sale of goods and is relieved from the need to provide the credit terms which his customer requires; if the arrangement is disclosed, the factor may carry out the administrative functions and collect direct, and—if the client does not guarantee payment by the customer—the client is protected against bad debts. In practice the agency was normally undisclosed and the client collected on behalf of the factor and guaranteed payment; the object of the arrangement was to provide funds only.

The arrangement, the nature of which derives much from the origins of **1–06** modern factoring,[5] has the merit of simplicity of concept. It is perceived to have the merit that, where the client has charged its assets to a lender, no arrangement was necessary to release any assets from the charge; it is also perceived that the sales by the client to the factor would be considered to be normal commercial transactions. In addition, by the absence of any reservation of title in the factor's purchase from his client, the factor may avoid any claim by the client's supplier to the goods[6] or the debts.[7] However, the agreement by the client to sell goods only through the agency of the factor gives the factor no proprietary rights to the future debts to be owed by the customers as is the case in an assignment of all future debts in a factoring agreement of the "whole turnover" type.[8] As a result, if the client sells some goods direct or through the agency of another financier, the factor has only a personal claim against the client for breach of contract; the factor cannot claim ownership of the resulting debts. Furthermore, it has been rejected by most practitioners because the factor, as principal in the sale to the customer, is a party to the contract of sale and, accordingly, liable for any breach and for defects in the goods themselves. Furthermore, difficulties have been encountered in devising suitable forms of documentation.[9] In the purchase of the *debts*, the assignee, although being in no better position than the

---

[5] See para.1–11 below.
[6] See para.8–43 below.
[7] See paras 8–48 *et seq.* below.
[8] See para.7–10 below.
[9] See, *e.g. Welsh Development Agency v The Export Finance Company Limited* [1992] B.C.C. 270.

seller, is not subjected to liability under the contracts of sale giving rise to the debts.[10]

1–07   Several devices have been used for documentation of this arrangement but none has proved satisfactory; for example:

> (i) the factor agrees to be a principal in a contract of sale only where the debtor has been informed of the agency, has acknowledged it and has agreed not to hold the factor liable; or
>
> (ii) it is provided in the documentation that the factor is to be principal only for such sales in relation to which the client proves to have performed all its warranties and other obligations under the contract of sale.

Method (i) above is of doubtful legal validity as regards the exclusion of the factor's obligations and would, in any case, be unsuitable for a discounter owing to the disclosure. Method (ii) was upheld by the Court of Appeal as not detracting from the concept of the agency for reasons of uncertainty[11]; but it is now considered too complicated to be satisfactory. However, it may well be possible to solve this problem by providing in the agreement between the factor and the client that:

> (i) in respect of any contract of sale with its customers, the client would act as agent for the factor in the client's relations with the factor; but
>
> (ii) as regards the relations between the client and his customer, the client would be principal.

This dual capacity has judicial approval.[12]

Another alternative

1–08   As regards the provision of funds, lending against a fixed charge on the book debts of the client might have the same practical effect as factoring by the purchase of the debts and payment on account for them by the factor on

---

[10] See para.9–44 below.

[11] *Welsh Development Agency v The Export Finance Company Limited* [1992] B.C.C. 270.

[12] See *Aluminium Industrie Vaassen B.V. v Romalpa Aluminium Ltd* [1976] 2 All E.R. 552 at 563, where Roskill L.J. is reported as saying: "I see no difficulty in the contractual concept that, as between the defendants [*the buyer*] and their sub-purchasers, the defendants sold as principals, but that as between themselves and the plaintiffs [*the seller*], those goods which they were selling as principals within their implied authority for the plaintiffs were the plaintiffs' goods which they were selling as agent for the plaintiffs to whom they remained fully accountable. If an agent lawfully sells his principal's goods, he stands in a fiduciary relationship to his principal and remains accountable to his principal for those goods and their proceeds".

invoice date. At one time, the advantages and disadvantages of each form would have been evenly divided.[13] Lending on security would overcome the difficulties of prohibitions of assignments in contracts between sellers and buyers of goods and services,[14] and of conflicts with other chargees.[15] On the other hand, a purchase and sale of the debts provided for the factor the benefit of direct recovery from the debtors (as opposed to the need to appoint a receiver), the absence of the need for the client to register a charge (where the client is a company) and payment of charges by the client without deduction of tax. From the client's point of view at one time, a perceived advantage was that the finance was "off balance sheet".[16]

At one time, some practitioners of factoring were considering a change to   **1–09** lending on security. The introduction of the administration procedure by the Insolvency Act 1986 and the advantages of the present system to a factor whose client is in administration[17] now appear to have caused the scales to come down firmly on the side of buying the debts. This seems likely to remain the position in spite of the changes in accounting standards,[18] whereby factoring ceases to be off balance sheet as far as the client is concerned.

2. THE ORIGINS AND A BRIEF HISTORY

"There are many ways of raising cash besides borrowing. One is by selling   **1–10** book debts ..."[19] The selling of debts to "raise the wind" is as old as commerce itself, and some writers of the history of factoring have traced the practice back to Babylonian times 5000 years ago.[20] However, for the development of modern factoring, as described in the next chapter of this book, it is necessary to go back only to the last century. A brief consideration of the origins and history is of help to an understanding of factoring in all its variations and the avoidance of some of its misuse and the difficulties occasioned thereby. Factoring in the United Kingdom appears to have developed from two sources: from the activities of mercantile agents in the United States and of banks in continental Europe.

---

[13] For a full discussion of this alternative see paras 13–02 *et seq.* below.
[14] See paras 9–36 to 9–38 below.
[15] See Ch.8.
[16] For the up to date position see paras 5–17 *et seq.* below and the relevant passages of Financial Reporting Standard 5 contained in App.11.
[17] See paras 11–29 *et seq.* below.
[18] See n.16 above.
[19] *Chow Young Hong v Choong Fah Rubber Manufactory* [1962] A.C. 209, *per* Lord Devlin at 216.
[20] see for example, "Factoring 5000 Years", one of a Series of Studies in finance history published by Svenska Finans AB in 1974.

The start of modern factoring in the United States

1–11 The early factors, as their name implies, were mercantile agents. Up to the latter part of the nineteenth century and before the rapid advances made in systems of transport and communication, it was common for any manufacturer or merchant selling outside his immediate locality to employ mercantile agents. Such agents (or "factors", as they were known) took their principals' goods physically and held them on consignment, marketed and sold the goods and collected payment from the customers on behalf of the principals. They were rewarded by a commission and had a prescriptive right to deduct that commission and any other charges and expenses from amounts held by them for their principals by reason of collection from customers. Some of the factors were *del credere*[21] agents who guaranteed to the principals due payment by each customer.

1–12 It was natural that during the important period of colonisation by European countries from the sixteenth century onwards the exporters of consumer goods from the mother countries should look to the establishment of mercantile agents in the colonies to assist their exports. The exporter would have little knowledge of the market and the customers, and it would be necessary to maintain stocks in the country of the customers in order to provide for prompt delivery of orders. The developments and rapidly increasing standards of living in the eastern seaboard of the United States made increasing demands on exporters from the United Kingdom and Europe. Many great factoring houses flourished there and, in time, were in a position to assist their principals with finance by making loans against the goods sent on consignment to them secure in the knowledge of the prescriptive right of a mercantile agent to reimburse himself out of the proceeds of the sale of the goods. Later, such rights were validated by statute in several states by the adoption of Factors' Acts which gave the factor a right of lien on his principal's goods to secure his advances and other sums owed to him.

1–13 The factors provided in essence six services: marketing, storage and distribution, administration, collection from customers, protection against bad debts and finance. Towards the end of the nineteenth century the improvement in communications and in the speed of the transport of goods made it unnecessary for the manufacturers and merchants to send goods on consignment; the goods sold by sample could be despatched direct to the customer. For similar reasons, the principals could also dispense with the services of marketing provided by the factors. However, the principals wished to retain the comfort of the protection that they were receiving from their factors in guaranteed collection from their customers; some also needed the finance. Thus, modern factoring of debts was created by the

---

[21] An agent who guarantees the third party's obligations to the agent's principal.

6

substitution of the assignment to the factor of debts arising from direct sales by his client (formerly his principal for the sales by the factor as mercantile agent). As owner of the debts, the factor would retain the right to collect which he formerly enjoyed as a mercantile agent; as owner of the debts, the monies which he collected from customers became his property so that he was able to reimburse himself for the funds which he had laid out for the purchase of the debts assigned to him. The factor would no longer be required to find the customers, but the details of the customer when found would be submitted to him for credit approval; the factors' knowledge of local businesses, in which they had acted as agents for many years, would still be invaluable to their clients.

The development of factoring of debts in the United States

The change in the function of the early factors in the United States took **1–14** place in an uncertain background of law. The new relationship (formerly between the principal and agent) as assignor and assignee had to be established under the common law by judicial decisions, and by the fourth decade of this century there were sufficient precedents available in New York and the New England states for the factors there to be able to provide their services with some confidence. For the most part, notice to the debtor was necessary to validate the assignments against the rights of third parties and any countervailing claims of the debtor. For this reason, invoice discounting (or confidential factoring without disclosure to the debtor, as described in the next chapter) was not feasible. Later, in response to growing demand by businesses and finance houses for a method by which the latter could finance the debts of the former, many of the states adopted statutes by which the assignment, either by way of outright sale or by way of security, could be validated otherwise than by notice to the debtor. In some cases, the validation was by reliance on a written instrument of assignment or by the marking of the client's ledgers.

More importantly, some of the states introduced the provision for the **1–15** registration of the assignments. Such statutes were the basis for those parts of Art.9 of the Uniform Commercial Code which deal with the perfection of security interests in intangibles including debts.[22] Under the Uniform Commercial Code (of which Art.9 has now been adopted by every state), assignments of future debts can be perfected by registration to secure fluctuating advances. Even if the factoring is based, as it usually is, on the outright sale and purchase of debts, the arrangement must be registered, *as if it were* a security right, in order to be valid against the claims of third parties or a trustee in bankruptcy of the client. Such arrangements have created a much more certain background of law in which a factor may

---

[22] Or "accounts" as they are referred to in the US.

7

operate, and it is significant that since the adoption of the Uniform Commercial Code by most states in the 1950s factoring and, in particular, "accounts receivable financing"[23] has increased rapidly. In the early 1960s, factoring, as practised in the United States, was transferred to England, like a tender seedling, and embedded into a basis of law and commercial practice which was scarcely prepared to receive it; and this (including the absence of any comprehensive code to cover such arrangements and security rights) accounts for the many uncertainties which are documented in the second part of this book. It also accounts for the difficulties encountered by practitioners in its early years here.

Another source of factoring in the United Kingdom

1–16   In many countries in Continental Europe it had been customary for banks who had not the advantage of the peculiarly English security right, the floating charge, to finance the trade debts owned by their customers by advancing money against the delivery of copy invoices to the banks. The exact form of documentation appears to have varied considerably, but it is probable that, in many cases, the taking of assignments of the debts represented by such invoices would not have given the banks security against the claims of third parties or in the bankruptcy of the customer. In many jurisdictions,[24] notice to the debtor in some form or another would have been necessary to have perfected the assignments for these purposes. No doubt the banks would have relied on evidence of the likely cash flow available to liquidate the advances.

1–17   By the early part of the 1950s, in the absence of interest in such business by the clearing banks, many small and several larger finance houses in London and some of the larger provincial cities had entered the market of discounting "invoices" on a similar individual basis. The banks continued to rely on their well tried practice of taking floating charges. Some of these finance houses were originally manufacturing concerns with cash to spare, which may have been persuaded by the higher returns apparently available from providing finance in this way than were available from the mundane activities of the manufacture of goods. Such concerns were mainly in the textile and furniture trades for which the service had been largely provided by the banks in continental Europe; at least one major furniture manufacturer sold its business entirely and turned to the discounting of trade debts.

1–18   It is probable that the discounters took their cue from the continental practice. The arrangements were similar to those practised on the continent: the trader presented his copy invoices to the discounter with a document

---

[23] As invoice discounting on an undisclosed basis is known in the US.

[24] Including France until 1982 when the enactment of the Loi Dailley made provision for the "cession" of book debts to banks without notices to the debtors.

offering the debts to the discounter for sale; no notice was given to the debtor and the trader guaranteed payment by the customers by a specific number of days after invoice date. The discounter paid a percentage (less his charges) on account and relied on his having an assignment of the debts represented by the invoices (owing to the very liberal rules relating to equitable assignments in England) and on the trader's undertaking to pass on to the discounter payments received from the customers. In practice, arrangements for the discounter to recover his investment varied, and very often there would be a monthly settlement by which recoveries from customers and amounts payable by the trader for recourse were set off against advance payments to be made against new invoices.

In considering their security in these arrangements, the discounters were **1–19** probably influenced to some extent by a false analogy with the discounting of bills of exchange. The analogy is false because a bill, representing a sum certain in money accepted by the debtor, gives the discounter as a holder in due course the right to payment free from any defence, counterclaim or set-off which the debtor may have against the creditor as drawer of the bill. The situation with an invoice is quite different: many trade debts are the resulting balance of debits for amounts payable by the debtor for goods and services (represented by invoices), credits for counter-claims by the debtor (whether or not represented by credit notes) and deductions for discounts and other allowances. An invoice does not tell the whole story and, in the absence of notice to the debtor of the assignment, the discounter may be faced additionally with justified deductions by the debtor in respect of equities arising after the discounting of the debt purportedly represented by the invoice.[25] Thus, some of the early discounters, who discounted debts on the basis of individual invoices, were faced with losses when the net indebtedness of the debtors emerged, on the insolvency of clients, as far less than the face value of the invoices.

The early discounter's feelings of insecurity, arising from these losses, **1–20** were increased by claims by liquidators of client companies that the arrangement was in fact a disguise for the substance of the transaction: lending against the security of the debts. As an unregistered charge, the discounter's rights to the debts would be void against the liquidator. These claims for the most part failed. However, discounters were advised that, to be safe in this respect, all their dealings with their clients must be consistent with the outright purchase of the debts rather than the taking of a security right over them. It was therefore, important that the sums collected from customers, being the discounter's property, should be passed on to the discounter in their original form. Unlike payments made to meet a bill of exchange on its maturity, payments on open credit terms do not always relate to particular invoices. Some customers in the trades in which invoice

---

[25] See Ch.9.

discounting was acceptable were in the habit of paying round sums on account, and, as not all invoices were discounted, payments could often not be appropriated to particular discounted invoices. Accordingly, the actual payments could often not be passed on to the discounter, and a weekly or monthly settlement was made.

1–21   The result of such influences was to cause a number of small discounters to withdraw from the provision of the service altogether. A few looked to greater security by providing their services for the whole of a client's sales and by requiring notices to the debtors for payments to be made direct to the discounter. By such means, the discounter would have greater control, would avoid many cross-claims by debtors and would be seen to be purchasing the debts and not lending against them. In effect, they started to provide a factoring service much as it had evolved in the United States, although not many of them accepted the risk of loss by reason of the financial inability of debtors to pay.

The two sources of factoring merge

1–22   From these two sources, factoring developed in the United Kingdom in the 1960s on similar lines, responsive to the market which looked to the factoring services increasingly for a source of funds rather than for the administrative services of sales accounting and collection and for protection against bad debts. Most of the early practitioners who had looked to the United States for guidance still provided the full service including protection against bad debts, whereas others looked to direct collection from debtors as an enhancement of their security and tended to concentrate their marketing on the provision of finance alone.

3. MORE RECENT DEVELOPMENT[26]

Developments in the United States

1–23   Whilst factoring was developing in the United Kingdom in the early 1960s on a disclosed basis with notices to the debtors and direct collection from the customers, paradoxically in the United States the financing of trade debts by way of the undisclosed discounting of invoices (without any form of administrative service or protection against bad debts) developed more strongly. The development of this type of facility, normally labelled "accounts receivable financing", had been encouraged by the adoption of

---

[26] See table in App.1. Care should be taken in assessing the figures in this table because in the US only the full service is included in "factoring" and the Italian figures include factoring carried out by "captive" factors of large corporations.

the Uniform Commercial Code[27] by all states except Louisiana at that time. This trend has appeared to continue.

Factoring on a disclosed basis, without recourse to the client as regards **1–24** the inability of the debtor to pay by reason of his insolvency, had developed strongly in the trades for which the early functions of mercantile agents had been traditional.[28] These were in the main businesses dealing in textiles, clothing and footwear, furniture, toys and other (mainly non-durable) consumer goods. However, by the 1960s, the provision of this service in such trades was reaching a point of saturation. Attempts by United States factors to develop their services outside these trades do not appear to have been altogether successful. The reason for this difficulty seems to be the absence of a file of credit information on debtors and prospective debtors outside the traditional trades. Whilst factors in the United Kingdom, for this aspect of their services, rely to a large extent on the insurance principal of a spread of risks and, in some cases, on credit insurance as a form of reinsurance, factors in the United States relied on a close knowledge of their customers and the receipt of financial information direct from them. In trades where most of the suppliers use factors, it would be natural for the debtors to co-operate with the factors to establish and maintain credit ratings.

In breaking into other trades and industries, factors in the United States **1–25** find themselves caught in an inextricable circle. In order to establish files of credit information, great expense is necessary, and, before they have such files, they are unable to market the service and achieve the income to provide for such investment. The difficulties and expense in establishing such files arises from the reluctance of debtors to provide financial information when they have no need to purchase from a client using a factoring service. Another difficulty, which has been met by those attempting to extend their services into other fields, is the reluctance of debtors in such other trades and industries to deal with factors direct and to make payment to them. This may seem surprising in view of the ineffectiveness of a prohibition by a debtor on the assignment of debts under the law in the United States.[29] However, it appears that for a factor to pursue such a claim through the courts would be time consuming and expensive; and the commercial considerations, such as the likely reluctance of the debtor to purchase from a supplier using factoring in the future, would probably preclude such a step. Even were the debtor to accept that payment had to be made to the factor, the factor would not have the leverage that he has in the traditional trades to obtain prompt payment: the effect on the debtor's credit standing of delayed payments.

The difficulty in breaking away from the traditional trades has been **1–26** aggravated by the pressure on profit margins caused by severe competition

---

[27] See para.1–15 above.
[28] See para.1–11 above.
[29] See para.12–33 and Ch.12, n.64 below.

11

among factors in those trades. The pressure on margins is the result of the restriction; and the reluctance to invest in the development in other areas is the result of the poor profitability. Thus, the development of "accounts receivable financing" continues to be the main thrust of the expansion of factoring in its wider sense in the United States as it is now in the United Kingdom. It is unlikely that accounts receivable financing is included in the figures for the United States in the table in App.1.

1–27 In spite of this difficulty, in more recent years severe competition has created the need for factors to look for clients in a wider range of trades and industries. A further impetus to diversification has been the development of factoring across national borders. First, in international factoring the factor of an exporting client will often use the services of a correspondent factor in the importer's country to guarantee and to collect the debts.[30] The developing use of factoring by exporters to United States (especially of electronic and engineering products from the Far East) was thought to be a compelling element in the extension of factoring to these trades. In order to provide the services expected from them by their overseas correspondents, the United States factors would need to broaden the base of their operations. Secondly, the demand from exporters has induced the use of worldwide credit insurance to support export factoring without the use of correspondent factors in the countries of the debtors.

Developments in Continental Europe

1–28 In Europe, factoring has developed strongly in the last four decades on the basis of a provider of finance for domestic business and for international trade as a provider of finance and the protection against bad debts. With the exception of Germany, Belgium and the Netherlands, the main emphasis in the early years has been on the type of factoring, whether disclosed to the debtors or not, on a full recourse basis whereby no protection against bad debts was given. For the practitioners the absence of the expense of establishing a credit information base outweighed the slightly smaller income generated by the absence of the additional service of protection against bad debts; from the point of view of the users of the service there seemed to be little demand for protection against bad debts, partly on account of the widespread use of credit insurance which had been introduced many years earlier.

1–29 In more recent years, many of the factors have added non-recourse facilities, partly because they felt better equipped to do so in view of accumulated know-how of local markets, partly because users have become more nervous about creditworthiness of customers—a reflection of economic uncertainty and increased bankruptcy levels. While credit insurance

---

[30] See the description of factor's "chains" in Ch.6.

remains very popular, the combined service of finance and risk protection by a factor has made factoring companies very competitive.

Developments have not been regular across all the countries: the early **1–30** rapid development of factoring in Scandinavia (especially in Sweden) in the 1960s and 1970s gave way to faster growth in Italy and subsequently in Spain and the United Kingdom. In Germany the impetus towards non-recourse factoring was the result of a decision of the courts that recourse factoring was to be considered as if it were the lending on the security of the debts. As a result, the factor was at a disadvantage as compared with the non-recourse factor in a conflict, over the rights to the debts, with a supplier to his client who had reserved title to goods until paid.[31]

The growth of factoring in Italy has been assisted by the establishment, by **1–31** each of some large purchasers of goods and services, of a captive factoring company to which its suppliers of goods and services are obliged to sell the debts arising from such supply in order to receive prompt payment. This has been referred to by some factors as "reverse factoring".

The demand for factoring from exporters is a demand, not only for **1–32** finance, but also for an assurance of prompt payment without the risk of default. The exporter may be fully versed in the credit standing of his debtors and of the law and practices in relation to the collection of debts in his own country, but, in many cases, wishes to rely on a factor where he is selling to another country. In some of the smaller countries, such as Belgium and the Netherlands, where the domestic markets are small, the development of international factoring has tended to be proportionately greater than in the larger markets. This has applied not only to the factoring of exports of the factor's own clients but also to their acting as correspondent factor for those factors in other countries who are exporting. In order to provide this service, it has been necessary for the factors in such smaller countries to establish credit information bases, and such a library of credit information is best established on the basis of a good domestic non-recourse factoring business.

Nevertheless, the large volumes of international factoring can be found **1–33** primarily in the major trading markets: Italy, France, Germany and the combined Benelux countries.

With the recent accession to the EU of most of the Central European **1–34** countries, international factoring with an emphasis on export factoring will prove to be more and more popular in that part of Europe.

For Western European countries, import factoring will probably grow **1–35** faster than export factoring as many of those countries are becoming exporters of "services" (not always so suitable for factoring) and importers of all typical "consumer goods" (typically very factorable and coming more and more from lower wage countries, with Asia as best example).

---

[31] See Ch.12, n.28.

Developments in Asia

1–36   It is well known that vast quantities of consumer goods are exported from countries in South East and East Asia to Europe and North America. Up to the beginning of the last decade, the main instrument of payment was the letter of credit; by means of such an instrument, the exporter was assured of payment by importers of whose credit standing he may have had little knowledge. More recent developments in communications and the handling of cargo have created situations in which letters of credit are not the most suitable terms of payment. Furthermore, many importers are reluctant to be committed to pay for goods which they have not had an opportunity to inspect and before they have the documents of title to the goods and thus an assurance of delivery; in some cases, the importers have been able to use their bargaining position to insist on terms of payment against the delivery of documents of title or of open credit. Even the former terms appear to have become less popular. In order to provide such terms and at the same time to obtain, not only finance, but also an assurance of prompt payment, exporters in such countries have turned increasingly to factors. Thus, export factoring appears to have been the chief impetus to the establishment of a well developed factoring industry. The largest volumes of export factoring are nowadays generated by Taiwan, Hong Kong, Japan and Singapore. Many predict, however, that China's export factoring volume will grow rapidly to perhaps the world's largest market for such services. All major Chinese banks, presently 13 in total, have established (export) factoring departments, and, although they still have to go through a considerable learning curve, figures are already increasing rapidly.

1–37   The latest trend for the factors in Asia is to use their acquired knowledge about export factoring to start offering domestic factoring as well and to open up for import factoring.

1–38   The latter is particularly visible in Asia's most developed economies: Japan, Taiwan and Singapore. Wage levels have increased there to a point that the countries are becoming more and more net-importers rather than net-exporters.

Developments in the United Kingdom

1–39   The early reluctance of the factors in the United Kingdom to provide their services on an undisclosed basis owed much to the feeling that, against an uncertain background of law, with disclosure to the debtors they would be less likely to be attacked in the courts as providing loans on the security of debts in disguise. As a result of requiring notice to the debtors and direct collection from them by the factor, the full non-recourse service was provided by most and, in marketing, emphasis on the administrative service and protection against bad debts had equal prominence with the provision of finance. However, the marketing of factoring in this sense was severely

14

impeded by the widespread use of credit insurance in the traditional trades, for which factoring and invoice discounting had been used and the reluctance of potential clients to agree to the disclosure of the relations with a factor to their customers. This resistance to the disclosure of the use of the service was increased by the selling by some of the early factors of the service (sometimes fully on a recourse basis) to businesses for which it was not suitable and by some smaller entrants into the field whose administration and collection functions were not up to the perceived standards. The result of this misuse of factoring (which is more fully documented in Ch.2) was the spread of bad reports among potential users and a growing antipathy in some sections of the accountancy profession to which potential users looked for advice. Unfortunately, the successful achievements of some of the factors in enabling their clients to grow rapidly and soundly by a proper use of the service were not well documented.[32] In this way, factoring had a slow start in the 1960s and, by the start of the next decade, some of the promoting shareholders of the early factoring companies (merchant banks and confirming houses) disposed of their interests.

At about that time the clearing banks started to take an interest in factoring and now, either by acquisition or the starting up of a new company, nearly every one of the major UK banks has become the owner of a factoring company. More recently, there has been intense interest in factoring (particularly for the provision of finance on an undisclosed basis) on the part of overseas banks and other financial institutions and their acquisition or setting up of companies in this field. Although these companies in the main still provided non-recourse factoring, the inclusion within the range of financial services of the banks of factoring in all its forms was seen as a form of asset based finance and not so much as an administrative service or an alternative to credit insurance. Such an emphasis in the marketing has probably arisen from the need of a bank to earn a return on its deposits rather than to be a provider of a pure service. In recent years, the growth of the businesses of most bank-owned factors has been in invoice discounting with recourse. **1–40**

The interests of the banks in factoring and the establishment over the last decade of a large number of smaller factoring companies has led to a substantial growth of factoring in all its forms. However, the smaller companies rarely provide protection against bad debts and for the most part do not provide any administrative service; it is probable that the necessary investment in a credit information base and in systems is not attractive to them. For this reason, and possibly because the banks may be more interested in putting their funds to use than in providing the other services, in the last few years invoice discounting (including agency factoring in which, although on a disclosed basis, the factor does not provide any administrative service) has **1–41**

---

[32] See Ch.2.

overtaken all the other forms of factoring combined. A more recent development is that some factoring companies, regarding the market for the full service or simple finance by way of invoice discounting as saturated, have developed a number of other financial services to be provided in conjunction with factoring in one form or another. These other financial products have included stock finance, confirming, finance for management buy-outs and even minority share holdings. There have also been instances of the establishment of captive factors by large purchasers of goods and services as developed in Italy and described in para.1–31 above.

1–42   Unlike the position in some other countries in Europe and the Far East, international factoring does not appear to have increased its share of the market. Certainly, the interest in the factoring of exports from the United Kingdom is not as marked as it was in the days of the early factors when many in the wool trade in Yorkshire used a factor for their sales to North America. The pattern of exports from the United Kingdom is now such that most of the goods and services exported are not suitable for factoring.[33]

4. THE FULL SERVICE AND VARIATIONS

1–43 An examiner of students of factoring once set the following question: "Describe and compare the two types of factoring agreement at present in general use". He should not have been surprised that he received several different answers all of which were correct. The students may have correctly taken the question to refer to any of the following:

(1) Recourse and non-recourse factoring agreements.

(2) Agreements for factoring with or without disclosure to debtors.

(3) Agreements for factoring with direct collection by the factor or collection by the client on behalf of the factor.

(4) Agreements which include or do not include the availability of finance by way of early payment by the factor.

(5) Agreements whereby the factor pays for each purchased debt (less any earlier payments) on a fixed maturity date or when payment is received from the debtor.

(6) Agreements which themselves provide for the assignment of the debts or which merely provide for each debt to be offered to the factor.[34]

---

[33] See Ch.2.
[34] See paras 7–08 *et seq* below.

As many factoring agreements combine features of some or all of these **1–44** differences, there are a large number of combinations and permutations in the forms of factoring offered by practitioners. The difficulty in the task of describing these different forms briefly is compounded by the absence of uniformity among practitioners in the labels used for the same type of factoring and the provision by different practitioners of different types under the same labels. This chapter contains a description of the complete, or full, service and the main variations. A table of variants at the end of the chapter may help to dispel some of the confusion caused by the differences in the labels. Any of the variations may be provided in either way described in (5) or (6) above, and these differences are described in subsequent chapters.

The full service

Factoring in its full form, or old line (*i.e.* traditional) factoring, has been **1–45** described earlier in this chapter[35] where a definition accepted in the United States was reproduced. However, to describe it in even more precise terms, it is a continuing relationship between a factor and a supplier (the client) of goods and services to trade customers in which the factor purchases all or substantially all of the trade debts of his client arising from such sales of goods or the provision of such services as they arise in the normal course of business. The client in return for agreed fees and finance charges is thereby relieved:

(a) from the need to administer and control a sales ledger and collect amounts payable from the debtors;

(b) from losses arising from the inability of a debtor to pay; and

(c) from the provision of trade credit to the debtors, to a substantial degree.

The transfer of ownership of the debts is normally accompanied by the submission to the factor of copies of invoices representing the debts sold. In some cases, the factor may require the submission of originals to the factor for onward transmission to the debtors, accompanied by copies for retention by the factor. Many factors now arrange for their larger clients to notify debts to the factors by electronic means and some do not even insist on the input to be supported by hard copies of invoices or credit notes.

The factor, in turn, is responsible to the client for the purchase price of the **1–46** debts assigned. The purchase price is normally the amount payable by the debtor after the deduction of any discount or other allowance allowed to the

---

[35] See para.1–02 above.

debtor and, in some cases, after deduction of the factor's charges.[36] The factor will credit the account of the client in his records with such purchase price of debts sold, and, as a corollary, the client may charge all his sales to one account—that of the factor. The client will now look to the factor alone to collect the proceeds of his sales. The final date for payment of the purchase price will be either a fixed number of days after invoice date (often referred to as the maturity date) or when collection has been effected from the debtor. These alternatives are described more fully in Ch.3.

1–47   To the extent that the factor has given approval of the debts, he purchases the debts without recourse to the client as regards the debtor's failure to pay owing to insolvency. The client thus receives full protection against bad debts provided that he does not sell to any debtor not approved by the factor or to an extent greater than the approval given.

1–48   By making an early payment (sometimes referred to as a prepayment or an initial payment) on account of a substantial part of the purchase price of each debt as soon as it is created and purchased, the factor provides the finance to meet the trade credit requirements of the client's debtors. Some factors make such a prepayment by way of an advance secured by their right to set it off against the full purchase price when due, whereas others provide for prepayments by part payments of the purchase price itself. The effect is exactly the same in each case. The factor will make a retention of part of the purchase price of each debt so that, in aggregate, he will hold a sufficient balance to provide for any debt to be charged back to the client by way of recourse for the non-payment of an unapproved or disputed debt. However, the balance credited for the purchase price of debts purchased less the retention may normally be drawn by the client by way of prepayment at short notice.

Recourse factoring

1–49   Although most forms of factoring other than the full service are provided with full recourse to the client in respect of the failure of the debtor to pay for any reason, "recourse factoring" normally describes the service by which the factor provides finance for the client and carries out the functions of sales ledger administration and collections, but does not protect the client against bad debts. The factor has full "recourse" (the right to have payment guaranteed or the debt repurchased by the client) for debts unpaid for any reason, including insolvency of the debtor. Thus, the variation is effected by the simple expedient of providing that, in respect of every debt purchased by the factor, he shall have the right to sell it (or part of it) back to the client for the amount for which he credited the purchase price originally in addition to his charges (or be guaranteed payment in full by the client) to the extent that

---

[36] In many cases now the administration or service charge is recovered by the factor by a debit to the client's account; see para.10–49 below.

the debtor shall not have settled it within an agreed period from the invoice date. The period often agreed is three months or 90 days from the end of the month in which the invoice is dated. Such a period postulates that in many trades and industries, in which the normal usage is for payment to be due at the end of the month following that of the invoice, the factor must collect payment within two months of the due date or the recourse may come into effect. It is usual to provide that the factor will refrain from exercising his right of recourse for a specified further period in payment of an additional charge by the client, usually referred to as the "refactoring charge".[37] In such a case, however, the factor may require that an additional retention be maintained against the purchase price of further debts purchased so that in effect the client will have repaid the amount paid by the factor against, or on account of, the purchase price of the unpaid debts.

In this way, in respect of debts that are seriously overdue, the client will **1–50** remain relieved from the collection function but the finance for such debts may be withdrawn. If the debt becomes irrecoverable, the recourse is then finally exercised. It is apparent that the factor, in such a case, does not have the ultimate responsibility for collection. Approvals of credit are given by the factor on debtor accounts for the purpose of specifying the amount of finance available against them or as an advisory service to the client or for both reasons.

Agency factoring

This variant of the service is sometimes referred to as "bulk factoring", **1–51** but, as virtually all factoring relates to the whole of a client's sales with the submission to the factor of batches or schedules of debts in bulk, the term "bulk" could be applied to all forms. The term "agency" is now usually used to denote the form for which the Germans use the more descriptive term "Eigen-Service Factoring" ("Own Service Factoring"). This form of factoring is further removed from the full service in that the factor, although requiring disclosure to the debtors, takes no responsibility for the administration or collection of the debts and the factoring is fully on a recourse basis. In some cases, directions are given to the debtor to pay direct to the factor; in others, although notice of the assignment is given to debtors, they are instructed to pay to the client as the factor's agent. In the latter cases, the client is obliged to hold the monies recovered in trust for the factor and to pay them into a bank account of the factor.

In all cases, the client administers the sales ledger and enforces payment **1–52** from debtors as agent for the factor. Thus, this form of factoring is usually referred to as "Agency Factoring" or "Agency Discounting". The purpose of the arrangement is purely for financing the trade credit requirements of

---

[37] see para.3–34 below.

the client's debtors and the notice to them to pay the factor is to improve the factor's security. The service provided is, therefore, no more than that obtained by means of invoice discounting,[38] and for that reason it is commonly referred to as "Disclosed Invoice Discounting".

1-53   This system is used where the client's pattern of trade consists of a large number of small debtor accounts but where he does not meet the standards of financial standing or administration required for consideration of an invoice discounting arrangement. However, although the foregoing is the usual nature of agency factoring, at least one leading factoring company provides this service on a non-recourse basis, subject to approval of debtor accounts. Another recently developed variant has been described as a half-way house between recourse and agency factoring. Under that arrangement, the factor retains responsibility for the administration of the sales ledger but allows the client to carry out collection procedures.[39]

Invoice discounting or confidential factoring

1-54   For those clients who need finance for the trade credit requirements of their debtors, but no administrative service or protection, another service is provided extensively by factors. By the simple expedient of releasing the client from the need to notify the debtors to pay direct to the factor and by providing that all debts sold to the factor should be subject to full recourse, factoring is changed to a purely financial service sometimes referred to as "confidential factoring" or, more commonly, "invoice discounting". In the early days of invoice discounting, debts represented by individual invoices were sold to factors. This system gave rise to some difficulties: it was not always possible for the client to pass on to the factor the payment for the invoice in its original form as the payment might be made after deductions for cross-claims or combined with payment of other invoices.[40] In recent years, the service of invoice discounting has more usually been provided on a "whole turnover" basis by including all the client's sales or all to particular customers. The client maintains the sales ledger and collects from debtors on behalf of the factor to whom the ownership of the debts has been transferred and arrangements are made for the proceeds of collections to be paid by the client direct to the factor's bank account.

Undisclosed factoring

1-55   The term "undisclosed factoring" is sometimes applied to an "invoice discounting arrangement", as described above; but it is usually taken to

---

[38] See para.1–54 below.
[39] It is referred to as "CHOC" (Client Handles Own Collections), for a purist a misnomer: the collections are the factor's and not the client's because the debts belong to the factor.
[40] See also para.1–19 above.

denote an arrangement for invoice discounting whereby the factor will provide protection against bad debts to a limited extent by specifying that an agreed percentage (normally 80 per cent) of any approved indebtedness shall be without recourse as regards credit risks. The arrangement limits the protection to such a percentage so that the client, who maintains the ledger and collects from debtors, has some incentive to carry out these duties with efficiency. In some cases, however, factors have been known to accept that the full amounts of approved debts should be without recourse and thus to provide the same protection against bad debts as in the full service.

Maturity factoring

The above are the principal forms of factoring in which the factor pro- **1–56** vides finance by making prepayments of part of the purchase price of the debts purchased by him. Where finance is not required, an arrangement, used increasingly by small businesses as an alternative to credit insurance, comprises full administration of the sales ledger, collection from debtors and protection against bad debts. This service, often called "maturity factoring", is provided without any financial facility. The arrangement is that of the full service but without the facility for prepayment by the factor to the client and, accordingly, no finance charge is levied. Payments for the debts purchased are made either:

(1) after a fixed period based on expectation of the average period of credit to be taken by debtors (often referred to as the "maturity period") from either invoice date or the date of the transfer of the debts to the factor and the submission of copy invoices; or

(2) on receipt of payment from each debtor or, in respect of approved debts, the earlier insolvency of the debtor.

The system in (1) above offers attractions to the client in that he may calculate his cash flow in advance as soon as sales are effected to approved accounts. On the other hand, the factor may tend to make a liberal estimate of the maturity period and, in many cases, will reserve the right to adjust it in accordance with actual experience from time to time. The second method has the advantage of flexibility in allowing for changes of terms of payment by the client and requests to the factor for allowing latitude to debtors.

Recourse factoring or invoice discounting combined with credit insurance[41]

Apart from the forms mentioned above, co-operation with credit insurers **1–57** may be used for the benefit of the client. First, almost the equivalent to the

---

[41] For a more detailed analysis of the use of credit insurance by factors see Ch.14.

full service may be obtained by the use of recourse factoring combined with a credit insurance policy; secondly, the equivalent of undisclosed factoring may be achieved by the use of credit insurance combined with invoice discounting.

1–58   If a business prefers the protection against bad debts offered by a credit insurer (or if he is already a policy holder and does not wish to give up the policy) but is looking for the finance for the trade credit requirements of his customers, this co-operation between a credit insurer and a factor may be the answer to these requirements. In the case of recourse factoring, where the client is looking for relief from administrative burdens, the factor should agree to administer the policy (making all returns and paying the premium and other charges on behalf of the client) so that the client is relieved from these burdens; otherwise the equivalent of the full service will not be achieved. In all cases, the factor's position will be more secure if he carries out these functions; if he does not he will not know if the client has breached the policy conditions in these respects so that the insurer may not then be bound to meet a claim. In such a case, the factor's reliance on recovering from the insurer in respect of an insolvent debtor may be ill-founded.

Co-operation between factors and bankers

1–59   It may sometimes be agreed between a bank and its customer that the customer should continue to use the bank's facilities for the financing of its trade debts whilst taking advantage of a factor's services. In such a case, the bank's security may be improved by the factoring arrangements and the bank's reliance on the administration and the monitoring of the debts by the factor combined with certain undertakings from him. The advantage to the bank's customer (the factor's client) will be that he will keep his full relationship with his or her banker and, owing to the bank's improved security, may obtain a better facility. The arrangement has advantages over a guarantee from the factor to the bank based on the factor's liability to the client for the purchase price of debts which he has purchased. First, repayment to the bank by the factor does not require a formal demand; it requires only a call (which may be by telephone) to the factor. Secondly, it does not require that the factor should rely on set-off for the recovery from the client (by reason of an indemnity) of his payment to the bank. By the use of this method, the bank may lend confidently on the actual level of the client's trade debts instead of relying on projections or returns from the customer which may give little indication of the quality of the debts, the likelihood of disputes or of returned goods.

1–60   An outline of such an arrangement is as follows:

> (1) The factor enters a full factoring agreement which his client (the bank's customer) and a prepayment facility is included.

(2) Arrangements are made with the client that either:

    (i) he is paid only on payment by the debtors (so that the factor's indebtedness to the client for the debts purchased is always approximately equal to the outstanding debts owned by the factor); or

    (ii) that the factor may make a substantial fixed retention based on the amount for which he would have made prepayments against the debts outstanding at the start of the arrangement.

(3) In either case, the amount retained (either an amount equivalent to all the debts outstanding at any one time or a fixed amount) will be held by the factor for the benefit of the bank. Such retention is a book debt owing by the factor to the client and, as such, it will fall within any charge on book debts created by a client company in favour of the bank. Alternatively (or if the client is a partnership or sole trader), any amount payable by the factor to the client, including the retention, may be assigned by the client to the bank. In the case of a company, the assignment, being by way of security, will be registrable. To support the charge or assignment, the client will have given irrevocable instructions to the factor by which all amounts payable by the factor under the factoring agreement are to be paid to the bank.

By relying on that security and certain undertakings from the factor, the **1–61** bank may lend to the client either the whole of the amounts which would have been available by way of prepayment or, where a fixed amount is withheld, that amount. The undertaking from the factor will be based on his or her obligation to pay to the bank all amounts payable by it to the client and on a special provision in the factoring agreement by which a request for a prepayment from the bank is deemed to be a request from the client. The undertaking in the case of a fixed retention will be to pay that amount to the bank whenever so requested by the bank.

The undertakings given where the amounts retained are equivalent to the **1–62** full amounts of outstanding debts are based on the amount which the factor would have paid if he had been making prepayments. Such reports may include the basis of the availability: the total of the amount of assigned outstanding debts and the amounts of unapproved and disputed debts within the total. On the basis of each report, the bank should be able to allow the client's borrowing to increase to the figure of the availability; in between reports, the borrowing should be reduced by payments from the factor equivalent to receipts from debtors (less the factor's charges). The undertaking by the factor will be equivalent, not to the latest availability, but to the highest balance remaining of any reported availability after deducting payments made to the bank since the date of it. In this way, the bank's security would not be affected by the report of an availability less than its outstanding advances; this might occur if the factor were to find that a large outstanding debt were to be the subject of recourse to the client by reason of a dispute.

1–63 On the insolvency of the client or at any time beforehand, if the bank wishes to recover its advances on the basis of this arrangement, the bank may call upon the factor to make a prepayment of the amount of its undertaking. The bank may then recover its advances without incurring the expense, inconvenience and delays caused by recovery through a liquidator or receiver. The arrangement eliminates all the shortcomings of the reliance on a charge (whether fixed or floating) on the trade debts themselves. The benefit of this arrangement for a banker is to enable him or her to follow more closely the fortunes of a fast growing business for which the traditional means of finance may not keep pace.

TABLE: FACTORING VARIANTS

TABLE: FACTORING VARIANTS

	Availability of Finance	Protection Against Bad Debts*	Notices to Debtors	Sales Ledger Administration	Collections	
Full Service	A	A	A	A	A	Any of these may be referred to as: "Notification Factoring"
Recourse Factoring	A	N	A	A	A	
Agency Factoring	A	N	A	N	N	OR
Maturity Factoring	N	A	A	A	A	"Disclosed Factoring"
CHOC	A	S	U	S	N	Alternatively:
Invoice Discounting	A	N	N	N	N	"Confidential Factoring" OR "Non-Notification Factoring"
Undisclosed Factoring	A	S	N	N	N	

* Any form which includes this element may be referred to as *"non-recourse factoring"*

Key: A = Always provided
 U = Usually provided
 S = Sometimes provided
 N = Never or rarely provided

CHAPTER 2

THE APPLICATION OF FACTORING TO MODERN BUSINESS

2–01 A client of a factoring company once mentioned to an executive of that company that the client had in the past used three different factors and had never had cause to complain and had received a good service from each. The response from the factoring executive was that the experience was the mark of a well administered business of the client. The service provided by a well established factor is a reflection of the administrative competence of the factor's client and the acceptability of its products; the factor must rely on the information passed to him by the client and cannot improve the quality of the debts created by his client.

2–02 Many businesses have been disinclined to consider factoring based on anecdotal experiences. Apart from the allegation of poor service (which in many cases may indeed be an indictment of the quality of the client rather than the factor), there have been two main criticisms. First, it is said that factoring is solely a means of finance suitable only for those businesses which do not meet the criteria of traditional lenders. Secondly, it is sometimes alleged that, once a business has entered into a factoring arrangement, it is difficult to terminate it and it may, in some cases, lead to financial difficulties. The first objection is to a large extent based on the disregard of the administrative services and protection against the default of debtors which may be provided and of the benefits of a facility which follows the growth of a developing business automatically; the benefit and use of these aspects of the service are dealt with later in this chapter. The second allegation has arisen very largely from the use of the wrong service or the wrong use of any one of the variants of factoring. In this chapter, therefore, there are described, not only some of the most suitable uses for factoring, but some of the limitations on its use and some of the consequences of its misuse.

26

1. THE USE AND MISUSE OF FACTORING

Factoring to finance the movement of goods

The true historical nature of short-term trade credit is that it is the means   **2–03**
of financing the movement of goods to buyers who, by selling them on to
sub-purchasers, will be able to liquidate automatically the credit granted to
them. Such onward sales may be of their goods in their original form or
incorporated into others. Any short-term credit granted by a supplier of
items to be used as capital equipment by the buyer is not self-liquidating; the
buyer will be in little better position to pay for the equipment at the end of
the credit period than at the beginning of it. The price of such equipment
will be liquidated only over a period of years by the profits generated by its
use and by provisions for its depreciation. As a result, such short-term credit
is not true credit as described above, but it is often a convenience to enable
the buyer to ensure that the equipment will perform the function for which it
was purchased. Factoring was not designed to fill in the period before
acceptance of the client's product by the customer, and any credit required
for the financing of such purchases should be found by leasing, hire-purchase or medium-term loans. Factoring was developed to fill the requirements of suppliers of goods for the granting of true self-liquidating short-
term trade credit to their customers; therefore, the service is most suitable
for the suppliers of raw materials, components and consumer goods. These
goods can be made, sold and forgotten; the debts arising from their sales can
stand by themselves and be fully collectible in the absence of the supplier.
Such goods, unlike goods sold to a user as capital equipment, are not often
subject to substantial after sales services or back-up; and the factor can be
reasonably confident of their acceptance by the customers because they are
likely to be of a repetitive nature so that the factor can judge the likelihood
of acceptance by his experience. Only with such confidence can the factor
pay out, at invoice date, a large proportion of the amount which he may
expect to recover; the factor, unlike other providers of debtor finance, does
not have the debtor's signature before paying out. Such confidence is
essential to a successful factoring arrangement; in the absence of such
confidence, the factor may impose additional safeguards which may detract
severely from the benefit of the service to the client.

Reference to the origins of factoring in the United States[1] should indicate   **2–04**
that the type of business that is most suitable for the service of a factor is the
type that would have been able to make use of the services of a mercantile
agent in the absence of modern methods of marketing and distribution. In
addition, factoring has been used most successfully for businesses providing
short-term services, such as the provision of temporary staff or cleaning or

---

[1] See paras 1–11 *et seq.* above.

inspection services, except when they are provided under long term contracts. Where the full service has been applied to businesses for which factoring is suitable, there have indeed been successes. An efficient factoring service, including finance automatically following the growth of sales, combined with a well managed supplier of goods and services, is an excellent combination to bring a proprietary company to the stage of public participation. The acid test of a successful factoring facility is: "can the additional working capital which a factor makes available allow the client to increase his profits?"

Failure of factored businesses to achieve profits

2–05   The successes mentioned above have been masked by the more notorious failures caused by the use of factoring by a flagging, unprofitable and badly managed business. In such a case, factoring will have been adopted purely for the funds generated by it. The charges of the factor may not be recovered by reduced administration in such a case, and the extra cost may well increase the losses. The usual result is to defer the ultimate failure so that, when it does occur, the assets available for creditors have been further dissipated. Time and again recourse have been made to a factor in such circumstances for what has become known as "last resort finance". Factoring a loss making business which continues to lose money is likely to hasten its demise. Only if it can be seen that the business is returning to satisfactory profitability should it resort to factoring; it is then that the extra breathing space may be of value. If factoring is to provide such a breathing space, then factoring without recourse will be of particular benefit to the client, who may not be in a position to absorb the loss occasioned by a substantial bad debt.

Factoring finance used for capital expenditure

2–06   A similar situation of frustrated expectations for both client and factor may arise when factoring is used as a means of financing capital expenditure. The additional funds generated by the prepayments made available to the client become locked up in fixed assets. The business is then in the position of being paid regularly for a large part of its sales immediately on despatch of the goods but will continue to take the normal period of credit from its suppliers. If the business had strained resources before the new investment and the start of factoring, the growth will still be inhibited because the working capital has been depleted and the investment in the new fixed assets will not be able to pay for its keep. If the business was financing comfortably before the new investment, any downturn in trade will now cause delays in payments to creditors; prepayments for this month's reduced level of sales will not be sufficient to cover expenses and creditors incurred at a higher level of trade in the previous months. This is a classical overtrading situation[2] in which the growth of the business must continue indefinitely (even if unprofitably) and any downturn avoided at all costs if financial difficulties are not to be met. The position can be avoided by using factoring with a financial facility for the purpose for which it was designed (to allow the more effective use of working capital) and by financing the capital investment by medium-term loans, leasing or capital.

No difficulty in terminating factoring if properly used

It is in the circumstances described above that the factor's client will find himself demanding a higher and higher level of prepayments—a level which the factor cannot safely meet. In the first case, the demand may be to finance continuing losses and in the second, after a downturn in sales, to meet the high level of creditors' claims previously incurred. It is in such situations that the client will find it difficult to terminate the arrangements. Where, however, a profitable business uses a factoring service for the relief of administration and protection against bad debts, no such difficulties will emerge. Furthermore, no difficulties will be encountered when the funds generated by a factoring agreement are used to finance working capital to support an increasing level of sales and to assist in producing higher profits resulting from lower unit costs. Then, the finance provided will probably not be used to the full at all times, allowing creditors to be paid up to date and advantage taken of special purchasing opportunities. If factoring is so used, at no stage should there be any difficulty in terminating the arrangement when this is necessary. **2–07**

Disregard of recourse by client

A difficulty may arise from a misunderstanding by the client of the nature of recourse factoring. It has been known for a concern, with the type of business for which factoring is quite suitable, to enter into such a recourse arrangement without full regard to the recourse provisions and to use the prepayments in such a way that the funds would be removed from working capital (by using the funds for investment in fixed assets or even to repay directors' loans in the client company). The result is that, when the factor exercises his right of recourse, no funds are available to repay the prepayments made in respect of the recoursed debt, and the factor must perforce make deductions from further payments in order to recover what is due to him. Thus, the planned cash flow may not materialise, and the client may find himself in difficulty. **2–08**

It is situations such as this that cause professional advisers to dissuade their clients from using factoring in any of its forms; a not uncommon **2–09**

---

[2] See paras 2–11 *et seq.* below.

complaint is that a factor will make his or her prepayments, but that the balance of the purchase price seems to be delayed indefinitely owing to the setting off of recourse against it. However, it is not the factoring arrangement that is wrong, it is the misuse of the funds generated and the failure of the client to understand that the funds provided under a recourse arrangement are not "non-returnable cash". Such arrangements are the equivalent, in substance, though not in form, of the borrowing of the money on the security of the debts and should be treated as such in financial planning. Similar disregard of the contingency of recourse is less likely to arise in the case of bulk or agency factoring or invoice discounting in which the client, and not the factor, has the responsibility for collecting the debts on behalf of the factor. With the presence in the client's offices of the sales ledger and credit control department, the impression of the managers of the business is not that (as has indeed happened) the debts have been sold, but that finance has been raised against the security of the debts. Where the factor has the appearance of responsibility to collect, the client may fail to discriminate between recourse and non-recourse. It is apparent that, if recourse factoring is used where there are exposures concentrated on few debtors of relatively high value, it should be used in conjunction with credit insurance with an undertaking from the factor not to exercise recourse whilst awaiting payment from the insurer. On the other hand, such additional problems of recourse factoring may be avoided where the business has a good spread of debts owing by debtors of good credit standing.

Factoring no panacea for debtors of poor quality

2–10   Businesses that sell traditionally to trades and industries in which the expectation of bad debt losses is exceptionally high will not find a solution to this problem through factoring or credit insurance. These services can only spread the costs of such losses horizontally, across their many clients or insured, and by time over a period of years; they cannot therefore subsidise such a business in its regular high incidence of losses. Losses, other than those that are exceptional, have to be absorbed by a high margin of profit. Because the factor will need to keep his prepayments to a relatively low level so that his retention may be sufficient to cover the expected high level of bad debts, the client will be disappointed with the level of finance provided and he may well have planned for more. Even where the full non-recourse service is provided, the factor will be unlikely to accept, in return for a small percentage on sales values, such higher than average risks, and this will be reflected in the level of his credit approvals.

Factoring and overtrading

2–11   The benefits of factoring, the relief from administrative burdens and bad debt losses and the availability of finance, linked to sales volume without formal limit, are especially valuable to, and appreciated by, businesses which are growing vigorously. The service enables such a business to increase its sales rapidly, confident in the knowledge that the resulting trade credit requirements of its customers will be met. In this way, growth takes place without overtrading as might well not be the case if the business relied on traditional finance tied to a limit based on an historical financial position. On the other hand, to take the view—as some have—that factoring leads to overtrading, is a false syllogism; because many who are overtrading turn to factoring, factoring is not on that account a cause or encouragement to overtrade. Certainly, as demonstrated earlier, factoring, in any form, will not help those who are already overtrading in the classical sense: selling on shorter terms than they are buying so that growth is imperative at any cost (even at a loss) to keep the business alive. Indeed, if any form of factoring with finance is used in such circumstances and the funds generated used for investment in fixed assets, then the difficulties may be aggravated as is described above.[3]

2–12 Overtrading in its widest sense is usually taken to mean the carrying on of a business which is too large for the resources available for its support. The availability of immediate funds, without recourse, geared to the value of the debts created by the sale of acceptable goods to creditworthy customers, should enable a business to plan for growth with the resources automatically available. Thus, provided that the resources generated are used wisely as working capital to finance profitable sales and creditors are paid in due time, the growth may take place without overtrading. The factoring facility will provide the basis for achieving increased profits, which themselves can form the basis for the raising of additional resources. It seems that a more potent cause of overtrading is the reluctance of traditional providers of capital and lenders to provide a business with the necessary resources until profits have been earned and ploughed back and a healthy net asset position achieved. In this way, businesses are tempted to try to achieve the profits without the resources to support the necessary sales volume. Factoring will break into this vicious circle, providing the necessary resources in the first place so that the increased sales may be achieved and profit earned.

2–13 However, it is often overlooked that the key to the avoidance of over-trading is the non-recourse element in the full service. Only with this protection, and without the danger that the funds taken by the client may have to be repaid, may the client plan confidently for rapid growth. Otherwise, the business must continually provide for the contingent liability to repay the factor (or more usually for an interruption in cash flow when the factor takes the repayment against sums currently due to the client) in the event of a debtor failing to pay after due date.

---

[3] See para.2–06 above.

2. THE BENEFITS OF THE SERVICES

Sales ledger administration and collection

2–14   The importance of good sales ledger administration is not always appreciated by business-people and even accountants. This may arise from the emphasis placed by members of the accountancy profession on management and financial accounts. However, it is apparent that a sales ledger is the basis for the cash flow of a business. Apart from compliance with statutory requirements, a business needs its sales ledger to know exactly how much is owed by any one customer, to enable it to send clear statements to and to collect from customers and to provide information for the control of credit. In order to achieve such aims, it is essential that the ledger should be kept on an "open item" basis whereby all specific invoices, unpaid parts of invoices (representing unauthorised deductions by the debtors) and unallocated credit notes and payments are listed. Many small businesses seem unable to keep their sales ledgers on this basis even with the advent of data processing packages specially designed for this purpose; many such businesses kept their ledgers on the basis that items brought forward from previous months are shown as a balance. Such a balance may include deductions made many months previously and may be the result of the deduction of unallocated or round amount payments. The result is often the masking of disputed items whilst the debtor has been paying more recent items promptly. The longer this situation is allowed to develop the bigger is the eventual write-off for disputes which cannot be satisfactorily settled at a late stage.

2–15   An open item system will highlight such disputes; the necessity of allocating payments as they come in will create a discipline to resolve disputes and deductions promptly. Many small businesses, even with systems that provide for open item accounting, have not the time or the resources to enjoy the benefits of the system because, in most cases, all the appropriation of payments and credit notes to invoices cannot be carried out automatically by the system. Even in some of the most advanced systems, only payments which clear individual invoices without deduction can be appropriated automatically. By the use of full, maturity or recourse factoring[4] any business has the benefit of an open item system with prompt allocation of payments and credits by well trained and experienced personnel. The management of the business using such services is relieved from the burden of the supervision of these tasks and is usually provided with regular clear reports of outstanding debts analysed by the age of the invoices and highlighting disputed items.

2–16   The supervision of overdue sales ledger accounts and the collection from

---

[4] See Ch.1.

debtors, which is vital for the cash flow for most small businesses, are often part time tasks of management or personnel who have many other functions. In many small or medium-sized businesses the employment of a full time credit controller may not be justified. Often these tasks tend to be the Cinderella of the accounting function and are not given the importance which they deserve until cash flow problems remind the management of them. It may then be difficult to make the necessary allocations and bring the accounts up to date. By the use of full, maturity or recourse factoring,[5] the debts purchased by the factor should be collected by personnel skilled in keeping the credit taken by customers to a minimum whilst avoiding prejudice to customer relations. In particular, in full factoring or maturity factoring, the factor has the ultimate responsibility for the collection of the debts approved by the factor in respect of which there is no recourse to the client; in providing such service, the factor has the incentive to collect promptly in order to avoid the risk of the debtor's default. In many cases, the factor will reduce the credit taken by debtors and ageing profile of the sales ledger and in this way will, not only improve the cashflow, but also reduce interest costs and bad debts.

The use of factoring to avoid bad debts

Insurance for merchants and manufacturers against losses caused by the default of their customers was introduced into the United Kingdom early last century. For many years credit insurance, as this type of insurance is known, did not have general acceptance. It was surprising that, although it was usual for businesses to effect insurance in respect of current assets against many risks (some of them indeed rare), it was not often considered prudent to insure debts against the risk of the insolvency of debtors, which is something that is occurring every day. It was more surprising because in the circulation of working capital it is at the stage of becoming a debt that, with added value and profit margin included, an item has reached its greatest value. However, during the last recession the higher incidence of insolvency greatly increased the perception of the danger of the interruption of cash flow caused by such an event. Sometimes the default of a large customer has been the cause of the failure of the supplier itself—this has been referred to as the "domino effect". It starts with the insolvency of a large company which hitherto appeared soundly financed and which has many independent suppliers; the failure of some of the suppliers has in turn been the cause of the insolvency of some of their own suppliers. Thus, credit insurance is, in particular, an instrument for stability in a recession. **2–17**

In considering the use of credit insurance, some prospective insured consider the expense of it only in relation to the past incidence of bad debts. **2–18**

---

[5] *ibid.*

Regular small losses are part of the cost of running a business, and the inclusion of them in an insurance arrangement is, in effect, a "pound swapping" arrangement with additional costs of administration. It is against the large unexpected losses that insurance is essential in many types of business; it is when such a loss occurs that management consider the loss to be bad luck, whereas it is the result of bad management—the failure to effect insurance. Even if a bad debt reserve of a size sufficient to absorb the loss is held there is unlikely to be held additional liquid resources to represent such reserve and to replace the lost cash flow. The loss may be aggravated by the loss of work in progress and of a sales outlet. Such losses arrive unexpectedly and may cause considerable difficulty; on the other hand, the cost of credit insurance or factoring is predictable and may be budgeted for in costing the price of products.

2–19 In spite of the recent more widespread recognition of the importance of credit insurance, there is still little recognition among businessmen and their professional advisers of the benefit of this aspect of the services of the non-recourse factors. The benefit of this protection may be obtained without any finance for those who wish to continue to rely on their traditional sources of finance by the use of maturity factoring. For a small or medium-sized business there may be considerable advantages in the use of a factor as compared with the use of credit insurance. The principal advantage is that the money lost by the interruption of the cash flow, caused by the default of the customer, is immediately replaced in full (to the extent of the factor's approval); the business does not have to wait for the settlement of the claim and the insurer's indemnity is usually between 75 and 90 per cent of the insured debt and not the full amount. Such settlement may, in some cases, be deferred until official insolvency, followed by the obtaining by the insured of admittance of his proof in the insolvent estate and a period for consideration of the claim by the insurer. In the case of full factoring, a substantial part of the purchase price of the debt (its amount less the factor's charges) will already have been paid when the invoice was issued, and the balance will be paid on the date of the insolvency.

2–20 Another advantage is the relief from the administration of the policy. In a typical credit insurance arrangement, periodic returns of turnover and of overdue accounts are required and the claims procedure requires additional paper work. Furthermore, factors do not often require additional fees for the approval and maintenance of credit limits; these costs are merged into the cost of providing the full administrative functions. It has on some occasions emerged that the savings engendered by the relief from administrative and collection functions by the use of the full service or maturity factoring[6] can cover the factoring administration charges so that the protection against bad debts may be provided for virtually no fee.

---

[6] See para.1–56 above.

There are naturally many businesses for which such protection is not **2–21** necessary; they may have such a wide spread of customers that the business is self-insuring in this respect or they may sell only to government departments. However, when the decision has been taken that protection is necessary, then a careful review of the costs and benefit of insurance and non-recourse factoring should be made. In some respects, credit insurance has advantages over the services offered by factors: cover for work-in-progress is sometimes available and some insurers will stay on risk in respect of a disputed claim against a debtor, whereas a factor will normally effect recourse in respect of a debt the subject of a dispute which is not settled within a few months.

The benefit of the finance generated by prepayments

The following statement on the finance generated by factoring sum- **2–22** marises the benefit of this aspect of factoring services and comes from a completely disinterested source:

> "Factoring is without doubt today one of the most effective ways for a small or medium-sized business selling raw materials or consumer goods or providing services to finance the trade credit it grants to its customers. True, it may rely on its own resources or on credit provided by the bank or on that provided by its own suppliers but inflation coupled with high interest rates and the current low supply of risk capital have led many businessmen to seek the alternative forms of finance such as factoring, with the many services which it offers."[7]

Before the Second World War, merchants and manufacturers financed the **2–23** credit to be granted to their customers partly by using their own capital resources, which were augmented by the ploughing back of profits, and partly by the credit granted to them by their own suppliers. In the years since the war, high rates of taxation combined to reduce the supply of internally generated resources. The deficiency could not be filled entirely by the credit granted by suppliers (themselves often suffering from the same forces). The problem was aggravated for those near the end of the chain of supply between raw materials and retailers where the customary periods of credit tended to be longer. For these reasons there has been an increasing dependence on bank finance especially by way of overdraft. However, since banks' facilities are determined to a large extent by criteria other than the value of the prospective level of trade debts outstanding from time to time, they do not have the mechanisms in place to monitor the value of book

---

[7] From the report of the secretariat of UNIDROIT (see para.12–24 below) following a second meeting of the representatives of governments for the consideration of a draft convention to harmonise the laws relating to factoring for international trade.

debts regularly, and young vigorously growing businesses have not always been able to obtain sufficient finance to realise their full productive capabilities. A bank might well expect its customer to reach a sufficient level of trade and, thus, of profitability and thereby produce the profits and the assets to support the required level of finance; but, without the availability of the finance to support the required level of trade, the business cannot reach it.

2–24   It is the function of the factor to cut into this inextricable circle. The factor's provision of finance by way of prepayment (for example, 80 per cent) of the purchase price of debts created automatically follows the growth of the business without formal limit.[8] This enables a factor's client, without sufficient internally generated funds to support a higher level of trade, to plan for growth in the knowledge that the factor will exactly match to the extent of, say, 80 per cent the funds required for the trade credit to be granted to his customers. Particularly in the case of the full service, the factor undertakes to buy without recourse every debt arising from the sale of acceptable goods (or the provision of acceptable services) to creditworthy customers. The client is then required to fund only the remaining part (in this example 20 per cent) and the agreed percentage may match his gross profit margin. For a business with new products or markets to develop, such an arrangement will enable it to support the additional turnover and to produce the higher profits; in the case of a manufacturing business, the extra sales volume may well reduce unit costs. In this way, the factor's charges may be easily absorbed without taking account of savings engendered by the saving of administrative tasks and the avoidance of bad debts.[9]

3. LIMITATIONS ON THE USE OF FACTORING

Post-invoice contractual obligations of client

2–25   The factor's ability confidently to provide funds at the time when goods are delivered or services completed, without the debtor's intimation that he has accepted the goods and services, depends, not only on his experience of the acceptability of the goods and services in question, but also on the absence of substantial continuing obligations of the client under the contract of sale or for services. Where there remain continuing obligations, then, in the event of the insolvency of the seller or the cessation of the business for

---

[8] In recent years some factors have imposed on their clients a funding limit. This has the effect of removing one of the principal benefits of factoring here described. However, in order to mitigate this effect such limits are often referred to and dealt with as "review limits" and fixed at an amount unlikely to be reached on the basis of cash flow forecasts for the year following the start of factoring.

[9] See also the case histories in para.2–30 below.

other reasons, the factor will be faced with counter-claims from the debtor, which, in some cases, may well have the effect of reducing the amount payable by the debtor to nil.[10] The factor will in most cases have no positive liability to the debtor, but the indeterminate amount of such likely cross-claims has the effect of limiting the use of factoring. In addition to the unsuitability of factoring to the provision of most items purchased by the debtors for use as capital equipment (in respect of which the client may be responsible for warranties and service after invoice date), factors normally find themselves unable to provide their services to contractors in the construction industry.[11] In neither of these industries is the factor able to make a confident assessment of the acceptability of the products based on previous sales; in most cases every product differs from others produced by the same supplier.

There are many other goods and services provided on the basis of contracts continuing over several months or even years. In the case of a business of which this is the normal pattern of trade, the factor may well take the view that to provide for the counter-claims, arising from claims for damages for failure to complete such a contract, should preclude the provision of any form of factoring which includes finance by way of payment on account of the purchase price of the debts on invoice date.[12] On the other hand, there are cases in which the problem can be overcome by the expedient of agreements between the prospective client and his debtors by which the contracts are made divisible and the goods or services represented by each invoice are regarded as provided under a separate contract.[13]   **2–26**

Effect on client of use beyond limitations

It may be thought that the use of factoring beyond its limitations is a matter that will affect the factor only and that, if he is prepared to accept the risks of such possible cross-claims by debtors, it should not be to the detriment of the client. However, when it is apparent to the factor that he may be faced with such difficulties in making an early recovery, the result may well be a restriction in pre-payments and even a complete interruption to the client's cash flow. The difficulties may even result in poor administration by the client and be reflected in difficulties in collection from debtors; by reason of the debtors' cross-claims, the failure of debtors to accept the goods and services or modifications (in the case of machinery for capital equipment), the required collections may be the responsibility of the client. Even in the case of non-recourse factoring, the factor may no longer be responsible for the default of the debtor and the disputed debt may be subject to recourse;   **2–27**

---

[10] For a full analysis of the effect of such cross-claims see paras 9–15 *et seq.* below.
[11] See paras 9–50 *et seq.* below.
[12] *ibid.*
[13] See para.9–56 below.

for it is normal for factors to have the right of recourse in respect of a debt the subject of a defence or counterclaim which is not settled within a reasonable period (sometimes defined as 60 days). To the client the resulting disservice is apparent; the restriction in the prepayments may cause an aggravation of the deficiency of working capital which may have initially caused its management to look to factoring. The business may well have embarked on planned growth on the understanding that the agreed percentage of sales would be available on despatch of its products; but, owing to its being unable to warrant that it had completed all its obligations under its contract of sale,[14] it may then find that prepayments by the factor are withheld only because, in accordance with trade practice, there may be much to be done after invoice date.

2–28   Difficulties cannot be attributed to the services themselves but only to the way in which they are used; to blame the services would be equivalent to blaming the concept of a motor car for the cause of an accident, rather than the way in which it is driven. The image of factoring can only benefit by a thorough consideration of its proper use and the difficulties caused by its misuse described above. Much of the adverse comment on factoring has been caused by the acceptance by factoring companies of the wrong type of client in the wrong circumstances for the wrong reasons; this has not always been the result of any misunderstanding by the management of factoring companies but sometimes of pressure by shareholders on managers to widen their marketing outside the industries that are usually considered suitable in order to increase profitability more rapidly. In most cases, the factoring company has not suffered; it has been able to protect itself by reducing its prepayments. But the image of factoring has been impaired. Only by a full ventilation and discussion of the misuse of the services, can the criticisms of the service be rebutted and the undoubted benefits and value of factoring and some of its variations be brought to the attention of the business community and professional advisers.

4. BUSINESSES WHICH MAY BENEFIT MOST FROM FACTORING

2–29   From the foregoing, it is apparent that, to be suitable for factoring, the contracts of sale of the prospective client should give rise to debts which, not only represent the full performance of the contract (without further or continuing obligations on the part of the supplier), but which also are strictly numerable as to value by reference to the contracts and are free from the likelihood of counterclaims. Ideally, the debts should be such that they stand by themselves as fully payable without any back-up from the client;

---

[14] A standard warranty in any well drafted factoring agreement.

such debts arise from the supply of a product colloquially referred to as "sell and forget". There are many businesses the sales of which give rise to such debts; for example, the sale of a specific number of tables or chairs at a specific price unrelated to any other contract for sale would give rise to such strictly computable debt. On the other hand, a contract for public relations services or other consultancy based on certain performance and results over a specific period might not give rise to a strictly computable amount of debt. It is often not recognised that some invoices issued by service and contracting companies represent only the supplier's idea of what he should be paid (they have been sometimes described as the hopes and aspirations of the supplier) and do not necessarily coincide with the debtor's opinion of what he owes. In the provision of special purpose machinery, the amounts payable may become the result of negotiations between engineers on each side, particularly when modifications to the machinery are necessary; in the case of shopfitting and similar work, the end result may seem to the customer different based on his expectations from the specification and plans.

The benefit of factoring to businesses with good growth prospects

Within the limits of suitability there is a large number of situations in **2–30** which factoring may be of particular benefit. The most usual case is that of a well managed business with a good and acceptable product of which the growing sales will outstrip the financial support of traditional lenders. The finance provided by a factor, which automatically follows the growth of the outstanding book debts, enables the business to plan for an increase of sales without having to make frequent applications to its bankers supported by cash flow forecasts, budgets and other financial information; the management of the business may concentrate on producing and selling. Furthermore, the acceptance by the factor of the administration of the sales ledger, which may be greatly increased, and the credit assessment of new customers will be of especial benefit in such a case. Examples of the assistance given by a factor in such circumstances are as follows:

Example 1

A company, which had started with capital of £10,000, after two years of trading had a net worth of about £15,000 and had achieved a sales volume of £150,000. Its bankers were willing to lend on overdraft a sum which would match the net worth. The company was then introduced to a new market for its products and the exploitation of the new market would quickly result in an increase of sales to £400,000 and outstanding book debts of about £65,000. The banker suggested to the company that it should use factoring and as a result of the use of a factor the additional funds were found to finance the book debts; the use of the full service enabled the company to sell into the new market without increasing its accounts staff and gave it confidence in the avoidance of bad debts in a market in which it had little experience. Ten years later the company's annual turnover was £7,000,000 and net pre-tax profits about £350,000. The principal director was sure that this could not have been achieved without factoring, but his successful use of it was based on his never having used all the resources available from his banker and his factor to the full at any time.

Example 2

A holding company owning subsidiaries in several different trades owned a company selling products to the building industry. At a time of rapid expansion of the subsidiary's sales, the holding company's chairman was looking for some way of funding the subsidiary's growth automatically. At the time, the subsidiary's outstanding book debts amounted to £80,000 and, on enquiry at its bankers as to how much would be available on overdraft when the book debts reached £500,000, it was suggested that the chairman should not ask hypothetical questions. To a similar question, a factor replied that, provided that the debts arose from the sale of acceptable goods to reasonably creditworthy customers, then the factor would provide £400,000 by way of prepayments for those book debts. The management of the subsidiary could not see any saving in the factor's administration of the sales ledger which was a function performed by personnel with other duties; but they decided on the full service for the protection against bad debts. After several years, when outstanding book debts had risen to well over one million pounds, the finance by way of prepayments was no longer required; but the company decided to continue to use the factor's services, not only for the protection against bad debts, but also because the sales ledger and collection functions had grown to such an extent that to carry out such tasks themselves would cost the company more than the factor's charges. Another reason for this company staying with their factor, like many others even when they no longer take any prepayments, is for the comfort of having a facility in place in case of unexpected changes or opportunities.

The benefits of factoring in the development of new products

2–31   A business person may be very well versed in the credit standing of customers in his or her own trade or industry. However, when a new type of product is developed or the business diversifies by the purchase of other businesses, there may be a completely different type of customer to be served. It has been known for businesses to be restrained from diversification by fear of the unknown credit risks. Such uncertainties may even arise from the simple change in the pattern of trade so that sales which hitherto had been made to a relatively small number of wholesalers are to be made to a large number of small retailers. In all such cases the use of a factor will enable the business to exploit its new opportunities with confidence. In the case of a switch of sales from wholesalers to retailers the acceptance of the administrative function by the factor will also assist this development. Factoring was used in such circumstances by a company dealing in precious metals, the sales of which were for the most part to a small number of customers in the jewellery business well known to the company and its executives. A development in the electrical and electronic industry created a demand for the company's products there so that it had the potential to sell to any company in these industries. The number of actual customers increased by many times the original number and the sales volume would develop substantially. For these two reasons alone factoring would have been justified but the main impetus was the factor's approval of customers in the new fields in which the factor was experienced; in this way the company was able to develop its business with confidence in relation to finance, administration and protection. Businesses moving into new markets, especially overseas, may have no knowledge of their new customers and their credit ratings. Non recourse factoring can assist in providing credit limits and debtor protection.

Factoring and seasonal trades

In businesses which have most of the sales concentrated in one or two **2–32** short periods during any year, the working capital requirements during those short periods may be quite out of proportion to the capital resources of the business and consequently to the amount of finance available from traditional sources which are looking at balance sheet ratios. Such a disproportion applies particularly to the trade debts of manufacturers who may attempt to spread their sales by offering long credit outside the peak selling period. For example, a lawn mower manufacturer may offer terms of payment to its customers by which payment for all sales from December through to May are to be made at the end of June; in this way the distributors would have an opportunity to sell the products at the start of the grass cutting season before being obliged to pay. The resulting high value of debts, which may be well out of line with other balance sheet items, may be safely financed by the purchase of the debts by a factor relying on experience of the acceptability of the product and on the profitability of the supplier without regard to the balance sheet ratios.

There are many other examples of such seasonal peaks of outstanding **2–33** book debts in consumer goods trades, particularly in the clothing industry which traditionally experiences two seasons: Spring and Autumn. An importer of such goods may have the goods which he imports financed largely by a bank's opening letters of credit on his behalf and releasing the goods to him for onward sale on a letter of trust; but the bank may require repayment of the amounts laid out for the purchase of the goods as soon as they are sold. The employment of a factor in such circumstances may enable the importer to finance the goods right through to the ultimate payment from the customers of the sub-sales. In order to provide factoring to businesses of a marked seasonal nature without obliging the client to incur unnecessary costs, some factors will provide the service on an intermittent basis to cover only the periods of the seasonal peaks. This is arranged by a continuing agreement by which the factoring procedures are brought into effect for specific months by notice from the client to the factor.

Factoring and the relief of administrative burdens

2–34   Maturity factoring has often been adopted for the protection it offers against bad debts together with the relief from the tasks of sales accounting and collections from debtors by businesses which have no need of the financial benefit. It has sometimes been found advantageous for a business to accept the administrative function alone and the savings together with the protection against bad debts have outweighed the cost of the service. The following is an example of such a saving:

Example 3

A small company in the foundry industry, watching its competitors invest in expansion in the late 1970s, expected a recession in the industry. In view of the growth of capacity in the industry and the expected fierce competition together with a recession, it decided to cut its overheads to the minimum and to reduce its office staff from three to one; it expected to be able to cope with some of the additional work itself. Unfortunately, it had just not enough time for all the administrative tasks and, naturally, the following up of overdue accounts and collections from debtors fell into arrears because there was no particular deadline for these tasks. It considered the alternatives of a new member of staff or maturity factoring; the cost of each was about equal when the overheads were taken into account. The advantage of factoring was that the factor was always there to carry out these tasks, whereas there would have to be cover for the extra member of staff during absence for vacation and sickness. After several years of the use of maturity factoring it emerged that the cost had been no more than the cost of the additional personnel would have been; additionally, the factor had absorbed some bad debts so that the protection against bad debts had been provided for him at virtually no expense.

The choice of a suitable service

2–35   When it is considered that factoring might be suitable to assist in the financing or administration of a business, or both, it is important that the business should choose the right service to meet the particular situation. Finance for growth alone may be achieved by invoice discounting if it is used by a well established company with adequate reserves and efficient accounting procedures. A company exploiting new markets or a new product may be better served by the full service so that it is relieved from unfamiliar risks and trade usages. A business that is growing fast on a small capital base also needs the full service. In addition to the finance and administrative function it needs the assurance that it will not be set back by an interruption to its cash flow by customer defaults.

CHAPTER 3

THE FACTOR'S RELATIONS WITH HIS CLIENT

3–01 This chapter deals with the relations, the communication and the accounting between the factor and the client. The factor's main requirement from this aspect of factoring is that it should be ensured that the debts which he has purchased are payable at the value at which they are notified or offered to him without his need to enlist the support of the client. The factor will also wish to rely on the client's support in collecting the debts should this be necessary by reason of the debtor's defence or counterclaim or because there remain after invoice date further obligations of the client to the debtor[1]; and, in the case of invoice discounting and in some cases of agency factoring,[2] he must have confidence in the sales ledger administration of the client. The factor also needs to specify the rates at which he is to be remunerated for the functions which he carries out. From the client's point of view, the procedures should provide for payment in accordance with his perception of the finance to be generated by his sale of the debts to the factor; and he will wish to have confidence in the factor's reports and accounting with him so that he may have sufficient information for the proper conduct of his business. The client will also need to know the exact circumstances in which he will be required to repurchase any debt from the factor by reason of the exercise of recourse by the factor. The legal relationship by which these matters are regulated is described in the second part of this book[3]; here the administrative procedures of a typical factoring arrangement are described.

3–02 Any of the types of factoring described in Ch.1 may be provided under an agreement which simply provides for the offer of each debt to the factor as it arises (a "facultative" agreement) or under an agreement which itself binds the debts as being assigned to the factor without further formality (a "whole turnover" agreement).[4] In the former case, each debt must be the subject of

---

[1] See paras 2–25 and 2–26.
[2] See paras 1–54 and 1–51 respectively.
[3] See, in particular, Ch.10.
[4] For a description of the two types and an explanation of the difference between them see Ch.7, and especially paras 7–08 to 7–11 below.

an individual offer normally evidenced by the delivery of copy invoices, by which such debts are represented, to the factor; in the latter case, the invoices are merely "notified" to the factor as an accounting function because the debts will have already vested in the factor upon their coming into existence.[5] In order to avoid prolixity in this chapter, the sending of invoices or copies to the factor by the client will in all cases be described as a notification whether the sending of them constitutes an offer or not.

1. PROCEDURES IN FULL, RECOURSE AND MATURITY FACTORING

The start of factoring

When the agreement between the factor and his client has been executed, **3–03** and the factor and the client are ready to start the arrangement, it is first necessary for the two parties to prepare for the details on the client's sales ledger at the prospective starting date to be entered into the factor's records. It is usual for the factor to purchase the debts outstanding at the starting date; if he does not there will be confusion among debtors as to whom to pay until the outstanding debts are cleared. Furthermore, subsequent credits allowed to, or deductions made by, debtors relating to the outstanding debts may be applied by the debtors against amounts owing to the factor for later invoices.

If the arrangement is for non-recourse factoring (*e.g.* full or maturity **3–04** factoring), then, at the earliest opportunity, the factor must make a review of the debtors currently served by the client in order to assess their credit standing and to determine the level of his approvals. The approvals are usually based on a credit limit for each debtor and, in respect of debts at any time within that limit, the factor will have no recourse if the debtor fails to pay by reason of his insolvency.[6] For this purpose, the client is usually expected to prepare a list of all his debtors paying meticulous attention to names and addresses in view of the number of concerns whose names tend to be similar. The factor will then make his assessment of each debtor on the basis, not only of the information available to him from his own files or from status reports and files at the Companies Registry, but also relying to some extent on the client's own experience of payments from the debtors. As this exercise sometimes takes place a few weeks before the debts themselves are taken on by the factor (in order to allow the factor time to make his assessments), it is important that the client should *from that time* send in to the factor applications for credit approvals and not wait until the starting

---

[5] As to when a debt comes into existence for this purpose see para.7–12(2) below.
[6] See paras 3–11 *et seq.* below for a description of the methods by which approvals are given.

date. The client should apply for a limit as soon as they take an order. If they wait until the goods are delivered, it may be that the factor will not grant a limit and no prepayment or credit limit will be made available, so resulting in a hole in the cash flow. It has not been unknown for the starting date to be delayed with a consequent change in the make up of the outstanding debtors, whereupon the factor may not be in a position to give immediate approval to some of the debts; if prepayments[7] are to be made only in respect of approved debts, then the initial cash flow expected by the client may not be forthcoming. For this reason, among others, factors have sometimes started the non-recourse arrangement with sales after the start of factoring and accept the initial outstanding debts with full recourse to the client; in this way it is often hoped to arrange for an earlier start.

3–05   In order to transfer the existing debts to the records of the factor and to make the first arrangements for payments to be made direct to the factor the client must bring his ledger up to date to the close of business on the day before the starting date and prepare statements for his debtors. The statements are prepared in duplicate and one copy is sent to each debtor with a notice of the assignment and instructions to pay to the factor; the statement is often accompanied by an introductory letter the legal effect of which is analysed in Ch.8. The other copy may be sent to the factor as a notification of the initial outstanding debts, but in some cases the factor may require copies of the individual invoices not least so that he may be in a position to send any copies required to debtors. In any event, if the sales ledger has not been kept on an open item[8] basis by the client, the ledger will need to be analysed so that each balance represents only specific invoices before it can be taken on by the factor. On the basis of the statements, the copy invoices or the analysis, the factor will create his own sales ledger accounts and credit the client with the purchase price of the debts which is the total invoice value (less any outstanding credit notes) less the factor's discount charges.[9]

3–06   If prepayments are to be provided (i.e. otherwise than in maturity factoring), the client will be at liberty to draw against the credit less the agreed retention; that retention is a percentage of debts eligible for prepayments, which is inverse to the prepayment percentage in addition to the equivalent of any debts not so eligible. Such ineligible debts will include those disputed or seriously overdue and, although in some cases the factor will be prepared to make prepayments in respect of debts whether approved for credit or not, in others ineligible debts will include those not approved for credit.

---

[7] See para.1–48 above.
[8] See para.2–14 above.
[9] See para.3–35 below. For the reason for not treating the factor's other charges as a deduction in computing the purchase price of the factored debts see para.10–49 below.

Continuing arrangements

From the start of factoring the client will invoice his customers in the **3–07** usual way, but the invoices are to bear a notice that the debts represented by them have been purchased by and assigned to and are payable only to the factor. It is considered that the notice should refer to the "purchase" by the factor in order to make it clear that the debt has been the subject of an outright assignment by way of sale and purchase; in the words of a well-known judgment, the debtor should be made aware that the debt has been "made-over" to the factor.[10] A typical notice is as follows:—

"The debt represented by this invoice has been purchased by and assigned to and is to be paid to .... [*Insert name and address of factor*] of .... or direct to their bank account at:

[*name and address of bank*]

Sort Code: ....

Account Number: ....

Your obligations in respect of this debt will be discharged by payment only to ... [*insert name of factor*] who should be advised of any disagreement or claim in respect of the debt or the invoice."

The invoices are to be notified to the factor in convenient batches, but **3–08** only after delivery of the goods or completion of the relevant service. Such notification is normally by the submission of copies of the invoices but some factors require to have the originals sent to them for onward transmission to the debtors so that they may ensure the delivery to debtors of the assignment notices. The notification normally constitutes a warranty that the debt is then a legally binding obligation of the debtor without the possibility of any defence or counter-claim.[11] The notification will also constitute other warranties; in particular, that the debt has arisen from a contract of sale providing for payment on terms approved by the factor, in a currency approved by the factor and otherwise as approved by the factor. The factor and the client must agree on such terms at the outset so that the factor's terms on which he purchases the debts are properly assessed.[12] In particular, it is important that the maximum settlement discount to be allowed to the

---

[10] *Wm. Brandt's Sons & Co v Dunlop Rubber Co Ltd* [1905] A.C. 454, *per* Lord MacNaghton at p.462. See also para.8–08 below.
[11] See para.10–12 below.
[12] See paras 10–14 *et seq.* below.

debtor should be approved by the factor at the outset so that the factor's retention[13] may be fixed at a level to absorb such a reduction in the amount recoverable from debtors.

3–09   The amounts of the invoices are debited to the particular debtors' accounts by the factor and the client is credited. As a corollary, the client will notify the factor of credit notes issued, which have the effect of reducing the amount payable by the debtors. The amounts of these credit notes will be credited to the relevant debtor accounts and debited to the client's account, thereby reducing *pro tanto* the amount payable by the factor to the client. Most factors now expect that the client should place a debtor's account number on each invoice and credit note so that the input to the factor's data processing system can be effected without delay; this assists the factor in updating the accounts daily and in providing up-to-date feedback of information to the client. Now, in many cases the factor's debtor accounts for particular clients are updated by input from a terminal in the client's office.

3–10   The client may continue to draw the agreed prepayment percentage of the value of notified invoices less the factor's charges and less the value of any notified credit notes. In addition, the factor will also pay the balance of the purchase price of debts which have been settled by payment by the relevant debtors. In effect, the client may draw up to the balance credited to him less the retention as described in para.3–06. If a payment is made by a debtor, the outstanding debts are reduced by the same amount; the retention, which includes a percentage of the outstanding debts eligible for prepayment and the full amount of ineligible debts, is then automatically reduced and that releases the unpaid purchase price of the debt which has been paid. Some factors will pay the balance of the purchase price, not on payment of the debt, but a fixed number of days after the invoice date or after the end of the month in which the debt has been invoiced. This latter system, which normally only applies in the case of non-recourse factoring (full or maturity factoring), has the advantage to the client that he can budget his cash flow more exactly.

Approvals

3–11   Approvals of debts in full and maturity factoring are given for the purpose of specifying debts which the factor will accept without recourse as regards the failure of the debtor to pay by reason of insolvency. In recourse, factoring approvals are not given for this purpose because every debt is purchased by the factor with full recourse; they may be given as an advisory service as regards the credit standing of the debtor or to determine the eligibility of the debt for prepayments. This difference and the fact that,

---

[13] See paras 5–38 and 10–02 *et seq.* below and 1–48 and 3–06 above.

whilst some non-recourse factors will make prepayments only in respect of approved debts, others may prepay in respect of approved and unapproved may have caused some confusion. As a result, the term "eligible" is now sometimes used to label a debt in respect of which a prepayment will be made leaving the term "approved" to denote "without recourse".

Whichever the reason for the approvals, they may be determined in any of the following ways: **3–12**

(a) by establishing in respect of each debtor a credit limit within which the total indebtedness of that debtor at any time is deemed to be approved;

(b) by specifically approving debts arising from individual contracts of sale;

(c) by the establishment of limits in respect of each debtor for monthly deliveries whereby any deliveries in excess of such a limit will rank as unapproved;

or by a combination of any two or all the above methods.

The advantage of method (a) is its flexibility in that it allows for irregular deliveries and for invoices in respect of deliveries, that have been made whilst the limit is full or exceeded, to drop into the limit to the extent that a debtor payment or credit note creates an availability within it; on the other hand, under method (c), to the extent that any invoice exceeds the periodic delivery limit, such invoice remains unapproved. Each of the methods has a disadvantage as compared with others. Method (a) will only enable the client to ensure that all the outstanding debts are protected if he has sufficient information to know the up-to-date state of all the debtor accounts at all times[14]; only with this information can he control the deliveries so that the outstanding debts remain within credit limits. Method (b) imposes an undue administrative burden on both parties, unless the business of the client consists of a relatively small number of orders of large amounts. Method (c) has the advantage of allowing the client to make his deliveries without reference to the state of the account. However, it has the disadvantage of inflexibility: if deliveries are not spread regularly, there may be unapproved debts arising from one month's sales whilst the outstanding is less than the factor would in total be prepared to approve. **3–13**

It is necessary for the factor to protect himself from a deteriorating financial position or impending insolvency of a debtor by reducing or cancelling a credit limit of either type referred to above, but naturally such cancellation or reduction should not affect deliveries of goods made or **3–14**

---

[14] See para.3–15 below and particularly regarding the provision of information by electronic means.

services completed before receipt by the client of notification of it. If this were not so, the client could not confidently effect his deliveries or perform services in the certainty of protection against a bad debt. In this respect it is unfortunate that some factors, in their agreements, take the right to refuse to accept any debt offered to them (or to have any debt repurchased by the client on its notification under a whole turnover type of agreement)[15]; a client might make a delivery within a limit only to find that, because the debtor had called a meeting of creditors between the delivery and the raising of the invoice, the factor had declined to accept the invoice and that consequently the client was not protected. With the use of specific approval of individual orders (method (b) above), the factor should have no need to have the right to withdraw an approval; he will normally stipulate that the approval is conditional on delivery within a period (*e.g.* 60 days), and it will naturally be expected that the client will not release any goods on notification of any official insolvency of the debtor.

Reports and feedback of information to client

3–15   Whereas in the United States factors tend to take the view that the client should not be concerned with the state of the sales ledger provided that they are obtaining approval in respect of every invoice and are looking to the factor alone for payment, factors in the United Kingdom have been constrained by market forces to furnish their clients with the fullest up to date information regarding customer accounts. This applies notwithstanding the fact that it is to the factor's account with the client that the client must look for his incoming funds because the factor has become the client's only debtor as regards that part of the client's business within the scope of the factoring arrangement. This feedback of information is particularly important if approvals are given by means of limits of outstanding indebtedness.[16] Accordingly, most factors in the provision of the full service or recourse or maturity factoring, whereby the client is relieved from the administration of the sales ledger, provide at the minimum monthly lists of outstanding debts analysed by the due dates for payment of the items. Such lists often provide additional information regarding disputed items, the current credit limit for each debtor and a note of how much is unapproved and consequently with recourse to the client. Although such a list will be invaluable as a guide to the pattern of the client's sales and the payment habits of the customers and will allow the client to locate the problems of slow payments where these are indicated generally by an increase in the value of debts in relation to sales, the sending of such a list once a month, or even once a week, may in many industries not provide the instant

---

[15] See para.7–10 below.
[16] See paras 3–13 and 3–14 above.

information necessary to enable the client to decide whether or not to release a delivery. As a result, most factors now provide a terminal in the client's office by which the client may have access, among other things, to any account on the sales ledger.

2. PROCEDURES IN AGENCY FACTORING AND INVOICE DISCOUNTING

The start of the arrangement

In the case of undisclosed factoring (or invoice discounting without **3–16** recourse),[17] or in some cases of agency factoring in which the factor is accepting debts without recourse, the procedures described in para.3–04 above must be adopted to enable the factor to make detailed credit assessments of all but the smallest debtors. In the usual case of invoice discounting or agency factoring with full recourse to the client, many factors do not assess individual debtor accounts, but protect themselves against the insolvency of debtors by relying on a good spread of the business and a provision to protect themselves against undue concentration of a large proportion of sales on individual debtors.[18] In such a case, the procedures for a detailed examination of each individual debtor account is not required. Other factors will expect to establish credit limits for all the debtors over a certain size in order to provide for the eligibility of debts for prepayments, or the factor may rely on a credit insurance policy and the limits approved under it.[19]

In no case, however, will it be necessary for the ledger to be transferred to **3–17** the factor's records because it is the essence of these arrangements that the client retains the sales ledger function carrying it out as agent for the factor who has become the owner of the debts. However, the clients can download its sales ledger information to the factor electronically on a daily or weekly basis with the knowledge that it cannot get lost in the post. The factor will nevertheless expect the ledger to be kept on an open item system so that he may ensure that the administration of it and the control of credit are up to the standards which he requires; in some cases this may entail an analysis of the ledger and a change of system to enable the client to qualify for the service and this alone may be of benefit to the client. In most cases the factor will rely, for the notification of the debts outstanding at the start, on a copy of the client's sales ledger control account showing the position in total together with an aged list of debtors; that is a list of balances on the sales

---

[17] See para.1–55 above.
[18] See para.3–24 below.
[19] See Ch.14.

ledger analysed by the due dates of the invoices. The aged list will assist the factor in determining which debts may be disputed and which debtors need examining from the point of view of credit assessment. The factor will credit the client with the full value of the debts outstanding at the start of factoring and allow the client to draw the agreed percentage of that credit after deducting from it the total of ineligible debts (*i.e.* disputed debts, debts in excess of any specified credit limit or more than specified number of days overdue). In effect, the amount of the ineligible debts becomes a part of the factor's retention; the remainder of it is the percentage of the aggregate amounts of eligible debts that remains after deducting the prepayment percentage from 100 per cent.

Continuing arrangements in invoice discounting and agency factoring

3–18   In most such arrangements, the factor will not expect to be notified by the provision of the individual invoices. The client will usually send a notification of total sales, returns, discounts allowed and other adjustments each week and the factor will make available the agreed percentage of the net amount of such notification (less his charges) and the equivalent of the remaining percentage of the debts settled by customers during that week. At the end of each month the factor will be furnished with an up to date aged list of debtors on the basis of which he will be able to adjust that part of the retention representing ineligible debts; for example, this enables the client to have the benefit of a drawing against any disputed amount in respect of which the dispute has been settled in his favour, but it creates a new retention against any new dispute. The factor will also be furnished with a copy of the client's sales ledger control account at the end of each month so that he may reconcile these figures with his own records and most factors arrange for occasional visits to the client's offices by members of the factor's staff in order to be reassured of the correctness of the records and the effectiveness of the control of credit. The client will be required to furnish the factor regularly with a copy of the client's purchase ledger so that the factor may check for any suppliers cross-claims against a purchase from the client.

Recovery of payments from the debtors

3–19   In confidential invoice discounting, notices to the debtors of the assignments of the debts is not required except in the case of a serious breach of the agreement by the client or its insolvency. Accordingly, unlike the position in disclosed factoring, the proceeds of the debts do not flow automatically to the factor. In order to enable the factor to make recoveries from the debtors, it is provided that collections by the client are held in trust for the factor and are made available to the factor either by being paid into a trust account, in the name of the client but for the benefit of the factor, or by being paid in by the client direct to the factor's own account through the branch of the factor's bank nearest to the client. In both methods the charges for the collection of cheques are borne by the client either by inclusion in the factor's charges to the client or, in the case of a trust account, by instructions to the bank to debit such charges to the client's normal account. In order to enable the client to pay direct to the factor's account cheques made payable to client (including cheques crossed "account payee" and consequently not transferable[20]) without the task of endorsing them, the bank will normally accept an indemnity and instruction from the client or an indemnity from the factor. Such an indemnity is also usually given in the case of disclosed factoring in view of the number of debtors who persist in sending their cheques made payable to the client.

There are two methods by which the factor may recover payments from the debtors in agency factoring. Often, although the client is administering the sales ledger and sending out statements and reminders to debtors, the notices by the client to the debtor may be in the usual form by which the debtor is instructed to pay to the factor direct; in this method, the factor will recover direct from the debtors as in the case of full or recourse factoring. Alternatively, if the factor wishes not to carry out the function of processing the incoming remittances, the debtor may be sent a notice of assignment but be instructed to pay the client as agent for the factor; the funds are then passed to the factor in the same way as in invoice discounting as described above. The disadvantage of the first method is that, in order to enable the client to administer the sales ledger and follow up for payments, the factor must keep the client constantly informed of payments; this is normally done by the daily sending of copies of remittance advices from debtors. In the second method, the notice must be somewhat equivocal and it detracts considerably from the benefits to the factor of such notices.[21] As such notice must mention the agency of the client, it is important that it should also include a notice that the client is not authorised to bind the factor in any way. **3–20**

3. DISPUTES AND CONCENTRATION IN ALL TYPES OF FACTORING

The disposal of disputes

It is important that both the factor and the client should be aware at the earliest stage of any failure of a debtor to accept the goods or service and the invoice by which it is represented giving rise to a debt sold to the factor. A **3–21**

---

[20] Cheques Act 1992, s.1 and see para.10–35 below.
[21] See para.8–09 below.

factor normally has the right to include the amount of any such disputed or queried debt in his retention and, ultimately, to have the debt repurchased by the client. If the client fails to inform the factor at the earliest time of such disputes or queries, the factor may lose confidence in the debts notified to him and may require some increase in his retention and this may lead to the factoring arrangement as a whole being subject to criticism as not providing the amount of finance which was envisaged at the outset. On the other hand, if the client is not informed of any dispute notified by the debtor to the factor, but not to the client, there will be a delay in the resolution of the disputes and such delays often impede such resolution. Furthermore, in the case of any form of non-recourse factoring, it is not unusual for the agreement to provide for the factor to be no longer responsible for the credit risk in respect of a debt which is, or has been, disputed even if it is approved. For these reasons and because disputes may hamper collection efforts in respect of undisputed debts on the same account, the importance of early disposal of disputes is of prime importance to the satisfactory working of the factoring arrangements.

Dispute notices

3–22   In the full service or recourse or maturity factoring, it is very often only on a demand for payment being sent by the factor that the debtor notifies that he has not accepted the goods or service or the invoice. In such case it is a normal procedure for the factor to send to the client a notice specifying the debtor, the invoice and the reason for the withholding of payment together with a copy of any relevant communication from the debtor. The factor will expect then to be kept informed regularly of the progress of the efforts of the client to settle the matter. If payment is not made by the debtor or a credit note is not issued by the client within a reasonable period, normally in domestic trade a matter of months, then the debt will be the subject of recourse.

The exercise of recourse

3–23   Even when a debt becomes the subject of the right of recourse, it is not advisable for any factor who has accepted the sales ledger function to give effect to the recourse and reassign the debt to the client until such time as it is clear that it should be credited out of the sales ledger. Whilst retaining the debt on his records and refraining from giving notice of any reassignment, the factor will, in most circumstances, be fully protected. In the full service or maturity factoring, it is normal for disputed debts, even if previously approved, to become unapproved and consequently the factor will no longer be responsible for the credit risk; and where prepayments have been made, he will normally have the right to make a retention in respect of the disputed item against the next debts notified to him. The early exercise of recourse in respect of disputes means that, until the disputed items are to be credited, the factor is not performing the whole sales ledger function, which may have been a reason for the acceptance of factoring by the client. More important to the factor is the aggravation caused to debtors who, having received an introductory letter by which they are informed, in strong terms, that payments for the client's supplies must be made to the factor, are then given notice that certain invoices are to be paid to their supplier, the client. Such aggravation is believed to have been the cause of the prohibition of assignments in the purchase orders of some large and powerful buyers of goods and services. It has then been known for such concerns to agree to make payments to a factor only on terms that payments must be made to the factor until the arrangement comes to an end. The right of recourse in respect of debts, which should still be kept on the ledger account, naturally arises more often in the case of recourse factoring in which recourse may be exercised at a specified time related to the date of the invoice whether the debt is disputed or not.

Concentrations

Closely allied to the problem of disputed debts is any concentration of a   **3–24** large proportion of the client's sales to one or a few debtors; it is likely to be a problem to a factor who is making prepayments. If a dispute arises in relation to a substantial part of the indebtedness of a debtor which constitutes as much or more than the retention held by the factor, the factor may consider the need to withhold payments against further invoices notified to him by the client. Such a step may put the client into acute difficulty by virtually stopping the cash flow of the business. In most cases, the matter would be settled by a compromise allowing the client sufficient resources to carry on his business, but the factor has to make a difficult decision as to whether the dispute may or may not indicate that all the products of the client are subject to some fault. Sometimes the withholding of payment by a large debtor may arise from an extraneous disagreement between the debtor and the client unconnected with the debt owing to the factor; or the debtor may hold up payment of the whole account on the grounds of one faulty delivery. In all such cases, the factor may find himself in the awkward position of having to make a judgement on the merits of the case and in having to decide between his own and his client's interests.

It is usually considered advisable for a factor to avoid finding himself in   **3–25** such a position by providing at the outset of the factoring arrangements that he will not be obliged to make prepayments in respect of any indebtedness of any one debtor which exceeds a specified percentage of the aggregate of outstanding debts purchased by him from the client. Such arrangements are referred to as "concentration limits" and are becoming more usual, particularly in recourse and agency factoring and invoice discounting. In full factoring or undisclosed factoring without recourse, the factor can protect himself by not making prepayments in respect of debts over credit limits. Most factors and invoice discounters will accept concentration limits of up to 20 per cent, but above this figure they will only approve a higher limit based on payment experience, the debtor's financial profile and the quality of the client's product or service as determined by the credit note percentage.

4. SOME NORMAL EXCLUSIONS FROM THE ARRANGEMENTS

3–26 Although factoring is normally arranged to include the whole of a client's sales (or in some cases the whole of the sales in a particular market or of a particular branch or division of the client) and although this applies whether the agreement is on a whole turnover or facultative basis,[22] there are certain debts which the factor may wish not to have notified to him. The principal type of debt of which the factor does not require notification comprises debts in respect of which the client cannot give all the warranties and undertakings required by the factoring agreement[23]; such debts include:

(1) debts arising from sales to the client's own suppliers which may result in a set-off available to the debtor against the factor[24];

(2) purported debts arising from contracts for delivery on sale or return;

(3) debts arising from sales on terms more liberal than those approved by the factor.

Other debts which are normally excluded from the arrangement include debts arising from sales to associates of the client and sales of goods to individuals for their personal or domestic use.

3–27 The exclusion of such debts from the factoring arrangements where the agreement is on a facultative basis[25] is a simple matter; the factor either requires that they should not be offered to him or he declines to accept them. In the case of an agreement of the whole turnover type,[26] a paradox arises: the agreement itself effects the transfer of ownership to the factor of all debts existing at the starting date and arising thereafter and the client is required to notify every debt. If the client notifies any such debts, he is deemed to have warranted that which he cannot warrant; if he does not notify them he is in breach of the agreement in that respect. The problem may be overcome

---

[22] See para.3–02 above.
[23] See Ch.10.
[24] See Ch.9.
[25] See para.7–08 below.
[26] See para.7–10 below.

by providing that any such debt shall be notified separately from other debts, that such separate notification shall not be deemed to constitute any warranties and that the factor shall have no obligation to make prepayments but shall have the right of recourse in respect of the debts included in them. The client should be required to state clearly in any such separate notification the reason why all the usual warranties cannot be given in respect of the debts included in it.

5. THE FACTOR'S CHARGES

The factor's charges to his client in most cases consist of an administration charge (or service or factoring charge or commission) and a discount for prepayments. In most cases the factor will endeavour to cover all the functions which he performs, except for the finance by way of prepayments, in the administration charge. However, in some cases, additional charges for specific aspects are made; in particular, in the case of export sales, any bank charges for the collection of cheques or the exchange of currencies into sterling are usually charged additionally to the client. Where a client's pattern of business is such that he needs to apply frequently for the opening of new accounts or credit approvals on them and the number is out of proportion to a relatively small volume of sales, the factor may charge for the maintenance or opening of such accounts. **3–28**

There is, however, an important exception to the absorbing by the factor (within the administration charge) of the cost of all the functions of and related to sales accounting. It is normal that the costs of legal proceedings for the recovery of a debt or part of a debt, which is subject to recourse, should be borne by the client. **3–29**

The administration charge

By whatever expression the charge is labelled, it is normally calculated *ad valorem* as a percentage on the notified value of the debts included in the factoring arrangements before the deduction of any discounts, credit notes or other allowances granted to the debtors. The charge is usually to cover the functions undertaken by the factor (*e.g.* sales accounting or the acceptance of the risk of bad debts) and as a commitment fee for the provision of finance following the growth of the business without formal limit. As a result, the charge will vary widely according to the nature of the factoring service provided. **3–30**

In the case of invoice discounting or agency factoring with full recourse, whereby the client retains the accounting function as agent for the factor, in addition to acting as a commitment fee the charge will often cover only the additional bank charges which the factor may bear by the collection of cheques into his own bank account. However, some factors have arranged **3–31** for global insurance to cover them and their clients against the loss of the debts by reason of the destruction of the records by fire or other perils. Such insurance is necessary to protect the factor against the loss of documentary evidence of the debts (orders and delivery receipts) even if there is adequate back up for the data. It also protects the client because the debts lost in such circumstances would be the subject of recourse. The cost of such insurance is sometimes included in the administration charge. In invoice discounting or agency factoring the percentage charge is often a fraction of one per cent.

3–32   Where any form of non-recourse factoring is provided, the administration charge must include an element to cover the risk of bad debts and this element is related to the appropriate credit insurance premium and, thus, varies according to the industry, the spread and quality of the debtors and the average period of credit taken by debtors. This element in the charge may be kept down by the expedient of providing that only the excess over a fixed small amount in respect of any one bad debt loss will be accepted by the factor without recourse; by this means, there will be avoided the "pound swapping" of a higher administration charge against the factor's acceptance of the normally expected small losses. For the full service, recourse factoring or maturity factoring, in which the factor carries out the sales ledger function, the charge must cover the administration of the sales ledger and the collection of payments; this element will vary according to the number of invoices, credit notes, payments and debtor accounts for a given volume of sales. For the full service the charge typically varies between 0.5 and 2.5 per cent according to the variables mentioned above and the total volume of sales of the client; the charges for any variation of the service (such as recourse factoring), where the client retains some of the functions, should be somewhat less.

Minimum and additional administration charges

3–33   It is natural that the cost to the factor of carrying out the sales ledger administration and collection functions, as well as providing finance by way of prepayments, is to some extent reduced proportionately to the sales volume by the scale of the operation. It is much less expensive for the factor to provide his services to five clients each with a sales volume of £10 million than to 50 whose turnover is only £1 million each. For this reason, two variations of the strict application of an *ad valorem* method of calculation are often used. The first is the agreement of a minimum aggregate charge; by such a provision, if the aggregate value of debts sold to the factor during any specified period (month, quarter or year) should not produce a specified aggregate of charges, then the client is obliged to pay an additional fee to make up the difference. Normally, such charge would be based on an annual turnover but charged on account monthly and adjusted at the end of the year. Secondly, in order to provide a downward sliding scale of total charge as the client's volume of sales increases, it is sometimes arranged for the client to pay a fixed fee each month and for the *ad valorem* charge to be fixed at a percentage less than normal. The latter method of charging is more usual in invoice discounting where the factor takes on no administrative function; indeed there are factors who will charge a fixed administration charge only for that service or rely only on the discount charge and waive any administration charge.

Refactoring charges

In many recourse factoring arrangements, it is provided that the factor **3–34** will normally exercise his right of recourse in respect of any debt which remains outstanding a specific number of days after invoice date or after the end of the month in which the invoice is raised. In this way, the factor is obliged to carry out the sales accounting function and collection for a limited period. In many such cases, in order to relieve the client of all these functions, the factor will be prepared to continue to account for any debt and his or her efforts to collect it after the date when recourse is due and, for the continuation of the acceptance of these functions, the factor will make an additional *ad valorem* charge in respect of each such debt retained for each month in which it remains outstanding.

The discount charge

The business of purchasing debts payable *in futuro* with the immediate **3–35** payment of part or all of the purchase price has, on several occasions, been distinguished by the courts from the lending of money on the security of the debts.[27] Such discounting of debts postulates that the purchaser will be recompensed for his providing finance for the period from early payment until settlement of the debt by deducting a discount in the calculation of the purchase price of the debts. The courts have also recognised that "the amount of the discount is no doubt often calculated by reference to the amount of interest which the payer calculates his money would have earned if he had deferred payment to the due date".[28] However, it has also been considered that, as opposed to interest which accrues from day-to-day, a discount is fixed as a deduction from the purchase price at the time of the purchase.[29] As it is important to the factor that all his procedures should be consistent with the purchase of debts,[30] some of the early factors in the United Kingdom, also taking their cue from American practice, calculated the discount to be applied to the purchase of every debt in advance to a fixed

---

[27] See paras 7–19 *et seq.* below.
[28] *Chow Yoong Hong v Choong Fah Rubber Manufactory* [1962] A.C. 209, *per* Lord Devlin at p.217.
[29] *ibid.*
[30] See paras 7–19 *et seq.* below.

maturity date. The maturity date was established by reference to the average period of credit taken by the debtors of the client over the previous one or two years. The discount was deducted from the notified value of each batch of invoices by reference to the weighted average of the invoice dates; the client was then allowed back interest on the undrawn part of the purchase price. This method of calculating the discount provided certainty for the client and a discipline for the factor to keep his collections within the agreed maturity date.

3–36   The system was found to create a certain amount of conflict between the client and the factor. It did not allow for flexibility to the client in the granting of terms; the client gained no benefit from sales on shorter terms and the factor would be reluctant to agree to latitude to a favoured customer of the client. Furthermore, it meant that, in order to keep the ledger as a whole within the limits of the maturity date, the factor needed to exercise recourse in respect of a disputed debt as soon as the dispute was notified with the disadvantages outlined in para.3–23 above. Some clients considered that their factors were using undue pressure on their customers for early payment (in order to obtain payments before the maturity dates) and were thereby causing them loss of business. For these reasons and owing to the difficulty of making an accurate forecast of the payment habits of debtors in the business environment of the United Kingdom (as opposed to the more disciplined payment habits of debtors in the United States), the discount charge is now normally calculated on a day-to-day basis at a rate per cent per annum on the amount of each prepayment until it is recovered by settlement of the debt by the customer. For practical purposes the charges are normally calculated in aggregate. According to the accounting method used, the calculation may be on the balance on a current account or on the difference between the aggregate of outstanding debts and the unpaid balance of the purchase price of those debts owed by the factor to the client; the amount on which the charge is calculated is often referred to by factors as the "funds in use". Although the charge is specified as a discount to be deducted in calculating the purchase price of the debts, it cannot be calculated in advance. For administrative purposes, the purchase price is credited to the client's account before the deduction of the charge and the charge is normally debited monthly.

3–37   From a review of the cases, in which discounting has been distinguished from lending,[31] it seems reasonable to infer that, apart from the method of calculating the finance charge, there are other distinguishing features. Of these, a principal test is whether or not (as there must be in the case of lending on security) there is an equity of redemption[32]; and, in this respect and in every other respect, most factoring arrangements are consistent with

---

[31] See Ch.7, n.49.
[32] This is explained in para.7–22 below.

the purchase of the debts. In view of the practical and commercial convenience of charging the discount on a day-to-day basis, most factors now
charge their finance charge in this way, relying on the other distinguishing
features of their activities to ensure that they are in practice purchasing
debts.[33]

The method is acceptable to the client in its providing flexibility for him in **3-38**
the granting of credit. The factor does not need the discipline of a fixed
maturity date to encourage him to obtain early settlement of debts; competition and the additional risk of the debtor's default are two spurs to the
factor's performance in this respect. The factor also may wish to keep his
funds in use in each client's business to the minimum in order that he can
provide his services as widely as possible for the investment of a given
amount of funds.

Collection date or maturity date

Although most factors now calculate the discount charge on a day-to-day **3-39**
basis, there are two separate methods of determining the "funds in use" on
which the charge should be calculated. The two methods derive not from a
difference as to the concept of funds in use: in both cases, this is the difference between the aggregate notified value of outstanding debts and the
unpaid balance of their purchase prices. It is the amount paid on account by
the factor in addition to any charges to his client less his recoveries from
debtors. The different methods of calculation derive from two separate
concepts as to when a debt ceases to be outstanding for this purpose. The
first concept is that a debt remains outstanding until it is paid by the receipt
of cleared funds into the bank account of the factor (the collection date).
The second concept is that a debt ceases to be outstanding on a maturity
date; such maturity date is normally calculated in the manner referred to
above[34] and it might be expected that this method would have the disadvantages of that early method of charging.[35] However, the difference is
that factors who now employ the maturity date system of charging reserve
the right to make additional discount charges on any excess of outstanding
debts and to make an allowance for any shortfall; it is often also provided
that the factor should be able to adjust the maturity period during the
currency of the agreement. Furthermore, although the initial amount of the
discount could be calculated in advance, it is often calculated on a day-to-
day basis to avoid the need to credit back interest in respect of undrawn
funds. Closely allied to this question is the date for the payment of the
balance of the purchase price of debts, that is the purchase price after
allowing for any prepayment. Such payments are made either on the

---

[33] See also paras 7–19 *et seq.* below.
[34] See para.3–35 above.
[35] See para.3–36 above.

collection date or the maturity date to coincide with the method used for the calculation of funds in use.[36]

6. CLIENT ACCOUNTS AND PAYMENT BY THE FACTOR

3–40   There are two methods of accounting between the factor and his client which are in use or have been used and which are consistent with the factor's purchase of and ownership of the debts. One of these methods is suitable for payment of the balance of the purchase price of each debt on the collection date[37] and the other for payment on a maturity date.[38] The importance of a system of accounting between the factor and the client which is consistent with the purchase of debts as opposed to lending on the security of them is apparent from the remarks in para.3–35 above.

Accounting: payment on collection date[39]

3–41   In this system there is one account between the factor and his client and this is kept strictly in accordance with the purchase of debts by the factor. The account, normally labelled the "current account",[40] is kept in the same way as a purchase ledger account kept by a purchaser of goods which would have entered on it credits for the goods purchased and debits for payments by the purchaser for the supplies and which would show a balance representing the amount owed by the purchaser. The current account therefore has credited to it the purchase price of the debts purchased by the factor; the purchase price is the notified invoice amount of debts less any settlement discount or other allowance to the debtor and less, in some cases, the factor's charges. As the amount of any discount or allowance and the amount of the factor's discount charge cannot be ascertained until some time after the notification of the debt, the credit on notification is usually of the notified amount less the administration charge only and the other items to be deducted are debited as soon as ascertained. Also credited is any other amount payable by the factor to the client; *e.g.* any amount recovered by the factor in relation to a debt which has been repurchased by the client by reason of recourse.

3–42   The following items are debited to the current account:

---

[36] See above.
[37] See para.3–39 above.
[38] *ibid.*
[39] See App.2.
[40] For the advantage in law of keeping the accounts by this method, see paras 10–02 and 10–03 below, and *Re Charge Card Services Ltd* [1987] Ch.150.

(1) Any payments (including prepayments) made by the factor to or on behalf of the client.

(2) The amounts by which the purchase price of any debts are to be reduced or extinguished whether such amounts are represented by credit notes or not; such amounts may arise by reason of recourse or discounts or other allowances granted to debtors.

(3) Any part of the factor's charges which have not been deducted from the notified amount of any debt in making the credit to the account.

(4) Any other amount payable by the client to the factor (for example, amounts payable to the factor for supplies to the client by another client of the factor and consequently assigned to the factor).

The balance in credit on the account at any time represents the unpaid balance of the purchase price of the debts notified to the factor. The client will be at liberty to draw that balance subject to the agreed retention (a percentage, inverse to the prepayment percentage, of the debts eligible for prepayment in addition to the equivalent of the full amount of any that are not eligible).

Availability reports

Whilst most clients now have on-line access to their accounts with the factor, a hard copy of the current account is normally submitted to the client once a month. **3–43**

The availability of funds at any time (the amount which the client may draw by way of prepayment on account of the purchase price of the debts sold to the factor) is the excess of the balance on the current account in the client's favour over the retention at that time. The retention is the equivalent to a percentage of the debts outstanding which are eligible for prepayment at that time in addition (normally) to the full amount of those that are disputed or otherwise ineligible for prepayment. The amount of the availability is made known to the client on a daily basis.[41] As such information is required frequently, it is made known by some factors by on line access for the client to the factor's computer data; some factors also have facilities for the client to request by similar means the transfer of funds. **3–44**

The memorandum account

This account which may be labelled "the discounting account" or (perhaps more aptly) simply "funds in use" is referred to as a memorandum **3–45**

---

[41] See App.3.

account because *it is not an account in the accepted sense of the term showing the position between two parties and arising from the transactions between them.* The current account shows the position between the factor and his client; the individual debtor accounts show the position between the factor and the debtors. The memorandum account is debited with payments by the factor to, or on behalf of, the client and with the factor's charges and credited with payments from debtors. There should be entered on the account any entry in the factor's records which does not affect both the current account with the client and an account with a debtor; consequently no credits for invoices or debits for credit notes or discounts or for the recourse of debts are entered on it. The balance should represent the difference between the net total of the sales ledger for the particular client (*i.e.* after deduction of any credit balances) and the credit balance on the current account. The account represents the extent to which the outstanding debts are financed by the factor, while the credit balance on the current account represents the amount which remains to be financed by the client. The purpose of the account is for the calculation of the discount charge on the daily balance. If a credit balance emerges on the account, the factor may credit to the client a discount allowance.

Accounting: payment on a maturity date[42]

3–46   Payment of the balance of the purchase price of each debt on a fixed maturity date provides the client with the advantage of the ability to forecast his cash flow more accurately than where payment is made on the collection date. A typical system of accounting between the factor and the client, where this method of payment is used, consists of three accounts and is as follows:

3–47   **(1) A sales ledger control account.** This is not part of client accounting; the debts purchased by the factor are owned by him and the sales ledger comprises the accounts between the factor and the debtors. However, the account is used as part of the accounting information provided to the client in place of the memorandum account used in the system described above and partly also in place of availability reports. All entries on the factor's sales ledger in relation to the business of the particular client (comprising in the main invoices and credit notes notified to him and payments received by him) are entered on the account in aggregate. The balance on the account at any time represents the net total of the factor's sales ledger in respect of debts purchased from the client.

3–48   **(2) Debts purchased account.** The gross notified invoice value of debts is credited to this account as soon as they are notified to the factor; the

---

[42] As this system is rarely used in the UK now, no example has been shown in the appendices.

corresponding debit will have been to the sales ledger control account. There are no other entries on this account, except for the transfer to the credit of the current account described below by debit to this account of the notified value of each batch of invoices on their maturity date. The balance in credit on the account represents the aggregate notified value of debts purchased by the factor from the client which have not reached their maturity dares irrespective of any payment by the debtors or credit note issued by the client.

(3) The current account. The notified value of the debts purchased by the factor is credited to this account when they have reached their maturity date. The account is debited with any payments (including prepayments) to or on behalf of the client. It is also debited with all the other items chargeable to the client as are listed in para.3–42 above. It is apparent that, as payment of the balance of the purchase price of debts (after deducting prepayments) is payable under this system on their maturity dates, a nil balance on this account would indicate that no prepayments had been taken in respect of the outstanding debts; any debit balance will represent the aggregate amount of prepayments drawn against the debts remaining outstanding. **3–49**

If the aggregate value of outstanding debts as notified to the factor and represented by the balance on the sales ledger control account is larger than the balance on the debts purchased account (representing the total of notified unmatured debts), then collections are being made on average after the maturity date. As a corollary, if the balance on the sales ledger control account is less than the balance on the debts purchased account, the collections are being made, on average, before the maturity dates. It is therefore possible to determine the actual funds in use by putting the three accounts together. By adding to the current account balance the difference between the sales ledger control account balance and the debts purchased account balance (if the former is larger), or deducting the difference (if the former is smaller) the result will be the amount of funds in use. For this purpose, the accounts may be combined as follows: **3–50**

Example 1

Current account balance-debit (prepayments and charges uncollected)	£100,000
Sales ledger control account-debit (net total of sales ledger)	£350,000
Debts purchased account-credit (total of unmatured debts)	£325,000
Funds in Use	£125,000

In the above example the client has been paid £100,000 before the maturity of the debts and the funds in use have been increased by £25,000 because this is the extent to which the client has been paid on maturity for debts not paid by the debtors.

Example 2

Current account balance-debit (prepayments and charges uncollected)	£100,000
Sales ledger control account debit (net total of sales ledger)	£310,000
Debts purchased account-credit (total of unmatured debts)	£325,000
Funds in Use	£85,000

In this example the actual total of the sales ledger is less than the aggregate value of notified debts as they would have been if they had remained, on average, outstanding until the maturity dates; they are being collected on average faster than had been estimated and the amount of funds provided by the factor is to that extent less.

Calculation of discount charge

3–51   In the system by which payment of the balance of the purchase price is payable on maturity, the discount charge may be calculated on the balance on the current account which represents the aggregate of prepayments in respect of debts whose maturity dates have not arrived (whether they have been paid or not). However, in order to provide for flexibility, many factors using this system will make an adjustment for average payments earlier or later than the maturity dates. The combination of the accounts under this system provides an equivalent to the memorandum account[43] under the arrangements where the balance of the purchase price is to be paid on the collection date. Therefore, in order to avoid separate adjustments, the discount charge is often calculated on a day to day basis on the balance of the combined account. Thus, the client will gain the benefit of fast collections and suffer the penalty of delays in debtor payments as he does when payment is made on collection. If the current account had been in credit to a greater extent than any excess of the sales ledger control over the debts purchased account, then the funds in use are a negative amount. In such

---

[43] See para.3–45 above.

case, it is not unusual for the factor to allow the client a discount allowance on the negative balance.

Availability[44]

By reference to the current account and the debts purchased account, the client using this system will be able to ascertain the extent to which he has drawn prepayments and the amount of the unpaid balance of the purchase price of debts. But, in order that he may be able to determine the retention and thus the amount available to him from time to time, he will need to know the balance on the sales ledger account; in most cases it will be necessary for the client to have a report, as described in para.3–43 above, because he will need to know the amounts of ineligible debts outstanding in respect of which there may be a full retention. Where this system of accounting is used, the amount of the availability may be made known to the client at any time by direct access to the factor's computer data as in the case of the first system described above.

3–52

Accounting: another system

A very simple method of accounting now appears to be in common use among factors providing recourse or agency factoring or invoice discounting. The factor maintains two accounts. First, he maintains a sales ledger control account in the name of the client on which are recorded in total all the transactions on the accounts of debtors. The other account is the "current account" to which are debited payments made to, or on behalf of, the client and the factor's charges; to this account are credited payments from the debtors notwithstanding that they are factor's recoveries. As a result, the current account will reflect the same balance as the memorandum account described above,[45] but in this case it is regarded as an account between the factor and his client. As is the case in both the other accounting systems described above, in order to know the availability of funds which he may draw, the client will, in most cases, need an availability report based on the total of eligible and ineligible debts outstanding.[46] In this system the discount charge is normally calculated on the balance on the current account which represents the funds in use. Although the method of accounting is simple, for its use in England and Wales (or any country whose law in relation to these matters is based on English law), the disadvantage is that it should be viewed in the light of the comments in paras 7–19 to 7–25 below. An account with the client, on which payments by the factor (to the client) are debited and payments received from *debtors* are

3–53

---

[44] See also para.3–43 above.
[45] See para.3–45 above.
[46] See para.3–43 above.

credited, appears to record a situation in which the sums received from the debtors belong to the client and not the factor and that the factor is recovering from *the client*, as a repayment, the funds which he has paid in purchasing the debts. In this system the current account is the equivalent of the amount overdrawn from time to time on a current account with a bank. If the debts have been purchased outright by the factor, then such recoveries are the factor's monies and should not be credited to a client account other than a purely memorandum account which is *not* an account between the parties. However, in order to overcome this difficulty, most factors using this system in the UK show the equivalent of the daily balance on the sales ledger control account as a credit balance on an account with the factor, a "debts purchased" balance; it is apparent that the sales ledger control account if reversed, as to debits and credits, will show as a credit balance in favour of the client the value of debts purchased by the factor and remaining outstanding. The entries of the proceeds of the debts to the credit of the sales ledger control account and, at the same time, as a debit to reduce the value of the outstanding debts purchased will together represent a transfer from debts purchased to the current account of debts paid. The balance on the current account, representing the payments made by the factor against the outstanding debts only, must be deducted from the balance of debts purchased to show the unpaid balance owing by the factor to the client at any time.[47]

Methods of payment

3–54   For many years after the introduction of factoring into the United Kingdom, the usual method of payment (whether a prepayment or a payment on the maturity or collection date) was by cheque direct to the bank account of the client. In the early days, most factoring companies calculated the discount charges from the dates of the cheques sent in payment to the client (not the dates when they were presented to the factor's bank) until the clearance of the debtors' cheques. As interest rates increased, this question of the value dating of the cheques was of concern to the clients and prospective clients. As a result, several of the factors changed their practice and began to allow for the value dating of the cheques sent in payment to the client in the calculation of the discount charge. Others overcame the problem to some extent by paying by telegraphic transfer to the client's bank; however, this was not entirely satisfactory owing to the cost of such method of transferring funds and the limit below which such method is not acceptable to the banks. At present, practices vary[48] but many of the leading factors will now transfer funds electronically and ensure that their discount

---

[47] See App.4.
[48] See para.5–08 below.

charge is calculated from the date of receipt of funds by the client. Routine payments are very often made by Bankers' Automated Clearing System (BACS) which is a low cost method of transferring funds providing credit of cleared funds to the client on the second day after the payment has been initiated. For the provision of value on the same day Clearing House Automated Payment System (CHAPS) may be used; in this case, the cost is usually covered by a specific charge to the client.

CHAPTER 4

THE FACTOR'S RELATIONS WITH THE DEBTORS

4–01 In most circumstances there are no contractual relations between the factor and the debtors. The factor's rights to collect payment from the debtors derives purely from the purchase of the debts by the factor and their assignment to him. It would be possible for the factor to become a party to the client's contracts of sale with a debtor by means of a novation (an agreement among the client, the debtor and the factor) substituting the factor as a party in place of the client; but such an arrangement would be administratively impracticable because it would require the debtor's execution of the novation agreement in each case and the factor has no wish to become a party to the contracts of sale and thereby accept responsibilities as well as rights under them. Such considerations also influenced some early factors in changing from factoring arrangements by which, instead of buying the debts, the factor bought the goods (the subject of a sale by his client) from his client and resold them through the client as the factor's agent. In a few cases, such an arrangement had been used to provide a commercial effect similar to factoring; by paying 80 per cent of the price of the goods immediately to the client and allowing credit to the debtors, the factor relieved his client from the need to provide trade credit.[1]

4–02 The factor's rights, deriving from his purchase of the debts, and the debtor's countervailing rights are analysed in Ch.9; this chapter deals with the usual procedures for the collection of payment of the assigned debts from the debtors in any case in which the factor has responsibility for this function (*i.e.* full, recourse or maturity factoring). These procedures start in the client's office with the acceptance of orders and the production of the source documents (invoices and credit notes), continue in the factor's office with the sales accounting and collection and, if such collection procedures fail, may finally end in legal proceedings.

---

[1] See also paras 1–05 and 1–06 above.

1. NORMAL COLLECTION PROCEDURES

The client's terms and conditions of sale

Provided that there is no agreement between the client and the debtor, **4–03** whether in the contract of sale or otherwise, by which any debt arising from a contract of sale between the client and the debtor should not be assigned,[2] the factor obtains, by the assignment of the debts to him, the absolute right to be paid without the need for the consent of the debtor.[3] However, the factor obtains no better rights than those of the client under the contract of sale. The factor may collect only according to the agreed terms. Accordingly, it is necessary for the factor to examine carefully his client's standard terms of sale, particularly as regards the due dates for payment and maximum settlement discounts to be allowed and to be advised of any variations. It is normal for the factor to have stipulated in his factoring agreement the most liberal credit terms to be allowed by the client and for the right to approve any other terms; as a purchaser the factor should be able to determine precisely the rights that are to be assigned to him.

Many large buyers, such as mail order houses, department stores and **4–04** government departments will purchase only on their own standard terms of purchase and it is essential that these should be examined in respect of customers existing at the outset of factoring and arising thereafter. Unfortunately, where the buyer purchases on his standard terms and the seller (the factor's client) considers that the sale was on his own standard terms of sale, it is not always an easy matter to determine whose terms prevail. This has been referred to as the "battle of the forms".[4] A buyer may order goods on his own standard-term conditions, and, as likely as not, the seller will purport to accept the order on his standard terms, which in all probability will be inconsistent with those of the buyer. The approach of English law is to say that the seller's "acceptance" of the buyer's order is a counter-offer (since to be effective an acceptance must be the "mirror image" of the offer, *i.e.* must be unqualified[5]), and, if the buyer proceeds with the contract without further comment, he is taken to have assented by conduct to the counter-offer thus made. This is so even if the buyers conditions had contained a clause providing that those were to override any inconsistent provisions in the seller's terms: for ex hypothesi, the seller, in invoking his own conditions, has rejected the buyers clause.[6] In short, English law adopts the "last shot" approach. Acceptance by conduct applies to a counter-offer as

---

[2] For the effect of such a ban on assignments see paras 9–36 to 9–38 below.
[3] See para.7–06 below.
[4] *Butler Machine Tool Co Ltd v Ex-Cell-O Corporation (England) Ltd* [1979] 1 All E.R. 965, CA.
[5] *Tinn v Hoffman & Co* (1873) 29 L.T. 271.
[6] See Goode, *Commercial Law* (3rd ed., 2004), p.87, as at p.142, n.21.

much as to an original offer, and is inferred from the counter-offerees subsequent acts in furtherance of the transaction.[7] However, in many cases, the events would not have followed this pattern, and, ideally, the client should obtain the customer's signed acknowledgement of his standard terms of sale before trading begins. It might well be possible for such a document to be included in any new customer's application for credit terms so that such terms would be granted only if the acknowledgement were to be signed.

The raising of source documents

4–05   At the outset, and during the currency of the factoring agreement on the opening of any new debtor account by the factor, it is essential that he should ascertain the exact legal name of the debtor (*i.e.* the name of the sole proprietor, partners, members or company where a trading name is used). Such information should be readily available to the factor's client; in accordance with the provisions of the Business Names Act 1985, the full names of the partners or individual owning the business and an address for the service of legal proceedings must be shown on most form of business communication from the debtor and be exhibited at its principal place of business. Similar provisions apply to the registered name of any company and its registered office, whether or not it is using a business name other than the name under which it is registered.[8] In view of the probable clog on recovery proceedings, which may be caused by the absence of the identity of the owner or owners of a debtor's business, factors should not accept as approved for credit or eligible for prepayment any debt in respect of which these details are not made available to him by the client. It is also important, not only from the point of view of the factor, but also for the client's benefit, that the exact terms and conditions of any sale should be determined and that any invoice (and the copy sent to the factor) should accord with those terms. If meticulous attention is not paid to these matters, aggravation may be caused to debtors by incorrect due dates on the factor's statements and requests for payment of items which are not due and this may result in damage to customer relations. Such errors may also result in delays in collection procedures and, ultimately, in a defence on the part of the debtor when proceedings for recovery are taken. The invoices (and the copies sent to the factor as notifications of the debts) purchased by him or with the offers to sell the debts will bear a notice of the assignment of the debts to the factor and instructions to pay the factor direct. Such notices should be printed on the invoice forms or, in the case of computer produced invoices, printed by the computer. It has been the practice of some factors to arrange for the notices to be placed on the invoices by means of sticky labels, but this

---

[7] *Butler Machine Tool Co Ltd v Ex-Cell-O Corporation (England) Ltd* [1979] 1 All E.R. 965.
[8] Companies Act 1985, ss.348, 349 and 351.

procedure may lead to omissions. If sticky labels are used, the Factor should receive a photocopy of the top copy original invoice as despatched in order to see that the notice of assignment has been endorsed.

The client should also ensure that credit notes for agreed allowances and **4–06** returned goods are promptly sent out to debtors and notified to the factor. It is also important that, on any such credit note that relates to a specific invoice, the invoice, in question should be identified so that the credit note may be properly allocated by the factor on the open item system, as described in Ch.2. If items that should be credited are left on the ledger, and thus on any statement sent to the debtor, payments may be delayed by queries from the debtor.

Collection from the debtors

The debtor, having been notified by the invoice (and in most cases by an **4–07** introductory letter from the client) of the factor's ownership of the debts, will then expect to receive a statement and requests for payment from the factor. Having been notified the correct details of the dates and amounts of the invoice and their due dates for payment, the factor will include these details in the input to his computer. The resulting sales ledger accounts, kept on an open item system as described in Ch.2, will produce clear statements listing the individual invoices and their due dates. It is advisable for the factor to include on each debtor statement a notice of assignment, not only as a reminder to the debtor, but also as some support for evidence of the debtor's receipt of notice. If the debtor denies receipt of notice, naturally the burden of proof of its actual receipt is on the factor and without an acknowledgement or, in the absence of its despatch by recorded delivery or by hand, evidence of the receipt of the invoice bearing a notice may not be a simple matter. The sending of such regular, prompt and correct statements is the foundation of the factor's procedures for the collection of payments by debtors; although some large concerns disregard statements and pay against invoices, many such business concerns still expect to receive a statement each month before making payments.[9]

From the data taken from the copy invoices and the input of cash receipts **4–08** and credit notes, lists of overdue accounts may be produced for the factor's staff from which they will be able to determine the next stage in the collection procedure. Such procedures, comprising several letters of increasing severity, are very often determined by agreement with the client at the outset and revised from time to time. Such agreement may cover the form of the letters, their timing and any special treatment to be given to particular customers. In this way, it is possible to ensure that such procedures are not

---

[9] For the current developing practice of large concerns by which invoices are sent to customers by electronic means see paras 4–58 and 4–60 below.

out of line with normal practices in the particular trade; and by this means the client may be able to influence to some extent the keeping of the funds in use (and consequently the discount charges) to a minimum without damaging customer relations. In the case of some larger buyers of goods and services, the factor may have to follow up for payment for a number of clients; in such cases, it may be that letters will not be effective and the client's staff may build up a relationship with the purchase ledger department of the buyer by telephone calls for payment of the supplies of several clients. By the creation of such relationship queries and disputes, which are often the cause of delays in payments, may be cleared up rapidly. Requests and demands for payment by fax or e-mail very often have more effect than letters.

4–09 Where, as is sometimes the case, standard letters are produced by the factor's computer at the prescribed number of days overdue, in case it is necessary in subsequent legal proceedings to show exactly what demands have been made, at the minimum there should be a record of the text of the standard letter and evidence of the addressee and the date on which it was sent. For a similar reason, careful notes should be kept of any telephone calls. The lack of any complaint about the goods may be useful evidence later. In the case of any letter sent by fax, evidence of its transmission should be available; such evidence of transmission to the right debtor is particularly important if the letter includes a notice of the assignment. Both sent and received emails should be either stored or printed off and placed on the file.

4–10 It is well known that many debtors resent demands (or even polite requests) for payment after the date when payment is due. Such an attitude seems illogical particularly from buyers who would be more than a little upset if the seller was late in delivering the goods and would make their feelings known to the seller in blunt terms. The due date for payment of supplies is part of the contract terms and, by paying late in breach of his obligations, the buyer inflicts the damage of increased finance charges on the seller. As such feelings do in fact exist, it is of the utmost importance that the factor's records show details of every invoice, correct in accordance with the contract of sale, so that no unjustified demands are made on the debtors. Such meticulous correctness must be founded on first class administration in the client's office as well as that of the factor and on close co-operation between the two. If any such unjustified demand is sent the reputation of both client and factor may suffer. The delays in paying suppliers by large and powerful buyers has been the subject of much publicity in recent years. This publicity combined with lobbying on behalf of small businesses has resulted in the enactment of statutory provisions for interest on overdue trade accounts. The Late Payment of Commercial Debts (Interest) Act 1998 (came into full effect on August 7, 2002). Suppliers may claim interest and administration charge for late payment.

4–11 The Act applies to contracts for the supply of goods or services where both parties are acting in the course of business with the exception of consumer credit agreements, contracts intended to operate by way of security and other contracts specified by statutory order. The rate of interest is set at 8 per cent over the Bank of England base rate, a rate high enough to deter debtors from financing themselves by such late payments and to enable sellers to carry such overdue debts by finance on normal overdraft terms. Such interest runs from the agreed due date for payment or, if none, from the 30th day after the goods are supplied or service completed or the invoice date if that is later.

Although the parties are unable to contract out of the statutory provi- **4–12** sions (unless the supply contract provides for a substantial remedy for late payment), the lack of use suggest it has not been the answer that the proponents of this legislation sought. The cost of credit to be granted by a supplier must be reflected in the price of the goods sold; if the buyer has the bargaining power to delay payments without being met by a refusal on the part of the seller to supply further at the same price, then the buyer, faced with a possible demand for interest, would have the power to reduce the price paid or to stipulate a later due date for payment. It is unlikely that a small supplier will risk upsetting a good customer by a demand for interest unless the supplier's product is such that it is essential to the buyer; and in that case payments are unlikely to be delayed in the absence of interest.

A supplier is not obliged to claim the interest and has six years within **4–13** which to decide whether to make a claim. In practice, such interest and administration charge is only applied in a collect out following the failure of the client where there is no ongoing business relation with customers to nurture.

A better influence on the payment habits of the customers, for a supplier **4–14** with an acceptable product at an attractive price, is for the supplier to make it clear at the outset (*i.e.* when the order is taken) that supplies will continue only if payments are made promptly. In the case of such a supplier who is the client of a factor, the factor should be requested to remind the buyer's accounts payable department of this requirement at the earliest stage and that the client's invoices are to be given priority for payment.

The next steps

When persuasion, cajolery or threats have failed to produce payment, **4–15** then it is quite usual for the client to be consulted. For administrative convenience the client may waive consultation and, except in relation to certain specified debtors, leave it to the factor to take legal proceedings in such circumstances. However, in many cases consultation with the client may serve to avoid legal proceedings and the mark of a good collection system is the ability to obtain payment without resort to solicitors. The client may assist recovery at this stage by:

(1)   holding up delivery of further supplies; and/or

75

(2) adding his own persuasion to that of the factor.

4–16   The courts deprecate the use of petitions for the winding up of companies or for the bankruptcy of individuals for the purpose of debt collection; the express purpose of the requirement for advertisement of a winding up petition, not less than seven days before the hearing, is to ensure that the winding up is available to all creditors and not solely for procuring payment of the debt owing to the petitioner. However, the threat of such a petition may often bring payment without the need for the factor to have recourse to legal proceedings. It seems reasonable that a creditor faced with persistent refusal to pay without reason on the part of a business of some substance should not remind the debtor of the creditor's rights in this respect. A petition for the winding up of a company may be founded on an inability to pay its debts[10] and it is deemed to be unable to pay its debts if it has neglected to pay or secure or compound to the reasonable satisfaction of the creditor a debt exceeding £750 for three weeks following the service at its registered office of a demand in the prescribed form.[11] Inability to pay debts may be based on other evidence[12] and it may well be that an unsatisfied demand for payment within a shorter period (especially if preceded by persistent reminders) may suffice for such evidence. In the case of an individual, who is domiciled and then present in England and Wales and has carried on business there within the previous three years, a petition for bankruptcy may be founded on the individual's inability to pay (or his having no reasonable prospect of paying) a liquidated debt of more than £750.[13] As in the case of a company, inability to pay may be based on the failure to pay or secure or compound within three weeks after the serving of a statutory demand.[14] In either case, therefore, the issue of a statutory demand may be used in suitable cases as pressure to bring about payment.

The use of bills of exchange to settle factored debts

4–17   In some trades it is normal practice for the credit granted by suppliers to their customers to be covered by bills of exchange drawn by the buyer and accepted by the debtor. Naturally, if the bulk of the sales of a supplier of goods is to be sold on such terms, the supplier may be able to obtain the funds which he requires for the trade credit granted to customers by discounting the accepted bills and it is unlikely that he would use a factor for the other functions. However, it is not uncommon for a factor's client to

---

[10] Insolvency Act 1986, s.122(1).
[11] *ibid.*, s.123(1)(a). The demand is known as a "statutory demand" and for its form and content see Insolvency Rules 1986 (SI 1986/1925), r.4.5.
[12] *ibid.*, s.123(1)(e).
[13] The amount may be changed by statutory instrument.
[14] Insolvency Act 1986, s.268(1)(a). For the form and content see Insolvency Rules 1986 (SI 1986/1925), r.6.1.

have some customers who will accept bills. The use of bills will largely avoid the time-consuming debt collection procedures outlined above and such convenience will outweigh the additional administrative tasks in the obtaining acceptance of the bills in the first place; if a bill is not met on first presentation, in the absence of a request by the debtor for an extension (normally by the replacement of the old bill by a new one with a later maturity), then more often than not it is a case for immediate legal proceedings to obtain payment.

According to the terms agreed between the client and the debtor, the bill **4–18** will be drawn either at invoice date or at the end of the month in which the invoice is raised. In factoring arrangements, the bills are sometimes drawn by the factor who would then have the task of sending the bill to the debtor and procuring the debtor's acceptance of it; and the client may regard these tasks as being the proper functions of the factor. However, in many cases, the client himself draws the bill, obtains the debtor's acceptance of it and sends it to the factor duly endorsed in his favour. In some cases, the factor will expect not to make a prepayment of the purchase price of a debt, arising from a contract of sale which provides for payment by a bill, until he has received the accepted bill endorsed in his favour; the factor, having taken the bill in good faith and for value, will then be a holder in due course[15] and protected against the debtor's defences and counterclaims of which he had no prior notice. If the client omits to endorse the bill, the factor may do so on the client's behalf in accordance with a power of attorney which is usually given by the client in the factoring agreement.[16] However, although the factor may have arranged with his bankers to collect for him negotiable instruments made payable to the client without endorsement,[17] in the case of bills of exchange (other than sight drafts), it is as well for the factor to arrange for their endorsement in order that he may have the rights of a holder in due course.[18] For this reason, many factors arrange for the endorsement of all cheques and sight drafts also if the insolvency of the client is pending; by becoming a holder, in due course, the factor expects to mitigate the impact of disputes and counterclaims of the debtors.

The practice of "self-billing" by buyers

An increasing number of large buyers including most mail order houses **4–19** and "catalogue" sellers have adopted a practice by which the seller's invoice is disregarded and payment is made on short terms on the basis of the buyer's own orders and records of goods received and accepted against the

---

[15] Bills of Exchange Act 1882, s.29(1).
[16] See paras 10–46 and 10–47 below.
[17] Including cheques crossed "account payee" and consequently not transferable (Cheques Act 1992, s.1); see para.10–35 below.
[18] See n.15 above.

orders. The buyers raise their own internal document to take the place of a seller's invoice and their remittance advice, consequently, makes no reference to invoice numbers. Where there are a large number of relatively small transactions relating to consumer goods, rejections and deductions are not infrequent; then, it is often almost impossible for the factor to reconcile the remittance advices to the debtor account based on his client's invoices. There have been attempts to overcome the difficulties by the use of notifications by the client to the factor of delivery notes or other documentation of which the reference numbers may be quoted by the buyer. However, it seems that no satisfactory solution has yet been found. Certainly, the advantage of having a large debtor of satisfactory credit standing will be outweighed by the additional administrative burden incurred by the factor in dealing with this problem. Furthermore, in order to avoid the accumulation of a large number of unallocated deductions or disputed items on such an account, which in view of the short terms may be a high percentage of the outstanding balance, the factor should make arrangements whereby his client will promptly accept a charge back of the buyer's deductions and debit notes. If such accounts are included in invoice discounting or agency factoring, it is advisable for the factor to monitor carefully the client's handling of the appropriation of payments, deductions and debit notes from the buyer. It is also the practice of many of such large buyers to prohibit the assignment of the debts arising from their purchase contracts. Consequently, where the factoring is on a fully disclosed basis, it is as well for the factor to obtain the buyer's consent to the assignment and its agreement to pay direct to the factor and to make arrangements by which the factor may identify the invoices paid. In such a case, it has been known for the buyer to require an undertaking from the factor that *all* payments are to be made to him; this precludes reassignment to the client by the factor of debts which are the subject of recourse.

A final step before legal proceedings

4–20   It is apparent that efficiency in the collection function, which is of benefit to both the factor and his client, depends on efficiency not only in the factor's office but also in the client's; unless the basis on which the sales ledger is constructed is correct and the terms are clearly agreed between the client and the debtor, even the most efficient factor may have difficulty in collecting. Inefficiency or negligence on the part of the client may also cause difficulties at a later stage. The failure of the debtor to pay may appear to the factor to be without reason, but it may have nothing to do with dilatoriness or shortage of liquid resources; it may arise from a reason (either justifiable or not) known to a client which has not been communicated to the factor. For example, the debtor may have paid the client by reason of a prohibition of assignments in the contract of sale or because he had overlooked the assignment notice; or the debtor may not have accepted the goods. In such circumstances, if the client is negligent and has failed to inform the factor, legal proceedings (or a threat of them) may be a cause of much aggravation and unnecessary expense. In order that the position should be clarified, it is often advisable, especially in the case of a large creditworthy debtor, to bring the matter to the notice of a senior official by telephone or by a letter sent by facsimile for his attention. If the telephone is used, the call should be confirmed by one of the other means. It may be that the accounts-payable department of the debtor had not thought it necessary in such circumstances to respond to the factor's pressing letters or calls and the management may be quite unaware that the company may be considered a slow payer. In many cases, the unpleasantness of unnecessary proceedings has been avoided by these means.

2. MATTERS TO BE CONSIDERED BEFORE LEGAL PROCEEDINGS

Who may sue

In Ch.7 arrangements for transferring the ownership of debts to the factor **4–21** from the client, who creates them by the supply of goods or services, are described. It was there predicated that such debts were not normally transferred to the factor by assignments in statutory form[19] (normally referred to as legal assignments) but by assignments in equity only; and the reasons for this normal procedure are also explained there. However, although the absence of a legal assignment in no way detracts from the factor's right of ownership, there is a procedural difference when it comes to legal proceedings for the recovery of the assigned debts.[20]

In the case of a legal assignment completed by notice to the debtor, the **4–22** factor as assignee may sue in his own name alone,[21] but where the assignment is valid in equity only, even when notice of that assignment has been received by the debtor, then the client as assignor and the factor as assignee should be joint plaintiffs. The purpose of the rule appears to have been founded on the requirement of the courts to have all three parties before them following the merging of the administration of the courts of equity and common law.[22] Such a requirement would certainly be necessary where only part of a debt has been assigned and that is possible in equity but not if the assignment is to be in accordance with the statute. Accordingly, it has often been the practice for a factor, who wishes to avoid the complication of

---

[19] In accordance with the provisions of the Law of Property Act 1925, s.136; and see para.7–05 below.
[20] See para.7–06 below.
[21] Law of Property Act 1925, s.136 and see para.7–05 below.
[22] See para.7–04 below.

joining his client in any proceedings for the recovery of debts, to have the transfer of the ownership to him of the debts perfected by a legal assignment; in most factoring agreements, the factor would have the right to such perfection and indeed to execute the form of assignment himself by virtue of a power of attorney in the agreement.[23] Often, however, a factor, having only an equitable assignment of a debt but of the *whole* of it, will take the proceedings in his own name alone relying on the rules of the court procedures by which no action should fail for want of a joinder.[24] This procedure may avoid the delay and the cost[25] of the legal assignment; but the factor runs the risk that the case may be put back if the court orders the client as assignor to be joined as a party to the proceedings.

Further steps before proceedings—identification of the debtor

4–23 By the time that solicitors have been instructed, whether the factoring is on a disclosed or undisclosed basis,[26] notice of the assignment of the debt will have been given to the debtor. If the assignment is to be perfected in statutory form, a further notice will have to be given to complete that assignment. The advantage of early notice is that the notice fixes the rights of the three parties (particularly as regards the debtor's rights of set-off and counterclaim)[27] and prevents the debtor from discharging the debt by a subsequent payment to the client. In the case of disclosed factoring, where notice is carried on the invoice, for evidential purposes such notice should be confirmed as often as possible in subsequent communications to the debtor (*e.g.* on statements and requests for payment).

4–24 The full details of the case to be passed to the solicitor for the purpose of proceedings must include the amount of the debt, the invoice date and the date on which payment was due according to the contract of sale or service, as well as the client's and the debtor's full legal name and address.[28] Where either of them is a company, the registered office should be included. The use by a debtor of a trading name, as opposed to the name or names of the natural person or persons or the company owning the business, may cause problems and delays. If the trading name only is given, then there may be an

---

[23] See para.10–38 below. "There is a rule of practice that the assignor should be joined but that rule will not be insisted upon where there is no need; inparticular if there is no risk of a separate claim by the assignor ..." *Raiffeisen Zentralebank Oesterreich AG v An Feng Steel Co Limited per* Mance L.J. [2001] W.L.R. 1344 at 60. There will be a good case for a joiner if, for example, the assignor disputes the assignment or if the assignment relates to only part of the debt; then all parties should be before the court.

[24] Historically, RSC, Ord.15, r.6 and CCR, Ord.15, r.1, now replaced by the CPR whose "overriding" objective supports such an approach, particularly CPR 1.1(2) (d), but the CPR does not reproduce the former clear guidance of the RSC and CCR.

[25] See paras 7–04 *et seq.* below.

[26] See "Table of Factoring Variants" at end of Ch.1.

[27] See para.8–08 below.

[28] See para.4–05 above.

error in identifying the person to be sued with consequent delay and further aggravation. Furthermore, if the trading name only is the subject of the proceedings, then on an attempt to execute on goods after judgment the debtor may avoid the execution by claiming that the goods are owned by a company. Accordingly, to avoid delays in establishing the correct legal name of the debtor, it is important that this should be established when the account is opened.[29] It is also advisable for the factor to check once again the details of the order, particularly as to the due date for payment and delivery, before instructing solicitors to avoid as far as possible any defence by the debtor in relation to these matters. It is also important that the factor should be aware that there are no trade customs or a course of dealing indicating that the credit to be allowed has not been exceeded.

The CPR[30] has by Practice Direction prescribed pre-action protocols for **4–25** many areas of litigation which have been approved by the Head of Civil Justice. They outline the steps parties should take to seek information from and to provide information to each other about a prospective claim. The object is to encourage early exchange of information which might enable the parties to agree a settlement without proceedings. Non compliance will be reflected in subsequent directions and orders for costs. There is at present no protocol for debt recovery; nevertheless it is still good practice for the claimant or their solicitor to send a detailed letter of claim to the prospective defendant and to wait a reasonable period for the defendant to respond before issuing proceedings. Parties now have a positive obligation in accordance with the overriding objective (CPR r.1.1(2)) and must help the court further this objective (CPR 1.3). From a practical point of view, a solicitor's letter, indicating to the debtor that the factor is serious regarding the threat of proceedings, may elicit payment from the debtor without the cost of such proceedings. Furthermore, if proceedings result in immediate payment by the debtor, the Court may refuse to award to the factor legal costs up to the prescribed amount if no such letter has been sent.

Payment by instalments

Sometimes in order to avoid legal proceedings, on receipt of a demand **4–26** from the factor or the solicitor, the debtor may offer to pay by instalments. If the factor wishes to consider accepting such an offer, he should carefully bear in, mind the following:

(1) The agreement for instalments should always be in writing.

(2) The agreement should contain an admission and precise details of

---

[29] *ibid.*
[30] The Civil Procedure Rules 1998 (CPR) are made under the Civil Procedure Act 1997. Accordingly they are "rules of court" as defined by the Interpretation Act 1978. The CPR constitute a single set of rules replacing the Rules of the Supreme Court (RSC) and County Court Rules (CCR).

the debt to which it relates including the exact amount and references to the invoices by which the debt is represented. In some cases, particularly when there have been arguments regarding the amount of the debt or any counterclaim, it may be advisable to obtain the debtor's agreement to submit to judgment on an undertaking by the factor not to enforce it whilst the instalments continue to be paid promptly. Such a procedure will obviously avoid delay in enforcement if there is any breach of the instalment arrangements.

(3) It is important that the precise amount of the instalments, the intervals and the date of the first payment should be stipulated (for example: first payment on December 10, 2005, and thereafter on the 10th day of each subsequent calendar month).

(4) For the benefit of the client, where the discount charges are calculated until the collection date,[31] and otherwise for the benefit of the factor, the agreement should provide for interest at a rate at least matching the discount charge.

(5) It is essential that the agreement for instalments should provide for the full unpaid amount to become immediately due and payable on any default by the debtor. Otherwise, the factor may be left in a position of having to sue for each instalment as it becomes due.

(6) If the debtor is a limited company, then instalment arrangement should, if possible, be guaranteed personally by the directors, shareholders or other interested third parties. If the debt is substantial, the possibility of taking a charge to secure it over assets of the company or any property of the guarantors should be considered. In the case of individuals or partnerships, a charge on property should also be considered.

(7) Finally, it is advisable to have the instalments represented by postdated cheques or accepted bills of exchange. If the latter are taken and drawn by the client and endorsed in favour of the factor, the factor's position as a holder in due course may serve to avoid any further dispute being raised by the debtor.[32]

4–27 A statutory demand sent by the factor[33] may well bring about an offer of payment by instalments, and, in any case, the three week period following the issue of the demand should be used for negotiations towards a settlement of the debt without resort to a petition for winding-up (or bankruptcy in the case of an individual) or other proceedings.

---

[31] See paras 3–35 *et seq.* above.
[32] See para.4–18 above.
[33] See para.4–16 above.

Winding-up or bankruptcy proceedings

If a statutory demand has been made on a company or individual, or if a **4–28** petition for winding-up of a company or bankruptcy of an individual has been threatened and there are other grounds for showing that the company or individual is unable to pay its debts, then consideration should be given to whether or not to proceed with the petition. If, in the case of a company or partnership, a winding up petition has been advertised or, in the case of an individual or partnership, it is known that a bankruptcy petition is pending, and the company, partnership or individual owes to the factor an overdue debt, then it is advisable for the factor to give notice of support[34] to the petition. In the absence of such notice, if the petitioning creditor's debt is settled, the factor will be left to start his own proceedings; but, in the case of the factor's notice of support, the debtor will have to settle with the factor as well as the petitioner in order to avoid the possibility of a winding-up order or bankruptcy as the case may be. An acknowledgement of the notice of support should be obtained from the petitioner or his or her solicitor together with an undertaking not to agree to the dismissal of the petition without consulting the factor.

If on the petition for winding-up or bankruptcy (as the case may be) or on **4–29** giving notice of support to another's petition the debtor offers to settle the debt, then the factor should also insist on his costs being paid in order to settle the matter. Furthermore, there are advantages in arrangements for payment in settlement to be made by a third party (*e.g.* a director of a corporate debtor). In the case of the factor's petition, there may be supporting creditors or in the case of the factor's notice of support, there may be still further supporting creditors; if settlement is not made with all of these, the winding-up or bankruptcy order may well be made. Now, where a company is being wound-up by the court, any disposition of its property made after the date of the petition (the commencement of the winding-up)[35] is void; similarly, all such dispositions of a bankrupt's property after the date of the bankruptcy petition are void.[36] Consequently, the liquidator or trustee in bankruptcy may claw back any such payment made by the debtor after the petition, notwithstanding that it was made for the purpose of avoiding winding-up or bankruptcy respectively, if an order is made on the petition or the substituted supporting creditor. On the other hand, it is doubtful if any payment by any third party in such circumstances could be rendered void.

---

[34] Insolvency Rules 1986 (SI 1986/1925), r.4.16 and r.6.23 respectively.
[35] Insolvency Act 1986, s.129.
[36] *ibid.*, s.127 and s.284 respectively.

3. LEGAL REMEDIES

Litigation

4–30   A winding-up or bankruptcy order will not bring about payment of the debt but only the factor's right to participate ultimately *pari passu* with other unsecured creditors. Therefore, if all other efforts to obtain payment as described above have failed and if the factor knows of no reason why the debt or any sum due to the factor from the client or any guarantor should not be paid, then the factor will have no alternative but to resort to legal proceedings for its recovery. A contested action is a civilised battle. It is played out according to the rules of law but involves persuasion, tactics and strategy. The factors case should be prepared in detail so as to present it in the strongest light either to the courts for trial or to the other side for the purposes of negotiating a favourable settlement. The manner in which the case is handled can make or break the factor's case. Rules of court exist to ensure the proper conduct of litigation, including the exchange of statements of case defining the issues, disclosure and production of relevant documents. Within the factors own documentation together with the law applicable on assignment and set-off are a myriad of provisions and rules. These together with the rules of court must be thoroughly mastered and the rights and benefits they confer be fully utilised.

4–31   Litigation is adversarial, that is to say, the court adjudicates only on the issue which the parties present to it and upon the evidence which the parties choose to call. This places a heavy burden on the lawyers on both sides. The factor should therefore ensure that the lawyer chosen to pursue their claim has a thorough understanding of the legal framework within which the factor operates and knows of the content of the factor's agreement and security documentation.

The Civil Procedure Rules

4–32   Civil procedure has undergone considerable change by virtue of the Civil Procedure Rules (CPR) which took effect from April 26, 1999. The CPR comprises the code governing civil procedure in County Courts, the High Court and the Courts of Appeal.

4–33   The concept underpinning the CPR is that of "the overriding objective of enabling the court to deal with cases justly".[37] This must be given effect to by the court when making decisions[38] and by actively managing cases[39] and

---

[37] CPR 1.1.

[38] CPR 1.1(2): by ensuring that the parties are on an equal footing, saving expense, dealing with the case in a proportionate, expeditious and fair manner; and by allotting an appropriate share of court resources to it.

[39] CPR 1.4 which includes encouraging use of alternative dispute resolution.

by the parties.[40] Its purpose is to achieve more open litigation. Gone are the days of tactical ambush. Indeed, even before the start of litigation, parties are required by pre-action protocols to seek and provide information to each other. Penalties may be imposed where there is a failure to comply with pre-action protocols.[41] Currently no protocols exists for money claims but parties are wise to apply the spirit of the protocol by providing to the opponent all relevant information necessary to understand the factor's case before commencing proceedings. The factor should therefore ensure that his solicitor has all the information needed at the very start of the process including a full set of copy documents where action is to be taken in reliance upon those documents.

The Litigation Process

Factors will instruct skilled lawyers to handle their affairs who have at **4–34** their finger tips *inter alia* The White Book published annually, the authoritative text on Civil Procedure. The factor needs to know that the outcome he expects from the litigation will be achieved but not every detail of the process. However, to have a general appreciation of some of the aspects of litigation which are most use to the factor is helpful. What follows is a brief resume of those matters.

(i) *Default judgement*

If the defendant has not filed an acknowledgement of service or a defence **4–35** and 14 days have expired since the particulars of claim were issued or if the defendant has filed an acknowledgement of service but has not filed a defence and 28 days have expired, then the Factor can apply for a default judgment.[42] In such cases, there is no hearing and obtaining the default judgment is simply an administrative act. It is possible for a default judgment to be set aside or varied.[43]

(ii) *Summary judgment*

In most actions by the factor to recover from its client the unpaid balance **4–36** on the factoring account or from the guarantor of this sum, with the skilful application of the provisions within the factor's documents success at summary judgment is possible. The summary judgment procedure enables

---

[40] CPR 1.3.
[41] PD—Protocols, para.2.
[42] CPR 12.3.
[43] CPR Pt 13.

the court to give the factor judgment if satisfied that the defence put forward has no real prospect of success.[44]

4-37 Summary judgment can be applied for only after the defendant has filed either an acknowledgement of service or his defence. It is necessary to complete an application notice and serve this, together with all relevant evidence on the other party and the court, giving notice of 14 days before the hearing[45]; the respondent has to file and serve any evidence in reply seven days before the hearing.[46] If the applicant responds to the respondent's evidence, the reply evidence must be filed at least three days before the hearing.[47]

4-38 A very useful tool to achieve summary judgment is the use of a conclusive evidence clause which can be found in most modern factoring agreements and the Factor's standard surety documentation. In the absence of such a clause, existing for the benefit of the factor and being relied upon, the factor is faced with the lengthy task of proving to the court's satisfaction how precisely the sum claimed has been calculated. This is potentially difficult for factors whose agreements have a number of different charging provisions and the computer software used is not readily able to produce historical data in support of the present balance due. The conclusive evidence clause contained within the factoring agreement and contract of surety provides that a notice in a certain form, or a demand by the factor, shall be conclusive evidence as between factor, client and surety, see *Bache & Co (London) Ltd v Banque Vernes et Commerciales de Paris* [1973] 2 Lloyds Rep. 437. In that case, the Court of Appeal held that the guarantor must usually pay the sum certified to be due, and if it subsequently transpires that he paid too much, he can initiate separate proceedings against the creditor for its return.

4-39 The judgment of the Court of Appeal in the case was firmly founded on the rationale that: "the commercial practice of inserting conclusive evidence clauses is only acceptable because the bankers or brokers who insert them are known to be honest and reliable men of business who are most unlikely to make a mistake".[48] This approach has recently been followed the *Society of Lloyds v Terence William Fraser* [1999] 1, Lloyds Rep. IR 156, where the wording of the relevant clause was: "For the purposes of calculating the amount of any Name's Premium as set out in clause 5.1(b) and the amount of any Name's Premium discharged by the transfer of assets or the amount realised through the liquidation of Funds at Lloyd's for application in or towards any Name's Premium, the records of and calculations performed by the (MSU) shall be conclusive evidence as between the Name and (Equitas)

---

[44] CPR 24.
[45] CPR 24.4(3).
[46] CPR 24.5(1).
[47] CPR 24.5(2).
[48] As *per* Denning J. at 440.

in the absence of any manifest error". The Court of Appeal reconsidered conclusive evidence clauses and confirmed the following at p.178:

"1. the figures contained in such a certificate are to be taken as correct unless:

(i) in their own terms they manifestly cannot be correct; or

(ii) if by pointing to some other piece of evidence the person subject to the clause can demonstrate that they clearly cannot be correct in some respect;

2. the burden of proof is on that person to show manifest error;

3. that person is not entitled to inspect and check the accuracy of the records in the possession of the other party or the figures derived from them, even if it is otherwise impossible to ascertain whether there has been any manifest error, as such an exercise involves a contradiction of the express wording and intention of such clauses."

It means that the factor's client and any guarantor may not look behind the certificate produced to satisfy the conclusive evidence clause or indeed rely upon other financial statements. Used correctly, the conclusive evidence clause is a powerful tool.

(iii) *Interim injunctions*

The factor will from time to time need urgent action to protect his **4–40** position as the owner of the debts it has purchased from, for example, the client in breach of the agreement collecting and banking the proceeds of debts he has sold or perhaps the debtors paying the client notwithstanding the sale of the debts to the factor. In situations such as these an injunction may be an appropriate remedy.

Before an interim injunction will be granted, the claimant must show that **4–41** there is a pre-existing cause of action against the defendant.[49] Thereafter, the claimant must satisfy the requirements laid down in *American Cyananid Co v Ethicon Ltd* [1975] A.C. 936 that:

(a) there is a serious question to be tried;

(b) damages would not be an adequate remedy for the claimants, who would suffer irreparable harm if the injunction were not to be granted; and

(c) should the defendants succeed at trial, he would be adequately

---

[49] *The Siskina* [1979] A.C. 210.

compensated for any loss suffered by the undertaking in damages to be given by the claimant as a condition of grant of the injunction.

Applications can be made before the claim form has been issued, in urgent cases or where it is in the interests of justice to do so, whether or not notice should be given to the other side depends on whether there is true impossibility in giving such notice.[50]

(iv) *Freezing injunctions*

4-42 More and more factors are the target of dishonest business men and fraudsters. Where large fraud is discovered, swift action may be needed by the factor to freeze the assets of the perpetrators in the hope that the assets frozen may be used to meet any subsequent judgment. The freezing injunction is to prevent the defendant from rendering a judgment against him, nugatory by transferring his assets abroad or otherwise dissipating these prior to trial. This remedy is statutory.[51]

4-43 Before granting a freezing injunction, the court will usually require to be satisfied that:

(a) the claimant has "a good arguable case"[52] based on a pre-existing cause of action[53];

(b) the claim is one over which the court has jurisdiction[54];

(c) the defendant appears to have assets within the jurisdiction[55];

(d) there is a real risk that those assets will be removed from the jurisdiction, or otherwise dissipated, if the injunction is not granted[56]; and

(e) there is a balance of convenience in favour of granting the injunction.[57]

The court can also order disclosure or the administration of requests for further information to assist the claimant in ascertaining the location of the defendant's assets.

4-44 In exceptional cases, the court will be prepared to grant a worldwide

---

[50] *Bates v Lord Hailsham of St Maryleborne* [1972] 1 W.L.R. 1373.
[51] CPR 25.1(1)(f); Supreme Court Act 1981, see 37(J).
[52] *Aiglon Ltd v Gall Shan Co Ltd* [1993], 1 Lloyds Rep. 164.
[53] *The Veracruz* [1992], 1 Lloyds Rep. 353.
[54] *The Siskina* [1979] A.C. 210.
[55] *Third Chandris Shipping Corp v Uni-Marine SA* [1979] Q.B. 645.
[56] *Montecchi v Shimco (UK) Ltd* [1979] 1 W.L.R. 1180.
[57] *Barclay-Johnson v Yuill* [1980] 1 W.L.R. 1259.

freezing order.[58] The relief granted by a freezing injunction does not give the claimant security in the frozen assets so as to place him in a preferential position compared to the other creditors,[59] and the court will not usually refuse to allow the defendant to use his assets as he wishes in the running of his business and for ordinary daily living or to discharge his ordinary debts[60] or legal expenses.[61] Moreover, the rights of secured creditors are unaffected,[62] as are accrued rights of set off.[63]

As with interim injunctions, the Court has a discretion over whether or not to grant a freezing injunction, provided it is just and convenient.[64] The purpose of the freezing order requires that they be made without notice. The claimant must give an undertaking as to damages, must notify the defendant, and affected third parties, and must indemnify any third party for expenses incurred in complying with the order.[65]

The Freezing Injunction is a valuable weapon for preventing those who   **4-45** defraud or attempt to defraud the factor for enjoying the fruits of their fraudulent activity.

The enforcement of judgments

With an unsatisfied judgment, apart from proceedings for winding up or   **4-46** bankruptcy of the debtor, the factor has a number of choices open in order to enforce the judgment. The procedures open to him include the following:

(1) Execution may be levied on the debtor's goods by a writ *fieri facias* in the High Court or a warrant of execution in the County Court. If the debtor trades in more than one place, it may be advisable for the sheriff or bailiff to attend at more than one or all; in this way, delays, in starting again after finding premises to be empty, may be avoided. If more than one sheriff or bailiff is instructed, each must know of the other's taking part in the proceedings.

(2) As a judgment creditor, the factor may obtain a third party debt order on a person who is indebted to the debtor. The object of the order is an attachment of monies owed to the judgment debtor. An order is made on the application to the court by the judgment creditor (who can show that there is a sum owing by the Third Party to the debtor) and is served upon the third party; the order

---

[58] *Babanaft International Co SA v Bassatne* [1990] Ch. 13.
[59] Supreme Court Act 1981, s.37(1).
[60] *Lightline Ltd v Edwards* [2003] B.C.L.C. 427.
[61] *Polly Peck International Plc v Nadir (No.2)* [1992] 4 All E.R. 769.
[62] *The Coral Rose* (No.3) [1991] 1 W.L.R. 917.
[63] *The Cretan Harmony* [1978] 1 Lloyds Rep. 425.
[64] *The Theotokos* [1983] 2 All E.R. 65.
[65] *Z Ltd* [1982] 1 All E.R. 556.

has the effect of restraining the third party from parting with any money owed to the debtor and orders his appearance in court on a given day (normally not less than eight days later). Unless the Third Party can show reason why he should not pay the attached debt to the judgment creditor, the order will then be made, and the debt must be paid over to the judgment creditor. Such orders are often served on banks in respect of credit balances on debtors' bank accounts, but, to be effective, the account must be in credit when the order is served. Attempts have been made to make third party debt orders against factors who provided factoring services for debtors of other factors, but usually these attempts fail; either there is no availability on the debtor's account with the factor because the debtor has drawn up to the hilt or, in some cases, the debtor's factoring agreement provides that such an order is one of the events that gives the factor the right to withhold payments.

(3) The factor with a judgment against a debtor may apply to the court for a charging order on any real property of the debtor. In this way, the factor will become a secured creditor subject to the rights of the holder of any prior security on the property. Any such charge should be registered. It must be remembered that it is often the case that the debtor owns the property with another, in which case the charging order will only attach to the debtor's share of the beneficial interest in the property and the co-owner's share will be left free of the charge. It is possible, once a charging order has been obtained, to seek an order for sale of the property concerned, but this is at the discretion of the court taking into account the position of any co-owner.

(4) At all times, when obtaining and executing judgments obtained, the factor should remember to include amounts relating to the applicable interest under the County Courts Act 1984 or the Supreme Court Act 1981 or the Late Payment of Commercial Debts (Interest) Act 1998.

4–47 The steps to be taken will naturally depend upon the factor's assessment of the property of the debtor available to satisfy the judgment, but whichever route he chooses he should act quickly. The intervention of winding up or bankruptcy of the debtor may well forestall the factor's efforts at self-help. If another creditor of the debtor hears of the impending execution, attachment or charging order, feeling aggrieved that all creditors are not to be treated on a pro rata basis, he may take steps for winding-up or bankruptcy. Any creditor who has issued execution against any goods or land of a company or has attached any debt due to it may not retain the benefit of the execution or attachment, unless it is completed before the commencement of the winding up of the company or the court in its discretion orders otherwise.[66] In the case of a winding-up by the court, the commencement is the date of the petition[67]; in voluntary winding-up, the commencement is not until the member's resolution to wind-up but, if the creditor has received notice of a meeting at which a resolution to wind the company up is proposed, the date on which he had notice is substituted for the commencement of winding-up for this purpose.[68] For the purpose of these provisions the completion of the execution or attachment is as follows:

(1) in relation to goods, the seizure, sale or the making of a charging order;

(2) in relation to a debt, receipt of the debt; and

(3) in relation to land, seizure, the appointment of a receiver or the making of a charging order.

In most cases of the bankruptcy of an individual the factor, attempting to levy execution on or attach the property of the debtor, will be met by a similar bar to his recovery once a petition for bankruptcy has been presented. At any time, while proceedings on the petition are pending, the court may stay any action, execution or other legal process against the property of the debtor.[69]

Partnerships

Although in English law a partnership has no corporate existence, the **4–48** Insolvency Act 1986 has introduced provisions for the winding-up of insolvent partnerships as if they were companies and these rules are discussed in Ch.11.[70] Therefore, the factor's rights in relation to execution of the property of a partnership must be viewed, not only in relation to the partners as a collection of individuals, but also in relation to the partnership as a whole in a case in which it is to be wound up as if it were a company.

4. INSOLVENCY OF THE DEBTOR

The effects of the most usual forms of insolvency on the rights of the parties **4–49** with whom the insolvent company, partnership or individual has contracted are described in Ch.11. These forms are:

---

[66] Insolvency Act 1986, s.183.
[67] *ibid.*, s.129.
[68] *ibid.*, s.183(2)(a).
[69] *ibid.*, s.285(1).
[70] See paras 11–71 *et seq.* below.

(1) administrative receivership of a company;

(2) administration of a company partnership;

(3) the winding up of a company or partnership by the Court;

(4) the voluntary winding-up of a company;

(5) the bankruptcy of an individual or the partners of a partnership; and

(6) a voluntary arrangement in the case of a company or partnership or individual.

It will be noted from the discussions of these effects in Ch.11 that the rights of a creditor to obtain payment are in all cases obstructed.

The appointment of an administrative receiver

4-50   If, as is usual, the charge under which an administrative receiver has been appointed covers all the property of the debtor company, the factor will be unable to enforce any judgment against it because all his property will be in the possession of the receiver. In such circumstances, virtually the only remedy that is open to the factor is to petition for the winding-up of the company. This course will not bring about any prospect of payment of the factor's debt nor, indeed, of an earlier distribution (pro rata with other unsecured non-preferential creditors) because any liquidator appointed by virtue of any winding-up will be unable to take possession of the property of the company until the receiver has been discharged. However, such a petition may be considered for the following purposes:

(1) where it may seem possible for the charge to be avoided in the winding-up of the company,[71] to enable a liquidator to investigate such a course of action; or

(2) where the directors have taken no steps to wind the company up voluntarily, and the discharge of the receiver is impending to ensure a pro rata distribution of assets available to unsecured creditors.

In any such circumstances, careful consideration must be given to the position of the company because a winding-up order may be prejudicial to the ultimate return to unsecured creditors by hampering the receiver's efforts

---

[71] *e.g.* pursuant to the provisions of the Insolvency Act 1986, s.245 or as a transaction at an undervalue (see para.11–70 below), or if the charge is void for lack of registration under s 395 of the Companies Act 1986.

to carry on the company's business and to sell the business as a going concern.[72] Since the enactment of the Insolvency Act 1986 and the provisions therein for an administrative receiver to consult with and provide information for unsecured creditors,[73] such decisions may be taken in the light of the best available information.

Unconnected with the question of recovery from a debtor company in receivership but related to it in time is the consideration by the factor of approving credit for a receiver who is carrying on the business of the debtor company. In carrying on such a business, a receiver will often require supplies from the source previously available to the company. Unless it is otherwise provided in the contract for the purchase of goods, an administrative receiver is personally liable on it.[74] Accordingly, if there is no exclusion of liability, the factor may look to the standing of the receiver personally, as well as the availability of assets of the company to the receiver, in assessing the request for approval. If, as is now often the case, the receiver excludes personal liability, the factor will be able to consider only the position of the business of the company in receivership. **4–51**

Voluntary arrangements

The effect on creditors' rights of recovery under a voluntary arrangement will depend on the terms of the arrangement. When the arrangement becomes effective,[75] the terms of it are binding on every person who had notice of and was entitled to attend the meeting of creditors at which the proposal was approved; and this would normally include the factor as a creditor. Such arrangements may provide for no immediate payment or payment by instalments over a period, or for payment of part only of each debt; but it is likely that all unsecured non-preferential creditors will be treated rateably. It is likely also that, having been bound by the terms of the arrangement, the factor would be unable to take any further proceedings for recovery whilst it remained in force; in any case, on a report of the decision of the meeting by the supervisor,[76] the court is likely to stay any winding-up proceedings which have already been commenced. **4–52**

Administration

As described in Ch.11, there are now two routes for a company to become the subject of an administration. A court order for appointment of an administrator can still be obtained, but much more commonly the **4–53**

---

[72] See para.11–35 below.
[73] Insolvency Act 1986, ss.46–49.
[74] Insolvency Act s.44(1)(b).
[75] See para.11–79 below.
[76] *ibid.*

out-of-court route will now be used. But whichever procedure is adopted, the effect is to put in place an immediate moratorium preventing unsecured creditors, such as a factor, from bringing court proceedings for the recovery of his debt[77] or exercising any other remedy, including the bringing of a winding-up petition without the consent of the administrator or the court. The remedies will revive once the administration comes to an end.

Winding-up and bankruptcy

4–54   From the time of a petition for the winding-up or bankruptcy of a debtor and, in most cases, following the notice of a meeting of creditors of a debtor company, the factor will be unable to enforce any judgment.[78] After a winding-up or bankruptcy order in relation to his debtor, the factor will be unable to start or continue any proceedings for the recovery of this debt.[79] In the case of a voluntary winding-up, the property of the company must be applied, after payment to preferential or any secured creditors, to a *pari passu* distribution to unsecured creditors[80]; furthermore, following notice of the meeting no execution or attachment may be enforced.[81] Therefore, the factor will have no further remedy available to him except to petition for winding-up by the court; such action may be taken if the factor is dissatisfied with the prospective conduct of the voluntary winding-up. However, the court is likely to take into account the views of all unsecured creditors, who appear at the hearing, in coming to a decision whether to make an order or to let the voluntary winding up continue.

5. RECOVERY FROM GUARANTORS

4–55   If a debt owing to a factor is guaranteed by a third party, such as a director of a debtor company, amounts recovered from the guarantor do not have to be deducted from the factor's proof of debt in the bankruptcy or winding-up of the principal debtor until the position has been reached that, by reason of payments from the guarantor and dividends from the insolvent estate, the factor has received payment in full.[82] The reason for this is that, until the guarantor has paid the guaranteed debt in full, he has no right to be subrogated to the factor's right to prove in the estate of the principal debtor, and there can, therefore, be no double proof for the same debt. For this reason, it is important that, when taking a limited guarantee, the factor

---

[77] See para.11–48 below.
[78] See para.4–47 above.
[79] See paras 11–54 and 11–62 respectively.
[80] Insolvency Act 1986, s.107.
[81] See para.4–47 above.
[82] *Re Sass* [1896] 2 Q.B. 12 and see also Goode, *Legal Problems of Credit and Security* (3rd ed., 2003) para.8–18.

should ensure that the form of guarantee covers the *whole* debt (subject to a limitation of liability on the part of the guarantor) rather than *part of the debt*. In the latter case, the guarantor would be subrogated to the right to prove on payment of the whole of the part guaranteed, and this would result in the inability of the factor to maintain his proof for that part. In addition, a guarantor of part only of a larger debt, who had paid the full amount of that part, may share rateably with the creditor in any security given for the whole of the debt.[83]

In the event of the bankruptcy or winding-up of a guarantor, the factor **4–56** will be able to submit proof in the estate of the guarantor for the amount of the debt as reduced by any payment made by either the guarantor or the principal debtor *before* the submission of that proof; but he will not be required to reduce his or her proof in respect of sums received from the principal debtor afterwards.[84] In the event of the bankruptcy or winding-up of both principal debtor and guarantor, the factor will be able to maintain his proof for the full amount, notwithstanding any dividend from either. Naturally, the factor will be unable to maintain any proof in either of the foregoing situations once he has received 100 pence in the pound. As a result of these rules, it is as well for the factor to get his proof in to the insolvent estate of a guarantor at the earliest possible stage in his recovery proceedings.

If the factor has obtained the guarantees of more than one party for the **4–57** same debt, it is usually the case that each guarantor will have a joint and several liability for the debt. In such a situation, the factor must exercise caution when negotiating with a single guarantor to reach "full and final settlement" with that individual. If the factor agrees to accept from one of a number of co-guarantors that a specific sum is accepted in full and final settlement, the effect of this would be to release the other co-guarantors from their liability, unless:

(1) the agreement reached can be construed purely as an agreement not to pursue that individual; or

(2) the factor reserves the right to pursue the remaining guarantors.

Otherwise, it is suggested that the co-guarantors, if pursued, would lose their rights of contribution from the settling individual who could raise a defence that he no longer has a liability for the debt owing to the agreement reached with the factor.[85] However, this difficulty for the factor may be avoided by

---

[83] *Re Butlers Wharf Ltd* [1995] B.C.L.C. 56.
[84] *Re Amalgamated Investment & Property Co Ltd* [1985] 1 Ch. 349 and see Goode, *op cit.*, p.8–32.
[85] *Deanplan Ltd v Mahmoud* [1992] 3 All E.R. 945.

providing in the instrument of guarantee that any release or compromise with one of the guarantors shall not affect the liability of the others.

6. ELECTRONIC DATA INPUT AND DIRECT DEBITS

4–58 In recent years, there has been a tendency for some large buyers of goods and services to require that their suppliers should send invoice data electronically for entry in the buyers purchase ledger records without any hard copy invoice. This poses two problems for the factor. First, the factor of a client on whom this system has been imposed will be expected to accept electronic input to his records instead of the usual copy invoices and credit notes for notifications or offers of debts. Such a system should pose no problem as regards the assignments which are almost invariably equitable[86] but postulates a high degree of trust on the part of the factor.

4–59 Secondly, the factor will have a problem of ensuring that the notices of assignment will be conveyed to the buyers; it is unlikely that the buyer's system would provide for the notice to be received and recorded. Some factors have considered reliance on introductory letters[87]; but it is not certain that such letters are not effective as notices except for debts in existence at the dates of the letters.[88]

4–60 A further development has been the requirement of clients, whose debtors have been paying by direct debit by automated input to their bank accounts, to continue to have their customers' payments made in this manner after the start of factoring. This may be the case if goods or services or hire is on a regular basis. If the factoring arrangement is on a disclosed basis, whereby the factor is responsible for collection from the debtors, there seems to have been no difficulty for the factor to arrange with his bankers for the system to be put into operation, provided that the factor gives an indemnity to his bank in respect of repayments it must make for any amount that is shown to have been incorrectly debited to the debtor's bank account or the subject of a dispute. Such an undertaking is on a standard form of indemnity used by banks generally. In such a case, the factor should obtain a counter-indemnity from his client, and it will be apparent that, before agreeing to such an arrangement, the factor should make a careful estimate of the likely incidence of such repayments based on the business standards of his prospective client.

---

[86] See para.7–06 below.
[87] See paras 8–12 *et seq.* below.
[88] *ibid.*

7. CONSTRUCTION INDUSTRY TAX DEDUCTION SCHEME

Under this scheme contractors in the construction industry are obliged to **4–61** deduct tax at the standard rate from all payments to their sub-contractors with the exception of any sub-contractor of whose tax affairs HM Revenue & Customs is satisfied and who is in possession of the relevant certificate from HM Revenue & Customs.[89]

If a factor decides to provide factoring to a sub-contractor in the con- **4–62** struction industry (in spite of the other difficulties that may arise described in para.2–25 above), then the factor must be aware of the effect on his recoveries of this scheme. HM Revenue & Customs booklet, I.R. 14/15 dated December 1998, sets out the tax deduction scheme in plain language and, in particular, contains lists of operations that are included in, and those that are excluded from, "construction".[90] The following is a summary of the effect of the scheme on factors and discounters:

(1) The debtor is obliged to deduct tax at the standard rate from any payment to a sub-contractor in respect of work done in the construction industry unless the sub-contractor (as payee) holds (or the sub-contractor *and* the nominee, if payment is to be made to a nominee, each hold) a certificate from HM Revenue & Customs giving exemption from the deduction of tax. In the case of a company, the certificate is referred to as "CIS5", and in the case of an individual or partnership as a "CIS6".[91]

(2) There are two methods by which the debtor may be satisfied that it may pay without deduction of tax:

(a) production of the certificate by the sub-contractor to its debtor; or

(b) *in the case of a company only*, the production of a certifying document, signed by a director or the secretary of the sub-contractor, certifying that the sub-contractor holds a CIS5 and giving details of it ("the certifying document method").[92]

(3) A factor is unlikely to be entitled to such a certificate: one of the

---

[89] From April 6, 2007 a new construction industry scheme is to be introduced under which tax certificates will be abolished in favour of a system of registration.

[90] Under the new scheme contractors will include companies not in the construction industry, but whose average annual expenditure on "construction operations" in the three year period before their last accounting date, exceeds £1 million.

[91] From April 6, 2007 all contractors and sub-contractors who wish to be paid gross must register with HM Revenue & Customs.

[92] Under the new scheme the debtor is required to verify with HM Revenue & Customs the sub-contractor's payment status unless an exception applies.

conditions to be satisfied by a company is that its business must consist of, or include, construction operations or the furnishing of labour in construction operations. Therefore, simply as "a nominee", a factor cannot receive payment without the deduction.

(4) However, a special concession is made for factors *provided that the certifying document method is used*. This means that there is no way in which a factor may receive payment without deduction of tax if the factoring agreement is with a sole trader or partnership because that method may only be used by sub-contractors that are companies. For sole trader or partnership clients and those clients which are companies but which do not wish to use the certifying document method, it may be possible to provide an invoice discounting facility under which payments made gross by the debtor can be paid to a bank account controlled by the factor. However, if the client fails to procure payment in the manner described, under an invoice discounting arrangement the factor will not be able to collect from the debtor in his own name. Whilst this may cause some practical difficulties for the factor, he should be able to rely on the power of attorney in his factoring agreement to collect the debts or, in the case of a company, his charge over the debts and other assets and rights to appoint a receiver or administrator to whom the debts can be paid and then collected by the factor.

(5) The special arrangements, by which the factor may receive payment without deduction, is available only if payment is to be made by cheque or credit transfer into a bank account operated by the factor for the sub-contractor's legally [sic] assigned debts. Such a bank account must be designated with the name of the factor *and the name of the sub-contractor*.[93]

From the above it is clear that, in order to provide factoring services for a company being a sub-contractor in the construction industry with reasonable safety, a factor must, not only have more than the usual confidence in the reliability and administrative ability of the client, but must also allow, in assessing the factoring charges, for the factor's own additional administrative work in monitoring the client and running a separate bank account.

---

[93] From April 6, 2007 factors as nominees will be able to receive payments gross if their clients are so entitled.

CHAPTER 5

MUTUAL REVIEWS: THE FACTOR AND THE CLIENT

The use of factoring, the relations between the factor and his client and the **5–01**
operational procedures have been described in previous chapters; the legal
relations between the parties are described in the second part of this book.
This chapter discusses the considerations to be taken into account by the
factor and the client before entering into an agreement. In reviewing any
proposal for factoring, the prospective client's professional advisers,
accountants and solicitors, have an important role. It has been said that
factoring is like a marriage whereas other forms of business finance, such as
leasing or hire purchase, are more like flirtations. A business is likely to have
only one factor and the relationship should last a long time; it may have
several leasing or hire-purchase agreements in place at the same time.
Accordingly, great care must be taken by both parties before a decision is
made to enter into the agreement; the wrong decision made in haste may be
the cause of some of the difficulties described in Ch.2.

1. THE PROSPECTIVE CLIENT'S ASSESSMENT

Businesses seeking additional finance

First, it is important that a business that is looking solely for additional **5–02**
finance should look critically at its own financial position with the independent advice of a professional accountant to ensure that the finance
generated by a factoring arrangement will be a suitable answer. It is
important that such finance should not be used for capital expenditure; it
should be used to provide the additional working capital required for any
increase in trading generated by additional capital expenditure.[1] If the
business is unprofitable or heading for insolvency, factoring will be unlikely
to assist; in most such cases, it will merely postpone the final failure whilst

---

[1] See para.2–06 above.

assets available for creditors are further dissipated.[2] Only if there are good prospects for the business to return to profitable trading within a short period will factoring be of assistance. In order to ensure the positive use of the finance to be provided by a factoring arrangement, cash flow forecasts and extrapolations of revenue accounts should be prepared comparing the likely position over the next one to three years with and without the assistance of a factor. Then, before considering the use of factoring, it should be seen that the business will be profitable, with a positive cash flow, after absorbing the costs of the factoring arrangements.[3] In an ideal situation, the funds provided would enable the factor's client to achieve an increase in sales volume and thus reduce unit costs. Furthermore, in making projections of cash flow and profitability it should not be assumed that the maximum allowable prepayments should always be drawn. The most successful use of factoring has rarely been based on using funds to the full at all times; reliance on such full use may be a cause of some difficulty if planned sales are not achieved or if a substantial debt does not rank as eligible for the prepayment of a part of its purchase price.

The factor's other functions

5–03   A business with adequate credit insurance or a pattern of debtor portfolio that makes it self-insuring may not require the credit protection afforded by full or maturity factoring[4]; and if it is efficient in sales accounting and credit control, then it may not require to hand these functions over to a factor. In such a case, invoice discounting or agency factoring[5] will provide the finance which it is seeking from factoring. However, in many cases, it is likely that one of the other variants of factoring may be more beneficial by relieving the client from the bad debts and the administrative functions. Examples of such use of factoring (for example, by a business exploiting new products or markets which may result in unfamiliar risks[6]) are described in Ch.2. If the factoring is to be used to finance rapid growth, it is as well for the prospective client to consider a form of non-recourse factoring[7] or to use credit insurance in conjunction with invoice discounting or recourse or agency factoring. In this way, the danger of a setback to the plans for expansion, or even financial difficulty, by reason of a substantial bad debt may be avoided.[8]

5–04   The use of factoring otherwise than for the provision of finance is not often considered, particularly by professional advisers. However, there are

---

[2] See para.2–05 above.
[3] See para.3–28 above.
[4] See paras 1–45 and 1–56 respectively above.
[5] See paras 1–54 and 1–51 respectively above.
[6] See para.2–31 above.
[7] See "Table of Factoring Variants" at end of Ch.1.
[8] See para.2–13 above.

many cases in which it may be fully justified and beneficial; neither the prospective user nor the adviser should be deterred from considering such use only on account of the general view that factoring is just another means of "raising the wind". Such considerations should particularly apply in the case of small businesses which need protection against bad debts; businesses with sales volumes of less than several million are often not attractive to credit insurers and their terms may not compete with those of a factor when due allowance has been made for the factor's relieving the business from administrative tasks.[9] The handing over to a factor of the functions of sales accounting and collection from customers and the acceptance by the factor of bad debts has been proved to be of economic benefit by the examples of many businesses which, having accepted full factoring for the finance provided, continued to retain it when they no longer required the finance. All these considerations should be taken into account in choosing the right variant.

Choice of factor

Having decided on the type of factoring that will meet his needs, a pro- **5–05** spective client will then have a choice of factoring companies. In making the choice, the prospective client must first consider the credit standing of the factoring companies among which the choice is to be made; factoring, as it is at present usually practised in the United Kingdom, constitutes the sale by the client to the factor of his trade debts. Having sold the debts to the factor and having been paid on account of the purchase price, the client is an unsecured creditor for the balance. There are a number of good factoring companies offering their services throughout the United Kingdom, but surprisingly many prospective users enter into agreements after negotiations with one only. In some cases, this failure to look further afield arises from the recommendation by a bank to its customer that a factoring company owned by the bank should be used; in such a case, the customer may believe that his relations with the bank may be impaired if he looks elsewhere. However, even if ultimately the bank's own factoring company is to be used, it is advisable for the prospective user to check the terms offered by at least one other factor and its method of operation to ensure that what is offered is as suitable as can be obtained elsewhere. The apparent terms offered by factoring companies for the same business vary widely; and, more significantly, even if the apparent terms are identical the resulting cost may vary owing to differing methods of calculation of the charges and, in some cases, the addition of other charges.

In most circumstances, the prospective client should select two or three **5–06** likely factoring companies and investigate their terms, method of operation

---

[9] e.g. as described in para.2–34 above.

and the provisions of their agreement in detail. The proposed arrangement will be likely to include the whole of the sales of the business and consequently its cash flow; accordingly a great deal of care in the selection will not be out of place. At an early stage a specimen of each factor's standard contract should be obtained. Many businesses which are seeking a factoring service leave this consideration until they have made up their minds which factor to use; they may then pass the standard form to their solicitors for a review almost as a formality. This is a mistake; factoring agreements and their operational requirements vary widely and at that late stage it may be difficult to procure an amendment to a standard document. If, however, the factor is aware that there are still competitors in the field the amendment of a provision, unacceptable to the prospective client, may be more readily forthcoming. In particular the matters mentioned in the succeeding paragraphs *together with the normal operational procedures* should be carefully examined. The operational procedures may often be considered at a visit to the factor's offices; most reputable factors are prepared to show a prospective client their systems at first hand and, if required, to refer the prospective client to an existing client for an impartial view of the effect of that particular factor's methods of operation.

The factor's charges[10]

5-07   Many businesses, which have adopted factoring in the past, have, even with the guidance of their professional advisers, chosen purely on the basis of the apparent cost of the administration charge as a percentage of turnover and the finance charge as a percentage of funds used. The choice is not so simple. It is necessary to look at the basis of the calculation of the charges. For example, some factors, in providing recourse factoring, make an additional charge in respect of any debt which remains unpaid a specific number of days after due date. This is sometimes referred to as a refactoring charge[11] and it is often not taken into account by the client in assessing the cost. There are often cases, especially for small businesses, where a minimum annual administration charge[12] is pitched at a level which, when compared with the achieved sales volume, will make the arrangement quite uneconomic for the business in question. However, in view of the unbounded optimism of most small businesses such a minimum charge may have been compared at the outset with a sales level quite unlikely to be achieved. It is here that the professional adviser should counsel caution.

5-08   The method of calculation of finance charges[13] varies considerably. Whether the basis of ultimate payment by the factor for debts purchased is

---

[10] See also paras 3–28 *et seq.* above.
[11] See para.3–34 above.
[12] See para.3–33 above.
[13] See paras 3–35 *et seq.* above.

when collection is made from the debtors or on a fixed maturity date, it is important that it should be made clear to the prospective client when the finance charge will start to run. Some factors have started the calculation of the finance charge on the date on which a cheque is sent to the client; as it is natural for the factor to allow several days for clearance of cheques received before the finance charge ceases to run, the result is that the client is charged for a period during which he has no use of the funds. This may be the case even where ultimate payment of the purchase price is on a maturity date, because the factor will normally have the right to charge his finance charges for the extra days beyond the maturity date taken on average by the debtors and, in making this calculation, the maturity date will be extended by a period for the clearance of cheques. The best practice, now very often followed, is for cheques sent by the factor to be value dated for clearance, in the same way as cheques received, or for funds to be transferred electronically so that the client does not start paying a finance charge until cleared funds are at his disposal. Where finance charges are levied on the extra days, a comparison solely of the percentage charge may be entirely misleading.

The simple percentage of the administration charge may also not give a **5–09** correct estimate of the cost; it is necessary for the prospective client to know which of the administrative functions are to be accepted by the factor for that charge and which are to be charged for separately. Nobody would decide on the purchase of a motor car, for example, by simply comparing prices and not quality and performance or, in particular, which of the accessories are optional extras and have to be paid for separately. However, many business people have chosen a factor simply on price; not only have they not considered the basis of calculation of the charges, but also they have not taken into account, for example, that, whilst most factors which provide non-recourse factoring will absorb debt collection costs on approved debts, in recourse factoring such costs are normally an additional charge to the client.

The factor's right to variations

The original basis of the factoring arrangement may on the face of it seem **5–10** attractive, but a close examination of the standard factoring agreement may disclose that the factor has the right in certain circumstances, or even at his entire discretion, to alter certain elements in the arrangement. These elements may include the percentage of prepayments and, in the case of final payment on a maturity date, the maturity period. In both cases, if alterations are made during the course of the agreement to the detriment of the client, then the main reason for which he may have entered into the agreement, a guaranteed cash flow, may be impaired. Some factors even take the right to alter, at their entire discretion, the administration and discount charge during the currency of an agreement. If the factor takes the right to make such changes unilaterally in the duration of the agreement, then the agreement should provide that any change must be the subject of reasonable notice and the client should have the right to terminate the agreement if the change is not acceptable.

Arrangements for termination

5–11   In Ch.2 above it was suggested that the reluctance of some people in business to use factoring was based on their experience that, once a business had adopted it, there might be some difficulty in terminating the arrangement when it was no longer required. It was pointed out that these experiences were probably based on the use of the wrong variant of the service or the use of the service in the wrong circumstances. In all circumstances, however, it is most important at the outset for the prospective user to find out exactly what arrangements may be made for termination. It has been known for a factor to provide for a long period of notice by the client (up to 12 months or more) and a minimum period for the agreement of up to three years if he wishes to terminate. If such a period of notice is stipulated and provision is made for no prepayments during that period, then obviously the client may have some difficulty in arranging for termination; to obtain a replacement of the finance provided from a bank or another factor, the debts must be freed immediately from the existing agreement by which they are bound. A reputable factoring company, which is confident in the excellence of its service, should not need to incorporate into its factoring agreement draconian provisions for termination in the absence of insolvency or a serious breach of the agreement on the client's part; such a factoring company will be confident that the client will not wish to cease using his services merely to seek another similar arrangement.

Method of dealing with credit approvals

5–12   If protection against bad debts is sought by the prospective client or it is considered advisable as a precaution against overtrading, the factor's method of providing this protection should be examined. A comparison with usual credit insurance practice as regards this aspect will be instructive. For example, many factors follow credit insurance practice in providing that cancellation of a credit limit will not affect deliveries already made by the client, even if a copy of the relevant invoice has not yet been received by the factor at the time of the cancellation. On the other hand, in some factoring contracts, the factors take the absolute right to refuse to purchase any debt until such time as the copy invoice has been received and accepted. In such circumstances, the client may have made a delivery of goods in the knowledge that it is within an approval given by the factor, but may be faced with a refusal by the factor to accept the debt on the subsequent submission of the copy invoice. The method of division of any recoveries after the insolvency of the debtor is also a matter which should be considered;

although most factors take the right to appropriate payments by solvent debtors to debts approved for credit in priority to those that are not approved, once the debtor is in liquidation or bankruptcy dividends and other recoveries should be shared rateably. Where approvals are given by the establishment by the factor of credit limits in relation to individual debtors, factoring agreements normally provide that factors should be obliged to consider upward adjustments only upon application by the client. However, it is now the practice of some factors to review limits on every account on which there is an excess outstanding over the limit regularly (*e.g.* monthly) in the absence of any such application. Some factors may additionally adjust limits upwards to accommodate increased business on well rated accounts by automatic changes in the overnight update of data.

Disputed accounts

A factor cannot take responsibility for dealing with disputes with, and **5–13** rejections by, the client's customers, whether they arise from the goods or services themselves or from the invoices or the terms of the contract of sale or service. A factor will have the right of recourse to the client in respect of any debt which cannot be collected for such reasons. Such a right of recourse postulates the obligation of the client to repurchase the debt; the prospective client and his adviser should ensure that the factor will allow adequate time for such difficulties to be settled by the client before such right of recourse is exercised. Some factors now take the view that, even if a dispute is not settled within a reasonable time, recourse should not be exercised but that the factor should await settlement of the debt by payment or the issue of a credit note or a combination of both. If the factor adopts this course, he may protect himself by stipulating that, at the time when the factor had the right to exercise recourse, the disputed debt becomes unapproved even if it has previously been approved, so that it is no longer eligible for credit protection or prepayment. The advantage of this system is that it avoids the need to tell the debtor that the debt has been reassigned; some large buyers from factored suppliers have objected to the position arising whereby certain invoices are to be settled direct to the supplier whilst most others are to be paid to the factor.[14]

Guarantees and indemnities

Not infrequently, when a factor is requested to provide his services, **5–14** including prepayments, for a company in a group, he may require guarantees and indemnities from other group companies; and, in the case of an independent company, he may require them from directors or shareholders

---

[14] See para.3–23 above.

in a personal capacity. The main purpose of such requirements is to provide for the factor to be reimbursed in the event that, on the insolvency of the client company, he is unable to recover from the debtors the prepayments which he has made. Many such guarantees and indemnities are very widely drawn and would even cover the factor against inability to recover if his loss arises from the failure of the debts to vest in him owing to a defect in his documentation. On the other hand, a usual practice now is for the factor to be satisfied with an indemnity covering losses arising only from breaches of the factoring agreement by the client company. Such losses, for example, might be occasioned by the banking by the client company in its own bank account of debtors' cheques, purportedly in settlement of debts purchased by the factor, or from the failure of the client to deliver to the debtor goods which conform to the details on the copy invoice notified to the factor. The rationale of the requirement for such a restricted form of indemnity is that the events, which may give rise to the factor's losses and are covered by the indemnity, are within the control of those who manage the business of the client company; they are naturally quite outside the control of the factor. However, if a wider form of indemnity is expected, then the prospective guarantor or indemnifier may well consider if he is prepared to be responsible for the factor's losses arising from:

(1) the failure of the debts to vest in the factor owing to a defect in the factoring agreement;

(2) a claim to the debts by a receiver owing to the failure of the factor to have obtained a waiver from a bank holding a charge on the debts[15]; or

(3) the insolvency of any debtor.

In the case of any form of non-recourse factoring, it is apparent that (3) should be excluded; the whole object of a non-recourse arrangement is for the factor to accept the credit risks in respect of approved debts and, in respect of unapproved, he should avoid loss by declining to make any prepayment. Even in the case of factoring with full recourse to the client, it is arguable that in some circumstances the factor, being an expert in matters of trade credit, should be in a better position than the guarantor to protect himself.

5–15   The form of guarantees and their enforcement are matters beyond the scope of this treatise and references should be made to specialist works on the subject or specific legal advice. However, mention must be made of the careful consideration to be given by a factor taking a guarantee from a person who is likely to be influenced by the client (or a director or principal

---

[15] See paras 8–77 et seq. below.

shareholder of it, if it is a company), or is under duress and has little or no interest in the subject matter of the guarantee. In such a case, unless the factor ensures that the guarantor is aware of the need for independent legal advice, the guarantee is likely to be unenforceable owing to the factor's implied knowledge of the circumstances. Such a person is likely to be, but by no means limited to, the wife or cohabitant of the main director or shareholder of the client. This is the result of the decision in *Barclays Bank Ltd v O'Brien*,[16] in which it was indicated that "the wife attend a private meeting (in the absence of the husband) with a representative of the creditor at which she is told the extent of the liability as surety, warned of the risk she is running and urged to take independent legal advice". If such a procedure is followed by a factor, then careful notes should be made of the meeting. As a result of that case, there is no doubt that, to be absolutely safe, the factor's best protection is a confirmation from an independent solicitor that advice as to the meaning and effect of the guarantee has been given to the prospective guarantor. A review of some cases, which have been considered by the Court of Appeal since the *O'Brien* case, suggests that the steps propounded in the *dicta* in the case are not exclusive. These cases indicate that informing the guarantor of the need to take independent legal advice should relieve the beneficiary of the guarantee of responsibility even if that warning is not heeded.

2. THE ACCOUNTING CONVENTIONS

All the considerations mentioned above in the chapter should be taken into account by a professional adviser to a prospective user of factoring. The standard documentation should be reviewed at an early stage and the actual operational procedures and accounting arrangements should be seen at first hand. If the person advising a prospective client is also the auditor, an examination of the factor's accounting procedures at this stage may well be a help later on when the audit of the client's annual accounts is to be undertaken. Most factors are quite willing to demonstrate to professional accountants the factoring systems, the returns made to clients and the accounting procedures. The auditor may then be able to assess whether the systems, returns and accounts will be satisfactory to him as an auditor. **5–16**

Present factoring practice postulates the transfer of the ownership of the debts to the factor whichever variant of the service is used. As a result, in accordance with the accounting conventions, as they were before the promulgation of Financial Reporting Standard 5 by the Accounting Standards Board, those debts appeared in the balance sheet of the factor and not that of the client. There appeared as a debt, in the balance sheet of the client, the **5–17**

---

[16] [1994] A.C. 180.

unpaid balance of the purchase price of the debts purchased by the factor; this is the amount of the purchase price of the outstanding debts (*i.e.* the amounts payable by the debtors less the factor's charges) less the amounts already paid on account of the purchase price by way of prepayment. This balance remains as a debt owing to the client subject to the factor's rights of retention and set-off. The accounting conventions, by which the factor's ownership of the debts the subject of a factoring agreement, is recognised in the balance sheet of his client, are no longer accepted in the case of any form of factoring in which the client retains a significant interest in the debts sold to the factor. This would apply to any form of factoring described in this book because at the minimum the client retains an interest in the time of the collection of the proceeds of the debts by reason of the continuance of the discount charge until that time.[17] Furthermore, even in the case of any form of factoring without recourse, there are likely to be debts which are not approved and are subject to recourse; the client also has the responsibility for the collection of any debt which is the subject of a dispute with the customer or of a breach of any warranty or undertaking given by the client in the factoring agreement. In any form of factoring, in which all debts are subject to recourse if not paid for *any* reason, the client's interest is substantial owing to his obligation to pay (either by way of repurchase of the debt or by way of a guarantee of payment[18]) if the debtor fails to do so. Finally, most factoring agreements now provide for an obligation on the part of the client to repurchase all debts previously purchased by the factor and remaining unpaid on the termination of the agreement Thus, in all forms of factoring the client will usually have a significant potential interest in all outstanding debts.

Financial Reporting Standards

5–18   The current conventions have been promulgated by the Accounting Standards Board in Financial Reporting Standard[19] to which reference should be made for a full understanding of the principles on which the standards are based.[20] The purpose of the Accounting Standards Board is to ensure that company accounts show the substance and true commercial effect of transactions and not necessarily their legal form. The standard provides that an asset may be omitted from the balance sheet[21] of a company, which has sold the asset, only if the company retains no significant interest or risk in relation to the asset. Otherwise, the asset must be shown in

---

[17] See para.3–35 above.
[18] See paras 10–28 *et seq.* below.
[19] "Reporting the Substance of Transactions".
[20] A full copy of "Application Note C-Factoring of Debts" is contained in App.11 of this book; this shows the application of the standard to the accounts of clients of factors.
[21] Referred to as "derecognition".

the balance sheet at its full value and the purchase price or other finance received must be shown either as a liability ("separate presentation") or as a deduction from the value of the asset ("linked presentation"). Thus, if linked presentation were considered to be requisite for a client who had sold its debts to a factor, the position might be shown as follows:

Trade Debts	500,000	
Less		
Amount received from factor	380,000	£120,000

Such presentation is considered requisite only in a case in which the financier may look only to the asset financed to recover his funds and has no reserve rights against the company in the event of a shortfall.

"Derecognition" will never apply to factoring or discounting arrange- **5–19** ments as carried out in the UK at present because in all cases the client retains the significant benefits and risks in the assigned debts mentioned above. In the case of some non-recourse arrangements, a "linked presentation" may be applicable; but for that to apply, the factor should have no reserve rights against the client. However, a linked presentation will rarely be requisite even in non-recourse arrangements because most factors provide for full recourse of all debts on termination of the factoring agreement or on the insolvency of the client. Except in the rare cases in which a "linked presentation" would be appropriate, "separate presentation" must apply.[22]

3. THE FACTOR'S ASSESSMENT OF THE PROSPECTIVE CLIENT

Some of the mischief caused by the use of factoring for an unsuitable **5–20** business or at the wrong time was described in Ch.2; in Chs 3 and 4 it was demonstrated that a successful factoring operation depends, not only on the efficiency of the factor, but also on that of the client's own office administration. It is therefore important for the factor to make a thorough review of every prospective client's business before offering any variant of factoring. If the factor does not, he runs the risk that the arrangement will not be successful; and the blame for the unsuccessful outcome will probably be laid at the door of the factor's own operations (which may be impeccable) or even of "factoring" in general. For the purpose of such a review, it is normal for a

---

[22] See App.11.

first exploratory discussion to take place between a new business executive of the factor and an executive director or principal of the prospective client.

The survey

5–21   If, as a result of such a meeting, a *prima facie* case can be made out on both sides for the proposed factoring arrangement, then the factor will normally expect to carry out an investigation of the prospective client's business; this is referred to as a "survey". Apart from determining the suitability of factoring in the particular case, the purposes of the survey, combined with the initial and any other meetings, are as follows:

(1)   to assess the quality of the debtors and thus the likely risks of the failure by the factor to collect in the purchased debts and, in the case of non-recourse factoring, to determine how much to include in the factor's charges for this risk in relation to approved debts;

(2)   to assess the administrative function to be taken over by the factor and how much the factor should charge for this element;

(3)   to assess the strength of the client's business and the prospect of its profitable operation whilst the factoring arrangements are in place;

(4)   to ensure that the factor will obtain ownership of the debts purported to be sold to him free from any charge or other encumbrance or claim by any third party[23]; and

(5)   to determine the extent to which the factor's ability to collect the debts purchased by him will be frustrated by disputes, returns and allowances and other cross-claims by debtors.

The best practice is for terms to be quoted only after the survey has been carried out because, even if there is a clear indication of suitability on both sides, suitable terms can be arrived at only after an in depth study of the nature and pattern of the prospective client's business. Unfortunately, severe competition and pressure on management to produce fast growth in recent years appear to have reduced the survey to something of a formality for some factoring companies who have consequently entered into agreements with unsuitable businesses or at the wrong time; the result has been some of the unhappy events described in Ch.2. The matters to be studied are described in the succeeding paragraphs of this chapter. Some of them may be considered at the initial meeting or on the survey or at other times before an offer is made; the timing depends on the factoring company's own organisation and new business strategy.

---

[23] The encumbrances most often met are described and their effect is analysed in Ch.8.

Independent enquiries

Naturally the factor will make the normal independent enquiries **5–22** regarding a prospective client. In relation to a company, such enquiries have in the past included a search at the companies' registry regarding the capital and constitution of the company, its shareholders and officers and any charges on its property. In all cases, the factor is likely to obtain status reports on the prospective client and, in the case of a newly established business, to make extensive enquiries regarding the previous business activities of the directors and shareholders or principals. The examination of financial accounts of the past few years and up-to-date management accounts will assist the factor in assessing the financial strength and future prospects of the business.

The product

Possibly the most important condition for a successful factoring opera- **5–23** tion is that the client's product should be acceptable to its customers, in good demand and of such a nature that there will be little (or ideally nothing) in the way of post-invoice contractual obligations on the part of the client. The nature and acceptability of the product will affect, not only the degree to which the factor will be faced with credits and allowances granted to the debtors by the client and claims for set-off and abatement by the debtors,[24] but also the credit risk as regards the debtors. There is little doubt that debtors will pay more promptly for goods that are essential to their businesses and cannot be obtained elsewhere than for goods or services which are widely available; furthermore, a supplier with a product which is competitively priced and in good demand should be able to command customers of good quality. Where the business of the client is more than usually liable to disputes or is liable to substantial contractual obligations after the delivery of the goods,[25] payments by debtors may well be delayed pending testing of the product or completion of the further obligations. Any such delays in payment will increase the credit risk.

In Ch.2 there are described the difficulties that may result both for the **5–24** factor and the client from the provision of factoring to certain types of business. It is not possible to list the types of business that are suitable and those that are unsuitable because even within the same trade or industry there are considerable variations of practice. There are also many areas in between complete suitability and unsuitability and, although of prime importance, the product is not the only matter to be taken into account. There are, however, two important principles to be considered:

---

[24] The effect of such claims on the ability of the factor to collect is analysed in Ch.9.
[25] See paras 2–25 *et seq.* above.

111

(1)   the nearer the product is to being simple and repetitive without any post-invoice contractual obligations, the more likely is the factor to be able to avoid disputes and cross-claims; and

(2)   the greater the competition in the trade or industry the more likely is the factor to be faced with poor credit risks.

5–25   As regards the first of these principles, many factors in the United Kingdom and Europe have disparaged their counterparts in the United States for not developing factoring widely outside the traditional industries: textiles, clothing, footwear, toys and similar consumer goods. However, that may be the result of long experience and there is little doubt that some outside the United States have become overconfident as regards the suitability of certain types of business; there have certainly been examples of factors' inability to collect from debtors on the insolvency of their clients solely by reason of the type of product or service provided by the client.

5–26   A particular difficulty has been experienced where the client's business includes the sale of products made from special tooling (or moulds) produced and retained by the client. In some cases, the client will recover the cost of the special tooling by including an element to cover it in the price of the products and, in such a case, the tooling will probably remain the property of the client and there will be no problem as regards the factoring arrangements. However, in most cases, the tooling is invoiced separately and becomes the property of the debtor. If the debt for the mould or tooling is accepted by the factor, then it is advisable that no payment on account of the purchase price of that debt should be made until some of the products have been accepted by the debtor. Even when the mould or tooling has been paid for by the debtor, difficulties may be met on the insolvency of the client if other debts are then owing by the debtor: the debtor may well decline to pay unless the tooling is delivered to him[26] and the person charged with the administration of the client's insolvent estate may decline to release it. It is likely that the debtor would have no right in the liquidation or bankruptcy of the client to set off his claim to the tooling against a debt for goods sold and delivered to him, but the debtor may not be easily persuaded to pay promptly in such circumstances. On the other hand, if the person administering the estate of the insolvent client is cooperative and the debtor is keen to place the tools with other moulders, then prompt payment of his debt to the factor may be induced by the release of the tools.

---

[26] In order that set-off should apply in the bankruptcy or liquidation of the debtor both claims must be claims as will result in payment of money and not claims for the return of goods in specie; see para.9–12 below.

The terms and conditions of sale or service

Closely allied to the consideration of the goods or service provided by the **5–27** prospective client is a review of the client's terms and conditions of sale. The importance of such a review in relation to collections from the debtor has been referred to in Ch.4 and the question of the debtor's countervailing rights is dealt with fully in Ch.9. It will be apparent from a study of Ch.9 that the factor must be particularly vigilant in those cases where, because of competitive pressures, the prospective client must accept the debtor's terms and conditions of purchase in place of his own terms of sale. The following are some of the matters to which special consideration often has to be given:

(1) prohibition on the assignment of debts arising from the contract of sale or service[27] will enable the debtor to obtain a good discharge by paying the client. If sales to a debtor who includes such a term in his purchase contract constitute a large part of the total, then it may be advisable for the factor to procure a waiver from the debtor.

(2) Contractual set-off provisions that are wider than those arising in equity[28] are often included in such terms.

(3) Where orders constitute more than one delivery, the factor should consider whether the contracts are entire or divisible, and it may be necessary to procure the inclusion of a "cut-off clause".[29]

(4) The reservation of title to goods sold until payment has been received may well assist the factor in his assessment of the credit risk, but he should ensure that such terms do not detract from his right to payment on due date for which provision is made. Where the client sells goods, purchased subject to reservation of title, in their original form, it may be necessary for the factor to exclude such terms in the client's conditions of sale.[30]

(5) If goods are delivered on consignment or terms of sale or return or sale or exchange and debts are notified to the factor on delivery, the factor will not have a definite due date on which he can recover from the debtor. The factor may be able to accept the debts when a firm sale has been effected, but such arrangements call for additional monitoring by the factor in order to ensure that the debts which he has purchased are in fact collectable and not subject to return or exchange. The factor as assignee cannot be in a better

---

[27] See paras 9–36 and 9–37 below.
[28] See paras 9–09 *et seq.* below.
[29] See paras 9–51, 9–56 and 9–57 below.
[30] See para.8–43 below.

position than the client as regards his relations with the debtors; it may, therefore, be necessary for the prospective client's standard terms to be amended before factoring starts.

5–28   The factor should also consider the following special classes of debtor:

(1)   Government departments including agents for the government such as area health authorities.[31]

(2)   Debtors closely associated to, or under, common control with the prospective client. Such associates, including directors or employees of the prospective client, do not effectively provide for an independent source of recovery for the factor.

(3)   Individuals purchasing for their own personal, domestic or family use.

Debts incurred by any such debtor and those arising from some of the special terms mentioned above (in particular any debts arising from sales on a sale or return basis) are often excluded from the factoring arrangements. Furthermore, where a debtor is also a regular supplier, it may well be advisable to exclude such debts, unless an agreement between the *factor* and the debtor not to effect set-off can be concluded[32] However, the factor, whose arrangement is of the whole turnover type[33] should consider whether it would not be to his advantage not to exclude them but to release the client from the obligations to notify them to the factor and to give notice to the debtors. By such means the factor may own the debts and the release of the obligation to notify is based on the rationale that the client cannot give the factor the requisite warranties in relation to them.

Encumbrances on debts

5–29   In Ch.8 it is argued that a factor should not be concerned with the terms on which the client is purchasing from its suppliers[34]; unlike his complete information regarding the debtors, the factor has no information regarding the suppliers from whom the client may purchase from time to time. In this respect he must rely on the warranties in the factoring agreement that the debts notified to him will be free from any counter-claim in respect of purchases by the client from the debtor and that such debts will not be held in a fiduciary capacity on behalf of any supplier. However, it is as well for the factor to examine the purchase ledger to assess as far as he can the

---

[31] See paras 9–33 and 9–35 below.
[32] See para.9–20 below.
[33] See para.7–10 below.
[34] Paras 8–28 *et seq.*

114

degree to which cross trading, giving rise to claims by debtors to set-off, may be endemic in the particular business. Where there may be a significant incidence of set-off, it may be advisable to stipulate that the client should provide periodically lists of creditors for comparison with the debtors. This is considered essential in an invoice discounting arrangement.

The factor should make a search at the Companies Registry to determine **5–30** whether there are any registered charges affecting the debts to be factored. The factor may well be in a stronger position in a conflict with a chargee if his agreement was entered into before the creation of the charge.[35] A search before the execution of the factoring agreement showing that no charges have then been registered is not conclusive that no charges are in existence; a charge may have been created before the factoring agreement becomes effective[36] and registered afterwards but within the requisite 21 days. Most factors are able to monitor the registration of such charges by on-line facilities with a credit reporting organisation. Otherwise, a further search should be made after 21 days. To be absolutely safe in this respect, the factor should make no prepayments until 21 days have elapsed since the execution of the agreement, but owing to competitive pressures such a precaution is now considered impracticable. Enquiries should also be made as to whether any debts are likely to represent the proceeds of goods released to the prospective client on the strength of a letter of trust by which such proceeds are held in trust for a banker or other financier. If in the course of these enquiries any encumbrances on the debts to be factored emerge, then the factor's rights to the debts should be settled by a waiver from the other party or by a priority agreement.

Management and administration

The factor's administration of the sales ledger and his ability to collect **5–31** from the debtors depends to a large extent on the reliability of the client in sending the right goods to the right customers and in producing invoices that are meticulously correct. It is, therefore, important that the factor should carefully review the administrative arrangements in the client's offices. In particular, it should be ensured that there are adequate controls to deal with:

(1) the acceptance and processing of orders;

(2) in the case of manufacturing, the putting of the ordered products into production;

(3) the raising of invoices;

---

[35] For a review of such conflicts see Ch.8.
[36] See para.7–10 below.

(4) disposal of disputes and claims by debtors;

(5) the approval and issue of credit notes; and

(6) the retention and availability of evidence of the delivery of goods and the completion of services.

4. THE FINANCIAL STRENGTH OF THE PROSPECTIVE CLIENT

5–32 It is probable that before the survey the factor will already have examined audited accounts of the business for its last completed and previous two or three financial years. However, such accounts may not give an absolute indication of the up-to-date position and prospects of the business. There are many in the factoring industry who consider that a factor, in his consideration of a new client, should not be too concerned with this aspect; their view is that, if the factor's rights to collectable debts owing by creditworthy debtors are secure, the failure of the client will not be the cause of a loss. It is therefore often considered that the detailed investigation of the viability of the business of a prospective client will cause them to miss a great deal of new business which will not be outweighed by the saving of the additional expense of a fast turnover of clients. The better view, however, is that:

(1) the acceptance of businesses that are likely to fail increases the factor's expenses, by reason of the cost of setting up new sales ledgers and the recovery of the debts on old ones;

(2) such increase in costs may be reflected in the charges of the factor to all clients; and

(3) such an attitude tends to lend credence to the allegations that a factor is a relatively expensive financier of last resort.

As a result, the best practice is for an examination of the up-to-date financial position of the prospective client, his prospects, the viability of the business and the benefits which will accrue to it from the use of factoring. For this purpose, apart from financial accounts, the examination will often include:

(1) up-to-date management accounts;

(2) an analysis of trade creditors by age;

(3) the checking that amounts payable for PAYE, VAT and national insurance have been settled satisfactorily; and

(4) a consideration of cash flow forecasts.

5. ASSESSMENT OF DEBTORS

The quality and spread of debtors

Unless the number of debtors is unusually small, it is not normally pos- **5–33** sible or commercially acceptable to make a detailed investigation of all the debtors at the stage when a survey is conducted. To check the credit standing of several hundred debtors is expensive in staff time and in the cost of information. At this stage, therefore, the factor will obtain an indication of the general quality of the debtors by examining:

(1) the quality of the largest 12 or 20 regular customers;

(2) the incidence of the placing of accounts for collection with a debt collection agency or solicitor;

(3) the average period of credit taken by the debtors (usually referred to by factors as the "debt turn") over a period of at least one year and the comparison of this with the debt turn normally expected in the particular trade or industry; and

(4) the ageing of the debtors to ensure that there are no disputes which have not been resolved.

The debt turn

The debt turn—the average period of credit taken by debtors—may also **5–34** be an indication of acceptability or otherwise of the product. It may, however, be the result of the absence of good collection procedures by the prospective client—the very reason for his seeking the assistance of a factor. An allegation that a poor debt turn is the result of the lack of diligence should not be accepted by the factor at face value; a careful investigation may reveal some serious disputes, poor credit risks or even special arrangements such as consignment sales or long credit terms. The calculation of the debt turn may be carried out in a number of ways; but the most usual is to compare the average of month end totals of debts outstanding with the gross sales value:

$$\frac{AD \times 365}{S} = \text{Debt turn in days}$$

Where AD = average total debts at each month end over one year and S = gross sales value for the year.

The calculation can, however, conceal distortions caused by the inclusion of:

(1) large disputed accounts;

(2) bad debts which have not been written off;

(3) accounts on which special terms have been agreed; or

(4) associated company current accounts.

If possible, these distortions should be eliminated by excluding such accounts from the sales value and the totals of debts. The calculation may also be somewhat distorted by any delay in the issue of credit notes. In spite of the drawbacks of this method of calculation, it has the advantage of simplicity. It may not give a true absolute figure owing to the taking of the average of outstanding debts on the basis of end of month figures, because in many cases these are regularly the highest each month; if terms are monthly account, payments usually come in early in the second month after invoice date. It does, however, give a reasonable though crude indication of a trend and a comparison with others in the same type of business. By other methods, the details are more difficult to extract and may also be distorted by special circumstances.

6. ASSESSMENT OF THE FACTOR'S TERMS

The discount charge

5–35   Having come to the conclusion that the business is suitable for the particular variant of factoring under consideration, the factor must assess the discount and administration charge to be quoted. The discount charge will be based on the cost of funds to the factor, the attractiveness of the business to him and the risk of any loss which he may suffer if the client becomes insolvent. His assessment of the risk of loss will depend on the strength of the prospective client's financial position and quality of its management and the likelihood of disputes and cross claims from debtors; in the case of any recourse arrangement, the quality of the debtor portfolio will also be germane to this assessment.

The administration charge

5–36   In the case of invoice discounting or agency factoring[37] in which the factor does not take over any administrative function, the administration charge will reflect only the factor's requirement for remuneration as a commitment fee for making available the funds in addition to the cost of administration of the client's accounts, the reconciliation of the sales ledger control and his

---

[37] See paras 1–54 and 1–51 respectively above.

periodic visits to inspect the accounting records. In any case, where the factor carries out the sales accounting function, the charge must include element to cover this and the collection from the debtors. In order to be able to assess the appropriate charge at his survey of the prospective client's business, the factor will extract some statistics relating to these functions. The most usual figures considered for this purpose are:

(1) the number of invoices and credit notes issued for a given volume of sales;

(2) the number of remittances received from debtors for that volume of sales and, in particular, the proportion of remittances that may be appropriated automatically to invoices;

(3) the number of active debtor accounts and the number of new debtor accounts opened (or old ones reopened) each month;

(4) the incidence of settlement discounts; and

(5) the incidence of any other special features such as carriage charges or returnable pallets.

The non-recourse element

If the factor is providing any form of factoring without recourse as **5–37** regards the failure of approved debtors to pay by reason of their insolvency, then he must include within his administration charge a percentage to cover the risk to him of the insolvency of approved debtors. Unlike a banker who tends to avoid the risk of loss by taking adequate security except in the case of businesses of first class standing, the factor providing non-recourse factoring seeks to accept the risk of loss but to be adequately remunerated for doing so. He will avoid unusually high risks by declining to approve the debtor concerned, but he will expect to accept the credit risks which are normal in the trade and industry. His assessment of this element in the charge will depend on his knowledge of the expected percentage of losses in the particular trade, the record of losses sustained by the prospective client over the past three to five years and his review of the general quality of the debtors and his calculation of the debt turn.[38]

The prepayment percentage

At this stage the factor must also consider what percentage of the pur- **5–38** chase price of the debts sold to him he should withhold until payment by the debtors; this retention is to provide for the set-off of recourse. The converse

---

[38] See paras 5–33 and 5–34 above.

is his maximum prepayment or early payment on account of the purchase price. In order to assess a reasonable percentage for this purpose, the factor must take into account to what extent the invoiced amount of sales is not recovered from debtors (otherwise by reason of bad debts) in the normal running of the sales ledger. This unrecovered percentage will include settlement discounts, returns and allowances, quantity discounts and disputed accounts to be credited. On his survey the factor will take out figures to calculate the percentage of these items to sales over a period of at least a year; he will then need to add to that percentage for the risk that, if the client becomes insolvent, there may well be an increase in the rejection of goods, particularly if the client's business includes an element of post-invoice contractual obligations.

5-39   The matters described above are those that a factor will usually review before offering any variant of factoring; in particular types of business there may be others that the client will need to take into account. In the case of some of the variants, less emphasis may be placed on some aspects, but in most cases all should be taken into account; even if the factor is not taking on the sales ledger function, he should be aware of the workload because he may have to accept it if the client's administration deteriorates or if the client gets into financial difficulties. At all times, when considering the client's business, the factor should keep in his mind's eye the possibility of having to collect the debts without the assistance of the client.

CHAPTER 6

INTERNATIONAL FACTORING

A factoring arrangement will normally be designated by practitioners as **6–01** "international" if the client (as supplier of goods or services) and the person responsible for the payment for the goods and services are situated in different states. Such a designation is virtually in accordance with scope of the application of the UNIDROIT convention[1]; the application of that convention is limited to receivables arising from contracts of sale of which the parties are in different States. The UNCITRAL convention[2] applies, not only to receivables that are international (*i.e.* when the assignor and the debtor are in different States), but also to international assignments where the assignor and the assignee are in different states no matter where the debtor may be. However, for the purpose of determining that factoring transactions are international in character, the situation of the factor does not appear to be relevant: the factor may be in the state of the client or the debtor (or there may be a factor in each) or it may be in a third state. Even in the rare case of a factoring contract between a factor in one state and the client in another in respect of domestic sales of the client, it is probable that the factoring contract would be considered to be domestic. The special legal aspects to be taken into account in international factoring are described in Ch.12; in this chapter the principal methods of dealing procedurally with international factoring transactions are considered.

The requirement in international factoring of procedures different from **6–02** those in domestic business arises from differences in language, law and business practice. Among the most important of these matters are the law and practice relating to the collection of debts and those relating to the financing of businesses. Although there are many overseas states where English is the language of communication and commercial law and practices are almost identical with those in England, the factoring of exports to, or imports from, such countries is treated by English factors as international. On the other hand, in spite of the marked difference between English and

---

[1] See paras 12–24 *et seq.* below and App.5.
[2] See paras 12–35 *et seq.* below.

Scottish law relating to factoring transactions,[3] it is natural that business between England and Scotland should be treated as domestic business.

1. THE TWO FACTOR SYSTEM

6–03   In the early days of modern factoring, whilst its practice was virtually limited to the United States and Canada, little thought had been given to the special difficulties that might arise in the factoring of debts arising from sales across national borders. Special difficulties do not even appear to have arisen in the factoring by factors in the United States of debts arising from exports to that country from the United Kingdom; and this probably arose because these difficulties often arise from the factor's lack of knowledge of the law and practice relating to the collection of debts in another country and the factor in such cases would have been collecting in his own country. However, when factoring was introduced into Europe, factors in the United States saw the opportunity of developing factoring for export transactions by using a correspondent factor in the importer's country. At the same time, factors in Europe, where international trade consisted of a larger part of the sales of typical prospective clients, were faced with the problems mentioned above together with need to obtain fast and reliable credit information. These needs gave rise to the "two factor system" and the creation of worldwide groups of correspondent factors normally referred to as "chains".

The use of the two factor system

6–04   By the two factor system the client enters into an agreement, to include his export sales, with a factor, usually in his own country, so that for his domestic and export business he has to deal with only one factor. The client's factor ("the export factor"), having made arrangements with correspondent factors ("the import factors") in the countries of the client's customers to accept the credit risk on the debtors and to be responsible for collection, then sub-assigns the purchased debts to the import factors. The export factors remains responsible to the client for all aspects of the service and will normally provide finance by way of prepayments. The import factor, dealing with debtors in his own country, will be responsible for the credit risk in respect of approved debts and for collection; having no contractual relations with the client, he will be responsible for these matters to the export factor who in turn will be responsible for them to the client. Naturally the export factor will be responsible to the import factor for the acceptance of recourse (*e.g.* for a disputed debt) and the export factor will

---

[3] See paras 7–26 *et seq.* below.

look for it in turn to the client. In recent years, some factors have accepted the duties of impact factor in respect of debtors situated in countries other than their own. A factor is likely to do this for a neighbouring country where the law and commercial practices are well known to him.

The establishment of chains

Chains of correspondent factors were established for the purpose of **6–05** promulgating common rules to cover the relations between import and export factors[4] and for the accounting arrangements between them. The rules normally cover such aspects of the business as:

(1) the acceptance by the import factor of a new client;

(2) the acceptance of the credit risk by the import factor and cancellations of approvals for future shipments;

(3) the settlement of disputes and recourse;

(4) warranties by the export factor regarding the value and validity of the assigned debts and of the validity of the assignments; and

(5) the time and method of payment by the import factor for the assigned debts.

The export factor must ensure that his own factoring agreement with his client is consistent with these rules to the extent that he has no liability to the import factor for which he cannot look to the client and that he is not exposed to risks as regards failure of the import factor to collect for which he cannot look to the import factor. The accounting rules should include the provision of frequent accounts by the import factor to the export factor showing the position between the two parties and frequent returns showing payments received, disputed items and the state of the debtor accounts.

The past chains (known as "Closed Chains") limited their membership to **6–06** one factor in each country; the members of such chains tended to be associated by common shareholders. Now there are only two chains, Factors Chain International ("FCI") and the International Factors Group ("IFG"), and both are open chains accepting a number of members in any one country. Although some members of the chains are associated by common shareholdings, that is not a condition of membership. Some members belong to both chains. FCI, the larger chain, has made vigorous efforts to expand membership outside Western Europe and North America and now has about 180 members in 50 countries including many in Eastern Europe, Asia, on the Pacific Rim and in Central and South America. The wide member-

[4] See App.6.

ship allows for competition by factors for import business in any country in which there is more than one member.

Procedures under the two factor system

6–07   A typical two factor system works like this[5]:

(1) At the outset, the export factor obtains from the client the normal information obtainable on a survey[6] of the client's business.

(2) The export factor passes to each import factor the following information relating to the client's business in the import factor's country:

    (a) nature of goods or services provided;
    (b) estimated sales volume;
    (c) terms of payment;
    (d) number and type of debtors;
    (e) expected number of invoices and credit notes for the stated volume of sales.

(3) Each import factor considers the information and indicates his terms (administration charge for his part of the service).

(4) On receipt of all quotations from import factors the export factor will be able to determine his own terms.

(5) When the arrangement starts, the procedure for the client is exactly the same as for sales within the United Kingdom,[7] except that:

    (a) the notice of assignment on his original invoices directs the debtors to pay to the appropriate import factor in the language of the debtor; and
    (b) the client may have to supply an extra copy of each invoice to the export factor for onward transmission to the import factor.

(6) On notification or acceptance of each debt the export factor transfers it to the appropriate import factor electronically.

(7) The import factor is then responsible for collections and accounts to the export factor who, in turn, accounts to the client.

(8) Where the arrangements are for factoring without recourse details of the debtors, together with required approvals, are submitted by

---

[5] See App.7.
[6] See paras 5–21 *et seq.* above.
[7] See Ch.3.

export factor to import factor. The import factor usually gives his approvals by the establishment of credit limits on debtor accounts. The export factor gives the equivalent approval to the client. In such a case, it is usually arranged that the import factor will pay at the latest 90 days after due date for any unpaid approved debt except:

(a) if the failure to pay arises from a denial by the debtor of his liability to pay or a counterclaim by the debtor; or
(b) if the debt is subject to a breach of warranty by the seller or export factor.

(9) The import factor will take no responsibility for disputes, but will assist in their settlement if required.

Naturally, on a reciprocal basis, factors in the United Kingdom act as import factors for overseas factors in respect of sales by their clients to customers in the United Kingdom.

Advantages and disadvantages of the two factor system

The advantages for the parties in the use of the two factor system are as follows: **6–08**

(1) In spite of having indirectly handed over the function of sales accounting and collection to an expert in the law and business practices of the country of the debtor, the *client* has only one factor to whom to look for his factoring services. Even if his exports are spread among a number of countries, he will receive only one account and the communications from his factor in his own language and according to the business practices of his own country.

(2) It may also be possible for the *client* to receive the benefit of a lower discount charge if this is generally available in the country of the debtor. This result may be achieved by arranging for the import factor to make prepayments for the debts sub-assigned to him at the rate of discount charge in effect in his own country; the benefit would then be passed on by the export factor to the client. In such a case, as the export factor is responsible for his client, it would be necessary for the export factor to give the import factor an indemnity against failure to recover owing to disputes or breach of warranty on the party of the client.

(3) The *export factor* is in a position to offer expert collection in a large number of countries without having to obtain experience of the law and practice of those countries. He is relieved from the need to deal with debtors in their own language and of the

misunderstandings which sometimes arise from translations. He may rely on credit approvals given by factors who are experts in the credit conditions of their own countries. Furthermore, although it is not the responsibility of the import factor to resolve disputes between the client and the debtor, he would normally be expected to help with their disposal; in the absence of a correspondent in the debtor's country, this may be difficult for a factor particularly in the insolvency of his client.

(4) There is also the advantage to the *debtor* in his being able to pay to a person in his own country and to receive communications from his creditor in his own language. It is also helpful for a debtor to be able to communicate with such a person regarding any disputed item.

6–09 There are also disadvantages in the system. The overall cost will probably be more than if a single factor[8] (whether in the country of the exporter or of the debtor) is used, because the two factors must share the administration charge and, however efficient the system, there must be some duplication of records. The transmission of funds from the debtor may be slower than if the export factor is paid direct by the debtor, because the import factor may await cleared funds in his bank account before paying the export factor; and for smaller items settlements may be made weekly or two weekly.

6–10 For the *import factor* such business is often not attractive. The exports of the client may be scattered over a large number of countries so that the sales volume to each is relatively small and the cost to the import factor of dealing with a client account for such small volume may be disproportionate. He may have to deal with only a few accounts and may not receive sufficient remuneration to accept the exposure of the credit risks. This disadvantage of the two factor system has sometimes been aggravated by the practice of some factors in using direct import factoring where there are substantial sales to an individual country. For this reason also and owing to the more widespread understanding of the laws and practices for other countries, some factors, particularly in Western Europe, use direct export factoring without the intervention of an import factor for debtors in neighbouring countries. A view has been expressed that the two factor system is now tending to become more limited to intercontinental trade and commerce.

Mitigating the exchange risk by the two factor system

6–11 The risk to a client, selling in the currency of the debtor's country, by reason of the fluctuation of exchange rates between the dates of shipment and payment, may be largely eliminated by the use of the two factor system

---

[8] See paras 6–14 to 6–20 below.

and prepayments by the import factor. If, in reliance on an indemnity from the export factor in respect of any recourse, the import factor makes pre-payment of the *whole* of the purchase price on shipment of the goods in the currency of the invoice (in which he should be reimbursed by collection from the debtor), then the export factor may sell that currency immediately upon receipt. The client would then have available to him the sterling equivalent of the invoice value at the spot rate ruling shortly after shipment date.

Improvements in the two factor system

The disadvantage of the two factor system caused by the duplication of **6–12** records was in the past aggravated by the reluctance of export factors to rely fully on the returns from import factors of the sales ledger records. In theory, the export factor should not need to keep the sales ledger because the debts have been sold to the import factors and the export factors should rely on the import factors' accounting and reports. However, export factors often feel the need to maintain a sales ledger updated by the reports of payments, which they receive from the import factors, in order to be in a position to provide prompt feedback of information to the clients. Such a need is particularly relevant when the factor offers on line access to his records through a terminal in the client's offices.[9] Considerable efforts have been made to overcome this problem: systems have been evolved for mes-sage switching through a satellite by which invoices and credit notes may be notified to the import factor and instant updating of debtor accounts by the import factor may be relayed to the export factor.[10] On the adoption of such systems by at least one member in every country in which a chain is represented the problem is largely overcome.

Although reports of receipts from debtors may be made instantaneous by **6–13** such advanced systems, the problem of the receipt by the import factor of cleared funds (so that he may credit his client for the purpose of accruing discount charges) remains intractable. The most obvious remedy for this problem is a multi-party, multi-currency, set-off arrangement, similar to that adopted by the world's airlines many years ago. The matter appears to be under study by at least one of the chains. In the meantime, the rules of FCI provide for the immediate transfer of funds by the import factor on the receipt of a cheque and the export factor undertakes to reimburse the import factor if any such cheque is returned unpaid.

---

[9] See para.3–15 above.
[10] Such instant updating of the export factor's records is now universally applied by at least one of the chains; see reference to "EDIFACToring" and the "Interfactor EDI Rules" in arts 26 and 28 of the Code of International Factoring Customs in App.6.

2. OTHER SYSTEMS FOR INTERNATIONAL FACTORING

The single factor system

6–14   This system, which has been sometimes more aptly described as the "one-and-a-half factor system", was designed as a solution to some of the perceived defects in the two factor system. The intention of its protagonists is to modify the two factor system in order to avoid the delay in payments to the client of the purchase price of debts where such payment is to be made by the export factor on receipt of payment from the debtor; such delay may arise in the two factor system by reason of the debtor's payment having to pass additionally through the hands of the import factor.[11] The system may also have the effect of overcoming some of the duplication of administrative tasks which is a feature of the two factor system.[12] The system is sometimes adapted for use in international invoice discounting.[13]

6–15   By the single factor system the use of the import factor is dispensed with for normal routine collections from and payments by the debtor. However, the import factor acts to protect the export factor against the risk of the insolvency of the debtor, to collect seriously overdue debts and to assist with the resolution of disputes. The inception of the arrangement is exactly the same as under the two factor system.[14] There is however a difference in the operation of the arrangement as follows:

(1)   There is at the date of shipment of the goods no sub-assignment to the import factor; the debts for the time being remain in the ownership of the export factor. As a result, the notice on the invoices is for payment direct to the export factor who is responsible for collection.

(2)   The import factor, having given credit approvals[15] will be responsible for the failure of the debtor to pay an approved debt by reason of his financial inability to do so.

(3)   If any debt remains unpaid for an agreed number of days after its due date for payment (or in respect of an approved debt on any earlier insolvency of the debtor), that debt will be assigned by the export factor to the import factor. The import factor will thereafter be fully responsible for collection of that debt (if approved) and will use his best efforts to collect it (if unapproved).

---

[11] See para.6–09 above.
[12] See paras 6–09 and 6–12 above.
[13] See paras 6–23 and 6–24 below.
[14] See para.6–07 above, sub-paras (1) to (4).
[15] See para.6–07 above, sub-para.(8).

(4) As in the two factor system, the import factor will be responsible to pay in respect of any approved debt unpaid 90 days after the date on which it is due for payment except in the case of a dispute or counterclaim or a breach of warranty. The period mentioned in sub-paragraph (3) above is sometimes specified as 60 days; this period will give the import factor an opportunity of 30 days in which to collect before becoming liable to pay the export factor. If the period is specified as 90 days, the import factor will have the invidious duty of having to pay before having had an opportunity to communicate with the debtor and to ensure that there is no reason, other than financial inability, for the non-payment.

Although by the single factor system the import factor's tasks are limited **6–16** to the acceptance of the credit risk and the collection of difficult accounts, there are some disadvantages. First, the normal collection procedures by a factor, who may not fully understand the business practices of the debtor's country and who may have some difficulties with the language, are less likely to produce results of the standard of collections by the import factor. Secondly, the debtor may be confused by his receiving two notices of assignment: the first to the export factor on the invoice and the second after the agreed period when the import factor takes over. If proceedings for recovery are necessary, such double notice may induce the debtor's lawyers to require evidence of the assignments. Thirdly, the import factor may be less liberal in the giving of approvals than when he has the responsibility for collection from invoice date.

Direct import factoring

It has often been arranged for a client with a substantial volume of export **6–17** business with one country to factor his debts with a factor in that country. This was the method of factoring used by the early factors in the United States. Naturally it would not be a good solution for an exporter whose exports are spread among a number of countries, because it would then result in a multiplicity of agreements according to different laws and a multiplicity of factors using different systems of operation. Its advantages are simplicity and the use by the client direct of a factor who has the knowledge and experience to deal efficiently with credit approvals and collections in his own country. Provided that there is no problem of communication between the client and the factor and the client is competent to deal with a foreign factor, it is an almost ideal solution where the client is looking for collection and protection against bad debts only without any finance by way of prepayments. Indeed, in some cases members of chains[16]

---

[16] See para.6–05 above.

have made arrangements with a correspondent factor to take on a direct basis the client's business in the correspondent's country in return for an introductory commission. The purpose of such an arrangement is to avoid delays in the transmission of information and funds.

6–18   Where the client is looking for finance for his export sales, the factor may find it difficult to monitor the operations of his client without a correspondent in the country of the client with the knowledge of local law and business procedures. This would be the case especially in the event of the insolvency of the client where the factor's ownership of the debts might be challenged by a creditor or the person charged with the task of administering the insolvent estate of the client. It is also necessary for the factor to consider all the legal problems of the assignments of debts across national boundaries which are described in Ch.12; he should ensure that his agreement is binding on the client and third parties in the insolvency of the client according to the law of the client's country as well as that of his own. It is possible also that there may be regulatory impediments in the factor's country to the giving by him of finance by way of prepayments.

Direct export factoring

6–19   Before the establishment of the international chains,[17] it was normal for factors, whose clients wished to include exports within the factoring arrangements, themselves to handle those functions delegated to the import factor under the two factor system. Some factors still handle exports on this basis and the system has the advantage of simplicity for the client; he has to deal with only one factor with one system of procedures and accounting and that factor is in his own country. There is no problem of communication and the information on the state of debtors' accounts does not have to pass through two hands; payments are received direct by the factor and not through an import factor. A factor experienced in export documentation may even assist with this aspect of exports and with collections against shipping documents and letters of credit.

6–20   For the factor, however, there are a number of problems in direct export factoring. First, he must give careful consideration to all the problems relating to conflicts of law in relation to his purchase of the debts free from encumbrances.[18] In this connection he would be well advised to ensure that his assignments and the procedures for them conform to the laws of the debtor's countries as well as those of his own; this is not a light task if his client's business is spread among a large number of countries. Secondly, there are the following commercial matters to be considered:

---

[17] *ibid.*
[18] See Ch.12.

(1) *Credit risks:*
The assessment of credit risks in relation to debtors outside the United Kingdom is difficult without a detailed knowledge of the country of the debtor and its business practices and accounting conventions. The usual answer to this problem is credit insurance. However, the assignment of a credit insurance policy to the factor is not a complete answer to the problem.[19]

(2) *Collections from debtors:*
Collection by a factor in a country other than that of the debtor may be impeded by the following difficulties:

(a) Letters in a language foreign to the debtor may be disregarded or sent to be translated while payments are still withheld.

(b) It might be difficult to deal with general correspondence relating to the collection procedures.

(c) In countries which still maintain exchange control the regulations are often used as an excuse for delays in payment; these delays may be genuinely aggravated by a change in the payee and the channel of payment.

(3) *Disputes:*
There is little doubt that the incidence of disputes and of the non-acceptance of invoices is higher in international trade than in domestic business. This arises *(inter alia)* from misunderstandings regarding contract terms, owing to language problems, regarding trade customs and damage and loss of goods in shipment by sea and air. There is less inclination on the part of debtors to report such disputes to a factor in another country; if the dispute has been notified to the seller, it does not seem necessary to go to the length of reporting it to another organisation in the same country. If it is reported, then it may be in a language that is not understood and, by the time it is translated, valuable time in which to recoup from the client may be lost. It has been known that, without the intervention of a correspondent factor in the country of the debtor, only at the stage of legal proceedings was the factor made aware of the dispute.

Foreign correspondents

From the foregoing it should be apparent that, in order to operate direct **6–21** export factoring successfully, a good correspondent in each country in which a debtor is located must be available to effect collection when any debt becomes seriously overdue and such correspondent must be familiar

---

[19] For a full discussion of the use of credit insurance for this purpose see Ch.14.

with the extra difficulties which arise when collection is on behalf of an assignee. The correspondent must be familiar with developments in the legal concepts relating to the protection of the assignee against the claims of third parties including those arising in the insolvency of the client. In this connection, it should not be overlooked that these matters will probably fall to be considered according to the law of the debtor's country. Such a correspondent must be available at short notice to assist with the resolution of disputes arising from contracts of sale. Attempts have been made to establish a chain of such correspondents outside the factoring industry; but owing to the specialised knowledge required and the economics of establishing procedures for a few *ad hoc* problems, from time to time, it is doubted if any solution can be found better than membership of a chain and the use of a correspondent within the chain.

3. CURRENCY RISKS IN INTERNATIONAL FACTORING

6–22 There are necessarily some currency risks associated with exporting. Exporters are often obliged by the force of competition to quote prices and to invoice in the currency of the country of their debtor's domicile. An exporting client of a factor may be protected against the risk of fluctuations in the currency in which he has invoiced between invoice date and payment in one of three ways:

(1) He may arrange with his bank to sell the currency forward and with his factor to remit to him, on payment by the debtor, in the currency of the invoice.

(2) He may arrange for the factor to credit him in sterling at the rate of exchange ruling on the date when he notifies or offers the currency debt. The exchange risk will then be the factor's responsibility.

(3) He may arrange with the factor, under the two factor system, that the correspondent factor in the debtor's country will make prepayment immediately upon receipt of the copy invoice so that the proceeds may be sold immediately by the export factor and the client paid in his own currency.[20]

4. INVOICE DISCOUNTING

6–23 In view of the rapid growth of the demand for, and the provision of, invoice discounting and other forms of factoring on a confidential basis without

---

[20] The procedure is explained in para.6–11 above.

notice to the debtors in many countries of the world, serious consideration has recently been given to the extension of these services to export sales. In the past, several invoice discounters in the United Kingdom have extended this service to the exports of clients without any special precautions; but they have done so on a limited basis whereby the export sales are a small proportion only of total sales. In this way, debts that are difficult to collect may be recoursed to the client and absorbed by the retention held by the factor.[21] If it is proposed to offer factoring or invoice discounting where exports are all or a large proportion of the sales of the prospective client, then all the considerations mentioned above[22] in connection with direct export factoring should be considered very carefully; the difficulties will be magnified by the absence of notice. It is likely that notice to debtors to pay the factor direct would be given only when the client is in financial difficulty or insolvent. Experience in domestic discounting and factoring has demonstrated that a client's difficulties are likely to be known to customers who will then be more reluctant to pay promptly and may delay until they have ensured that they will have no cross-claims against the client. Such difficulties may be compounded in the case of a factor giving notices for the first time; the factor will need to act quickly and notices in his own language may not be understood immediately so that the debtors may continue payments to the client whilst a translation is being obtained. This problem may be partly overcome by the holding of the factor, from the start of factoring, of a stock of letters signed by the client giving notice of the assignments in the languages of the debtors.

In spite of the difficulties mentioned above, several factors are now **6–24** offering invoice discounting for exports to a number of overseas countries. Very often the risk of the failure of the debtor to pay is covered by the client's credit insurance policy to which the factor may become joint insured. However, that precaution will not help the factor in the event of the insolvency of the client and the impeachment of the factor's unencumbered ownership of the debts under the applicable law which may not be that of the factor's or the client's country. Accordingly, before embarking on the discounting of debts owed by foreign debtors, any factor would be well advised to consider the matters discussed in Ch.12. To be safe the assignments should be valid, not only under the law governing the factoring agreement, but also under the law governing the contract of sale out of which the debt arose and the law of the country in which the debtor is situated.

In recent years, the single factor (or one and a half factor) system **6–25** described above[23] has been adapted for invoice discounting (with or without recourse) and used to overcome some of these problems. The only change to

---

[21] See paras 1–58 and 3–06 above.
[22] See paras 6–19 and 6–20.
[23] See paras 6–14 to 6–16 above.

the system as described is that no notice of an assignment is given to the debtor until the import factor takes over at the agreed time after the due date of the invoice. Until then, the client handles the collection as agent for the export factor as in normal domestic invoice discounting.

5. BACK-TO-BACK FACTORING

Back-to-back arrangements between two factors

6–26 Back-to-back factoring is usually an extension of the two factor system: its object is to overcome the difficulty created by the channelling by an exporter of all his sales to one country through a distributor. Very often the distributor is a subsidiary or associate of the exporter; in those and other cases, the result is often that the amount of credit required by the distributor is far higher than can be granted by the import factor on the normal unsecured basis. In many cases, the import of the client's products is the only business of the distributor. The difficulty of accepting the credit risk is overcome by the entry into a factoring agreement by the distributor with the import factor and the use of the balance owing by the import factor for debts purchased as security for the credit granted.

6–27 A typical back-to-back arrangement works like this:

(1) The export factor enters into a factoring agreement, covering the full service, with the client (exporter) and makes arrangements with an import factor to act as his correspondent factor.

(2) The import factor enters into a factoring agreement with the distributor for his domestic sales. This agreement may be for any form of factoring in which prepayments are available. However, the normal arrangements will be varied as follows:

(a) Prepayments are not normally taken; they may, however, be limited to a very small percentage to cover the distributor's overhead expenses.

(b) The import factor and the distributor agree that, at any time at the discretion of the import factor, the amount due to the import factor for the supplies by the client (indebtedness assigned to him by the export factor) may be set off against amounts due to the distributor under the domestic factoring arrangements. It is thought that the right of set-off would be available to the import factor in the insolvency of the distributor.[24]

---

[24] See para.9–12 below.

(3) The approvals given to the export factor by the import factor will be made in one of two ways:

    (a) on the basis of the position on the distributor's account with the import factor; or

    (b) on the basis of firm orders from approved debtors received by the distributor for goods to be shipped.

Alternatively, the import factor may accept all debts from the export factor with recourse but undertake not to exercise any recourse to the extent that he has available rights of set-off.

(4) The exports from the client to the distributor will then be factored through the two factor system in the usual way, except that settlement by the distributor to the import factor (and consequently the import factor to the export factor) will depend upon his sub-sales and the position on his account with the import factor.

It will be appreciated that the system may be difficult to bring into operation when the distribution arrangement is just starting. Until goods have been imported and sold, the import factor has no basis for his approvals (other than evidence of firm orders) as he has nothing owing to the distributor. This lacuna can be overcome only by the exporting client accepting that his first sales will be with recourse.

Back-to-back arrangements by a single factor

An arrangement similar to back-to-back factoring is sometimes entered   **6–28** into without the assistance of an export factor. In such a case, the factor enters into a domestic factoring agreement with a distributor and agrees to accept instructions to pay a percentage of the purchase price of each invoice to the supplier. The supplier may or may not be in the same country as the distributor. Difficulties have been encountered by factors in accepting such instructions and confirming them to the supplier. The percentage to be paid to the supplier will be the invoice value less the importer's mark-up. The balance payable to the importer may not be sufficient to cover the importer's overheads owing to a high incidence of recourse for returned goods. The importer may allege that the recourse arises from deficiencies on the part of the supplier and should be deducted from payments to him.

The purpose of such arrangements is to give the supplier confidence in the   **6–29** granting of credit to the distributor; the factor may, therefore, not be in a position to make such deductions owing to the form of his confirmation to the supplier. If it is part of the proposed arrangements that such confirmation should be given to the supplier, then it is advisable that the instructions should be for all payments to go to the supplier (or to an account under the joint control of the supplier and the distributor). It will then be up to these two parties to divide the amounts so paid. As such difficulties may be compounded when there is more than one supplier, these arrangements should be made only with a distributor of the goods of one supplier.

CHAPTER 7

THE LEGAL STRUCTURE OF FACTORING AND TRANSFER OF OWNERSHIP OF THE DEBTS

In its simplest form, which is the provision of funds by way of invoice   **7–01**
discounting without any form of service or protection to the client, factoring
is in substance no different from lending against the security of debts.
However, the judiciary has on several occasions distinguished in law the
provision of funds to a business by a purchase of debts (which is the method
almost invariably used by factors in the United Kingdom) from the lending
of money.[1] This chapter and the next cover the legal relations between the
factor and his client; and in this chapter the legal structure of the arrangement for the transfer of ownership of the debts is described.

1. TRANSFER OF OWNERSHIP BY ASSIGNMENT

The factor's principal demand of the law is that he should obtain unen-   **7–02**
cumbered ownership of the debts which he has purchased in such a way that
he may have the sole right to collect them in full; in this way, he should be
able to recoup the funds he provides to the client for the purchase price of
the debts. Naturally the principal requirement of the client from the factoring agreement is that he should be paid the full purchase price (the
amount payable by the debtor less the factor's charges) at the time stipulated according to the particular variation of the service to be provided.

Debts which are the subject of factoring arrangements belong to a class of   **7–03**
property known as "choses in action", the ownership of which cannot be
enforced by possession as is the case with chattels. In a small proportion of
cases, the debt may be represented by a bill of exchange or other negotiable

---

[1] "There are many ways of raising cash without borrowing. One is by selling book debts ..."
Chow Yoong Hong v Choong Fah Rubber Manufactory [1962] A.C. 209. See also, *e.g. Re George
Inglefield Ltd* [1933] Ch. 1 and *Lloyds and Scottish Finance Ltd v Cyril Lord Carpets Sales Ltd*
[1992] B.C.L.C. 609.

instrument (a documentary intangible) the ownership of which may be transferred by endorsement and delivery; but most factored debts are not so covered and are pure intangibles. As a result, in order to enforce his ownership of the debts, the factor must have transferred to him the sole right to collect from the debtor using, if necessary, legal proceedings. Such transfer is effected by an assignment, which is an agreement by a creditor to transfer his rights in relation to a debt to a third party and the latter's agreement to accept those rights without necessarily the consent of the debtor.

Historical background to assignments

7–04   Common law has never recognised the transfer of ownership of pure intangibles except by means of a novation requiring the consent of the debtor. Before the Judicature Act 1873, the common law courts were influenced by:

(1)   the personal character of the obligation of the debtor; and

(2)   the fear that the purchase of dubious claims at a large discount by wealthy people might flood the courts with contentious litigation.

Although courts of equity recognised such assignments, proceedings for the recovery of debts had to be pursued in the common law courts. As a result, it was necessary for the assignee to recover from the debtor by using the assignee's name and, if the latter refused to co-operate, to obtain an order for the assignor to do so from the court of equity before starting proceedings in the common law court. Since 1873, when the Judicature Act combined the administration of the courts of equity and of common law, this cumbersome procedure has been unnecessary provided that all three parties, the debtor, the assignor and the assignee, are before the court. If the assignor co-operates in the action, the assignor and assignee will be joint plaintiffs in the action; if he does not, then the assignee must proceed against the debtor and assignor as joint defendants.[2]

Assignments in statutory form

7–05   Section 25(6) of the Judicature Act 1873 gave statutory recognition to assignments of debts provided that they conformed with its requirements. The provisions were substantially re-enacted by s.136 of the Law of Property Act 1925. A formal assignment in accordance with the statute is normally referred to as a "legal assignment" to distinguish it from other

---

[2] *Holt v Heatherfield Trust Ltd* [1942] 2 K.B. 1.

assignments still recognised in equity.[3] The requirements of the statute are that it should be in writing under the hand of the assignor, it should be an absolute assignment of the whole debt (and not by way of charge only) and express written notice of it should be given to the debtor. No particular form of notice is specified by the statute except that it must be in writing. The statute provides for "notice" to be given and not "a notice" so that it does not need to be a separate document; it may be included in a letter.[4] From the few decided cases on the matter it seems clear that, at the minimum, the notice must state that there has been an assignment, what has been assigned and to whom it has been assigned. The notice does not need to include the date of assignment; but if it does and the date is incorrect, then the notice is invalid.[5] An assignment, complying with these requirements and being completed when notice has been received by the debtor,[6] has the effect (subject to equities having priority[7]) of transferring to the assignee:

(1) the legal right to the debt;

(2) all legal and other remedies for the debt; and

(3) the power to give a good discharge for the debt without the concurrence of the assignor.

Therefore, providing that there are no equities having priority (either by way of countervailing rights of the debtor[8] or third party claims[9]) a legal assignment would give the factor what he requires: The unencumbered sole right to collect from the debtor.

Equitable assignments

Any assignment of a debt or other legal *chose in action* which does not fulfil these requirements will be valid in equity provided that the intention of the parties is clear and value is given. Such an equitable assignment need not be in writing. Notice to the debtor is not a necessary prerequisite to the transfer of ownership; but notice is important in relation to competing interests.[10] It is probable that notice to the debtor alone, provided that it was made with the knowledge of, or made known to, the assignee, would **7–06**

---

[3] See *Wm. Brandt's Sons & Co v Dunlop Rubber Co Ltd* [1905] A.C. 454 at 461 where Lord Macnaghton said with reference to the Judicature Act 1873: "The statute does not forbid or destroy equitable assignments or impair their efficacy in the slightest degree".
[4] *Van Lynn Developments Ltd v Pelias Construction Co Ltd* [1969] 1 Q.B.607.
[5] *ibid.*; *Denney, Gasquet and Metcalfe v Conklin* [1913] 3 K.B. 177; *W.F. Harrison & Co Ltd v Burke* [1956] 2 All E.R. 169.
[6] *Holt v Heatherfield Trust Ltd* [1942] 2 K.B. 1.
[7] See para.8–04 below.
[8] See Ch.9.
[9] See Ch.8.
[10] See paras 8–07 to 8–09 below. See also Oditah, *Legal Aspects of Receivables Financing* (1991), p.131.

constitute an equitable assignment.[11] An equitable assignment may be of part of a debt only or by way of a charge.

7–07   However, whether an assignment is legal (in statutory form) or equitable, provided that the substance of the transaction is for the outright sale and purchase of a debt, such assignment will have the effect of transferring ownership absolutely. The statute has in no way detracted from the efficacy of equitable assignments and the position in relation to them remains exactly as it was before 1873.[12] The difference is purely procedural: the assignee has the right to sue in his own name alone for recovery from the debtor only if the assignment is legal. Otherwise, proceedings should be in the joint names of the assignor and the assignee.[13]

2. TYPES OF AGREEMENT COMMONLY USED

Facultative agreements

7–08   The two types of factoring agreement almost invariably used by factors were at one time influenced by stamp duty on written assignments of debts. At the start of factoring in England, the most commonly used was the facultative type. It is termed facultative because, although the client is bound by the agreement to offer every debt arising from sales in the normal course of its business (or of a particular division of the business or in a particular market), the factor may accept or decline to accept any debt. Thus, as far as the factor is concerned, the arrangement is purely optional. This type of agreement was based on long usage in the block discounting of hire purchase and instalment credit debts and on the practice in the United States. The absolute right to decline any debt was thought to give the factor better security; if the prospects of recovery from the debt were doubtful he need not have the responsibility of paying for it. However, the same protection can be effected in an arrangement in which the factor buys all debts in other ways.[14]

7–09   It was also considered at one time that, by using such an agreement, the factor could have assignments in the statutory form in respect of every debt. Now the normal arrangement is for the factor to be deemed to have

---

[11] See, *e.g. Alexander v Steinhardt Walker & Co* [1903] 2 K.B. 208, where instructions to the debtor, to pay the assignee, of which a notification was sent the same day to the assignee constituted a good assignment notwithstanding that the assignor's bankruptcy intervened before either of the communications had been received.

[12] *Wm. Brandts Sons & Co v Dunlop Rubber Co Ltd* [1905] A.C. 454 at p.462.

[13] See para.7–04 above. However, in practice it is not unusual for factors to take proceedings in their own name alone under an equitable assignment which has been notified to the debtor; unless the debtor objects the action should not fail for want of a joinder (see, *e.g.* RSC, Ord.15, r.6).

[14] See para.7–12 below.

accepted the offer and purchased the debt either by not declining the offer within a stipulated period or by paying an amount on account of the purchase price on receipt of the offer. The factor will obtain ownership of the debts in equity by such an informal assignment.[15] The facultative agreement itself gives the factor no real rights as regards the debts; but, apart from containing the factor's contractual right to have the debts covered by the agreement offered to him, the agreement also includes the rights and obligations of the parties in relation to every debt upon its being assigned to the factor by a separate act.

Whole turnover agreements

Common law has never recognised a present assignment of property not yet in existence or in the ownership of the assignor. Therefore, were it not for the assistance which equity provides for the factor, a whole turnover agreement, by which the client agrees to sell and the factor agrees to purchase all debts arising in the client's business, would require a new act of transfer by the client when each debt arose. However, by the equitable doctrine, by which that which ought to be done is done, the ownership of future property can be transferred by a present agreement. Once consideration has passed, such an agreement is effective to assign debts as they come into existence without further formality or act of transfer.[16] There is but one other stipulation for such an agreement to be effective: the subject matter, as it comes into existence, must be identifiable from and bound *by the agreement itself*.[17] The inclusion within the scope of the agreement must not be based on a later act of appropriation. The agreement need not cover *all* debts of the client; it may apply to a certain division or product or market (as long as the debts are clearly defined), but not, for example, to debts owing by such debtors as the client may wish to include from time to time. **7–10**

Until the factor has given valuable consideration, an agreement of the whole turnover type is effective as a contract only and does not give effect to the transfer of ownership of any future debt without a further act of transfer, even if it is executed as a deed by the client. A commitment to give the consideration is not sufficient to give effect to the assignments because equity will not enforce specific performance of a contract to pay money; for the assignments to be enforced and asserted against third parties the consideration must be executed.[18] However, once consideration has passed, the factor will take, as regards any debt (identifiable as falling within the scope of the agreement by reference to the agreement itself) on its coming into **7–11**

---

[15] See para.7–06 above.
[16] *Holroyd v Marshall* (1862) 10 H.L. Cas. 191.; *Tailby v Official Receiver* (1888) 13 A.C. 523.
[17] *Tailby v Official Receiver* (1888) 13 A.C. 523.
[18] *Holroyd v Marshall* (1862) 10 H.L.Cas 191, and see Goode, *Some Aspects of Factoring Law* (1982) J.B.L. at p.242.

existence, the same right and interest as if it had actually belonged to the client at the time when the agreement was made.[19] In such a case, no independent act of assignment is required. However, what constitutes consideration for this purpose in relation to assignments by way of purchase is not entirely clear; the decided cases relate to the assignment of future property by way of security for monies advanced by the assignee to the assignor where there was no commitment for further advances.[20] It is now generally accepted that, for this purpose under an agreement of the whole turnover type, one payment to the client or one credit to the client's account should be sufficient because the agreement is a single indivisible contract for the sale of the debts to which it relates.[21]

Advantages of whole turnover

7–12   From the factor's point of view, the advantages[19] of a whole turnover type of agreement are as follows:

(1) The agreement will define the class of debts to which the agreement applies and all those debts vest in the factor whether or not they are notified to him. The factor may protect himself against paying early on account of the purchase price of debts, of which he has doubt, by either or both of the following:

    (a) a provision by which debts are approved for early payment and by which payment for unapproved debts is made only upon their collection;

    (b) the right to require the client to repurchase any debt in relation to which the client is in breach of any warranty (*e.g.* if the debt is disputed or subject to set off). In a situation in which the factor's client is insolvent and the factor has doubts about the collection of all the funds laid out by way of early payment, it is better for the factor to own additional debts for which he has not paid (even if such debts are disputed or encumbered or doubtful of collection) than to own no such additional debts at all.

(2) Debts created up to the time of the appointment of a receiver or administrator to a client or the commencement of the bankruptcy or winding up of a client vest in the factor whether or not such debts have been notified to him or the debtor[22] and whether or not they have been invoiced. In this connection an existing debt is

---

[19] *Tailby v Official Receiver* (1888) 13 A.C. 523.
[20] See, *e.g. Tailby v Official Receiver* (1888) 13 A.C. 523.
[21] See Goode, *op. cit.* at p.242 and *Commercial Law* (3rd ed., 2004) n.41 on p.747.
[22] *Gorringe v Irwell India Rubber and Gutta Percha Works* (1886) 34 Ch.D. 128.

usually considered to be a debt arising out of an existing contract, whether or not it has been earned by the performance of the contract by the supplier.[23] The principle applies to debts earned by performance of the contract of sale or service by the supplier between the date of a petition for the supplier's bankruptcy or winding-up and the bankruptcy or winding-up order (as the case may be) in spite of the relation back of the bankruptcy or winding-up to the date of the petition; the disposition of the debts has taken place at the time when the agreement became effective.[24] However, this principle does not apply to any debt arising out of the delivery of goods or the performance of services by a trustee in bankruptcy or liquidator of an insolvent client even if the debt arose from a contract in existence at the date of his appointment.[25] It also seems likely that, based on the analogy of the position in bankruptcy, the principle would not apply to debts earned by performance by an administrative receiver.

(3)   Once an agreement of this type has started and the first credit or payment by the factor has been made, in the absence of compliance by the client of his obligations to notify the debts to the factor and to give notice to the debtors, the factor may himself give such notice and collect the debts. This would assist the factor if the client fraudulently discounted the same debts elsewhere without the factor's knowledge.[26] On the other hand, a facultative type of agreement, constituting a series of independent transactions, does not bind the subject matter as it comes into existence and, in the absence of offers and notices to the debtors, the factor has no such right *in rem*, but only a personal right against the client for damages; and he has no right for specific performance. The factor would, therefore, only have a personal right against the client for breach of warranties and undertakings if, instead of offering the

---

[23] *Hughes v Pump House Hotel Co Ltd* [1902] 2 K.B. 190. See also Goode *Commercial Law* (3rd ed.) pp.631 *et seq. cf. Burford Midland Properties Ltd v Marley Extrusions Ltd* [1994] B.C.C. 604 in which it was held that for the purposes of a voluntary arrangement in accordance with Pt I of the Insolvency Act 1986, rent payable under an existing lease in respect of any period after the date on which the arrangement became effective, was, not only not an existing debt, but was not a debt in any sense, *i.e.* not even a future debt. It was held that such rent was essentially "a right of property". By analogy, for the purposes of a factoring agreement of the whole turnover type and any conflicts with third parties it is most likely that the debtor's obligations under existing contracts, being rights of property, will belong to the factor. For avoidance of doubt it is advisable for the expression "debt" in any factoring agreement to be defined on the lines of the following: "any obligation of the debtor incurred under a supply contract whether or not payment has been earned by performance".
[24] See para.11–58 below.
[25] *Re Jones (ex p. Nichols)* (1883) 22 Ch. D. 782; *Re Collins* [1925] 1 Ch. 556; *Wilmot v Alton* [1897] 1 Q.B. 17, CA; and see Wood, *English & International Set-off* (1989), paras 7–173 to 7–176.
[26] The factor relying on the rule in *Dearle v Hall* (see para.8–02 below) would be able to defeat the claims of the other discounter.

debts to the factor, the client charged them to a bank or sold them to a third party.

(4) As a whole turnover agreement is a *present* assignment of future debts, upon the creation of any debt falling within the scope of the agreement (provided that some part of the consideration for which the agreement provides has passed), the rights of the factor to the debt take effect as from the date of the agreement.[27] Accordingly, the factor with this type of agreement is in a strong position to rebut the claims of any person who seeks to encumber the debts of the client after the agreement has become effective by the first payment or credit by the factor. The factor, whose agreement is of the facultative type, is often in a much weaker position. For example, such a subsequent encumbrancer might be a bank in whose favour the client creates a fixed charge on book debts and, in the case of a facultative agreement, the factor, in many cases, would be unable to accept any further offers of debts except subject to the charge.[28]

7–13 It is sometimes claimed that an agreement of the whole turnover type, the existence and effect of which is notified to the client's customers at the outset, will give the factor advantages in relation to the preclusion of the set-off of certain of the debtor's countervailing rights and in the factor's claim to priority under the rule in *Dearle v Hall*.[29] It is unlikely that these advantages exist in the present state of the law and the questions are discussed in detail in Ch.8.

7–14 A disadvantage to the factor of the facultative type of agreement arises from the factor's need to control the timing of assignment notices to debtors.[30]

3. SOLE TRADERS AND PARTNERSHIPS

7–15 The only disadvantage of a whole turnover type of agreement is that, if it is entered into with a sole trader or partnership, it should be registered under the Bills of Sale Act 1878. It is provided by s.344 of the Insolvency Act 1986 that a general assignment of existing or future book debts or any class of

---

[27] "The rule of equity which applies to the assignment of future choses in action is, as I understand it, a very simple one. As soon as they come into existence, assignees who have given valuable consideration will if the new chose in action is at the disposal of the assignor, take precisely the same right and interest as if it had actually belonged to him, or had been within his disposition and control at the time when the assignment was made". *Tailby v Official Receiver* (1888) 13 A.C. 523 *per* Lord Watson at 533.
[28] See para.8–28(2) below.
[29] (1828) 3 Russ. 1 and see para.8–03 below.
[30] See 8–07 below. A specimen of a whole turnover type of agreement is contained in App.8.

them made by a person, who is subsequently adjudged bankrupt, is void against the trustee in bankruptcy as regards book debts not paid before the bankruptcy petition unless the assignment has been so registered. An agreement of the whole turnover type described in para.7–10 constitutes a general assignment for this purpose; as a result, in the absence of registration, the factor with an agreement of this type may expect, in the bankruptcy of his client, to lose all the debts purchased by him and outstanding at the date of the petition. It is further provided by the section that the expression "general assignment" does not include an assignment of book debts due at the date of the assignment from specified debtors or of debts becoming due under specified contacts. As a result, there is no need for the registration of assignments under an agreement of the facultative type.

7–16 In order that a factoring agreement should be so registered, it must be executed by the client in the presence of a solicitor after the solicitor has explained the nature of the assignment contained in the factoring agreement. The solicitor then completes and signs an attestation clause on the factoring agreement to the effect that the agreement has been executed before him after he has explained the assignment. The solicitor then prepares an *affidavit* to that effect which is sworn in the presence of another solicitor. The *affidavit* together with a copy of the executed agreement must then be registered at the Bills of Sale Registry at the High Court within seven days of the execution of the agreement.

7–17 The section re-enacts in substance s.34 of the Bankruptcy Act 1914 with a re-arrangement of the text and an amendment of the effective time (for the debts to be paid in order to escape the provisions) consequent upon the abolition of the concept of acts of bankruptcy. The insolvency of partnerships is provided for under the subordinate legislation—the Insolvent Partnerships Order 1994.[31] Under the order, one of the methods of dealing with an insolvent partnership is by winding it up as if it were an unregistered company and the provisions as to winding up under Pt.V of the Insolvency Act 1986 apply with necessary amendments. There is no provision, for the avoidance of a general assignment of book debts in the Act in relation to the winding-up of companies whether registered or unregistered. However, the provisions for winding-up a partnership is permissive and not mandatory and the property of the partners may be administered in bankruptcy; in particular, where all the partners are individuals and none is a limited partner and bankruptcy orders are made against of them on their own petitions, then the trustees of the various estates administer the partnership property and this procedure is not a winding-up as an unregistered company.[32] Furthermore, although the section refers to an assignment by "a person"; by the Interpretation Act 1978[33] "a person" includes "a body of

---

[31] SI 1994/2421.
[32] The Insolvent Partnership Order 1994 (SI 1994/2421) and see para.11–74 below.
[33] s.5 and Sch.1.

persons corporate or unincorporate". Accordingly, an assignment under an agreement of the whole turnover type with a partnership must be registered under the Bills of Sale Act 1878 in order to avoid the risk of a claim by a trustee in bankruptcy to debts outstanding at the date of the petition. Registration only perfects the assignments so that they may not be rendered invalid by a subsequent bankruptcy of the assignor; registration does not have any significance as regards the priority of the assignment against competing assignees or other third parties.[34] Registration must be renewed once in every five years. However, by s.11 of the Act, renewal is not necessary by reason only of a transfer to another assignee; this means that a new registration is not necessary only on account of a change to another factor.

7–18   In rare cases a factor may wish to enter into a factoring agreement with a limited partnership registered in accordance with the Limited Partnership Act 1907. Such a partnership must include at least one general partner who is responsible for the partnership's obligations in full[35] and at least one limited partner whose liability is limited to his contribution to the partnership.[36] The management of the business of a limited partnership is in the hands of the general partners, and the limited partner may not take part in its management[37]; if he does, he will be liable in full for the obligations of the firm.[38] A limited partner will not be required to execute the factoring agreement and have his execution attested by a solicitor, as described in para.7–16 above, because all the powers of management of the firm's business are vested in the general partners and, if he did so, he might be considered to have taken part in the management of the partnership and made himself fully liable. Furthermore, in the event of the bankruptcy of the firm, it is most unlikely that the limited partner would himself become bankrupt; the object of his being a limited partner is to avoid such a misfortune. The death or bankruptcy of a limited partner does not dissolve the partnership.[39]

(All references to partnerships in this book are to partnerships other than those incorporated under the Limited Liability Partnership Act 2000 ("LLP"). The relations of a factor with an LLP are in all respects the same as those with a company.)

---

[34] See Goode, *Legal Problems of Credit and Security* (3rd ed., 2003) para.3–31.
[35] Limited Partnership Act 1907, ss.4(2) and 7. Such partnerships should not be confused with Limited Liability Partnerships to be formed under the proposed new legislation for that form principally for the organisation of professional firms.
[36] Limited Partnership Act 1907, s.4(2).
[37] *ibid.*, s.6(1).
[38] *ibid.*
[39] *ibid.*, s.6(2).

4. LENDING ON SECURITY DISTINGUISHED FROM PURCHASE

It is important to distinguish the normal basis for factoring by the outright **7–19** purchase of debts from the lending (as by bankers) on the security of debts. Although it would be possible to provide the full service and its variants with financial facilities by means of lending money on the security of a fixed charge on the client's book debts,[40] normal factoring arrangements in the United Kingdom are based on the sale and purchase of the debts and the vesting of them in the factor. As a result of the outright sale and purchase, the debts cease to be the property of the client and, in the case of a client incorporated under the Companies Acts, there is, at present, no way of registering a security interest in them such as there is in the United States under the Uniform Commercial Code.[41] The arrangement certainly does not constitute a charge because the ownership has passed to the factor; consequently, no registration is necessary or would be acceptable to the registrar under Pt XII of the Companies Act 1985.

In view of this absence of registration and as the lending on security of **7–20** book debts and the purchase of them, together with prepayments, appear to be very similar in substance, it is most important that the distinction should be kept firmly in mind by the factor when dealing with an incorporated client. If an agreement for prepayments on account of the purchase price of debts sold to the factor were to be held by the courts to mask a true transaction of lending on the security of book debts, it would be registrable.[42] In such an event, not being protected by registration, the factor would be unable to recover in competition with the rights of a liquidator, an administrator or any creditor of the company[43] with an interest in the charged property.[44]

Where invoice discounting or agency factoring are the services provided **7–21** and the client not only guarantees payment of the debts sold to the factor, but also collects them for him, there is, in particular, a very fine line between the purchase and a loan on security. It is, therefore, as well for the factor to ensure that, not only his documentation and communications both with the client and the outside world, but also his procedures and accounting are compatible with the outright purchase of debts.

Where an agreement for the sale and purchase of debts or of goods has **7–22**

---

[40] For a more detailed analysis see paras 13–02 *et seq.* below.
[41] U.C.C., s.9 501/527.
[42] Companies Act 1985, s.395.
[43] Companies Act 1985, s.395(1). For this purpose the expressions "a liquidator" and "an administrator" means respectively "the company in liquidation" and "the company in administration". *Smith (Administrator of Cosslett (Contractors)) Ltd v Bridgend County Borough Council* [2002] A.C. 336.
[44] *Re Ehrmann Bros Ltd* [1906] 2 Ch. 697 and see para.8–30 below.

been challenged as being in substance lending on the security of such debts or goods, two questions have been considered by the courts: do the documents represent the true intention of the parties? And does the substance of the transactions differ from their form? From a study of the relevant cases,[45] it seems possible to extract three main tests to be applied in any such challenge in order to determine whether or not an agreement for the purchase of debts is, in substance, a charge on book debts. These are as follows:

(1) Equity of redemption

In the case of a charge (including a mortgage), the borrower has "an equity of redemption"; that is the right to the ownership of the charged assets free of the charge on the discharge of his obligations to the lender. This is certainly not the same as the right which factor may take in his agreement to have the debts repurchased by the client on the happening of certain specified events. A right given by the factor to the client, as seller of the debts, to repurchase them would not by itself be conclusive that the transaction was one of lending on security and not of sale and purchase; an option to repurchase is not the same as an equity of redemption.[46] On the other hand, a right given to the client to have the debts transferred back to him free from any encumbrance on repayment of all payments made and amounts charged to him would constitute an equity of redemption.[47]

(2) Rights on realisation of the charged property

In the case of a loan on security, the lender, on realising the charged assets, has to account to the borrower for any excess over the amount of the borrower's obligations to him; and as corollary, if the asset does not realise the amount of the obligations, the borrower is still liable for the shortfall. In the case of an outright purchase, the purchaser is owner and any profit or loss on realisation attaches to him. The profit to the factor as purchaser should be the difference between the amount paid for the debt and its realisation; from this point of view, the definition of the purchase price as "the amount payable by the debtor less some, if not all, of the factor's charges" and the immediate credit of the purchase price are consistent with purchase.

---

[45] *Olds Discount Co Ltd v John Playfair Ltd* [1938] 3 All E.R. 275; *Re George Inglefield Ltd* [1933] Ch. 1; *Chow Yoong Hong v Choong Fah Rubber Manufactory* [1962] A.C. 209; *Lloyds and Scottish Finance Ltd v Cyril Lord Carpets Sales Ltd* [1992] B.C.L.C. 609; and more recently, *Curtain Dream plc v Churchill Merchanting Ltd* [1990] B.C.C. 341 and *Welsh Development Agency v The Export Finance Company Ltd* [1992] B.C.C. 270.

[46] See *Manchester Sheffield & Lincolnshire Rly Co v North Central Wagon Co* (1888) 13 App.Cas. 554, 557–568. See also the *dicta* of Browne-Wilkinson V.-C. in *Welsh Development Agency v Export Finance Co Ltd* [1990] B.C.C. 393 at 408H.

[47] *cf.* Oditah, "Financing Trade Credit: *Welsh Development Agency v Exfinco*" (1992) J.B.L. 541 at 549, where it is argued that such a provision described as a "reverter or relinquishment clause" is not fatal to a claim for the transaction to be one of sale and purchase.

A factor is unlikely to realise any other profit. On the other hand, in the cases of debts purchased with recourse, he is protected by the client against any loss by reason of short payment (or no payment) by the debtor; but such arrangements have been present in cases where the purchase of debts was upheld as such.[48] It is clear that the factor's protection is the obligation of the client to repurchase the debt or to guarantee payment; neither of these are the same as the obligation to repay the money paid to the client by the factor to the extent that it is not recovered by collection of the debts. It also seems clear that a non-recourse factoring agreement should undoubtedly pass this test.

(3) Discount or interest

A discount charge has been said to be fixed and paid once and for all in advance and interest to accrue from day to day. To be consistent with the purchase of a debt, the debt should be "discounted" by the application of a fixed discount to the purchase price at the outset.[49]

Administrative convenience has dictated that most factors now calculate **7–23** or adjust their discount charges on a day to day basis.[50] It is therefore important that the substance of the arrangement (as well as the form) in all other respects should be consistent with the sale and purchase of debts and demonstrate that it is the true intention of the parties. It is likely that the most important test of a security right (as opposed to outright purchase) is the inclusion of an equity of redemption.[51] Accordingly, the factor should never give his client the absolute right to have reassigned to him any of the debts sold to the factor on repayment only of the payments made by the factor to the client. It should also be noted that a provision in an assignment by which all rights in respect of the subject matter of the assignment remained with the assignor until certain events occurred was an influence in a decision of the court that the assignment was not an absolute assignment, but by way of charge[52]; even where the client is appointed agent to administer the sales ledger and collect the debts,[53] it should be specified in

---

[48] "It is now well established that factoring or block-discounting amounts to a sale of book debts, even though under the relevant agreement the purchaser of the debts is given recourse against the vendor in the event of default in payment of the debt by the debtor". *Welsh Development Agency v Export Finance Company Ltd* [1992] B.C.C. 270, *per* Lord Dillon at p.273 and see, *e.g. Olds Discount Co Ltd v John Playfair Ltd* [1938] 3 All E.R. 75 and *Lloyds and Scottish Finance Co Ltd v Cyril Lord Carpet Sales Ltd* [1992] B.C.L.C. 609.
[49] *Chow Yoong Hong v Choong Fah Rubber Manufactory* [1962] A.C. 209; *Lloyds and Scottish Finance Ltd v Cyril Lord Carpets Sales Ltd* (1979) 129 N.L.J. 366. However, this test does not appear to be decisive; see *Re George Inglefield Ltd* [1933] 1 Ch. 1 where the calculation of the finance charge does not appear to have been considered.
[50] For an analysis of this aspect of factoring practice see paras 3–35 to 3–39 above.
[51] *Curtain Dream plc v Churchill Merchanting Ltd* [1990] B.C.C. 341 *per* Knox J. at 351.
[52] "*The Halcyon the Great*" [1984] 1 Lloyds Rep. 283. See also Oditah, *Legal Aspects of Receivables Financing* (1991), at p.108.
[53] See paras 1–51 to 1–55 above.

the factoring agreement that the right to collect remains with the factor and that the agency is to procure collection for the benefit of the factor and not to collect.

7–24   Words such as "advance", "loan" or "interest" should be eschewed in favour of "prepayment", "early payment" or "discount".[54] However, it would appear that the word "finance" would not be an influence because finance may be provided equally by selling assets.

7–25   There appears to be no recently reported case in which a liquidator or creditor has upset an arrangement for the sale by a trading company of its book debts to a financier as being in substance loans on the security of the debts. Indeed there are several cases in which such an attempt has failed[55] and the courts accepted that the agreements between the parties reflected the true nature of the transactions in spite of the compatibility of certain of the practical arrangements with the lending of money. However, it may well be that in some future case arising from factoring (particularly invoice discounting or agency factoring) the circumstances may be distinguished. The court may then make its decision on the basis of the substance of the arrangement as evidenced by internal and external communications of the factor and its procedures and accounting arrangements with its client. If commercial expediency dictates procedures and accounting which are more consistent with lending on security, the mischief cannot be cured by the agreement itself.

5. SPECIAL CONSIDERATIONS FOR SCOTLAND[56]

Where Scots Law may apply

7–26   Although this book in the main is confined to a description of the law in England and Wales, a note on the position in Scotland may serve to remind practitioners that they should not assume that their standard agreement drafted for use in England and Wales will be effective for use in Scotland. For that purpose it is advisable to take advice from a Scottish legal adviser. What constitutes business in Scotland is itself a difficult question. A company incorporated in Scotland will be subject to the jurisdiction of the Scottish courts in winding-up, but it may have carried out most of its

---

[54] cf. Oditah, *Financing Trade Credit: Welsh Development Agency v Exfinco* (1992) J.B.L. 541 at 550.
[55] e.g. *Re George Inglefield Ltd* [1933] Ch. 1; *Olds Discount Co Ltd v John Playfair Ltd* [1938] 3 All E.R. 275; *Chow Yoong Hong v Choong Fah Rubber Manufactor* [1962] A.C. 209; *Lloyds and Scottish Finance Ltd v Cyril Lord Carpets Sales Ltd* [1992] B.C.L.C. 609.
[56] The following paras (7–26 to 7–47) were written by R Bruce Wood WS of Morton Fraser, Solicitors, Edinburgh.

business in England. Similarly, an English registered company may carry out business in Scotland and have Scottish debtors. The various contracts between these companies and their respective debtors may have been entered into under Scots law or English law or a mixture of both. The leading case on factoring questions in Scotland, *Tay Valley Joinery Limited v CF Financial Services Ltd*,[57] itself had to address this problem. In that case, the invoice discounting agreement was governed by English law, but the parties accepted and the judges agreed that the efficacy of the transfer of the debts due by Scottish debtors had to be tested under Scots law rules.

Frequently the contract of sale entered into by the factor's client with a **7–27** debtor will be silent as to the governing law of that contract. Therefore, vexed conflict of laws questions can arise as to what the proper law of a debt is. However, this issue has been simplified since the *Tay Valley* case by the Contracts (Applicable Law) Act 1990,[58] which applies between England and Scotland in much the same way as it applies between the United Kingdom and other European countries. That Act incorporates the text of the Rome Convention, which, *inter alia*, prescribes the laws which are to apply in a purchase of book debt. It draws a distinction between the contract between the assignor and the assignee on the one hand (in our case, the invoice finance agreement) and the contract between the assignor and the debtor on the other hand (in our case, the book debt). The invoice finance agreement may be governed by whatever law suits the parties, and their choice of law will be upheld; however, it is provided[59] that the assignability of the book debt and the efficacy of any purported transfer of the book debt made under the invoice finance agreement as against persons other than the assignor and assignee will be tested according to the requirements of the proper law of the debt or possibly the law of the country where the debtor is, the situs of the debt. Thus, in simple terms, if a book debt is governed by English law, its transfer should only have to satisfy English law requirements, but, if a book debt is governed by Scots law, its transfer may have to satisfy the stricter requirements of Scots law which are set out below.

In light of the foregoing, it might be thought tempting for a factor to **7–28** approach his client at the outset of a proposed transaction and suggest that he change his documentation to provide that in future all his the debts would be governed by English law, thus avoiding the stricter Scottish requirements. Although the matter remains untested in this particular context,[60] there is an exception in the 1990 Act whereby the proper law will be disapplied if it arises from a choice of law made contrary to the public

---

[57] 1987 S.L.T. 207.
[58] For its application in England and Wales see Ch.12.
[59] Rome Convention, Art.12.2.
[60] But see *English v Donnelly* [1958] S.C. 494, where the submission of a hire purchase agreement with exclusively Scottish contacts to English law was ruled ineffective as being contrary to public policy, being an attempt to evade the provisions of a Scottish statute.

policy of an interested state.[61] It is thought that the strict requirements of Scots law regulating the transfer of ownership in book debts may involve just such public policy considerations, namely, the policy inherent generally in civil law based legal systems (of which Scots law is one) to render ineffectual transfers of property which are concealed from the transferor's creditors. There will, however, be many genuine cases where it is perfectly reasonable to choose English law as the proper law of the debt contract. Factoring companies must, however, be alert to the dangers that in their normal business with English clients, those clients may have Scottish debtors, with or without a clear choice of law in the contract. Furthermore, no matter what the proper law of the debt may be, where the client is Scottish, insolvency proceedings in respect of it will be carried out under Scots law, which will therefore be the system under which the efficacy of the factor's title in competition with claims by the client's creditors will be investigated. Also, where the debtor is Scottish and another creditor of the client seeks to do diligence (*i.e.* in English terms, carry out execution) by way of arresting the debt in the debtor's hands, difficult questions can arise, no matter what the proper law of the debt, if the debtor has no prior notice of the factor's interest.[62]

7–29   In any case of doubt, it is suggested that, in view of the very loose rules regarding the validity of equitable assignments in England and the more difficult position in Scotland explained below, an agreement giving unimpeachable beneficial ownership of the debts to the factor under Scots law should be used. However, where the client is English, an English liquidator dealing with an English factoring agreement may well not notice the potential problem. Several factors now have styles of agreement which, in the same document, govern the acquisition of debts with English debtors by English law and of debts with Scottish debtors by Scots law.

7–30   Traditionally, because of the public policy of Scots law described above, Scots law, like many continental European legal systems, has placed more difficulties in the path of the invoice financier than was the case in English law. As we shall see, two recent House of Lords' decisions in Scottish cases have gone a long way to assist the invoice financier in Scotland. To understand their impact, we must now turn to consider what is required to transfer the ownership of debts in Scots law. The recent abolition of stamp duty has also helped immeasurably the carrying on of invoice finance business in Scotland, as we shall see.

Transfer of ownership of debts in Scotland

7–31   In Scots law ownership is usually said to be indivisible (though, as we shall see, an ordinary trust arrangement involves some qualification to this).

---

[61] Rome Convention, Arts 7 and 17.
[62] See para.7–40 below.

Furthermore, equitable doctrines relating to the assignment of debts are unknown to Scots law. In Scotland there are three stages to the transfer of the ownership of a debt: first, there is the contract by which the parties agree to sell and buy the debt; secondly, there is the assignation[63] or document of transfer by which the debt is conveyed by the assignor to the assignee; and thirdly, there is a need for intimation (notification) of the transfer to the debtor. The first two stages in this process are frequently telescoped together[64] and the effect of the assignation is to complete the personal right to the debt in the assignee as between the assignor and the assignee. To effect the assignation there must be some form of conveyance or words of transfer; unlike in England, no assignation will be assumed from the fact that, for example, an offer to sell a debt has been accepted verbally or otherwise. Strictly speaking, that conveyance need not be written,[65] but, as the assignee's title depends on its existence, difficulties of proof dictate that in practice it must be in writing or something equivalent to it, such as electronic transmission.

This personal right is not "ownership". Intimation to the debtor is   **7–32** required to give the assignee a good title against third parties including other creditors of the assignor, the assignor's liquidator or trustee in bankruptcy and any other future assignee of the debt who takes the debt in good faith from the assignor and intimates it to the debtor prior to the intimation of the first assignee's assignation to the debtor. Once this intimation is given, the assignee has ownership of the debt.

The next question concerning the assignation is whether or not it is   **7–33** competent to assign future debts not yet in existence or whether the assignation is only valid if the debts being assigned are already in existence. The competence of such an assignation of future debts has sometimes been doubted.[66] Because of this, current styles of invoice finance agreement usually provide, first, for an immediate express assignation of all debts comprised in the whole turnover arrangement, followed by a corroborative specific assignation later when the debt is in existence (which, for convenience, is often combined with the procedure for the client notifying the factor of the debts being purchased from time to time). So, in case any future court should decide that a debt cannot be assigned until it exists, that further assignation is demanded under the invoice finance agreement at or after that point in time.

However, recent court decisions indicate virtually conclusively that an   **7–34**

---

[63] In Scots law "assignation" is used instead of "assignment". There is no other significance to the differing terminology.

[64] As they are in English law. But whereas in England, equity implies an assignment from contractual words of sale and purchase, in Scotland there have to be actual words of conveyance to operate an assignation and it is the earlier contractual stage which may be implied and not explicit.

[65] Since the Requirements of Writing (Scotland) Act 1995.

[66] e.g. Gloag and Irvine, *Law of Rights in Security* (1897), p.441.

assignation of future debts is valid. First, in one recent case[67] the Inner House of the Court of Session accepted as competent assignations of future debts, but stressed the need for the accurate identification of what it was that was being assigned. Moreover, the validity of the assignation of future debts seems to be the premise (although it is not explicit) upon which the normal form of agreement proposed by Professor Halliday[68] (and approved in *Tay Valley*) was structured. But of most significance here is the very recent House of Lords' decision in *Buchanan v Alba Diagnostics Limited*.[69] This was a patents case, which turned on the efficacy in Scots law of a present assignation of the rights to improvements made in future to the invention which was the subject of a patent. This assignation was held to be valid in respect of those future improvements. Now in Scots law patents and book debts are both examples of the same legal class of property, namely, incorporeal moveable property and, therefore, though the case is not directly in point, it can be regarded as being to all intents and purposes indistinguishable. In any event, the old Scots law doctrine of "accretion" on which the decision is based, applies to the acquisition of future property rights generally. It may therefore be concluded that, for the future, the current practice of insisting on a written notification of Scottish debts by the client as soon as they come into existence (a great nuisance for factors otherwise dealing with notifications electronically) is needlessly cautious and that reliance may safely be placed on the assignation of present and future debts contained in the invoice finance agreement.

7–35   The abolition of stamp duty on assignations of debts is further good news for factors transacting business in Scotland. Stamp duty was a far greater problem for the factor in Scottish practice than in England because of the need, explained above, for an assignation, almost certainly written, of the debt. Thus, the previous simple English device of the offer of debts by the client followed by oral acceptance by the factor, establishing in England an equitable assignment without the need for a stampable instrument, was not available in respect of Scottish debts. Factors, therefore, had to arrange for and accept an offer of the take-on debts, which included a written assignation of those debts, and thereafter sequential assignations of new debts as they came into existence. Factors then generally left such assignations unstamped and took the risk of having to stamp any assignation relating to any particular debt, the payment of which had to be enforced in court, at a later date and pay a penalty and interest for late stamping. Likewise, they had to hope that the point of non-payment of stamp duty was not taken in a more general context against the factor by a liquidator or other insolvency practitioner in relation to a claim in the client's insolvency. With the abolition of stamp duty, that major risk issue for the factor in Scotland has now

---

[67] *Gallemos Ltd (In receivership) v Barratt Falkirk Ltd* (1990) S.L.T. 98.
[68] Halliday, *Conveyancing Law and Practice in Scotland* (2nd ed., 1996 (Vol.1)), at para.8–64.
[69] [2004] RPC 34: *Times*, February 12, 2004.

disappeared. Any new problems with stamp duty land tax are the same as they are in England.

Having obtained the appropriate assignation, there then falls to be con-   **7–36** sidered what constitutes intimation in Scots law, upon the giving and receiving of which the assignee's title will be perfected. Text books on the subject in the past have tended to refer to effective intimation being given either in the form of a notice in duplicate, the duplicate copy of which has been acknowledged by the debtor and returned to the assignee or, as an alternative, an old style notarial declaration. Even the former is clearly considerably more formal than the normal practice of factoring companies and is likely to be commercially unacceptable. More recent indications, however, are that the courts will only seek to be sure that the debtor has been properly made aware of the transfer and, as long as he has been, then they will not require anything formal by way of intimation.[70] The intimation has to be given before the effective date of the appointment of a liquidator to a corporate client or of a trustee in bankruptcy to an individual client.[71] If the intimation is given later than that, then the debt will form part of the client's insolvent estate. The difficulties here are obviously greater with invoice discounting where it is not intended that the sale of the debt should be intimated to the debtor.

Creation of trusts in respect of book debts

From the above it appears that there is a problem to be solved. How is the   **7–37** factor to protect itself against any lack of title, pending valid intimation being given to the debtor—in particular, can invoice discounting safely be carried on in relation to Scottish debts? One method which has been successfully adopted is to provide that, in relation to every debt sold by the client to the factor, once an assignation of the debt has been granted, while a personal right only to the debt is vested in the factor, pending an intimated assignation, the client shall hold the title to the debt in trust for the factor.

The use of the concept of trust to protect a purchaser of property who has   **7–38** paid for but not received title, has had a stormy passage through the Scottish courts over the last 25 years,[72] but, after a number of rejections in a variety of circumstances, the principle was approved in the Second Division of the Court of Session in *Tay Valley*.[73] That case confirmed the view that debts may become the subject matter of a trust without the owner divesting himself of them by means of an intimated assignation. It also repeated the

---

[70] *e.g. Libertas-Kommerz GmbH* 1978 S.L.T 222 at 225, *per* Lord Kincraig.
[71] The same used to be true in relation to a receiver appointed to a corporate client; but see now para.7–46 below.
[72] See the excellent outline given in Drummond Young, *the Law of Corporate Insolvency in Scotland* (3rd ed., 2004), Ch.12.
[73] See n.57 above.

rule that it was possible for a person—the settlor or truster (the factor's client)—to make himself trustee of his own property for the benefit of another—the beneficiary of the trust (the factor)—provided that the property was dedicated to the trust by (i) a properly constituted instrument of trust and (ii) some physical act equivalent to the delivery, conveyance or transfer which would have been required had there been a separate, independent trustee.[74] The *Tay Valley* case is important as being the only detailed Scottish exploration of a factoring or invoice discounting relationship. The decision is often difficult to apply because the factoring agreement there was governed by English law (as was the trust) and at least one of the judges was strongly influenced by that. Academic doubt has been expressed in relation to the decision[75] and it is open to question whether parties with no valid connection with English law could choose English law as the proper law to evade the public policy principle of Scots law that, if a person wants to isolate property from his creditors, he must go through some public act to do so.[76] Nevertheless, even without the dubious device of purporting to govern the trust by English law, there appears now to be conclusive Scottish authority for the proposition that, if a seller having received the purchase price of an asset declares that he holds the asset in trust for the buyer and gives notice of this trust to the buyer, then the asset will not be attachable by the seller's creditors in the seller's insolvency. This principle was noted by the House of Lords in *Sharp v Thomson*[77] and confirmed by that House in *Burnett's Trustee v Grainger*.[78] Strictly speaking, this issue is *obiter* to the decision in *Burnett's Trustee*, but their Lordships' view on the subject is clear, even to the point of Lord Hoffman expressing consternation that a supposed strict rule of Scots law should be so easily evaded by a private, unpublicised trust. In any event, the trust question in this situation was expressly ruled on by the House of Lords in the much older case of *Heritable Reversionary Co Limited v Millar*.[79] None of these cases has anything to do with debts or factoring, but there is no reason to believe the position is any different in relation to the sale or purchase of debts.

7–39   It can be regarded as established, therefore, that a trust, properly drafted in Scots law form, will protect the factor against the liquidator, administrator or the trustee in bankruptcy of the factor's client.[80] Does that trust

---

[74] This rule was established in the House of Lords in *Allans Trustees* 1971 S.L.T. 62 and applied commercially in *Clark Taylor & Co Limited v Quality Site Development (Edinburgh) Ltd* 1981 S.L.T. 308.
[75] *e.g.* See George L Gretton: "Ownership and Insolvency: *Burnett's Trustee v Grainger*" [2004] Edin. L. R. Vol.8, p.389.
[76] See n.60 above.
[77] 1997 S.L.T. 636.
[78] 2004 S.L.T. 513.
[79] (1893) 19R (HL) 43.
[80] But see para.7–43 below.

also protect the factor against another creditor of the client, who has arrested the debt in the debtor's hands? Subject to the practical difficulty mentioned in para.7–40 below, if the trust is valid, there seems no reason why it should not prevail over the rights of the arresting creditor. Where an arrestment is laid on the debtor in respect of the debt, the arresting creditor should raise an action for payment (known technically as an action of furthcoming) to obtain payment from the debtor. The factor would be entitled to participate in that court action and it is thought that the court would accept the argument that the client held the debt only as trustee and not in his own right and, therefore, the debt comprises trust property which is not available to be attached in execution of a claim for obligations owed by the client in his own right. This remains untested in this specific context, but it is believed that the foregoing legal analysis should be sound.

The practical difficulty for the factor, competing in effect with an arresting **7–40** creditor, may be that the debtor may be willing to pay out the arresting creditor, with the consent of the client, without waiting for an action of furthcoming. The debtor will not know of the trust if the client does not mention it in connection with consenting to the release of the arrested funds. The client should, of course, make such mention of the trust and withhold consent or be in breach of his duties as trustee. Also, if an action of furthcoming is insisted upon by the arresting creditor, despite his knowing of the trust, and the factor (or the client as trustee) has to intervene in the action to vindicate the trust, legal costs may soon swallow up the debt. There is, therefore, much to be said for a factor, even in a confidential arrangement, being very ready in Scotland to give notices of assignation to debtors at the first hint of trouble.

We can also note in passing a related issue. Following a decision in *Style* **7–41** *Financial Services v Bank of Scotland*,[81] the Court of Session appears to have accepted a wide concept of trust in relation to the operation of bank accounts, which could assist in undisclosed cases. According to the decision in that case, if the invoice discounting agreement is intimated to the bank where the account, to which the debts are being paid, is held, then, even though that account is in the client's name, the bank will have been made aware of the fiduciary nature of the receivables and amounts in credit on the account will be payable to the factor. This limited protection may be useful where for any reason no proper trust has been created.

The question remains—given that some equivalent of delivery is required **7–42** to complete the trust in relation to debts when the client is both truster and trustee, what is sufficient to constitute such an equivalent to delivery? Although the three judges in *Tay Valley* (which was concerned with invoice discounting) all concluded for somewhat differing reasons that the agreement before them, together with the normal invoice discounting procedures,

---

[81] 1996 S.L.T. 421.

had the effect of vesting beneficial ownership of the debts in the factor, it is clear for the future that the key to the successful establishment of a trust is intimation to the beneficiary of the dedication of the debts to the trust. It is important not to confuse this intimation with the quite separate intimation to the debtor which is necessary to perfect an assignation and the factor's own title. Here, the court is concerned only with the mechanisms required to set up a valid trust where the truster and trustee are the same person (the client). The beneficiary is, of course, the factor and, therefore, it is to the factor (not the debtor) that intimation of the dedication of the debts to the trust has to be made. The normal practice in Scotland is to include, in the text of the invoice finance agreement, an acceptance by the factor that there has been intimated to him, as beneficiary, the creation of the relevant trust. However, to avoid any question being raised as to whether such intimation can be validly given before the debts are in existence, it is normally also provided that, in the course of the ongoing relationship, each schedule of debts given by the client to the factor notifying debts periodically purchased will incorporate an intimation of the dedication of those debts to the trust, pending the passing of full title to the factor. There seems to be no reason why such a notice could not validly be given electronically.

7–43 There are some further problems which have to be borne in mind with this trust route. First, part of the judicial hostility in cases prior to *Tay Valley* arose from the casual manner in which the trust was alleged to have been created. Although the court in *Tay Valley* blessed the simple style of trust clause contained in the text book model to which they referred,[82] their relaxed attitude may well have been partly attributable to the English dimension to the case and it is now regarded as a safer view that a more robust style, clearly indicative of a declaration of trust and the dedication of property to that trust, should be used. Secondly, when drafting the trust it should be borne in mind that, as the client is the trustee, provision will have to be made for the reinforcement of the trust for the benefit of the beneficiary upon the insolvency of the client/trustee. This may be done, for example, by incorporating a power of attorney into the trust in favour of the factor as beneficiary and allowing the beneficiary as attorney for the trustee to transfer debts out of the trust into the factor's own name.

7–44 To bolster any remaining anxieties the factor may have, the factor may, as in England, look for security as collateral cover for the invoice finance facility. With corporate clients, this may take the form of a floating charge. However, the following points should be borne in mind. The Bill of Sale Acts do not apply to Scotland and Scots law has no equivalent, but nor is a chattel mortgage valid in Scotland other than over a ship or aircraft. Most importantly, a fixed charge over book debts is impractical in Scotland, as notice of the charge has to be given to each debtor before the charge is

---

[82] Halliday, see n.68 above.

effective in relation to the relevant debt. The trust route, which can be used by an invoice financier to protect his right to a purchased debt pending the giving of notice and the vesting of title to the debt, cannot be used to protect his position pending the giving of notice where he has not purchased the debt but merely taken a charge or security over it.

The factor and the client's receiver

There used to be a further concern with the trust, namely, while it prevails **7–45** against the liquidator, administrator or trustee in sequestration of the client, there was an argument expressed in academic circles[83] that the trust may not prevail in certain circumstances against the rights of a receiver appointed in respect of the client. Accordingly, it was an invariable practice of factors in Scotland to take a floating charge from a corporate client, having priority of ranking over other floating charges in relation to the debts, so that any receiver's claim to defeat the trust would be negated by the factor's prior floating charge. (Bear in mind that in Scotland receivers can only be appointed under floating charges[84] and only companies can grant floating charges. Thus, the hardening of the case law in favour of the validity of the trust gives considerable comfort in relation to invoice discounting facilities made available to partnerships and sole traders—such persons cannot grant floating charges, but nor can they be made subject to a receivership.)

However, while such academic concern may still exist, it has become **7–46** irrelevant. As a result of the House of Lords decision in *Sharp v Thomson*,[85] the factor is now adequately protected against the client's receiver and no longer has to rely on the trust device to achieve this protection. That case was not a factoring case; rather, it was a conveyancing case. It concerned the purchaser of a house who had paid the price for the house and obtained from the seller a disposition (or conveyance) of the title to the house, but had not yet been able to register that conveyance in the Land Register, when the company selling the house went into receivership. The receiver claimed that the purchaser had no title because he had no real right by virtue of the lack of registration and was therefore an ordinary creditor for repayment of the price in the company's insolvency. The court referred to the wording of the Insolvency Act 1986, which governs the rights of receivers in Scotland, and noted that it restricted the receiver's powers to property in which the company had a beneficial interest at the time of the receiver's appointment. Accordingly, the court held that the receiver had no rights in respect of company property which the company had sold and been paid for, and which the company had conveyed away, but where the purchaser had as yet

---

[83] See, *e.g.*, *Trusts and Floating Charges by K G C Reid 1987 S.L.T.* (News) 113.
[84] And, as in England, now only under floating charges granted prior to the Enterprise Act 2002.
[85] 1997 S.L.T. 636.

no real right because the final step the purchaser required to take to perfect that real right (registration in the Land Register) had yet to take place. This was not property in which the company had such a beneficial interest.

7-47   The analogy with invoice discounting is seemingly irrefutable. The factor has paid the price; the debt has been sold and assigned; all that has not happened is the intimation to the debtor which perfects the real right. It follows that the factor has nothing to fear from a receiver in respect of debts which the factor has purchased, provided they have at least been assigned to the factor. As already mentioned, the modern Scottish forms of factoring or invoice discounting agreements will contain an assignation of all future debts, which, on the basis of *Buchanan v Alba Diagnostics Ltd*,[86] should be sufficient to take advantage against a receiver of the decision in *Sharp v Thomson*.

---

[86] [2004] UKHL 5—see n.69 above.

CHAPTER 8

THE EFFECT OF NOTICE TO THE DEBTOR
AND CONFLICTS WITH THIRD PARTIES

In Ch.7 the methods by which ownership of the debts, which are the subject **8–01** of a factoring agreement, is transferred to the factor were explained. It was there asserted that the factor's most important demand of the law is that he should be able to obtain that ownership unfettered by claims of other parties to rights or interests in the debts purchased by him; any such rights or interests of third parties may well prevent the factor from collecting the full amount (or even any amount) from the debtors so that he may be unable to recover the monies he has laid out in the purchase of the debts.

Questions of the priorities of such rights and interests in choses in action **8–02** are some of the most difficult in English law. These difficulties appear to have arisen from the development of non-possessory forms of consensual security in equity over personal property without any comprehensive statutory regulations relating to priorities such as is to be found in the Uniform Commercial Code in the United States. Such claims of others to rights or interests in the debts may be based on assignments, security rights (such as charges on the property of companies) or equitable tracing rights. In this chapter the effect of notice to the debtor, which has an important bearing on such conflicts and factor's position in relation to such claims are considered.

1. THE RULE IN *DEARLE v HALL*

The general rule which regulates the priorities between competing assignees **8–03** of the same debt is based on the case of *Dearle v Hall*[1] and has stood the test of time for over 180 years. The rule is that the assignee whose notice of assignment is first in time has priority provided that at the time of the assignment to him, which he took in good faith, he was not aware of any

---

[1] (1828) 3 Russ 1.

earlier assignment to a competing assignee[2]; and an assignee, having after the time of his assignment become aware of an earlier assignment, may still obtain priority by giving notice first.[3] In order to determine the first in time, the relevant date is that on which the notice is received by the debtor and not that on which it is sent.[4] If a debtor receives, on the same day, notices from each of two independent assignees of the same debt then the earlier assignment will be preferred; it appears that the law does not take notice of a portion of a day for this purpose.[5] The case of *Dearle v Hall* related to equitable assignments of equitable interests; and it appears to have statutory recognition, as regards equitable interests, owing to a reference to it in s.137 of the Law of Property Act 1925.

8–04   In a conflict between an assignee under an equitable assignment, which has been notified to a debtor, and a subsequent assignee whose assignment is in statutory form where the later assignment was taken in good faith, for value and without notice of the earlier equitable interest the rule will come to the assistance of the first assignee. This is so in spite of the usual rule that an equitable interest is subordinated to a subsequent legal interest obtained in good faith and without notice; it is the consequence of the statutory provision for the requisites of an assignment whereby the right of an assignee are "subject to the equities having priority over the right of the assignee".[6]

8–05   Where the conflict is between two assignees who have both taken valid assignments in statutory form, there can be little doubt that the first to complete his assignment by notice to the debtor must have priority. It is the date of the notice with effect from which the following are transferred to the assignee:

(1)   the legal title to the debt;

(2)   all legal and other remedies for the debt; and

---

[2] For the failure of a subsequent assignee who was aware of a prior assignment at the time of his assignment, to obtain priority by giving notice first, see *Re A D Holmes* (1885) 29 Ch.D. 786. For the failure of a receiver under a floating charge to obtain priority (on behalf of the chargee) by giving notice of the crystallisation of the charge in similar circumstances, see *Re Ind. Coope & Co Ltd* [1911] 2 Ch. 223.

[3] "It is not a question of what a man knows, when he does that which will better or perfect his security, but what he knows at the time when he took his security and paid his money". *per* Cotton L.J. in *Mutual Life Assurance Society v Langley* (1886) 32 Ch.D. 460 at 468.

[4] *Johnstone v Cox* (1881) 16 Ch.D. 571 affirmed 19 Ch.D. 17 and in relation to the notice of an assignment in accordance with Law of Property Act 1925, s.136 see *Holt v Heatherfield Trust Ltd* [1942] 2 K.B. 1 at 5.

[5] *Johnstone v Cox*, see n.4 above.

[6] Law of Property Act 1925, s.136(1); see also *E. Pfeiffer Weinkellerei-Weineinkauf GmbH & Co v Arbuthnot Factors Ltd* [1988] W.L.R. 150 at p.162. *cf. Oditah, Legal Aspects of Receivables Financing* (1991), pp.154 *et seq.*, where he argues trenchantly that the rule does not apply to such a conflict and that such an earlier equitable assignment is not an equity covered by s.136(1). The rule also applies to an equitable assignment of a legal *chose in action*; see *Compaq Computer v Abercorn Group Ltd* [1991] B.C.C. 484 at 498–500.

(3) the power to give a good discharge for the debt without the concurrence of the assignor.[7]

For the same reason he will prevail in a conflict with an assignee whose assignment is equitable and has not been notified to the debtor. However, in both cases the rule will apply only if the claimant under it has acted in good faith and taken his assignment without knowledge of the earlier assignment. If this is not the case, the first assignee must succeed.

It appears, therefore, that in all cases of conflicts between assignees, **8–06** whose assignments are either equitable or in statutory form, the priority rule is the same: the first (acting in good faith without knowledge of an earlier assignment) to procure receipt by the debtor of notice of his assignment has the right to collect and give a good discharge for the debt. It seems that part of the reasoning behind the rule is that notice to the debtor is a deterrent to the fraud of multiple assignments of the same debt; accordingly, it is considered that an assignee who fails to give notice promptly is somehow negligent and deserves to be displaced by a later assignee who gives notice first.[8] As physical possession of an intangible is not possible, notice is considered to be the nearest equivalent to it. The rule is also logical and commercially sound; if the priorities followed any other rule the debtor, on receipt of notice of an assignment, would be put on enquiry in every case to ascertain that there was no other assignment having priority.

2. THE EFFECT OF NOTICES OF ASSIGNMENTS IN FACTORING ARRANGEMENTS

The foregoing description of the effect of the rule in *Dearle v Hall* empha- **8–07** sises the importance to the factor of getting out his notice as early as possible after the assignment of each debt. In the case of a factor who uses the whole turnover type of agreement[9] for any form of disclosed factoring, the notice may be sent by means of a legend on the invoice direct by the client to the debtor; in normal commercial practice the debt will be in existence before the invoice is despatched to the debtor and the assignment will already have been effected automatically on the coming into existence of the debt.

---

[7] Law of Property Act 1925, s.136(1).
[8] See *Re Dallas* [1904] 2 Ch. 385 from which it also appears that: (i) as between those whose notices are received on the same day priority is determined by the date of the assignment; and (ii) a notice received by a bank after business hours is considered to have been received on the following day.
[9] See para.7–10 above. But see also para.4–59 above regarding difficulties in relation to the sending of notices caused by the electronic transmission of invoices.

8–08 On the other hand, where the factor uses a facultative type of agreement,[10] the assignment of each debt takes effect only when the offer of it has been made by the client and accepted (or deemed to be accepted) by the factor. Unless, therefore, the factor arranges for originals of invoices, bearing the assignment notices, to be sent to him for onward transmission to the debtor, he cannot be certain that the notice has been received by the debtor *after* the assignment has been made. An assignment according to the statute[11] cannot be completed by notice before it is made, and it seems doubtful if the notice of an equitable assignment, received by the debtor before the assignment has been made, would be valid for the purposes mentioned above or in Ch.9. Although notice to the debtor alone, provided that it is in respect of an irrevocable alienation of the debt, will constitute an equitable assignment,[12] in the case of a facultative agreement it is not clear that there is to be an assignment until the offer of the debt to be assigned has been accepted by the factor. Accordingly, notice received by the debtor before the offer of the debt has been accepted by the factor is likely to be of no effect.

8–09 In addition to assisting the factor in his claims to priority against competing interests in the debts, receipt of notice by the debtor also:

(1) fixes the rights of the parties in relation to the debtor's countervailing rights[13];

(2) prevents the discharge of the debtor by subsequent payment to the client[14];

(3) avoids changes in terms in the contract of sale (which have not been authorised by the factor) being enforceable against the factor[15]; and

(4) enables the factor to take proceedings for recovery of the debt in his own name.[16]

---

[10] See para.7–08 above.

[11] Law of Property Act 1925, s.136.

[12] *Alexander v Steinhardt, Walter & Co* [1903] 2 K.B. 208 and see Oditah, *op. cit.*, at p.145. But see Wolff, "*Assignment Agreements under English Law*" (2005) J.B.L. pp.473 to 493, where it argued that it is uncertain whether an assignment without the agreement of, or at least notification to, the assignor is effective to transfer ownership of the debt.

[13] See Ch.9.

[14] *Wm. Brandts Sons & Co v Dunlop Rubber Co Ltd* [1905] A.C. 454.

[15] *Brice v Bannister* (1878) 3 Q.B.D. 569. This case related to a stop order on monies held in court; but such a stop order is usually considered analogous to a notice to a debtor for such purposes. See also para.9–16 below and the *dictum* of James L.J. in *Roxburghe v Cox* (1881) 17 Ch.D. 520.

[16] Although strictly the assignee under an equitable assignment must join the assignor as co-plaintiff, in view of the rules of the courts that an action should not fail for want of a joinder (see, *e.g.* R.S.C., Ord.15, r.6), it is often effective for the factor to take proceedings in his own name alone, without the formality of an assignment in statutory form, provided that notice has been given to the debtor. However, the court may require all three parties to appear and this is likely if the debtor takes the point that the assignment is not in statutory form.

It is, therefore, apparent that it is in the interests of the factor's security to ensure that notices are received by the debtors at the earliest possible time after each debt is assigned. In invoice discounting or undisclosed factoring the factor is in greater danger of detractions from his security; an invoice discounter may well lose the proceeds of debts, the subject of his discounting agreement, to an assignee who was unaware of that agreement but who gave notices to the debtors first. The requirement that the client should mark all the records relating to the discounted debts to the effect that they have been assigned is, for this reason, an important safeguard; it is usual for a prospective purchaser of debts to inspect these records.

Although written notice is necessary for the purposes of s.136 of the Law **8–10** of Property Act 1925, for the purposes of fixing the rights of the parties in the case of an equitable assignment oral notice is sufficient provided that there is evidence of it.[17] Accordingly, notice by facsimile is effective for this purpose at the time that the transmission is received. It is also probable that notice by facsimile would suffice for the purposes of the Law of Property Act. There are no rules as to the form of the notice of an equitable assignment[18]; in *Wm. Brandt's Sons & Co v Dunlop Rubber Co*[19] it was said that all that is necessary is that "the debtor should be given to understand that the debt has been made over by the creditor to some third person". However, it is now considered that it must be made clear, not only that the debtor is to pay the assignee, but also that payment to the assignee alone will give the debtor a good discharge. A simple instruction to pay the factor may be taken to indicate that the factor is collecting purely as an agent; that would not preclude a discharge to the debtor by payment to the assignor.[20]

The benefit to the factor of (2) above will not apply in agency factoring if **8–11** it is conducted so that the debtor's payments are sent to the client.[21] Payment by a debtor of his indebtedness to the creditor's agent, whose agency ostensibly extends to the collection of his principal's debts, will discharge the debtor. If the factor appoints his client as agent and the creditor is instructed to pay the client, then the factor cannot expect that the debtor will bear the risk of the client's failure to account to the factor. This is the disadvantage of operating agency factoring whereby directions are given to the debtor to pay to the client who will collect as agent for the factor. It is probable that a notice including instructions to pay the client as agent for the factor would

---

[17] See Oditah, *Legal Aspects of Receivables Financing* (1991), at pp.130 *et seq.*
[18] For notice for the purposes of an assignment in accordance with s.136 Law of Property Act 1925 see para.7–05 above.
[19] [1905] A.C. 454 *per* Lord Macnaghten at 462.
[20] See *James Talcott Ltd v John Lewis & Co Ltd and North American Dress Co Ltd* [1940] 3 All E.R. 592 where the notice was held to be insufficiently plain for the factor to able to collect from the debtor who had already paid the supplier. In that case the notice was as follows: "To facilitate our accountancy and banking arrangements, it has been agreed that this invoice be transferred and payment in London funds should be made to James Talcott Ltd, 6–8 Sackville Street, London W1. Errors in this invoice should be notified to James Talcott Ltd immediately".
[21] See para.1–51 above.

in theory give the factor the other benefits mentioned above and that is the reason for the usual inclusion in the notice that the agency is for collection and no other purpose. However, it may well be that, in proceedings against a debtor in reliance on (1) or (3) above, the debtor might claim that the notice was not clear and unambiguous because, in spite of the assignment, it directed payment to the client. A purported notice of an assignment, which gave instructions that until the happening of a specified event all payments were to be made to the assignor and "all such other rights and benefits" shall accrue to the assignor, was held not to be a valid notice of an assignment for the purposes of s.136 of the Law of Property Act 1925 owing to its suspensory nature.[22] It is, therefore, possible that notices of assignments in agency factoring that direct payments to the client until the factor intervenes might, by analogy, be held not to be valid for equitable assignments. It is safer for the factor to have the payments made direct to him and appoint the client as agent for the purposes only of keeping the sales ledger and "procuring" that payments are made direct to the factor[23]; in this case, the notice to the debtors will give unambiguous instructions to pay the factor.

Introductory letters

8–12   An interesting question arises regarding notices to debtors and prospective debtors of the existence and effect of an agreement of the whole turnover type[24]; the question is whether such notices are effective (for the purposes of the rule in *Dearle v Hall* or for any of the purposes mentioned in para.8–09 above) as regards all future debts. It is usual practice for the factor at the outset of such an agreement to send out (or to procure that the client should send out) to all the customers (and to each prospective customer during the currency of the agreement) a letter giving notice in such terms. Typically, such a letter, which is often termed an introductory letter,[25] would give notice to the customers that from the date of the letter and until further notice all debts arising from supplies by the client are automatically assigned and become payable to the factor; such a letter might also remind the customer that consequently no new claim by the customer against the client may be set off against any such assigned debt.

8–13   There are a number of a reported cases which are considered to be authority for the view that a notice of assignment to a debtor is effective for the purposes of determining priorities only as regards debts in existence at

---

[22] *Gatoil Anstalt v Omennial Ltd (The "Balder London")* [1980] 2 Lloyd's Rep. 489.
[23] See para.11–51 above.
[24] See paras 7–10 to 7–11 above.
[25] As regards the validity of such a letter for the other purposes mentioned in para.8–09 in relation to future debts see paras 9–22 *et seq.*

the time of receipt of the notice by the debtor. These cases[26] related to multiple assignments by army officers of amounts payable to them by the government on their having resigned their commissions. The sums payable were made available through the army agents; and any notice received by the agents before receipt of the funds and their becoming payable by the gazetting of the officer's resignation was considered to be ineffective for this purpose. The notice to be effective had to be to some person "bound by some contract or obligation, existing at the time when the notice reaches him, to receive and pay over, or to pay over, if he has previously received, the fund".[27]

It seems possible, however, that the facts of the cases quoted above can be **8–14** distinguished from a factor's claim to priority against a competing assignee on the grounds of an introductory letter on the principle of the rule in *Dearle v Hall*.[28] The position might appear to be entirely different particularly in the case of a running and continuing account. An agreement binding the debts as they come into existence is a present assignment (albeit of future debts) and notice of the agreement, once it is effective, is notice of an assignment already made[29]; the assignment is made by the agreement itself but is inchoate until each debt to which it refers comes into existence. It seems also that such an agreement together with such a notice may be one of the equities referred to in s.136(1) of the Law of Property Act 1925.[30] However, in the present state of the law, a factor may not rely on introductory letter as notice for the purpose of the rule except as regards debts in existence at the time of receipt of the letter by the debtor.

3. CONFLICTS WITH CHARGEES

Some general points

Most companies which are looking to factoring as a means of financing **8–15** their businesses are likely to have, at some time, bank or other borrowing; and any such facility is likely to be granted on the security of a debenture comprising a general charge covering all the assets of the borrower including its debts. It is natural therefore that a factor, providing his services for a company and requiring that the debts which he purchases should be free from such an encumbrance, should consult any such chargee to arrange for

---

[26] See, *Johnstone v Cox* (1881) 16 Ch.D. 571; the cases were reviewed in *Re Dallas* [1904] 2 Ch. 385.
[27] *Per* Lord Selborne L.C. in *Addison v Cox* (1872) 8 Ch. App. 76 at 79.
[28] See paras 8–03 *et seq.* above.
[29] *i.e.* it is *not* a notice relating to an assignment not yet in existence; see para.8–08 above.
[30] See para.8–04 above.

a waiver or priority agreement at the outset; and the factor is likely to know of any valid charge affecting any debts of his prospective client (otherwise than in the circumstances described in para.8–19 below) by reason of his enquiries made before the start of factoring.

8–16   Before considering the factor's conflicts with chargees, there are two special points to be considered in connection with a factor's knowledge of a duly registered charge over the debts of a prospective or existing client.

8–17   First, for the purpose of the rule in *Dearle v Hall,*[31] the holder of a charge on debts of a company is usually considered to be in a position analogous to that of an assignee, notwithstanding that a charge, unlike a mortgage, does not constitute a transfer of ownership of the charged property[32]; but the rule may not assist the factor against the holder of a duly registered earlier charge. Due registration of a company charge is deemed to constitute notice, at the minimum, of the existence of the charge to those who would reasonably be expected to search the register,[33] and the factor with such constructive notice of the charge is not then acting in good faith without knowledge of the prior right of the chargee.

8–18   Secondly, the doctrine of constructive notice has usually been considered to relate only to the existence of the charge but not to the contents of the instrument.[34] Thus, where an instrument of charge included a covenant by the chargor not to discount or factor its debts, the factor is not fixed with constructive notice of the covenant in the absence of actual knowledge of it[35]; and this appears to be the case even if the particulars of the covenant are shown on the file at the registry, because such particulars have not been included in the matters, which, by law, have to be shown. On the other hand, there was an academic view that, as such a covenant is usual now in any charge over book debts, the factor may be deemed to have inferred knowledge of it by reason of failing to make such enquiries as he should reasonably be expected to make.[36] By analogy with that view, it seems more

---

[31] See para.8–03 above.

[32] See, *e.g. Business Computers Ltd v Anglo African Leasing Ltd* [1977] 1 W.L.R. 578 in which Templeman J. (as he then was) describes the floating charge created by the plaintiff as an "incomplete assignment to the Debenture Holders of the assets" of the plaintiff.

[33] For a full discussion of the extent of the effect of this doctrine, see Goode, *Commercial Law* (3rd ed., 2004), pp.662 *et seq.* and Goode, *Legal Problems of Credit and Security* (3rd ed., 2003), para.2–29.

[34] *Wilson v Kelland* [1910] 2 Ch. 306 and *Siebe Gorman & Co Ltd v Barclays Bank Ltd* [1979] 2 Lloyds Rep. 142. See also Gough, *Company Charges* (1996), pp.355 *et seq. cf.* the *obiter dicta* of David Neuberger Q.C. in *Ian Chisholm Textiles Ltd v Griffiths* [1994] B.C.C. 96 at 106c.

[35] Such actual knowledge might be by way of sight of the instrument of charge or by actual sight of a note on the file at the Companies Registry by reason of a search.

[36] *i.e.* by his having wilfully shut his eyes to the obvious. See Farrar, "Floating Charges and Priorities" (1974) 38 Conv. 315. For a contrary view, see Gough, *Company Charges* (1996), p.357, n.12 and McCormack, *Registration of Company Charges* (1994), at p.145, where he discusses his proposition (10). See also Goode, *op.cit.*, para.2–27.

likely that the factor could be held to have inferred knowledge of restrictions on the dealing with debts and their proceeds in the case of a *fixed* charge on debts of their client; a fixed charge of itself postulates such restrictions if the charge is to be established as such and not merely so termed.[37] If these arguments are accepted, then such inferred knowledge of the covenants or restrictions in a charge may be attributed to a factor whether his knowledge of the charge is actual, constructive or inferred.

Circumstances may arise in which the factor is unaware of the charge **8–19** affecting the debts which are the subject of the factoring agreement, and, on the insolvency of his client, a conflict may arise. For example, a registrable charge may be created by the client before the start of factoring but be registered after the start within the requisite 21 days of its creation; and it is the date of creation of the charge, and not its registration, that governs its priority.[38] Other circumstances in which a factor may well not know of a charge on the debts which he is factoring are as follows:

(1) The charge may be on debts other than book debts (which, if not a floating charge or for the purpose of securing an issue of debentures, is not subject to registration) and it is conceivable that a debt, which is not a book debt,[39] may be included in a factoring agreement.

(2) A negotiable instrument given to secure a book debt of a company and deposited to secure advances to the company is not to be treated as a charge on that book debt for this purpose.[40]

As regards a shipowner's lien on sub-freights, it has been held in a number **8–20** of cases that such liens constitute registrable charges. However, more recent judicial and academic opinion is that the liens are not charges at all but purely personal rights which enables the holder of the lien to intercept payment of the sub freight. Accordingly, a factor, who is contemplating the factoring of freights payable to one who holds a ship on charter from its owner, should make careful enquiries regarding the existence of such liens.

---

[37] *National Westminster Bank plc v Spectrum Plus Ltd* [2005] 3 W.L.R. 58. The authorities that such a restriction is not necessary (*Re Atlantic Computer Systems plc* [1990] B.C.C. 859 and *Re Atlantic Medical Ltd* [1992] B.C.C. 653) appear to have been decided on their particular facts; the property charged in both cases consisted of instalment credit agreements such as sub-leases and hire purchase agreements. See also para.13–26 below.

[38] See Goode, *Commercial Law* (3rd ed., 2004), p.662.

[39] A book debt is usually considered to be a debt of such a nature as it would normally be entered in the books of a company even if it is not so entered. See, for example, *Paul & Frank Ltd v Discount Bank Overseas Ltd* [1967] Ch. 348; see also *Coakley v Argent Credit Corporation plc* (June 4, 1998, unreported). McCormack, *Registration of Company Charges* (1994), at pp.40 *et seq.*

[40] Companies Act 1985, s.396(2).

The liens may already be in existence and, in the light of this later opinion, valid and taking priority without registration.[41]

8–21 In the following paragraphs the priorities in any conflict between a factor and a chargee, in relation to charges created both before and after the start of factoring, are examined.

Prior floating charge (duly registered)

8–22 A floating charge has been described as a present security over a class of assets which the chargor may manage in the normal course of business[42] and by which it is contemplated that, until some step is taken by the chargee or some event provided for in the charge document occurs (usually referred to as crystallisation), the chargor may carry on its business in the usual way.[43] This means that the company may (subject to any covenants in the instrument of charge) dispose of its assets in the normal course of business free of the charge. Therefore, in the now unlikely event of the creation by a company of a floating charge containing no covenants against the discounting or factoring of its debts, the factor would be at liberty to buy the company's debts free from the charge until crystallisation of it in spite of knowledge of the charge whether actual, inferred or constructive; it seems likely that the sale of debts to a factor would be considered "in the normal course of business". At one time it was considered that any activity of a company, provided that it was not *ultra vires* its memorandum, was in the normal course of its business[44]; now that the doctrine of *ultra vires* is ineffective as regards third parties dealing in good faith with a company,[45] it would seem even more likely that factoring would be considered to be in the normal course of a company's business. However, in the typical case in which the chargee is a bank and the charge contains the usual covenants, it would be unwise of the factor to rely on his lack of actual knowledge of those covenants owing to the possibility of his inferred knowledge of them.

8–23 Whether or not knowledge of the restrictive covenants would impeach the factor's proprietary rights to the debts which he has purchased for full

---

[41] See Goode, *Legal Problems of Credit and Security* (3rd ed., 2003) para.1–25. *cf. Agnew v Commissioner of Inland Revenue* [2001] 2 A.C. 710 at 722 where Millett expressed the view that a lien on sub-freights was merely a personal right to intercept them and not a proprietary right so that it would be difficult to characterise such a lien as a charge. A Privy Council decision on appeal from the New Zealand Court of Appeal. The decision was approved in the House of Lords in *Smith (Administrator of Cosslett (Contractors) Ltd) v Bridgend County Borough Council* [2002] A.C. 336.

[42] See Goode, *Commercial Law* (3rd ed., 2004), p.678.

[43] *Evans v Rival Granite Quarries Ltd* [1910] 2 K.B. 979; *Re Yorkshire Woolcombers Association* [1903] 2 Ch. 284 at 295.

[44] *Re Borax Company* [1901] 1 Ch. 326 and see also *Re Ind. Coope & Co Ltd* [1911] 2 Ch. 223.

[45] Companies Act 1985, ss.35A and 35B.

consideration is not certain[46]; but, at the very least, the factor would be liable to the chargee for procuring the chargor's breach of the covenant, and the courts are likely to restrain a person from enforcing his rights so as to cause a breach of a prior agreement of which he had knowledge.[47] Therefore, if in such a case the factor had entered into an agreement without any waiver or consent from the chargee, it is possible that the breach of a purely contractual provision in the charge may not prevent a valid transfer of proprietary rights by the assignments to the factor; but the factor may well be restrained from enjoying the proceeds of the debts contrary to the interests of the chargee whose covenants have been breached.

Prior fixed charge (duly registered)

A fixed charge constitutes an agreement between a creditor who holds the   **8–24** charge and the debtor by which the charged assets are put aside so that the proceeds of them are to be used for the satisfaction of the debt to the creditor in priority to any other use. Until 1979 it was not considered conceptually possible for there to be a fixed charge on debts, the proceeds of which must flow through a business to enable it to continue to trade. However, starting with the decision in *Siebe Gorman* in that year and continuing with a number of other cases, it was established that a fixed charge on debts was possible provided that the debts and their proceeds were placed under the control of the holder of the charge.[48] In this way, those proceeds could be used to discharge the claims of the holder of the charge. Without that control the charge would not be invalid altogether but would rank as a floating charge until its enforcement and that would mean that the holder would rank behind preferential creditors after the satisfaction of which often nothing is left for creditors.

From that time the degree of control necessary to constitute a charge on   **8–25**

---

[46] For a decision that such a restrictive covenant is purely a matter of contract and does not affect subsequent encumbrancers even if they have notice of the restriction see *Griffiths v Yorkshire Bank plc* [1994] 1 W.L.R. 1427 at 1435 E and F. The consequence of this decision should be that, if the factor had entered into an agreement without any waiver or consent from the chargee, a breach of the purely contractual provision in the instrument of charge would not prevent a valid transfer to the factor of the proprietary rights to the debts; but some doubt has been expressed regarding that decision see, for example, Berg "Charges over Book Debts" [1995] J.B.L. 434, n.17 and Goode, *Legal Problems of Credit and Security* (3rd ed., 2003), para.5–40.

[47] *Encyclopaedia of Banking Law*, 4124 (from which it appears that, for the purpose of the assignee's liability to the beneficiary of the covenant, actual, or possibly inferred knowledge, is necessary, but that constructive knowledge will not suffice) and *Manchester Ship Canal Co v Manchester Racecourse Co* [1901] 2 Ch. 37. See also Oditah, *Legal Aspects of Receivables Financing* (1991), p.112.

[48] *Siebe Gorman & Co Ltd v Barclays Bank Ltd* [1979] 2 Lloyds Rep. 142. That case has now been overruled in *National Westminster Bank plc v Spectrum Plus Ltd* [2005] 3 W.L.R. 58 because the countervalue of the proceeds of the charged debts remained at the disposal of the charger. However, it remains possible to create a fixed charge on the present and future debts of a company provided that arrangements are in force so that the debts and their proceeds are unconditionally appropriated for the discharge of the obligation which the charge secures.

debts as fixed continued to be a matter of some uncertainty and conflicting decisions in the courts until the recent *Spectrum* decision in which the *Siebe Gorman* case was held to be wrongly decided.[49] The effect of that decision of the House of Lords is that, for a charge on debts to be fixed, the company creating the charge must be unable to dispose of, or deal with, the charged debts except for the benefit of the charge holder who must have absolute control of the proceeds; the charged asset and its proceeds must be unconditionally appropriated as security for the discharge of the secured obligations to the chargee. It was also clearly stated in the judgment that it was not enough to provide in the charge document that the proceeds must be paid into a specified bank account of the chargee; the account into which they are paid must in fact be blocked. Whether the account is in credit in favour of the chargor or overdrawn, the chargee should have no right to use the countervalue of the proceeds paid into the account. This has implications for all holders of charges on debts that are labelled as fixed, especially for clearing banks, because, even if all proceeds of the debts are in fact paid into the customer's account with the bank, that alone will not constitute control. There must be a means of blocking the withdrawal or other use of the countervalue; and such blocking in the case of a bank account in credit may be difficult.

8–26   Although, by its very nature, such a charge should preclude the chargor from disposing of the charged debts and from dealing with the proceeds otherwise than under the control of the chargee, it must be presumed that awareness of the nature of a fixed charge was not imputed to the assignee which was a trading company. However, now that the nature of fixed charges is more widely known and as factoring companies may be considered to be more aware of these matters, it may be that a factor with actual or deemed knowledge of a charge, recognised to be fixed according to the above criteria, created before his agreement was entered into, but ignorant of any covenants in the instrument of charge, would be considered to have inferred knowledge of the restrictions which arise from the nature of the charge itself. If in such circumstances the factor were to purchase debts, covered by the charge, without a waiver or release from the chargee, it is likely that on the insolvency of the client/chargor he would be restrained from enforcing his agreement and ownership of the debts against the interests of the chargee.[50] In such circumstances he would be unable to recover any of the proceeds of the debts until the satisfaction (from such proceeds) of all amounts owing by the chargor to the chargee at the time of the conflict (subject to the limitation of the charge) and not only such amounts (still outstanding at the time of the conflict) as were owing to the chargee at the dates of the assignments; and, if the factor had actual or

---

[49] See n.37 above.
[50] See n.47 above.

inferred knowledge of the restrictions on the chargor—his client, he may well be liable to the chargee for assisting the chargor to breach the covenants.

Subsequent registered charges

Factoring agreements invariably provide that the client should not create **8–27** any charge which affects or may affect the debts included in the agreement. Nevertheless, it frequently happens that whilst a factoring agreement is in operation, the client will give a debenture including a charge on its debts to its bankers without any consultation with the factor. One must presume that the absence of consultation in such circumstances is the result of a mis-understanding of the nature of a factoring agreement on the part of both the client and the bank. If the client becomes insolvent and both the bank, by reason of its charge, and the factor, by reason of its prior agreement, claim the proceeds of the debts, the rule in *Dearle v Hall*,[51] although not assisting the factor owing to actual or inferred knowledge of the charge, may possibly assist the bank: if the bank were quite unaware of the factoring agreement and the factoring was on an undisclosed basis, it is possible (but unlikely) that the bank might, through a receiver, get notices to debtors first and obtain priority. It is therefore important that a factor, particularly in an undisclosed arrangement should ensure that any bank or finance company providing facilities to the client is aware of the factoring agreement.

Unless the bank is able to rely on *Dearle v Hall*[52] (which is most unlikely **8–28** owing to factoring, including invoice discounting, procedures), the result will depend to some extent on the nature of the factoring agreement and the position is likely to be as follows:

(1) In the case of an agreement of the whole turnover type,[53] there are a number of grounds on which the factor should be able to claim priority (whether the bank's charge is fixed or floating) as follows:

(a) The agreement itself constitutes a present assignment binding the debts as they come into existence; under such an assign-ment of future debts the assignee will take precisely the same right and interest in the debts, when they come into existence, as if they had been at the disposal of the assignor at the time when the assignment was made.[54] As the charge with which the factor is in conflict was not in existence at the time when

---

[51] See para.8–03 above.
[52] *ibid.*
[53] See paras 7–10 to 7–11 above.
[54] *Tailby v Official Receiver* (1888) 13 A.C. 523.

the assignment to the factor was made, the debts vest in the factor free from that charge.

(b) A charge on intangible personal property takes effect in equity only; a charge on debts cannot be effective as a legal charge.[55] Accordingly, the charge must be subject to the prior equitable rights of the factor, and this appears to be the case whether the bank or other chargee knew of the factoring agreement when it took its charge or not.

(c) Any charge on debts created by the factor's client, while the factoring agreement is in operation, must be in fact a floating charge even if it is described in the instrument as fixed. All proceeds of the debts purchased by the factor will have been, and are to be, paid direct to the factor (or in the case of invoice discounting made directly available to the factor) and will have been, and will be, at all times under the control of the factor.[56] Under a floating charge, the client has the ability to sell his property in the normal course of his business and he will be free of the charge. As the client was already factoring his debts when the charge was created, the sale of the debts to the factor is in the normal course of his business.[57] No covenant in the charge against the factoring of debt can be effective; an undertaking not to do something already done (the assignment in the agreement itself) is clearly of no effect.

(2) Less certain is the position of the factor with a facultative type of agreement.[58] Certainly in the case of a subsequent fixed charge, the factor, having inferred knowledge of the charge, might be precluded from buying any more debts except subject to the charge if the bank was unaware of the factoring agreement when the charge was created. This is because the agreement itself gives the factor no real rights to the debts but only a personal right against the client to have the debts offered free from encumbrances; the factor's real proprietary rights arise only as regards each debt when it has been offered to the factor and accepted. In the case of a floating charge,

---

[55] Nor can an assignment of a debt purporting only to be by way of a charge be a legal assignment; Law of Property Act 1925, s.136(1).

[56] "As stated in *Re Armagh Shoes* [1982] N.I. 59 at 62B, the contract constituted by the debenture must be construed by reference to the facts as they were, or might be foreseen to be, at the time it was executed and not by reference to the subsequent conduct of the parties: see *James Miller & Partners Ltd v Whitworth Street Estates (Manchester) Ltd* [1970] A.C. 583". *per* Morritt J. in *William Gaskell Group Ltd v Highley* [1993] B.C.C. 200 at 205C. At the time when a charge is created by a company, which already has a factoring agreement in place, it cannot be contemplated that the company has the ability to comply with the usual covenants in the instrument of charge.

[57] See para.8–22 and n.44 above.

[58] See para.7–08 above.

the position seems even more uncertain. Even if it could be shown that with inferred knowledge of the charge the factor had inferred knowledge also of the usual restrictive covenants, he would not have known of them when he entered into his agreement because they did not then exist. Until crystallisation the charge does not attach to the debts. As a result, the conflict is between two personal contractual rights: the rights of the chargee (not as such), but under the covenants (as negative pledges), and the rights of the factor to have the debts offered to him. In such circumstances, if neither one was aware of the other's rights when he entered into his own contract, it seems that the first in time (the factor) should prevail provided that his notices reached the debtor before those of the crystallisation of the charge.[59]

Naturally, if the bank had knowledge of the factoring agreement when it **8–29** took its charge, there seems little doubt that the factor's ownership of the debts, which he has purchased, should not be flawed by the charge. It seems clear that the bank, having taken its charge on the debts which it knows to be the subject of contractual rights, may be restrained from exercising its own rights under the charge in such a way as to interfere with those contractual rights.[60] This principle would apply to both types of factoring agreement but it would be unnecessary to rely upon it in the case of a whole turnover type[61] as the debts are already bound by that earlier agreement.

Unregistered charges

The priorities in a conflict between a factor and a chargee, whose charge **8–30** was not registrable, would in most cases be governed by the rule in *Dearle v Hall*.[62] However, where either one was aware of the other's prior rights, then it seems that the prior right must succeed and the giving of notices to debtors first will not assist the one whose rights have arisen later in time.[63] If the charge is registrable, but unregistered, under the existing law, the charge will be void against a creditor, an administrator or the liquidator of the company which created the charge (*i.e.* the factor's client)[64]; *such an*

---

[59] But see Oditah, *Legal Aspects of Receivables Financing* (1991), at p.112 where he argues that a restrictive covenant is not a "naked equity" that does not bind third parties.
[60] *Swiss Bank Corporation v Lloyds Bank Ltd* [1979] Ch. 548 at 573, where Browne-Wilkinson J. (as he then was) reviewed the case of *De Mattos v Gibson* (1858) 4 De G. & J. 276. The decision in the *Swiss Bank* case was reversed in the Court of Appeal but the principle appears to remain.
[61] See paras 7–10 and 7–11 above.
[62] See para.8–03 above.
[63] See n.2 above.
[64] Companies Act 1985, s.395(1). See also *Smith (Administrator of Cossett (Contractors) Ltd) v Bridgend County Borough Council* [2001] 3 W.L.R. 1347, where it was held that the scope of the section was not restricted to claims which a liquidator or an administrator could bring in their own names but applied also to claims by the company itself in liquidation or administration.

unregistered charge is not void altogether.[65] Unless the factor is able to rely on *Dearle v Hall,* his problem in such a case, in seeking priority over the unregistered charge, is that he is not normally a creditor of the client; in normal circumstances, the factor is a debtor of the client for the unpaid balance of the purchase price of the factored debts. In order to claim priority over the unregistered charge, the factor must become a creditor of his client. If his agreement so provided, he may also become a creditor to the extent of his funds in use by exercising the right to have the client repurchase all the debts on the basis that the ownership does not pass to the client until the repurchase price has been paid. However, a claim to priority over the unregistered charge may be made only by a liquidator (for all creditors), a secured creditor or one having a similar interest in the charged property.[66] It is not entirely clear whether, in these circumstances, the factor's claim as owner would be such that the factor's claim would succeed; for, if the factor is owner of the debts, then they are not part of the property of the client in which the factor has an interest.[67] If a factor takes a charge and it is duly registered, his priority over an unregistered charge will not be affected by any knowledge on the part of the factor of the existence of the unregistered charge when he took his charge; the priority depends on the statute which does not provide for a requirement of good faith.[68]

4. CONFLICTS WITH HOLDERS OF NEGOTIABLE INSTRUMENTS

8–31 A bill of exchange accepted (or a cheque drawn) by a debtor in discharge of a debt is a payment conditional upon the instrument being met; but the creditor's rights of action and remedies are suspended, when the instrument has been taken by the creditor, until its maturity. Thus, if a cheque is given or a bill accepted by the debtor before notice of the assignment of the underlying debt has been received by the debtor (even if the assignment took place earlier), then the holder of the instrument, would have the right to payment and the debtor would have no liability to the assignee; until notice the debtor is at liberty to settle with the assignor and, once the instrument

---

[65] See, *e.g. Re Ehrmann Bros Ltd* [1906] 2 Ch. 697; *Re Ashpurton Estates Ltd* [1983] Ch. 110.
[66] *Re Ehrmann Bros Ltd* [1906] 2 Ch. 697.
[67] In *E. Pfeiffer Weinkellerei-Weineinkauf GmbH & Co v Arbuthnot Factors Ltd* [1988] 1 W.L.R. 150 the point does not appear to have been specifically argued and it seems that both parties accepted the factor's *locus standi.* See also *McCormack, Reservation of Title* (1995), at p.100. If the factor were to obtain the legal title to the debts without notice of the unregistered charge by taking an assignment according to Law of Property Act 1925, s.136 he should have priority; but this is unlikely in normal factoring procedures. For the factor's ability to achieve priority by taking a charge as collateral security or otherwise, see Ch.13.
[68] *Re Monolithic Building Co* [1915] 1 Ch. 643; *Midland Bank Trust Co Ltd v Green* [1981] A.C. 513.

has been taken by the creditor, his rights against the debtor other than in the bill, being suspended, cannot be assigned.[69]

However, when notice of the assignment of a debt has been received by **8–32** the debtor, no cheque given or bill accepted thereafter by the debtor will detract from the rights of the assignee of the debt. Notice of an assignment in statutory form completes the transfer to the assignee of all rights to the debt including the power to give a good discharge[70]; and in the case of an equitable assignment after receipt of notice, the debtor is unable, either by payment or in any other way, to detract from the rights of the assignee.[71]

If such an instrument taken by the creditor in discharge, or purported **8–33** discharge, of a debt owing to him, is negotiated to a third party, who takes it before it is overdue (complete and regular on the face of it) in good faith and for value without notice of any defect in the title of the drawer (*e.g.* by reason of a previous assignment of the underlying debt) then the person to whom the instrument has been negotiated will have the right to have the instrument paid on presentation.[72] This will be so even if the bill was accepted (or the cheque given) after receipt of notice of the assignment of the underlying debt to another person; as the assignee in such a case would have the right to payment,[73] the debtor would have to pay twice for the same debt. Naturally, if the bill was accepted or the cheque drawn before the notice of the assignment was received, the assignee would have no right to payment. The same considerations (as apply to a person to whom a negotiable instrument has been negotiated) would appear to apply to the position of a person who has advanced money on the security of a negotiable instrument deposited with him in any conflict with an assignee of the debt to which the instrument relates. As such a security right created by a company is exempt from registration,[74] a factor should make searching enquiries, before starting a factoring agreement, regarding the practice of his prospective client in dealing with negotiable instruments.

Furthermore, although most agreements for factoring or invoice dis- **8–34** counting provide for the automatic assignment to the factor of any such instruments taken by the client in respect of the assigned debts, during the whole period of any such agreement which is on an undisclosed basis the factor must be on his guard against the discounting or pledging of negotiable instruments by his client.

---

[69] *Bence v Shearman* [1898] 2 Ch. 582.
[70] Law of Property Act 1925, s.136.
[71] See para.8–09 above and *Wm. Brandts Sons & Co v Dunlop Rubber Co Ltd* [1905] A.C. 454.
[72] Bills of Exchange Act 1882, s.29(1).
[73] See para.8–09 above.
[74] See para.8–19 and n.40 above.

5. NEGATIVE PLEDGE *SIMPLICITER*

8–35   It is now quite common for lenders to companies, whose credit-worthiness is at the higher end of the scale, to take, instead of security, a covenant from the borrower that it will not, until the loan is discharged, create any form of security over its property. Such covenants, often termed "negative pledges", sometimes include a restriction on the disposal of assets of the borrower otherwise than in the normal course of business. Such a restriction might well include an undertaking by the borrower specifically not to sell his debts or accounts receivable by way of factoring or discounting. If such a specific undertaking is not included, the question arises as to whether factoring or discounting would be considered to be in the normal course of business; it seems likely but not certain that it would.[75] However, assuming that the covenant is a clear prohibition of factoring or discounting, what is the position of the factor who enters into a factoring agreement with the covenantor?

Negative pledge simpliciter

8–36   It seems clear that if the factor, with knowledge of the covenant, enters into a factoring agreement with the person who has given the covenant, then the position would be similar to that where the covenant was in an instrument of charge: at the minimum; the factor as assignee would be liable to the beneficiary of the covenant for assisting in or inducing its breach.[76] For this purpose it would be necessary for the factor to have actual knowledge; constructive notice is not enough[77] and it is difficult to see how the factor could have inferred knowledge in such a case. In the case of a facultative type of agreement,[78] each debt is offered to the factor as it comes into existence, and the factor has no real right to any debts until he has accepted it. Thus, if the factor entered into such an agreement in ignorance of, and after the date of, the covenant, but subsequently became actually aware of its existence, the conflict would be between two purely contractual rights. It is arguable that in such a situation the factor would be unable to accept any further debts without becoming liable to the beneficiary of the covenant; it seems that the rights of the one whose equity was earlier in time must prevail. In the case of a whole turnover type of agreement,[79] for the factor to be liable, his knowledge would have to have arisen before he entered into his agreement because the type of agreement is indivisible.

8–37   As regards the possible impeachment of the factor's proprietary rights in

---

[75] See para.8–22 and n.44 above.
[76] See para.8–23 and n.47 above.
[77] *Encyclopaedia of Banking Law*, 4124.4.
[78] See para.7–08 above.
[79] See paras 7–10 and 7–11 above.

such circumstances, similar considerations appear to apply as in the case of a prior floating charge which includes such a covenant.[80] It is indeed clear that a negative pledge does not create any consensual security interest in favour of its beneficiary[81]; he will have no real rights over any of the assets of the covenantor when a conflict arises with the factor and he cannot be in a better position than he would have been but for the breach of the covenant.[82]

However, as an assignment is often considered analogous to a security **8–38** right for the purposes of resolving such conflicts,[83] it might be thought that the *De Mattos v Gibson* principle[84] would be applied if the interest of the beneficiary of the covenant were to be affected by the factoring agreement; if this were to be so, the factor might be unable to enforce his agreement and effect recoveries to the extent that such recoveries affected the rights of the beneficiary of the negative pledge. If the detrimental effect on the beneficiary was by way of his receiving a smaller dividend in the liquidation of the covenantor than would otherwise have been the case (the most likely scenario), then it is difficult to see how this principle could be applied without benefiting *all* unsecured creditors of the covenantor; as the covenant bestows no security or real right on the beneficiary, any proceeds of the debts, which did not go to the factor, would be claimed by the liquidator. As a result, in those circumstances, the remedy for the beneficiary of the covenant would perforce be by way of a claim for damages.

6. RESERVATION OF TITLE

The background

Of all such potential conflicts, that which at one time gave factors most **8–39** concern is the conflict with a client's supplier who is claiming the proceeds of the sub-sales of the client because ownership of the goods has been reserved to the supplier until payment for them has been made. Such concern has arisen not because the supplier's claim is likely to derogate from the factor's unencumbered ownership of the proceeds as debts purchased by the factor under the factoring agreement (and such improbability may be apparent from the discourse in the succeeding paragraphs); the concern seems to have arisen from the conceptual difficulties relating to equitable tracing rights in

---

[80] See paras 8–22 and 8–23 above.
[81] Moxton, "*Negative Pledges & Equitable Principles*" [1993] J.B.L. 458.
[82] See Goode, *Legal Problems of Credit and Security* (3rd ed., 2003) paras 1–71 *et seq*. and particularly para.1–78 for an analysis of negative pledges in favour of unsecured creditors.
[83] See n.32 above.
[84] (1858) 4 De G. & J. 276 and n.63.

commercial transactions and the absence until recently of case law bearing directly on such a conflict where the supplier is relying on such a right.

Reservation of title

8-40   The facts in *Pfeiffer Weinkellerei-Weinenkauf GmbH & Co v Arbuthnot Factors Ltd*[85] might appear to have dealt with such a conflict; but in that case the supplier's claim was based on a term in his contract of sale by which the proceeds of the sub-sales by the buyer (the factor's client) were assigned to the supplier. The assignment, being by way of security and unregistered, was void as against the factor who was considered to be a creditor of the buyer.[86]

8-41   The practice of reserving title to goods sold until payment for them has been received by the seller, in its simplest form without any stated term by which the proceeds of any sub-sale are to be held by the buyer for the seller, has long been established in commerce and industry in England and Wales; but it did not appear to come to the general notice of grantors of trade credit or to members of the accountancy and legal professions until attention was drawn to it by reports of the *Romalpa* case[87] and commentary on it in the late 1970s.

8-42   This case broke new ground, not because the terms in the sale contract were effective to retain in favour of the seller ownership of goods still held by the buyer in their original state, but because the Court of Appeal, upholding the decision of the judge in the court of first instance, recognised that the buyers, being in a fiduciary position in relation to the sellers, were under a duty to account to them for the proceeds of sub-sales. Such proceeds were, accordingly, not available to the receiver of the buyer. In that case it was conceded on behalf of the defendants that they held the goods as bailees; and this seems to be a unique feature of the case.

Terms reserving ownership of the goods in their simplest form, without any attempt to attach proceeds or goods other than those for which payment has not been made, are usually referred to as "simple reservation of title". More comprehensive terms purport to reserve to the supplier, until payment has been received for all goods supplied, any of the following:

(1)   any goods supplied by the supplier to the buyer (even those for which payment has been made) or any work in progress or finished goods into which the goods supplied have been incorporated ("extended reservation of title"); or

---

[85] [1988] 1 W.L.R. 150.
[86] See para.8–30 and n.67 above.
[87] *Aluminium Industrie Vaassen B.V. v Romalpa Aluminium Ltd* [1976] 1 W.L.R. 676.

(2) the proceeds of the sub-sales of the goods or even of goods into which the goods supplied have been incorporated ("prolonged reservation of title").

The effect on factors where the client's purchases and sales are both subject to reservation of title[88]

In the consideration of a conflict between the unpaid supplier and the factor who has purchased the debts, created by the onward sale of the supplier's goods from the buyer (his client) who has become insolvent, the first question is whether the buyer has given his customer (the factor's debtor) a good title by the sub-sale. If the sub-sale did not give the debtor a good title, then the debt purchased by the factor would be of little value to him because the debtor under the sub-sale would be unlikely to pay for goods which might be claimed from him by the unpaid supplier. The position will in many circumstances be covered under the following statutory exceptions to the normal rule that *nemo dat quod non habet*: **8–43**

(1) s.25(1) of the Sale of Goods Act 1979 combined with s.2(1) of the Factors Act 1889 provides, *inter alia*, that, where a person, having bought or agreed to buy goods, obtains possession of the goods with the consent of the seller and delivers them under a sale or other disposition to a third person who receives them in good faith and without knowledge of the rights of the true owner, then that sale or disposition shall be as valid as if expressly authorised by the true owner; and

(2) s.9 of the Factors Act 1889 (which has not been repealed) includes a provision which is similar to, but wider than, that in the Sale of Goods Act; it applies also where the delivery to the third person is under "an agreement for sale".

Accordingly, where the factor's client, having been in possession of the goods with the consent of his supplier, purports to transfer title to the debtor who takes the goods without knowledge that the client's purchase was subject to reservation of title, then the debtor will have obtained a good title to the goods.

Many such terms in sale contracts specifically authorise the onward sale of the goods by the buyer as principal as *between himself and the ultimate customer*. Where the terms are silent on this matter, such authorisation must surely be implicit because the contracts are contracts of sale, and not straightforward bailment contracts, and, except in the case of capital equipment or goods to be consumed by the buyer in the course of his **8–44**

---

[88] A situation often referred to by those in the business of factoring as "double ROT".

business, it must usually be envisaged that the goods are to be sold on in their original form or incorporated in other goods. In this connection it is of interest to note that in the *Pfeiffer* case[89] Phillips J. remarked that it seemed to him inappropriate to describe the relationship of a seller and a buyer in possession to whom title has not yet passed as that of bailor/bailee and he added that such relationship would not have the same incidents as a classic bailment.

8–45   Where the contract giving rise to the sub-sale by the factor's client himself provides for the reservation of title until payment has been made, the debtor, who has not paid for the goods, cannot rely on the above statutory provisions whilst the goods remain in their original form. The effect of the statutory provisions referred to above is to make effective the sale or agreement for sale by the factor's client; but, if the agreement for sale provides that title is not to pass until payment then, in the absence of payment, title will not have passed.[90] In the absence of payment by the factor's client and by the debtor, the supplier may be able to recover the goods.

8–46   If the debtor has a good title to the goods, then the supplier's claim must be to the proceeds which the factor will claim to have purchased as a factored debt. However, before dealing with such a conflict, it is necessary to consider the factor's position where the original supplier claims, not the proceeds, but the goods purchased by the debtor under reservation of title and held by the debtor in their original form. In such a situation the supplier may be able to recover the goods from the debtor and the factor will be unable to obtain payment from the debtor. The risk to a factor of such a claim by the client's supplier is perceived to be small; first, in most cases, the supplier will not know the identity of the debtors under the sub-sales, and, secondly, by the time a claim by a supplier is made, it is probable that the debtor will have either used the goods in manufacture or sold them. In the absence of knowledge of the terms on which the clients may be purchasing from day to day, factors, in all but the most unusual circumstances, rely on the warranties by their clients that the assigned debts are free from any claim by a supplier. However, owing to the almost invariable practice of the inclusion of reservation of title in terms of sale throughout commerce and industry in the United Kingdom, it would be difficult for factors to monitor and enforce such a warranty in practice.

8–47   In any well drawn factoring agreement the factor has the right to approve the terms and conditions in the contracts out of which the assigned debts arise. Although in most cases the risk described in paras 8–43 to 8–45 above is small, where a factor's client is selling goods in their original form and such goods are traceable (*e.g.* by being serially numbered), then the factor

---

[89] *E. Pfeiffer Weinkellerei-Weineinkauf GmbH & Co v Arbuthnot Factors Ltd* [1988] 1 W.L.R. 150.
[90] *Re Highway Foods International Ltd* [1995] B.C.C. 271.

should consider whether to prohibit the client's use of reservation of title in his terms of sale. In doing so, the factor will need to weigh the balance between:

(a) in non-recourse factoring, the ability to recover the goods in the insolvency of the debtor; or

(b) in recourse factoring, the likely resistance of the client to such a prohibition; and, on the other hand, precluding the risk referred to above.

The position where the debtor has a good title to the goods

On the premise that the supplier cannot recover his goods from the **8–48** ultimate customer under the sub-sale (the factor's debtor) because the ownership has passed to the latter (which, as explained in paras 8–44 and 8–45 above, is most likely), it seems that the supplier will have two hurdles to overcome in order to have a valid claim to the proceeds of the sub-sale. Before reviewing these two hurdles, there are two points to be considered in relation to any such conflict. First, there are the practical matters. In the normal course of businesses of the nature of those that might be likely to use factoring services, there is very often a stream of a large number of relatively small transactions and it is rare that such detailed terms can be agreed at the time when an order is placed by the buyer; very often, such orders are placed and accepted orally and the subsequent endorsement of the reservation of title provisions on the invoice will not be effective as a term of the supply contract. Furthermore, in such a stream of transactions, it is very often not possible to trace into a sub-sale the particular goods for which payment has not been made.

Secondly, it has been suggested that a factor, who is unaware that his **8–49** client has been purchasing goods on terms including a reservation of title provision and effecting sub-sales of such goods and including the proceeds as debts within the factoring agreement, may be deemed to have inferred knowledge of such terms of purchase. This may be relevant where the factor is relying on the rule in *Dearle v Hall*[91] by which, in a competition between two assignees of the same debt, priority goes to the one whose notice has been received first by the debtor; for that rule is subject to the qualification that he must have been unaware of any earlier assignment at the time when he made his commitment.

There may be rare cases in which the factored client is known to be a **8–50** distributor for one or a few suppliers of whose long term contracts the factor is likely to be aware. However, in most cases, the factor could hardly be expected to examine every one of his client's purchase contracts in the

---

[91] (1828) 3 Russ 1 and see para.8–03 above.

continuing stream of transactions. Even if he might be aware from his initial survey that such terms have been agreed with one or more of the suppliers, he is not to know from whom, and on what terms, his client may subsequently make purchases. Most factors rely on warranties, given by the client in the factoring agreement, that such terms do not apply; and, on these grounds, it was accepted, in two cases relating to such a conflict,[92] that the factor had no actual or inferred knowledge of the reservation of title provisions of the client's supplier.

8–51   In order to lay claim to the proceeds, the supplier must first show that the goods themselves remained in his ownership until title passed to the customer under the sub-sale, either by reason of the statutory provisions[93] or in accordance with a term in the supplier's contract of sale. Since the *Romalpa* case[94] there have been a number of cases in which suppliers, whose terms of sale included reservation of title provisions in their prolonged form, have sought to establish their ownership of goods into which the goods, which they supplied, have been incorporated[95] or to goods supplied by them which had been worked on in the course of manufacture.[96] In all such cases, the supplier has failed in his claim except where the goods supplied had not been irretrievably mixed with other goods and could be simply traced and detached from the other goods.[97]

8–52   It seems from a review of the cases concerned that it would be virtually impossible to construct conditions of sale which would reserve to the seller ownership of the products into which his goods had been incorporated without either creating a charge (which, unless registered, would be void against creditors, an administrator or a liquidator of the buyer, as described in para.8–30 above) or by giving the seller the free benefit of the buyer's labour and other materials; it is doubtful if any buyer could agree to the latter.[98] Therefore, it is most unlikely that a factor, who included within his factoring arrangements the proceeds of a sub-sale of goods purchased by his client on terms which included such reservation of title, would be faced with a claim by the supplier to such proceeds unless the goods:

---

[92] *E. Pfeiffer Weinkellerei-Weineinkauf GmbH & Co v Arbuthnot Factors Ltd* [1988] 1 W.L.R. 150 and *Compaq Computers Ltd v The Abercorn Group Ltd* [1991] B.C.C. 484.

[93] See para.8–43 above.

[94] *Aluminium Industrie Vaassen B.V. v Romalpa Aluminium Ltd* [1976] 1 W.L.R. 676.

[95] See, *e.g. Borden (UK) Ltd v Scottish Timber Products Ltd* [1981] Ch. 25; *Re Bond Worth Ltd* [1980] Ch. 228; *Clough Mill Ltd v Martin* [1985] 1 W.L.R. 111. For a case in which the reservation of title claim by a supplier of an animal to an abattoir was held to be ineffective on the death of the animal see *Chaigley Farms Ltd v Crawford, Kaye & Grayshire Ltd (t/a Leylands)* [1996] B.C.C. 957.

[96] *Re Peachdart Ltd* [1984] Ch. 131.

[97] *Hendy Lennox Ltd v Graham Puttick Ltd* [1984] 1 W.L.R. 485.

[98] For a full exposition of this aspect of reservation of title see Goode, *Proprietary Rights and Insolvency in Sales Transactions*, pp.83–86. See also Hicks "When goods become new species" (1993) J.B.L. at p.485 and *Modelboard Ltd v Outer Box Ltd* [1992] B.C.C. 945.

(a) retained their original form; or

(b) incorporated into other products, retained their original form and were separable and clearly identifiable.[99]

Assuming that the goods are so unchanged or separable and identifiable, **8–53** the supplier must then show unequivocally that the buyer has been placed in a fiduciary capacity as regards the proceeds. It seems that the courts will not import such terms into the contract of sale where no such terms exist. A proceeds clause alone will in all probability not invest in the supplier an equitable right to trace; such a contractual arrangement appears to be the creation by the buyer of a security right in favour of the supplier. It must be shown from the circumstances of the transaction and the whole of the terms that such a fiduciary relationship exists; for example, in the *Romalpa* case (unusually) it was accepted on behalf of the buyer that it was a bailee.[1] Such contract terms merely confirm the fiduciary position of the buyer as regards the proceeds which has already existed by reason of the nature of the transaction.

In *Re Andrabell Ltd*[2] the supplier's claim failed because: **8–54**

(1) there was no provision for separate storage of the goods before they became the subject of a sub-sale;

(2) there was no acknowledgement by the buyer of a fiduciary relationship; and

(3) the terms did not provide for a duty to account for the whole of the proceeds of the sub-sale but only an amount equivalent to the amount owing by the buyer to the supplier.

In another case,[3] the supplier's right to the proceeds has been held to **8–55** constitute a security right and to be a registrable charge by reason of its being "defeasible or destructible" upon payment by the buyer. This was also one of the grounds for the factor's claim to priority to be upheld in *Compaq Computer Ltd v The Abercorn Group Ltd.*[4] In that case, *Compaq Computer Ltd* (the supplier) claimed the proceeds of its customers' sub-sales on the grounds of the terms of supply which included prolonged reservation of title; the factor had included those proceeds within invoice discounting arrangements with the customer which had also created two charges on book debts in favour of the factor. The judgment included the following which should be of comfort to factors in such a conflict:

---

[99] *Hendy Lennox Ltd v Graham Puttick Ltd* [1984] 1 W.L.R. 485.
[1] *Aluminium Industrie Vaassen B.V. v Romalpa Aluminium Ltd* [1976] 1 W.L.R. 676.
[2] [1984] 3 All E.R. 407.
[3] *Tatung (UK) Ltd v Galex Telesure Ltd* (1989) 5 B.C.C. 325.
[4] [1991] B.C.C. 484.

(1) Under its agreement with its customer (the factor's client), the supplier's rights to the proceeds of the customer's sales constituted a charge on (or assignment by way of security of) the customer's book debts; in particular, as the proceeds remained trust monies only so long as sums remained owing to the supplier, the supplier's rights were "defeasible".[5]

(2) The charge was void as against the factor (who had become a creditor of its client) by reason of the absence of its registration under s.395 of the Companies Act 1985. The factor had priority by reason of its two duly registered debentures which included charges on the debts comprising the proceeds of the sales of the dealer and which, presumably, were held by the factor as collateral security for the client's obligations under the factoring agreement.[6]

(3) As the supplier's agreement with the customer regarding the proceeds of the sub-sales had the characteristic of a charge or assignment by way of security, the factor, having given its notices to the debtors, would have priority over the supplier's rights relying on the invoice discounting agreement (even without the benefit of the charges) and the rule in *Dearle v Hall*.[7] If a customer, having purchased on terms included prolonged reservation of title, is obliged to account to the supplier as the supplier's bailee or agent for all monies received by the customer arising from the sub-sales of goods supplied by the supplier and, if that were to be all, then the customer would hold the proceeds of the sub-sales in a fiduciary capacity. However, provision would then need to made in the terms of sale for the customer's remuneration (which is generally not included in such terms). In other words, how does the customer get its mark up? Furthermore, such terms of sale seem always to include strict payment terms whereby the customer is obliged *additionally* to pay for the products.

8–56   The conflict of such payment terms with the provision for the *whole* of the proceeds to be held in trust for the supplier was analysed by Michael Hart Q.C. sitting as a Deputy High Court Judge in *Modelboard Ltd v Outer Box Ltd*.[8] He said that it would be astonishing if the supplier may keep the whole of the proceeds of the sub-sale and also sue for price payable by the customers. He felt that it would also make no commercial sense if the supplier

---

[5] "Once it is accepted that the beneficial interest in the proceeds of sale was determinable on payment of debts, [the supplier] is faced with the difficulty that the rights and obligations of the parties were in reality and in substance characteristic of those of the parties to a charge and not those in a trustee/beneficiary or other fiduciary relationship". *per* Mummery J. *ibid.*, at 495.
[6] For an analysis of the benefits of such charges, see Ch.13.
[7] (1828) 3 Russ 1 and see para.8–03 above.
[8] [1992] B.C.C. 945 at 949–950.

were to be entitled to the whole proceeds of the sub-sale, but not to the purchase price of the goods. He considered that no customer would be likely to agree to such a windfall for the supplier because the customer would make no profit nor receive any compensation for his expenses. He also mentioned a third possibility: that it was implied that the supplier would be obliged to repay to the customer an amount equivalent to the latter's gross profit. However, he considered that the only possibility, which met the requirement of commercial reality and did not require contractual obligations to be implied, was that the supplier was entitled to have recourse to the proceeds of resale as security for the discharge of the price payable by the buyer. Accordingly, he concluded that the terms constituted a charge on the resale price to secure the supplier for the purchase price, notwithstanding that no words of charge were used.[9]

Therefore, in order that a right to trace should be upheld, the transaction **8-57** must clearly be that of bailment or agency and, in view of the inconsistencies between such relationships and the relationships under contracts of sale, this is almost impossible to achieve by the supplier in normal, commercial sales transactions. It is doubtful whether it would be commercially possible, other than in rare cases, for the supplier to ensure the separate storage of the goods and the payment of the proceeds into a special bank account.

Finally, even if in rare cases the supplier can establish his rights to the **8-58** proceeds of the sub-sales by the factor's client, a strong argument that the proceeds to be attached are the monies paid to the client by the factor, by way of payment of the purchase price of the debts assigned to him, is as follows:

(1) It must be envisaged by the supplier that the client (his buyer) would effect a sub-sale of the goods (even if it is not explicitly provided for in the supplier's terms);

(2) The client would have given the debtor a good title and would, as between himself and the debtor, have the right to collect payment; and

(3) It is quite normal commercial practice to arrange for collection of trade debts by receiving payment from a factor in return for the transfer to the factor of the right to collect payment from the debtor.[10]

---

[9] *Re Kent & Sussex Sawmills Ltd* [1947] Ch. 177 at 179; *Re Welsh Irish Ferries Ltd* [1986] Ch. 471 at 478; and *Compaq Computer Ltd v Abercorn Group Ltd* [1993] B.C.C. 484 at 493.
[10] In this connection it may be of interest that in Germany, where these practices have been in general use in commerce far longer than in England and Wales, in such a conflict these arguments were adduced in favour of a non-recourse factor to whom the court awarded priority (BGH WM 1977, 1198; 1982, 37 and 1350); see Klaus Bette, "Die Kollision der Factoringzession mit anderen Forderungsabtretungen", at p.212 in *Factoring Handbuch* (3rd ed., edited by Prof. Dr K.F. Hagenmueller, Heinrich J. Sommer and Dr Ulrich Brink; published by Fritz Knapp Verlag).

Position of factor summarised

8–59   From the foregoing, it seems that, in order to ensure that his rights to debts purchased should not be encumbered by claims to the debts by suppliers to his client, the factor should in all cases ensure that his client has given him a warranty that the debts falling within the scope of the factoring agreement are not the result of sub-sales of goods purchased on the basis of prolonged reservation of title. In the event of the client breaching this warranty, it seems that the factor has nothing to fear in those cases in which his client is a manufacturer, unless the goods purchased by the client are identifiable after the sub-sale and can readily be returned to their original form.

8–60   If the goods are passed on in their original form and the client also sells on terms which provide for reservation of title, the factor will need to consider the risk of a supplier's claim to the goods in the hands of a debtor. The factor may then consider it necessary to decline to approve the client's sales on such terms. If, however, the supplier's claim is to the proceeds, in most cases the supplier's claim will constitute an assignment by way of security or some other form of security right created by the client as buyer. In the case of a corporate client, the supplier's claim will normally fail as against the factor because that security will be registrable but is likely to be unregistered. Almost invariably notice of the assignment by the factor will have been given first, in the case of disclosed factoring, on the invoice and, in the case of confidential factoring, at the first signs of financial difficulties. In the absence of knowledge of the supplier's claim at the time when the relevant assignment to the factor became effective,[11] the factor would be able to rely on the principle of *Dearle v Hall*[12] and obtain priority over the supplier's assignment or charge.

8–61   If the factor were to become aware of the unregistered charge (constituted by the prolonged reservation of title in the terms on which his client had purchased), then he would be able to claim priority by:

>   (i)   procuring that his client repurchase the debts and so becoming a creditor for the repurchase price; and

>   (ii) taking a charge on the debts (to secure his client's obligations to him under the factoring agreement) and duly registering it.

His registered charge should then have priority over the unregistered charge of his client's supplier. It is from the foregoing apparent that, in normal circumstances, a factor is likely to be in a stronger position if he is unaware

---

[11] See para.8–50 above.
[12] (1828) 3 Russ 1 and see para.8–03 above.

of any terms on which his client purchases and relies upon warranties in the factoring agreement.

There remains those cases in which the supplier's claim is based on an **8–62** equitable tracing right, and for the reasons explained above these are likely to be rare. In such cases, the application of the rule in *Dearle v Hall* is not certain. The authorities are not clear as to the resolution of a conflict between a supplier, claiming by way of equitable tracing the proceeds of a sub-sale by his buyer, and an assignee of those proceeds, where the assignee is seeking to rely on the rule in *Dearle v Hall*.[13] Academic opinion seems to be divided as to whether the rule would apply, although there are strong arguments that it does.[14] Therefore, in such cases, the factor may be at some risk, as regards debts still outstanding when the conflict arises, even in the absence of knowledge of the terms agreed between the supplier and his client.

As regards debts already paid to the factor by the time when the supplier **8–63** asserts his claim, it appears that the factor should obtain priority, provided that the factor has received the payments in good faith without knowledge of the supplier's terms. It appears that money passes into the legal ownership of a purchaser in good faith and the legal ownership displaces the equitable right of the supplier.[15]

The decided cases indicate that it is almost impossible to construct a **8–64** prolonged reservation of title clause in terms of sale which, in relation to the proceeds of the customer's sub-sales, will constitute a valid trust of those proceeds, unless the customer is to act as sales agent for the supplier. However, there can be no standard procedure for the factor for every situation in "traversing legal territory judicially described as 'a maze, if not a minefield' ".[16] On reviewing every prospective client, the factor must decide if the nature of the business is such (*e.g.* distribution of products in their original form for a regular supplier) that he should examine the terms on which the prospective client purchases. If he does, and the trust provisions are defeasible and the payment terms strict, then there would be little risk for the factor to provide his services supported by a charge on debts that do not vest in him. In the rare event of the terms and the performance of them providing for a clear trust of the proceeds, then the factor should obtain a waiver. In all other cases, the factor is likely to be in a stronger position without knowledge of terms of supply to his prospective client.

---

[13] This question was explored in depth in *Compaq Computer Ltd v Abercorn Group Ltd* [1991] B.C.C. 484 but a decision on the point was unnecessary because Compaq's claim to the proceeds was held to be an assignment by way of a charge or, if not, an equitable assignment.
[14] Goode, *Commercial Law* (3rd ed., 2004), p.752, n.69. See also McCormack, *Reservation of Title* (1995), pp.154 *et seq.*, and, by analogy, see Goode, *Legal Problems of Credit and Security* (3rd ed., 2003), para.5–36.
[15] *ibid.* and see Oditah, *Legal Aspects of Receivables Financing* (1991), at pp.153–154.
[16] *per* Mummery J., *Compaq Computer Ltd v Abercorn Group Ltd* [1991] B.C.C. 484 at 486.

7. OTHER CONFLICTS

Goods released on trust receipt

8–65   In order to finance the movement of goods, especially for their import, banks and other financiers often take security by means of a pledge by the trader of the documents of title to the goods which is treated in law as a pledge of the goods themselves. The pledge, if it does not depend on a written agreement but is purely a possessory security, does not require registration at the companies registry (if the trader is a company) nor as a bill of sale (if it is not). It is usually necessary for the trader to take physical possession of the goods and to sell them in order to repay the advances made by the lender. So that the lender's security should not be lost before the advances have been repaid, the lender will often release the documents to the trader against the provision of a trust receipt by the trader. By the trust receipt the trader undertakes to hold in trust for the lender, not only the goods until sold, but also the proceeds of their sale. It has been held that a trust receipt for such purposes constitutes a continuation of the pledge and that, furthermore, the lender's rights to the proceeds do not require registration at the companies registry or as a bill of sale (as applicable).[17]

8–66   It is, therefore, apparent that if a factor's client has made such an arrangement and either offers or notifies to the factor the proceeds, to which such a trust receipt relates, the factor may well take the assignment of the proceeds as debts falling within the scope of the factoring agreement. He might be completely unaware of the pledge or the trust receipts. On the insolvency of the client, the lender might well claim that the assignment to the factor was invalid on the basis that the proceeds, being held by the trader in trust, were not property of the trader capable of being assigned by it. On the other hand, as it is probable that the factor will have given notice to the debtor first, he might claim priority on the basis of the rule in *Dearle v Hall*.[18] However, as in the case of a conflict between a factor and a supplier to the client on *Romalpa*[19] type terms[20] (claiming by way of equitable tracing), it is not clear that the rule applies because it is not a conflict between two assignees.

8–67   Although there are similarities in the positions of a lender in such a case and the supplier who has reserved title to the goods sold to the factor's client, the position is in most cases not exactly the same. In the case of the trust receipt, the trust relating to the proceeds of sale is based on a well established principle (and does not require registration), whereas, in the case of the

---

[17] *Re David Allester Ltd* [1922] 2 Ch. 211; *North Western Bank Ltd v John Poynter Son & MacDonalds* [1895] A.C. 56.
[18] (1828) 3 Russ 1 and see para.8–02 above.
[19] *Aluminium Industrie Vaassen B.V v Romalpa Aluminium Ltd* [1976] 1 W.L.R. 676.
[20] See paras 8–39 *et seq.* above.

Romalpa type terms,[21] the existence of a trust may well not be established.[22] Although conflicts between factors and holders of trust receipts have arisen in practice, it appears that they have in all cases been resolved without recourse to litigation (possibly by compromise); as there appears to be no reported case on the point nor any authoritative published comment on it, a resolution of the problem remains a matter of uncertainty.[23]

The liens of a carrier

The question of a carrier's lien on goods, despatched by a client to a **8–68** debtor, is not strictly a question of conflict between the factor and the carrier relating to rights to debts purchased by the factor. On the insolvency of the client, there may well be an unpaid carrier who has a general lien on such goods in respect of which the client had responsibility for delivery to the debtor's premises. Such a claim to the goods will obviously impair the factor's right to recover any related debt. Factors often accept notifications or offers submitted as soon as goods have been placed in transit in the United Kingdom to debtors. If the carrier seized the goods, the debtors would not pay and the client would be in breach of his warranty that the debts were *bona fide* obligations of the debtors.

This aspect may not be a too serious problem in the case of domestic sales **8–69** in relation to which delivery may take only two or three days. Even if the carrier's charges for all his sales are the client's responsibility, the aggregate of unpaid debts may well be fully absorbed by any retention made. Indeed, in many cases, in the event of insolvency and an insufficient retention, it may sometimes be worthwhile for the factor to settle with the carrier in order to release the goods to the debtors and recover the indebtedness. However, in the case of export sales in circumstances in which the client is responsible for carriage and freight charges, the amounts payable may be considerable and, in view of the longer transit time, the aggregate of the outstanding invoices represented by goods which have not reached the debtors may be a large proportion of the whole. Furthermore, this aspect needs to be considered carefully in the case of an importing client whose business is such that the goods are despatched from his overseas supplier direct to the customers. In such a case, the factor should accept responsibility for the debts only when the underlying goods have been placed in transit in the United Kingdom to the debtors.

---

[21] See nn.19 and 20 above.
[22] See para.8–55 and n.5 above.
[23] See also para.8–63 and n.13 above regarding the uncertainty of the application of the rule in *Dearle v Hall* in such a conflict.

The rights of a mercantile agent

8–70   A mercantile agent (or factor in the original sense) has a prescriptive right, born of long usage in the law merchant, to a lien on his principal's goods in his possession and on the proceeds of the sale of those goods effected through his agency. As a result, if a client sells to the debtors through a mercantile agent, it is likely that the agent's lien would attach to the proceeds (*i.e.* the debts) in priority to the factor's rights to debts resulting from the agent's sales on behalf of the client. The factor's rights to any such debt under the assignment to him cannot be better than the client's rights at the time of the assignment. This question does not appear to have been decided in the courts in the United Kingdom and it would not appear to be a serious matter for factors in their domestic businesses because few businesses employ mercantile agents in this country. To be a mercantile agent, for this purpose, the agent must sell in his own name without disclosing that of his principal.[24] However, the priority of a mercantile agent in these circumstances has been accepted in international trade in Europe. A factor should be on his guard if his client factors his exports and is likely to use a mercantile agent. Agreement between the factor and the agent should be reached at the outset. Obviously, if the agent is adamant about retaining his rights and the client persists in using him, then the client will be unable to warrant that these debts are free of encumbrances and they will have to be excluded from factoring.

Factoring of sub-rentals in respect of real property

8–71   It has sometimes been proposed that a corporate lessee of real property, who has granted a sub-lease of it, should include the sub-rentals within a factoring agreement. The difficulty for the factor in purchasing such sub-rentals within the scope of his agreement is the risk that, on the insolvency of the client, the superior landlord might claim the benefit of them.[25] This is another conflict for the determination of which there is no clear authority; it is not entirely certain whether the statutory provision gives the landlord priority over any person with existing rights to the sub-rentals. In *Rhodes v Allied Dunbar Pension Services Ltd*,[26] where the conflict was between the landlord and a receiver for a mortgagee of the property, the Court of Appeal gave judgment in favour of the landlord on the grounds that:

(i)   the deed of debenture did not have the effect of an equitable assignment to the bank of the right to future payments of rent by the sub-tenants;

---

[24] *per* Lord Denning in *Rolls Razor Ltd v Cox* [1967] 1 Q.B. 552.
[25] In accordance with the Law of Distress Amendment Act 1908, s.6.
[26] [1989] 1 All E.R. 1161.

(ii) the bank had not taken possession of the property so that the lessee remained at all times entitled to the sub-rentals; and

(iii) the receiver was, by the instrument of the mortgage, deemed to be the agent of the lessee.

Although these circumstances would not apply in the case of an assignment of the right to future sub-rentals under a factoring agreement, it can be inferred from the judgment that such an assignment would be overridden by a s.6 notice.[27] The section was intended to enable the undertenant to pay the sub-rentals direct to the superior landlord and so avoid distraint upon the undertenant or forfeiture of the head lease with probable termination of the undertenancy. This purpose would be defeated if the right to receive the sub-rentals could be removed from the superior landlord.[28]

Factoring of sub-rentals of leased equipment

Sub-rentals that may more usually become the subject of factoring **8–72** agreement are the rentals payable to a lessee of equipment whose business is the hiring out of such equipment. It is not uncommon for the lessor of such equipment, in consideration for consent to the hiring out, to require the lessee to assign to the lessor the proceeds of such sub-hire as security for payments under the lease. If the lessee, being a company, is a party to a factoring agreement by which such proceeds are purchased by the factor, then the priorities should be determined in accordance with the principles which apply to a conflict between a factor and a bank holding a charge upon the debts of the factor's client.[29] If the factor's client is a sole trader or partnership, the rule in *Dearle v Hall* should apply.[30]

It has been known in such a case that the lessor's documentation provides **8–73** that the assignments are in accordance with the statute[31] and for the lessor to claim, as a purchaser of the legal title in good faith and for value, priority over the factor's equitable title to the proceeds of the sub-hire. Such a claim seems unlikely to succeed. First, the agreements to create the assignment will

---

[27] "Likewise, in my view, in the case of a person, including a mortgagee, who takes not an assignment of a headlease, but a sub-term carved out of the headlease. Such a person acquires an estate which from its inception is subject to the rights conferred on superior landlords and undertenants by ss.6 and 1". *per* Nicholls L.J. in *Rhodes v Allied Dunbar Pension Services Ltd* [1989] 1 All E.R. 1161 at 1168.
[28] See also Oditah, *op. cit.*, at p.163.
[29] See paras 8–15 *et seq.* above. Such a charge on the proceeds is likely to be a fixed charge; *Re Atlantic Computer Systems plc* [1992] Ch. 505 and *Re Atlantic Medical Ltd* [1992] B.C.C. 653 was held but *cf. Royal Trust Bank v National Westminster Bank plc* [1996] B.C.C. 613 at 619–620, where Millett L.J. expressed the view (albeit *obiter*) that a charge on hire-purchase and lease-purchase agreements and leases was a floating charge owing to the ability of the chargor to use the proceeds of the charged property in the normal course of its business.
[30] (1828) 3 Russ. 1, and see para.8–03 above.
[31] Law of Property Act 1925, s.136.

in many cases be made before the equipment has been hired out and so relate to future debts; such assignments will be effective in equity only. Secondly, in accordance with the factoring agreement (whether on a disclosed or undisclosed basis), the proceeds of the sub-hire will be paid by the debtors for the benefit of the factor. Until the lessor intervenes and gives notices of his assignments to the debtors, his assignments will be incomplete as legal assignment.[32] This is unlikely to happen before the lessor is aware of the prior factoring agreement. Thirdly, to comply with the statute, an assignment must be absolute and not by way of a charge.[33] It has been held that the fact that an assignment is taken by way of security (being a mortgage and not simply a charge) is not fatal to its nature as an absolute assignment[34]; but the authorities also show that, when the surrounding circumstances are taken into account, although expressed as a mortgage, the assignment may be in fact by way of a charge.[35]

Factoring for travel agents

8-74   Up to now it had been thought that the debts arising from sales of air tickets by travel agents could not be sold by the agents of their own volition to factors because their agreements with the carriers provided that the agents should sell strictly as agents and were to collect the proceeds on behalf of the carriers. It was thought that the carriers had the beneficial ownership of the debts representing the proceeds of the sales. The same considerations were normally considered to apply to sales of package tours and holidays by the agents. It was considered probable, but not entirely certain, that, where the agent had paid to the carrier the full amount payable by the ultimate customer under any contract with that customer (which may have included more than one item), the agent would have been subrogated to the rights of the carrier so that it would then be collected from the customer for its own account. It would have been possible for the agent to assign those rights to the factor; but it was unlikely that the agent would have paid the carrier before it had itself collected from the customer. In any case, the agent would have been unable to give the factor a legal assignment of the resulting debt. Such sales would have in many cases formed the bulk of the business of a travel agent and such businesses had been considered unsuitable for factors.

8-75   However, from an examination of the *dicta* in *Re* ILG Travel Ltd,[36] it appears that factors should not decline such business without careful

---

[32] *ibid.*
[33] *ibid.*
[34] *Tancred v Delgoa Bay & East African Rly Co Ltd* (1889) 23 Q.B.D. 239.
[35] *Mercantile Bank of London v Evans* [1899] 2 Q.B. 613 and see Oditah, *op. cit.* at 108.
[36] [1996] B.C.C. 21.See also *Henry v Hammond* [1913] 2 K.B. 515 for the principle that a person, described as a trustee, who is entitled to mix the trust money with his own is a debtor and not a trustee.

consideration of the particular contractual relations between the agent and its suppliers. That case related to the question of set-off between ILG Travel Ltd (in liquidation) and the travel agents selling the package tours on behalf of ILG; for that purpose, it was necessary to determine the status of the monies collected by the agents from the customers. Although the liquidator contended that certain provisions of the agency agreements established a "bare trust" of those monies, it was decided that the obligations under these provisions constituted an equitable charge because the agents were entitled to deduct from the collections sums due to them from ILG. Consequently, there was a debtor/creditor relation between the agents and ILG and, as a result, the debts owing by customers were due to the agents in their own right. Despite an alternative reason given for the decision in that case, the first reason should be authority that a trust provision in a carrier's contracts with travel agents, if similarly constructed, will be held to constitute a charge which, if not registered, will be invalid against the claims of the agent's factor (as a creditor of its client) who factors the proceeds of the ticket sales.[37] In *ILG Travel* the question of registration of the charges did not arise because none of the travel agents was insolvent.

Apart from reliance on this case (and many of the agreements between the travel supplier and the agent may be distinguished), it now seems that, in any case in which the agent is obliged to pay the supplier on a specific date whether or not he has recovered from the customer, the trust will be unlikely to hold up as a bare trust. In such a case, the trust will be considered defeasible, and, accordingly, a security right to secure payment by the agent to the supplier and registrable as a charge.[38] Consequently, the trust (if, as is likely, it is not registered) will be ineffective against the claims of a factor relying on a charge on the debts. **8–76**

8. WAIVERS AND PRIORITY AGREEMENTS

In the foregoing paragraphs of this chapter indications have been given of some of the cases in which the factor should obtain at the outset from a third party, who may have a security right or interest in the factored debts, a waiver of such right or interest. In the case of a facultative agreement, such a waiver, or an agreement as to priorities, should be sought even if the third party's rights or interest arises during the currency of the agreement, because under that type of agreement the factor's real rights to each debt **8–77**

---

[37] For the position of a factor as creditor in such a conflict, see the factor's position in relation to a supplier of goods seeking to establish a trust of the proceeds of his buyer's sub-sales; see paras 8–39 *et seq.* above.
[38] See, by analogy, *Compaq Computers v Abercorn Group Ltd* [1991] B.C.C. 484; *Tatung (UK) Ltd v Galex Telesure Ltd* (1989) 5 B.C.C. 325; *Modelboard Ltd v Outer Box Ltd* [1992] B.C.C. 945 at 950.

come into existence only when the debt has been offered to and accepted by him. On the other hand, in the case of an existing whole turnover agreement and the creation of a new charge (or a new assignment) by the client in favour of a third party, a waiver is in most cases not necessary because the factor's rights should have priority.[39] However, in such a case, in order to avoid any misunderstanding and invidiousness, the factor should on notice of the charge immediately seek acknowledgement from the third party that it is aware of the factor's prior rights. The difference between a waiver and an acknowledgement has practical significance: in the case of a request for a waiver, the third party may seek to impose some conditions. Indeed, it has not been unknown for a bank, on being asked to confirm its understanding of the position in such circumstances, to offer a waiver in which a limitation is imposed on the aggregate amount of the factor's prepayments outstanding at any one time or to stipulate its ability to terminate the waiver by notice. The bank would thus cause a breach by the client of the pre-existing factoring agreement.

8–78   Such waivers (or letters of release as they are sometimes termed) will normally specify that the third party:

(1) confirms that it is aware of the factoring agreement and its terms;

(2) consents to the agreement and agrees that the debts sold to the factor under the agreement shall be free from *any* security right in the third party's favour;

(3) stipulates that the waiver does not preclude its taking security rights over any amount that may become payable by the factor to the client (or that for avoidance of doubt an existing charge on book debts attaches to such amounts payable)[40];

(4) reserves the right to terminate the waiver in certain circumstances[41] (for example, crystallisation of its charge or on notice to the factor).

In addition to the foregoing, the factor should procure the inclusion of the further confirmations mentioned below. First, it is important that the factor

---

[39] See paras 8–27 and 8–29.

[40] Some of the banks have recently been anxious to take a specific charge on the factors indebtedness to the client because it may be construed that, having waived *all* its rights to the debts, the bank may have no claim under its existing charge to any balance available after the factor has recovered his prepayments.

[41] But see Goode, *Legal Problems of Credit and Security* (3rd ed., 2003), para.5–55, where he distinguishes the position in relation to a whole turnover type of agreement from that of a facultative agreement and indicates that in the case of a whole turnover agreement the waiver should be permanent because the agreement commits the factor to future purchases. However, in any case whether or not this condition is to be included depends on the nature of the security and the bargaining strength of the parties.

should understand the significance of the stipulation in (3) above. As the charges taken on book debts (and the factor's indebtedness to his client is undoubtedly a book debt[42]) may, notwithstanding the *Spectrum* decision, be fixed, actual notice to the factor of such a charge may well preclude set-off by him, against his indebtedness to the client, of certain of the client's subsequent liabilities.[43] The notice has the same effect on the rights of the factor (as debtor) as notice of the assignment of his indebtedness.[44] The most important of such rights of set-off relates to recourse and it is probable that, as any recourse would in most circumstances arise from the same agreement as that giving rise to the indebtedness (and be closely connected with it) or be dealt with as an item on a current account,[45] the right to set off such recourse would not be affected by notice of the charge. To avoid any doubt, the factor would be well advised to make certain that the stipulation in (3) above is hedged by the following proviso:

> "but the chargee's rights under any such charge shall at all times be subject to all rights of defence and set-off which the factor may have against the company, whether arising before or after notice of such charge."

Secondly, factors should also not overlook the need to have included in the waivers consents to their purchasing the related rights referred to in paras 10–24 to 10–27 and the release of such rights from any charge. Thirdly, it should be made clear that termination of the waiver does not affect the factor's rights to debts and their related rights in existence at the time of such termination.

Form of waiver

Waivers are sometimes in the form of agreements between the parties. **8–79** This is necessary where, as is not uncommon now, the factor takes a charge in conjunction with its factoring agreement either to catch those debts purportedly assigned to the factor, which fail to vest in him for technical reasons, or over other assets as collateral security or for both reasons.[46] In the case of debts charged to the factor, the bank cannot simply waive or release its rights to the debts and attach any surplus by charging the factor's indebtedness to the client; it must retain its charge on the debts and agree

---

[42] See n.40 to para.8–19 above.
[43] See Lightman & Moss, *The Law of Receivers and Administrators of Companies* (3rd ed., 2000), paras 16–033 *et seq.*
[44] See para.9–21 below.
[45] See paras 9–17 and 10–02 below.
[46] See Ch.13.

with the factor as to priorities.[47] The effectiveness of a waiver in the form of an agreement will depend upon the presence of consideration flowing from the factor unless it is by way of a deed. The usual consideration would be based on the fact that the factor had entered into the factoring agreement at the request of the third party which was to give the waiver; the provision of factoring service would be presumed to improve the fortunes of the client and consequently the security of the third party. Alternatively, the factoring agreement may have enabled the third party to reduce his exposure to risk.

8–80   More often, however, a waiver is drafted not as an agreement but as a letter informing the factor of a fact. The fact is the consent given to the client by the third party for the client to enter into the factoring agreements by which the debts are to be sold to the factor free from any encumbrances in favour of the third party. If the factor were to make the agreements to his detriment and be met by a demand from the third party that the factor give up his rights to the debts, it would seem that the third party would be stopped from denying the consent.

8–81   As waivers are rarely executed as deeds, the question of the authority of signatory should not be overlooked. It is most likely that the signature of any official of a major commercial bank, having the status of branch manager or higher, may be relied upon; over a long period the banks have accepted the validity of waivers signed in this way and may be considered to have held out such officials as having that authority. At the minimum, such officials would be clothed with the ostensible authority to sign such waivers.[48] However, to be safe, the factor should ensure that:

(1) a waiver given by an individual or partnership is executed as a deed; and

(2) a waiver given by a corporate body (other than a Member of the London Clearing Banks) is either by way of a deed or supported by a certified copy of a board resolution authorising the giving of the waiver.

Waivers and assignees of security rights

8–82   The question has arisen as to whether or not an assignee of a security right would be bound by a waiver given by the original holder of the security right. For example, a finance company holding a fixed charge on book debts of a company to secure a fixed sum debenture, might after having given a waiver to a factor, assign the debenture together with the security right for value; this might occur if a guarantor of the liability of the company paid off

---

[47] As to agreements regulating priorities see Ch.13 and App.9.
[48] *First Energy (UK) Ltd v Hungarian International Bank Ltd* [1993] 2 Lloyd's Rep. 194 and see Brown, "The Agent's Apparent Authority: Paradigm or Paradox" (1995) J.B.L. 360.

the indebtedness under the debenture and took the assignment. Would the assignee who had taken the assignment in ignorance of the waiver be bound? There appears to be no case giving direct authority on the question, but the view of a leading academic is that the assignee would not be bound.[49] Consequently, the factor should procure that a note of the waiver be endorsed on the instrument of charge.

9. WHERE THE RULE IN *DEARLE V HALL*[50] DOES NOT APPLY

This chapter would not be complete without reference to two possible conflicts, between factors and third parties claiming the debts the subject of a factoring agreement, where this rule has no application. The first is the claim of a judgment creditor of the factor's client who seeks to enforce his judgment by a Third Party Debt order[51] on a customer of the client. In such a case, the factor will succeed, provided that the indebtedness of the customer, which is the subject of the order, has been assigned to the factor before the garnishee order *nisi*. The order can attach only to a debt with which the factor's client, as judgment debtor, may honestly deal.[52] The factor's rights will prevail even in the absence of notice of the assignment to the customer[53]; once the debt has been assigned to the factor, there is no indebtedness to the client and there is nothing to which the order may attach. Consequently, in the case of a factoring agreement of the whole turnover type,[54] under which the debts vest in the factor upon their coming into existence, the factor will be unaffected by any attempt by a creditor of the client to execute his judgment by a garnishee order on any debts the subject of the factoring agreement. In the case of a facultative agreement,[55] the factor will be protected only if the offer of the debt, the creditor seeks to attach, has been accepted before the time of the order *nisi*. **8–83**

The other circumstances in which the rule does not apply arise in the event of a claim to the factored debts by a liquidator or trustee in bankruptcy of the factor's client. In such a case, the factor's rights will depend on the timing of his assignments and not the notices of them. The assignments must **8–84**

---

[49] Goode, *Legal Problems of Credit and Security* (3rd ed., 2003) para.5–56, where he suggests that to forestall such a situation the factor, on receiving a waiver, should procure that a note of it is placed on the instrument of charge. *cf. Python (Monty) Pictures Ltd v Paragon Entertainment Corporation* [1998] E.M.L.R. 640, where a sub-assignee of copyright was bound by a side letter between the assignor and assignee of it although the sub-assignee was ignorant of the side letter.
[50] (1828) 3 Russ 1 and see para.8–03 above.
[51] See para.4–46 above.
[52] *Holt v Heatherfield Trust Ltd* [1942] 2 K.B. 1.
[53] It seems beyond argument that the absence of notice does not affect the efficacy of the transaction as between assignor and assignee". *per* Atkinson J., *ibid.*, at p.5.
[54] See paras 7–10 and 7–11 above.
[55] See para.7–08 above.

have been made before the commencement of the winding-up or bankruptcy as is more fully explained in Ch.11.[56]

10. OFFICE HOLDER'S WRONGFUL COLLECTION OF DEBTS

8–85 Some of the conflicts that may arise between a factor and an office holder (administrative receiver, administrator, liquidator or provisional liquidator) of an insolvent corporate client were described earlier in this chapter. Where there is such a conflict (or even where there may be no conflict but the office holder is awaiting a report on the factoring agreement by his legal adviser), it has been known for the office holder to collect, or attempt to collect, the debts of which the unencumbered ownership has passed to the factor. If the office holder succeeds in collecting any such debts, then he will not be protected by s.234 of the Insolvency Act 1986 which exempts an office holder from liability from loss and damage resulting from "seizure or disposal" of property which is not the property of the company except by reason of his negligence.[57] He will be liable to the factor for loss and damage resulting from his collection of the debts which are the property of the factor; the terms "seizure" and "disposal" do not include the collection of debts. Furthermore, he will not have any lien on the proceeds for his expenses of such collection as is the case with the seizure and disposal of other property.[58]

11. PARTNERSHIPS AND SOLE TRADERS

8–86 This chapter has so far dealt mainly with conflicts which may arise in relation to clients of factors which are companies. Where there is a conflict between a factor, using an agreement of the whole turnover type, of a client which is a sole trader or a partnership and another factor or another assignee of such a client, then the former factor cannot rely on registration of his agreement under the Bills of Sale Act 1878[59] for priority over the other factor or assignee. Registration has the effect only of perfecting the factor's rights to the debts and prevents the avoidance of the assignments under the factoring agreement on the bankruptcy of the client.[60]

---

[56] See paras 11–58 and 11–63 respectively.
[57] *Welsh Development Agency v The Export Finance Corporation Ltd* [1992] B.C.C. 270 *per* Dillon L.J. at 295f, and see Lightman & Moss, *The Law of Receivers and Administrators of Companies* (3rd ed., 2000), para.6–02.
[58] Insolvency Act 1986, s.234(4)(b).
[59] See paras 7–15 *et seq.* above.
[60] See Goode, *Legal Problems of Credit and Security* (3rd ed., 2003), para.3–31.

CHAPTER 9

SET-OFF AND THE DEBTOR'S COUNTERVAILING RIGHTS

There are few more important principles of law in commercial and financial **9–01**
dealings than the principle of set-off. Debts and other intangibles make up a
large part of the assets of most businesses many of which rely on set-off to
protect themselves as if it were a security right. It is not a security right; but
its effects are in many circumstances analogous. Certainly to a factor these
principles are (with the exception of the rules relating to assignments) the
most important elements of the law. The factor is affected by these principles
in two ways: they provide him with a method safely to recover amounts
payable to him by his client, in particular in relation to recourse,[1] and they
may detract from his rights to recover from debtors funds that he has
provided to his client by way of prepayments.

1. THE NATURE AND CLASSIFICATION OF SET-OFF

Unfortunately, the importance of the subject is matched by its difficulty and **9–02**
complexity. This is demonstrated in Philip Wood's massive book[2] in which
he identifies seven different heads of set-off. The grey area in the law and the
conceptual difficulties, aggravated by differences in terminology, have created a subject too vast to be dealt with in this book otherwise than by way of
a synopsis and those who require a more detailed analysis are referred
elsewhere.[3]

---

[1] See Ch.10
[2] Wood, *English & International Set-Off*.
[3] For example, Derham, *The Law of Set-off*, (3rd ed., 2003) and Goode, *Legal Problems of Credit and Security* (3rd ed., 2003), Ch.VII para.3–31, and see n.2 above.

The nature of set-off

9–03 Set-off is a means by which a debtor who has a monetary cross-claim against his creditor may use that cross-claim to discharge or reduce *pro tanto* his admitted liability to the creditor. Set-off should be distinguished from a substantive defence, such as is available to a buyer where the seller has not earned payment by delivery of goods in conformity with the contract of sale; a substantive defence may be available, for example, to a defendant who claims that payment has already been made or that a condition precedent to the creditor's right to payment has not been fulfilled. Whether a monetary cross-claim amounts to a set-off is a "matter of law", whether or not it has been pleaded as a defence or a counterclaim.[4] Set-off should also be distinguished from the common law doctrine of abatement. This doctrine allows the defendant, who has purchased goods or contracted for work, to defend himself in an action against him for the full price by showing that what the plaintiff has delivered or performed is worth less, *at the time of delivery or performance*, than was provided for in the contract by reason of the plaintiff's breach of the contract.[5]

9–04 The relations of parties to a current account, although often included in the doctrine of set-off, may be distinguished from it because in the case of a true current account the parties have no claims on each other for the items individually debited and credited; there is only a single claim, one way or the other, for the resulting balance from time to time. This differentiation is important for the factor in relation to his ability to recover the repurchase price of debts the subject of recourse in the insolvency of his client.[6]

9–05 In considering the effect of set-off, it is important to distinguish between the situation where set-off is only a procedural shield against the claim of a creditor and those cases in which it is a substantive defence. In the former case, there remain in existence two independent opposing debts, but, for convenience, claim and counter-claim are heard in the same proceedings; the two debts remain independent until judgment is given. Where set-off is a substantive defence, it may be set up outside any court or analogous proceedings as an immediate answer to a creditor's claim. The difference is not purely academic; it has practical implications. If set-off is purely a procedural matter, then the consequences will be as follows: it will not prevent a creditor against whom the cross-claim is to be set off making any self-help available to him in respect of his whole claim. The most usual nature of such

---

[4] *Hanak v Green* [1958] 2 Q.B.9. However, the Civil Procedure Rules now expressly provide that, where a defence contends he is entitled to money from the claimant and relies on this as a defence to the whole or part of the claim, the contention may be included in the defence and set-off against the claim, whether or not it is also a Part 20 (or counter) claim: CPR r.16.6.
[5] *Mondel v Steel* (1841) 8 M. & W. 858; *Gilbert-Ashe (Northern) Ltd v Modern Engineering (Bristol) Ltd* [1974] A.C. 689; and see Goode, *Legal Problems of Credit and Security* (3rd ed. 2003), paras 7–15 and 7–71 and Derham, *The Law of Set-Off*, ss 2.87 *et seq.*
[6] See para.10–02 below.

self-help is the reliance on default provisions in a contract such as the right
to terminate the contract or recover goods or other chattels or to appoint a
receiver or administrator. The existence of a cross-claim (which may be set
off only in proceedings) would not prevent a creditor, to whom only the
balance between the claim and cross-claim has been tendered, relying before
proceedings on any such default provisions. Where set-off may operate as a
substantive defence or only a procedural shield is indicated in the paragraphs which follow and which describe the types of set-off.

The classification of set-off

In spite of the many differing circumstances in which the rights to set-off **9–06**
arise, the doctrine is usually considered under four heads.

(a) Statutory or independent set-off

As the statutes of set-off have been repealed[7] and presumably to avoid **9–07**
confusion with set-off in insolvency[8] (which is itself governed by statute and
statutory instruments), the expression "independent" has been coined for
this category of set-off.[9] The statutes were introduced to avoid a multiplicity
of actions, and, in spite of their repeal, their effect, which is procedural,
remains.[10] Set-off under these procedural rules may apply to claims and
cross-claims which have no connection and are entirely independent.
However, for the rules to apply both the claim and cross-claim:

(1) must be monetary claims[11]

(2) must be ascertained liquidated claims representing debts accrued
     due (but not necessarily due for payment) at the time of the
     pleadings[12]; and

(3) must lie between the same persons in the same right.[13]

Although the importance of independent set-off has declined since the
development of the doctrine of equitable set-off, it remains important where

---

[7] Civil Procedures Acts Repeal Act 1879, s.2.
[8] See paras 9–12 and 9–14 below.
[9] Wood, *English & International Set-Off*; the expression has been adopted by the courts; see for
example *Aectra Refining & Marketing Inc v Exmar NV* [1994] 1 W.L.R. 1634; *Metal Distributors
(UK) Ltd v ZCCM Investment Holdings Plc* [2005] 2 Lloyds Rep. 37.
[10] Supreme Court Act 1981, s.49(2) and CPR r.16.6.
[11] There is an exception to this requirement which does not seem relevant to a treatise on
factoring; see Derham *The Law of Set-Off*, (3rd ed., 2003), s.2.14, and Goode, *Legal Problems of
Credit and Security* (3rd ed., 2003), p.153.
[12] *B Hargreaves Ltd v Action 2000 Ltd* [1993] B.C.L.C. 1111.
[13] See Goode, *op. cit.*, paras 7–36 *et seq.*

claim and cross-claim are not connected to the extent that the latter doctrine would apply.

(b) Equitable set-off[14]

9–08   Equitable set-off, which is now generally considered to take effect as a substantive defence,[15] is wide in scope; it is not a condition of its application that the cross-claim should be for a liquidated sum which has accrued or become due. On the other hand, it will only be applied where the claim and cross-claim arise out of transactions which are closely connected; it is not essential that they should arise out of the same contract and the closeness of the connection has been the subject of judicial consideration in a large number of cases in which the decisions fall on either side of a line which is difficult to define.[16] It will not be available in every case where the claim and cross-claim arise from the same contract; for example, it is regarded as an established rule of law that set-off is not available to the owner of a cargo in respect of his claim for damages (against the shipowner for breach of contract) and his obligation to pay for freight.[17] It remains debatable whether or not that for the doctrine to apply the cross-claim must "impeach" the claim to the effect that it would be inequitable to allow the plaintiff to obtain judgment for it in full.[18] Although some more recent cases seem to have somewhat widened the scope of the availability of the remedy, it appears that for it to apply the following requirements remain:

(1)   whether or not the claim and cross-claim arise out of the same contract they must be closely connected, and the cross-claim must be such that it would be inequitable not to allow credit for it;

(2)   in most circumstances the cross-claim must be a monetary claim; and

---

[14] Now often referred to as "transaction set-off" owing to the need for a close connection between claim and cross-claim; see for example Goode, *Principles of Corporate Insolvency Law* (3rd ed., 2005), *Aectra Refining & Marketing Inc v Exmar NV* [1994] 1 W.L.R. 1634; *Metal Distributors (UK) Ltd v ZCCM Investment Holdings Plc* [2005] 2 Lloyd's Rep. 37.

[15] Goode, *Principles of Corporate Insolvency Law* (3rd ed., 2005), paras 7–54 *et seq.*, p.175, where Professor Goode states that equitable set-off takes effect as a substantive defence in those cases where that is not precluded by contract and where he considers, nevertheless, that it is not self-executing but that some form of notice is necessary to bring it into effect. See also Goode, *Legal Problems of Credit and Security* (3rd ed., 2003) p.262; Derham, *The Law of Set-Off*, (3rd ed., 2003), ss.4.29 *et seq.*

[16] For a full review of the cases see Wood, *English & International Set-Off* (1989), paras 4–51 *et seq.* and Derham, *The Law of Set-Off*, (3rd ed., 2003), ss.4.29 *et seq*; see also *Aectra Refining and Manufacturing Inc v Exmar NV* [1994] 1 W.L.R. 1634.

[17] "*The Dominique*" [1989] A.C. 1056. For a discussion of this rule and its extension to carriage of goods by road see para.9–41 below.

[18] *Rawson v Samuel* (1841) Cr. & Ph. 161, 178. See *Bim Kemi AB v Blackburn Chemicals Ltd* [2001] 2 Lloyd's Rep. 92, *per* Potter L.J. at 201, discussed by Goode, *Legal Problems of Credit and Security* (3rd ed., 2003) p.269–270; Derham, *The Law of Set-Off*, (3rd ed., 2003), ss.4.03–4.07.

(3) the claim and cross-claim must be between the same persons in the same right.[19]

(c) Contractual set-off

By agreement, two parties may extend almost without limit the right and **9-09** availability of set-off in respect of their respective claims against each other. Such an agreement may be relied on by either party not merely as a procedural defence against the claims of the other; the cross-claim will operate in a substantive manner to reduce or extinguish the claim of the other party *pro tanto* before any judgment or analogous proceedings. In effect, the dealings of the two parties, which are the subject of the set-off agreement between them, are considered to give rise to only one debt after a merger of the opposing claims. If the agreement extends the right of set-off to contingent claims, then to give effect to the right, a two stage process is necessary. First, the party setting up the contingent claim will be able to suspend payment until his cross-claim becomes liquidated; then he will be able to set off the liquidated sum.[20]

Such contractual arrangements may include the combination of accounts **9-10** between the parties which for accounting convenience have been kept separately; although a banker has a prescriptive right to combine all the current accounts of a customer,[21] for others (such as a factor) to have such a right, it would seem necessary to provide for it in a contract.

As a corollary to contractual set-off, it is possible to exclude set-off by **9-11** agreement between the parties; but such an agreement will not be effective in the bankruptcy or winding-up of either party when the rules of insolvency set-off are effective, because these statutory provisions cannot be waived or renounced by contract.[22] Furthermore, until the rules relating to insolvency set-off apply between the debtor and the assignee, a provision in the assignor's contract with the debtor that the debtor will not raise claims against an assignee is enforceable. Such an agreement not to set off may be relied upon by an administrative receiver.[23] However, a provision to exclude

---

[19] See Goode, *Legal Problems of Credit and Security* (3rd ed., 2003), para.7-53.
[20] Goode, *Legal Problems of Credit and Security* (3rd ed., 2003) p.248-249; *c.f.* Derham, *The Law of Set-Off* (3rd ed., 2003), s.16.02.
[21] *Garnett v McKewan* (1872) 27 L.T. 560 which was approved in *Halesowen* (see n.22).
[22] *British Eagle International Airlines Ltd v Compagnie Nationale Air France* (1975) 1 W.L.R. 758; *National Westminster Bank Ltd v Halesowen Presswork and Assemblies Ltd* [1972] A.C. 785. But see Richard Bethel-Jones, "Contracting out of Set-Off Rights" Journal of International Banking Law, Vol.9 Issue 10, p.428, where it is argued that the exclusion of set-off by agreement might be effective in the insolvency of one of the parties provided that it was for the benefit of the insolvent estate. For confirmation that a debtor and creditor may by agreement exclude set-off (until the winding up or bankruptcy of one or the other intervenes), see *Hong Kong & Shanghai Bank v Kloeckner* [1989] B.C.L.C. 776 and *Coca-Cola Financial Corporation v Finsat International Ltd* [1998] Q.B. 43.
[23] *John Dee Group Ltd v WMH (21) Ltd (formerly Magnet Ltd)* [1997] B.C.C. 518.

set-off in a contract by a customer or upon standard written terms of business may be unenforceable if it is held to be unreasonable under ss.13(1)(b) and (c) of the Unfair Contract Terms Act 1977;[24] in relation to consumer contracts such terms are also subject to the test of fairness under the Unfair Terms in Consumer Contracts Regulations 1999.[25]

(d) set-off in insolvency

9–12   The rules of set-off to be applied in the bankruptcy or winding-up of either of the parties are contained respectively in the Insolvency Act 1986[26] and The Insolvency Rules 1986.[27] The rules cannot be excluded nor modified by agreement between the parties[28] nor by any multilateral arrangement among a group of traders for the netting of debit and credit balances.[29] They provide that, as between the person in bankruptcy or winding-up and a creditor claiming in the estate, only the balance (if any), after an account has been taken of what is due from each to the other, is provable or payable to the trustee or liquidator. The rules apply when:

(1) there have been mutual credits, mutual debts or other mutual dealings between the creditor and the insolvent person before the commencement of bankruptcy or the company goes into liquidation (as the case may be);[30]

(2) the claims on both sides are such as would be provable in an insolvent estate and as would result in a claim for payment of money (*e.g.* as opposed to a claim for the return of goods *in specie*); and[31]

(3) the sums due from the insolvent person to be included in the account taken must have been *due* before the other party had notice of a bankruptcy petition (or, in the case of a company, a winding-up petition or the calling of a meeting of creditors) of the insolvent person.[32]

---

[24] *Stewart Gill Ltd v Horatio Myer & Co Ltd* [1992] 2 All E.R. 257.
[25] Sch.2, para.1(b) (SI 1999/2003).
[26] s.323.
[27] SI 1986/1925, r.4.90.
[28] See n.22 above.
[29] *British Eagle International Airlines Ltd v Compagnie Nationale Air France* [1975] 1 W.L.R. 758. Part VII of the Companies Act 1989, and the regulations made under it (S.I.1991, No.880) make provision for the modification of the law relating to insolvency in respect of default in certain financial markets and some netting arrangements remain valid in the insolvency of a member of the market (and in some cases of a client of the member).
[30] Insolvency Act 1986, s.323(1) and Insolvency Rules 1986, r.4.90(1).
[31] *Rose v Hart* (1818) 8 Taunt. 499.
[32] Insolvency Act 1986, s.323(3) and Insolvency Rules 1986, r.4.90(3), and see para.9–11 below.

The mutuality of the dealings mentioned in (1) above means that the debts must be due to and by the parties in the same right. For example, the rules will not apply where the claim on or by one of the parties only is as trustee or is for the return of money advanced for a special purpose[33]; nor will the rules apply where a claim is against joint debtors and the cross-claim is by one only of such debtors.[34] It will be noted from the foregoing that it is not necessary for the claims of both parties to be closely connected as it is for equitable set-off to apply; nor do the claims need to be for liquidated sums as is the case in independent set-off.[35] Insolvency set-off will apply to a claim against the insolvent party by an assignee provided that his assignment was made before he had notice of the calling of a meeting of creditors for the purposes of winding-up or a petition for bankruptcy or for winding-up of the person by whom the assigned debt is owing; if the assignment was not made before that time then the debt would not be *due to the assignee by the requisite time*.[36]

The provisions substantially re-enacted s.31 of the Bankruptcy Act 1914 **9–13** and its extension to the winding-up of companies.[37] However, the 1986 Act and rules provide that the debt on which the solvent party is claiming must be "due" before he had notice of certain events portending the insolvency; and this replaced the old provision by which the credit from which the debt arose must have been granted before notice of the specified events. Consequent upon the enactment of the 1986 Act and the making of the Rules, there was some uncertainty as to the precise meaning of these provisions. Certainly the word "due" does not mean due for payment, but due in the sense of "in existence"; but the uncertainty, in particular, related to the question as to whether a contingent liability of the insolvent party could be set off against an actual liability to the trustee or liquidator. The question had been a matter of controversy before the Act, notwithstanding the view of the Insolvency Law Review Committee that there was no doubt that set-off in such circumstance was available.[38] It is now beyond doubt that in this context "due" means "owing" or "incurred" and that there has been no substantive change in the law.[39] It is also generally accepted that a claim by the solvent party, which is contingent at the time when the claimant has notice of any of the events referred to above, is subject to the insolvency set-off provisions provided that it is in existence and capable of being

---

[33] See, *e.g. Barclays Bank Ltd v Quistclose Investments Ltd* [1970] A.C. 567.
[34] See *Lindley & Banks on Partnership* (18th ed., 2002) paras 27–83 *et seq.*
[35] See para.9–00 above.
[36] See n.32 above and Wood, *op. cit.*, paras 7–29 *et seq.*
[37] Companies Act 1985, s.612.
[38] *Insolvency Law and Practice* (Cmnd. 8558 (1982) para. 1356).
[39] See nn.26 and 27 above and Wood, *op. cit.*, paras 7–235 and 7–236.

quantified, as for proof of debt, at the time *when the account is taken*.[40] Insolvency set-off affects the substantive rights of the parties; it does not require the causes of action to be merged in proceedings but is self-executing upon an account being taken and that is when the liquidator or trustee in bankruptcy adjudicates on proofs.[41]

9–14 It should be noted that the only corporate insolvency procedure in respect of which the self-executing provisions of the Insolvency Rules are always applied, is winding-up. Prior to the enactment of the Enterprise Act 2002, the insolvency set-off contained in Rule 4.90 of the Rules did not apply to a company in administration.[42] However, the enactment of the Enterprise Act 2002 has introduced new provisions relating to set-off and insolvent companies, particularly in relation to administrations. Sums due from a company to another party will not now be taken into account for set-off purposes if, at the time they became due: (a) that other party had notice at the time they became due that a meeting of creditors had been summoned under s.98 of the Insolvency Act 1986; (b) the liquidation was immediately preceded by an administration and the sums became due during the administration; or (c) the liquidation was immediately preceded by an administration, and the other party had notice, at the time that the sums became due, that an application for an administration order was pending, or any person had given notice of intention to appoint an administrator.[43] A specific provision has also been introduced for administrations, whereby an administrator is obliged to take an account of what is due from each party to the other in respect of mutual dealings and set-off, but only where he has given notice of his intention to make a distribution.[44] Until an administrator has given such notice, the normal principles of equitable or independent set-off will apply.

2. THE DEBTOR'S DEFENCES AND COUNTERCLAIMS

9–15 In Ch.10 the warranties normally given by the client are described. One of the most important of these is that by which the client undertakes that every

---

[40] Derham, *The Law of Set-Off*, (3rd ed., 2003) s.8.07. and in particular s.8.26, where he rebuts the suggestion that a claim, which is likely to emerge as a debt but in respect of which the contingency has not occurred when the claimant had notice of the relevant events, may not be subject to insolvency set-off on the grounds that such contingent claims are provable based on an estimate; and see Goode, *Legal Problems of Credit and Security* (3rd ed., 2003), paras 7–91 *et seq.*
[41] See *Stein v Blake* [1996] A.C. 243.
[42] *Isovel Contracts Ltd v ABB Building Technologies Ltd* [2002] 1 B.C.L.C. 390.
[43] Insolvency Rules 1986, r.4.90(3), as inserted with effect from 15 September 2003 by Sch.1, para.19 of the Insolvency (Amendment) Rules 2003 (SI 2003/1730).
[44] Insolvency Rules 1986, r.2.85 and r.2.9.

debt sold by him to the factor shall be payable by the debtor as a valid collectable debt free from any defence or cross-claim. Accordingly, if the factor is unable to collect any debt that he has purchased, by reason of such a claim by the debtor, he will have the right to be indemnified by his client or to exercise his right of recourse. However, reimbursement from the client can normally only be obtained by set-off against the balance owing to the client in respect of other debts purchased. In a continuing agreement the level of the factor's retention, as a minimum balance, may well be sufficient to absorb any debts which are subject to recourse for this reason. It is in the situation of the insolvency of the client, when the debtors are likely to look more closely at their rights, that the level of these defences and claims for set-off increases. Such difficulties on the insolvency of clients have been the cause of many significant losses to factors since the service was introduced into this country. It is therefore important that a factor should be fully aware of the rights of the debtor in such a case. In the event of the insolvency of the client, it may well be possible that a debtor may raise a defence or cross-claim that he may consider commercially justifiable but which, on examination, is not tenable in law.

The general rule is that the factor, as assignee, can be in no better position **9–16** as regards his right to recover from the debtor than the client was at the time when the debtor had received notice of the assignment; as assignee, he takes the assignment subject to equities. An example of this principle is contained in the words of James L.J. in *Roxburghe v Cox*[45]:

> "Now an assignee of a chose in action takes, subject to all rights of set-off and other defences which were available against the assignor, subject only to this exception, that after notice of an assignment of a chose in action the debtor cannot by payment or otherwise do anything to take away or diminish the rights of the assignee as they stood at the time of the notice."

Accordingly, if a defence relating to defects or deficiencies in the very goods or service, that give rise to the debt in question, is raised by a debtor, the factor will be in no better position than the client (against whom, in the case of goods, a defence would be available to the debtor under Sale of Goods Act 1979, s.53(1)(a)). The defects or deficiencies must have been in existence at the time when the debt was assigned.

Equitable and independent set-off by debtor against factor

As regards equitable set-off, the general view is that the debtor will be able **9–17** to set off, in reduction or cancellation of the factor's claim for payment, any

---

[45] (1881) 17 Ch. D. 520.

cross-claim arising out of the same contract as that which gave rise to the factored debt or out of a contract that is "closely connected" with the contract which gave rise to the assignee's claim.[46] There are some exceptions to the general rule and circumstances in which a cross-claim, contingent at the time when notice is received by the debtor, may not qualify for equitable set-off and thus not be available for set-off by the debtor against an assignee's claim arising under the same contract.[47] The close connection is the essential feature of the rule and the cross-claim must be such that it would be inequitable for the assignee to succeed on his claim without allowing the set-off.[48] However, in factoring normal trade debts, it seems most unlikely that a factor would be met with a cross-claim arising out of the contract giving rise to the factored debt which did not qualify. It is probable, but not certain, that, for such a cross-claim to qualify for set-off, it must be due and payable before proceedings are started by the factor on the assigned primary claim.[49] The close connection does not appear to extend to a cross-claim arising from the creditor's tort; for in *Stoddart v Union Trust Ltd*[50] it was held that the debtor could not set off his cross-claim, which was for damages for fraudulently inducing his entry into a contract, against an assigned debt arising out of the very contract.[51]

9–18   In respect of a counterclaim arising out of any other contract or on any other grounds (where independent set-off is claimed as available to the debtor), the generally accepted rule is that the notice of the assignment fixes the rights of the parties. As a result, after receipt of the notice, the debtor cannot set off against the factor a debt which comes into existence subsequently, even though it arose out of a liability that existed before the notice; but the debtor may set off against the factor a cross-claim that accrued due as a liquidated and ascertainable debt before the notice even if not payable until after it.[52] Independent set-off is confined to debts which, at the time when the defence of set-off is filed, were due and payable and either liquidated or in sums capable of ascertainment without valuation or estimation. For a thorough review of the law relating to the rights of a debtor in respect of set-off against an assigned debt, reference should be made to the judgment of Templeman L.J. (as Templeman J.) in *Business Computers Limited v Anglo-African Leasing Limited*.[53] After a detailed review of the authorities he summarised the position thus:

---

[46] *Business Computers Ltd v Anglo-African Leasing Ltd* [1977] 1 W.L.R. 578; *"The Nanfri"* [1978] 2 Lloyds Rep. 132; *"The Raven"* [1980] 2 Lloyds Rep. 266 at p.272.
[47] See Wood, *English and International Set-Off*, paras 4–51 and 16–22.
[48] See para.9–08 and n.18 above.
[49] See Wood, *op cit.*, para.16–22.
[50] [1912] 1 K.B. 181.
[51] Such a claim may be set-off in insolvency if it arises out of a dealing between the parties: *Tilley v Bowman* [1910] 1 K.B. 745; Derham, *The Law of Set-Off*, (3rd ed., 2003), ss.8.44–8.45).
[52] For a full discussion, see Derham, *The Law of Set-Off* (3rd ed., 2003), ss. 17–38—17–46.
[53] [1977] 1 W.L.R. 578.

"The result of the relevant authorities is that a debt which accrues due before notice of an assignment is received, whether or not it is payable before that date, or a debt which arises out of the same contract as that which gives rise to the assigned debt, or is closely connected with that contract, may be set off against the assignee. But a debt which is neither accrued nor connected may not be set off even though it arises from a contract made before the assignment."

It is apparent that, apart from the question of defences raised on account of defects in the goods or services supplied, the factor must be on his guard in relation to some ancillary transactions between the client and his debtors. The most common cause of such counterclaims are claims for set-off for goods supplied by the debtor to the client; if these goods were supplied before the assigned debt on which the factor is claiming arose, the debtor may well be able to set off notwithstanding that the two claims arose from entirely independent contracts.

The effect of contractual set-off on the factor as assignee[54]

The factor's rights as assignee of a debt will not be affected in any way by **9–19** any contract between the client and the debtor extending the common law or equitable rules of set-off where that contract has been entered into *after* the debtor received notice of the assignment of that debt.[55] The position, where the client and the debtor enter into such a contract *before* notice has been received by the debtor, is not so clear. The normal equitable principles, that an assignee takes subject to the equities and cannot be in a better position than the assignor is at the time of notice to the debtor, would appear to indicate that the factor would be fully bound by such contract terms.[56] In *Watson v The Mid Wales Railway Company*[57] set-off of a cross-claim relating to rent not accrued due was not allowed against the assignee of a bond, although the contract giving rise to the rent was in existence at the time of notice of the assignment to the debtor. However, the *dicta* in the case indicate that, had the payment of the rent been made a charge on the bond (*i.e.* or if it had been agreed that the rent should be set-off against the debt), then the set-off might have been allowed. Where an assignor and a debtor had agreed, before the debtor had received notice of the assignment, to set off future claims, it is considered that the assignee would not be affected by transactions arising between the debtor and the assignor *after* the debtor

---

[54] For a full discussion, see Derham, *The Law of Set-Off* (3rd ed., 2003), ss.17–38 —17–46.
[55] *Roxburghe v Cox* (1881) 17 Ch. D. 520.
[56] *Mangles v Dixon* (1852) 3 H.L. Cas. 702; see also Derham, *The Law of Set-Off*, (3rd ed., 2003), s.17.2.
[57] (1867) L.R. 2 C.P. 593.

had received the notice; but there appears to be no reported case on the point.[58]

9–20   If the contract between the client and the debtor is to exclude or restrict the application of set-off,[59] the client's rights under such an agreement are unlikely to be available to the factor unless the debtor specifically agrees (*i.e.* by a new contract or a novation). It is possible, but not certain, that the debtor might be deemed to have waived his right of set-off if he had received and not demurred at notice implying that the factor had taken his interest in the debt for value relying on the agreement not to set-off.[60] Therefore, if the factor wishes to protect himself against the countervailing rights of the debtor as described below, it is advisable for him to make an independent agreement with the debtor not to set-off any cross-claims against the assigned debts. Such an agreement would not stand up in the insolvency of the debtor,[61] but it would do so in the insolvency of the client (if the debtor were not insolvent); and it is when the client is insolvent that the factor most needs this protection because he may not then be able to recover from the client in respect of the client's breach of the usual warranty that the debt is free from encumbrance.

3. THE EFFECT OF NOTICES ON THE DEBTOR'S COUNTERVAILING RIGHTS

9–21   In para.8–09 the effect of notice to the debtor was described, and it was demonstrated that the ability of the factor to collect from the debtor would be assisted by procuring notice as early as possible. From the preceding paragraphs it is apparent that the sooner the notice is received by the debtor, the more likely is the factor to be able to defeat any claim of the debtor to independent set-off or set-off in the client's insolvency[62]; receipt of notice by the debtor fixes the rights of the parties in these respects. It should not be overlooked in this connection that where an assignment is purportedly made in breach of a contract term prohibiting the assignment of a debt arising from that contract, then the assignment is invalid[63]; accordingly, any notice given in such a case will be of no effect, and the debtor will have available to him all rights of set-off as if there had been no notice.

---

[58] See, *e.g.* Goode, *Legal Problems of Credit and Security* (3rd ed., 2003), para.7–26 and Wood, *English & International Set-Off*, para.16–36.
[59] See para.9–11 above.
[60] See also paras 9–26 and 9–27 below.
[61] See para.9–11 above.
[62] See para.9–29 below.
[63] *Helstan Securities Ltd v Hertfordshire County Council* [1978] 3 All E.R. 262 (approved by the House of Lords in *Linden Garden Trust Ltd v Lenesta Sludge Disposals Ltd* [1994] 1 A.C. 85 417), and see paras 9–36 to 9–39 below.

Introductory letters and the debtor's countervailing rights

The effect of the usual method of notice by procuring the endorsement of **9–22** it on the invoice has been described in para.8–07; and the effect of letters informing debtors of the automatic assignment to the factor of all future debts of the client (introductory or "take on" letters) in relation to an agreement of the whole turnover type[64] was discussed in paras 8–12 to 8–14. It was there concluded that, in the present state of the law, such letters may not be of any effect in respect of debts not in existence at the time when they are received by the debtor for the purpose of the factor's claim to priority under the rule in *Dearle v Hall*.[65] There remains to be considered if such a letter would be effective in respect of future debts as regards the countervailing rights of the debtor. There appears to be no specific authority for the view that a notice of the assignment of a debt, not then in existence, is ineffective to intervene in the debtor's right of set-off against such debt when it comes into existence. The cases quoted above[66] do not provide any specific authority because:

(i) they related to prospective interests in a trust fund and not to future debts; and

(ii) all except one dealt with conflicts between competing assignees and not the rights of the debtor.

In the one case in which the question of the debtor's countervailing rights was concerned the court considered that such a notice was ineffective as regards the debtor's rights. However, that was not a necessary part of the judgment and accordingly not a binding precedent; the debtor's set-off was allowed because its claim was in existence before he received notice.[67]

As none of the reported cases related to trade debts the circumstances of a **9–23** Canadian case[68] may seem persuasive to the contrary. In that case, at the start of a factoring agreement the client sent to the debtor, the defendant in the case, a letter informing the latter of the existence of the factoring agreement (and incidentally giving notice of the assignment of the debt then owing to the client). Notwithstanding the admitted receipt of that letter, following the subsequent insolvency of the client the debtor, in paying the factor, deducted from his debt to the factor amounts owed in respect of the debtor's supplies to the client. The factor claimed that, by reason of the notice given in the letter, the debtor was not entitled to impair the factor's right to payment in full by a claim to set off an independent debt

---

[64] See para.7–10 above.
[65] See para.8–03 above.
[66] See Ch.8, nn.26 and 27.
[67] *Roxburghe v Cox* (1881) 17 Ch. D. 520 at 527.
[68] *Canadian Admiral Corporation Ltd v L.F.* Dommerich & *Co Inc* S.C.R. 1964 at 238.

unconnected with the contract which gave rise to the debt assigned to the factor. The trial judge gave judgment in favour of the factor, and this was upheld in the Ontario Court of Appeal. However, the decision was reversed in the Supreme Court, but only on the grounds that the factoring agreement did not bind the debts as they came into existence, but merely provided that each debt of the client should be offered to the factor; thus, when each debt came into existence, there was no automatic assignment arising from the agreement itself.

9–24   In this connection there might also be considered the analogy between this type of agreement, binding the debts as they come into existence without any further formality, and a present fixed charge attaching to future book debts as they come into existence. It seems likely that actual notice to a debtor of such a fixed charge created by his creditor on present and future book debts would have the same effect, as regards set-off by the debtor, as notice of an assignment of such indebtedness as it came into existence.[69]

9–25   It has also been argued that an assignee *ought* to be able to protect himself against the debtor's rights of set-off with a notice such as is contained in a factor's "take on" letter.[70] Rory Derham has persuasively argued that the principle in *Dearle v Hall* should not apply to set-off, and that, as far as the debtor is concerned, his conscience should be affected as from the time that he becomes aware of the assignment. This is because notice for the purpose of establishing priorities between competing assignees serves a different function to notice for the purpose of set-off. Notice is given to the debtor, because it is regarded as the method by which the assignee gets in possession of the debt, with the first to obtain possession having priority. In the case of set-off, notice defines the point at which the debtor's conscience is affected, which has nothing to do with the possession of debts. Derham concludes that the debtor's conscience can be affected whether the debt is present or future.[71] Nonetheless, a factor would be unwise to rely on a "take on" letter to protect him, in relation to debts not then in existence, against any right to independent set-off (*e.g.* in respect of goods sold by the debtor to the factor's client) that may accrue to the debtor after receipt of the letter. However, for most purposes English law treats as an existing debt any obligation to pay arising out of an existing contract, even if payment has not been earned by the other party's performance.[72] Thus, the debts for which the factor have given notice at the date the debtor receives the "take-on" letter should include debts arising from orders received and accepted by his client, whether or not the client has raised an invoice.

---

[69] See Lightman & Moss, *The Law of Receivers and Administrators of Companies* (3rd ed., 2000), paras 16–033 to 16–039.

[70] See Wood, *op cit.*, para.16–119.

[71] Derham, *The Law of Set-Off* (3rd ed., 2003), s.17.20.

[72] See, *e.g. Brice v Bannister* (1878) 3 Q.B.D. 569; *Ex p. Moss* (1884) 14 Q.B.D. 310; *G. & T. Earle v Hemsworth R.D.C.* (1928) 140 L.T. 69.

Notices and the debtor's implied waiver and estoppel

It occurs not infrequently that a debtor will not raise the question of set- **9–26** off (particularly in relation to an independent cross-claim) until some difficulty emerges in his relations with his creditor, or the latter appears to be in financial difficulties. A debtor may continue for many months to pay to a factor the exact amount of assigned debts without raising the question of a debt owed to the debtor by the client which may have been in existence for some time past. When the debtor finally applies the set-off and deducts the indebtedness of the client to him from his payment to the factor, the factor may well consider that the debtor has impliedly waived the right of set-off. By the debtor's silence the factor has been led to believe that the debts which he had purchased would be free from encumbrance and he has thereby been induced to make prepayments against their purchase price which he may not be able to recover in full; if the client then becomes insolvent, the factor may be unable to recover from the client in respect of the latter's breach of warranty.

It seems, on the analogy of an estoppel, that silence can only be con- **9–27** sidered as having induced a change of position if the silent party had, in the particular case, a duty to speak,[73] and there is good authority for the proposition that it is the duty of the assignee, in a situation as described in the preceding paragraph, to make enquiries and not of the debtor to volunteer the information.[74] Nonetheless, if a debtor sees a factor continuing to make payments to his client in ignorance of the debtor's right of set-off and if the other conditions of estoppel are satisfied, the debtor may not be allowed from asserting his right.[75] As a result, it seems that a factor may be helped in such a situation if his assignment notices have included words on the lines of the following: "and [name of factor] should be advised immediately of any claim or dispute affecting this debt".

4. INSOLVENCY SET-OFF AND THE FACTOR

(a) The debtor's insolvency

If a debtor is bankrupt or in liquidation, the insolvency set-off provi- **9–28** sions[76] will not operate as regards the factor's claim on the debtor and any

---

[73] See generally Wilken and Villiers; *The Law of Waiver, Variation and Estoppel* (2nd ed., 2002).
[74] *Mangles v Dixon* (1852) 3 H.L. Cas. 702.
[75] *ibid. Spiro v Lintern* [1973] 1 W.L.R. 1002. See also Wood, *English and International Set-Off* (1989), paras 16–87 and 16–88 and 13.2.13. For an example of a case in which on the particular facts of the case the debtor was held to have the duty, on receipt of notice of the assignment, to draw the attention of the assignee to the prohibition, see: *Orion Finance Limited v Crown Financial Management Services Ltd* [1994] B.C.L.C. 607 at 622–633. The case was the subject of an appeal but not on this part of the decision.
[76] See paras 9–12 to 9–14 above.

cross-claim which the debtor may have against the client because there is no mutuality. However, the factor will be met with such cross-claims as would have been available to a solvent debtor; these may affect the factor's right of proof of debt and consequently the amount of any dividend to which he may be entitled from the debtor's estate. The cross-claims of a debtor in bankruptcy or liquidation which will be applied to reduce (or extinguish) the proof of the factor as assignee are all those which would be available (by way of equitable set-off or independent set-off) to a solvent debtor against an assignee.[77]

9–29 In any case, where the debt is subject to recourse, the factor will be affected by an impairment of his proof (by reason of a cross-claim by the liquidator or trustee in bankruptcy) if he is unable to recourse the shortfall to the client; this would happen if the client is insolvent and there are insufficient sums owing by the factor to the client against which the recourse may be set off. If the debt is not subject to recourse (otherwise than by reason of the cross-claim), the factor would in any event have the right to recourse the amount of the debt on his books for which proof is not accepted; in such a case, the application of the set-off may be of positive benefit to the factor in not having to accept a bad debt loss for the full amount of the debt.

9–30 If the factor's claim against the insolvent debtor arises out of a contract which includes a term which prohibits the assignment of the debt,[78] then the assignment is ineffective to transfer the right of proof to the factor. Insolvency set-off will apply in such a case as if there had been no assignment; the client will, accordingly, benefit by the set-off of his liability to the debtor against the "assigned" debt. The factor will be able to recourse the debt to the extent of the set-off even if the agreement is on a non-recourse basis; but, if the client is also insolvent (and the recourse is of no benefit to the factor), then the amount which he can recover through the client's right of proof of debt will be reduced to the extent of the set-off.

(b) The client's insolvency

9–31 If the debtor is not insolvent, the bankruptcy or liquidation of the client will not directly affect the rights of the factor and the debtor *inter se*; the rules of insolvency set-off apply only to the mutual indebtedness of a party in bankruptcy or liquidation and his creditor or debtor. However, it is in such a situation that the debtor is most likely to rely on any equitable or independent set-off available to him against the factor as assignee. It is probable also that any pre-existing agreement between the client and the debtor not to set off their mutual claims on each other will be ineffective to

---

[77] See paras 9–16 *et seq.* and Wood, *English & International Set-Off* (1989), para.16–132 and Derham, *The Law of Set-Off* (3rd ed., 2003) s.17.301.
[78] See paras 9–36 *et seq.* below.

prevent the debtor exercising those rights. The set-off rights available to the debtor are those which would have been available to him against the assigned debt if the client had been solvent.[79] As in the case of the debtor's insolvency, if the debt on which the factor relies has arisen from a contract which includes a prohibition against its assignment, then the debtor will be able to disregard the assignment and insolvency set-off will apply between the client and the debtor. In such a case, the factor may recover the debt only through the client's express or constructive trust,[80] and the amount of the recovery will be reduced to the extent of the set-off.

However, where the client is bankrupt and the factor delays in suing the debtor, the debtor may lose his right of set-off. The insolvency set-off provisions will not apply for want of mutuality, and the debtor will only have a right to an equitable or independent set-off if the claim against the client is still in existence.[81] Upon discharge from his bankruptcy, the client will be released from his bankruptcy debts, whereupon the debtor's claim against the client will cease to exist, so that it cannot be set-off against the factor's claim.[82] This is likely to be of increasing importance due to the reduction of the period within which a bankrupt is discharged from bankruptcy from (in most cases) from three years to one year in all cases, or less if the official receiver files the requisite notice.[83]   **9–32**

(c) Set-off by and against the Crown

The rights of set-off between the Crown and a solvent person are governed by the Crown Proceedings Act[84] and the Civil Procedure Rules,[85] the general effect of which is *inter alia* that without permission of the court set-off is not available to or against the Crown: **9–33**

(1) if the claim and counterclaim relate to different government departments; or

(2) the Crown is sued or sues in the name of the Attorney General.

---

[79] See Wood, *English & International Set-Off* (1989), paras 16–122 to 16–131 and Derham, *The Law of Set-Off* (3rd ed., 2003), s.17.28.

[80] See para.9–37 below.

[81] A claim that has ceased to exist cannot be the subject of a set-off: *Aries Tanker Corp v Total Transport Ltd* [1977] 1 W.L.R. 185.

[82] Insolvency Act 1986, s.281(2) and Wood, *England and International Set-Off* (1989) 894–895 and Derham, *The Law of Set-Off* (3rd ed., 2003), s.17.29. Derham suggests that a debtor faced with the prospect of losing the benefit of the equitable defence should apply before the assignor's discharge for a declaration and a permanent injunction to restrain the future action by the assignee against him, although he notes this is unsupported by authority.

[83] Insolvency Act 1986, s.279. The original s.279 was replaced on April 1, 2004 by s.256 and Sch.19 of the Enterprise Act 2002 (SI 2003/2903). Transitional provision is made by Sch.19 to deal with bankrupts who are subject to a bankruptcy order made prior to April 1, 2004.

[84] s.35(2).

[85] C.P.R., Sch.1, R.S.C., Ord.77, r.6.

However, where the other party is in bankruptcy or liquidation, the insolvency provisions[86] apply. They are mandatory; they apply where the claims by and against the Crown are through different departments and they also apply in relation to a claim under a statutory provision (*e.g.* for taxes) and a contractual claim.[87] An attempt was made in Scotland by a liquidator of a Scottish company to obtain payments from the Ministry of Defence free from cross-claims by the Department of Trade and Industry and HM Revenue & Customs. But that attempt failed and the court held that the Crown was an "indivisible entity" and applied the insolvency rules of set-off then in force in Scotland.[88] The Insolvency Law Review Committee[89] recommended that there should be no set-off by and against different government departments, nor between contractual and statutory claims by and against the same department; but the law remains as stated above.

9–34   It has usually been considered that a factor whose client's customers include government departments must watch carefully the liabilities of his client for taxes and other sums owing to the Crown. However, in the bankruptcy or liquidation of such a client, any debt owing by a government department and vesting in the factor would be subject to insolvency set-off in respect of amounts accrued due to the Crown, before the assignment of that debt had been completed by notice to the department concerned; in order that insolvency set-off should apply, there must be mutuality in relation to the claim and cross-claim,[90] and the assignment destroys the mutuality.[91] It therefore seems that any claim for set-off by the Crown in such a situation would be by way of independent set-off. In that case, the provisions of s.35(2) of the Crown Proceedings Act 1947 and the C.P.R. Sch.1, R.S.C., Ord.77, r.6, will apply.[92] Thus, in any proceedings where the Crown claims to set off amounts due from a factor's client for duties and taxes against the claim of a factor for an assigned debt due by another department of the government, the Crown can only assert the right to set-off with the permission of the Court.

9–35   However, in many cases a factor will be faced with a valid claim by the Crown to exercise his rights in respect of insolvency set-off; and this will apply to debts accruing due to the Crown *after* as well as before notice of the assignment to the factor of any debt due by the Crown. This difficulty for the factor arises from the practice of government departments almost invariably to include, in their purchase contracts, the terms forbidding the

---

[86] Insolvency Act 1986, s.323 and Insolvency Rules 1986, r.4.90.
[87] *Re D. H. Curtis (Builders) Ltd* [1978] Ch. 162; *Re Cushla* Ltd [1979] 3 All E.R. 415 and more recently in the House of Lords in Secretary of State for Trade and Industry v Frid [2004] 2 W.L.R. 1279 (2004) 2 W.L.R. 1279.
[88] *Smith v Lord Advocate* 1981 S.L.T. 19.
[89] *Insolvency Law and Practice* (Cmnd. 8558 (1982), paras 1342 to 1347 and 1362).
[90] See para.9–12 above.
[91] See para.9–31 and n.79 above.
[92] See para.9–33 above and Wood, *English & International Set-Off*, para.12–179.

assignment of claims against them under such contracts.[93] Unless the factor had obtained a waiver of the prohibition, the notice to the debtor of an assignment in breach of such a term would be ineffective. Sometimes such a waiver has been given on the understanding that the assignments shall be of the ultimate sum owing to the factor's client after taking into account a deduction of all sums owing by the client to government departments arising both before and after notice of the assignments. In this way, the department, which has been requested to give the waiver, will seek to extend the Crown's rights contractually. Such a contractual set-off provision would not be affected by the insolvency of the client because the agreement is between the factor and the government department neither of which is insolvent.

5. CONTRACTUAL TERMS PROHIBITING ASSIGNMENTS

Closely connected with the question of the debtor's countervailing rights is **9–36** the right of a debtor to refuse to deal with the factor where the purported assignment to the factor arises from a contract in which there is a prohibition against the assignment of the right to payment under it. It is well established that such a purported assignment will not give effect to the transfer to the assignee of the right to be paid by the debtor.[94] If a factor includes such a debt within his factoring agreement, the debtor may disregard any notice of assignment and decline to deal with the factor. As a result, the debtor's payment to the client in such circumstances will give him a good discharge, and he will have the same rights of set-off as if the debt had not been subject to the factoring agreement. That principle has been confirmed in the House of Lords[95] in the course of which judgment it was said that "an assignment of contractual rights in breach of a prohibition against such assignment is ineffective to vest the contractual rights in the assignee".[96] The judgment also removed one uncertainty: it is now certain that in most circumstances a prohibition in a purchase contract against the assignment of "the contract" (without more) includes a prohibition against the assignment of the creditor's rights arising out of the contract and renders ineffective any assignment of the contractual right to be paid.

In the *Helstan case*[97] it was held additionally that an assignment made in **9–37** breach of such a prohibition was void altogether and ineffective as between the assignor and assignee. If this were to be the law then a factor, not only

---

[93] See para.9–36 below.
[94] *Helstan Securities Ltd v Hertfordshire County Council* [1978] 3 All E.R. 262; see generally McCormack, *Debts and Non-Assignment Clauses* [2000] J.B.L. 422.
[95] *Linden Garden Trust Ltd v Lenesta Sludge Disposals Ltd* [1994] 1 A.C. 85.
[96] *ibid.*, at p.109.
[97] See n.94 above.

would be unable to obtain payment direct from the debtor in respect of a debt purported to be so assigned, but also, in the insolvency of his client, may have no rights to the proceeds which would form part of the insolvent client's estate. However, it is generally considered that the judge's decision (that the assignment was void as between assignor and assignee) was not a necessary part of the judgment in the case and, accordingly, is to be treated as *obiter* and not binding. There is strong support for the view that the debtor has no legitimate interest in prohibiting the alienation of the bare right to the proceeds of a debt.[98] In relation to this question the House of Lords judgment in the *Linden Garden* case,[99] although including *dicta* favourable to the rights of the assignee to have the proceeds held for his account by the assignor, has not removed the uncertainty; the *dicta* were not a necessary part of that decision. It seems clear that such a prohibition in a contract (in the absence of clear words to that effect) cannot affect a contractual undertaking by the factor's client to make over to the factor the proceeds of payments to be made under the contract. However, it is still not absolutely certain whether such an undertaking has the effect of creating a constructive trust of the proceeds so that they are taken out of the property of the assignor available to a liquidator, receiver or trustee in bankruptcy. Although case law, even this decision in the *Linden Garden* case, is not conclusive, the 1888 decision in *Re Turcan*[1] is persuasive as to a constructive trust of the proceeds for the benefit of the factor. That case related to the transfer of the benefits of an after-acquired insurance policy to trustees of a marriage settlement; the rights of the trustees to the proceeds were held to be valid against the claims of the executor of the assured notwithstanding such a prohibition in the policy. Although reference was made to the case in the judgment in the *Linden Garden* case without casting any doubt on it, the House of Lords had to consider only the direct relations between the assignee and the debtor. In a more recent case,[2] it was held that there could be no objection to the creation of a trust in favour of a third party of the fruits of a contract containing a provision against its assignment unless there were also a prohibition against such a trust; and it has been mooted that, if there were such a prohibition, it might be invalid on grounds of public policy.

9–38   Owing to the preponderance of judicial and academic opinion, which is favourable to the factor's rights, it seems almost inconceivable that any

---

[98] See Goode, "Inalienable Rights?" [1979] M.L.R. 558; and Oditah, *Legal Aspects of Receivables Financing* (1991), pp.260–262.
[99] *Linden Garden Trust Ltd v Lenesta Sludge Disposals Ltd* [1994] 1 A.C. 85.
[1] (1888) 40 Ch. D. 5.
[2] *Don King Productions Inc v Warren* [2000] Ch. 291. See also *Hendry v Chartsearch Ltd* [1998] C.L.C. 1382, a Court of Appeal judgment; in that case, Millett L.J. appeared to be in no doubt (at p.1394) that, in relation to an assignment of contract rights made in contravention of a prohibition in the contract, it was effective as between the assignor and the assignee but ineffective between the assignee and the other party to the contract.

liquidator or receiver of a factor's client would succeed in a claim to invalidate the factor's ownership of the proceeds of a factored debt on the grounds of such a prohibition in the contract of sale giving rise to the debt. To guard against the grain of uncertainty which remains, any well drawn factoring agreement will include an express trust of the proceeds.[3] In some cases, additional protection has been provided for the factor by the creation by the client of a charge on factored debts which fail to vest effectively in the factor.

Thus, the more serious mischief to the factor (that he may have made a payment to his client and received no debt in return) may be mitigated but, as the notice of a void assignment is of no effect, the factor is in the position of having rights to a debt which at any time may be impeached by payment by the debtor to the client, by subsequent changes in the contract of sale or service or by the coming into existence of subsequent claims by the debtor against the client. The factor's ability to recover from debtors, who have contracted with the factor's client on these terms, may in some cases be restored by the debtors' sometimes overlooking their contract terms and making payment to the factor. There seems little doubt that, if the debtor has established a pattern of paying the factor in respect of invoices bearing a notice of assignment, the debtor would be deemed to have waived the prohibition. Owing to the adverse effect on the factor's security of such a prohibition in the supply contract, factors often request the debtor to waive the prohibition. This is particularly the case where the debtor is an important customer of the client. Very often the consent is given to the assignment of the bare amount payable under the supply contract or of the ultimate amount payable after providing for all the debtor's countervailing rights; in the latter case, the notices of the assignments would have no effect on the debtor's right of set-off. If the consent can be construed as applying only to sums ascertained and established as payable, then the factor has no right to arbitrate or litigate to establish the amount due and payable where that is in dispute.[4] **9–39**

6. ASSIGNMENT OF CROSS-CLAIM

It is not unusual for parties to trade with one another, and this may give rise to various questions in relation to set-off. Take the following situation: a supplier (S) supplies goods to his customer (C) and C supplies goods to S. In **9–40**

---

[3] See para.10–35 below.
[4] *Flood v Shand Construction Ltd* Vol.81 Build. L.R. 31. "The party to whom a contractor pays a sum which he is bound to pay may well be a matter of indifference to him. The same is not necessarily true of the party against whom he finds himself defending a claim in arbitration". *Yeandle v Wynn Realisations Ltd (In Administration)* (1995) 47 Con. L.R. 1 *per* Sir Thomas Bingham M.R. at 13.

reduction or extinction of any claim by S, C may be entitled to rely upon his cross-claim by way of equitable set-off, if the claim and cross-claim are sufficiently closely connected; if not sufficiently closely connected, then C will have to rely upon independent set-off in judicial proceedings. If S assigns the debt owed by C to a factor (F1), then F1 can recover the debt from C subject to any defences that C may have at the date he received notice of assignment. However, if C also assigns the debt owed to him by S top another factor (F2), then S is liable to F2, and C is liable to F1 for the full amount of the relevant debts. Set-off will not be available as they have divested themselves of the chose in action that would otherwise have constituted the defence by way of set-off. As S and C will have assigned the debts for value, they could not expect to rely upon the outstanding claims by way of set-off, even if they have not, in fact, received the full value of the debts.

7. TRANSACTIONS INSULATED AGAINST SET-OFF

Freight and carriage charges

9–41   The rules of equitable set-off[5] do not apply to freight for the carriage of goods by sea (as distinguished from charter hire for the use of a ship), whether or not the claim for payment of the freight charges has been assigned. Freight charges are payable in full free from any claim against the carrier for defective performance of the contract. That principle is well established[6] and appears to have its origin in the supposition that, if the master of a ship did not recover the freight charges in full, he could not pay the seamen's wages. It is not certain whether the principle applies to cross-claims that are independent of the claim for payment of the freight charges; and Derham[7] argues that the better view is that it does not because independent set-off is a creature of statute, not equity. Certainly, the principle does not apply in the case of the insolvency of either of the parties as insolvency set-off is mandatory and self-executing.[8]

9–42   The insulation of freight charges from set-off as described above may not appear of much assistance to factors who rarely provide their services for shipowners or charterers. However, domestic road transport is a business that is frequently served by factors and the question as to whether the rule should apply to domestic carriage of goods by land arose in the High Court in *United Carriers Ltd v Heritage Food Group (UK) Ltd.*[9] In that case, the

---

[5] See para.9–06 above.
[6] *"The Dominique"* [1987] A.C. 1056.
[7] Derham, *op. cit.*, 55–22.
[8] *Stein v Blake* [1996] A.C. 243.
[9] [1995] 2 Lloyds Rep. 269.

defendant admitted the carrier's claim for the carriage charges but sought to set off cross-claims for short delivery and other breaches of contract on the part of the carrier. It was held that, although the rule in relation to carriage of goods by sea was of great antiquity and had little relevance to modern carriage by road, the court was bound by precedence and that the rule by which the carriage charges were insulated should apply. If the set-off of claims for damages cannot apply against the claim by the carrier, it cannot apply against the carrier's factor as assignee. This judgment must be of assistance to factors in providing their services to such businesses; in the insolvency of the client it is equitable set-off of claims for damages, and not insolvency set-off, that most commonly affects the recoveries because insolvency does not affect the position between the factor and the debtors. The rule will also apply in the case of carriage of goods by road under the Convention on the Contract for the International Carriage of Goods by Road.[10]

Cheques and direct debits

It is a long established rule of English commercial law that unliquidated **9–43** cross-claims or defences (except in exceptional circumstances such as fraud, invalidity or total failure of consideration) are not available against the holder of a negotiable instrument. The reason for this concept has been that there should be no detraction from the value of the negotiability of the instruments which have been considered to be almost equivalent to cash; they may be used by the holder, by endorsing them over to a third party (for example by discounting a bill of exchange), to raise funds for the purpose of discharging his own liabilities.[11] The rule has been extended to direct debits. A cancellation by debtor of a direct debit in favour of its supplier on the grounds of cross-claim for damages for an alleged breach of contract was treated by the Court of Appeal as analogous to the countermanding of payment of a cheque. This was justified by reference to the modern commercial practice of treating direct debits in the same way as payment by cheque, *i.e.* as the equivalent of cash. As a result, no equitable set-off of the cross-claim was allowed.[12] The decision of the majority has been criticised on the basis that cheques give rise to new rights whereby a recipient can sue upon the cheque itself, whereas, where a direct debit is cancelled, the person entitled to the money must sue on the underlying contract.[13] It is not clear

---

[10] See Derham, *The Law of Set-Off*, (3rd ed., 2003) s.5.02 *et seq.*
[11] For a case in which set-off of an unliquidated claim for damages was not allowed against the first holder of a bill of exchange: *Nova (Jersey) Knit Ltd v Kammgarn Spinnerei GmbH* [1977] 1 W.L.R. 713.
[12] *Esso Petroleum Co Ltd v Milton* [1997] 1 W.L.R. 938.
[13] See criticisms in *Chitty on Contracts* (29th ed., 2004), Vol.1, para.34–389; A. Tetterborn, Note (1997) 113 L.Q.R. 374; *Paget's Law of Banking* (12th ed., 2002), para.17.161. It is not clear whether the no set-off rule should not apply to cheques.

whether the no set-off rule should not apply to cheques crossed "account payee only", as they are no longer transferable instruments.[14]

8. POSITIVE LIABILITY OF THE FACTOR TO THE DEBTOR

9-44 Although a factor may have his own claim against a debtor reduced or extinguished by the debtor's countervailing rights, he incurs no positive liability to the debtor under the contract that gave rise to the assigned debt. As the bare assignee of the amount payable by the debtor, he is not a party to the contract. Furthermore, it is also generally accepted that in most circumstances, once the debtor has paid the assigned debt to the factor, any claim by the debtor against the client, whether arising out of the contract that gave rise to the assigned debt or not, must be against the client. The factor is considered in most cases to have no liability to repay to the debtor; it has been said that, although an assignee takes subject to equities, he is not subjected to them. The burden of performance of the client's contract with the debtor can be shifted on to the shoulders of the factor only by a novation accepted by all three parties; but this has the effect of cancelling the old contract between the client and the debtor and creating a new one between the factor and the debtor.[15] Such an arrangement is not part of the functions of a modern factor. However, novation is an important principle in trade finance as the trade financier may be requested to purchase or sell goods on his own behalf where the client has already entered into the relevant contract. If the client did not enter into the contracts as agent for the financier, then the financier is obliged to become a party to the contract with the consent of the other contracting parties.[16]

Position of the factor arising from total failure of consideration

9-45 A factor cannot be liable on the contract giving rise to the debt that has been assigned to him as there is no privity of contract between him and the debtor. However, a factor may be liable to repay a debtor who has made payment in relation to an invoice that purports to evidence a debt. This might occur where an invoice has been issued and either no goods or services have been supplied, or services supplied were lawfully rejected by the debtor for non-conformity with the contract. The debtor may then be entitled to repayment from the factor on an action for money had and received, which is based on the quasi-contractual principle of restitution. If the factor is

---

[14] s.81A of the Bills of Exchange Act 1882, inserted by s.1 of the Cheques Act 1992; *Paget's Law of Banking* (12th ed., 2002), para.17.162 and J.K. McLeod, "*The Unbanked Payee*" (1997) 113 L.Q.R. 133 AT 156.
[15] e.g. *The Blankenstein* [1985] 1 W.L.R. 435; *The Aktion* [1987] 1 Lloyd's Rep. 283, 310–311.
[16] See paras 1–05 to 1–06 above; *e.g. Welsh Development Agency v Export Finance Co* [1992] B.C.C. 270.

obliged to repay the debtor, then he may be exposed to a loss in circumstances where:

(1) he has paid his client against the invoice representing the transaction in question;

(2) his client has become insolvent; and

(3) his retention is insufficient to cover his recourse on the basis of the client's breach of warranty.

However, when faced by a claim by a debtor, a number of defences may be available to the factor.

First, the debts may have been payments due and payable by the debtor in **9–46** advance of the performance of the contract by the assignor. Although most factors require that in relation to all debts assigned the client has fully performed its obligations under the contract, the debtor's rights may only extend to a claim on the contract, in practice many invoices are raised and paid for in advance of services being rendered. If so, and the client has failed fully to perform the contract, the debtor's rights may only extend to a claim on the contract against the client as assignor.[17] Nonetheless, Lord Goff has conceded that it is still "a matter of debate" whether in exceptional circumstances "a plaintiff may have a claim in restitution when he has conferred a benefit on the defendant in the course of performing an obligation to a third party".[18] Secondly, where there is a course of dealing between the parties whereby the client raises invoices in advance of performance (*e.g.* payment for services payable weekly or monthly in advance), then the debtor may be estopped from asserting that he is entitled to recover payments made in advance on non-performance, subject to proving the elements of the estoppel. Thirdly, the factor may be able to rely upon the defence of change of position.

The basis of his defence would be that the debtor's payment or course **9–47** of payments had led him to believe that the debtor had accepted in full the obligation to pay the invoice in question and that, accordingly, he was bound to pay and had paid the client the purchase price of the debt in full. This defence is now well established in English law and available to a person who has changed his position in good faith and where it would be inequitable that he should make restitution.[19] In such a case, there can be no

---

[17] *Pan Ocean Shipping Co Ltd v Creditcorp Ltd ("The Trident Beauty")* [1994] All E.R. 470, HL.

[18] *ibid.*, at 475.
[19] *Lipkin Gorman (a firm) v Karpnale Ltd (formerly Playboy Club of London Ltd)* [1991] 2 A.C. 548; and see Goff and Jones, *The Law of Restitution* (6th ed., 2002), Ch.40. On the relationship between the defence of change of position and estoppel by representation, see *Scottish Equitable plc v Derby* [2001] 3 All E.R. 808; *National Westminster Bank plc v Somer International UK Ltd* [2002] Q.B. 1286; and the discussion in Goff and Jones, *The Law of Restitution* (6th ed., 2002), paras 40–12 and 40–13.

question of the factor being unjustly enriched by having been paid for nothing: in fact, he has paid his client in relation to the invoice and is unlikely to be able to recover the advance.

The factor's liability for credit balances

9–48   Not infrequently credit balances emerge on the accounts of debtors in the records of factors. The question of the responsibility of the factor for payment of any such credit balance to the debtor is the subject of much uncertainty and disagreement even between the factors themselves. Such uncertainty and disagreement arise because in most cases a credit balance is created by the issue by the client to the debtor, and the acceptance by the factor, of a credit note representing a value exceeding the debit balance on the debtor's account. It is clear that a credit balance created by a debtor's payment, either duplicated or mistaken as to amount, is repayable by the factor who has received the payment as money paid by mistake.

9–49   The view that the factor has no responsibility for credit balances created by the issue of credit notes is based on the doctrines of the assignee's avoidance of any liabilities under the sale contract. However, apart from the position which may arise if the credit note has been issued in recognition of total failure of consideration,[20] there are cogent arguments in favour of the factor's liability. First, if the credit note creates a credit balance, it must surely be in recognition of an earlier overpayment because a defect or deficiency in the goods or services did not emerge until after payment. It is then possible that the debtor could claim that the resulting balance represented his having paid too much in the first place by mistake of fact. His mistake was to assume that the goods or services were in order at the time when he paid; although the credit note was issued later, it represented the facts in existence at the time of payment.[21] Secondly, the debtor might claim that by a course of dealing the factor had given ostensible authority to the client to issue credit notes which adjusted the factor's own account with the debtor.

9. LONG TERM CONTRACTS FOR THE SUPPLY OF GOODS OR SERVICES

9–50   The countervailing rights of the debtor against the factor as assignee, especially in relation to substantive defences[22] and equitable set-off,[23] have

---

[20] See para.9–45 above.
[21] *cf.* Oditah, *Legal Aspects of Receivables Financing* (1991), at pp.47–49.
[22] See para.9–03 above.
[23] See para.9–08 above.

had the effect of restricting the field of trades and industries in which the factor may safely provide any form of factoring in which prepayments are available to the client. Such countervailing rights may detrimentally affect the factor's ability to collect the full amount of an assigned debt where such a debt arises under a continuing uncompleted contract for the supply of goods or services. The client may have sold and delivered goods or completed services under such a contract and invoiced them and, in good faith, have offered or notified to the factor the debt representing such goods or services; and the factor may have made a prepayment on account of the purchase price of the debt. If the client then fails to deliver the remainder of the goods or complete the remainder of the services for which the contract provides (for example, for reason of his insolvency or a strike or *force majeure*), the factor will in all probability then be met by a cross-claim by the debtor. The cross-claim will be for breach of the same contract as that which gave rise to the factored debt, being a defence by way of equitable set-off that may arise at any time, notwithstanding the receipt of notice of assignment by the debtor. Naturally, in a continuing arrangement for factoring, an occasional experience of such an uncompleted contract is unlikely to be a problem; the recourse, which is available to the factor owing to the client's breach of warranty that the debt is free from such a cross-claim, may be set off by the factor against amounts payable by him for further debts purchased from the client. The difficulty for the factor will be serious if the bulk of the client's business relates to long term contracts and the client becomes insolvent. For this reason factors tend to eschew such businesses.

Long term contracts for services

The consequences of the failure by the client to complete a contract for services depends on whether the contract is entire or divisible. Under an entire contract the debtor had no liability for payment until performance of the whole contract has been completed. A divisible contract will provide for payment for part performance. Whether a contract is divisible or entire depends on the terms of the contract itself and, if provision is made for the invoices to be issued periodically, by the supplier of services, then in the absence of any specific provision in the contract the presumption may be that the contract is divisible. However, unless the terms of the contract are examined carefully by the factor, he will not know to which type of contract the debts notified or offered to him are related. The effect on the factor may well be as follows: **9-51**

(1) If the contract is entire the debtor will not be obliged to pay any part of the invoice already issued, unless the whole contract is substantially completed.[24] Even if the contract is substantially

---

[24] *Bolton v Mahadeva* [1972] 1 W.L.R. 1009; *Hoenig v Isaacs* [1952] 2 All E.R. 176.

completed, the debtor will be able to set off, as against the factor's claim for payment, a counterclaim for breach of contract because the claim and counterclaim arose from the same contract and are closely connected.[25]

(2) If the contract is divisible, the debtor will be obliged to pay the invoice for part performance provided that the invoice relates to a separable part of the contract; but the debtor will be able to set off his counterclaim for breach of contract.[26]

9–52   The debt which is not payable by the debtor because it relates to part (but not substantially the whole) performance of an entire contract will be subject to recourse to the client who will be in breach of warranties given in the factoring agreement. For the same reason, such a debt arising under a divisible contract or relating to the substantial completion of work under an entire contract, which is subject to a counterclaim for damages, may be recoursed to the client. In the one case, the debt is not a legally binding obligation of the debtor and in the other is subject to a counter-claim; in both cases, the client will have warranted otherwise.[27]

Contracts for the supply of goods

9–53   Where there is a contract for the sale of goods to be delivered by instalments, which are to be invoiced and paid separately, it is a question to be determined by a construction of the contract whether any defect or default in any one or more of the deliveries may give the debtor the right to repudiate the whole contract or only the right to a claim for compensation.[28] However, the normal presumption, in the absence of anything to the contrary in the contract, is that each delivery according to the contract is to be invoiced and paid for separately. In this respect the factor may be somewhat better off in relation to a debt arising from a contract for the sale of goods than in relation to one arising from a contract for services. Furthermore, if the debtor has accepted one or more of the instalments of goods and not the whole quantity contracted for, the factor may well be able to rely on the Sale of Goods Act 1979 and to claim payment of the price of the goods as a part delivery accepted by the debtor.[29] However, the factor's claim in relation to a contract of sale will be subject to a counterclaim by the debtor if the client

---

[25] *Government of Newfoundland v Newfoundland Railway Co* (1888) 13 A.C. 199; *Roxburghe v Cox* (1881) 17 Ch. D. 520; *Business Computers Ltd v Anglo-African Leasing Ltd* [1977] 1 W.L.R. 578.
[26] *ibid.*
[27] See Ch.10.
[28] Sale of Goods Act 1979, s.31(2).
[29] s.30(1).

wrongfully fails to deliver a further instalment.[30] The position will be exactly as described above[31] in respect of an incomplete divisible service contract.

An uncertainty that very often affects the factor's consideration of a long **9–54** term contractual arrangement between a client as supplier of goods and a debtor is the practice of some purchasers by which the goods to be purchased are specified but the exact quantity (or even the price) is subject to periodic call off. Such arrangements are common among large retail chains. The specification of the product, and often its price, are agreed with the manufacturer, but the quantities to be supplied are called for direct to the manufacturer by branches as required. Depending on the circumstances, the main agreement entered into with the manufacturer may be a binding agreement to supply goods on demand at a fixed price for a certain period of time, in which case individual calls for the supply of goods may simply be a trigger which binds the client to supply the goods at the price agreed. Alternatively, if the main agreement does not contain provision as to price, then it will probably not be binding, but will operate as a letter of intent. In such cases, individual calls for the supply of a specific quantity of goods at a specific price will, upon acceptance by the client, take effect as separate contracts. In both cases, the factor would be able to accept the debts arising from such deliveries without anxiety.

A further difficulty for the factor may arise where, although all the goods **9–55** arising under an individual and separate contract have been properly delivered by the client and accepted by the debtor, the client becomes insolvent and the debtor refuses to pay in full claiming that servicing of the goods or other back-up is no longer available to him. Where there had been a contract for such services between the client and the debtor, it is likely that set-off of a cross-claim would be available to the debtor; even if the contract for the services were to be separate from that for the supply of the goods, it is likely that they would be considered to be closely connected.[32] If the goods are of such a nature that after sales service is implicit or usual (and the example of office equipment such as photo-copiers is sometimes mentioned in this connection), then the debtor may have a cross-claim for the absence of implied service even if it had not been the subject of a specific contract; but in relation to other goods (such as raw materials, components or non-durable consumer goods) such a presumption of after sales service is most unlikely. However, whether the service is the subject of a contract or implied, the debtor would have to formulate his cross-claim at the time when payment for the goods becomes due and, if there is no apparent defect in the goods, such a cross-claim is unlikely to be of substantial value.

---

[30] Sale of Goods Act 1979, s.51(1).
[31] At para.9–51 above.
[32] See para.7–17 above.

Cut-off clauses

9–56   In view of potential difficulties arising from the client's long term contracts with his debtors, where such contracts are a normal part of the client's
business or where an individual contract of such a nature constitutes a large
part of the client's business, it is advisable for the factor to stipulate that the
debts arising from such a contract will be approved and eligible for prepayment only if a "cut-off clause" is included in the contract. The purpose
of such a clause is to divide the contract so that each delivery may be
deemed to constitute a separate contract. An example of such a clause in a
contract for services would be:

> "This contract is divisible. The work performed in each month during
> the currency of the contract shall be invoiced separately. Each invoice
> for work performed in any month shall be payable by the customer in
> full, in accordance with the terms of payment provided for herein,
> without reference to and notwithstanding any defect or default in the
> work performed or to be performed in any other month."

Or, in a contract for the sale of goods:

> "This contract is divisible. Each delivery made hereunder:
>
> (i)   shall be deemed to arise from a separate contract, and
> (ii) shall be invoiced separately and any invoice for a delivery
>   shall be payable in full in accordance with the terms of pay-
>   ment provided for herein without reference to and notwith-
>   standing any defect or default in the delivery of any other
>   instalment."

Undertaking from the debtor direct

9–57   Alternatively, it may be possible for the factor to obtain from a debtor
who is anxious to maintain continuity of supply from the client an undertaking on the following lines:

Re: XYZ Limited ("the Company")

> "In consideration of your continuing your factoring services for the
> company we hereby undertake to pay in full the amount of any invoice
> for goods sold to us (services completed for us) by the company and
> accepted by us without any deduction or set-off in relation to any claim
> we may have or expect to have against the company in respect of any
> goods (services) provided or to be provided by the company which are
> not the subject of the said invoice."

CHAPTER 10

THE FACTORING AGREEMENT—PAYMENT TO THE CLIENT BY THE FACTOR AND OTHER TERMS

In Ch.7 it was postulated that the factor's principal requirement in the   **10–01**
factoring agreement was that the debts which he purchases from his client
should vest in him free from the rights and interests of third parties; the
methods by which this is achieved were described in Chs 7 and 8. From the
client's point of view, the most important provisions are those which relate
to the obligations for the factor to pay him for the debts which he sells to the
factor. The converse of such provisions is the protection of the factor
against paying to the client more than he will ultimately collect from the
debtors after a deduction for his charges.[1] The factor will be obliged to pay
to such an extent if the balance owing to the client for the price of debts
purchased (the factor's retention) is insufficient to absorb all the amounts
subsequently to be set off by the factor for the repurchase price of debts to
be recoursed; in the insolvency of the client (and in the absence of collateral
security), the factor will be unsecured for the balance. These and the miscellaneous provisions peculiar to a factoring agreement are discussed in this
chapter.

1. PAYMENT TO THE CLIENT AND THE FACTOR'S RETENTION

The case for a current account

Although the accounting methods and provisions for payment of the   **10–02**
purchase price of debts as described earlier[2] vary among factoring companies, it is now not unusual that the arrangements should be made by way of

---

[1] Except, in the case of an approved debt in non-recourse factoring, solely by reason of the
insolvency of the debtor.
[2] See Ch.3.

the credit of the purchase price to a current account and the debit thereto of all amounts paid by the factor to the client and all amounts to be charged to the client.[3] These debits include the repurchase price of debts the subject of recourse and the amounts of credit notes (issued by the client with the authority of the factor). The provisions for payment to the client are then by way of drawing by the client against the balance on the current account subject to the maintenance of the agreed retention. If the agreement were to provide that the purchase price of each individual debt is to be paid separately, then the factor would have to rely on set-off of individual transactions (albeit arising out of the same or a closely connected contract), rather than having all the transactions merged in a current account to give rise to one debt.[4] In such a case, if the client were insolvent, then the factor would have to rely on the insolvency set-off rules.[5]

10–03   The advantage to the factor of providing for payment to the client by way of drawing against a current account was amply demonstrated in the case of *Re Charge Card Services Ltd*,[6] the importance of which to factors is such that a synopsis of part of Millett J.'s judgment is set out here. The case raised two questions and the second, which is of general interest to factors, was as follows[7]:

The liquidator of the client company challenged the right of the factor to hold (after the commencement of the winding-up) a retention against further charges to arise and, more importantly, against the potential liability of the liability of the client for recourse in respect of any debts for which the factor had paid and which might remain unpaid by the debtors 120 days after the invoice date. There were two prongs to the liquidator's attack. First, the liquidator claimed that the factor's right to retain the unpaid balance of the purchase price of purchased debts, for the purpose of applying it against further amounts to become payable to the factor by the client, was a security right and a charge on a book debt and was void against the liquidator for want of registration.[8] Secondly, the liquidator claimed that the rules relating to set-off in insolvency[9] did not allow the

---

[3] This is the accounting system described in para.3–36 above and *not* that described in para.3–48 above.

[4] See para.9–04 above.

[5] See paras 9–12 to 9–14 above.

[6] [1987] Ch.150.

[7] The first question is of interest only to a factor who is again likely to provide his services to a credit card company. It related to the possible liability of customers, who had used a credit card to settle an account, to pay the dealer when the credit card company had failed to pay him owing to its winding-up. Fortunately for the factor it was decided *on the particular facts of the case* that the indebtedness of the customers to the credit card company (assigned to the factor) could be sustained. The dealer's only remedy was to prove as a creditor in the estate of the credit card company. The case went to the Court of Appeal (but only in respect of the first question) which upheld the decision of the Court of First Instance.

[8] Companies Act 1985, ss.395 and 396 and see para.8–30.

[9] See paras 9–12 to 9–14 above.

factor to set off, against the actual liability of the factor to the client for the balance of the purchase price of debts, the liability of the client company for recourse the very existence of which (in addition to its amount) was at the commencement of liquidation contingent only.

It was held that the liability of the factor to the client was not the purchase **10–04** price of each debt but the balance of a current account to which the purchase price was credited and other items debited.[10] Therefore, there was no question of set-off because there were no independent obligations capable of being set off; the arrangement gave rise to a single liability the ultimate balance on the account.[11] It was further held that the retention was security for the factor; but it was security (in the widest sense of the word), by means of a contractual arrangement, against overpayment by the factor.[12] The right to retain a balance on the current account was not a registrable charge because there was no property capable of being the subject matter of a charge; the only asset was the amount due under the agreement and this already took account of the retention.[13]

The factor was entitled under the agreement to require on notice the **10–05** repurchase by the client of all debts remaining outstanding. As such notice had not been given, the repurchase price was not then available to be debited to the account and it was conceded on behalf of the factor that this was a matter of set-off. For this reason, and in case he were to be wrong regarding the retention, the judge made a thorough review of the authorities relating to the availability of set-off of a contingent claim against the estate of a bankrupt individual or company in liquidation. Following this review he held that set-off was indeed available even if the existence as well as the amount of the liability of the insolvent estate was contingent. It was also held that the factor's right to hold the retention as security could not constitute a charge in favour of the factor because it was conceptually impossible for a debt to be charged in favour of the debtor himself; but that doctrine has now been definitively rejected by the House of Lords in another case.[14] However, that decision of the House of Lords does not affect the remainder of the judgment.

As regards the application of insolvency set-off to contingent claims **10–06** against a client in winding-up or bankruptcy, the decision in the case[15] has been a comfort to factors. Although the case related to events before the coming into effect of the provisions of the Insolvency Act 1986 and the

---

[10] See para.10–02 above.
[11] [1987] Ch.150 at 174.
[12] ibid.
[13] ibid.
[14] *Morris v Rayners Enterprises Incorporated; Morris v Agrochemicals Ltd* [1997] B.C.C. 965.
[15] *Re Charge Card Services Ltd* [1986] 3 All E.R. 289 (first instance); [1987] Ch.150 at 174.

Insolvency Rules 1986 relating to set-off in bankruptcy and winding-up respectively,[16] those provisions made no substantive change to the law.[17]

10–07   In view of the House of Lords rejection of the conceptual impossibility of a charge on a person's own indebtedness to another ("a charge back"), factors must now bear in mind the difference between contractual set-off and a charge back as follows:

> (1) contractual set-off provides for the debtor (in this case the factor) to satisfy in whole or in part his indebtedness to the creditor (the client) by applying against that indebtedness the factor's cross-claims against the client; and
>
> (2) a charge back arises where the creditor (the client) agrees that his claim on the debtor (the factor) may be held to secure the factor's claims against the client.

The distinction arises because in (2) the client no longer has an unencumbered beneficial ownership of the balance of the purchase price of the factored debts.

10–08   In order to avoid the risk that the holding of a retention is a charge back (and thus registrable as charge on a book debt), the factor should not provide in his agreement that it is for the purpose of security for the client's obligations. In place of such provision the factor should account to the client on a current account (to which the purchase price of debts is credited and the payments to the client debited) and require that a "minimum balance" be retained by the client on the current account. The minimum balance to be held may be equivalent to a percentage of approved and the full amount of unapproved debts outstanding from time to time. Such an arrangement (a "flawed asset") is not unusual in relation to credit balances on bank accounts. For recovery of items not taken into account in the current account balance (*e.g.* the client's contingent liability for recourse), the factor should then rely on contractual set-off otherwise than in the winding-up or bankruptcy of the client when insolvency set-off would apply. Contractual set-off should be available to the factor in the case of an administration order in relation to the client and the priority of such set-off over any rights a holder of a charge on the client's assets should be dealt with in every waiver letter. To be quite safe and to guard against developments in the law relating to insolvency set-off, factors may well consider a consequential change to any charges on book debts which they normally take as collateral security by including a charge over the retention and, if it

---

[16] s.323 and r.4.90 respectively; see also para.9–12 above.
[17] *Stein v Blake* [1995] 2 All E.R. 961; and see also para.9–13 above.

is not at present their practice to take such charges, to take a separate charge over it.[18]

Provisions for set-off and combination of accounts

Whether the factor provides for his obligations for payment to the client **10–09** by way of a current account, as described above, or for payment of the purchase price of each debt individually, it is usual to provide for the set-off of any amount owing to the factor by the client against such obligations. The set-off provisions should extend to any contingent or prospective liability of the client and, where there is a current account between the factor and the client, it should be provided that the factor may make a reasonable estimate of any contingent liability that cannot be exactly determined and debit the current account therewith. As the factor's accounting with his client is often conducted on more than one account, provision should also be made for the combination of these accounts at the option of the factor at any time. The set-off provisions should be extended to cover any liability of the client to the factor otherwise than under the factoring agreement and include, for example, liability to the factor as a result of an assignment to the factor by another client of a debt arising from supplies to the former client by that other client.

Prohibition of assignment of the client's rights

The set-off rights of the factor referred to above may be affected by the **10–10** intervention by assignment by the client of his rights under the factoring agreement including the factor's indebtedness to the client.[19] Consequently, a factor will usually be protected against such intervention by the usual provision in factoring agreements that the client may not assign or create a charge over all or any of his rights under the agreement, including his right to payment from the factor, without the consent of the factor.

2. WARRANTIES AND UNDERTAKINGS BY THE CLIENT

Warranty of the validity and value of debts

Among all types of agreement for the financing of debts, whereby the **10–11** debts are taken by way of purchase or for security, factoring is unique in

---

[18] See para.13–22 below.
[19] *Mangles v Dixon* (1852) 3 H.L. Cas. 702 and see also *Watson v Mid Wales Railway Company* [1867] L.R. 2 C.P. 593 where the set-off was not allowed but in which the principles relating to the intervention of an assignee in a contract for set-off were indicated. See also paras 9–19 and 9–20 above and Ch.11.

that the factor most usually is unable to rely on the debtor's acceptance of the obligation to pay. In other arrangements of a similar nature (*e.g.* leasing, block discounting or forfeiting) the financier will have available to him a document signed by or on behalf of the debtor before parting with his funds. On the other hand, the factor has perforce most usually to rely on an invoice which represents only the client's interpretation of what the debtor must pay in accordance with the contract of sale or service. Although the general experience of commerce and industry is that in only a very small proportion of cases will the debtor not accept the invoice, there are inevitably, in the case of most businesses, a number which are not accepted. Whether such failure by the debtor to accept the invoice is justified or not and whether the invoice is incorrect by reason of mistake, inefficient administration in the client's office or by reason of fraud, the factor must protect himself.

10–12   It is no part of the factor's service to protect the client against trade disputes; and the factor must avoid, if possible, the payment for debts represented by overstated invoices and, if he should pay, then he must be able to recover his payment by recourse to the client. It is therefore normally provided in the factoring agreement that the client should warrant the validity and value of the debts offered and the agreement will provide that any debt, in respect of which there is a breach of such a warranty, should be subject to recourse. Such warranties normally provide that:

(1)   the goods which gave rise to the debt have been delivered (or the services completed) and that they conform to the contract between the client and the debtor; and

(2)   the debt is a legally binding obligation of the debtor for the amount stated in the invoice and that the debtor will accept the goods and the invoice therefor without any dispute, deduction, defence, cross-claim or set-off.

10–13   A reduction in the amount payable by the debtor may arise out of contractual arrangements between the client and the debtor even when the goods delivered or services provided and the invoice all comply with the contract of sale. It may arise from purchases by the client from the debtor[20] or because the goods have been delivered on a "sale or return" basis and these should be covered by the warranty mentioned above.[21] It may be based on an established agreement for the giving of quantity discounts based on the value of goods taken over a stated period; such a discount would be calculated at the end of the period and apply retrospectively. It is likely that the deduction would be available to the debtor against the factor as assignee in view of its close connection of an outstanding debt with the previous

---

[20] For the debtor's countervailing rights in such a case see paras 9–17 and 9–18 above.
[21] Item (2) in para.10–12 above.

debts arising from the sales to which the discount related; as a result, when such a discount is allowed, there may well be a substantial deduction from the next payment to be made to the factor. Although such deduction should be covered under the warranty relating to the value of the debt (described above), it is normally considered advisable to include in the agreement an undertaking by the client not to purchase from any debtor without first informing the factor and to disclose any contractual arrangements by which the amount of the debt may be reduced below the amount of it as notified or offered.

Warranties regarding terms in the contract of sale or service

Factoring is normally provided only for businesses that sell on short terms **10–14** of payment and the factor's charges and his assessment of risks is based on the terms on which he expects the client to sell. Furthermore, the factor must ensure that the sum which he recovers from the debtor is not diminished by reason of payment in a depreciating currency or an unusually large settlement discount. As a result, he will expect warranties that each debt offered or notified to him arises out of a contract which:

(1) provides for payment on terms not more liberal than have been approved by the factor;

(2) does not provide for discounts greater than he has approved; and

(3) provides for payment in a currency approved by him.

Assignability of debts and freedom from encumbrances

It is naturally necessary that the client should warrant that the debts **10–15** offered or notified are such that he has the absolute right to assign them and, in order that the factor should avoid conflicts of the type referred to in Ch.8, the factor will expect that the client should give warranties and undertakings regarding the freedom of the debts from any encumbrance. Although the factor may be expected to make a search at the companies registry before the start of factoring, there are several types of encumbrance that escape the requirement of registration but may affect the debts sold to the factor by the client[22]; and these may include the tracing rights of the client's suppliers whose terms include prolonged reservation of title.[23] The client should give warranties and undertakings that no encumbrances (other than as disclosed to the factor) exist at the outset, that none will be created during the currency of the factoring agreement and, in particular, that no contract for the

---

[22] See para.8–19 above.
[23] See paras 8–39 to 8–64 above and in particular para.8–43 in relation to the client's sales *and* purchases on terms which reserve title to goods.

237

purchase of goods will enable the supplier to have any claim on or interest in any debt arising from the onward sale of such goods. The client should also warrant that every debt sold to the factor will be unencumbered.[24]

Warranties in connection with variations of contracts of sale

10–16   Having sold and delivered goods in accordance with a contract of sale, correctly invoiced them and sold the resultant debt to the factor, the client may seek to vary the contract of sale. This might occur if the debtor asked the client to take some goods back and the client was disposed to agree. If this occurred on a large scale with a number of debtors, the factor might be put in a position where he would be unable to collect from the debtors all that he had paid on account of the purchased price of debts sold to him. In their arrangements with their clients, factors recognise that credit notes must sometimes be issued. In every business errors occur and, to a limited extent, the wrong goods or faulty goods may be delivered or invoices be incorrect. However, the conscious decision to vary a contract should not be made by a client without the consent of the factor, once the debt arising out of the contract has vested in the factor. The factor will expect an undertaking from his client not to vary or cancel any contract in such circumstances.

Undertaking to co-operate in recovery proceedings

10–17   Where the debts vest in the factor by an equitable assignment and it is necessary for him to take legal proceedings for recovery, it may be necessary for him to join the client or to use his name.[25] A further undertaking required from the client is that he will, if so requested by the factor, co-operate with the factor in recovery proceedings, whether through the courts or otherwise. Furthermore, in the case of invoice discounting, undisclosed factoring, agency factoring or "CHOC", the factor requires the client to undertake to act promptly and efficiently in procuring the collection of debts; the client, having sold the debts to the factor, is to ensure that they are paid promptly for the benefit of the factor.

Warranty to disclose

10–18   Although the credit protection element of a factoring agreement is analogous to a policy of credit insurance, a factor does not have the protection that an insurer has by reason of the insurance policy belonging to a class of

---

[24] It should be noted that in *E. Pfeiffer Weinkellerei-Weineinkauf GmbH & Co v Arbuthnot Factors Ltd* [1988] 1 W.L.R. 150 and in *Compaq Computer Ltd v The Abercorn Group Ltd* [1991] B.C.C. 484 the factor was assisted because he relied on such a warranty and was unaware of the contractual terms of a supplier in respect of prolonged reservation of title.
[25] See para.7–04 and Ch.7, n.13 above.

contracts that are *uberrimae fidei*. Under such contracts it is assumed that one party (in the case of insurance the prospective insured) is in possession of most of the material facts regarding the subject matter of the contract; accordingly, that party is obliged to make a full disclosure of such facts. Failure to do so makes the contract voidable at the option of the other. A factoring agreement is not a contract *uberrimae fidei*. In order to place himself in a position equivalent to that of a credit insurer the factor should require a warranty from the client that, before making the agreement, the client has disclosed any fact or matter known to the client which might have influenced the factor's decision whether or not to enter into the agreement or to approve any debt for credit or for a prepayment on account of its purchase price or to accept any person as a guarantor of the client's obligations. The agreement should also include an undertaking by the client to disclose any further such fact or matter arising during the currency of the agreement.

Other usual provisions

The following are further warranties and undertakings of the client and **10–19** miscellaneous provisions often included in a factoring agreement:

(1) a warranty that the debtor, by whom every debt offered or notified to the factor is owing, has an established place of business and is not an associate of the client;

(2) an undertaking to comply with the standard procedures promulgated by the factor from time to time for operation of the agreement;

(3) an undertaking by the client to pay all carriage and shipping charges, for which the client is responsible, in relation to the goods giving rise to a debt offered or notified to the factor and all bank charges in relation to collection of foreign debts and all other debts in respect of which the factor has full recourse to the client (unapproved debts);

(4) an indemnity from the client to the factor in respect of the costs (including legal costs) of collection of such unapproved debts and any such costs of or incidental to the enforcement of the provisions of the factoring agreement; and

(5) an authority for the factor to rely on any communications whether oral or in writing purportedly sent to the factor by on behalf of the client in spite of the absence of, or any defect in, the authority of the sender.

239

Inability of client to give warranties

10–20   Without any fault on the part of the client, from time to time there may arise debts in relation to which the client is unable to give every warranty and undertaking contained in the agreement. For example, the debtor may have a cross-claim against the client arising from a previous transaction. In the case of an agreement of the facultative type,[26] the client will be obliged to make this known to the factor who may then decline to accept the debt or do so on terms whereby his payment for it is reduced. In the case of an agreement of the whole turnover type,[27] a paradoxical situation may arise: the agreement provides that every debt is to be assigned to the factor automatically and the client is obliged to notify every debt to the factor as it comes into existence; but, on the other hand, such notification is usually deemed to constitute a warranty by the client that the debt is free from such a cross-claim. Whether or not the client notifies the debt, he will be in breach of one or other of the terms of the factoring agreement. To resolve this difficulty some factors have provided that any debt, in relation to which the client is unable to give all the warranties and undertakings in the agreement, shall be notified separately with a note of the circumstances; the factor will then be able to designate the debt as not eligible for finance or subject to immediate recourse.

3. CREDIT NOTES AND CREDIT BALANCES

10–21   Although the factor expects the client to undertake that no event will occur that will reduce the liability of the debtor to pay an amount less than that specified in the offer or notification to the factor, even in the best regulated business such events sometimes occur. Mistakes are made in invoicing, in manufacture and in the despatch of goods; and sometimes for commercial reasons it seems requisite for the client to agree to take goods back. In the normal routine of factoring concerning, as it normally does, a continuous stream of relatively small transactions, the factor will by a course of dealing allow the client to make such adjustments to the value of the debts (already owned by the factor) by the issue of credit notes to the debtor.

10–22   It is apparent that the recognition of such a right of the client by a course of dealing leaves the factor in danger of its abuse by the client. In order to protect themselves against over zealous invoicing and the consequent issue of substantial credit notes after the factor has paid on account of the debts represented by such invoices, it is the practice of some factors to provide in their agreements that the client should issue credit notes only with the

---

[26] See para.7–08 above.
[27] See para.7–10 above.

consent of the factor. Others find this practice commercially unacceptable and administratively burdensome; but, even in this case, it is essential that the factor should take the right in the factoring agreement to impose such a restriction on the client in the event that the factor should find that the client is misusing his authority to issue credit notes. The provision, when put into effect by notice to the client, would require the client to send the originals of credit notes to the factor who would issue them to the debtors only when the factor had approved them.

There is a widespread view that the client, and not the factor, is respon-   **10–23** sible for credit balances arising on the accounts of debtors in the records of the factor.[28] This view has led to claims by liquidators or trustees in bankruptcy of insolvent clients to have such credit balances credited back to them in the expectation that the claimant will prove as an unsecured creditor. It is in most circumstances more likely that the factor himself is liable[29] so that, by acceding to the liquidator's or trustee's claim, the factor may leave himself exposed to a double payment in respect of each such balance. For the avoidance of doubt, the factor should include in the factoring agreement authority for payment to the claimant. If such credit balances are dealt with as they arise the difficulty in the insolvency of the client will not arise. The factor has no reason not to pay; in the case of a credit note, he has been already reimbursed by the client by reason of the debit of amount of the credit note to the client's account and, in the case of an overpayment, he will have received the funds.

4. TRANSFER TO THE FACTOR OF ANCILLARY RIGHTS

There are a number of rights which are closely connected with every debt   **10–24** purchased by the factor. Although the debt, being the right to receive payment for goods or services supplied, is usually the principal right of the client under his contracts of sale or service, there are other important rights of the client under such contracts. These include rights of lien and to stop goods in transit, the right in certain circumstances to rescind or terminate the contract, the right to accept returned goods and, in many cases, the right to retain title to the goods until the debtor has paid for them.

It is usual for the factoring agreement to provide that the following   **10–25** should automatically be transferred to the factor on purchase of any debt:

(1) all the client's rights under the relevant contract of sale or service (including the right to the ownership of any goods which have been returned or rejected by the debtor);

---

[28] See paras 9–48 and 9–49 above.
[29] *ibid.*

241

(2) all instruments of payment taken or available to the client in or on account of settlement of the debt;

(3) the benefit of any credit insurance policy in respect of the debt;

(4) the benefit of any guarantee or indemnity given by a third party in respect of the debtor's obligations under the contract of sale or service; and

(5) the ownership of all books, computer data, records and documents on or by which the debt is recorded or evidenced.

The ownership of the last item is usually considered advisable in order to avoid a situation in which a trustee, liquidator, administrator or receiver of an insolvent client refuses access to the papers which may be required as evidence to enable the factor to collect the debts which he has purchased. Since the enactment of the Late Payment of Commercial Debts (Interest) Act 1998, some factors have included the right to statutory interest in the ancillary rights transferred to them along with the debts. This would enable the factor to claim such interest if it became necessary for the recovery of the funds in use. However, although factors may agree to collect such interest as an additional service, it is unlikely that any factor will take full responsibility for collecting it or make prepayments against its collection.

10–26   It is not advisable for the agreement to provide, in all circumstances, for the automatic transfer of ownership of goods which the client sells subject to reservation of title until payment. Such automatic inclusion of goods in the purchase of debts and related rights may detract from the factor's ability to recover value added tax included in bad debts.[30] Secondly, it would bring the factor automatically into the chain of ownership and may in some circumstances subject him to claims in respect of liability for defects in the product; as the factor would in many cases not have the opportunity to inspect every sale contract in a continuous stream of small transactions, he might be unaware that the ownership of the goods had passed through his hands. In order to avoid such potential liability for the factor without his knowingly accepting it, it is advisable for the agreement not to provide for the automatic transfer of ownership of the goods, but to provide for the right to have ownership transferred to him if he should think it requisite; this would apply to goods before title had passed to the debtor. However, title to all returned or rejected goods should be automatically transferred to the factor. By the realisation of such goods the factor may be able to recover his funds in use in the event that a substantial proportion of the debts are irrecoverable by reason of returns of goods.

10–27   It is important that the factoring agreement should provide that the purchase price of a debt (normally equivalent to the net amount payable by

---

[30] See paras 10–55 and 10–56 below.

the debtor less the factor's discount charge so far as it applies to the debt) should be payable for the sale by the client to the factor, not only of the debt itself, but also of these ancillary rights including the rights to goods. Otherwise, it could be alleged that those rights are transferred not by way of sale but by way of security; in the case of a company client, this could be considered to be a charge requiring registration. It should also not be overlooked that in any letter of waiver or priority agreement it should be provided that, not only the debts, but also the ancillary rights are released from the charge in respect of which the waiver is to be given.[31]

5. RECOURSE

In order to recover from the client (normally by way of debit to the client's account with the factor or by way of set-off[32]) the amount of any debt (or part of a debt), which the factor cannot recover from the debtor, the factor must provide for recourse to the client in respect of such debts. The inability to recover from the debtor may be by reason of: **10–28**

(1) the debtor's insolvency or the failure of the debtor to pay by a specified number of days after the due date for payment (except in the case of an approved debt in a non-recourse agreement);

(2) an unauthorised deduction or discount taken by the debtor;

(3) the failure of the debtor to accept the goods or services and the invoice for them in full; or

(4) a breach of some other warranty by the client.

The recovery from the client by recourse may be structured in the agreement by any one of the following three methods: **10–29**

(1) by the guarantee by the client of due payment by the debtor in respect of debts the subject of recourse;

(2) by a requirement that such debts should be repurchased for a repurchase price equivalent to the amount specified in the relevant notification of offer; or

(3) by a requirement that the client should repay to the factor any prepayment made by the factor on account of the purchase price of the debt.

---

[31] See paras 8–77 and 8–78 above.
[32] See paras 10–02 and 10–03 above.

If the recourse is by way of repurchase, the purchase price must be based on the notified or offered amount (and not the amount payable by the debtor), because the former will have been the basis for the credit to the account of the client while the latter may well be less. The advantage of the third method is that the debt remains in the ownership of the factor, whereas on a repurchase or the payment by the client as guarantor title to the debt would normally revert to the client.

10–30   Where a debt is the subject of recourse by reason of the winding-up or bankruptcy of the debtor and:

(1)   the client is also being wound-up or is bankrupt; and

(2)   the retention is insufficient to cover the recourse;

the factor may be in a better position to recover the amount of the recoursed debt if the recourse is framed as a guarantee by the client rather than by way of repurchase.

10–31   In the winding-up or bankruptcy of a principal debtor, the creditor (in this case the factor) is not obliged to deduct, from the amount of his proof in the estate of the debtor, any payments received (whether before or after the commencement of the winding up or bankruptcy) from the guarantor (in this case the client) until the guarantor has paid 100 per cent. The reason for this rule is that the creditor's proof for the full amount of the debt does not offend against the rule against double proof in the debtor's estate for the same indebtedness; the guarantor has no right to be subrogated to any of the creditor's rights (including the right to prove in the debtor's estate for the part of the debt in respect of which he has paid) until he has discharged the guaranteed debt in full.[33] Furthermore, although the creditor is obliged to deduct from his proof against the estate of the insolvent guarantor (the client) sums received from the debtor before the submission of his proof, he is not obliged to adjust his proof in respect of sums received afterwards.[34] Therefore, if the factor submits his proofs in the estates of both the debtor and the client promptly, he may receive dividends calculated on the *full amount* of the debt as specified in his proofs from both estates until he has recovered, in aggregate, 100p in the pound. This point does not affect the advantage of the third method of exercising recourse mentioned above by which the factor recovers the purchase price of the debt but retain s the debt itself.

10–32   It is unlikely that there are analogous principles in relation to the repurchase of a debt. However, almost the same result may be achieved by providing that, on the repurchase by the client of a debt the subject of

---

[33] *Re Sass* [1896] 2 Q.B. 12; see also para.4–56 above.
[34] *Re Amalgamated Investment & Property Co Ltd* [1985] 1 Ch.349; see also para.4–57 above.

recourse, the ownership of the debt shall remain vested in the factor until the repurchase price has been fully discharged.

6. SECURING THE FACTOR'S RIGHTS AND INTERESTS TO DEBTS AND ANCILLARY RIGHTS[35]

Assignments in statutory form

In Ch.7 it was explained that factors do not normally take assignments of the purchased debts in statutory form[36] but rely on equitable assignments. It was also postulated that the absence of a statutory form of assignment did not detract from the factor's rights in any way because the difference is purely procedural.[37] However, as the factor may in some circumstances deem it necessary that his title to any debt should be perfected in legal form for procedural reasons, it is normally provided in the agreement that the client should execute and deliver to the factor such documents as may be necessary for this purpose. It should also be provided that the client should execute such documents and do such things as may be requisite to transfer title to any ancillary rights[38] and to any of the underlying goods in respect of which the factor may be entitled to ownership. **10–33**

Creations of trusts by the client

The widespread practice of buyers of goods and services, who purchase on their own standard terms, to include in such terms provisions prohibiting the assignment of the debts arising from their purchases was described in Ch.9.[39] The effect of such prohibitions on the factor's rights to debts assigned in breach of such terms was also discussed there. It was concluded that the more serious mischief that a factor might not be able to claim the proceeds of a debt assigned to him in such circumstances was most likely to be avoided. It is most likely that such proceeds would be held by the client in a constructive trust for the factor. However, as a precaution it is normal for factors to include a provision within the factoring agreement itself whereby the client holds any debt, which is the subject of an assignment to the factor but fails to vest absolutely in the factor, in trust for the factor. The efficacy of such a provision does not appear to have been tested and it will not **10–34**

---

[35] See also Ch.13 regarding factor's use of charges as collateral security.
[36] Law of Property Act 1925, s.136.
[37] See para.7–07 above.
[38] See para.10–25 above.
[39] See paras 9–36 to 9–38 above.

prevent the purchaser (as debtor) obtaining a valid discharge by ignoring the notice of the assignment and paying the client.[40] Such a trust provision should apply also to the ancillary rights purchased by the factor.[41]

Provisions for and recovery of funds paid by debtor to client

10–35   Once notice of the assignment of a debt to the factor has been given to the debtor and in the absence of a prohibition of assignments in the contract giving rise to the debt, the debtor is obliged to pay the factor; payment to the client who supplied the debtor will not give him a valid discharge. If the debtor pays to the client in these circumstances (an *indirect* payment[42]), the factor is entitled to recover the amount so paid by a second payment from the debtor; this is so whether the assignment is in statutory form[43] or equitable.[44] However, because a certain number of debtors continue to make indirect payments even after receipt of notices of assignments and, owing to the practice in confidential factoring or invoice discounting arrangements of appointing the client as the agent of the factor to collect from the debtors, such indirect payments must be provided for in the factoring agreement. The usual provisions are that:

(1)   the identical monies, cheques and other instruments representing such indirect payments must be passed on to the factor by the client immediately upon their receipt; and

(2)   pending their delivery to the factor such monies and instruments are to be held by the client in trust for the factor.

In order to reinforce such trust provisions and to provide for payments by means of credit transfers direct to the client's bank account, it is usual for the factor to require that the client should instruct his banker to hold in trust for and remit to the factor any such receipts. It is apparent that in purchasing the debt the factor has vested in him the right to collect it and, accordingly, the proceeds are his property; thus, the trust is implicit even if it were not to be explicitly provided for. The efficacy of the creation of such a trust has been upheld by the court.[45] In order that a provision in the factoring agreement for the client to pass on to the factor "the identical cheques" should be of practical value to the factor, it is now necessary that the client should provide the factor's bank with clear instructions to collect for

---

[40] *ibid.*
[41] See paras 10–24 to 10–27 above.
[42] So called by many factors because a *direct* payment must be the payment to the person who is entitled to receive it: the factor as assignee.
[43] Law of Property Act 1925, s.136.
[44] *Wm. Brandts Sons & Co v Dunlop Rubber Co Ltd* [1905] A.C. 454.
[45] *International Factors Ltd v Rodriguez* [1979] Q.B. 351.

the benefit of the factor any such cheques made payable to the client. This is the result of the almost universal use in the United Kingdom of cheques crossed "account payee" which are now not transferable.[46] In such cases, the bank may, additionally, require an indemnity (to cover any claim on the bank from the "true owner" of any such cheque) from the client or the factor or from both of them. The factoring agreement must include an undertaking by the client to furnish such instructions and indemnity.

The factor will have no need to recover by a second payment from the **10–36** debtor if he can recover from the client and, in most circumstances, the provisions in the factoring agreement are effective so that the remittances representing indirect payments reach the factor through the client. However, if, in breach of the trust provisions, such a remittance is paid by the client into his own overdrawn bank account and the client becomes insolvent, the factor will first look to his retention and the possibility of recoursing the debt by way of set-off against any balance of the purchase price of other debts owing to the factor.[47] In addition, the factor has available to him (apart from the right to a second payment from the debtor) two other possible avenues for recovery.

Recovery from third parties

The factor will, in the case of a corporate client, look for recovery first to **10–37** any guarantor or indemnifier. If the client is a partnership, then all the partners (except in the case of a limited liability partnership or any limited partner of a limited partnership) are jointly and severally liable to the factor. In the absence of any guarantee or indemnity of a corporate client (or if all the guarantors and indemnifiers are themselves insolvent), the factor may be able to recover from any solvent director or other officer of the client who can be shown to have knowingly assisted in the breach of trust. A factor was successful in one such case[48] against a solvent director of a client company in liquidation in his personal capacity. Before the commencement of the winding-up the director had caused the company to pay into its own bank account a cheque made payable to the client which had been sent by the customer to settle a factored debt. The director was held liable to the factor in tort and it was no defence that it would have been open to the factor to have recovered direct from the customer, which had received notice of the assignment, by second payment.

In an analogous, but more recent, case,[49] the Privy Council held the **10–38** controlling director of a travel agency to be liable as an accessory to the breach of trust by the agency. The agency had used, for its own purposes,

---

[46] Cheques Act 1992, s.1.
[47] See paras 10–28 et seq. above.
[48] See n.45 above.
[49] *Royal Brunei Airlines SDN BHD v Philip Tan Kok Ming* [1995] 2 A.C. 378.

monies held by the agency in a fiduciary capacity for the airline. It was held that it was not necessary to show want of probity on the part of the trustee (in that case, the travel agency) provided that the accessory had acted dishonestly with actual or inferred knowledge of the breach. For this purpose, inferred knowledge means wilfully averting ones eyes or wilfully refraining from making enquiries; to show lack of care or negligence is not sufficient.

Recovery from the client's bankers

10–39   It may well be that none of the guarantors or indemnifiers or any officers, against whom knowing assistance of the breach of trust might be alleged, are solvent. The factor may then in some circumstances be able to recover the misapplied proceeds of customer payments from the bank into which the proceeds have been paid. The factor's chances of recovery from the bank depend largely on the state of the bank account when the monies are paid in and the subsequent conduct of the account.

(a)   Where the monies remain in a credit balance on the client's bank account

10–40   If the proceeds of the misapplied payments have not been withdrawn by the client or applied to reduce the client's overdraft, which is most unlikely in the insolvency of the client, the factor should be able to recover the proceeds by a common law claim for money had and received. In such a situation the bank is not a *bona fide* purchaser of the money for value; it has given no value. On collection of the misapplied cheques or receipt of the credits the money passes into the ownership of the bank which becomes a debtor to its customer (the factor's client) on its account with the bank; but this does not affect such a claim. The factor need only show that the bank has received the trust monies without any consideration and it is not necessary to show that the bank still possesses them.[50] Alternatively, the factor may recover the proceeds by a proprietary claim in equity. It is a prerequisite to the operation of such a remedy that a fiduciary relationship exists with regard to the monies claimed; the factor's claim is based on the obligation of his client to hold such proceeds in trust. The advantage of such a claim is that the factor may follow the monies into a mixed fund and charge the fund with the return of the monies claimed.[51]

(b)   Where the monies are no longer in a credit balance on the client's account with the bank

10–41   Unfortunately the bank account of the transgressing insolvent client is unlikely to be in credit. However, if the bank has not given value, the factor

---

[50]   *Agip (Africa) Ltd v Jackson* [1991] 3 W.L.R. 116 and *Lipkin Gorman (A Firm) v Karpnale Ltd* [1991] 3 W.L.R. 10.
[51]   *Agip (Africa) Ltd v Jackson* [1991] 3 W.L.R. 116 at 131.

may also be able to trace the monies through the bank account to others to whom it has been transferred, provided that it can be identified and no value has been given for it by such other parties.[52] The most usual situation will be that the proceeds of the misapplied payments will have been used to honour cheques drawn by the factor's client or used by the bank to reduce the client's overdraft. In either case, the bank, as a *bona fide* purchaser for value of the legal title to the monies, will be able to resist the factor's common law claim or its equitable proprietary claim. Furthermore, the principles of equity do not allow the tracing of monies through an overdrawn bank account whether the account was overdrawn before or after the monies were paid in.[53]

However, there still remains the possibility that the factor may recover **10–42** from the bank as constructive trustee of the proceeds of their misapplied customer payments if it can be shown that the bank, before it collected or received the proceeds, knew of the breach of trust on the part of the client. The courts will not extend the responsibilities of trustees and their liabilities for breach of trust to their bankers, unless, with knowledge of the trustee's lack of probity, they receive some part of the trust funds or assist in the trustee's dishonest act.[54] The question then is what degree of knowledge must be ascribed to the bank in order to fix it with the liability of a constructive trustee. It is here that the courts, having distinguished between a knowing *recipient* and one who knowingly assists the dishonest act—that is *an accessory*.[55]

It now appears that liability as a knowing recipient will not depend upon **10–43** dishonesty of the recipient, but will be strict liability based on receipt and actual or *constructive* knowledge.[56] However, the bank will be treated as a recipient only if it has received some benefit from the receipt. This means generally that it will be so treated only if it has applied the funds received to a reduction in its customer's overdraft. Where the bank has received no such benefit, it may be treated as an accessory, provided that it had actual or inferred knowledge of the client's breach of trust before it collected the cheques or received the transfers representing the proceeds and acted with dishonesty. It now appears to be established that the knowledge must be *actual* knowledge or:

(i) knowledge that the bank would have obtained but for wilfully shutting its eyes to the obvious; or

---

[52] *Banque Belge pour l'Etranger* v *Hambrouk* [1921] 1 K.B. 321.
[53] *Bishopsgate Investment Management Ltd* v *Homan* [1994] 3 W.L.R. 1270.
[54] *Barnes* v *Addy* (1874) 9 Ch. App. 244.
[55] *Royal Brunei Airlines SDN BHD* v *Philip Tan Kok Ming* [1995] 2 A.C. 378. See also *Twinsectra Ltd* v *Yardley* [2002] A.C. 164 in which their Lordships appeared to rely heavily on the *Royal Brunei* case.
[56] *per* Lord Millett *Twinsectra Ltd* v *Yardley* [2002] A.C. 164 at para.105.

      (ii) knowledge that the bank would have obtained but for wilfully failing to make such enquiries as an honest and reasonable man would make.

For this purpose, it appears that dishonesty means more than mere negligence or recklessness, but acting with conscious impropriety; and such impropriety may include deliberately closing ones eyes, or deliberately failing to ask questions, to avoid learning something that one would rather not know.[57] In particular, it should be noted that an example of such impropriety is the participation in a transaction in the knowledge that it includes misapplication of trust assets to the detriment of the beneficiary of the trust (*i.e.* in the circumstances here considered, the factor).[58]

10–44   The bank is likely to have strong grounds to defend against such a claim. Unless the bank had been notified by the factor of particular items that are trust monies before the bank was required by the client to collect them or before the relevant credits came in (*i.e.* actual knowledge on the part of the bank), it is likely to claim that knowledge of the existence of the factoring agreement (even if it is said to cover the client's sales) should not be sufficient to fix the bank with inferred knowledge because:

      (i) in a stream of frequent relatively small transactions the bank cannot as a practical matter be expected to examine every cheque or credit and it should be able to rely on s.4 of the Cheques Act 1957 (which gives bankers protection in respect of a cheque collected in good faith for a customer even where the customer's title to the cheque is defective);

      (ii) the bank is entitled (and in fact obliged) to treat its customer's mandate at its face value except in extreme cases;

      (iii) in the absence of knowledge of fraud it must comply with the mandate; and

      (iv) the bank cannot be expected to be suspicious of its customer.

Conclusions regards claims against third parties other than guarantors or indemnifiers

10–45   The factor's rights to recover from third parties is clear except in the situation which most frequently arises: where no recovery from directors or other guarantors is possible and the bank has a defence of *bona fide* purchaser of the legal title of the monies for value. The principal uncertainty

---

[57] *per* Lord Nicholls *Royal Brunei Airlines SDN BHD v Philip Tan Kok Ming* [1995] 2 A.C. 378 at p.389 and quoted approvingly by Lord Hoffman in *Twinsectra*.
[58] *Royal Brunei Airlines SDN BHD v Philip Tan Kok Ming* [1995] 2 A.C. 378.

arises from the fact that all the cases, in which a bank's liability as constructive trustee has been considered, have concerned substantial sums of money represented by few transactions. It is not clear what the court's attitude would be in the case where the bank was aware of the factoring agreement but not of the particular items; would the court consider that the bank had closed its eyes to the obvious? It seems unlikely and, in any case, it is now standard practice for bankers to insist on a disclaimer of responsibility (except as regards specific items of which it has been put on notice) in the granting of waivers. In view of the most recent cases and the limitation of the degree of knowledge required to create the bank as a constructive trustee (unless it is a dishonest recipient), factors should not be confident of recovering from this source. However, as the chance of recovery increases with the degree of knowledge, it is advisable for factors to make their client's bankers aware not only of the factoring agreement *but also its terms and in particular the trust provisions.* Factors will also need to continue to monitor their clients with the utmost vigilance.

Factor to have power of attorney

It may be necessary for the factor to act quickly without having to call **10–46** upon his client to deal with the formalities for securing and perfecting his rights and interests. In the case of an insolvent client, an officer with authority to sign may not be available nor may the trustee, liquidator, receiver or administrator wish to co-operate. Therefore, it is normal, either within the factoring agreement itself or by a separate document, for the factor and the directors and other officers of the factor to be appointed jointly and severally to be the attorney or attorneys of the client for the purpose of executing any document requisite for this purpose. In this way, the factor may (for example) effect a legal assignment or assignation in his own office and give notice or intimation to the debtor without delay. Such powers normally include the authority:

(1) to institute or defend proceedings in the client's name;

(2) to complete and endorse negotiable instruments in the name of the client where such instruments relate to factored debts;

(3) to resolve disputes with the client's customers and to complete the client's uncompleted contracts of sale or for services; and

(4) to do such other things as are requisite to procure the performance of the client's obligations under the factoring agreement.

Any such power of attorney should be stated to be irrevocable. Where an **10–47** irrevocable power of attorney is given to secure a proprietary interest, the power is not to be revoked:

(1) by the donor unilaterally without the consent of the donee; or

(2) by the death of the donee, or in the case of an incorporated donee, by its winding-up or dissolution.[59]

Thus, with an irrevocable power of attorney in the factoring agreement the factor may continue to perfect his title to debts, already vested in him, to negotiate instruments and to complete the client's contracts from which factored debts have arisen after the bankruptcy, liquidation of or the appointment of a receiver or administrator to his client.

7. VALUE ADDED TAX

10–48 Factoring agreements usually provide that the value of the debts purchased by the factor should include the amount of any value added tax payable by the debtor which is applicable to the goods and services giving rise to such invoices. In effect, the factor is, when paying the purchase price of debts to the client, including in his payments the client's output tax. VAT may affect the factor in two other aspects of the business and may need to be provided for in the agreement.

VAT and the factor's charges

10–49 In the past the authorities have taken a view of the substance of factoring transactions where the factor has the responsibility of administering the accounts in respect of the factored debts. As a result, in such cases (which have been referred to by HM Revenue and Customs as "mainline factoring"), it has been accepted that the factor provides a service which is a taxable supply and the position as regards the factor's charges has been as follows:

(1) value added tax at the standard rate is applied to the administration or service charges; and

(2) the discount charges, being for the provision of finance (albeit by way of early payment on account of the purchase price of the debts sold to the factor), are charges for exempt supplies.

10–50 More recently it had been mooted that, as the ownership of the factored debts vests in the factor, his accounting for, and collection of, the debts is for himself and not the clients. On this reasoning, the administration or service charge should not be taxable. However, there are significant interests

---

[59] Powers of Attorney Act 1971, s.4.

in the collection of the debts retained by the client: the incidence of the discounting charges (which normally accrue until collection) and, in the case of recourse factoring, the avoidance of bad debt losses. In this respect the factor is providing a service to his client; and this supports the view that value added tax should continue to be applied to the administration or service charges, provided that such charges are actually charged to the client *and not effected as a reduction from the value of the debts in determining their purchase price.*

The sale of debts by the client to the factor is a supply; but it is an exempt supply.[60] It is apprehended that the recourse of a debt, if effected by way of repurchase by the client and not by way of a guarantee by the client of payment of the debt, would also by an exempt supply by the factor to the client.　**10–51**

A factor providing this type of factoring service is partially exempt, and the taxable inputs must be allocated between taxable and exempt outputs (according to the regulations in force[61]); only input taxes attributable to taxable supplies by the factor will be recoverable. The regulations provide for the recovery of input tax in full where it can be specifically identified as relating to a taxable outward supply and for no recovery where the input specifically relates to an exempt supply (or relates to an activity other than a taxable supply). The remainder of the inputs are to be allocated to taxable and exempt supplies proportionately or by some other method considered by the commissioners to be fair and reasonable.　**10–52**

It is in most circumstances impracticable to allocate the factor's taxable inputs (such as telephone charges and computer supplies) between the administration of debtor accounts and the accounts relating to the provision of funds to the client. Accordingly, virtually all the factor's input taxes need to be allocated by some method to be agreed between the factor and the Commissioners. Some factors whose business is entirely of the nature, which is referred to above[62] as "mainline," have been able to obtain agreement that the recovery should be proportionate to the number of data processing transactions for each of the activities.　**10–53**

All charges for all other forms of factoring, including invoice discounting and agency factoring, are exempt; and where the factor provides only such services, no input tax will be recoverable. If the factor provides both types of service, then he will need to reach agreement with HM Revenue and Customs as to a fair and reasonable method of allocation.　**10–54**

---

[60] EC 6th Directive, Art.13B and see H.M.C.E. leaflet 701/29/92 para.3. In a recent case, *Capital One Bank Europe PLC v Revenue & Customs Commissioners* (VADT19238) (2005), assignments of receivables were held not to be supplies at all; but that case may be distinguished from the assignments under a factoring agreement because it related to assignments by way of security and not a sale and purchase as in a factoring agreement.

[61] Value Added Tax Act 1994, ss. 4(2) and 26(3).

[62] At para.10–49 above.

Value Added Tax bad debt refunds

10–55   The procedure now in force for refunds of value added tax included in bad debts provides that such a refund will be available to a business which has accounted for, and paid tax on, any such supply made for a consideration in money if:

(i) the whole or any part of the consideration has been written off as a bad debt;

(ii) at least six months has passed since the due date for payment of the supply; and

(iii) the amount to be paid for the supply is at least equal to the open market value.[63]

The amount of the refund is the amount of value added tax included in the written off consideration. Such a refund is available only if the supply was made at, or at less than, its open market value and, in the case of goods, title has passed from the supplier.

10–56   The relief is available only to the supplier of the taxable goods and services. The factor, although having paid the client the equivalent of the output tax in his payment of the purchase price of the debt,[64] is unable to recover it if the debtor is insolvent. If the debt has been purchased by the factor with recourse to the client, then the client will be obliged either to repurchase the debt or to pay the amount of it to the factor under his guarantee of due payment by the debtor. In the latter case, the debt will become vested in the client by subrogation and, in either case, the client will be able to recover the tax for himself. In the case of debt purchased without recourse, it is normal for the factoring agreement to provide for the repurchase of the debt by the client where the relief is available so that the client may recover the relief. However, in order to achieve the purpose of the non-recourse arrangement for protection of the client against bad debts, it is necessary that there should be no consideration for the repurchase other than an undertaking to pass on to, and meanwhile in trust for, the factor by the client of any recoveries in respect of the debt including the tax refund and any dividends from the estate. If the repurchase is affected on this basis then, although the client has been paid by the factor for the debt and has not paid the factor for the repurchase, the client will be able to write off the unrecovered consideration for the goods or services and thus qualify for a refund. The reason for this is that the consideration which the client has received from the factor in the first place is *not* the consideration for the

---

[63] Value Added Tax Act 1994, ss.36(1) to 36(4); Finance Act 1997, s.39 and Finance Act 1998, s.23.
[64] See para.10–48 above.

supply but for the assignment of the debt. However, in order that this should apply, it is important that the factoring agreement should not provide for the automatic purchase of the underlying goods by the factor along with the debt[65]; if the agreement so provided, then the consideration paid by the factor would be consideration for the goods in addition to the debt and there would be no write-off by the client. These arrangements enable the factor to recover indirectly the value added tax included in his bad debts.

The cash accounting scheme and the factor's client

The cash accounting scheme[66] for value added tax which applies to small **10–57** businesses allows the business to account for output tax on the receipt of payment for the supply of goods and services instead of at invoice date. This is of great benefit to such small businesses because, not only does the timing difference provide for later payment of the VAT, but the arrangement also relieves them from having to claim refunds in respect of bad debts. In the past HM Revenue and Customs were willing, for the purposes of the scheme, to look upon factoring as if the factor made loans to the business; as a result a factor's client using the scheme accounted for VAT only on receipt of payment from customers by the factor. By the amendment to the scheme, which took effect from August 1, 1997, VAT must be brought into account for the full invoice value when each debt is assigned to the factor. This will mean a substantial impact on the cash flow of some small businesses using factors.

8. THE CONSUMER CREDIT ACT 1974 AND FACTORING

In order to consider the possible effect of the provisions of the Consumer **10–58** Credit Act 1974 on a factor's agreement with his client and on his relations with debtors, three points must be borne in mind. First, a consumer credit agreement under the Act exists where credit not exceeding £25,000[67] is provided to an individual (which includes a partnership); secondly, "creditor" includes an assignee[68]; and thirdly, the Act does not regulate a consumer credit agreement for fixed sum credit under which the number of payments to be made by the debtor does not exceed four and those

---

[65] See also para.10–26 above.
[66] A taxable person will be eligible to operate the scheme if he has reasonable grounds for believing that his taxable turnover (excluding VAT) in the year just starting will not exceed £350,000. VAT Regulations 1995 (SI 1995/2518), reg.58(1).
[67] Consumer Credit Act 1974, s.8(2) and Consumer Credit (Increase of Monetary Limits) (Amendments) Order 1998 (SI 1998/996).
[68] Consumer Credit Act 1974, s.189(1).

payments are to be made within 12 months of the date of the agreement.[69] Those conditions will apply to virtually all debts the subject of an agreement for the factoring of trade debts.

The effect upon the factor's relations with the client

10–59   The purchase of debts is considered not to constitute the extension of credit to the seller of the debts provided that he has no *repayment* obligation. Even if the seller (the factor's client) guarantees payment by the debtor under provisions for recourse in the factoring agreement,[70] it is not considered that provision of credit is involved; in such a case, the recourse is for *payment* of the debt and not for *repayment* of an advance. It is likely (but not certain) that the framing of the rights of recourse under the agreement as a repurchase (and not a guarantee)[71] would not be considered a repayment obligation in this respect. Therefore, as far as the factor's relations with his client are concerned, provided that:

(1)   he provides his factoring or discounting services only for corporate clients; or

(2)   his agreement provides for the purchase of debts, he does not make loans and his recourse is framed as a guarantee, the agreements will be outside the scope of the Act and accordingly will not be regulated (even if his unrecovered prepayments never exceed £25,000).

10–60   If the factor provides his services for partnerships and sole traders and his recourse is framed as a repurchase, it is possible (but unlikely) that his agreement could be considered as a "personal credit agreement"[72] and fall within the scope of the Act. In such a case, the credit would be considered to be "running account credit".[73] However, it is most unusual in these days for a factor to enter into any agreement under which no more than £25,000 would be outstanding by way of unrecovered prepayments at any time, and such an agreement would be outside the definition of a "consumer credit agreement" and, accordingly, would not be regulated.[74]

10–61   In circumstances where the funds to be provided by the factor will at some time exceed the limit, this must be apparent from the outset. In this connection, the fact that the factor has not placed a prepayment limit of £25,000

---

[69] *ibid.*, s.16(5); Consumer Credit (Exempt Agreements) (No.2) Orders 1985 (SI 1985/757), art.3(1)(a)(i).
[70] See para.10–29 above.
[71] *ibid.*
[72] Consumer Credit Act 1974, s.8(1).
[73] *ibid.*, s.10(1)(a).
[74] See para.10–58 above.

or less on the client is not sufficient to take the agreement outside the scope of regulation on these grounds alone; a consumer credit agreement will be a regulated agreement if:

> "*at the time that the agreement is made* it is probable, having regard to the terms of the agreement and any other relevant considerations, that the debit balance will not at any time rise above £5000."[75]

This limit has been subsequently raised to £25,000 by statutory instrument.[76] If the agreement is to avoid regulation on the grounds of this limit, it should also avoid provisions by which the charges to the client increase or other provisions favourable to the factor come into effect if that limit is exceeded.[77]

The factor's relations with debtors

Although the Act includes assignees as creditors,[78] the contracts giving rise to the factored debts will not constitute regulated agreements if they are payable, as is usual in factoring or invoice discounting, in one amount in each case.[79]   **10–62**

Ancillary credit business[80]

It is usually considered requisite for a factor or invoice discounter to obtain a licence for each of the following ancillary businesses[81]:   **10–63**

(1) Debt adjusting (generally negotiating with a creditor or the owner of goods on hire on behalf of the debtor or hirer regarding the discharge of his obligations).

(2) Debt counselling (giving advice to debtors or hirers about the liquidation of debts under consumer credit or hire agreements).

(3) Debt collecting.

It is also considered advisable in most cases for a factor to obtain a licence for credit brokerage in view of possible introductions by their staff to other companies carrying on consumer credit or consumer hire business.

---

[75] Consumer Credit Act 1974, s.10(3)(b)(iii).
[76] Consumer Credit (Increase of Monetary Limits) Order 1998 (SI 1998/996).
[77] Consumer Credit Act 1974, s.10(3)(b)(ii).
[78] *ibid.*, s.189(1).
[79] See n.69 above.
[80] Consumer Credit Act 1974, Pt X.
[81] Consumer Credit Act 1974, s.146(6)(a) by which assignees are excluded from the exemption for regulation of this type of business.

10–64 If the factor is a *credit reference agency*, then it should be licensed for that ancillary business. Whether or not it is a credit reference agency is a question of fact; and it will be such an agency if it were to collect credit information *for the purpose of* furnishing other persons with it.[82]

Factoring transactions not normally subject to regulation

10–65 The preceding paragraphs are a summary of the probable effect of the Consumer Credit Act 1974 on factoring transactions. As it appears unlikely that such transactions will be regulated under the Act, no attempt has been made in this treatise to analyse or explain the provisions of the Act in more detail. If the factor's method of operation is such that his transactions are likely to be regulated, he will need to obtain detailed advice.

9. THE DATA PROTECTION ACT 1998 AND FACTORS

10–66 In essence the act provides that any business obtaining or maintaining data regarding individuals must comply with the principles laid down by the act. For this purpose "data" means information which is processed by means of equipment operated automatically or is recorded with the intention that it should be so processed or is or is intended to be part of a filing system. "Personal data" means data relating to a living individual who can be identified as relating to it. The principles require all personal data to be:

- fairly and lawfully processed;

- obtained only for specified and lawful purposes;

- adequate, relevant and not excessive;

- accurate and up to date;

- not kept for longer than is necessary;

- processed in accordance with individual's rights;

- safe and secure;

- not transferred to non—EU countries without adequate protection for freedom and rights.

10–67 The act applies to data only relating to individuals and not that relating to any corporate body (including any company or limited liability partnership

---

[82] *ibid.*, s.145(8).

incorporated under the Limited Partnership Act 2000 (an "LLP")). There-fore, so far as factors are concerned compliance with the principles will require regular monitoring on its part of the manner in which it uses information supplied to it by clients and which it gathers from third parties (for example, credit reference agencies) about any of the following:

- the factor's clients who are individuals or partnerships (other than LLPs);

- the clients' customers who are individuals or such partnerships;

- any individual guarantors; and

- directors or members of corporate clients.

The Data Protection Act and factoring agreements

Consequently, additional provisions are necessary in and relating to the **10–68** factoring agreements as follows:

Application for any agreements (including those with corporate bodies)

When application is made for a factoring agreement, the factor should **10–69** procure from the principal or each partner of the applicant (in the case of an applicant not being a corporate body) or, otherwise, each director or member of the applicant an acknowledgement and consent relating to any data held about that individual, which should include the following:

(1) that the individual acknowledges and consents that the factor may at any time obtain data from a third party including any credit reference agency about the individual;

(2) that the data will be held by the factor and used for the purpose of considering the application and, if an agreement is entered into, for the factor's consideration of the continuance of it and the terms of such continuance;

(3) that the factor may use the data for training or marketing purposes and that, for these purposes, may monitor and/or record telephone calls; and

(4) that the factor may pass any of the data to any group company, any of the factor's bankers, solicitors, accountants or insurers and to trade associations for the purpose of statistical analyses of financial services or for the prevention of fraud.

The applicant should also acknowledge that he knows that he should call a specific department of the factor if it wishes to have a copy of any data held by the factor about him or details of other parties from or to whom data may be passed. He should also acknowledge that he should apply in writing for such information and that a fee may be payable.

Provisions to be included in all factoring agreements

10–70   In all factoring agreements (including those with companies and LLPs), the factor should procure that the client warrants and undertakes, in relation to any living individual including a debtor or a partner, shareholder, director or other officer (or in the case of an LLP a member) of a debtor or a person who has, or may give, a guarantee or indemnity in respect of the obligations of a debtor under a supply contract that:

(1)   the client has strictly complied and will, until the end of the agreement and the discharge of all its obligations, strictly comply with the provisions of the Data Protection Act 1998 including the principles contained in the schedules to that Act; and

(2)   that the client has disclosed and will disclose to any such living individual that the client may at any time pass to the factor data which the client may hold in respect of that individual.

It appears that, in the case of invoice discounting or any form of undisclosed factoring, it is sufficient for compliance with the principles laid down by the act for the client to refer in such a disclosure to a debtor that the data has been passed to the client's "financier". It is apparent that the factor will need to approve the form of disclosure by the client to such individuals and to monitor the continued disclosure while the factoring agreement continues.

10–71   The following acknowledgements and consents are required in agreements with partnerships and sole traders for the purposes of the act but are also normally considered requisite in all other factoring agreements:

(1)   A confirmation by the client that by his entering into the agreement it has consented to the making by the factor of searches or other enquiries at credit reference agencies about the client and, if it is a company, its directors and other officers and, if it is an LLP, its members.

(2)   A confirmation by the client that it is aware that credit reference agencies may make a record of such searches which may be seen by others and used in their lending, credit and purchasing decisions about the client or any of the individuals referred to in point (1) above and that they be so used for the prevention of fraud or money laundering.

(3)   An acknowledgement that the factor my disclose any details of the

factoring agreement or any transaction under it or any other information held by the factor in name of the client to:

- any credit reference agency;
- any trade register for the purpose of credit decisions, fraud prevention or the tracing of debtors;
- any person who may provide a service to the factor (including his insurers) or who may act as his agents on the understanding that such information will be retained by any of them in confidence;
- any other person for the purpose of the factor's business;
- any assignee of the factor; or
- any guarantor or indemnifier of the client's obligations to the factor.

(4) An acknowledgement that the factor may monitor and/or record telephone calls with the client.

(5) The client's authority for the factor to provide the factor's bankers and auditors with such information in the factor's possession relating to the client's affairs as any of them may require at any time and for the factor to obtain from the client's bankers and auditors any information in their possession which factor may require regarding the state of the client's accounts or his financial affairs. This last authority will require the client to warrant that he has given the requisite authority to his bankers and auditors to provide the information.

Additional provisions for agreements with sole traders or partnerships (other than LLPs)

All sole traders and partners of partnerships (being clients of a actor) **10–72** should also acknowledge that they have the right to prevent the factor from getting in touch with any of them or passing information about them to others or using it for marketing purposes. The factor should undertake to comply with any such request. The client should also acknowledge that he has the right to be given details of any credit reference agencies and others from whom the factor may receive and to whom he may pass information about the client.

10. MISCELLANEOUS TERMS

Inspection and production of client's records and accounts

It is usual for any factoring agreement to include provisions whereby: **10–73**

(1) the client is obliged to submit to the factor copies of his annual accounts and other financial statements produced; and

(2) the factor is allowed to inspect the accounting records, together with supporting documents, of the client at the client's premises.

The provision for the submission of accounts in some cases may extend to monthly or quarterly management accounts, and to require their production if they are not otherwise produced. The provisions for the inspection of records and documents sometimes include only such records and documents as relate to the debts sold or to be sold to the factor. They would include copy invoices, orders, proof of delivery, remittance advices and correspondence with debtors. These records and documents may be necessary for the factor as evidence of the existence of debts in his collection procedures; the agreement will normally provide for their production and delivery to the factor and for the ownership of them to vest in him.[83] Some factors require the right to inspect any of the books, accounts, records and correspondence that they may in their discretion require to see and such wider provisions may be necessary for the factor to ensure that the debts sold to him are not subject to any set-off or other encumbrance. In the case of invoice discounting, where no notices are sent to the debtors, it is usual for the factor to require that a note should be made on all records held by the client relating to the debts that the debts have been sold to the factor. This provides some protection against a fraudulent second sale of the debts by the client.

Termination

10–74 The agreement usually provides for termination on notice of an agreed period by either side. It is also usual for the factor to provide that the agreement may be terminated immediately on notice on the occasion of events such as a serious or persistent breach by the client or the client's insolvency or his ceasing to carry on his business. It is also usual for the agreement to provide for its immediate termination upon the insolvency of a guarantor or a breach of an undertaking given by a third party on which the factor is relying. The position of the factor on the appointment of a receiver or administrator in respect of a client company or its winding-up or the bankruptcy of an individual client is dealt with in Ch.11.

Repurchase of debts on client's breach or insolvency

10–75 The factoring agreement should provide for the right of the factor to withhold all payments and (at the factor's option) for the repurchase by the

---

[83] See para.10–25 above.

client of outstanding debts vesting in the factor (at a repurchase price equivalent to the amounts notified or in the original offer) when any event occurs giving him the right to immediate termination *whether or not he has exercised that right*. This last provision is necessary because it is not always considered advisable for the factor to terminate the agreement; if the business is continuing, further debts may be created and be assigned to the factor. The right to require the repurchase of the debts is particularly important if the factor holds collateral security by way of guarantees or a charge on assets of a corporate client; the repurchase price of the debts will normally be a great deal more in aggregate than the unpaid balance of the purchase price owed to the client and will thus create a net actual liability to the factor on the basis of which the factor may call upon the guarantor to pay or enforce his collateral security. On the other hand, a factor, whose insolvent client is indebted to the factor on another account (*e.g.* for supplies to that client by another client of the factor), should not require such repurchase until that other indebtedness has been set off against any credit balance owing by the factor to the client.[84] Once the repurchase has been effected, the factor will become the client's creditor on the factoring account; there will then be nothing owing by the factor to the client against which to set off the debt on that other account.

Many factors include provisions for the client to pay additional charges in the event of a "termination event". Such events are those which normally give the factor the right to immediate termination of the agreement and include a serious breach of the client's obligations under the agreement, any form of insolvency of the client and the termination of his business. The additional charges may be, in the case of invoice discounting or agency factoring, an increase in the administration charge to cover the factor's expense of having himself to collect the debts; in the case of a factoring arrangement in which the factor has the duty to collect from the outset, the charge maybe an *ad valorem* fee on the sums collected after the event. It is important that, if the additional charge is to be brought into effect following a breach of the agreement by the client, it should be based on a reasonable estimate of the additional costs to be incurred by the factor; otherwise, it may be held by the court to be a penalty and unenforceable. A penalty is a provision for the payment of an additional sum designed to be a threat held over the head of a party to a contract to secure compliance by that party as opposed to a genuine pre-estimate of the other party's likely loss on a breach by that party.[85] The unenforceability of the penalty does not preclude the factor, as the innocent party, from recovering compensation for actual loss. It is also possible that a provision for the payment of a minimum annual

10–76

---

[84] See para.11–83 below.
[85] *Widnes Foundry v Cellulose Acetate Co* [1933] A.C. 20. For a fuller discussion of the topic of damages as a remedy for breach of contract see Goode, *Commercial Law* (3rd ed. 2004) pp.115 *et seq.*

administration charge[86] may be considered to be a penalty if the breach and consequent termination were to take effect very early in the relevant year so that the charge would be out of proportion to the likely damage to the factor. However, it is to be noted that default interest which exceeded the amounts due under an agreement by a moderate amount was held not to be a penalty[87]; it was the view of the judge that a 1 per cent increase was consistent only with the increase in the credit risk caused by the default.

---

[86] See para.3–33 above.
[87] *Lordsvale Finance plc v Bank of Zambia* [1996] W.L.R. 688.

CHAPTER 11

INSOLVENCY OF THE CLIENT

In this chapter there are considered the rights and obligations of the factor **11–01** both in respect of the continuation of the factoring agreement and in respect of debts already vesting in him on the occurrence of the most usual events on the insolvency of the client. These events are the appointment of an administrative receiver or administrator to a corporate client, the winding-up of a corporate client or a partnership and the bankruptcy of an individual client or partnership. Also, there is considered the effect of a voluntary arrangement by a client under Pts I and VIII of the Insolvency Act 1986.

The Enterprise Act 2002 has introduced profound changes to the insol- **11–02** vency regimes mentioned above, in respect of both companies and individuals. The most far-reaching may be the efforts to advance the administration procedure as the principal regime for rescuing of companies in financial difficulties. This is to be achieved by a two-pronged approach. There is now, with effect from September 15, 2003, a new out of court route into administration, intended to be quicker, cheaper and less bureaucratic, encouraging those involved to seek advice at any early stage when there is a better chance of achieving a rescue. The Government's stated intention was to move away from the administrative receivership, seen as destructive of value in businesses and essentially biased towards banks and other debenture holders, towards the administration which is a collective procedure having a primary purpose of rescuing the company as a going concern. To encourage the use of administrators it will no longer be possible for a debenture holder, whose charge was created after September 15, 2003, to appoint an administrative receiver subject to six exceptional cases which are unlikely to be met in factoring. The debenture holders only out of court option will now be to appoint an administrator under para.14 Sch.B1 of the Insolvency Act 1986, provided the charge is a "qualifying floating charge" as therein defined. A floating charge qualifies for this purpose if it is created by an instrument which either:

1.   states that para.14 applies to the floating charge; or

2.   purports to empower the holder of the floating charge to appoint an administrator of the company; or

3. purports to empower the holder to appoint an administrative receiver within the meaning given by s.29(2) of the Insolvency Act 1986; (or the equivalent in Scotland).

11–03   As part of the overall scheme Crown preference, that is the right of HM Revenue & Customs to be paid (within certain limits) out of the realisations from charges which as created were floating charges, has been abolished with retrospective effect in any corporate insolvencies commencing on or after September 15, 2003. Other non-Crown preferential debts are unaffected—in practical terms mainly obligations to employees up to certain limits and contributions to occupational pension schemes.

11–04   One consequence of these changes will be to give floating charge holders with pre September 15, 2003 charges a windfall in the form of the previously preferential Crown debt, whilst still allowing them to appoint an administrative receiver, who owes only limited duties to unsecured creditors and other stakeholders, such as guarantors.[1]

11–05   Linked to the abolition of Crown preference is a new concept of "top-slicing" which will apply to all formal corporate insolvency procedures where there is a floating charge created after September 15, 2003. This therefore includes the six exceptional cases where a floating charge holder will continue to be able to appoint an administrative receiver.[2]

11–06   Briefly, the appointed insolvency practitioner will be required to set aside, for distribution to unsecured creditors, a prescribed part of the net realisations of assets subject to any floating (but not fixed) charge. The amount of the prescribed part has been fixed by regulation as follows:

Net realisations less than £10,000	Nil
Net realisations less than £600,000	50% up to £10,000 plus 20% thereafter up to a maximum prescribed part of £600,000.

Apart from the prescribed minimum below which there is no top-slice distribution, the appointed insolvency practitioner has a discretion not to distribute if he considers the cost to be disproportionate to the benefit for unsecured creditors.

1. RECEIVERSHIP

11–07   It is unlikely that the appointment of a receiver in relation to a specific asset of a corporate client, other than the debt owed to the client by the factor

---

[1] *Standard Chartered Bank Ltd v Walker* [1982] 1 W.L.R. 1410, *Downsview Nominees Ltd v First City Corporation Ltd* [1993] A.C. 295, *Medforth v Blake* [2000] Ch. 86 [1999] B.C.C. 771.
[2] s.176A of the Insolvency Act 1986.

himself, will directly affect the rights and obligations of the parties to the factoring agreement; it may, however, be the cause of some other event that may affect them such as administrative receivership, the appointment of an administrator or winding-up. The effect of the enforcement of a charge over the debt owing by the factor to the client is dealt with below[3] but, as the appointment of a receiver by the court or under statutory powers[4] in relation to the affairs of a client is rarely met by a factor, this part deals only with the effect of the appointment in relation to a client company of an administrative receiver out of court by virtue of a floating charge.[5]

Administrative receivers

"Administrative receivers" are a special class of receivers created and **11–08** given powers and status by the Insolvency Act 1986.[6] The right to appoint an administrative receiver is limited to the holder of a charge which, *as created*, was a floating charge[7]; the appointment must be over the whole or substantially the whole of the company's property or of what remains after the appointment of a receiver to a specific part of the property.[8] In order to have the privilege of appointing an administrative receiver (and the right to forestall the making of an administration order[9] and the appointment of an administrator[10]), it is now not uncommon for a creditor of a company taking security on a specific asset to include a floating charge on all other assets of the company; and sometimes, in order not to preclude the raising of funds elsewhere by the company, such a charge may be specified in the instrument itself as ranking behind all other prior and subsequent charges on the company's assets.[11]

Effect of the appointment of an administrative receiver

Although the Insolvency Act 1986 has, in respect of administrative **11–09** receivers, extended the duties and powers which were previously conferred on receivers and managers appointed in respect of floating charges, in many

---

[3] See paras 11–27 to 11–32 below.
[4] Law of Property Act 1925, s.103. Goode, *Legal Problems of Credit and Security* (3rd ed., 2003), paras 4–02 *et seq.*
[5] For a full review of the law relating to all types of receivers of companies reference should be made to Lightman & Moss, *The Law of Receivers and Administrators of Companies* (3rd ed., 2000).
[6] Pt III and Sch.1.
[7] Insolvency Act 1986, s.29(2)(a).
[8] *ibid.*, ss.29(2)(a) and 29(2)(b).
[9] *ibid.*, ss.9(3) and 11 and see para.11–38 below.
[10] *ibid*, s.13.
[11] Sometimes referred to as "lightweight floating charges"; see Oditah, *Legal Aspects of Receivable Financing* (1991), pp.118–124 and Goode, *Principles of Corporate Insolvency Law* (3rd ed., 2005), p.257.

respects the case law which governed the rights and duties of the receivers and managers still applies to those of the administrative receivers. The charge will in most circumstances be fixed on real property, investments, intellectual property and debts and floating on other assets such as stock and work in progress.[12] The effect of the appointment will include the following:

(1) The floating element of the charge will *crystallise*, if crystallisation has not occurred beforehand on some other event giving rise to it according to the instrument of charge. The charge will thus become fixed on all assets and attach thereto.

(2) In the absence of a resolution for the winding-up of the company or of a court order to that effect, the receiver is deemed to be the agent of the company irrespective of any provision to that effect in the terms of the instrument of charge or of his appointment.[13] He is personally liable on any contracts entered into by him except where the contract itself otherwise provides.[14]

(3) Unlike the position in a winding-up, the directors' powers do not cease and they may continue to exercise them in relation to any property or rights of which the receiver has not taken possession to the extent that they do not interfere with the receiver's rights.[15]

(4) However, over property of the company in respect of which the administrative receiver has been appointed (or where such powers would derogate from the powers of the administrative receiver), the powers of the directors of the company are suspended.[16] The administrative receiver's powers will include the power to carry on the business[17] and to realise the assets of the company.[18] Whilst he is agent of the company, his powers are limited by the Memorandum and Articles of the company but a person dealing with him

---

[12] For the difference between fixed and floating charges see paras 8–22 to 8–24 above and Lightman & Moss, *The Law of Receivers and Administrators of Companies* (3rd ed., 2000), Ch.3.
[13] Insolvency Act 1986, s.44(1)(a).
[14] *ibid.*, s.44(1)(b).
[15] *Newhart Development Ltd v Co-operative Commercial Bank Ltd* [1978] Q.B. 814 at 819; *cf. Tudor Grange Holdings v Citibank NA* [1992] Ch. 53.
[16] *Re Emmadart Ltd* [1979] Ch. 540. The same principles apply under Scots law; see *Independent Pension Trustee Ltd v AW Construction Co Ltd* (1997) S.L.T. (OH) 1105.
[17] His power to do so after the commencement of any winding up of the company is not certain as he then ceases to be the agent of the company (*Gosling v Gaskell* [1897] A.C. 575); for the subsequent position see para.11–35 below.
[18] The powers are set out in Sch.1 to the Insolvency Act 1986 and by s.42(1) of the Act are deemed to be included in the instrument of charge by which he is appointed (whether or not they are so specified). For full details of his powers see Lightman & Moss, *the Law of Receivers and Administrators of Companies* (3rd ed., 2000), Chs 8 and 9.

in good faith and for value is not prejudiced by his acting *ultra vires*.[19]

Effect of appointment on company's pre-existing contracts

The extent to which an administrative receiver (in his capacity as such and **11-10** not personally) may be liable to perform the pre-existing contracts of the company, to which he is appointed, appears still to be developing in case law; some of the cases relating to the obligations of receivers and managers which were decided before the introduction of administrative receivers, having been quoted with approval in later cases, still apply.

The appointment of an administrative receiver does not terminate the **11-11** company's normal commercial contracts[20]; and an administrative receiver has no statutory right to disclaim unprofitable contracts such as is provided for liquidators by the Insolvency Act 1986.[21] Except in the circumstances mentioned below,[22] he may decline to perform any contract of the company in existence before his appointment provided that the repudiation does not affect his realisation of the company's assets or seriously damage its trading prospects.[23] In this respect, an administrative receiver is in a better position than the company itself; if it were not so the security under which he was appointed would be of little effect. In the event of his repudiation of a contract, the other party to it will rank only as an unsecured creditor of the company in respect of damages for the breach.

However, if an administrative receiver adopts a pre-existing contract **11-12** (unless it is varied by mutual consent of the parties), he must adopt all its terms: its burden as well as the benefit. For example, where a receiver adopted a contract for the carriage of goods of the company by road, it was held that the goods were subject to the carrier's general lien to secure a pre-existing debt of the company to the carrier in addition to the receiver's debt.[24] Where a receiver adopted a pre-existing contract for the supply of goods by the company, the customer was able to set off a pre-existing debt of the company to the customer against its debt to the receiver for that supply.[25]

Case law has not fully clarified the circumstances in which the court will **11-13** make an order for the specific performance by an administrative receiver of a pre-existing contract which he has declined to perform. As regards the exercise of any proprietary right, it is apparent that in normal circumstances

---

[19] Insolvency Act 1986, s.42(3). *cf.* Companies Act 1985, ss.35, 35A and 35B introduced by the Companies Act 1989, s.108.
[20] *Parsons v Sovereign Bank of Canada* [1913] A.C. 160.
[21] s.178.
[22] para.11–13 below.
[23] *Airlines Airspares Ltd v Handley Page Ltd* [1970] Ch. 193.
[24] *George Barker Transport Ltd v Eynon* [1974] 1 All E.R. 900.
[25] *Rother Ironworks Ltd v Canterbury Precision Engineers Ltd* [1974] Q.B. 1.

such an order will not be made and an administrative receiver will not be prevented from realising the charged property although, in doing so, he breaches a pre-existing contract of the company; otherwise, the priorities of secured and unsecured creditors would be reversed.[26] Such an order has, however, been made where a purchaser of land of the company had an equitable interest in that land by reason of a contract for its sale to the purchaser binding the company at the time of the administrative receiver's appointment.[27] An administrative receiver was held to be liable to respect another party's preemption right over machinery of the company where the exercise of such a right would not adversely affect the realisation of the company's assets and where damages would not have been an adequate remedy for the other party.[28] The conclusion to be drawn from such cases seems to be that the court will order specific performance only in order to secure to the other party real rights to property of the company which should have priority over the security held by the person who appointed the receiver.

11–14   Furthermore, where damages were considered by the court to be an inadequate remedy for breach by an administrative receiver of a supply contract, the High Court granted a mandatory injunction securing supply on the existing contractual terms by the company in receivership.[29] The case arose from the administrative receiver's disregard of the existing contract and attempt to enforce future supplies, essential for the customer's business, on terms more favourable to the company in receivership. The decision turned on the particular facts of the case but it raises issues (such as the effect of such a decision on the profitability of the receiver's trading) which are beyond our scope.

Factor's rights on the appointment: general

11–15   The factor's rights on the appointment of a receiver to take possession of the property of a client company will depend upon the terms of the factoring agreement. Most usually the agreement will provide for one or more of the following options by the factor:

(1)   to terminate the agreement forthwith by notice; or

(2)   with or without termination of the agreement:

---

[26] *Astor Chemicals Ltd v Synthetic Technology Ltd* [1990] B.C.L.C. 1 at 11.

[27] *Freevale Ltd v Metrostore (Holdings) Ltd* [1984] Ch. 199. In a case in the House of Lords, the same principle was applied under Scots law although it does not recognise equitable principles in relation to proprietary rights. In that case, a floating charge, on crystallisation, was held not to attach to land in respect of which a conveyance, executed by the chargor company and delivered to the purchaser before crystallisation of the charge, had not been *recorded in the Register of Sasines before that time*. *Sharp v Woolwich Building Society* [1998] B.C.C. 115.

[28] *Ash & Newman Ltd v Creative Devices Research Ltd* [1991] B.C.L.C. 403.

[29] *Land Rover Group Ltd v UPF (UK) Ltd* [2002] EWHC 3183.

(a) to refrain from making any further prepayments or other payments to the client until all funds in use have been recovered;

(b) to require that all prepayments should be repaid; or

(c) to have all debts vesting in the factor repurchased for their full invoice value on the basis that they shall not vest in the client until the full amount of the repurchase consideration has been received by the factor.

There is little prospect that, in the present state of the law, the court would make an order for the specific performance of a factoring agreement.[30] **11–16**

In the case of an agreement of the whole turnover type by which the future debts vest in the factor by virtue of an agreement in existence before the creation of the security under which the administrative receiver was appointed, it might be argued that, in the absence of termination of the agreement according to its terms, the factor has a proprietary right (superior to that of the security holder) to debts created by the receiver as agent of the company. On the other hand, all the resources from which such debts are created have been assigned for the benefit of the security holder by the receiver's appointment. If the receiver had been appointed under a charge taken by a person with actual knowledge of an existing factoring agreement (a contractual obligation inconsistent with the creation of the charge) without any consent or agreement by the factor in relation to the charge, then it is likely that the holder of the charge would be restrained from enforcing the charge[31]; in such a situation, the conflict would not arise and the factoring agreement would continue. In any other situation neither (2)(b) nor (2)(c) above will be of much immediate help to the factor. In both those cases, if the factor has prepaid in respect of the outstanding debts purchased, he is likely to become a *creditor*; in the former case, to the extent that his unrecovered prepayments exceed the retention (unpaid balances owed to the client), and in the latter, to the extent that the total amount credited by him in respect of the debts exceeds the retention. The receiver will not be responsible to him and the directors will have no rights in respect of assets with which they would need to deal, if they are to satisfy the factor's demand for repayment. In both cases, however, the factor will be in a position to make a demand on any guarantors without waiting for the final outcome-whether or not the funds in use will be fully recovered from payments by debtors. **11–17**

Whichever of the options above is available to and exercised by the factor, it is usual for the factor to be able to refrain from making further payments **11–18**

---

[30] See para.11–13 above.
[31] See para.8–28 and n.60 thereto above.

to the client until all funds in use have been recovered. The balance of the factor's account in favour of the client will normally be an asset subject to the charge and in the possession of the receiver[32]; accordingly, the amount ultimately payable to the client, after taking into account all recourse and any other set-off, will be payable to the receiver unless by that time he has obtained his discharge. In the event of the receiver's discharge before payment is to be made by the factor, then such payment will fall into the hands of any liquidator subsequently appointed. Invariably, there will be provision in the factoring agreement for additional fees to be charged to the account to compensate the factor for the loss of annual charges and costs caused by the client's insolvency. If these charges exceed a reasonable pre-estimate of loss, they may be challenged as a penalty, and thus irrecoverable by the factor.

Factor's position as regards existing debts

11–19 Assuming that the priorities have been regulated by a waiver or otherwise as described in Ch.8, in all cases the factor's rights *in relation to the debts and related rights*[33] *vesting in him* remain unaltered on the appointment of the receiver. In particular:

(1) the factor's powers to execute legal assignments and to endorse the client's name on negotiable instruments will be unaffected, provided that the power of attorney given to him in the factoring agreement is stated to be irrevocable[34]; and

(2) any trust provisions in the factoring agreement, by which remittances from debtors received by the client are to be held for the account of and sent to the factor, remain in effect.[35]

11–20 The factor may have available to him and may exercise the option of terminating the agreement and re-assigning to the client all outstanding debts. The re-assignment may arise from the nature of the factoring contract; if the contract is for recourse factoring, all the debts will have been purchased by the factor with full recourse. On the other hand, the re-assignment may arise from special provisions in the agreement which come into effect on insolvency as described above. The factor will be an unsecured creditor of the company for the repurchase price of the re-assigned debts except to the extent that the factor may exercise set-off against the unpaid

---

[32] See para.11–27 below.
[33] See paras 10–24 to 10–26 above.
[34] See paras 10–46 and 10–47 above.
[35] See para.10–35 above.

balance of the purchase price of the debts of which the ownership vested in the factor at the time of the receiver's appointment.

Where prepayments have been made and have not been fully recovered on **11–21** the appointment of a receiver, the factor will still be interested in collecting the outstanding debts in order to recover his funds in use. However, the advantage to the factor of having the right to sell the debts back to the client is that he will no longer be responsible for any credit risk. The term in the agreement will provide that the client should repurchase the debts at the amount originally notified or at which they have been offered and this would apply notwithstanding the recovery of a lesser amount; the debts will however, *remain the factor's property until the repurchase price of all of them has been paid.* As the client has no funds with which to pay, the payment must come from the factor's collection. So, in this way, or by a direct provision in the agreement cancelling the factor's responsibility for collection or credit risk on the occurrence of insolvency (including receivership) of his client, the factor may continue to collect for his own account until he has recovered the funds he has laid out by way of prepayments. At that stage he may have no further responsibility. In the absence of recourse provisions in the factoring agreement, in the case of the full service or maturity factoring, the factor will be responsible for the ultimate collection and the credit risk on all approved accounts even after his recovery of the funds in use.

Where the arrangements for factoring have included the administration of **11–22** the debtor accounts and collections, and the factor has the right to have the outstanding debts re-assigned, it may well be worthwhile for the receiver to make arrangements with the factor to continue to collect and record the debts. Such an arrangement will save the receiver from the administrative burden of taking on the sales ledger accounts and effecting collection. Such arrangements may often be made with a factor for little, if anything, in the way of an additional charge in return for efficient co-operation from the receiver's staff in providing some important administrative back-up from the client's records. Examples of this back-up are:

(1) the provision of proof of delivery of goods where this is required by a debtor;

(2) help in dealing with disputes or warranty claims relating to the goods.

No doubt the receiver will in any case appreciate that such co-operation is in his interest; the factor's recoveries are ultimately for the benefit of the estate of the client.

Position as regards existing debts not notified under agreement of the whole turnover type

11–23   Although the factor will normally have the right to terminate the agreement forthwith on the appointment of an administrative receiver to his client,[36] such a right is not normally given to the client; the receiver, as agent of the company, will be able to terminate only on the agreed period of notice. Therefore, unless the factor himself exercises the right of immediate termination, the agreement will usually remain in existence for some months. If the receiver declines to implement the provisions of an agreement of the whole turnover type,[37] then, assuming that the factor holds a valid waiver from the holder of the charge under which the receiver was appointed, or if the factoring agreement was created first, the factor will be able to exercise his rights of ownership and collection of any debts (together with their related rights) which have come into existence *and been earned by performance by the client* up to the time of the receiver's appointment.[38] As such debts vest in him, he may give notice to the debtors and demand payment from them whether or not the debts have been notified to him; if they have not been invoiced, the factor may invoice them himself by virtue of his irrevocable power to attorney.[39]

11–24   The application of this principle (by which an agreement to assign identifiable future property operates as an actual assignment when the property comes into existence[40]) to debts arising out of contracts in existence, but not earned by performance before the appointment of the receiver, is not certain. It may be covered by the terms of a waiver. If it is not so covered, or if the charge under which the receiver was appointed was created after the factoring agreement was already in existence and, accordingly, no waiver was necessary, the position would be as follows: the client's rights under contracts of sale in existence at the time of the receiver's appointment and any debts arising out of them should vest in the factor, but any goods or other resources available to fulfil the contract would have vested in the chargee when the crystallisation of the floating charge completed an inchoate assignment to him of the stock and work in progress.[41]

---

[36] See para.10–74 above.
[37] See paras 7–10 and 7–11 above.
[38] *Tailby v Official Receiver* (1888) 13 A.C. 523, and see para.7–12(2) above.
[39] See paras 10–46 and 10–47 above.
[40] *Holroyd v Marshall* (1862) 10 H.L. Cas. 191; *Tailby v Official Receiver* (1888) 13 A.C. 523; see also *G & T Earle v Hemsworth RDC* (1928) 140 L.T. 69 and para.7–10 above. As to when property (including debts) come into existence, see para.7–12 above and n.23 to that para.
[41] See *Business Computers Ltd v Anglo-African Leasing Ltd* [1977] 1 W.L.R. 578.

There appears to be no reported case on this point in relation to recei-   **11–25**
vership, but in such circumstances it seems likely that the court might apply
the bankruptcy principle by which assigned debts not earned by performance at the commencement of a bankruptcy belong to the insolvent
estate.[42] Any debts arising out of the receiver's own contracts (before any
winding-up of the company) are entered into by him as agent for the
company but are for the benefit of the chargee. After a winding-up order or
a resolution to wind up, they are entered into by him either as principal or as
agent for the chargee[43]; and the resulting debts are in no way bound by the
factoring agreement.

Position as regards existing debts not offered under an agreement of the facultative type

The appointment of a receiver does not terminate the company's con-   **11–26**
tracts and this includes the factoring agreement (unless terminated by either
party according to its terms), but the receiver may decline to perform the
contracts of the company existing at the date of his appointment.[44] As a
result, on the appointment of an administrative receiver to his client, a
factor with an agreement of the facultative type[45] has no remedy in the event
of a refusal of the receiver to offer further debts (including those invoiced
before the receiver's appointment) except a claim for breach of contract
against the company itself. For this he will be unsecured. He has no proprietary rights—in relation to such debts.[46]

The receiver's rights in relation to the factor's indebtedness to the client

Arrangements by which banks and other financiers may provide finance   **11–27**
on the security of the amounts payable by the factor to his client for purchased debts under a factoring agreement (the factor's debt) are now not
uncommon. In many cases, the factor's debt is only the unpaid balance of
the purchase price of debts after the factor has made prepayments; but in
others it may be arranged for the factor to pay only on maturity or collection of each debt so that the factor's debt will be approximately the
equivalent of all outstanding debts arising from the client's sales. The

---

[42] *Re Jones, ex p. Nichols* (1883) 22 Ch.D. 782 and see Wood, *English & International Set-off*
(1989), paras 7–173 to 7–175. In *G & T Earle v Hemsworth RDC* (1928) 140 L.T. 69 an assignee
of retention moneys succeeded against the claims of a receiver, but, although the retention
monies did not become payable until after the appointment of the receiver, they had been
earned by performance beforehand.
[43] See paras 11–35 and 11–36 below.
[44] See paras 11–10 to 11–13 above, and Lightman & Moss, *The Law of Receivers and
Administrators of Companies* (3rd ed., 2000), paras 8–006 and 8–007.
[45] See para.7–08 above.
[46] *ibid.*

security may be taken by way of an assignment to the bank or financier of the factor's debt or it may be by way of a specific fixed charge on it; and, in many other cases, the factor's debt, being a book debt,[47] would fall within a standard bank debenture which included a fixed or floating charge on book debts. Reference should be made to the discussion in Ch.8 on the effectiveness of a fixed charge over future book debts.

11–28   Following the *Charge Card Services Ltd* case[48] and the publicity it brought to the practice of factors to hold a retention as security (in its widest sense) for recourse, there have been some attempts by receivers appointed under charges, which include a factor's debt as charged property, to seek to obtain immediate payment of that debt (including the retention) and to deny the factor the right to set off any recourse or other items to be charged to the client after the receiver's appointment. The argument appears to be that, on the appointment of the receiver, the factor's debt is assigned for the benefit of the holder of the charge and that, once notice of the receiver's appointment has been given to the factor, the rights of the parties are settled[49] and no further independent set-off will be available to the factor as debtor. If the factor's claim were to be in respect of independent transactions, this argument might prevail and the factor's position would indeed be unsafe; if the bank's security is by way of assignment (and most probably also in the case of a fixed charge[50]), it would be the notice of the assignment or of a fixed charge that would preclude further set-off.[51] This would mean that the factor would be unable safely to continue the factoring arrangements after such notice which might be received by the factor even before the start of the factoring agreement. However, all such allegations can be rebutted because there is a line of cases which are good authority for the principle that, following the assignment of a debt, any cross-claims of the debtor, *i.e.* here, the factor, which have not accrued at the time of notice of the assignment but which arise out of the same contract as that which gave rise to the debtor's actual liability and are closely connected with it, can be set off against that liability.[52]

---

[47] See Ch.8, n.39, p.169.
[48] [1987] Ch. 150.
[49] *Roxburghe v Cox* (1881) 17 Ch.D. 520 and see para.9–18 above.
[50] See Lightman & Moss, *The Law of Receivers and Administrators of Companies* (3rd ed., 2000), paras 16–037 to 16–039. In the cases relating to a debtor's rights of set-off on the appointment of a receiver to his creditor the point as to the distinction between an assignment and a charge has not been taken and they have been treated as analogous; see Goode, *Legal Problems of Credit and Security*, (3rd ed., 2003), para.4–60, n.26.
[51] *Roxburghe v Cox* (1881) 17 Ch.D. 520, and see para.9–18 above. For this purpose it seems that actual notice would be necessary, *i.e.* not solely by reason of registration (see para.8–17 above).
[52] See, *e.g. Young v Kitchin* (1878) 3 Ex. D. 127; *The Government of Newfoundland v Newfoundland Railway Co* (1888) 13 A.C. 199; for the exercise (after the appointment of a receiver) of a right conferred by a contract of which the receiver has taken the benefit, see *George Barker Transport Ltd v Eynon* [1974] 1 All E.R. 900; and see para.9–17 above.

In the case of an agreement of the whole turnover type,[53] there can be no **11–29** doubt about the factor's rights in this respect; the purchase of all the debts, those for which the factor has to pay and those which are the subject of potential recourse, arise from the one agreement (the factoring agreement itself), and all such transactions are inextricably interwoven.

In the case of a facultative agreement[54] also, the factor's case seems sure. **11–30** It may well be considered that, as an agreement of this type does not itself give effect to assignments of the debts but provides only that they should be offered by the client, each assignment under such an agreement is the subject of a separate contract. Although there is no reported case bearing exactly on the close connection of transactions linked under the unifying influence of such a master agreement, it seems most likely that the connection in such a case would be considered to be close enough for the set-off to be allowed.[55]

In both cases, as it is usual for the factoring agreement to include pro- **11–31** visions for the set-off of such claims, the receiver would be likely to take the debt owing by the factor to the client subject to the factor's contractual rights in this respect; it seems well established that an assignee takes subject to any agreement for set-off in respect of transactions which have their inception before notice of the assignment.[56] Whilst owing no positive obligation to the factor, the beneficiary of the charge cannot take the benefit of the factoring agreement without the burden of it.[57] The holder of a charge "... could assert their position as assignees of the company's property ... only by themselves recognising and giving effect to the pre-appointment contractual rights ...".[58]

In spite of the factor's ability to rebut such allegations by receivers **11–32** appointed to client companies, it is advisable for the position to be clarified at the time when the factoring agreement is entered into or, in the case of a subsequent charge, when the charge is created. This may be done in the letter of waiver or acknowledgement.[59]

Summary of factor's rights

The factoring agreement remains in effect if it is not terminated according **11–33** to its terms; but the receiver is likely to have no obligation in respect of it. The factor cannot enforce any rights against the company itself because the

---

[53] See paras 7–10 and 7–11 above.
[54] See paras 7–08 and 7–09 above.
[55] For a decision regarding equitable set-off in a case concerning a series of contracts on similar terms, see *"The Angelic Grace"* [1980] 1 Lloyds Rep. 288.
[56] *Mangles v Dixon* (1852) 3 H.L. Cas. 702; *Smith v Parkes* (1852) 16 Beav. 115; see also Derham, *The Law of Set-Off*, (3rd ed., 2003) and Wood, *English & International Set-off* (1989), paras 16–33 *et seq.*
[57] *George Barker Transport Ltd v Eynon* [1974] 1 All E.R. 900.
[58] *ibid., per* Edmund Davies L.J. at 907.
[59] For a form of words which may achieve such clarification see para.8–78 above.

directors have no means to procure compliance with the terms. If the priorities having been properly regulated between the factor and the chargees, or if the factoring agreement has priority in relation to the debts and related rights by law,[60] then the factor may in most circumstances:

(1) exercise all rights of ownership and collection in respect of debts offered to and accepted by him or notified to him (according to the type of agreement);

(2) in the case of an agreement of the whole turnover type exercise such rights in respect of debts earned by performance of its contracts by the client up to the time of the receiver's appointment; and

(3) exercise his rights of set-off in respect of recourse, charges and other amounts payable by the client under the agreement.

In relation to the set-off of independent transactions, the factor in any event should be able to claim priority over the receiver on the basis of contractual set-off if the chargee was fully aware of the terms of the agreement before the factor received notice of the charge; however, this aspect should be dealt with by agreement (*e.g.* by a waiver) between the factor and the chargee when the factoring agreement or charge is created (whichever is later in time).[61]

Continuation of factoring by an administrative receiver

11–34   If the factoring agreement is not terminated according to its terms, it will continue to be effective as regards the client company itself but the factor will be unable to enforce its terms[62] as regards:

(1) in the case of an agreement of the facultative type,[63] debts not offered to the factor before the appointment[64]; and

(2) in the case of an agreement of the whole turnover type,[65] debts not earned by performance by the client company before the appointment.[66]

---

[60] See Ch.8.
[61] See para.8–78 above.
[62] See paras 11–10 to 11–25 above.
[63] See para.7–08 above.
[64] See para.11–26 above.
[65] See para.7–10 above.
[66] See paras 11–23 to 11–25 above.

If the receiver chooses to implement the agreement while he is agent of the company,[67] it will continue unaffected by his appointment. Without any variation he will have to accept, as set-off against the purchase price of new debts arising, positive liability of the client in relation to debts already vesting in the factor at the time of his appointment; such positive liability will arise if the balance owing by the factor for debts purchased before the appointment is not large enough to absorb, by way of set-off, all the amounts to be charged to the client in respect of such debts (including the repurchase price of debts the subject of recourse).[68] As a result, the receiver will wish to vary the existing arrangements so that a new client account is opened in respect of debts offered or notified by him, and so that any amount to be debited in respect of pre-receivership transactions is debited to the old account. As a consideration for such a change, the factor should obtain an undertaking from the receiver to use his best endeavours to dispose of disputes and claims by customers in respect of goods or services provided by the client both before and after his appointment. It may well be in the interests of the receivership to maximise the factor's recoveries in this way. The change may be made either by the creation of a new agreement between the receiver as agent of the company and the factor (and the termination of the existing agreement) or by an amendment to the existing agreement. In the former case, the receiver will be *personally* responsible for the obligations of the client under the contract unless the agreement specifically provides otherwise.[69] In the latter case, the amendment to the agreement is unlikely to bring about personal liability.

Termination of an administrative receiver's agency on winding-up

An administrative receiver's agency for the company ceases, in the case of **11–35** a winding-up by the court, on the making of the winding-up order and, in the case of a voluntary winding-up, on the resolution of the members.[70] He will never be the agent of the company if the company is already in liquidation at the time of his appointment.[71] If the instrument of charge in respect of which the appointment is made or the deed of appointment itself so provides, he will be the agent of the chargee; he may also be held to be the chargee's agent if he acts on the chargee's instructions.[72] Otherwise, he will act as principal,[73] and this is the case when the instrument of charge and the appointment make no provision in this respect.

---

[67] *i.e.* Before any winding-up order in respect of the company or a resolution to wind it up.
[68] See para.11–11 above.
[69] Insolvency Act 1986, s.44(1)(b).
[70] Insolvency Act 1986, s.44(1)(a).
[71] *ibid.*
[72] *American Express International Banking Corporation v Hurley* [1985] 3 All E.R. 564.
[73] For an analysis of the significance of the difference see Lightman & Moss, *The Law of Receivers and Administrators of Companies* (3rd ed., 2000), paras 11–036 *et seq.*

11–36   Whether the receiver is acting either as the chargee's agent or as principal, his power to deal with the property in the name of the company is not affected.[74] Whether he may then continue the business of the company otherwise than to the extent necessary for beneficial realisation of its property seems uncertain; for this reason, it is not uncommon for an administrative receiver, who wishes to carry on the business of a company in liquidation, to "hive down" the assets and undertaking to a newly formed subsidiary.[75]

11–37   Where an administrative receiver wishes to continue a factoring agreement while the client company is in liquidation, it would be advisable for the factor either to procure a personal warranty from the receiver that he is acting as principal or confirmation of the consent of the chargee as principal to the continuation of the agreement.

2. ADMINISTRATION[76]

Administration under Insolvency Act 1986

11–38   For the purpose of giving insolvent companies an opportunity for recovery, Pt II of the Insolvency Act 1986 introduced a new regime the Court supervised administration of such companies. This was initially only achieved by an administration order by the court, providing for the appointment of an "administrator" to an insolvent company, on the petition of the company, its directors, a creditor or creditors or all of them. The court might make the order if it considered that one of the following statutory purposes would be achieved:

(1)   the survival of the company or any part of its undertaking;

(2)   the approval of a voluntary scheme of arrangement under Pt I of the Act[77];

(3)   a compromise or arrangement between the company and its members or creditors (or any class of either of them) under s.425 of the Companies Act 1985; or

---

[74] *Sowman v David Samuel Trust Ltd* [1978] 1 W.L.R. 22.
[75] See Lightman & Moss, *The Law of Receivers and Administrators of Companies* (3rd ed., 2000).
[76] For a more detailed description see Lightman & Moss, *The Law of Receivers and Administrators of Companies* (3rd ed., 2000), paras 9–058 *et seq.* and Goode, *Principles of Corporate Insolvency Law* (3rd ed., 2005), Ch.10.
[77] See paras 11–79 and 11–80 below.

(4) realisation of the company's assets more advantageously than in winding-up.[78]

If there was an administrative receiver of the company in place when the petition was heard, no order would be made, unless either the receiver consented to the making of the order, or the court was satisfied that the charge in respect of which he was appointed would be liable to be avoided, released or discharged[79] on the making of the order. **11–39**

In para.11.02 the significant changes to the corporate insolvency regime were described, most importantly the new out-of-court route into administration. In order to give a fuller understanding, more details of the rationale behind the changes and the new regime itself need to be given. **11–40**

The list of disjunctive purposes for which an administration order could be granted has been replaced by a single purpose, namely the rescue of the company as a going concern. There is now a hierarchy of objectives so that, if this main purpose is not reasonably practicable and the proposed administrator thinks a better result for creditors as a whole would be achieved, he can act accordingly. Only if neither of these objectives can be achieved, and it will not necessarily harm the interests of creditors as a whole, then he must realise the company's property to distribute to one or more secured or preferential creditors. **11–41**

The out of court route is now available both to holders of qualifying floating charges (see 11.02) as well as the company and its directors, upon the filing of a notice of appointment. The company or its directors will need to declare that the company is or is likely to become unable to pay its debts. No such statement is required by the qualifying floating charge holder. **11–42**

The court procedure to appoint an administrator is still available, subject to a pre-condition that the Court must be satisfied that the order is reasonably likely to achieve the purpose of administration. This route will be the only one open to creditors other than qualifying floating charge holders. **11–43**

For pre September 15, 2005, qualifying floating charge holders the power of veto over the out-of-court appointment of an administrator is retained by appointing an administrative receiver instead. For post September 15, 2005, qualifying floating charge holders this power is reduced to the right to install or request (in a court application) its preferred administrator. The most senior qualifying floating charge holder has the right to trump the others. **11–44**

Even the out-of-court route requires a notice to be filed at court (any court having a High Court Registry). The reason for this seems to be to give the administrator court-approved status for the purpose of the European Insolvency Harmonization Regulations.[80] **11–45**

---

[78] Insolvency Act 1986, s.8.
[79] Pursuant to the Insolvency Act 1986, ss.238, 239 or 245.
[80] EC Regulation on Insolvency Proceedings 2000 (EC Regulation 1346/2000). This sets out common rules on cross-border insolvencies within the European Union. It came into force on May 31, 2002.

11–46   Following appointment, the administrator must make a statement setting out his proposals and send a copy to creditors as soon as reasonably practicable and in any event within 8 weeks. There is an automatic end to the administration after one year unless extended by the court or by agreement with creditors. Creditors meetings can be dispensed with and proposals approved by creditors in correspondence.

11–47   The powers of administration have been extended. A criticism of the pre Enterprise Act 2002 regime was the inability to make payments to pre-administration creditors, or distributions. Now the administrator will have discretion to make distributions to secured and preferential creditors, and to unsecured creditors with the leave of the court.

Effects of application for Administration Order or filing of notice of appointment or notice of intention to appoint Administrator.

11–48   When the company goes into administration (which for this purpose includes the filing of an administration application or notice of intention to appoint at the court), the effects are as follows:

A.1   No winding-up resolution may be passed;

A.2   No compulsory winding-up may be made (except on a public interest petition);

and without the consent of the administrator or permission of the court;

B.1   No step may be taken to enforce any security over the company's property;

B.2   No step may be taken to repossess goods under a hire-purchase agreement (including leasing conditional sale or reservation of title claim);

B.3   A landlord may not exercise a right of forfeiture by peaceable re-entry;

B.4   No legal process may be instituted or continued (including proceedings, execution, distress).

Effect of administration on debts vesting in factor

11–49   The prohibition on any steps to enforce any security on any property of the company, although extended to goods and chattels leased or on hire-purchase or conditional sale or subject to reservation of title, does not extend to the factored debts. As a result, the factor's rights in relation to the debts (and rights related to the debts such as guarantees, securities and negotiable instruments) already vesting in him remain unaffected. These rights will extend, in the case of an agreement of the facultative type, to debts offered to the factor before the appointment and accepted by him and, in the case of an agreement of the whole turnover type,[81] to debts earned by performance of the relevant contract of sale or services by the company before the appointment (whether or not notified or invoiced).[82] The position as regards these debts will be the same as on the appointment of an administrative receiver.[83] There are no reported cases to support this view but there is nothing in the statute to impeach the factor's rights to debts vesting in him prior to the appointment.

An interesting question arises as regards debts, not earned by performance but to arise under contracts in existence at the time of the order, in relation to a factoring agreement of the whole turnover type.[84] Such debts, being "in existence"[85] at the date of the appointment should vest in the factor, and the resources for the performance of the relevant contracts are still available to the company. This is unlike the position in administrative receivership where such resources are available only for the benefit of the holder of the charge under which the receiver was appointed. Although such resources are under the control of the administrator, they must be used for the benefit of the company as a whole and not, as in receivership, for the benefit of secured creditors.[86] The difficulty for the factor will arise if the administrator considers that it would not be to the company's benefit to perform the relevant contracts of sale so that the resulting debts vest in the factor; that would be the position if the factor were to set-off the purchase price of such debts against a pre-existing obligation of the client. In order to enforce his rights, the factor would have to obtain leave of the court. It seems likely that the court, having regard to the interests of the company as a whole, would exercise its discretion in support of the administrator's decision. **11–50**

Effect of the administration on factor's other rights

Although administration and administrators are the creation of statute, the legislators have not made any special provision for the rights and obligations of the factor and his client when an administration commences in respect of his client. Accordingly, the factoring agreement remains in force (unless it has been terminated according to its terms); but, in common with all other creditors, the factor is unable to enforce against the client in **11–51**

---

[81] See paras 7–08 to 7–10 above.
[82] Under an agreement of the whole turnover type all future debts are bound by the agreement itself whether or not such formalities have been completed; *Holroyd v Marshall* (1862) 10 H.L. Cas. 191; *Tailby v Official Receiver* (1888) 13 A.C. 523.
[83] See paras 11–27 to 11–32 above.
[84] See paras 7–10 and 7–11 above.
[85] As to when property (including debts) come into existence see para.7–12 above and n.23 to that para.
[86] *Astor Chemicals Ltd v Synthetic Technology Ltd* [1990] B.C.L.C. 1 at 12.

administration any positive liability which the client may have in favour of the factor without leave of the court, which is unlikely to be given.[87] As far as the balance owing to the client for the price of debts purchased allows, the factor will be able to exercise his rights of set-off. The exclusion of steps to enforce security and of proceedings against a company after an administration has begun does not apply to self-help by the application of equitable or contractual set-off.[88] Thus, the factor will be able to exercise all his rights to withhold payments (if his agreement so provides) and to set off his debt to the company against any recourse or charges payable to him. However, self-help in this connection does not extend to a counterclaim which is classed as "proceedings" and prohibited[89]; for this reason, the provision for a current account (in which all debits and credits are merged giving rise to one amount owing the balance of the account) and for a combination of accounts may well be to the factor's advantage.[90] His irrevocable power of attorney will enable him to perfect his ownership of debts vesting in him at the time of the administration and of any related rights.

Continuation of the agreement after the appointment of administrator

11–52   As the statute has not made any special provision in relation to an existing factoring agreement, to which a company in administration is a party, the factoring agreement will continue unless it has been terminated by either party. The factor will usually have the right under the agreement for immediate termination; but the administrator will in most cases need to give the requisite notice. In the case of an agreement of the facultative type,[91] if the administrator declines to cause the company to offer further debts, the factor will be unable to enforce his rights in this respect without leave of the court.[92] The position of a factor with an agreement of the whole turnover type[93] is less certain; the future debts created by the client's sales (until termination of the agreement) vest in the factor automatically by virtue of the agreement itself. Without any statutory intervention, it would appear that the vesting of debts created after the administration order will continue; unlike the position in receivership the resources of the company available for the performance of its contract of sales remain for the benefit of the company as a whole. In such a situation, the administrator may consider the continuation of factoring not to be in the best interests of the company. This would be the case if there remained substantial pre-administration liabilities

---

[87] Insolvency Act 1986, ss.11(3)(c) and (d).
[88] See Wood, *English v International Set-off*, para.7–20. (Insolvency set-off as provided for in the Insolvency Rules 1986 (SI 1986/1925) r.4.90 will not apply because the company is not being wound up.) See also Goode, *Principles of Corporate Insolvency Law* (3rd ed., 2005), p.307.
[89] *ibid.*
[90] See para.10–02 above.
[91] See paras 7–08 to 7–10 above.
[92] See paras 7–10 and 7–11 above.
[93] See paras 11–63 to 11–67 below.

of the company to the factor (*e.g.* for recourse) and the factor is likely to set these off against the purchase price of post-administration debts. It is, however, doubtful whether the court would support the factor if the administrator declined to recognise the vesting of such debts in the factor; the exercise of such vesting would be contrary to the spirit of an administration.[94] As a result, if the administrator considers it requisite to continue factoring, it would probably be in the interest of all parties for agreement to be reached by which the client account is ruled off and a new one started. As part of such agreement, the factor should obtain the administrator's agreement to procure that the company should settle disputes with customers and perform any continuing obligations under its contracts of sale giving rise to pre-administration debts. Unlike an administrative receiver, the administrator is not personally liable on any contract made or adopted by him.

3. WINDING-UP OF COMPANIES REGISTERED UNDER THE COMPANIES ACTS

The winding-up of companies is regulated by the Insolvency Act 1986 and **11-53** the Insolvency Rules 1986.[95] As regards the effect on a factoring agreement of the winding-up of a client, which is a company registered under the Companies Acts, little has been changed from the position as it was before the coming into effect of the Act. In the following paragraphs reference is to such a company as client; unregistered companies are rarely taken on as clients by factors, but reference to the regulations relating to the winding-up of partnerships is made later in this chapter.[96] For the purpose of this work the description of the procedures in, and effect of, winding-up and bankruptcy is limited to a synopsis and to that which affects the factoring arrangements of an insolvent client. For further information, reference should be made to the textbooks specialising on the subject.

The effect of winding up by the court (compulsory liquidation)

An order by the court for the winding-up of a company does not termi- **11-54** nate the company's contracts, but there are no means of enforcing their

---

[94] As regards a company's pre-existing contracts an administrator, whose duty is to manage the affairs of the company, is not in the same position as an administrative receiver, whose principal duty is to realise the charged property for the benefit of the person who appointed him. An administrative receiver will not be bound by a pre-existing contract if such compliance would give priority to the other party over the claims of unsecured creditors; but whether or not the Court will order such compliance by an administrator would appear to depend on the likely benefit to the company's business as a whole and the objectives of the administration. *Astor Chemicals Ltd v Synthetic Technology Ltd* [1990] B.C.L.C. 1.
[95] SI 1986/1925.
[96] See para.11-71 below.

continued implementation as all proceedings against the company are stayed except with leave of the court.[97] On the making of the order, the official receiver becomes provisional liquidator[98] and the directors' powers in relation to the property and the management of the company cease. Furthermore, on the making of the order, *the commencement of the winding-up is backdated to the date of the petition on which the order is founded* or any earlier resolution of the members for its winding-up.[99] The official receiver may (or shall if so requested by a quarter in value of the company's creditors) call separate meetings of members and creditors for the purpose of choosing a person to be liquidator in his place. The liquidator (whether the official receiver or another person) takes into his custody or under his control the company's assets in order to ensure that they are realised and distributed to the persons entitled thereto according to the Act and the Rules[1]; the court may on application by the liquidator order that all or any part of the company's property shall vest in the liquidator in his official name.[2]

Effect of resolution of members of a company to wind it up (voluntary liquidation)

11–55   As in the case of compulsory liquidation, the resolution of the members of a company to wind it up, whether following a declaration of solvency in relation to the affairs of the company (member's voluntary liquidation) or not (creditor's voluntary liquidation), does not terminate the company's contracts. However from the date of the resolution (the commencement of the winding-up[3]) the company must cease to carry on its business except for the purpose of its beneficial winding-up.[4] In a member's voluntary liquidation a liquidator is to be appointed by the members in general meeting; and on his appointment the directors' powers cease save as far as allowed by the members or the liquidator.[5] In a creditors' voluntary liquidation the liquidator is appointed by the nomination of the creditors unless they make no nomination in which case he is the person nominated by the members.[6] On his appointment the director's powers cease except so far as the liquidation committee (if one is appointed by the creditors) or the creditors allow.[7]

---

[97] Insolvency Act 1986, s.130(2).
[98] *ibid.*, s.136(2).
[99] *ibid.*, s.129.
[1] *ibid.*, ss.143(1) and 144(1).
[2] *ibid.*, s.145(1).
[3] *ibid.*, s.86.
[4] *ibid.*, s.87(1).
[5] *ibid.*, s.91(2).
[6] *ibid.*, s.100.
[7] Insolvency Act 1986, s.103.

Effect of winding-up on continuation of factoring agreement

As the commencement of a winding-up of any type or the appointment of **11–56** a liquidator does not automatically terminate the factoring agreement, it will remain in full force and effect unless it is terminated according to its terms. The factor will usually have the right to terminate it forthwith, but may be unwilling to do so and the liquidator on behalf of the company will need to give the requisite period of notice. However, in the case of compulsory or creditors' voluntary liquidation the factor will have no way of enforcing its continuance. In either case, it would be open to the liquidator to disclaim the agreement as an unprofitable contract[8] and the factor would be in the position of an unsecured creditor in respect of any claim for damages arising from its discontinuance.[9] In practice, as in both cases the business must cease except for the beneficial realisation of the assets, it is unlikely that many further debts would be earned by performance of contracts of sale or services; as a result, it is usual for factors to accept that the agreement will be discontinued except as regards their rights in relation to debts vesting in them on the appointment of a liquidator.

There appears to be no reason why a factoring agreement should not be **11–57** continued on the appointment of a liquidator in members' voluntary liquidation of a client company. If the liquidator declines to implement the provisions as regards any sales made by him (or disclaims it as an unprofitable contract[10]) then the factor should have his claim for the loss which he has suffered settled in full within twelve months from the commencement of the winding-up.[11] However even in a members' voluntary liquidation the business must not be carried on save for its beneficial winding-up.

Effect of winding up on debts vesting in the factor

A winding-up order in relation to a client of a factor or resolution to wind **11–58** it up will not affect the rights of the factor, whose agreement is of the whole turnover type,[12] to the ownership of the debts vesting in him at the time of the order or resolution. These debts will include, not only those notified to him, but also all those specified in the agreement and earned by the performance of the relevant contract of sale or service by the company before such time.[13] In respect of any such invoiced debts not notified to him, he may exercise all rights of ownership, including the giving of notice to the debtors and collection, because the assignment of them took place by virtue

---

[8] *ibid.*, s.178.
[9] *ibid.*, s.178(6).
[10] *ibid.*, s.178.
[11] *ibid.*, s.89.
[12] See paras 7–10 and 7–11.
[13] *Holroyd v Marshall* (1862) 10 H.L. Cas. 191; *Tailby v Official Receiver* (1888) 13 A.C. 523.

of the factoring agreement itself and does not rely on a further act of appropriation or other formality.[14] If any debts have been fully earned by performance but not invoiced by the time of the order or resolution, then the factor may invoice them by virtue of his irrevocable power of attorney.[15] The factor with this type of agreement will not be affected by the backdating of the commencement of a compulsory liquidation to the date of the petition[16] and the avoidance of dispositions of the company's property after the commencement[17] unless the factoring agreement first became effective after that time; the disposition of the debts will have been made by virtue of the factoring agreement itself.[18] Debts earned by performance by the liquidator in compulsory or creditor's voluntary liquidation will vest in the factor even if they arise under contracts in existence before the liquidator's appointment.[19]

11–59   The rights of ownership of the factor, whose agreement is of the facultative type,[20] in relation to debts vesting in him *at the commencement of the winding-up* will not be affected by a winding-up order in respect of his client or a resolution to wind it up. However, the debts vesting in him are only those offered to him and accepted by him before that time. He has no rights of ownership at all to any debts not offered to him even if they are earned by performance of the contract of sale or services before the commencement of the winding-up. Furthermore, in a compulsory winding-up the commencement is backdated to the date of the petition on which the winding-up is founded or any earlier resolution to wind up[21]; and any disposition made after that time is void except as otherwise ordered by the court.[22] The disposition of debts by the client under this type of agreement takes place when they have been offered *and* accepted;[23] as a result, the factor may be in a position of having accepted and paid on account for debts offered to him after a petition for the winding-up of his client and find that those debts do not vest in him; for the recovery of such payments he would be no better than an unsecured creditor unless set-off against an amount owing by him to the client is available to him. This situation could arise because a petition does not have to be advertised until seven days before the hearing[24] which could be many weeks after the date of the petition. In such circumstances, it

---

[14] See paras 7–10 *et seq.* above.
[15] Powers of Attorney Act 1971, s.4.
[16] Insolvency Act 1986, s.129.
[17] *ibid.*, s.127.
[18] *Holroyd v Marshall* (1862) 10 H.L. Cas 191; *Tailby v Official Receiver* (1888) 13 A.C. 523.
[19] *Re Jones ex p. Nichols* (1883) 22 Ch.D. 782 and see Wood, *English & International Set-off* (1989), paras 7–173 *et seq.*
[20] See paras 7–08 and 7–09 above.
[21] Insolvency Act 1986, s.129.
[22] *ibid.*, s.127.
[23] See paras 7–08 and 7–09 above.
[24] Insolvency Rules 1986 (SI 1986/1925), r.4.11.

would be advisable for the factor to procure that his client makes application,[25] before the petition is heard, to the court for validation of the assignments as being in the interests of the company; the benefit to the company might be the continuation of factoring enabling the company to continue its business at least until the hearing. It is most unlikely that such an application made after a winding-up order would succeed.

Provisional liquidators

At any time after the presentation of a petition for compulsory winding-up of a company and before the making of a winding-up order the court may appoint the official receiver or some other fit person to be a liquidator of the company provisionally.[26] The functions of the provisional liquidator will be such as the court may confer on him[27] and his powers may be restricted by the court.[28] The effect upon the factoring agreement of such an appointment will be the same as the appointment of a liquidator following a winding-up order,[29] unless the court makes some special restriction in the liquidator's powers in relation to it. The appointment will not affect the rights of the factor to debts then vesting in him and the backdating of the commencement of the winding-up (which affects factors whose agreements are of the facultative type[30]) cannot be effective until a winding up order is made.   **11–60**

4. BANKRUPTCY OF AN INDIVIDUAL CLIENT

The bankruptcy of an individual is regulated by Pt IX of the Insolvency Act 1986 and is brought about by a bankruptcy order made by the court on the petition of a creditor or creditors, of the individual or of the supervisor of or any person bound by a voluntary arrangement by the individual.[31] The bankruptcy commences on the date of the order and continues until the discharge of the individual.[32] Under far-reaching changes introduced by the Enterprise Act 2002, it is possible for a bankrupt to receive a discharge in as little as 12 weeks. Upon the making of a bankruptcy order, the official receiver becomes receiver and manager of the bankrupt's estate[33] and, upon   **11–61**

---

[25] Under the Insolvency Act 1986, s.127.
[26] *ibid.*, s.135.
[27] *ibid.*, s.135(4).
[28] ibid., s.135(5).
[29] See para.11–56 above.
[30] See para.11–59 above.
[31] Insolvency Act 1986, s.264.
[32] *ibid.*, s.278.
[33] *ibid.*, s.287.

the appointment of a trustee (either the official receiver[34] or an insolvency practitioner appointed by the creditors[35]), the bankrupt's estate vests in the trustee.[36]

Effect of bankruptcy on continuation of factoring agreement

11–62   The bankruptcy of an individual does not terminate or destroy the individual's contracts so that, unless the factoring agreement with the individual who becomes bankrupt is terminated by either party according to its terms, it will remain in effect. However, the factor has no way of enforcing its continuation because any action taken would be for damages for breach of the agreement and any such action would be likely to be stayed by the court,[37] and, furthermore, the trustee by notice may disclaim the agreement as an unprofitable contract.[38] In respect of any such claim for damages, the factor will be no better than an unsecured creditor.

Effect of bankruptcy of client on debts vesting in factor

11–63   The rights of the factor to the debts vesting in the factor on the making of a bankruptcy order are the same as those which apply in the case of a winding-up order of a company client as described above.[39] The factor whose agreement is of the whole turnover type[40] will be able to claim all debts earned by performance of the client before the bankruptcy order[41] and will be able to exercise his rights of ownership and collection of such debts even if not notified to him or invoiced. However, debts earned by performance of services or the delivery of goods by the official receiver (as receiver and manager) or the trustee (whether the official receiver or an insolvency practitioner), even if they arise out of contracts in existence before the commencement of bankruptcy, vest in the estate of the bankrupt and not the factor.[42]

11–64   The determination of which debts will vest in the factor, whose agreement is of the facultative type,[43] on the bankruptcy of his client is less straightforward. Certainly, he will not have ownership of any debt not offered to and accepted by him before the official receiver becomes receiver and manager of his client's estate on the making of the bankruptcy order, unless

---

[34] *ibid.*, ss.293(2) and 293(3).
[35] *ibid.*, ss.293(1) and 294.
[36] *ibid.*, s.306.
[37] Insolvency Act 1986, s.285.
[38] *ibid.*, s.315.
[39] See para.11–58 above.
[40] See paras 7–10 and 7–11 above.
[41] *Holroyd v Marshall* (1862) 10 H.L. Cas. 191; *Tailby v Official Receiver* (1888) 13 A.C. 523.
[42] *re Jones ex p. Nichols* (1883) 22 Ch.D. 782. See also para.7–12 above.
[43] See paras 7–08 and 7–09 above.

(which is unlikely) the official receiver or a subsequently appointed trustee continues to implement the factoring agreement. Dispositions of property of the bankrupt between the day on which the petition for bankruptcy is presented and the vesting of the estate in the trustee on his appointment are void except:

(1) to the extent that such disposition is made with the consent of or is ratified by the court; or

(2) the transaction took place before the commencement of bankruptcy (the date of the order) and was entered into by the other party in good faith and for value without notice that the petition had been presented.[44]

As a result of the foregoing, it seems likely that the factor with a facultative type of agreement will lose the ownership of any debt offered to him after he has notice of the petition for the bankruptcy of his client. This provision should not affect the factor with an agreement of the whole turnover type unless the agreement had not become effective before the date of the petition. Debts that are earned by delivery of goods or the performance of services up to the commencement of the bankruptcy (the date of the order) are bound and vest in the factor by virtue of an agreement of this type itself.[45]

A factor with an agreement of the whole turnover type which constitutes a **11–65** general assignment of book debts of a sole trader or partnership is likely to lose the ownership of all debts in existence at the date of the presentation of a petition for the bankruptcy of the sole trader or a partner if he has not ensured registration of the agreement within seven days of its execution under the Bills of Sale Act 1878.[46] An agreement of the facultative type under which the individual debts are offered to and accepted by the factor would not be caught by this provision in view of the exclusion of "debts due at the date of the assignment from specified debtors" from the definition of a general assignment.[47]

5. EFFECT OF CLIENT'S INSOLVENCY ON OTHER RIGHTS OF FACTOR

The effect of the winding-up of a company client and of the bankruptcy of **11–66** an individual client on the factor's other rights is similar. Provided that his

---

[44] Insolvency Act 1986, s.284.
[45] See paras 7–10 and 7–11 above.
[46] Insolvency Act 1986, s.344 and see paras 7–15 to 7–17 above.
[47] *ibid.*, s.344(3)(b).

power of attorney is stated to be irrevocable, it will remain unaffected by the insolvency of the client; and, as far as it is practicable, he will be able to continue to use the client's name in order to procure compliance with the obligations of the client as regards the debts in respect of which his rights of ownership are not impeached by the insolvency of his client as described above. The factor will thus be able to execute, on behalf of the client as assignor, assignments of such debts in accordance with the statute,[48] to sue in the client's name and to resolve disputes with debtors.

11–67   Furthermore, in view of the assignment to the factor of all rights under the relevant supply contracts along with the debts,[49] he will be able to exercise any lien on goods the subject of such supply contracts and to recover any goods of which the ownership has not passed from the client to the debtor.

Effect of the client's insolvency on set-off provisions

11–68   In both winding-up and bankruptcy of the client, the statutory provisions for set-off[50] take effect to replace any equitable, common law or contractual set-off available to the factor. Although set-off is not a security right, the factor needs to rely upon it for his security (in the widest sense of the word) in the insolvency of his client and it is then to the statutory provisions, and not those in his agreement, that he must look. In particular, it is important that he should be able to retain any balance owing to the client's estate, as at the commencement of bankruptcy or winding-up, and to apply by way of set-off a part or the whole of it for the discharge of the client's obligations to him. Such obligations will include any contingent liability of the client for recourse[51] that may subsequently arise in respect of any of the debts then outstanding.[52]

11–69   It is important that the factor should ensure that the provisions in his agreement for retention of amounts owing to the client and for recourse take into account the statutory provisions for set-off; no matter how widely the set-off provisions in his agreement they will be of no effect when he most needs them in the insolvency of his client. The statutory provisions for set-off in winding-up and bankruptcy will assist the factor where he is a creditor of his insolvent client as a result of his having purchased debts owing by that client from a supplier that is another client. Insolvency set-off will apply, against his indebtedness to the insolvent client for the unpaid purchase price

---

[48] Law of Property Act 1925, s.136.
[49] See para.10–24 above.
[50] Insolvency Rules 1986 (SI 1986/1925), r.4.90 and the Insolvency Act 1986, s.323 respectively and see paras 9–12 and 9–13 above.
[51] See paras 10–28 et seq. above.
[52] For a review of the question of set-off of the factor's contingent claims see paras 9–11 and 9–13 and 10–02 to 10–10 above.

of debts, in respect of his claim on the client provided that the assignment to the factor of his claim occurred before he received:

(i) in the case of a corporate client notice of a meeting of creditors; and

(ii) in any case notice of a petition for bankruptcy or winding-up.[53]

6. TRANSACTIONS AT AN UNDERVALUE

In the winding-up or administration of a company and in the bankruptcy of **11–70** an individual the Insolvency Act 1986 provides that the liquidator, administrator or trustee, as the case may be, may apply to the court to restore the position to what it would have been if the company or individual had not entered into a "transaction at an undervalue".[54] Such transactions include gifts and transactions under which the insolvent company or individual receives either no consideration or significantly less than it or he has provided in return[55]; and the provisions apply to gifts made to and such transactions entered into, whilst the company or individual is insolvent (or if the company or individual becomes insolvent by reason of the transaction),[56] within two years before the "onset" of the insolvency in the case of a company and five years of the petition in the case of an individual.[57] In the case of an individual, transactions within two years of the petition may be caught even if the individual was not insolvent at the time.[58] The "onset" of the insolvency is a new term used in the Act and it means the commencement of winding-up[59] or, in the case of an administration or a winding-up immediately following an administration, the presentation of a petition for an administration order.[60] However, the court will make no order in respect of any transaction at an undervalue entered into by a company if it is satisfied that it was entered into in good faith for the purpose of carrying on the business of the company and, at the time, there were grounds for belief that it would benefit the company.[61]

---

[53] See also paras 11–81 to 11–86 below.
[54] Insolvency Act 1986, s.238 and s.339 respectively.
[55] *ibid.*
[56] In the case of a company the Act refers to the company being "unable to pay its debts" which is defined in s. 123. In the case of an individual insolvency means inability to pay debts or a shortfall in the value of assets as compared with liabilities; see the Insolvency Act 1986, s.341(3). In both cases the transaction will be caught if the company or individual becomes insolvent by reason of the transaction itself; the Insolvency Act 1986, s.240(2)(b) and s.341(2)(b).
[57] Insolvency Act 1986, s.240 and s.341 respectively.
[58] *ibid.*, s.341.
[59] See para.11–54 above.
[60] Insolvency Act 1986, s.240(3).
[61] *ibid.*, s.238(5).

7. PARTNERSHIPS

11–71 The difficulty of dealing briefly with the position arising on the insolvency of a client which is an English partnership is due partly to the absence of a distinct legal personality of a partnership.[62] In law the factor, whose client is an English partnership, has a contract with each of the individual partners. The position is further complicated by the rules governing the insolvency of partnerships: the Insolvent Partnerships Order 1994.[63] The Order is based on the general concept that an insolvent partnership should be treated as far as possible as though it were a company and this concept no doubt owes its origins to the difficulty of dealing with the insolvency of a partnership of many partners across international borders when some of the partners are insolvent and some not. There appear to be six courses which may be taken in the case of an insolvent partnership:

(1) administration order relating to the partnership;

(2) partnership voluntary arrangement;

(3) winding-up of the partnership without the bankruptcy of any partner;

(4) winding-up of the partnership combined with bankruptcy of one or more partners;

(5) bankruptcy of partners without the winding-up of the partnership but with the partners' trustee dealing with partnership assets and liabilities; and

(6) bankruptcy of one, some or all of the partners without the winding-up of the partnership.

11–72 It is often the case (although rarely met by a factor) that one or more of the partners is a registered company and, in that case, reference to the winding-up of a partner should be substituted for bankruptcy in the options referred to in the preceding paragraph. The factor's rights will not be affected where there is no formal insolvency procedure for the partnership and one or more of the partners remains solvent; the factoring agreement should have provided for the joint responsibility of the partners and the solvent partner or partners will remain responsible to the factor. However,

---

[62] Under the Limited Liability Partnerships Act 2000 a partnership may now be incorporated with its own legal personality; the liability of individual members (partners) is limited to a requirement to contribute to its assets in the event of the LLP being wound up (New s.214A, IA 1986).

[63] SI 1994/2421.

the bankruptcy of any partner will in some cases bring about the dissolution of the partnership, and the position in such an event is described below.[64]

Formal insolvency procedures for partnerships

The rules[65] apply the insolvency procedures for companies in the Insol- **11–73** vency Act 1986 to insolvent partnerships with very few modifications. Accordingly, the rights of the factor in relation to the continuation of the agreement, to debts vesting in him and his other rights (including set-off) are the same as those which would apply if his client had been a company subject to an administration order, voluntary arrangement or compulsory liquidation instead of a partnership subject to bankruptcy proceedings.[66] It will often be the case that some or all of the partners as individuals are subject to concurrent bankruptcy proceedings or voluntary arrangements; but in the formal insolvency of a partnership it is to the partnership insolvency procedure that the factor must look to determine his rights.

Bankruptcy of all the partners without the winding-up of the partnership

The Insolvent Partnerships Order 1994 provides for insolvency proceed- **11–74** ings against all the individual partners of an insolvent partnership without involving the winding-up of the partnership.[67] These proceedings, which are by way of a petition for the bankruptcy of all of them by all of them jointly, may be taken when all the partners are individuals and none of them is a limited partner. The procedure does not involve the winding-up of the partnership and the trustees of the individual estates administer the partnership property.

In the case of bankruptcy of all the partners of a client of a factor, the **11–75** factor's rights as regards the agreement, the debts vesting in him and set-off and retention are the same as those applicable in the bankruptcy of an individual client.[68]

Dissolution of a partnership

Subject to express agreement to the contrary on the death or bankruptcy **11–76** of any partner a partnership will automatically be dissolved.[69] Furthermore, in the absence of express provisions, a partner may retire only by a

---

[64] See para.11–76 below.
[65] The Insolvent Partnerships Order 1994 (SI 1994/2421).
[66] See paras 11–56 *et seq.* above.
[67] SI 1994/2421.
[68] See paras 11–56 *et seq.* above.
[69] Partnership Act 1890, s.33.

dissolution of the firm. If the partnership agreement provides for its continuation then, subject to the exercise by the factor of any provision in the factoring agreement for the factor to terminate it immediately, it will continue and the outgoing partner or his estate will be liable for any obligation to the factor until he is released; this is the effect of the absence of a distinct legal personality in a partnership. Any incoming partner will not be bound by the factoring agreement unless he so agrees[70]; it is usual for a factor to provide in the factoring agreement that the existing partners should procure the execution by any incoming partner of a deed binding him to the terms of the agreement. Such arrangements are usually made by a novation including a power of attorney from the new partner.

11–77   If the partnership is dissolved either automatically as described above or by an agreement between the partners, the factoring agreement, being an agreement between the factor and each of the individual partners, does not terminate automatically and all the former partners will remain jointly and severally liable to the factor. The dissolution will therefore not affect the factor's rights in relation to the debts vesting in him at the time of the dissolution, nor will it affect his rights of retention and set-off; if his power of attorney is stated to be irrevocable, he will be able to use the firm's name to procure the performance of the client in respect of the debts vesting in him.

11–78   After the dissolution of a partnership, the authority of each partner to bind the firm continues so far as may be necessary to wind up the affairs of the partnership and to complete contracts in existence at the time of dissolution.[71] If any partner has become bankrupt, his ability to bind the firm ceases,[72] but his estate remains liable for the partnership's obligations. It would therefore appear that the factoring agreement may continue (unless terminated according to its terms) as regards the debts arising from contracts of sale or services in existence at the time of the dissolution. Following a dissolution the factor may obtain a good discharge by paying to any one of the partners what is due to a client which comprised a partnership.[73]

8. VOLUNTARY ARRANGEMENTS

11–79   The Insolvency Act 1986 has provided for procedures by individuals[74] and companies[75] who wish to compromise with their creditors. These procedures are less formal, and should be less expensive, than the formalities for an

---

[70] *ibid.*, s.17(1).
[71] Partnership Act 1890, s.38 and see *IRC v Graham's Trustees* 1971 S.L.T. 46 (HL).
[72] *ibid.*
[73] Payment to any one of joint creditors discharges a debt; *Powell v Brodhurst* [1901] 2 Ch.D. 160.
[74] Pt VIII.
[75] Pt I.

arrangement by a company under the Companies Act 1985[76] or for the bankruptcy of an individual. The procedure is similar but not identical whether the arrangement is to be made by a company or an individual; in each case, the arrangement is based on a "proposal" in which an insolvency practitioner must be named as "nominee" who, if the arrangement is made, becomes the "supervisor" of the arrangement. The supervisor acts under the supervision of the court and may apply to the court for directions. In the case of a company, the proposal may be made by the directors or, where a company is being wound-up, by its liquidator or, after an administration order, by the administrator. In the case of an individual, the proposal may be made by the debtor or his trustee in bankruptcy or the official receiver. In each case, the proposal is put to a meeting of creditors and, if approved, it becomes effective. The supervisor must notify the court that the voluntary arrangement has been accepted and in the case of impending winding-up or administration or bankruptcy, and the court may stay such proceedings.

The position regarding the contracts of the subject of the arrangement will **11–80** depend on the terms of the arrangement itself and, where a company or individual is a party to a factoring agreement, it would be usual for the proposal to provide for its continuance or otherwise because the Act is silent on the question of the company's or individual's contracts. If the arrangement does not provide for the position of the factoring agreement, it should continue as a contract without further formality. The factor's and the client's rights and obligations in respect of debts vesting in the factor at the time when the arrangement becomes effective, should be unaffected except as provided for in the factoring agreement. However, if the factor should become an unsecured creditor (for example, by reason of his rights of recourse exceeding his retention or in respect of a claim for damages owing to discontinuation of the factoring agreement as a contract) and had notice of and was entitled to vote at the meeting, then to the extent of his unsecured claim he will be bound by the arrangement. In the case of a company, voluntary arrangement the meeting cannot adopt a proposal to vary the rights of a secured creditor unless he agrees so that, if a factor holds a charge as collateral security,[77] he may continue to rely on his charge to secure the client's obligations to him. Although in the absence of any provision in the arrangement itself the factoring agreement will continue as a contract, the position is not the same as regards the factor's proprietary rights under an agreement of the whole turnover type to debts created after the coming into effect of the arrangement. For example, in a company voluntary arrangement the directors must put the supervisor in possession of the company's

---

[76] ss.425–430.
[77] See Ch.13.

assets,[78] and the assets are trust assets in the hands of the supervisor.[79] Accordingly, whether the sale of further goods can create debts in respect of which the factor *automatically* has *proprietary* rights is not clear. If factoring is to continue and the continuation is not part of the arrangement itself, then it would be prudent for the factor to have written confirmation of the continuation from the supervisor.

9. FACTOR'S CLIENT AS DEBTOR

11–81   It is not unusual that a client ("client C") of a factor is a customer of another client ("client S") of the factor. Where client S supplies goods or services to client C and assigns the resulting debt to the factor under client S's factoring agreement, client C becomes a debtor to the factor on that separate account. The factor may then seek to apply part or the whole of any credit balance of the factoring account with client C in the discharge of the debt owing for supplies by client S. If client C is in financial difficulty and the debt owing by him was purchased by the factor without recourse, then the factor may avoid a bad debt by exercising such set-off. Even if the debt has been taken with full recourse, it may be important for the factor to exercise that right of set-off instead of recourse to client S; client S's account may not be in credit to the extent sufficient to accept the debit or his financial position may be such that the recourse would create difficulties.

Is the set off available to the factor?

11–82   In the absence of formal insolvency of client C, the proposed set-off should be available to the factor provided that its documentation has been properly drawn. First, the factoring agreement with client C should provide for the set-off and for the combination of all accounts held by the factor in the name of client C if the factor requires it. However, in any case in which a bank or other lender holds a fixed charge on the debt owing by the factor to client C, the factor should have procured the charge holder's agreement for the set-off to have priority over the charge; this should be documented either, if the charge is on all debts owing to client C, in any waiver held by the factor or otherwise in the factor's consent to the charge. Notice to the factor of such a fixed charge on the factor's debt to client C is analogous to notice of the assignment of that debt and, accordingly, is likely, without consent of the charge holder, to preclude the set-off against that debt of further independent transactions in priority to the charge.

---

[78] r.1.23(1) of the Insolvency Rules 1986 (SI 1986/1925), and this applies to any administrator or liquidator if either shall hold office at the time that the arrangement comes into force. Similar provisions apply in the case of an individual voluntary arrangement (r.5.21(1)).

[79] See for example *Re Leisure Study Group Ltd* [1994] 2 B.C.L.C. 65.

Factoring agreements normally now provide for the right of recourse in 11–83 respect of all outstanding debts on the insolvency of the client. Therefore, if the client is in bankruptcy, winding-up, receivership or administration and the factor intends to exercise the set-off in the circumstances described above, then it is essential that the factor refrains from exercising recourse of all the debts of client. If the factor were to do so, the debit back to the client of the amount of all outstanding debts would more than cancel out the debt owed by the factor to client C for the unpaid balance of the purchase price of debts; there would then be nothing against which to set off the debt owed to the factor for supplies by client S.

Provided that no such debit back has been effected, that set-off should be 11–84 available to the factor:

(1) in the administration of client C, because self help by the exercise of contractual set-off is not considered to be the enforcement of a security right or proceedings which are stayed on the appointment of an administrator;

(2) in the receivership of client C, because the factor's right to exercise contractual set-off should have been given priority over the rights of the holder of the charge on the factor's account with client C by the agreement of the charge holder (see above); and

(3) in client C's winding-up, because not only will set-off be available to the factor but it will also be mandatory under r.4.90 of the Insolvency Rules.

What if the set-off results in a balance owing to the factor?

If the debt owing by client to the factor as a result of supplies by client S is 11–85 larger than the debt owing by the factor to client C on the factoring account, then the factor is likely to look either to any guarantee or any charge held by it as additional security for the discharge of client C's obligations under the factoring agreement with client C. The question then arises whether any such charge (whether a simple fixed charge on debts or an all assets debenture) or any guarantee will cover such additional indebtedness of client C to the factor. In general terms the question is: can a creditor gather in under the protection of the security afforded by any guarantee or charge, by means of an assignment, debts which, but for the assignment, would be unsecured?

There appears to be no reported decision on this question in England; but 11–86 there are compelling indications from decisions in Australia and New Zealand (which may influence the English courts) that the answer would be "no" unless there were to be a specific provision in the guarantee or charge for indebtedness arising from such an assignment to be secured. It may be thought that an "all obligations" or "sweeping up" definition of the indebtedness to be covered by the security document would be held to suffice. However, even such wide expressions as "all monies now or hereafter owing or payable to the [factor] on any account whatsoever" are unlikely to assist the factor; it is probable that, in the absence of a specific reference, it would be held that it was not within the contemplation of the parties to the security documentation that such indebtedness of client C arising from sources unconnected with its own factoring agreement would be covered.

CHAPTER 12

SPECIAL CONSIDERATIONS FOR
INTERNATIONAL FACTORING

In domestic factoring the relations between the three parties—the client, the debtor and the factor—are governed by one legal system and the legal framework of the relations in England and Wales has been described in previous chapters. However, in international factoring, the law of at least two countries may affect any of these relations; it may be more than two because a factor may be situated in a country that is neither that of the client nor the debtor. **12–01**

This difficulty for factors who purchase debts arising from sales across national borders is compounded by the difficulty of determining which law is to apply to any particular aspect of a factoring transaction. These difficulties were recognised by the United Nations Commission on International Trade Law (UNCITRAL) which in 1995 set up a working group to study all aspects of assignments in the financing of international receivables and to produce a convention on "The Assignment of Receivables in International Trade".[1] That the uncertainties discussed in this chapter are not exaggerated was demonstrated by the first report of the working group where the following was given as a principal reason for this interest of the UN:

"... the present legal environment ... [is] characterised by divergences among legal systems with the effect that cross-border assignments (in which the assignor, assignee and the debtor were not in the same country) might be unenforceable against the debtor or might be challenged by creditors of the assignee ..."

The convention has now been finalised and approved by the General Assembly and is open for ratification or for accession by all member states. It is hoped that if it is adopted by most important trading states, factors may be able to finance debts with more confidence; but in the meantime careful consideration should be given to the rest of this chapter.

---

[1] See also paras 12–35 *et seq.* below and App.12.

1. MATTERS AFFECTING THE FACTOR'S RIGHTS TO FACTORED DEBTS

Conflicts of law

12–02   There is a conflict of laws where proceedings are to be brought by a party in one country against a party in another or in relation to a matter in another and there is a difference between the laws of the two countries. The term is also used to express the study of legal relations between parties in different jurisdictions and of the proprietary rights of persons to property in other jurisdictions. The choice of the law to be applied to these matters may create problems of great complexity and, in some respects, uncertainty. For a full explanation of the principles in relation to these questions, reference should be made to a work on the specific subject.[2] These complexities and uncertainties must be borne in mind in the consideration of rules likely to be applied under English law to the aspects of concern to a factor in international factoring. For this purpose, factoring is international when the factor's client and the debtor are in different jurisdictions; and this includes business transacted between England and Wales on the one hand and Scotland on the other.

12–03   The law to be applied to contractual rights, where they are to be considered in any jurisdiction within the EU, is now governed by the Rome Convention on the law applicable to contractual obligations ("the Rome Convention"); and the Contracts (Applicable Law) Act 1990 gave legal effect in the United Kingdom on April 1, 1991, to the principal parts of that convention. The application of the Rome Convention is not restricted to cases in which one or both of the parties are resident within the EU or where the contract has some connection with a state in the EU; it applies to any case coming before a court in a member state that has ratified it. The Rome Convention covers most forms of commercial contract; it does not apply to the obligations of parties to bills of exchange but, otherwise, the exceptions are unlikely to be relevant to the business of factoring. Presumably because an assignment, as between the assignor and the assignee, is characterised in most jurisdictions as a contract Art.12 of the Rome Convention covers the contractual rights and obligations arising under "Voluntary Assignments" as follows:

> 1.   The mutual obligations of assignor and assignee under a voluntary assignment of a right against another person ("the debtor") shall be governed by the law which under this convention applies to the contract between the assignor and the assignee.

---

[2] *e.g.* Dicey & Morris, *The Conflicts of Laws* (13th ed., 2000); Goode, *Commercial Law* (3rd ed., 2004) Ch.37; Moshinsky, "The Assignment of Debts in the Conflict of Laws" (1992) 109 L.Q.R. 591.

2.   The law governing the right to which the assignment relates shall determine its assignability, the relation between the assignee and the debtor, the conditions under which the assignment can be invoked against the debtor and any question whether the debtor's obligations have been discharged.

In the next paragraphs there follows an outline of the principles likely to be applied by an English court to the matters of interest to a factor in conflicts of law. However, should the forum in which such a matter is to be considered be in another jurisdiction (particularly in a jurisdiction outside the EU where the Rome Convention has no application), different principles might be applied.

Which law is to be applied to each of the undermentioned matters is of **12–04** concern to the factor:

(1)   the validity of the assignment as between the factor and the client and the law to be applied in resolving a dispute between the factor and his client or between the factor and a correspondent factor in a different jurisdiction (to whom debts have been sub-assigned);

(2)   the assignability of the debt;

(3)   the factor's rights to the assigned debts when a person has been appointed to administer the property and business of an insolvent client;

(4)   the validity of the assignment as against any third party seeking to attach the assigned debt;

(5)   the validity of the assignment as between the factor and the debtor and the countervailing rights of the debtor; and

(6)   the priority of rights between the factor and another assignee of the same debt.

Unfortunately, the answers to these questions are not always clear and this applies even where the forum is within the EU. First, the Rome Convention is intended to govern contractual and not proprietary rights (although it has some effect on the latter) and, secondly, courts in different countries of the EU have interpreted Art.12 of the Rome Convention differently. As a result, it now appears that the Commission may consider some amendments to it.

Before dealing with the aspects of the law which are of concern to a factor **12–05** in the consideration of his ability to recover the funds laid out by way of prepayments, three general points have to be made. First, it was at one time thought that a debt (being intangible) had no locality but the courts have now evolved rules for determining the situation of intangibles. Debts are now considered to be situated in the country in which the debtor resides because that is usually the place where the creditor may recover or enforce payment. For this purpose, the residence of a corporate debtor is in the country which has jurisdiction over it.[3] The fact that a debt *may* also be enforced in another place does not make that other place the *situs*. "The general rule is clear that the debt is situate where the debtor resides ...",[4] but this is the general rule only and it may in some circumstances be negatived by the terms of the contract out of which the debt arose, and, if the debt is not yet due for payment, it may have no locality because it cannot then be enforced.[5] Where the debtor has more than one place of business:

(1) if the debtor expressly provides for payment in one of them the debt will be situate there; or

(2) if the debtor does not so stipulate then the debt will be situate where payment would normally be expected in the course of business.[6]

Secondly, a study of the authorities relating to matters to be considered by factors shows it to be one of uncertainty and that generalisation may lead to wrong conclusions in particular cases. The facts of the cases that can arise have been described as "bewildering permutations and combinations".[7] In particular, a clear distinction must be made between the contractual rights and the proprietary rights of the parties arising from assignments of debts. Thirdly, the decision as to the applicable law will depend to some extent on the forum in which the case is heard because the characterisation of a "debt" is not the same in every jurisdiction. A factor buying a series of individual debts of moderate amounts is in no position to determine his probable rights in relation to all the conflicts that may arise in each case (particularly where his rights depend on the proper law of the contract giving rise to the purchased debt); the factor should, therefore, have regard to the precautions mentioned below. At least, he should be aware of the risks if he, for commercial reasons, decides to forego these precautions.

The assignability of the debt

12–06   By reason of Art.12.2 of the Rome Convention,[8] it is "the law governing the right" that determines whether or not a right is capable of being

---

[3] See Dicey & Morris, "*The Conflicts of Laws*" (13th ed., 2000) paras 22–026 *et seq.* and Moshinsky *op. cit.*, at p.591.
[4] *per* Upjohn J. in *Re Claim by Helbert Wagg & Co Ltd* [1956] Ch. 323 at 342.
[5] *Re Claim by Helbert Wagg & Co Ltd* [1956] Ch. 323.
[6] Dicey & Morris, "*The Conflicts of Laws*" (13th ed., 2000), para.22–029.
[7] Collins, "*Floating Charges, Receivers and Managers and the Conflict of Laws*" (1978) I.C.L.Q. 691 at 696.
[8] See para.12–03 above.

assigned; and here the expression "right" includes a debt. Although it has been mooted that in this article the law governing the right may mean the law of the jurisdiction in which the debt is situated,[9] it is generally accepted to mean the law governing the contract of sale giving rise to the debt. Where a contract of sale giving rise to a factored debt is governed by the law of a foreign debtor's country, then the factor should be put on enquiry as to whether the assignment of a debt is repugnant to the law of that country as it was in England (except in equity) before 1873.[10] Therefore, where the Rome Convention applies, the law governing the contract of sale will also determine the extent to which any term in that contract may cause an assignment of a debt arising from that contract to be ineffective.

Validity of assignments as between factor and client

The validity of the assignment as between the factor and his client and all **12–07** matters of a contractual nature arising between them, such as the warranties given by the client to the factor, will be governed by the proper law of the contract (*i.e.* the factoring agreement).[11] This means the system of law by which the factor and the client intended the factoring agreement to be governed.[12] In any well drawn agreement this will be clearly expressed; but, if it is not, the choice may be determined by the circumstances of the case if these demonstrate the choice with reasonable certainty. The Rome Convention[13] provides that, if no choice is demonstrated, the applicable law will be that of the country with which the contract is most closely connected. Rules for determining the close connection in certain circumstances are included. These provisions are in line with the law as it had previously developed in England and the applicable law (formerly in England usually termed "the proper law") of a factoring agreement should in most cases be determined by the provisions of the agreement itself. The chosen law does not have to be the law of any party to the agreement nor is the choice restricted to the laws of countries in the EU. The same principles should apply to any sub-assignment to a correspondent factor and to relations between a factor and his correspondent; but, in that case, the proper law may be difficult to determine when the parties operate under an international code of practice and not a bilateral agreement.

However, as will be seen from the succeeding paragraphs, it does not **12–08** necessarily follow from the effectiveness of the assignments as contractual rights under the proper law of the factoring agreement that the factor will be entitled to obtain recognition abroad. For example, in the United States the

---

[9] Moshinsky *op. cit.*, at p.597.
[10] See para.7–04 above.
[11] Rome Convention, Art.12(1).
[12] *ibid.*, Art.3.
[13] *ibid.*, Art.4.1.

use of an assignment as "security" (in the widest meaning of the expression) will only gain recognition if it is perfected by registration in the state in which the assignor (the client) has his principal place of business; where that place is in a territory where no registration is possible (*e.g.* England), then the assignor will be deemed to be located in Washington DC.[14]

Does Article 12.2 determine priorities?

12–09   Ever since the introduction of the provisions of the Rome Convention into national laws, there have appeared differences between the views of academics in individual countries as to the effect of Art.12.2 on the rights of an assignee against the claims of any third party including a person appointed to administer the insolvent estate of the assignee. In those jurisdictions in which a debt is characterised as a species of property (such as England and Wales)[15] it was considered that, since the Rome convention was to regulate only contractual rights, Art.12.2 could not affect the proprietary rights of the assignee and such third party. It was thought that the article was not about the assignee's right to the debt but only the conditions in which the assignee with a valid right to it could demand payment. On the other hand, those who regarded a debt purely as a personal right (such as Scottish lawyers) considered that, since the article provides that the law of the contract giving rise to the debt governs the "conditions under which the assignment can be invoked against the debtor", where, by reason of that law, the assignee may exercise his right to payment that is the end of the matter; no third party may intervene.

12–10   In 2001 the English Court of Appeal decided in favour of the latter view. In that case ("*the Mount 1*"),[16] a debt owing by a French insurer and assigned to an Austrian bank was claimed by a creditor who had attached the debt after the assignment. The insurance was governed by English law as was the assignment and notice of it was given according to English practice. On behalf of the attaching creditor, it was claimed that the conflict should be determined under French law because that was where the debt was situated and that the Rome Convention had no relevance to the proprietary rights to the debt. If French law applied, then the assignment was invalid because the notice had not been given by a bailiff. The court held that Art.12.2 of the Rome Convention now applied to determine the debtor's obligation to accept the assignment and that, as the underlying contract (the contract of insurance) was under English law, that law applied. Accordingly, the debtor had been duly assigned in equity and there was nothing for the creditor to attach.

---

[14] U.C.C., s.9–307(c).
[15] See, for example, *Fitzroy v Cave* [1905] 2 K.B. 364 at 372.
[16] *Raiffeisen Zentralbank Osterreich AG v An Feng Steele Co (the Mount 1)* [2001] 2 W.L.R. 1344.

The result of that case appears to be that, as the law now stands, Art.12.2, **12–11** being applied in England to determine the debtor's obligation to accept the assignment, will give to such an assignee the right to displace any claims by third parties. The case should be of some assurance to factors who include in their agreements with their clients debts owing by debtors in an EU country where the contract of sale is governed by English law. If any conflict with a third party in relation to such a debt were to be heard in an English court, the outcome should be the same as it would be in the case of a domestic English debt. This result is also likely, but not certain, where the jurisdiction is any other in the EU.

Validity of the assignments in insolvency of client

It is doubtful if the decision in *the Mount 1*[17] is to apply to a conflict between **12–12** a factor as assignee of a debt arising from a contract governed by English law and the liquidator or trustee in bankruptcy of the factors client. If the case were to apply, then the result would not be in accordance the usual view in English law that, in the insolvency of a client, the assignments to the factor must be valid in accordance with the law of the of the country in which the client is domiciled. For a company in the United Kingdom this is considered to be the country in which the registered office is located, because it is under the law of that country that the insolvency would be regulated.[18] However, that view may be rebutted; while the administration of the property which has passed to the trustee or liquidator is so governed, the question as to:

(1) what foreign property passes; and

(2) subject to what encumbrances such property passes;

may be governed by the law of the country where the debt is situate. In English law bankruptcy creates a trust of the bankrupt's property for the benefit of the creditors and the same principles apply in the winding-up of a company; the recognition of that trust in relation to any property must depend upon the *lex situs*.[19]

Furthermore, in practice English courts have no extra-territorial jur- **12–13** isdiction over the proprietary rights to property situated outside England and Wales. Therefore, in the winding-up or bankruptcy of the client the effectiveness of the factor's claims to debts owing by foreign debtors will

---

[17] See para.12–10 above and n.16.
[18] *Re Anchor Line (Henderson Bros) Ltd* [1937] Ch. 483.
[19] See Dicey & Morris, *The Conflicts of Laws* (13th ed., 2000), para.31–024. Also by analogy, *Peer International Corporation v Termidor Music Publishers Ltd* [2002] 2 W.L.R. 849 in which it was held that title to property situate in England was to be determined according to English Law. See also Goode, *Commercial Law* (3rd ed., 2004) p.1109.

depend upon whether the assignments in the factoring agreement are recognised and enforceable under the law of the country where the debtors are situated. Such failure to recognise the assignments might arise, for example, because the formalities relating to notice had not been complied with before the commencement of the liquidation or the law of that country did not recognise assignments of future debts without individual written assignments (as is the case in an agreement of the whole turnover type).[20] On the other hand, the opinion of some academics is that, although it may be accepted in relation to individual assignments that the law of the debtor's country governs the proprietary rights to an assigned debt, this view should not be supported in relation to bulk assignments of existing and future debts as in factoring and that in such cases the law to be applied is that of the country of the place of business of the factor's client.[21] If that were to be established, then the difficulties caused to factors by the uncertainties regarding the applicable laws in the insolvency of their clients would be much alleviated. However, to be safe, it is suggested that factors should ensure that transfer to them of proprietary rights to the factored debts are also effective in accordance with laws of the countries where the debtors have their businesses.

12-14   The English courts have normally considered that the appointment of an administrative receiver gives effect to an assignment of the property of the company in receivership to the chargee.[22] In the case of a client in receivership, any conflict between the factor and the receiver would be considered as between two assignees and probably determined as indicated below.

Conflicts between the factor and a creditor of the client seeking to attach a factored debt

12-15   The validity of the attachment of a debt (the equivalent to an English garnishee order) will be determined by the law of the country in which the debt is situate because it is generally thought that no other country can have jurisdiction over the debt for this purpose.[23] This does not mean that the law of the situs of the debt will necessarily resolve a conflict between an attaching creditor and an assignee of the debt. It seems clear now that, certainly where the conflict is to be determined in England and probably in

---

[20] See paras 7–10 and 7–11 above.
[21] See Goode, *op. cit.*, p.1109 and Moshinsky (1992) 108 L.Q.R. 591, pp.609 *et seq.*
[22] See, for example, *Business Computers Ltd v Anglo-African Leasing Ltd* [1977] W.L.R. 578.
[23] Dicey & Morris, *The Conflicts of Laws* (13th ed., 2000) para.24–072, where, however, it is suggested that the English courts may exercise jurisdiction where the garnishee is resident in another jurisdiction for the purposes of enforcing a judgement under the Brussels Convention of 1968 or the Lugano Convention of 1988.

most other countries of the EU, Art.12.2 of the Rome Convention will assist the assignee.[24] This means that a factor with an assignment perfected, in accordance with the law of the contract giving rise to the debt (for example, under English law where notice has been given to the debtor), will take priority over a subsequent attachment.

The preceding paragraph deals with the situation where the assignment to **12–16** the factor of the debt has been perfected before the debt is attached by a creditor of the factor's client. Where the attachment, valid according to the law of the country of the debtor's residence, has been perfected before the assignment, then the factor is likely to lose the debt. An example of the difficulty that may face a factor in this respect occurred as long ago as 1900. In that case,[25] priority was given to an unsecured creditor of an English company in receivership when the creditor had attached a debt owing to that company by a French debtor, notwithstanding that the debt fell within the ambit of a floating charge in relation to which a receiver had been appointed. After the receiver's appointment the creditor, holding a dishonoured acceptance of the company, complied with the formalities of French law for the attachment of the debt. Unlike the position under English law, the earlier crystallisation of the charge, in the absence of the required formalities for an assignment in France, did not have the effect of vesting the debt in the chargee under French law. The conflict between the receiver and the creditor was decided by an English court which applied the *lex situs* of the debt to the third party's claim. In such a conflict, the appointment of a receiver is considered to effect an assignment to the chargee of the company's property,[26] and the charge may be considered to be analogous to a factoring agreement.

The priority of competing assignments

The rule in *Dearle v Hall*[27] (by which priority is given to the first whose **12–17** notice has been received by the debtor provided that the former acted in good faith) has no influence outside those countries which have adopted English law or based their own law on it. In some jurisdictions priority goes to the assignee whose assignment is first in time. It is on this basis that in Germany the right of a seller, who has sold to the factor's client on condition that title to the goods and proceeds remain reserved to the seller,

---

[24] *Raiffeisen Zentralbank Osterreich Ag v An Feng Steele Co (the Mount 1)* [2001] 2 W.L.R. 1344, and see para.12–10 above.
[25] *Re Maudslay, Sons & Field* [1900] 1 Ch. 602, the principles of which may well still apply. See also *Maciocia v Alma Holdings Ltd* 1993 S.L.T. 730, where the court declined to recall an arrestment (made under Scottish law) of a debt owing by a Scottish debtor on the application of a factor whose invoice discounting agreement provided for an earlier assignment (in accordance with English law) of the arrested debt.
[26] See n.22 above.
[27] (1828) 3 Russ 1.

would prevail over the factor's title to the proceeds (as factored debts) unless the latter had purchased them without recourse.[28]

12–18 The law governing such conflicts cannot be the proper law of the assignment (the law by which the factoring agreement is governed) because the competing assignments may have been made and be governed by the laws of different countries; where there is competition, there is no reason why the law of one or other should be applied. The authorities have been divided as to whether such priorities are governed by Art.12.2 of the Rome Convention (and accordingly to be determined by the proper law of the contract giving rise to the debt) or to be determined by the law of the country in which the debtor is situated (the *lex situs*).[29] Following *the Mount 1*[30] it now seems certain that an English court is likely to apply Art.12.2 on the grounds that the article governs the conditions under which the assignment can be invoked against the debtor; the first assignment to satisfy those conditions should prevail because after it there is nothing left for the competing assignment to assign. In any case, if the law to be applied is of a country where registration or publicity is not required for the perfection of an assignment, then the factor will face additional difficulties in ensuring that there is no assignment earlier than his own.

Reservation of title by a client's supplier

12–19 Although there is no direct authority on the matter,[31] it is likely that the *lex situs* of the debt would be applied in a conflict between a factor and a supplier to the factor's client who is claiming a factored debt as proceeds of goods sold under prolonged retention of title.[32] First, the supplier's claim is likely to be based on the creation of a trust of the proceeds and the Rome Convention does not apply to the constitution of trusts. Secondly, the proper law of the contract giving rise to the debt cannot apply; the law governing the client's contract for the sub-sale may well be different from

---

[28] See BGH WM 1977, 1978, 1982, 37 and 1350.
[29] For example, the following appeared in a note, relating to the invocability of an assignment in relation to third parties, in the report of a group of experts which met in May 1998 to discuss the draft convention of UNCITRAL (see paras 12–35 *et seq.* below) on Receivables Financing: "... the Rome Convention makes no provision in this regard and the case law of Contracting States of this Convention varies as to the law applicable in such circumstances. Mention might be made here of a decision of the Netherlands Court of Cassation (*Hoge Raad*) of 16 May 1997 (case *Brandsma v Hansa Chemie Aktiengesellschaft*), according to which the law of the assignment contract designated by Article 12, paragraph 1, of the Rome Convention also applies to the effects of the assignment on third parties".
[30] *Raiffeisen Zentralbank Osterreich Ag v An Feng Steele Co (the Mount 1)* [2001] 2 W.L.R. 1344, and see para.12–10 above.
[31] In *E. Pfeiffer Weinkellerei-Weineinkauf GmbH & Co v Arbuthnot Factors Ltd* [1988] 1 W.L.R. 150, the question of conflicts of law was avoided by both parties agreeing that the case should be considered under English law.
[32] See paras 8–39 *et seq.* above.

that governing the supplier's sale to the client on which the supplier's claim rests.

The validity of the assignment as between the factor and the debtor and the debtor's countervailing rights

The obligation of the debtor to recognise the assignment and his coun-   **12–20** tervailing rights against the assignee are governed by the proper law of the debt which would in most cases be the law governing the contract of sale.[33] The importance of this to the factor will be apparent as soon as the factor attempts to collect from a foreign debtor. At that stage, if the law of the debtor's country governs the contract of sale, there may be claims by the debtor that he has no obligation to pay the factor (for example because the law of his country recognises a ban on the assignment in the contract of sale) or that on account of some countervailing or restitutionary right (unknown in English law) he is not obliged to pay. In the case of a ban on assignments, the safeguards sometimes used in England (*i.e.* trust provisions or charges[34]) may not be recognised in other countries.

Precautions to be taken by the factor

Whether the factoring is confidential or with notices to the debtors, all the   **12–21** difficulties mentioned above must be taken into account and precautions taken to keep the risks to a minimum. In invoice discounting the absence of notice at the outset aggravates the difficulties at a later stage when the factor finds it necessary to give notice to the debtors and himself carry out the collections. At the minimum, the following precautions are necessary in all cases:

(1) All underlying contracts of sale by the client should be governed by English law or any other law which recognises the assignments and the debtors' obligations in the same way as under English law.

(2) In addition, each assignment from the client to the factor should be valid under the law of the client's country and according to the law of the country of the debtor and the formalities relating under the latter should be complied with.

---

[33] Rome Convention, Art.12.2.
[34] See para.10–34 above.

Use of two factor system to alleviate the problems

12–22   It is commonly thought that by the use of the two factor system[35] all those problems will be overcome. The general view is that the export[36] factor will ensure that his rights to the debts are valid as regards his relations with the client and in its insolvency and that the import factor[37] will ensure that the debt is validly assigned as regards his ability to collect free from third party claims. However, it is doubtful if the import factor would accept responsibility if the circumstances were similar to those described in the *Maudslay* Case[38] mentioned above with the substitution of the export factor for the debenture holder. However, the two factor system at least gives the export factor the opportunity to be advised regarding the formalities of the law of the countries in which the debtors are situated. These formalities vary widely.

Direct relations between an English factor and a client outside England and Wales

12–23   If an English factor wishes to provide his services, including a prepayment facility, direct to a client outside England and Wales,[39] he must be sure that, on the insolvency of his client, the debts which he has purchased and for which he has paid on account remain vested in him and cannot be claimed by the insolvent estate; otherwise, he will be unable to recover the prepayments made. He must therefore ascertain the formalities for perfection of the assignments, valid in the insolvency of his client, in the country of his client. For example, an English factor, who used for a client in the United States a standard factoring agreement (with all the safeguards described in previous chapters of this book), would not be protected against claims to the factored debts by a trustee in bankruptcy in the United States, unless the factor had filed the agreement, as a security interest, in the state in which the client had its chief executive office.[40] From this it seems clear that, in order to be protected both in the insolvency of his client and against third party claims to the factored debts, a factor providing factoring services for cross-border sales of a foreign client (as in the case of an English client) should ensure that his agreement is valid for these purposes in both the country of the client and that of the debtors.

---

[35] An arrangement by which the client's factor, having purchased debts from the client, sub-assigns them to a correspondent factor in the debtors' countries and by which the latter will be responsible for the collection and credit risks. See Ch.6.
[36] Who purchases the debt from the client.
[37] Normally located in the debtor's country and to whom the debt is sub-assigned.
[38] See para.12–16 and n.25 above.
[39] *i.e.* not through an export factor in the client's country.
[40] U.C.C., ss.9–501/507.

2. UNIDROIT

The International Institute for the Unification of Private Law, more com- **12-24** monly known as UNIDROIT, was set up by the Italian government under the auspices of the League of Nations with the object of promoting the harmonisation of commercial law. It now has 59 States as members. The Council of the Institute, which is situated in Rome,[40] decided in 1974 to include within its work programme for the period 1975 to 1977 a study of the subject of assignments of debts in general and of the contract of factoring in particular. Following a preliminary study and the replies to a questionnaire sent to interested parties, including national factoring associations, it set up a restricted study group of academics and practitioners. The study group considered that owing to the great differences of legal systems the study should in the first place be restricted to the desirability of promulgating rules for factoring only of transactions across national borders. It was felt, however, that the adoption of such rules by national governments would eventually influence legislation for domestic transactions. It was also considered undesirable to formulate a standard factoring contract for use between any factor and his client because the relationship of the factor with his client, including that for international factoring falling within the framework of the proposed rules, should be a matter of freedom to contract between the parties.

At the outset it was appreciated that, although the mechanics of factoring **12-25** in its various forms are conceptually fairly simple, the converse is true of the law under which factoring arrangements operate in many countries. Furthermore, these problems are aggravated by the wide variations in the legal systems and national laws.

The study was followed by meetings of an enlarged study group and later **12-26** of "government experts", being in most cases representatives of justice or trade ministries of national governments. These were held during the years 1981 to 1987. At these meetings a draft convention, formulated by the study group, was discussed and amended in the light of comments and representations called for by the national governments from interested parties in their own countries. The draft convention was finally considered by a Diplomatic Conference of representatives of 55 countries held in Ottawa in May 1988 and hosted by the Government of Canada. The conference made some further amendments to the draft and then adopted it. The convention is known as "The Unidroit Convention on International Factoring".[41]

The convention came into force on May 1, 1995 and has received six **12-27** ratifications accessions.

---

[40] Via Panisperna, 28.
[41] See App.5.

Definition of factoring under UNIDROIT

12-28   The convention as finally drafted provided a narrow definition of factoring in order to avoid encroaching on other forms of financing of *choses in action*. To be a "factoring contract" and covered by the convention a contract must have three characteristics.[43] First, it must provide for the assignment to the factor of debts arising from contracts of sale or service other than goods bought primarily by the customers for their personal, family or household use. Although factoring is concerned principally with trade debts only, it was thought that to define it as such would have the effect of excluding many debts normally included in factoring contracts; examples of these are debts owing by professional people, universities and government departments. Secondly, it must provide for the factor to perform at least two of the following functions[44]:

(1)   finance including loans and advance payments;

(2)   maintenance of debtor accounts;

(3)   collection of debts;

(4)   protection against default by debtors.

Thirdly, the contract must provide for notices of the assignments to be given to debtors.

Application of the UNIDROIT convention

12-29   The convention is limited in its application to factoring of debts arising from sales between persons whose places of business are in different states; and it will apply when both those states and the state of the factor are contracting states (*i.e.* states which have acceded to the convention) or when both the sale contract and the factoring contract are governed by the law of a contracting state.[45] However, the application of the convention *as a whole* may be excluded by agreement between the factor and the client or between the client and the debtor.[46] In the latter case, the exclusion will apply only to debts arising after the factor has been given notice of it; if this were not so, the factor might be misled into accepting responsibility for debts on the basis of protection of the convention where there was no such protection. The convention also recognises the two factor system by the application of

---

[43] See App.5, Art.1, para.2.
[44] The word "services" in the original draft was replaced by "functions" because it was pointed out that the factor performs most of the functions of factoring for himself as owner of the debts and not as a service for his client.
[45] Art.2.1.
[46] Art.3.

the rules to a subsequent assignment by the factor and it avoids the need for two notices of assignment in respect of each debt in that system[47]; notice of the sub-assignment by a factor to a correspondent factor will serve also as notice of the assignment by the client to his factor.[48]

Substantive rules of the UNIDROIT convention

The convention provides *inter alia* as regards the validity of assignments: **12–30**

> (1) the effectiveness of agreements to assign future debts and debts of a particular character in bulk[49] (agreements of the whole turnover type[50]);
>
> (2) the effectiveness of provisions in factoring contracts for the transfer to the factor of rights deriving from the contract of sale including rights to the underlying goods[51];
>
> (3) the obligation of the debtor to pay the factor and the discharge of the debtor on such payment if he has received notice of the assignment given by the client or by the factor with the client's consent provided that the debtor is not at the time aware of a third party's prior right.[52]

For this last provision to apply the notice must reasonably identify the debts to which it relates and the *factor* to whom payment is to be made; it must also relate to debts arising under contracts of sale then in existence. Therefore, under the convention an introductory letter[53] will have no effect in respect of future debts.

As regards the countervailing rights of the debtor, the convention pro- **12–31**
vides that:

> (i) the debtor may set up against the factor all defences arising out of the contract to which the debt claimed by the factor related; and
>
> (ii) any right of set-off existing at the time when he received notice of the assignment.[54]

---

[47] Art.11.1.
[48] Art.11.2.
[49] Art.5.
[50] See paras 7–10 and 7–11 above.
[51] Art.7.
[52] Art.8.
[53] See para.8–12 above.
[54] Art.9.

These provisions are broadly in line with the law as it is known in England and described in this book.

12–32 The convention also deals with the rights of the debtor in relation to recovery from the factor in the event of failure of the client fully, promptly and satisfactorily to perform the contract of sale or service; the uncertainty in relation to this matter under English law has been described above. Under the convention[55] late or defective performance or total failure to perform by the client will not entitle the debtor to recover from the factor. There are however two exceptions to the rule: the debtor will be entitled to recover from the factor (to the extent of the debtor's right to recover from the client) a sum paid to the factor when the latter has not discharged his obligation to pay the client for the debt in question or when the factor has made payment for it in the knowledge of the client's default.

Prohibitions of assignments in contracts of sale

12–33 The most controversial provision in the convention, which was initially inserted at an early meeting in Rome, was based on the provision in the Uniform Commercial Code of the United States[56] by which a prohibition of the assignment of a debt in a contract of sale is not effective as regards the rights of an assignee of the debt. Such a provision was commended by a number of representatives in the meetings of government experts on the grounds that it would assist small exporting businesses to counter the greater bargaining power of large and powerful buyers by enabling the exporters to finance their export sales on open credit often insisted upon by the buyers. A number of others objected to the provision on the grounds that it interfered with the rights of buyer and seller freely to contract. It was pointed out to the objectors that the provision would not make the contract term entirely ineffective and that, if it was breached by a seller's assignment of the resulting debt to a factor, the buyer would retain the usual remedies available to him such as a right to damages for breach of contract. However, no general agreement was reached and only after considerable discussion was a compromise solution accepted by all the parties. By this compromise, the convention provided[57] that an assignment should be effective notwithstanding an agreement between the client and the debtor prohibiting such assignment; however, it also provided that an assignment in contravention of such an agreement would not be effective as regards the debtor if at the time of the contract of sale his place of business were to be in a contracting state which had made a declaration that this provision should not apply to debtors within its borders.[58]

---

[55] Art.10.
[56] ss.9–406(d)–(e). See also paras 9–36 *et seq.* above.
[57] Art.6.1.
[58] Arts 6.2 and 18.

Limitation of scope of UNIDROIT convention

It is to be noted that the rules themselves are somewhat limited in their **12–34** application. They do not cover domestic factoring arrangements nor do they govern arrangements between factors and their clients. In particular, no attempt was made to propose substantive rules for regulating priorities; this was held to be impossible without impinging on national laws relating to the regulation of companies, bankruptcy, banking and the registration and publicity of security rights. Furthermore, owing to the widely differing national views on the subject, not least between those whose concepts are based on common law and those who live under a civil code system, it was not even possible to formulate rules as to which law should apply in given circumstances: that of the debtor's country or that of the client's. Again the provision, by which contracting states may opt out of the making effective of assignments where there is a prohibition in the contract of sale, may severely limit the effectiveness of Art.6; based on experience in the United States the general adoption of this Article would have provided a reassurance for factors to provide their services with more confidence for the general benefit of smaller exporters and the encouragement of international trade. The fact that not even a conflict of laws rule could be formulated is an indication that the uncertainties regarding this aspect described at the start of this chapter have not been exaggerated.

3. UNCITRAL

In 1995 the United Nations Commission on International Trade Law **12–35** ("UNCITRAL") set up a working group study all aspects of "assignments of receivables in international trade" and for the consideration of a convention on the subject. The working group was composed principally of representatives of governments of states which are members of UNCITRAL and of other UN members together with observers from associations of interested practitioners such as banks and factors. The working group completed the draft of the convention in December 2000. It was revised and approved by the Commission in June 2001 and submitted to the general Assembly of the UN which approved it in December 2001. It is now open for accession by individual states and will come into effect, among those states which have signed or acceded to it, six months after signing or accession by a fifth state. Although the scope of the convention is very wide, applying to all forms of assignment of receivables including those owing by consumers, it is likely to have some advantages for factors over the UNIDROIT convention.[59] First, it will apply to all forms of receivables financing

---

[59] See paras 12–24 *et seq.* above.

by way of assignments including confidential invoice discounting and, secondly, it will deal with priorities among competing assignees and the validity of an assignment in the insolvency of a factor's client. The general intention of UNCITRAL in the drafting of this convention was to provide for certainty as to the applicable law so that the providers of credit for receivables financing may do so at the minimum cost for the ultimate benefit of those who require the credit.

Some Substantive rules of the UNCITRAL convention

12–36   The principal substantive rules the convention[60] which may affect factors will include the following:

(1) The convention will apply to: (i) any assignment of a receivable arising from a contract between the client, located in a contracting state, and a debtor located in another state; and (ii) any assignment of a receivable across national borders by an assignor in a contracting state (for example, by an export factor to an import factor in the two factor system[61] or where the client and the factor are in different states). However, the rules of the convention relating to the rights and obligations of the debtor will not apply unless the debtor is also in a contracting state. The convention will apply to any subsequent assignment (*i.e.* an assignment by an assignee to a further assignee) as is commonly the case in the operation of the two factor system.[62]

(2) Among the exclusions are assignments of bank deposits and or letters of credit or arising under certain banking and financial transactions; and the convention is not to affect the rights and obligations of persons under laws relating to negotiable instruments or interests in real property.[63]

(3) An assignment will not be ineffective solely because it is of future receivables provided that they can be identified as receivables to which the assignment relates.[64]

(4) An assignment of a receivable will be effective in spite of a prohibition against it in the underlying contract.[65] It is fortunate that this provision applies to certain receivables only (including substantially all trade receivables) so that it does not prevent a factor

---

[60] Of which the full text is set out in App.12.
[61] See paras 6–03 *et seq.* above.
[62] Art.1.
[63] Art.4.
[64] Art.8.1.
[65] Art.9.

from prohibiting the assignment of its debt to its client. However, governments may exclude from this provision contracts where the debtor is a government department or local authority and it is probable that many states will take advantage of their exclusion.[66]

(5) The notice of the assignment[67] to the debtor, which must be in writing including electronic means, may be sent by the assignor or the assignee; but after such notification a payment instruction may be sent only by the assignee. Furthermore, a notice or payment instruction may relate to future receivables and this will be of assistance to factors in making introductory letter[68] effective in international factoring.

(6) It is also provided that notice of a subsequent assignment by the first assignee will constitute notice also of the first assignment. This should be of assistance to import factors under the two factor system[69] in which the first assignment, from the export factor to the import factor, is not normally notified to the debtor.

(7) There are rules relating to the discharge of the debtor by payment before and after notification of the assignment and after notifications by competing assignees and subsequent assignees.

(8) The convention includes provisions for notification to the debtor to cut off, as against the assignee, the debtor's defences, rights of set-off and modification of the contract giving rise the assigned receivable.[70]

(9) The priority of the assignee against claims by competing assignees, creditors of the assignor or the assignor's insolvent estate are to be governed by the law of the state in which the assignor is located.[71]

(10) Personal and property rights securing payment of receivables are transferred without the need for a new act of transfer, unless the local law requires it in which case the assignor is bound to perform that act.[72]

As the above are only descriptive of the provisions, it is recommended that factors and their professional advisers should read the actual convention which is available from the Secretariat of UNCITRAL at the United Nations in Vienna.

---

[66] Art.40.
[67] Arts 13 and 16.
[68] See para.8–12 above.
[69] See paras 6–03 et seq. above.
[70] Arts 18 to 20 inclusive.
[71] Arts 22 et seq.
[72] Art.10.2.

The Wide Scope

12-37   The scope of the convention is extremely wide. Unlike the UNIDROIT convention it does not exclude receivables owing by consumers but only *assignments* of receivables to individuals for personal, family or household purposes. It includes, not only assignments of receivables which are themselves international in character because the assignor and the debtor are in different countries, but also assignments of purely domestic receivables across national borders. Examples of the latter would be the securitisation of blocks of hire purchase receivables or mortgages and their sale by a bank to a bank in a different country. The convention covers not only trade receivables but also receivables arising from project finance; for example, the provision of finance for a bridge in consideration of the assignment to the financier of the tolls over many years would be covered.

12-38   The needs of project finance or securitisation are in some respects different from those of the factor financing trade receivables. As a result it seemed at one time that some of the provisions might be slightly less favourable to factors than those of the UNIDROIT convention. However, in the later stages of the drafting these difficulties for factors have been resolved and, although in a conflict the UNCITRAL convention will prevail, that convention does not preclude the application of UNIDROIT to the rights and obligations of debtors where it is not covered by UNCITRAL.[73]

12-39   Therefore, it is now apparent that factors would benefit from the adoption of the UNCITRAL convention, not only because it covers assignments that have not been notified to debtors, but also because it provides clear guidance on the law to be applied in relation to a factor's conflicts with third parties.

Rights of the assignee against third parties

12-40   The convention will provide for priority among competing assignees and between an assignee and the assignor's creditors and the validity of the assignments in the insolvency of the assignor. In the early days of the preparation of the draft convention, it was proposed that these matters would be dealt with by a system of registration at first in a national register of the country of the assignor and later in an international register. These proposals met resistance from delegates of countries where a system of priorities based on registration is repugnant to their laws and commercial practices. The convention now provides that these matters should be regulated according to the law of the state in which the assignor is located and the convention includes three sets of optional articles dealing with priorities

---

[73] Art.38.2.

based on registration, the first in time or the first to give notice.[74] There are also fall back provisions to provide for a case in which a country accepts the convention but has no conflict of law rules.[75]

---

[74] See annex to the convention.
[75] See Ch.V of the convention.

CHAPTER 13

THE FACTOR'S USE OF COMPANY CHARGES

13–01 In Ch.1 it was indicated that, by lending against the security of debts, a factor could provide the equivalent of the finance generated by the usual structure of factoring (the purchase of debts). This chapter examines the advantages and disadvantages of such a legal form; there is also described in this chapter the use of charges by a factor as collateral or additional security where his agreement provides for the purchase of the debts.[1] Although the Companies Act 1985,[2] in dealing with the registration of charges, includes a mortgage within the expression "charge" and the Law of Property Act 1925[3] throughout includes a charge within the expression "mortgage", in the consideration of the matters referred to in this chapter the difference between a mortgage and a charge must be borne in mind. Whilst a mortgage comprises the transfer of ownership of the mortgaged property to the security holder subject to the mortgagor's right of redemption, a charge does not include any transfer of ownership; a charge gives the security holder the right to have his debt discharged out of the proceeds of the charged property.

1. THE ALTERNATIVE LEGAL FORM

13–02 The reason for the provision of factoring by means of the purchase of debts is largely historical. The use of this system was not based on any perceived advantage of this legal form. The service was based on the activities of factors in the United States[4] and, at the time when the service was introduced into the United Kingdom, lending by a factor without banking status would have been hampered by some restrictive provisions of the Money Lenders Acts now repealed. Furthermore, at that time the concept of a fixed

---

[1] See para.1–08 above.
[2] s.396(4).
[3] s.205(1).
[4] See para.1–14 above.

charge on debts had not been developed. A floating charge[5] would not have given the factor the confidence of recovering in full the funds he had lent owing to the well-known deficiencies of that type of security and, in particular, the provision for payment of preferential debts of a company in receivership out of the assets subject to a floating charge.[6] By the early 1980s it had been generally accepted that it was possible for a company to create a charge on its existing and future debts as a specific charge attaching to the existing debts on the creation of the charge and on future debts as they came into existence.[7] The possibility of changing to this form of legal structure was then considered seriously by at least one factoring company. However, the introduction of the administration procedure by the Insolvency Act 1986[8] caused the consideration of any such change to be abandoned.[9]

The House of Lords decision in the *Spectrum* Case[10] appears to have **13–03** provided certainty in the degree of control by a chargee of the charged debts that is necessary. Therefore, renewed consideration of lending on security instead of purchasing is considered appropriate and, accordingly, the advantages of each form are analysed below.

Advantages of Purchase:

(a) Direct recovery from debtors

In the event of the insolvency of the client there is no sudden impact on the **13–04** debtors of a change in the person to whom they are to pay; such a change may detract from efficient collection by causing the debtors to examine carefully their rights of defence or set-off. However, this advantage does not apply:

(i) where there is prohibition against the assignment of the debts[11]; and

(ii) in cases where the service is on an undisclosed basis until notice has been given.

---

[5] For a description of a floating charge, see para.8–22 above.
[6] Insolvency Act 1986, s.40 as amended by ss.251 and 386 of the Enterprise Act 2002.
[7] At that time relying principally on *Siebe Gorman & Co Ltd v Barclays Bank Ltd* [1979] 2 Lloyds Rep. 142; That case has now been overruled in *National Westminster Bank plc v Spectrum Plus Ltd* [2005] 3 W.L.R. 58 because the countervalue of the proceeds of the charged debts remained at the disposal of the chargor. However, it remains possible to create a fixed charge on the present and future debts of a company provided that arrangements are in force so that the debts and their proceeds are unconditionally appropriated for the discharge of the obligation which the charge secures.
[8] See paras 11–38 *et seq.* above.
[9] See para.13–10(g) below.
[10] *National Westminster Bank plc v Spectrum Plus Ltd* [2005] 3 W.L.R. 58.
[11] See paras 9–36 *et seq.* above.

(b) Intervention in the debtor's rights of set-off

13–05 The effect of early notice to the debtor (*i.e.* as soon as the debt is created and assigned), so as to prevent the creation of further countervailing rights of the debtor, is described in Ch.9. Although it is thought that notice to a debtor of a charge on his indebtedness may have a similar effect[12] and a charge on receivables will normally give the chargee the right to take an assignment of them, it is unlikely that such notices would be given, or such an assignment taken, at an early stage.

(c) Absence of requirement to register a charge in the case of corporate clients

13–06 It is thought by some factors that the perceived reluctance of company directors to accede to the registration of a security right gives a factor using the present usual system a commercial advantage.

(d) Accounting considerations: off balance sheet finance for client

13–07 In the past, it had been accepted as the standard practice for the balance sheet of the client to show only the total of the unpaid purchase price of the debts as a debt owing by the factor with, in any case where the factoring is wholly with recourse to the client, a note of the contingent liability for the recourse. Such treatment has the effect of decreasing both current assets and current liabilities and improving the apparent current ratio. However, these considerations no longer apply.[13]

(e) Payment of discounting charge gross by client

13–08 If the interest, in the case of lending (other than by a bank, building society or insurance company), is considered to be yearly interest (and not short interest), then the client would be required to deduct tax at the standard rate from such interest.[14] There is no statutory definition of "yearly interest" and from case law interest is generally considered to be short interest if it arises

---

[12] Lightman & Moss, *The Law of Receivers and Administrators of Companies* (3rd ed., 2000), paras 16–037 to 16–039.
[13] For the accounting conventions in respect of the client's balance sheet and accounts see paras 5–17 *et seq.* above and App.11.
[14] Income and Corporation Taxes Act 1988, s.349. By reason of the provisions of ss.82 and 83 of the Finance Act 1996, with effect from April 1, 1996 the disadvantage to a factor (if it is not a bank) of receiving interest after deduction of tax is not as serious as it was before then. Until those sections came into force the interest was taken out of the revenue accounts of the recipient and taxed under Sch.D, Case III which would create complications in reclaiming the tax against expenses. Now, although the factoring company will still have to receive interest after deduction of tax, it will be able to set off the income tax deducted against its mainstream corporation tax and, if that is not sufficient, to have the excess repaid.

under an obligation of a short term nature[15]; for example, on a loan made under an agreement that requires the loan to the be fully repaid within one year.[16] In the case of the purchase of a debt, the finance charge is in most cases a discount on the purchase of each debt, is not subject to the above rules and is received by the factor without any deduction of tax.

(f) The requirement of a service agreement

If the service to be provided is to be any form in which administration of the sales ledger and collection of the debts is to be carried out by the factor, these functions are the natural result of the purchase of debts by the factor. No service agreement whereby the factor carries out the administration and collection as the client's agent will be necessary as would be the case where the debts will still remain vested in the client until the factor enforces his security.   **13–09**

(g) Requirement for guarantee of payment

Where any form of factoring without recourse is provided, if the factor does not purchase the debts, then the factor must give the client a guarantee of due payment of the approved debts. The possibility that the guarantee might constitute credit insurance must be considered. If the factor is providing insurance to his clients, it will be carrying on a regulated activity for which it needs to be authorised under the Financial Services and Markets Act 2000; otherwise, it will be committing an offence. There is no statutory definition of insurance and such a continuing credit guarantee does not appear to have been considered specifically by the courts. Reference to case law indicates that there remains the probability of such an arrangement being caught.   **13–10**

(h) The effect of the appointment of an administrator

The bar to legal process provided for by the Insolvency Act 1986 from the time of an administration application[17] or the giving of notice of the intention to appoint or of the appointment of an administrator[18] affects the second lender but not the collection by the purchaser of the debts already vesting in him. This has generally been considered the most important of the   **13–11**

---

[15] See Whiteman, *Income Tax* (3rd ed., 1988), para.18–10.
[16] See, *e.g.* the following definition of "insurance" in case law: "First, the contract must provide that the assured will become entitled to something on the occurrence of some event. Second, the event must be one which involves some element of uncertainty. Third, the assured must have an insurable interest in the subject-matter of the contract". *Medical Defence Union Ltd v Department of Trade* [1980] Ch. 82, *per* Megarry V.-C at p.89.
[17] Insolvency Act 1986, para.44 of Sch.B1, and see para.11–48 above.
[18] Insolvency Act 1986, para.43 of Sch.B1, and see para.11–48 above.

advantages of the continued provision of factoring by way of purchase of debts.

The advantages of lending on security

(a) Prohibitions against assignments

13–12 Although a charge document will usually provide for the assignment of the charged debts if called for by the chargee, a charge on a debt is not *per se* an assignment and is, accordingly, not affected by such a prohibition in the contract giving rise to the charged debt. Accordingly, lending on security may mitigate any slight concern which a factor may have that, in the winding-up or bankruptcy of his client, he must rely on the co-operation of the liquidator or trustee in bankruptcy for the collection for the account of the factor of any debt assigned to him in breach of such a prohibition[19]; with a charge on the debts the factor may collect through his receiver.

(b) Registration may be helpful in the case of a conflict with another chargee

13–13 In some circumstances, the factor's priority over a charge on the debts of his client taken after the coming into effect of the factoring agreement may be in doubt if the holder of the charge had no knowledge of the factoring agreement at the time when he took his charge.[20] Even in cases where the factor is entitled to such priority, it may be difficult to establish it. For example, where the factor's agreement is on a whole turnover basis, the factor will have priority over a charge taken after the factoring agreement has become effective, unless the chargee can rely on the rule in *Dearle v Hall*[21]; but sometimes the bank or lender who has taken the charge will dispute this. Where the factor has registered a charge, the priorities between him and the subsequent chargee will be governed by well established principles.[22]

(c) Value Added Tax

13–14 The ownership of the debts, although charged to the factor, would remain vested in the client; the functions of book keeping and collection would be provided by the factor under a service agreement. Any doubt as to the service provided by a factor, in administering the sales ledger and collecting the debts,[23] would disappear. There should then be no doubt about the

---

[19] See para.9–36 above.
[20] See paras 8–15 to 8–29 above.
[21] See para.8–27 above.
[22] See Goode, *Legal Problems of Credit and Security* (3rd ed., 2003), Ch.V.
[23] See para.10–49 above.

application of output tax by the factor on his administration charge and thereby the recovery of input taxes.

(d) Insolvency of factor's client

Where the factor provides his funds by way of lending on security, there **13–15** should be fewer disagreements with liquidators or trustees in bankruptcy who are likely to accept more readily the concept and priority of a charge on debts than the purchase under a factoring agreement. In the case of the appointment of a receiver by the holder of another charge, these priorities should have been covered by an agreement to regulate the priorities. In the insolvency of the client there is no requirement (as there is in the case of a purchase of the debts) for the factor to collect the remainder of the outstanding debts after recovery of funds in use or to arrange for the reassignment of such debts to the client if his agreement provides for this.

(e) Conflicts with suppliers who have reserved title

Where a supplier sells with reservation of title to the goods sold until they **13–16** are paid for and purports to extend his rights to the proceeds of an onward sale of such goods, in most circumstances the arrangement is likely to be held to be a charge on the proceeds. If it is unregistered, under the existing law, the charge will be void against a creditor or the liquidator or the administrator of the company which created the charge (*i.e.* the supplier's customer)[24]; *such an unregistered charge is not void altogether.*[25]

If the factor has purchased the proceeds as debts under a factoring **13–17** agreement with the supplier's customer, the factor will seek to have priority over the unregistered charge. Factor's problem in such a case, if it has purchased the debts, is that it is not normally a creditor of the client; in normal circumstances, the factor is a debtor to the client for the unpaid balance of the purchase price of the receivables. In order to claim priority over the unregistered charge, the factor must become a creditor of its client; and, if his agreement so provides, he may become a creditor to the extent of his funds in use by exercising the right to have the client repurchase all the debts on the basis that the ownership does not pass to the client until the repurchase price has been paid.

However, a claim to priority over the unregistered charge, under the **13–18** present law, may be made only by a liquidator (for all creditors) or a secured creditor or one having a proprietary interest in the charged property.[26] It is not entirely clear whether, in these circumstances, the factor's interest would

---

[24] Companies Act 1985, s.395.
[25] See *e.g. Re Ehrmann Bros Ltd* [1906] 2 Ch. 697.
[26] See *e.g. Re Ehrmann Bros Ltd* [1906] 2 Ch. 697 and *Re Ashpurton Estates Ltd* [1983] Ch. 110 at p.123.

be such that, in the absence of a charge on the debts, the factor's claim would succeed.[27] As a lender secured by a registered fixed charge on the debts the factor should have no difficulty in establishing his priority.

The balance of advantage

13–19   It is probable that recent changes in the law and business practice may have detracted from any advantages of providing factoring by way of lending on the security of debts and increased the advantages of the purchase of them as follows:

    (a) Now that stamp duty is no longer applied to the assignment of debts, there is no longer an advantage provided by the absence of liability to stamp duty in the case of an instrument of charge. It was previously considered that the lending on security of the debts would avoid the need for the factor to construct his agreement with stamp duty in mind.

    (b) Compliance by the factor's client with Financial Reporting Standards are no longer widely considered to be a bar to the acceptance of factoring.[28]

    (c) In spite of changes in the law a factor purchasing debts may still avoid the moratorium on the enforcement of his security caused by an administration application or the giving of notice of intention to appoint or of appointment of an administrator to any of his clients (para.13–10 above).[29]

    (d) The advantage (if indeed it exists[30]) of being a lender on security in a conflict with a supplier who claimed factored debts on the basis of reservation of title may be resolved by the factor taking a charge over the debts of his client that remain in the ownership of the client, reassigning the factored debts to the client and relying on the charge.[31]

13–20   Consideration must also be given to the factor's business with partnerships and sole traders for which the factoring must be by way of assignments; it is unlikely that any factor would welcome the prospect of the two

---

[27] In E. *Pfeiffer Weinkellerei-Weininkauf GmbH & Co v Arburthnot Factors Ltd* [1988] W.L.R. 150 the point does not appear to have been specifically addressed.

[28] For the passages relevant to factoring, see App.11. See also para.13–08 above.

[29] Insolvency Act 1986, paras 43 and 44 of Sch.B1.

[30] See para.8–30 above.

[31] Such a charge is likely to be held to be a fixed charge owing to the procedures adopted by factors in all forms of factoring for dealing with the proceeds of debts. See *National Westminster Bank plc v Spectrum Plus Ltd* [2005] 3 W.L.R. 58.

systems running at the same time. On the other hand, in the case of invoice discounting (with recourse) for companies, the adoption of the alternative legal form might well be considered advantageous. It seems therefore unlikely that in the present state of the law receivables financing by way of the purchase of debts will change.

2. CHARGES AS COLLATERAL SECURITY

A factor may obtain most of the benefits of both legal forms by entering into a factoring agreement, which provides for the normal purchase of the debts by the factor, and, additionally, taking a charge on property of the client company as collateral security to secure the client's obligations under the factoring agreement. Most of the benefits of the alternative legal form would be additionally available to the factor by the inclusion, in the property subject to such a charge, of any factored debts of which the ownership failed to vest effectively in the factor for any reason.   **13–21**

Charges on factored debts which fail to vest in the factor

When the notion of taking charges by factors as collateral security originated, the property charged was limited to debts within the scope of the factoring agreement which failed to vest in the factor for any reason. The idea for factors, whose agreements were of the facultative type,[32] was to catch the debts within the ambit of the agreement which had not been offered to, and accepted by, the factor at the inception of any insolvency proceedings against the client or on the termination of the agreement. In the case of both facultative and whole turnover agreements,[33] there was perceived to be a danger that the factor might have no rights to the proceeds of any debt assigned in breach of a provision in the contract of sale banning such assignment.[34] It was considered that, if assignments were invalid, then the debts would remain part of the property of the client company and be charged to the factor. More recently, it has been considered that the factor is protected from this danger (that the proceeds of such a debt would not be available to the factor) by: **13–22**

(i) the probability that they will be the subject of a constructive trust[35]; and

(ii) the specific trust provisions in the factoring agreement.[36]

---

[32] See paras 7–08 and 7–09 above.
[33] See paras 7–10 and 7–11 above.
[34] See paras 9–36 to 9–39 above.
[35] *ibid.*
[36] See para.10–34 above.

However, it is now appreciated that such a charge has other advantages for the factor. First, such a charge taken as collateral security will give the factor advantages (b), (d) and (e)[37] of changing to the alternative legal form.

13–23 Secondly, such a charge will protect a factor in the event that a liquidator, administrative receiver or administrator of a client company seeks to invalidate the factor's ownership of the factored debts.[38] Such a challenge might also be made in the case of debts the subject of an agreement of the whole turnover type for which the factor had not paid the purchase price.[39]

13–24 A further challenge might be based on an allegation that the holding of a retention (of a part of the purchase price of each debt), against which to apply sums payable by the client, constitutes a registrable charge. Where such rights are drafted in the factoring agreement by way of a charge back[40] and not as a contractual set-off, such a challenge might be successful now that the House of Lords has overturned the conceptual impossibility of a charge on the charge holder's own indebtedness.[41] As a safeguard any charge on book debts taken by a factor should include a charge on all amounts owing at any time by the factor to the client.

Charges on other debts

13–25 Subsequently, factors have sought to find other collateral security in order to protect themselves against exposure as unsecured creditors arising from a shortfall of the retention to provide for recourse of debts, which are not collectable, on the insolvency of a corporate client. Such other security has most commonly been the extension of the charges to all debts outside the scope of the factoring agreement. Such other debts may be trade debts excluded from the factoring agreement (for example, export debts where the agreement covered only domestic business) or other amounts payable to the client including claims under insurance policies and for the recovery of value added tax. In order that such collateral security should rank ahead of the claims of preferential creditors, a factor resorting to a charge on such non-factored debts will require that the charge should be recognised as a fixed charge. Since 1990 there appeared, until recently, to be two conflicting lines of authority on whether or not it is an essential element of a fixed charge that the chargor should be deprived of his freedom to manage the charged assets and their proceeds in the normal course of his business.

13–26 However, it is now clear that in order to rank as a fixed charge a charge on debts must provide, not only that the chargor may not dispose of the debts without the consent of the chargee, but also that the debts and their

---

[37] See paras 13–13, 13–15 and 13–16.
[38] See para.7–25 above.
[39] See para.7–10 above.
[40] See para.10–07 above.
[41] *Morris v Rayners Enterprises Incorporated; Morris v Agrochemicals Ltd* [1997] B.C.C. 965.

proceeds must be unconditionally appropriated as security for the discharge of the secured obligations. This means that the proceeds of the debts must be paid either direct to the chargee or into an account under the control of the chargee with a ban on the use of those proceeds, or their countervalue, by the chargor in the normal course of its business.[42] It is also necessary that such procedures are carried out in practice. Consequently, factors, wishing to enhance their security by taking a fixed charge on debts outside the scope of the factoring agreement, will be hampered by the difficulty of arranging for the proceeds of those other debts to be paid into a bank account under the factor's control. However, for commercial reasons, it would be natural for a factor's client, when creating a charge in favour of the factor on debts outside the scope of the factoring agreement, to have resisted an under-taking in the instrument of charge to give up the client's control of the proceeds of the debts; the client has required that the proceeds should be immediately available to him for the general purpose of his business. Indeed, it seems likely that, if a chargee complied strictly with the requisite cove-nants in a fixed charge created on all his debts to secure indebtedness other than an overdraft (*e.g.* a fixed term loan or a contingent liability), the charge would *on its creation* stultify the business of the chargor and cause his failure; all cash flow would be held for the benefit of the holder of the charge leaving nothing for the chargor's business.[43]

Where there is a prior fixed charge on such debts in favour of a bank **13–27** (which in present circumstances owing to the degree of control that must be exercised by the bank seems unlikely), the factor's client would have cove-nanted to pay the proceeds into a blocked account under the control of the bank; thus, the client would be deprived of management autonomy over the proceeds. In order that the factor should have a second fixed charge he would have to provide in his documentation that compliance with such covenants in the instrument of the first charge would be deemed to be compliance with covenants in favour of the factor. It is now likely that all charges by factors on debts outside the scope of a factoring agreement will be held to be floating even if they are expressed to be fixed charges.

The use of floating charges by factors

The security provided by a charge taken as collateral security may be **13–28** enhanced by the inclusion of a floating charge on the remainder of the property of the factor's client. Such a floating charge if created after September 15, 2003 no longer gives the factor the right to appoint an *administrative* receiver with very wide powers for the benefit of the factor.[44]

---

[42] *National Westminster Bank plc v Spectrum Plus Ltd* [2005] 3 W.L.R. 58.
[43] See Alan Berg, "Charges over Book Debts" (1995) J.B.L. 433.
[44] Insolvency Act 1986, Sch.B1.

However, if it is a *qualifying* floating charge,[45] it gives the factor the right to appoint an administrator. Although an administrator's duties are to act for the benefit of a company as a whole including its unsecured creditors and not simply for the benefit of the person appointing him, it may well be in the common interest of an insolvent client company and the factor for an administrator to continue the business of the company.

13–29   In order not to preclude the raising of finance by the factor's client by granting security to a financier on property other than the debts, such a floating charge is sometimes created by an instrument which does not preclude the creation by the client of charges in priority to the floating element in the factor's charge.[46] Where any such prior charge is a floating charge or if there is already in existence a floating charge, then the factor should seek the co-operation of the holder of the first or prior floating charge and such co-operation should be the subject of a provision in any agreement for the regulation of the priorities.

3. PRIORITIES

13–30   Unlike the priority given to preferential creditors in the winding-up of Companies[47] and in receivership or administration over the claims of a holder of a floating charge on the assets of a company,[48] there is no statutory provision generally regulating the priorities of company charges which have been duly registered.[49] The date of registration, which is necessary for perfection of most company charges, is not an arbiter of their priorities. There are rules of common law and equity (with some intervention by statute) which depend, not only upon the dates of creation of the charges, but also upon whether they are legal or equitable and whether fixed or floating. These rules are further complicated by questions of both actual and constructive notice. It is proposed here only to indicate the rules that a factor should consider when taking one of the charges referred to earlier in this chapter as collateral security from a client company which has already created or proposes to create a fixed and floating charge on all its assets in favour of bank or other financier.[50]

13–31   The general rule is that the charges rank in order of their creation; for a person cannot give to another a better interest in his property than he

---

[45] see Ch.11, para. and Insolvency Act 1986, para.14(2) of Sch.B1.
[46] Often referred to as a "lightweight floating charge".
[47] Insolvency Act 1986 s.175(1).
[48] *ibid.*, s.175(2)(b).
[49] As regards the priority of a duly registered charge over a registrable, but unregistered, charge, see para.8–30 above.
[50] For a more detailed study See Gough, *Company Charges* (1996), Goode, *Legal Problems of Credit and Security* (3rd ed., 2003) Ch.V, Oditah, *Legal Aspects of Receivables Financing* (1991), Ch.6 and McCormack, *Registration of Company Charges* (1994), Ch.7.

possesses and, when giving a charge which is second in time on his property, that property must already be encumbered by the first created charge. However, this rule is subject to the following:

(a) a legal interest in property taken *bona fide* without notice of an earlier equitable interest in the same property will rank ahead of the equitable interest;

(b) generally a fixed charge taken over property subject to an existing floating charge will have priority provided that the fixed charge is created before the crystallisation of the floating charge; and

(c) the rule against tacking of new advances.[51]

These rules may be displaced by an agreement among the holders of the charges and the company which created the charges.[52]

In some cases, the collateral security taken by a factor over any land and **13–32** buildings or plant and equipment will be by way of floating charge only; unless the factor is taking a fixed charge or mortgage on such property,[53] he will not be much concerned with rule (a). Charges on debts and other choses in action take effect in equity only and an assignment of a debt by way of charge cannot constitute a legal assignment.[54]

Priority of fixed over floating charges

It is likely that any charge taken by a factor on debts which are outside **13–33** the scope of the factoring agreement will constitute a floating charge even if it is termed as fixed.[55] As regards priorities, in accordance with rule (b) referred to above, the result will be that any subsequent charge, which constitutes in fact a fixed charge, will have priority unless the instrument of the factor's charge contained a covenant against the creation of such a fixed charge and the holder of the later fixed charge had notice[56] of the covenant when he took his charge. However, an agreement between the parties may provide for the factor to have priority in respect of his floating charge on the debts. Such an arrangement will create a circularity problem as follows:

• the holder of the fixed charge has priority over preferential creditors under the general law;

---

[51] See Goode, *Legal Problems of Credit & Security* (3rd ed., 2003), paras 5–17 to 5–22.
[52] A specimen "Deed of Priorities" between a factor and a bank is contained in App.9.
[53] In which case reference should be made to the works mentioned in n.63 above.
[54] Law of Property Act 1925, s.136(1).
[55] *National Westminster Bank plc v Spectrum Plus Ltd* [2005] 3 W.L.R. 58.
[56] It seems that only actual notice of the restriction will suffice; see also para.8–18 above.

- the preferential creditors have priority over the factor's floating charge by statute[57];

- by the priority agreement the holder of the fixed charge has given priority to the factor.

A similar situation was considered by the Companies Court in *Re Portbase (Clothing) Ltd*,[58] where it was held that the effect of the priority agreement was to subject the fixed charge to the priority of the floating charge which remained subject to the prior statutory rights of the preferential creditors. As a result, *both* charges ranked after the preferential creditors. In order to avoid this result, where a floating charge is to take priority over a fixed charge, the priority agreement should provide for the holder of the floating charge to be subrogated to the rights and interests in the property of the holder of the fixed charge to the extent necessary to provide for the agreed priority.[59]

The rule against tacking

13–34   Tacking occurs when the holder of a first mortgage (which for this purpose includes a charge[60]) on any property to secure a fixed sum seeks to secure a further advance to the owner of that property by that first mortgage *after* the creation of a second mortgage on the same property in favour of a third party. The effect of tacking of mortgages (when permitted) is further to defer the rights of the holder of the second mortgage. The rules against tacking[61] apply except where the holder of the first charge has made arrangements with the second for tacking or where the holder of the first charge had no notice of the second when he made his fresh advance or where the first charge imposes an *obligation* on the holder of it to make fresh advances.[62] This rule may affect a factor with a first charge because, in normal circumstances, the factor is a creditor, and not a debtor, of his client. In order that the factor may be in a position to enforce the charge, it will be necessary that the client should be actually indebted to the factor for a liquidated sum for which he may make a demand; this is normally done by a recourse of all outstanding debts for which the factoring agreement may

---

[57] Insolvency Act 1986, s.175(2)(b).

[58] [1993] Ch. 388.

[59] *ibid.*, at 109, where Chadwick J. suggests that it would be open to the holder of a prior fixed charge to assign some or all of his rights and interests in the charged property to the holder of a subsequent floating charge; such an assignment was absent in the circumstances of the case. He also distinguished the facts in the case from those postulated in Goode, *Legal Problems of Credit and Security* (3rd ed., 2003), paras 5–60 *et seq.*; *Re Woodroffes (Musical Instruments) Ltd* [1986] Ch. 366 at 375, to which Goode refers in his comment on the *Portbase* Case at para.5–40.

[60] Law of Property Act 1925, s.205(1).

[61] *ibid.*, s.94(3).

[62] *ibid.*, s.94(1).

provide in the case of a serious breach by, or insolvency of, the client. However, it may well be that, before the factor exercises this recourse and becomes a creditor for the repurchase price of the debts, the client will have created a second charge on the property charged to the factor. In these circumstances, the holder of the second charge may claim that when he took his charge there was nothing owed to the factor and the recourse is in effect the tacking of a liability from the client to the factor. A covenant in the instrument of the factor's charge against the creation of any further charges on the charged property will help the factor in this respect if it can be shown that the second chargee had notice of it[63]; but, in present state of the law, whether a note of the restriction at the Companies Registry is sufficient for this purpose is not certain. Accordingly, as a protection against such a claim by the holder of a second charge on property charged to the factor, the factor should procure an agreement for priorities with the holder of the second charge. That agreement should provide *inter alia* that the agreed priorities will not be affected by any fluctuation on the client's accounts with the factor nor by the emergence on such accounts of a nil or credit balance at any time.

4. INVALIDITY OF CHARGES

If a factor takes a charge from his corporate client when it is already in **13–35** financial difficulties, he may find that a liquidator or administrator (an office holder) subsequently appointed to the client may endeavour to seek to establish the invalidity of the charge. The principal grounds for such a claim are as below, and, in each case, the company must be in liquidation or administration and the office holder must be able to show that the company was unable to pay its debts (as defined in s.123 of the Insolvency Act 1986) at the time of the creation of the charge or that it became unable to do so by reason of the charge:

(1) The office holder may apply to the court to restore the position if the charge is held to be a transaction at an undervalue.[64] For this purpose, the onset[65] of the insolvency must take place within two years of the creation of the charge. However, it seems unlikely (but not impossible) that a charge would be caught under this provision

---

[63] In such circumstances, the second chargee is likely to be liable to the factor for the tort of knowingly procuring a breach of the factor's contractual rights; see also paras 8–35 to 8–38 in connection with breaches of negative pledges.

[64] Insolvency Act 1986, s.238, and see para.11–70 above.

[65] The "onset" of the insolvency means, in the case of an administration or a winding-up following immediately on the discharge of an administrator, the date of the petition for the administration, application or the appointment and otherwise, in the case of winding-up, the commencement thereof; Insolvency Act 1986, s.240(3).

because the creation of the charge does not have the effect of diminishing the value of the company's assets; it only appropriates assets to meet the company's liabilities to the holder of the charge.[66]

(2) the office holder may apply to have the charge set aside as a preference if the onset of the insolvency takes place within six months of the creation of the charge.[67] For this purpose, the company must have done something or suffered something to be done to put the creditor in a better position and to have been motivated by a "desire" to bring about that result; but desire need not be the sole or dominant motive.[68] The factor might argue in his defence that when he took the charge he was not a creditor. In most such cases, it is likely that directors would have been influenced by a desire for the continuation of the factoring agreement.

(3) A *floating* charge may be invalid if created within 12 months before the onset of the insolvency of the company except to the extent that the consideration for the charge consisted of money paid or goods or services supplied to the company or the discharge or reduction of any indebtedness of the company.[69] It is most unlikely that payments made by the factor for the purchase of debts under the factoring agreement would qualify as payments made to the company for this purpose. It may well help a factor to rebut any such claim if he obtains up to date management accounts from the client, showing a solvent position, or other evidence of the client's solvency at the time when the charge is created.

---

[66] *Re Mistral Finance Limited (in liquidation)* [2001] B.C.C. 27; but it may constitute a preference (see sub-para.(2) below).
[67] Insolvency Act 1986, s.239.
[68] *Re M C Bacon Ltd* [1990] B.C.C. 78 at 87.
[69] Insolvency Act 1986, s.245.

CHAPTER 14

FACTORING COMBINED WITH CREDIT INSURANCE

Credit insurance may be and has been used by factors and their clients to **14–01** insure the factored debts against loss by reason of the insolvency of any of the debtors principally for the following reasons:

(1) as an enhancement of the factor's own security;

(2) to protect the factor in respect of large exposures or debts outside the UK.

The use of credit insurance raises a number of matters of consideration for the factor and the client which may affect both the terms of the factoring agreement and the policy of insurance. For this reason, the factoring agreement may require amendments, and, in all cases, the policies of insurance must be amended or contain adequate endorsements to recognise that although the client supplies the goods and services, the factor owns the resulting debts. Also, the wide-ranging provisions of the Financial Services and Markets Act 2000 ("FSMA 2000") regulate many types of activity in relation to contracts of insurance which restrict the way in which credit insurance is used in conjunction with factoring agreements.

1. FINANCIAL SERVICES AND MARKETS ACT 2000[1]

The FSMA 2000 contains what is defined as "the general prohibition", **14–02** which provides that no person may carry on a regulated activity in the United Kingdom or purport to do so, unless he is an authorised person or

---

[1] The FSMA 2000 together with subordinate legislation made under that Act is a complex body of law; for a detailed analysis, see Colinvaux & Merkin's *Insurance Contract Law* (looseleaf); and Clarke, *The Law of Insurance Contracts* (looseleaf).

an exempt person.[2] A person who has permission under Pt.IV of the FSMA 2000 to carry on a regulated activity is an authorised person for the purposes of the Act.[3] Breach of the general prohibition is a criminal offence which may be prosecuted by the Financial Services Authority.[4] An agreement made by an unauthorised person in the course of carrying on a regulated activity in contravention of the general prohibition is unenforceable against the other party,[5] and the other party is entitled to recover any money or other property paid or transferred by him under the agreement, and compensation for any loss sustained by him as a result of having parted with it.[6] Accordingly, it is essential that factors do not carry on any regulated activity, or if they do so, that they first obtain permission under Part IV of the Act.[7]

14–03 What is a "regulated activity"? In so far as is material, an activity is a regulated activity if: "it is of a specified kind which is carried on by way of business; ... and in the case of an activity of a kind which is also specified for the purposes of this paragraph, is carried on in relation to property of any kind".[8] "Specified" means specified in the Financial Services and Markets Act 2000 (Regulated Activities) Order 2001[9] and as amended by the Financial Services and Markets Act 2000 (Regulated Activities) (Amendment) (No.2) Order 2003.[10]

14–04 The FSMA 2000 and subordinate legislation provide that following activities are specified kind of activities:

(1) Effecting or carrying out a contract of insurance as principal[11];

(2) Assisting in the administration and performance of a contract of insurance,[12] unless such activity consists only of the provision of information to the policyholder or potential policyholder by a person in the course of carrying on a profession or business which does not otherwise consist of the carrying on of regulated

---

[2] Financial Services and Markets Act 2000, s.19.
[3] *ibib.*, s.31.
[4] *ibib.*, s.23.
[5] *ibib.*, s.26(1).
[6] *ibib.*, s.23(2).
[7] *ibib.*, ss.40–55.
[8] *ibib.*, s.22. s.22 is also expressed to be "supplemented" by Sch.2 to the FSMA 2000, which itself "specifies" a range of regulated activities and investments.
[9] SI 2001/544.
[10] SI 2003/1476, the material parts of which came into force on January 14, 2005. The order operates by introducing amendments to the 2001 order (SI 2001/544) and to the FSMA 2000 itself. Accordingly, references to articles are to the new or articles in the 2001 order or the Act.
[11] SI 2001/544, Pt II, Art.10(1) and (2).
[12] SI 2001/544, Art.39A as inserted by SI 2003/1476, Art.11.

activities, and may reasonably be regarded as being incidental to that profession or business[13];

(3) "Insurance mediation", meaning the activities of introducing, proposing or carrying out other work preparatory to the conclusion of contracts of insurance, or of concluding such contracts, or of assisting in the administration and performance of such contracts, in particular in the event of a claim.[14] However, the provision of information on an incidental basis in the context of another professional activity will not be considered as insurance mediation, provided that the purpose of that activity is not, among other things, to assist the customer in concluding or performing an insurance contract.[15]

It has not yet been decided whether any information provided by a factor to his client may reasonably be regarded as being incidental to the business of factoring or invoice discounting so that such activity is not a regulated activity requiring permission. No doubt the answer will depend upon the circumstances of the particular case. Nonetheless, as a precaution, factors should either apply for permission under the FSMA 2000 or cease carrying on any activity that may be a regulated activity.

2. MATTERS FOR CONSIDERATION

Even at this late stage in the development of credit insurance for factors and **14–05** their clients, it has been known for a policy not to provide the cover that is perceived by the factor and the client; and this may apply even if the policy has been specially tailored for use by a client of a factor. There are now believed to be about sixteen insurers offering credit insurance in the UK and the policy conditions vary widely. Therefore, whether the factor or the client or both are to rely on the policy, specific advice on the policies offered should be obtained. The matters mentioned below are a guide as to the special points to be addressed in relation to the insurance of factored debts.

Matters for consideration in all credit insurance policies

(a) Provisions relating to credit management

Credit insurers expect the insured to carry out his credit management **14–06** function in such a way as to minimise losses. For this purpose, some

---

[13] SI 2001/544, Art.72C(3)–(4), as inserted by SI 2003/1476, Art.11.
[14] SI 2001/544, Pt II, Art.2.3 of Sch.4, inserted by SI 2003/1476, Art.12.
[15] *ibid.*

insurers, having obtained an outline of the credit management system used by the prospective insured, rely on a general proviso in the policy that the insured shall exercise care and prudence in granting and withholding credit and effecting collection of the insured debts. Other insurers, having obtained exact details of the insured's normal follow up procedure for collections, provide in their policies that any variation in a particular case will give the insurer the right to reject the claim.

14–07 It is very difficult for an insured under a credit insurance policy to comply strictly with the policy conditions at all times in every minute detail. There are often cases in which strict adherence to the normal procedure may not be advisable; flexibility is a requirement of good credit management. To make the insurance arrangement workable, the factor should ensure that the insurer relies only on general details of the collection and other credit management arrangements of the insured and that it will reject a claim only where a variation of the arrangement significantly affected the risk.

(b) Time for payment of claims

14–08 Some policies provide for the payment of a claim, other than for protracted default, within a set period after the insured's claim against the insolvent debtor has been accepted by the person in whose hands the administration of the insolvent estate lies. Such a provision is applicable to the debtor's bankruptcy or winding-up; but administrators and receivers have no duty to consider and adjudicate the claims of unsecured creditors. Therefore, if the policy is to cover the risks of administration and receivership (as it usually does) then the due date for payment of claims should be within a set period, not only of acceptance of the claim by a liquidator or trustee, but, in the alternative, of submission of reasonable evidence of its validity. In some policies there is no provision for a due date for payment of claims, but only for the "ascertainment" of the loss. An insured will feel more secure if the policy provides for a due date for the payment of the claim.

(c) Changes in the terms of the policy

14–09 It is normal for a policy to give the insurer the right to vary it by increasing premium rates or cancelling cover in any specific market; this is necessary to protect the insurer against an unexpected deterioration of the political or economic conditions in the market. Such a variation or cancellation in respect of an important market may make the continuation of the policy of little value to the insured. If such a provision is included then the factor should procure that the insured should have the right to an immediate termination of the policy if the increase is unacceptable to him or the client.

340

(d) Period of risk coverage

Traditional credit insurance policies cover losses in relation to goods sold **14–10** and delivered or services provided within the period of the policy subject to the submission of a claim within a fixed period (often six months) after the end of the policy period if it is not renewed. With a policy structured on these lines, where the client's terms of payment do not exceed 60 days, a factor may reasonably rely on the policy as regards the risk of the insolvency of the debtor in respect of debts offered or notified to the factor up to the termination of the policy. If the terms are longer then the factor, having paid the client in respect of a debt coming into existence towards the end of the policy period, may find that the six months period has expired by the time collection procedures have been completed but failed owing to the insolvency of the debtor. As a result the insurer will be "off risk".

The position is similar in the case of "protracted default" where this is **14–11** covered by the policy. This is often defined as the debtor's failure to pay within 90 days of the original due date unless that has been extended by agreement between the insured and the debtor. Claims in respect of this risk are normally payable six months after the protracted default has occurred; thus, the insurer has an opportunity to collect the debt or determine that it is not collectable. Such claims normally relate to cases where legal proceedings to bring about insolvency are not considered worthwhile. Therefore, where the original terms of payment exceed 60 days the factor should in respect of either risk procure that the policy provides for a run off period longer than six months.

Increasingly insurers are issuing policies that cover insolvency or pro- **14–12** tracted default occurring within the policy period. In such cases, where the terms of payment are short (say up to 60 days), the factor will be uncertain about the protection afforded in respect of debts notified or offered after the first six months; losses in respect of debts arising after that may well be outside the policy period. If the terms are longer, then the policy may be of little value to the factor. Such a policy is probably not at all suitable for a factor who wishes to use credit insurance for the purpose of enhancing his security or of accepting a large debtor exposure with greater safety.

Matters for consideration in relation to policies issued to the factor's client

Credit insurance policies normally provide either that, for a claim to be **14–13** admitted, the relevant debt must rank for dividend purposes in the insolvent estate of the debtor *in favour of the insured* or that an insured loss means a debt owing to the *insured*. If the policy is issued to the client alone, then neither the client as insured (not being the owner of the debt) nor the factor (not being the insured) would be able to procure the admittance of a claim against the insurer unless the factor were to reassign the debt to the client.

The factor may well not wish to do so (particularly if the client is insolvent or if the factoring agreement has terminated) because the factor may then lose control over the salvage (*i.e.* dividends from the estate and other recoveries). This difficulty may be compounded by the usual undertakings regarding salvage required by insurers which are described below.[16]

14-14   In the insolvency of the client, even if the factor were to be willing to reassign the debt, the subject of the claim, the person having the duty to administer the estate of the client may have no reason to go through the administrative procedures for a claim which, being of benefit only to the factor as assignee, will have no benefit to the estate. This difficulty may be overcome by the factor's use of his power of attorney to make the claim on behalf of the client *provided that the power includes such authority*.

14-15   There are other difficulties which may be met by a factor and the client, where the policy is issued solely in the name of the client, unless suitable amendments are made. The following are the main matters to be considered in this connection.

(1)   If the factor is relying on the policy for security, he cannot be certain at all times that the client has complied in all respects with the policy conditions, breaches of which entitle the insurer to decline to settle a claim (*e.g.* prompt and accurate declarations of turnover and of seriously overdue accounts and prompt payment of the premium). A warranty from the client to cover these matters will be of little value to the factor in the insolvency of the client.

(2)   Most policies provide for warranties and undertakings by the insured in relation to the credit management function and, if factoring is on a disclosed basis (or in invoice discounting if the factor subsequently requires disclosure), the client, as insured, has put himself in a position of being unable to comply with the warranties and undertakings; the collection of debts is in the hands of the factor.

(3)   A further difficulty relates to the usual practice of some insurers to provide that, for the establishment of credit limits up to a specific amount (a "discretionary limit"), the insured should not apply to the insurer for credit approval but should justify the credit granted to a debtor by information or payments experience or both. In any case, where the factor carries out the sales ledger function, it would be difficult for him to provide the information for the client without becoming a credit reference agency for the purposes of the

---

[16] See para.14–22 below.

Consumer Credit Act 1974[17]; and the experience of payments is that of the factor and not of the insured.

(4) It has been known in recent years for an insurer to provide that its liability terminates completely on the insolvency of the insured. If the policy is taken out as an enhancement of the factor's security, then the inclusion of such provision will severely detract from the use of the policy to the factor.

Policy issued to the client and factor as joint insured

The factor may well be able to overcome the deficiencies described above **14–16** if it is a policy-holder jointly with the insured either under a policy so issued initially or by the addition of the factor to an existing policy by endorsement. Then the factor's rights to the ownership of the debts and to carry out the credit management functions will be recognised and it will be able to submit claims direct to the insurer as a policy holder. The policy will be for the respective rights and interests of the two policy holders. Therefore, even in the case of a policy wherein the factor is a joint insured, there should also be in place an assignment (accepted by the insurer if it is prohibited) to the factor of all the benefits of the policy which may accrue to the client. In this connection it has been the practice of at least one insurer to incorporate a term in the policy whereby the insurer is entitled to be discharged by paying the first named policyholder or to have the right to be discharged by paying any of the joint insured at the insurer's discretion; therefore, the assignment is essential for the factor in order that it may be certain of receiving payments from the insurer direct.

The principal disadvantage to the factor of joint insurance is that the **14–17** factor will be jointly liable for declarations of turnover and seriously overdue accounts and, in particular, for the payment of the premium and other charges. Accordingly, some factors have in the past found themselves, in the insolvency of the client, liable for unpaid premiums without the ability to recoup from the client. This disadvantage can be overcome by an arrangement by which the factor takes responsibility for these matters and debits the client's account with the amounts paid to the insurer by way of premium and other charges. The factor will require undertakings from the client to make the requisite reports to the factor in any case in which the factor does not carry out the sales ledger function.

Even with all these safeguards in place, the factor cannot be certain that **14–18** the client may have done or omitted to do something which may avoid the policy. For example, in the proposal form the client may have failed to disclose a material fact. Whether or not such a non-disclosure emerging after the payment of a claim to the factor would entitle the insurer to recover

---

[17] See para.10–64 above.

the claim payment from the factor would depend on the terms of the factoring endorsement. The following example is instructive:

> A few years ago a factor received a demand for repayment of a sum paid to him by the insurer in respect of a claim under a policy issued to the factor's client with an endorsement which for most (but not all) purposes made the factor a joint insured. The insurer had avoided the policy with effect from its beginning by reason of such a non-disclosure. The insurer claimed at first against the factor as joint insured; but owing to a defect in the factoring endorsement, the claim could not be sustained. The insurer then claimed against the factor as assignee of the benefits of the policy, not as a contractual right, but on the basis of restitution. As the factor had not changed his position (*i.e.* by making further payments to the client) on receipt of the claims payment, it was advised by counsel that he was liable to make the repayment.

It seems therefore that such a liability would arise under whichever method is used and that this is not a disadvantage of the joint insured method unless the factoring endorsement to the policy places more onerous obligations on the factor. This might be the case if it obliged the factor to repay whether or not he had changed his position.

14–19   A further disadvantage to the factor as a joint policyholder is that he is liable for all salvage even if it has been received by the client; however, as the insured may well require a similar undertaking as a condition of recognising the factoring arrangements where the client is sole insured, this may be perceived as not being a disadvantage of this method of operation.[18]

3. REQUISITE AMENDMENTS TO POLICY OR FACTORING AGREEMENT

Policy issued to client as sole insured

14–20   The benefits of the policy should be assigned to the factor but many policies include prohibitions against the assignment of their benefits. Acceptance by the insurer of the assignment must be obtained. In addition, at the minimum, if a policy is issued to the client alone, then it is clear from the foregoing that it will require amendment from the standard terms by endorsement to cover:

> (1) a recognition of the factor's right to an assignment of the debts and the sole right to collect them and carry out credit management functions;

---

[18] See para.14–22 below.

(2) agreement by the insurer that continued ownership of the debt by the factor shall not by itself preclude the admittance of a claim; and

(3) agreement by the insurer that the information received by the factor and the factor's experience of payments shall be admissible for the establishment of credit limits within a discretionary limit.

It should be noted that these amendments will probably be necessary to protect the client himself, as an insured, even if the policy is not taken out or required by the factor as an enhancement to the factor's security. However, it is likely that as a condition of agreeing to the above (or even to the assignment itself) the insurer will require certain undertakings from the factor particularly as regards salvage[19] and the disclosure of information. As a result, the factor is half way to becoming a joint insured without most of the advantages of that method.

Policy issued to client and factor jointly

Where the factor is joint insured, it is important that special terms **14–21** incorporating the following provisions should be added to the factoring or discounting agreement, particularly where the policy is required by the factor to improve his security:

(1) An undertaking by the client to procure the addition of the factor as joint insured.

(2) The right of the factor to terminate the factoring agreement if the policy is terminated.

(3) Warranties of the client in relation to completion of the proposal form and that there has been no act or omission which will invalidate the policy in any way.

(4) Undertakings by the client in relation to such acts or omissions in the future and of full compliance with policy conditions.

(5) Authority for the factor to make declarations to the insurer and to administer the policy generally, if the client fails to do so, but excluding any obligation for the factor to do so.

(6) A provision for payments by the insurer, in settlement of claims to be dealt with under the factoring agreement as if they were payments by debtors.

(7) An authority to pay over salvage to the insurer.

---

[19] *ibid.*

Salvage under policies issued to the client (either solely or jointly with the factor)

14-22   The obligation on the part of the factor for the insurer's share of any salvage in respect of the settlement of a claim (whether the salvage has been received by the factor or the client) will not cause any problem to the factor in an on-going situation; where the client has received the salvage, the factor may debit the account of the client with the amount payable to the insurer. However, dividends from insolvent estates are sometimes paid many years after the onset of the insolvency. By that time the client may himself be insolvent or no longer a client of the factor. In such a case, as joint insured, or if such responsibility is placed on the factor by the insurer as a condition of recognition of the factoring arrangements, the factor may have to pay the insurer without being able to recover from the client or, at the minimum, having some difficulty in the recovery. In order to preclude such difficulties, the factor should ensure that in the factoring endorsement or the conditions for acceptance of the assignment (as the case may be) the factor's liability for salvage is for sums actually *received* by or available to the factor. If this is not possible, then the factor will need to ensure that the assignment to it of the debt, the subject of the claim, is notified and acknowledged by the person having the duty to administer the debtor's insolvent estate and refrain from any reassignment of the debt to the client at any time.

14-23   In some circumstances such an undertaking required by the insurer, even if it relates only to sums actually received or available to the factor, may cause the factor difficulty if the sum received relates to a debt reassigned to the client before payment of the claim by the insurer; it may be difficult for the factor to determine whether the sum received related to a debt in respect of which a claim had been settled. This may particularly be the case if the client is no longer a client of the factor. The factor as assignor of the reassigned debt will hold any recoveries in trust for the client as assignee. Accordingly, to avoid any arguments regarding the ownership of the recoveries, the factor should hold irrevocable authority from the client to pay over to the insurer any sum of which the insurer shall demand payment as salvage; such authority should include the factor's right to rely upon any statement made by the insurer as to the amount of salvage due without the requirement to make further enquiries.

4. POLICIES ISSUED TO FACTORS AS SOLE INSURED

Requisite amendments to standard credit insurance policies

14-24   For a policy, designed for a supplier of goods and services, to be issued to the factor alone some amendments will be required. Such amendments will vary considerably in accordance with the terms and conditions of the particular policy and these now vary widely. At the minimum the amending endorsement should include the following:

(1) Recitals of:

    (a) the nature of the factoring agreement and the assignments to the factor of the debts to be covered;

    (b) the scope of the policy (whether debts arising from the businesses of all clients or only approved clients are to be included); and

    (c) the definition of an approved debt for the purpose of the policy (the insurance normally covers only debts accepted by the factor without recourse).

(2) An insured debt must be defined (subject to the normal restrictions in the policy) as a factored or discounted debt arising from supplies by a client.

(3) For the purposes of the policy a contract entered into by a client for the sale of goods or provision of services should be deemed to be a contract entered into by the factor.

(4) Terms of payment must be computed by reference to the time of delivery of goods or the completion of services by the client; but for other purposes "delivery" or "despatch" should be, in the case of a facultative type of factoring agreement,[20] the date of the assignment and, in the case of a whole turnover agreement,[21] the date of notification.

(5) Where the policy includes confidential invoice discounting business, then it must be provided that the granting and withholding of credit and the collection of debts may be carried out by a client as well as by the factor as the insured party and that any steps taken by a client to mitigate a loss shall be deemed to be steps taken by the insured.

(6) In taking the usual right to cancel or reduce any credit limit or to cancel cover in any market by notice to the factor as the insured, the insurer must allow the factor sufficient time to notify the client or clients that further deliveries on the account or to the market may not be covered.

---

[20] See para.7–08 above.
[21] See para.7–10 above.

14–25   Most policy conditions will entitle the insurer to cancel the policy with effect from its beginning if there has been a failure on the part of the insured to disclose a material fact. Most policies will require that knowledge of such a fact by the client shall be attributed to the factor. It is therefore of the utmost importance that the policy should provide that in such circumstances the cancellation of cover should relate only to the business of the defaulting client, rather than the insurer being entitled to avoid the whole policy. Otherwise, the factor may be in a position of having to terminate non-recourse business with all his clients on account of a default of one of them.

Credit Protection based on a policy issued to the factor

14–26   If a factor takes out a credit insurance policy to cover the risk of loss which he accepts from his clients in non-recourse factoring, then he must ensure that all warranties or undertakings given by him as the insured in the policy are covered by similar obligations of the client to him in the factoring agreement. For example, these would be likely to include the usual undertaking of the insured to exercise due care and prudence, to report the financial difficulties of any debtor and to take steps to minimise loss.

14–27   However, in circumstances where the client is to receive part of the commercial benefit of the factor's credit insurance, the factor must ensure that he is not providing the benefit to its client in any way that may be construed as credit insurance. The distinction is between insurance in its true sense, as opposed to the provision of bad debt protection through a factoring agreement supported by credit insurance obtained by the factor. The distinction is one of substance, and not form.[22] Whenever the factor has obtained credit insurance and seeks to ensure that the client receives some of the commercial benefit of the protection, it is therefore important to ensure that the factor always retains the insurable risk, being the risk of non-payment of the debts due under the contracts of sale or supply. Nonetheless, the factor should be entitled to pass to his client the benefit of monies received from an insurer in relation to insured debts by treating the payments as a reduction of the client's liability to the factor in relation to those debts. The factor can charge for this service by modifying the discount charge in relation to the particular debt, so that the cost is treated under the factoring agreement as part of the purchase price of the debts. This will not affect the debtor's liability to pay the whole of the debt, and to the extent that it pays out under a policy in relation to a claim, an insurer will acquire

---

[22] In deciding whether or not an agreement creates a contract of insurance, the court will consider whether the nature of the rights the parties intended their agreement to confer is such as to constitute an agreement for insurance, whatever label the parties have attached to it. A similar process is involved in construing a document to see whether it constitutes a fixed or a floating charge (*Agnew v Inland Revenue Commissioners* [2001] 2 A.C. at 725–726), or whether it creates a tenancy or a licence (*Street v Mountford* [1985] A.C. 809 at 826).

under the equitable doctrine of subrogation the factor's rights as assignee to sue the debtors.

The factor must not only ensure that the provisions concerning the **14–28** application of monies received from the insurer and the charge for the service are consistent with the sale and purchase of debts, but also that the provisions in the factoring agreement relating to "non-recourse" are a mirror image of the credit insurance policy. In particular, the regulations for giving and withdrawing credit approvals in the factoring agreement should be no more liberal than those in the policy, and the following provisions must be included:

(1) The circumstances in which the factor will forego recourse must be identical to the circumstances in which a claim will be admitted by the insurer.

(2) The appropriation of receipts from debtors (*i.e.* the priority of appropriation to approved debts) in the agreement must be identical to the provisions for the same in the policy.

(3) The factor's rights on the non-disclosure by the client of a material fact must be consistent with those of the insurer.

APPENDICES

APPENDIX 1

INDEX OF FACTORING TURNOVER GROWTH

Accumulative Turnover Figures for All FCI Members Compared to Worldwide Factoring Turnover (in Millions of EUR)

	EUR 2000	EUR 2001	EUR 2002	EUR 2003	EUR 2004	INCREASE 2004/2003
Invoice Discounting	55,787	67,759	74,815	77,516	97,543	25.84%
Recourse Factoring	58,605	60,925	63,830	73,169	89,808	22.74%
Non Recourse Factoring	144,208	152,738	156,510	177,173	191,467	8.07%
Collections	16,028	10,318	15,640	12,836	15,549	21.14%
Total Domestic Factoring FCI	274,628	291,740	310,796	340,694	394,367	15.75%
Export Factoring	15,906	13,310	14,649	21,606	32,405	49.98%
Import Factoring	7,447	7,853	8,069	8,915	11,160	25.18%
Total International Factoring FCI	23,353	21,163	22,718	30,521	43,565	42.74%
Grand Total FCI	*297,981*	*312,902*	*333,514*	*371,215*	*437,932*	*17.97%*
World Domestic Factoring	578,997	644,659	681,281	712,657	791,950	11.13%
World International Factoring	44,843	41,023	42,916	47,735	68,265	43.01%
World Total	*623,840*	*685,682*	*724,197*	*760,392*	*860,215*	*13.13%*

	USD 2000	USD 2001	USD 2002	USD 2003	USD 2004	INCREASE 2004/2003
Invoice Discounting	51,882	60,983	78,556	96,895	131,683	35.90%
Recourse Factoring	54,503	54,832	67,022	91,462	121,240	32.56%
Non Recourse Factoring	134,114	137,464	164,336	221,467	258,481	16.71%
Collections	14,906	9,286	16,422	16,044	20,992	30.84%
Total Domestic Factoring FCI	255,404	262,566	326,336	425,868	532,396	25.01%
Export Factoring	14,793	11,979	15,382	27,007	43,747	61.98%

353

Import Factoring	6,926	7,068	8,472	11,144	15,066	*35.20%*
Total International Factoring FCI	21,718	19,046	23,854	38,151	58,813	*54.16%*
Grand Total FCI	*277,122*	*281,612*	*350,190*	*464,019*	*591,209*	*27.41%*
World Domestic Factoring	538,468	580,187	715,345	890,821	1,069,133	*20.02%*
World International Factoring	41,704	36,921	45,078	59,669	92,158	*54.45%*
World Total	*580,172*	*617,108*	*760,423*	*950,490*	*1,161,290*	*22.18%*

Factoring Turnover by Country in 2004 in Millions of EUR

Nr. of Companies		Domestic	International	Total
EUROPE	3	Austria	3,138	554	3,692
	6	Belgium	10,500	3,000	13,500
	5	Croatia	28	0	28
	3	Cyprus	2,100	40	2,140
	11	Czech Republic	2,150	470	2,620
	9	Denmark	3,780	3,000	6,780
	5	Estonia	3,500	420	3,920
	4	Finland	8,800	367	9,167
	20	France	75,900	5,700	81,600
	20	Germany	35,000	10,000	45,000
	10	Greece	4,200	230	4,430
	21	Hungary	1,310	65	1,375
	1	Iceland	0	16	16
	9	Ireland	13,000	150	13,150
	40	Italy	113,000	8,000	121,000
	17	Latvia	140	15	155
	9	Lithuania	820	220	1,040
	1	Luxembourg	245	40	285
	4	Netherlands	12,900	6,700	19,600
	8	Norway	7,510	1,110	8,620
	10	Poland	3,200	340	3,540
	10	Portugal	14,200	500	14,700
	6	Romania	220	200	420
	7	Russia	1,100	30	1,130
	6	Slovakia	500	165	665
	3	Slovenia	170	15	185
	19	Spain	43,835	1,541	45,376
	64	Sweden	12,400	2,100	14,500
	5	Switzerland	1,000	400	1,400
	97	Turkey	6,400	1,550	7,950
	100	United Kingdom	182,000	2,520	184,520
	533	*Total*	*563,046*	*49,458*	*612,504*
AMERICAS	4	Argentina	90	11	101
	75	Brazil	15,450	50	15,500
	61	Canada	2,189	968	3,157
	20	Chile	4,000	200	4,200
	4	Costa Rica	180	0	180
	5	Cuba	5	185	190
	4	El Salvador	100	5	105
	14	Mexico	4,500	100	4,600
	4	Panama	200	1	201
	110	U.S.A.	77,050	4,810	81,860
	301	*Total*	*103,764*	*6,330*	*110,094*
AFRICA	1	Egypt	0	1	1
	3	Morocco	250	50	300
	9	South Africa	7,000	100	7,100
	3	Tunisia	165	20	185
	15	*Total*	*7,415*	*171*	*7,586*
ASIA	12	China	3,555	760	4,315
	10	Hong Kong	2,800	2,000	4,800

Nr. of Companies		Domestic	International	Total
0	Indonesia	0	0	0
8	India	1,450	175	1,625
2	Israel	35	120	155
15	Japan	71,856	679	72,535
1	Lebanon	40	1	41
12	Malaysia	700	30	730
1	Oman	8	0	8
0	Saudi Arabia	0	0	0
10	Singapore	2,200	400	2,600
1	South Korea	0	32	32
6	Sri Lanka	125	3	128
25	Taiwan	15,000	8,000	23,000
20	Thailand	1,470	30	1,500
3	United Arab Emirates	130	15	145
126	*Total*	*99,369*	*12,245*	*111,614*
AUSTRALASIA 25	Australia	18,123	58	18,181
4	New Zealand	233	3	236
29	*Total*	*18,356*	*61*	*18,417*
1004	*TOTAL WORLD*	*791,950*	*68,265*	*860,215*

Factoring Turnover by Country in 2004 in Millions of USD

Nr. of Companies			Domestic	International	Total
EUROPE	3	Austria	4,236	748	4,984
	6	Belgium	14,175	4,050	18,225
	5	Croatia	38	0	38
	3	Cyprus	2,835	54	2,889
	11	Czech Republic	2,903	635	3,537
	9	Denmark	5,103	4,050	9,153
	5	Estonia	4,725	567	5,292
	4	Finland	11,880	495	12,375
	20	France	102,465	7,695	110,160
	20	Germany	47,250	13,500	60,750
	10	Greece	5,670	311	5,981
	21	Hungary	1,769	88	1,856
	1	Iceland	0	22	22
	9	Ireland	17,550	203	17,753
	40	Italy	152,550	10,800	163,350
	17	Latvia	189	20	209
	9	Lithuania	1,107	297	1,404
	1	Luxembourg	331	54	385
	4	Netherlands	17,415	9,045	26,460
	8	Norway	10,139	1,499	11,637
	10	Poland	4,320	459	4,779
	10	Portugal	19,170	675	19,845
	6	Romania	297	270	567
	7	Russia	1,485	41	1,526
	6	Slovakia	675	223	898
	3	Slovenia	230	20	250
	19	Spain	59,177	2,080	61,258
	64	Sweden	16,740	2,835	19,575
	5	Switzerland	1,350	540	1,890
	97	Turkey	8,640	2,093	10,733
	100	United Kingdom	245,700	3,402	249,102
	533	*Total*	*760,112*	*66,768*	*826,880*
AMERICAS	4	Argentina	122	15	136
	75	Brazil	20,858	68	20,925
	61	Canada	2,955	1,307	4,262
	20	Chile	5,400	270	5,670
	4	Costa Rica	243	0	243
	5	Cuba	7	250	257
	4	El Salvador	135	7	142
	14	Mexico	6,075	135	6,210
	4	Panama	270	1	271
	110	U.S.A.	104,018	6,494	110,511
	301	*Total*	*140,081*	*8,546*	*148,627*
AFRICA	1	Egypt	0	1	1
	3	Morocco	338	68	405
	9	South Africa	9,450	135	9,585
	3	Tunisia	223	27	250
	15	*Total*	*10,010*	*231*	*10,241*
ASIA	12	China	4,799	1,026	5,825
	10	Hong Kong	3,780	2,700	6,480

357

0	Indonesia	0	0	0
8	India	1,958	236	2,194
2	Israel	47	162	209
15	Japan	97,006	917	97,922
1	Lebanon	54	1	55
12	Malaysia	945	41	986
1	Oman	11	0	11
0	Saudi Arabia	0	0	0
10	Singapore	2,970	540	3,510
1	South Korea	0	43	43
6	Sri Lanka	169	4	173
25	Taiwan	20,250	10,800	31,050
20	Thailand	1,985	41	2,025
3	United Arab Emirates	176	20	196
126	*Total*	*134,148*	*16,531*	*150,679*
AUSTRALASIA 25	Australia	24,466	78	24,544
4	New Zealand	315	4	319
29	*Total*	*24,781*	*82*	*24,863*
1004	*TOTAL WORLD*	*1,069,133*	*92,158*	*1,161,290*

Factoring Turnover Growth in 2004 in Millions of EUR

	1998	1999	2000	2001	2002	2003	2004
EUROPE							
Austria	1,832	2,007	2,275	2,181	2,275	2,932	3,692
Belgium	4,366	7,630	8,000	9,000	9,391	11,500	13,500
Bulgaria	0	2	1	2	0	0	0
Croatia	0	0	0	0	0	0	28
Cyprus	959	1,120	1,410	1,554	1,997	2,035	2,140
Czech Republic	468	780	1,005	1,230	1,681	1,880	2,620
Denmark	2,894	3,360	4,050	5,488	5,200	5,570	6,780
Estonia	213	470	615	1,400	2,143	2,262	3,920
Finland	5,230	5,630	7,130	7,445	9,067	8,810	9,167
France	44,255	53,100	52,450	67,660	67,398	73,200	81,600
Germany	20,323	19,984	23,483	29,373	30,156	35,082	45,000
Greece	596	850	1,500	2,050	2,694	3,680	4,430
Hungary	115	144	344	546	580	1,142	1,375
Iceland	21	100	125	26	16	25	16
Ireland	3,957	6,160	6,500	7,813	8,620	8,850	13,150
Italy	75,319	88,000	110,000	124,823	134,804	132,510	121,000
Latvia					Shown with Estonia	until 2003	155
Lithuania					Shown with Estonia	until 2003	1,040
Luxembourg	0	0	0	0	197	257	285
Netherlands	17,702	20,500	15,900	17,800	20,120	17,500	19,600
Norway	3,787	4,260	4,960	5,700	7,030	7,625	8,620
Poland	609	605	2,085	3,330	2,500	2,580	3,540
Portugal	5,545	7,450	8,995	10,189	11,343	12,181	14,700
Romania	20	37	60	98	141	225	420
Russia	0	0	0	0	168	485	1,130
Slovakia	179	160	160	240	240	384	665
Slovenia	14	35	65	71	75	170	185
Spain	9,936	12,530	19,500	23,600	31,567	37,486	45,376
Sweden	7,677	7,550	12,310	5,250	10,229	10,950	14,500
Switzerland	1,464	1,300	1,300	1,430	2,250	1,514	1,400
Turkey	4,043	5,250	6,390	3,947	4,263	5,330	7,950
United Kingdom	84,255	103,200	123,770	136,080	156,706	160,770	184,520
Total Europe	*295,778*	*352,214*	*414,383*	*468,326*	*522,851*	*546,935*	*612,504*
AMERICAS							
Argentina	1,026	1,481	1,715	1,017	71	70	101
Brazil	13,620	17,010	12,012	11,020	11,030	12,040	15,500
Canada	1,863	1,952	2,256	2,699	3,100	3,161	3,157
Chile	1,991	2,600	2,650	3,123	3,130	3,500	4,200
Colombia	85	50	0	0	0	0	0
Costa Rica	162	226	258	208	210	185	180
Cuba	0	185	108	113	120	93	190
El Salvador	0	0	0	123	157	102	105
Mexico	2,519	3,550	5,030	6,890	6,340	4,535	4,600
Panama	0	11	220	220	0	160	201
U.S.A.	70,059	88,069	102,268	101,744	91,143	80,696	81,860
Total Americas	*91,326*	*115,134*	*126,517*	*127,157*	*115,301*	*104,542*	*110,094*

AFRICA							
Egypt	0	0	0	0	0	0	1
Morocco	187	57	45	50	190	160	300
South Africa	3,957	5,340	5,550	5,580	5,860	5,470	7,100
Tunisia	54	73	60	171	153	210	185
Total Africa	*4,198*	*5,470*	*5,655*	*5,801*	*6,203*	*5,840*	*7,586*
ASIA							
China	11	31	212	1,234	2,077	2,640	4,315
Hong Kong	1,294	1,800	2,400	2,690	3,029	3,250	4,800
Indonesia	28	33	3	0	1	1	0
India	174	257	470	690	1,290	1,615	1,625
Israel	108	219	460	429	354	190	155
Japan	38,980	55,347	58,473	61,566	50,380	60,550	72,535
Lebanon	0	0	0	10	22	35	41
Malaysia	687	805	585	842	610	718	730
Oman	14	21	30	36	29	10	8
Philippines	10	10	0	0	0	0	0
Saudi Arabia	0	0	0	150	100	50	0
Singapore	1,510	1,970	2,100	2,480	2,600	2,435	2,600
South Korea	17,149	15,120	115	85	55	38	32
Sri Lanka	38	62	99	115	110	102	128
Taiwan	1,004	2,090	3,650	4,511	7,919	16,000	23,000
Thailand	715	1,010	1,268	1,240	1,274	1,425	1,500
United Arab Emirates	0	0	0	0	0	37	145
Total Asia	*61,723*	*78,775*	*69,865*	*76,078*	*69,850*	*89,096*	*111,614*
AUSTRALASIA							
Australia	3,319	5,100	7,320	7,910	9,527	13,716	18,181
New Zealand	162	184	100	410	465	263	236
Total Australasia	*3,481*	*5,284*	*7,420*	*8,320*	*9,992*	*13,979*	*18,417*
TOTAL WORLD	*456,506*	*556,877*	*623,840*	*685,682*	*724,197*	*760,392*	*860,215*

Factoring Turnover Growth in 2004 in Millions of USD

	1998	1999	2000	2001	2002	2003	2004
EUROPE							
Austria	2,153	2,013	2,116	1,963	2,389	3,665	4,984
Belgium	5,130	7,653	7,440	8,100	9,860	14,375	18,225
Bulgaria	0	2	1	2	0	0	0
Croatia	0	0	0	0	0	0	38
Cyprus	1,127	1,123	1,311	1,400	2,097	2,544	2,889
Czech Republic	550	782	935	1,102	1,765	2,350	3,537
Denmark	3,400	3,370	3,767	4,939	5,460	6,963	9,153
Estonia	250	471	572	1,260	2,250	2,828	5,292
Finland	6,145	5,647	6,631	6,701	9,520	11,013	12,375
France	52,000	53,259	48,779	60,894	70,766	91,500	110,160
Germany	23,880	20,044	21,839	26,436	31,664	43,853	60,750
Greece	700	853	1,395	1,845	2,829	4,600	5,981
Hungary	135	144	320	491	609	1,428	1,856
Iceland	25	100	116	23	17	31	22
Ireland	4,650	6,178	6,045	7,032	9,051	11,063	17,753
Italy	88,500	88,264	102,300	112,341	141,544	165,638	163,350
Latvia				Shown with Estonia		until 2003	209
Lithuania				Shown with Estonia		until 2003	1,404
Luxembourg	0	0	0	0	207	321	385
Netherlands	20,800	20,562	14,787	16,020	21,123	21,875	26,460
Norway	4,450	4,273	4,613	5,130	7,381	9,531	11,637
Poland	715	607	1,939	2,997	2,625	3,225	4,779
Portugal	6,515	7,472	8,365	9,170	11,910	15,226	19,845
Romania	24	37	56	89	148	281	567
Russia	0	0	0	0	176	606	1,526
Slovakia	210	160	149	216	252	480	898
Slovenia	17	35	60	64	79	213	250
Spain	11,675	12,568	18,135	21,240	33,145	46,858	61,258
Sweden	9,020	7,573	11,448	4,725	10,738	13,688	19,575
Switzerland	1,720	1,304	1,209	1,287	2,363	1,893	1,890
Turkey	4,750	5,266	5,943	3,552	4,476	6,663	10,733
United Kingdom	99,000	103,510	115,106	122,471	164,530	200,963	249,102
Total Europe	*347,539*	*353,271*	*385,376*	*421,489*	*548,974*	*683,669*	*826,880*
AMERICAS							
Argentina	1,206	1,485	1,595	915	75	88	136
Brazil	16,004	17,061	11,171	9,918	11,580	15,050	20,925
Canada	2,189	1,958	2,098	2,429	3,255	3,951	4,262
Chile	2,340	2,608	2,465	2,811	3,287	4,375	5,670
Colombia	100	50	0	0	0	0	0
Costa Rica	190	227	240	187	221	231	243
Cuba	0	186	100	102	126	116	257
El Salvador	0	0	0	111	165	128	142
Mexico	2,960	3,561	4,678	6,201	6,657	5,669	6,210
Panama	0	11	205	198	0	200	271
U.S.A.	82,320	88,360	95,110	91,570	95,700	100,870	110,511
Total Americas	*107,309*	*115,506*	*117,662*	*114,442*	*121,065*	*130,678*	*148,627*

AFRICA

Egypt	0	0	0	0	0	0	1
Morocco	220	57	42	45	200	200	405
South Africa	4,650	5,356	5,162	5,022	6,153	6,838	9,585
Tunisia	63	73	56	154	161	263	250
Total Africa	*4,933*	*5,486*	*5,259*	*5,221*	*6,513*	*7,300*	*10,241*
ASIA							
China	13	31	197	1,110	2,182	3,300	5,825
Hong Kong	1,520	1,805	2,232	2,421	3,001	4,063	6,480
Indonesia	33	33	3	0	1	1	0
India	205	258	437	621	1,355	2,019	2,194
Israel	127	220	428	386	588	238	209
Japan	45,802	55,513	54,380	55,409	52,899	75,688	97,922
Lebanon	0	0	0	9	23	44	55
Malaysia	807	807	544	758	641	898	986
Oman	17	21	28	32	30	13	11
Philippines	12	10	0	0	0	0	0
Saudi Arabia	0	0	0	135	105	63	0
Singapore	1,774	1,976	1,953	2,232	2,730	3,044	3,510
South Korea	20,150	15,165	107	77	58	48	43
Sri Lanka	45	62	92	104	116	128	173
Taiwan	1,180	2,096	3,395	4,059	8,313	20,000	31,050
Thailand	840	1,013	1,179	1,116	1,339	1,781	2,025
United Arab Emirates	0	0	0	0	0	46	196
Total Asia	*72,525*	*79,011*	*64,974*	*68,469*	*73,380*	*111,370*	*150,679*
AUSTRALASIA							
Australia	3,900	5,115	6,808	7,119	10,003	17,145	24,544
New Zealand	190	185	93	369	488	329	319
Total Australasia	*4,090*	*5,300*	*6,901*	*7,488*	*10,492*	*17,474*	*24,863*
TOTAL WORLD	*536,395*	*558,574*	*580,172*	*617,108*	*760,423*	*950,490*	*1,161,290*

CLIENT STATEMENT

DATE	PAGE
31/07/05	1

ACCOUNT

4498 GBP

FUNDS IN USE

Value Date	Debits	Credits	Balance
1/07			17.80
30/06		4.406,26	4,388.46CR
1/07			3,971.10CR
1/07	417.36		.00
1/07	3.971,10		
5/07	27.44		27.44
11/07	26.40		53.84
12/07		39.080,50	39,026.66CR
13/07	141.82		38,884.84CR
13/07	38.884,84		.00
15/07		13.492,53	13,492.53CR
18/07		11.456,25	24,948.78CR
19/07		10.955,12	35,903.90CR
19/07	24.948,78		10,955.12CR
20/07	21.02		10,934.10CR
21/07	111.59		10,822.51CR
22/07		11.519,71	22,342.22CR
22/07	10.822,51		11,519.71CR
25/07	11.519,71		.00
26/07	12.42		12.42
27/07		9.458,75	9,446.33CR
28/07	9.446,33		.00
29/07	109.04		109.04
31/07	242.05		351.09
31/07	0,08		351.17

CURRENT ACCOUNT

Ref. %	Description	charges	Debits	Credits	Balance
	B/F balance				75,428.97
	Payment value dated 300605				
	Adj. B/F Balance				75,428.97
	Invoice 47360.15less chg	417.36		46.942,79	122,371.76
	Payment Bank Transfer		3.971,10		118,400.66
6.500	Invoice 3113.75less chg	27.44		3.086,31	121,486.97
6.500	Invoice 2995.95less chg	26.40		2.969,55	124,456.52
	Debtor payments				124,456.52
	Invoice 16093.46less chg	141.82		15.951,64	140,408.16
	Payment Bank Transfer		38.884,84		101,523.32
	Debtor payments				101,523.32
	Debtor payments				101,523.32
	Debtor payments				101,523.32
	Payment Bank Transfer		24.948,78		76,574.54
	Invoice 2385.00less chg	21.02		2.363,98	78,938.52
	Debit note no. 106666	111.59	111,59		78,826.93
	Debtor payments				78,826.93
	Payment Bank Transfer		10.822,51		68,004.42
	Payment Bank Transfer		11.519,71		56,484.71
6.500	Invoice 1409.86less chg	12.42		1.397,44	57,882.15
	Debtor payments				57,882.15
	Payment Bank Transfer		9.446,33		48,435.82
6.500	Invoice 12372.75less chg	109.04		12.263,71	60,699.53
6.500	Min Mthly Admin (inc VAT)	242.05	242,05		60,457.48
6.500	Discount. Chg@ 6.50000%	.08	0,08		60,457.40

TOTAL DISCOUNTS	TOTAL INVOICES	TOTAL CREDITS
	85,730.92	

Fortis Commercial Finance UK

APPENDIX 3

CALCULATION OF AVAILABILITY

Total Outstanding.:	60,808.57		
Credit Balances:	0.00	Funding Retained:	0.00
No. of CR Balances:	0.00	Special User Retention:	0.00
No. of Debtors:	1	Accrued Disc Charge:	0.08
Funding Approved:	60,808.57	Penalty Disc Charge:	0.00
Funding Unapproved:	0.00	Conc %: 0 Value:	0.00
Disputed Balance:	0.00	Retention %: 15 Value:	9,121.29
Funds In Use:	109.04	Retention %: 100 Value:	0.00
Max Funds In Use:	250,000.00	Retention %: 100 Value:	0.00
Unprocessed Batches:	0.00	Total Retentions:	9,121.37
		Current A/C Balance:	60,699.53
		Availability:	51,578.16

Agreed Overpayment:	0.00	Availability:	0.00
Uncleared Drafts:	0.00		

Fortis Commercial Finance UK

APPENDIX 4

VENTURE FINANCE PLC

CLIENT BALANCE STATEMENT

EXAMPLE COMPANY NAME   Client No:
EXAMPLE STREET   Currency: STERLING
EXAMPLE TOWN   Business: Domestic
EXAMPLE COUNTY

EXAMPLE

DEBTS PURCHASED ACCOUNT   Page   1
STERLING

DATE	DESCRIPTION	REF	CREDIT	DEBIT	BALANCE
	OPENING BALANCE				1029336.50
20299	CASH			36660.88	992675.62
30299	INVOICES		541340.23		1534015.85
30299	CASH			233005.86	1301009.99
50299	INVOICES		79880.24		1380890.23
80299	INVOICES		7822.56		1388712.79
80299	CASH			103869.51	1284843.28
100299	CASH			11607.12	1273236.16
110299	CASH			250316.76	1022919.40
120299	INVOICES		12086.17		1035005.57
160299	DR NON-CASH ADJ		0.23		1035005.80
170299	CASH			11280.00	1023725.80
190299	CASH			55874.26	967851.54
	CLOSING BALANCE				967851.54

APPENDIX 4

EXAMPLE CLIENT LIMITED
EXAMPLE STREET   Client No: 0005
EXAMPLE TOWN   Currency: Sterling
EXAMPLE COUNTY   Business: Domestic

EXAMPLE

CURRENT ACCOUNT   Page   1

DATE	DESCRIPTION	REF	DEBIT	CREDIT	BALANCE
	OPENING BALANCE				783825.33
20299	CASH			36660.88	747164.45
30299	CASH			233005.86	514158.59
30299	FACTORING CHG	I0302	3789.38		517947.97
30299	FACT CHG VAT	I0302	663.14		518611.11
50299	FACTORING CHG	I0502	559.16		519170.27
50299	FACT CHG VAT	I0502	97.85		519268.12
80299	CASH			103869.51	415398.61
80299	FACTORING CHG	I0802	46.94		415445.55
80299	FACT CHG VAT	I0802	8.21		415453.76
100299	CASH			11607.12	403846.64
100299	PAYMENT		450000.00		853846.64
110299	CASH			250316.76	603529.88
120299	FACTORING CHG	I1202	72.52		603602.40
120299	FACT CHG VAT	I1202	12.69		303615.09
170299	CASH			12280.00	591335.09
180299	PAYMENT		50000.00		641335.09
190299	CASH			55874.26	585460.83
	CLOSING BALANCE				585460.83

366

EXAMPLE CLIENT LIMITED
EXAMPLE STREET   Client No: 0005
EXAMPLE TOWN   Currency: STERLING
EXAMPLE COUNTY   Business: Domestic

EXAMPLE

CLIENT BALANCE STATEMENT

19/02/99	DEBTS PURCHASED OPENING BALANCE		967851.54
19/02/99	LESS CURRENT ACCOUNT OPENING BALANCE		586460.83
19/02/99	NET CLIENT OPENING BALANCE		381390.71

The opening balance of the above account represents the amount standing to your credit in respect of debts bought from you and not yet paid by your customers. It will be due to you when the debts are paid, subject to any charges or adjustments.

UNIDROIT CONVENTION ON INTERNATIONAL FACTORING

THE STATES PARTIES TO THIS CONVENTION,

CONSCIOUS of the fact that international factoring has a significant role to play in the development of international trade,

RECOGNISING therefore the importance of adopting uniform rules to provide a legal framework that will facilitate international factoring, while maintaining a fair balance of interests between the different parties involved in factoring transactions,

HAVE AGREED as follows:

CHAPTER I—SPHERE OF APPLICATION AND GENERAL PROVISIONS

Article 1

1. This Convention governs factoring contracts and assignments of receivables as described in this Chapter.

2. For the purposes of this Convention, "factoring contract means a contract concluded between one party (the supplier) and another party (the factor) pursuant to which:

(a) the supplier may or will assign to the factor receivables arising from contracts of sale of goods made between the supplier and its customers (debtors) other than those for the sale of goods bought primarily for their personal, family or household use;

(b) the factor is to perform at least two of the following functions:

— finance for the supplier, including loans and advance payments;
— maintenance of accounts (ledgering) relating to the receivables;

— collection of receivables;

— protection against default in payment by debtors;

(c) notice of the assignment of the receivables is to be given to debtors.

3. In this Convention references to "goods" and "sales of goods" shall include services and the supply of services.

4. For the purposes of this Convention:

(a) a notice in writing need not be signed but must identify the person by whom or in whose name it is given;

(b) "notice in writing" includes, but is not limited to, telegrams, telex and any other telecommunication capable of being reproduced in tangible form;

(c) a notice in writing is given when it is received by the addressee.

Article 2

1. This Convention applies whenever the receivables assigned pursuant to a factoring contract arise from a contract of sale of goods between a supplier and a debtor whose places of business are in different States and:

(a) those States and the State in which the factor has its place of business are Contracting States; or

(b) both the contract of sale of goods and the factoring contract are governed by the law of a Contracting State.

2. A reference in this Convention to a party's place of business shall, if it has more than one place of business, mean the place of business which has the closest relationship to the relevant contract and its performance, having regard to the circumstances known to or contemplated by the parties at any time before or at the conclusion of that contract.

Article 3

1. The application of this Convention may be excluded:

(a) by the parties to the factoring contract; or

(b) by the parties to the contract of sale of goods, as regards receivables arising at or after the time when the factor has been given notice in writing of such exclusion.

2. Where the application of this Convention is excluded in accordance

with the previous paragraph, such exclusion may be made only as regards the Convention as a whole.

Article 4

1. In the interpretation of this Convention, regard is to be had to its object and purpose as set forth in the preamble, to its international character and to the need to promote uniformity in its application and the observance of good faith in international trade.

2. Questions concerning matters governed by this Convention which are not expressly settled in it are to be settled in conformity with the general principles on which it is based or, in the absence of such principles, in conformity with the law applicable by virtue of the rules of private international law.

CHAPTER II—RIGHTS AND DUTIES OF THE PARTIES

Article 5

As between the parties to the factoring contract:

    (a) a provision in the factoring contract for the assignment of existing or future receivables shall not be rendered invalid by the fact that the contract does not specify them individually, if at the time of conclusion of the contract or when they come into existence they can be identified to the contract;

    (b) a provision in the factoring contract by which future receivables are assigned operates to transfer the receivables to the factor when they come into existence without the need for any new act of transfer.

Article 6

1. The assignment of a receivable by the supplier to the factor shall be effective notwithstanding any agreement between the supplier and the debtor prohibiting such assignment.

2. However, such assignment shall not be effective against the debtor when, at the time of conclusion of the contract of sale of goods, it has its place of business in a Contracting State which has made a declaration under Article 18 of this Convention.

3. Nothing in paragraph I shall affect any obligation of good faith owed by the supplier to the debtor or any liability of the supplier to the debtor in

respect of an assignment made in breach of the terms of the contract of sale of goods.

Article 7

A factoring contract may validly provide as between the parties thereto for the transfer, with or without a new act of transfer, of all or any of the supplier's rights deriving from the contract of sale of goods, including the benefit of any provision in the contract of sale of goods reserving to the supplier title to the goods or creating any security interest.

Article 8

1. The debtor is under a duty to pay the factor if, and only if, the debtor does not have knowledge of any other person's superior right to payment and notice in writing of the assignment:

    (a)   is given to the debtor by the supplier or by the factor with the supplier's authority;

    (b)   reasonably identifies the receivables which have been assigned and the factor to whom or for whose account the debtor is required to make payment; and

    (c)   relates to receivables arising under a contract of sale of goods made at or before the time the notice is given.

2. Irrespective of any other ground on which payment by the debtor to the factor discharges the debtor from liability, payment shall be effective for this purpose if made in accordance with the previous paragraph.

Article 9

1. In a claim by the factor against the debtor for payment of a receivable arising under a contract of sale of goods the debtor may set up against the factor all defences arising under that contract of which the debtor could have availed itself if such claim had been made by the supplier.

2. The debtor may also assert against the factor any right of set-off in respect of claims existing against the supplier in whose favour the receivable arose and available to the debtor at the time a notice in writing of assignment conforming to Articles 8(1) was given to the debtor.

Article 10

1. Without prejudice to the debtor's rights under Article 9, non-performance or defective or late performance of the contract of sale of goods shall

not by itself entitle the debtor to recover a sum paid by the debtor to the factor if the debtor has a right to recover that sum from the supplier.

2. The debtor who has such a right to recover from the supplier a sum paid to the factor in respect of a receivable shall nevertheless be entitled to recover that sum from the factor to the extent that:

(a) the factor has not discharged an obligation to make payment to the supplier in respect of that receivable; or

(b) the factor made such payment at a time when it knew of the supplier's non-performance or defective or late performance as regards the goods to which the debtor's payment relates.

CHAPTER III—SUBSEQUENT ASSIGNMENTS

Article 11

1. Where a receivable is assigned by a supplier to a factor pursuant to a factoring contract governed by this Convention:

(a) the rules set out in Articles 5 to 10 shall, subject to sub-paragraph (b) of this paragraph, apply to any subsequent assignment of the receivable by the factor or by a subsequent assignee;

(b) the provisions of Articles 8 to 10 shall apply as if the subsequent assignee were the factor.

2. For the purposes of this Convention, notice to the debtor of the subsequent assignment also constitutes notice of the assignment to the factor.

Article 12

This Convention shall not apply to a subsequent assignment which is prohibited by the terms of the factoring contract

APPENDIX 6

GENERAL RULES FOR INTERNATIONAL FACTORING

(Promulgated by Factors Chain International—printed July 2005)

TABLE OF CONTENTS

SECTION I GENERAL PROVISIONS

Article 1 Factoring contracts and receivables

A factoring contract means a contract pursuant to which a supplier may or will assign accounts receivable (referred to in these Rules as "receivables" which expression, where the context allows, also includes parts of receivables) to a factor, whether or not for the purpose of finance, for at least one of the following functions:

- Receivables ledgering

- Collection of receivables

- Protection against bad debts

Article 2 Parties taking part in two-factor international factoring

The parties taking part in two-factor international factoring transactions are:

(i) the supplier (also commonly referred to as client or seller),
    the party who invoices for the supply of goods or the rendering of services;

(ii) the debtor (also commonly referred to as buyer or customer),
    the party who is liable for payment of the receivables from the supply of goods or rendering of services;

(iii) The Export Factor,

374

the party to which the supplier assigns his receivables in accordance with the factoring contract;

(iv) the Import Factor,

the party to which the receivables are assigned by the Export Factor in accordance with these Rules.

Article 3 Receivables included

These Rules shall cover only receivables arising from sales on credit terms of goods and/or services provided by any supplier who has an agreement with an Export Factor to or for debtors located in any country in which an Import Factor provides factoring services. Excluded are sales based on letters of credit (other than standby letters of credit), or cash against documents or any kind of sales for cash.

Article 4 Common language

The language for communication between Import Factor and Export Factor is English. When information in another language is provided an English translation must be attached.

Article 5 Time limits

Except as otherwise specified the time limits set forth in these Rules shall be understood as calendar days. Where a time limit expires on a non-working day or any declared public holiday of the Export Factor or the Import Factor, the period of time in question is extended until the first following working day of the factor concerned.

Article 6 Writing

"Writing" means any method by which a communication may be recorded in a permanent form so that it may be re-produced and used at any time after its creation. Where a writing is to be signed, that requirement is met if, by rules accepted among the parties, the writing identifies the originator of the writing and indicates his approval of the communication contained in the writing.

Article 7 Deviating agreements

An agreement in writing made between an Export Factor and an Import Factor (and signed by both of them), which conflicts with, differs from or extends beyond the terms of these Rules, shall take precedence over and supersede any other or contrary condition, stipulation or provision in these

Rules relating to the subject matter of that agreement but in all other respects shall be subject to and dealt with as part of these Rules.
(N.B.: Article 7 amended June 2004)

Article 8 Numbering system

In order to identify exactly all suppliers, debtors, Import Factors and Export Factors, an appropriate numbering system must be agreed upon between Export Factor and Import Factor.

Article 9 Commission/Remuneration

(i) The Import Factor shall be entitled to commissions and/or charges for his services on the basis of the structure and terms of payment as promulgated by the FCI Council from time to time.

(ii) The agreed commissions and/or charges must be paid in accordance with those terms of payment in the agreed currencies. A party delaying payment shall incur interest and the equivalent of any exchange losses resulting from the delay in accordance with Article 26.

(iii) In case of a reassignment of a receivable the Import Factor has nevertheless the right to the commission or charges.

Article 10 Settlement of disagreements between Export Factor and Import Factor

(i) All disagreements arising between an Export Factor and an Import Factor in connection with any international factoring transactions shall be settled under the Rules of Arbitration provided that both are members of FCI at the time of the inception of the transaction.

(ii) Furthermore any such disagreement may be so settled if only one of the parties is a member of FCI at the time of request for arbitration provided that the other party accepts or has accepted such arbitration.

(iii) The award shall be final and binding.

Article 11 Good faith and mutual assistance

Under these Rules all duties shall be performed and all rights exercised in good faith. Each of the Export Factor and Import Factor shall act in every way to help the other's interest and each of them undertakes to the best of his ability to assist the other at all times in obtaining any document that may assist the other to carry out his duties and/or to protect his interests. Each of the Import Factor and the Export Factor undertakes that each will inform the other immediately of any fact or matter which comes to his attention and which may adversely affect the collection of any receivable or the creditworthiness of any debtor.

SECTION II ASSIGNMENT OF RECEIVABLES

Article 12 Assignment

(i) The assignment of a receivable implies and constitutes the transfer of all rights and interest in and title to such receivable by any means. For the purpose of this definition the granting of a security right over a receivable is deemed to be its transfer

(ii) All assignments of receivables must be in writing.

Article 13 Validity of assignment

(i) The Import Factor is obliged, as regards the law of the debtor's country, to inform the Export Factor of:

    (a) the wording and formalities of the notice of assignment; and

    (b) any elements in an assignment that are necessary to safeguard the Export Factor against claims of third parties.

The Import Factor warrants the effectiveness of his advice.

(ii) The Export Factor, whilst relying on the Import Factor's advice under paragraph (i) of this Article as regards the law of the debtor's country, shall be responsible for the effectiveness of the assignment to him by the supplier and of his assignment to the Import Factor including their effectiveness against the claims of third parties and in the insolvency of the supplier.

(iii) If the Export Factor requests a particular assignment, enforceable against third parties, the Import Factor is obliged to act accordingly as far as he is able to do so in accordance with the applicable law, at the expense of the Export Factor.

(iv) Whenever the assignment of a receivable needs special documentation or a confirmation in writing in order to be valid and enforceable, at the request of the Import Factor the Export Factor must provide such documentation and/or confirmation in the prescribed way.

(v) If the Export Factor shall fail to provide such documentation or confirmation in relation to that receivable within 30 days of the receipt of the Import Factor's request, then the Import Factor may reassign such receivable.

(N.B.: Paragraphs (i) and (ii) amended June 2004)

Article 14 Validity of receivables

(i) The Import Factor must receive details of invoices assigned to him without undue delay and in any event before the due date of the receivable. In addition he must receive details of credit notes relating to such invoices.

(ii) The Import Factor may require that the original documents evidencing title, including the negotiable shipping documents and/or insurance certificate, are forwarded through him.

(iii) At the request of the Import Factor and if then needed for the collection of a receivable the Export Factor must promptly provide any or all of the following as proof and in any event within the following time periods:

(a) 10 days from the receipt of the request, an exact copy of the invoice issued to the debtor;

(b) 30 days from the receipt of that request:

(1) evidence of shipment;
(2) evidence of fulfilment of the contract of sale and/or services where applicable;
(3) any other documents which have been requested before shipment.

(iv) If the Export Factor:

(a) does not provide the documents referred to in Article 14 (iii); or

(b) fails to provide a reason for that delay and a request for further time, both acceptable to the Import Factor;

within the prescribed time limits, then the Import Factor shall be entitled to reassign the relevant receivable.

(v) The time limit for the Import Factor to be entitled to request these documents from the Export Factor shall be 270 days after due date of the receivable.

(N.B.: Paragraph (iv) added June 2004—previous (iv) moved to Paragraph (v), Paragraph (i) amended June 2005)

Article 15 Reassignment of receivables

(i) Any reassignment of a receivable under Article 13 (v) or Article 14 (iv) must be made by the Import Factor no later than the 60th day after his first request for the relevant documents, or the end of any extended time granted by the Import Factor.

(ii) In the event of any reassignment of a receivable permitted to the Import Factor under these Rules, the Import Factor shall be relieved of all obligations in respect of the reassigned receivable and may recover from the Export Factor any amount paid by the Import Factor in respect of it.

(iii) Every such reassignment must be in writing.

(N.B.: Paragraph (i) amended June 2004)

SECTION III CREDIT RISK

Article 16 Definition of credit risk

(i) The credit risk is the risk that the debtor will fail to pay a receivable in full within 90 days of its due date otherwise than by reason of a dispute.

(ii) The assumption by the Import Factor of the credit risk on receivables assigned to him is conditional upon his written approval covering such receivables.

Article 17 Approvals and requests for approvals

(i) Requests of the Export Factor to the Import Factor for the assumption of the credit risk must be in writing and must contain all the necessary information to enable the Import Factor to appraise the credit risk and the normal payments terms.

(ii) If the Import Factor cannot confirm the exact identification of the debtor as submitted to him he may amend these details in his reply. Any approval shall apply only to the exact identity of the debtor given by the Import Factor in that approval

(iii) The Import Factor must, without delay and, in any event, not later than 10 days from receipt of the request, advise the Export Factor of his decision in writing. If, within the said period, the Import Factor cannot make a decision he must, at the earliest, and before the expiry of the period so advise the Export Factor.

(iv) The approval shall apply up to the amount approved to the following receivables owed by the debtor:

    (a) those on the Import Factor's records on the date of approval;

    (b) those arising from shipments made or services completed up to 30 days before the date of request for approval;

and shall be conditional in each case, upon the receipt by the Import Factor of the invoice details and the documents as stipulated in Article 14.

(v) The approval of a credit line binds the Import Factor to assume credit risk on those receivables up to the approved amount for shipments made before cancellation or expiry date of the line.

Shipment occurs when the goods are placed in transit to or to the order of the debtor whether by common carrier or the debtor's or supplier's own transport.

(vi) A credit line is a revolving approval of receivables on a debtor's account with one supplier up to the amount of the credit line. Revolving means that, while the credit line remains in force, receivables in excess of the line will succeed amounts within the line which are paid by the debtor or the Import Factor or credited to the debtor. The succession of such receivables shall take place in order in which they are due for payment and shall be limited at any time to the amount then so paid or credited.

(vii) All approvals are given on the basis that each account receivable is in conformity with the terms of payment (with a permissible occasional variation of 100% or 45 days whichever period is shorter) contained in the pertinent information upon which such approval was granted.

(viii) The approval shall be given in the same currency as the request. However, the credit line covers receivables represented by invoices expressed not only in that currency, but also in other currencies; but in all cases the risk to the Import Factor shall not at any time exceed the amount of the original approval.

(ix) There shall be only one credit line for each supplier on each debtor and any new credit line shall cancel and replace all previous credit lines for the same supplier on the same debtor in whatever currency denominated.

(x) If it is known to the Import Factor that it is the practice of the debtor to prohibit assignments of receivables owing by him then the Import Factor shall so inform the Export Factor in giving his approval or as soon as it is known to the Import Factor if later.

Article 18 Reduction or cancellation

(i) For good reason the Import Factor shall have the right to reduce or cancel the credit line. Such cancellation (which expression includes a reduction) must take place in writing or by telephone (to be confirmed in writing). Upon receipt of such notice of cancellation the Export Factor shall immediately notify the supplier and such cancellation shall be effective as to shipments made after the supplier's receipt of such notice. On or after the sending of any such notice of cancellation to the Export Factor, the Import Factor shall have the right to send such notice also direct to the supplier, but he shall inform the Export Factor of such an action.

The Export Factor shall cooperate, and shall ensure that the supplier shall cooperate, with the Import Factor to stop any goods in transit and thus minimise the Import Factor's loss. The Export Factor undertakes to give the Import Factor all assistance possible in such circumstances.

(ii) On the effective date of the termination of the contract between supplier and Export Factor all credit lines are immediately cancelled without notice, but shall remain valid for any receivable relating to a shipment made and services completed before the time of termination provided that the receivable is assigned to the Import Factor within 30 days of that date.

(iii) When the cancellation of the credit line is effective as in paragraph (i) of this Article, or the credit line has expired then:

(a) the right of succession as described in paragraph (vi) of Article 17 ceases and thereafter, except as provided in sub-paragraphs (b) and (c) of this paragraph, any payment or credit (other than a payment or credit in connection with a transaction excluded in Article 3) may be applied by the Import Factor in satisfaction of approved receivables in priority to unapproved receivables;

(b) if any such credit relates to an unapproved receivable and the Export Factor establishes to the satisfaction of the Import Factor that the credit arose solely from the failure to ship or a stoppage in transit, the credit shall be applied to such unapproved receivable; and

(c) any monies subsequently received by the Import Factor resulting from a general distribution from the estate of the debtor in respect of receivables assigned by the Export Factor or the relevant supplier shall be shared between the Import Factor and the Export Factor in proportion to their respective interests in the amount owing by the debtor as at the date of the distribution.

(N.B. Paragraph (iii) (b) and (c) amended June 2003)

Article 19 Obligation of Export Factor to assign

(i) Subject to the provisions of paragraph (iii) of this Article the Export Factor must offer the Import Factor all receivables owing by debtors in the Import Factor's country which have been assigned to the Export Factor.

(ii) The Export Factor shall inform the Import Factor whether or not the Export Factor's agreement is to include the whole turnover on credit terms to the Import Factor's country.

(iii) In exceptional cases, the Export Factor may withhold from the Import Factor receivables in respect of any debtor, for which the Import Factor is not prepared to assume any risk or a substantial part of it or is prepared to do so only at a factoring commission unacceptable to the Export Factor, but this exception shall not apply to any debtor referred to in paragraph (iv) below.

(iv) When the Import Factor has approved a credit line on a debtor and an invoice owing by that debtor has been assigned to the Import Factor, then all subsequent receivables of that supplier in respect of that debtor must be assigned to the Import Factor, even when the receivables are only partly approved or not approved at all.

(v) When the Import Factor decides to cancel a credit line, the obligation for the Export Factor continues to exist until all approved receivables have been paid or otherwise provided for; in other words, until the Import Factor is "out of risk". However, after cancellation of the contract between the Export Factor and the supplier, further assignments of receivables cannot be expected.

SECTION IV COLLECTION OF RECEIVABLES

Article 20 Rights of the Import Factor

(i) By reason of the assignment to the Import Factor of full ownership of each receivable, the Import Factor shall have the right of bringing suit and otherwise enforcing collection either in his own name or jointly with that of the Export Factor and/or that of the supplier and the right to endorse debtor's remittances for the collection in the Export Factor's name or in the name of such supplier and the Import Factor shall have the benefit of all rights of lien, stoppage in transit and all other rights of the unpaid supplier to goods which may be rejected or returned by debtors.

(ii) If any cash, cheque, draft, note or other instrument in payment of any receivables assigned to the Import Factor is received by the Export Factor or any of his suppliers, the Export Factor must immediately inform the Import Factor of such receipt. It shall be held in trust by the Export Factor or such supplier on behalf of the Import Factor and shall, if so requested by the Import Factor, be duly endorsed and delivered promptly to him.

(iii) If the sales contract contains a prohibition of assignment the Import Factor shall have the same rights as set forth in paragraph (i) of this Article as agent for the Export Factor and/or the supplier.

(iv) If the Import Factor:

(a) is unable to obtain judgement in respect of any receivable assigned to him in the courts of the debtor's country by reason only of a term relating to jurisdiction in the contract of sale between the supplier and the debtor which gave rise to that receivable; and

(b) informs the Export Factor of that inability within 365 days of the due date of the invoice representing that receivable;

then the Import Factor may immediately reassign that receivable and recover from the Export Factor any amount paid in respect of it under paragraph (ii) of Article 24.

(N.B.: Paragraph (iv) amended June 2004)

Article 21 Collection

(i) The responsibility for collection of all receivables assigned to the Import Factor rests with him and he shall use his best endeavours promptly to collect all such receivables whether approved or unapproved.

(ii) Except as provided in Article 27 when the total amount of receivables owing by a debtor at any one time is approved in part:

(a) the Import Factor shall be entitled to take legal proceedings for the recovery of all such receivables without obtaining the prior consent of the Export Factor but the Import Factor shall inform the Export Factor of such action;

(b) if the Export Factor notifies the Import Factor of his disagreement with such legal proceedings, which are then accordingly terminated, the Import Factor shall be entitled to reassign all receivables then owing by the debtor and to be reimbursed by the Export Factor with the amount of all costs and expenses incurred by the Import Factor in such proceedings and the provisions of paragraphs (ii) and (iii) of Article 15 will apply to that reassignment; and

(c) except as provided in paragraph (ii) b) of this Article the costs and expenses of such legal proceedings shall be borne by the Import Factor and the Export Factor in proportion to the respective amounts of the approved and unapproved parts of the outstanding receivables.

Article 22 Unapproved receivables

(i) When all receivables owing by a debtor at any one time are wholly unapproved:

(a) the Import Factor shall obtain the consent of the Export Factor before incurring legal and other costs and expenses (other than the Import Factor's own and administrative costs and expenses) relating to their collection;

(b) such legal and other costs and expenses shall be the responsibility of the Export Factor and the Import Factor shall not be responsible for any loss and/or costs which are attributable to any delay in the giving of such consent by the Export Factor;

(c) If the Export Factor does not answer the Import Factor's request for consent within 30 days, the Import Factor is entitled to reassign the receivables then or any time thereafter;

(d) The Import Factor shall be entitled on demand to a deposit from the Export Factor to cover fully or partly the amount of the estimated costs to be incurred in the collection of such receivables.

SECTION V TRANSFER OF FUNDS

Article 23 Transfer of payments

(i) When any payment is made by the debtor to the Import Factor in respect of any receivable assigned to him he shall pay in the currency of the invoice the equivalent of the net amount received in his bank to the Export Factor immediately after the value date or the date of the Import Factor's receipt of the Bank's notification of the amount received whichever is later except to the extent of any previous payment under guarantee.

(ii) All payments, irrespective of the amount, shall be transferred daily via SWIFT.

(iii) Not later than the day of the transfer the Import Factor shall provide a report showing the allocation of the amount transferred.

(iv) The Export Factor shall repay to the Import Factor on his demand:

(a) any payment made by him to the Export Factor if the debtor's payment to the Import Factor was made by a payment instrument subsequently dishonoured (cheque or equivalent) provided that:

(i) the Import Factor notified the Export Factor of this possibility with the payment advice (payment under reserve); and

(ii) the Import Factor's demand has been made within 10 banking days in the Import Factor's country from the date of his transfer of the funds to the Export Factor; and

(iii) repayments demanded by the Import Factor will not affect his other obligations;

(b) without any time limit, any payment made by the Import Factor to the Export Factor in respect of any unapproved Receivable or unapproved part of a Receivable to the extent that payment by the debtor or any guarantor of the receivable is subsequently recalled under the law of the country of the payer and such recall is either paid or settled by the Import Factor provided that any such settlement is effected in good faith.

(N.B.: Paragraph (iv) (a) adjusted and Paragraph (iv) (b) added October 2002)

Article 24 Payment under guarantee

Except as provided in Articles 25 and 27:

(i) the Import Factor shall bear the risk of loss arising from the failure of the debtor to pay in full any approved receivable on the due date in accordance with the terms of the relevant contract of sale or service; and

(ii) to the extent that any such receivable shall not be paid by or on behalf of the debtor by the 90th day after the due date as described above, the Import Factor shall on such 90th day make payment to the Export Factor ("payment under guarantee").

(iii) For the purpose of paragraphs (i) and (ii) of this Article, payment by the debtor shall mean payment to any one of the Import Factor, the Export Factor, the supplier or the supplier's insolvent estate.

(iv) In the event of payment to the supplier or the supplier's insolvent estate the Import Factor shall co-operate with and assist in the debtor's country the Export Factor to mitigate any potential or actual loss to the Export Factor.

(v) If an approved receivable is expressed in a currency other than that of the corresponding credit line, in order to determine the approved amount that receivable shall be converted to the currency of the credit line at the rate of exchange ruling at the date on which the payment under guarantee is due. In all cases the risk of the Import Factor shall not exceed at any time the amount of the original approval.

Article 25 Prohibitions against assignments

(i) In respect of any approved receivable arising from a contract of sale or for services which includes a prohibition of its assignment the Import Factor's obligation for a payment under guarantee shall arise on the official insolvency of the debtor or when the debtor makes a general declaration or admission of his insolvency, but, in any event, not earlier than the 90th day after the due date as described in paragraph (i) of Article 24.

(ii) After any payment under guarantee in respect of any approved receivable referred to in paragraph (i) of this article the Import Factor shall have the sole right to claim in the insolvent estate of the debtor in the name of the supplier.

(iii) The Export Factor shall obtain from the supplier and deliver to the Import Factor any document that may be required by him for the purpose of making any claim as described in paragraph (ii) of this Article.

(iv) The provisions of this article shall apply, in spite of anything to the contrary elsewhere in these rules.

(N.B.: Paragraph (iv) added June 2003, Paragraph (i) amended June 2004)

Article 26 Late payments

(i) If the Import Factor or the Export Factor fails to make payment of any amount when it is due to be paid to the other he shall pay interest to that other.

(ii) Except as provided in paragraph (iii) of this Article, if the Import Factor does not initiate a payment to the Export Factor according to the requirements of Article 23 or Article 24, the Import Factor shall:

    (a) be liable to pay to the Export Factor interest calculated for each day from the date on which such payment shall be due until actual payment at twice the 3-months-LIBOR as quoted on such due date in the relevant currency, provided that the accrued amount of interest exceeds EUR 50; and

    (b) reimburse the Export Factor with the equivalent of any currency exchange loss suffered by him and caused by the delay in payment.

If there shall be no LIBOR quotation for the relevant currency, twice the lowest lending rate for such currency available to the Export Factor on such date shall apply.

(iii) If as a result of circumstances beyond his control the Import Factor is unable to make any such payment when due:

    (a) he shall give immediate notice of that fact to the Export Factor;

    (b) he shall pay to the Export Factor interest at a rate equivalent to the lowest lending offer rate available to the Export Factor in the relevant currency calculated for each day from the day when his payment shall be due until actual payment, provided the accrued amount of interests exceeds EUR 50.

SECTION VI DISPUTES

Article 27 Disputes

(i) A dispute occurs whenever a debtor fails to accept the goods or the invoice or raises a defence, counterclaim or set-off including (but not limited to) any defence arising from a claim to the proceeds of the receivable by any third party. However, where there is a conflict between the provisions of this Article and those of Article 25 the latter shall prevail.

(ii) Upon being notified of a dispute the Import Factor or the Export

Factor shall immediately send to the other a dispute notice containing all details and information known to him regarding the receivable and the nature of such dispute. In either case the Export Factor shall provide the Import Factor with further information regarding the dispute within 60 days of the receipt by the Export Factor or his sending it as the case may be.

(iii) Upon receipt of such dispute notice the approval of that receivable shall be deemed to be suspended.

If a dispute is raised by the debtor and the dispute notice is received within 90 days after the due date of the invoice to which the disputed receivables relates, the Import Factor shall not be required to make payment under guarantee of the amount withheld by the debtor by reason of such dispute.

If a dispute is raised by the debtor and the dispute notice is received after payment under guarantee, but within 180 days of the due date of the invoice, the Import Factor shall be entitled to reimbursement of the amount withheld by the debtor by reason of such dispute.

(iv) (a) The Export Factor shall be responsible for the settlement of the dispute and shall act continuously to ensure that it is settled as quickly as possible. The Import Factor shall co-operate with and assist the Export Factor, if so required, in the settlement of the dispute including the taking of legal proceedings.

(b) If the Import Factor declines to take such proceedings or if the Export Factor requires a reassignment of the disputed receivables so that proceedings may be taken in his or the supplier's name, then, in either case, the Export Factor is entitled to such reassignment.

(c) Whether or not any such reassignment has been made the Import Factor shall again accept as approved, within the time limits specified in paragraph (v) of this Article, such disputed receivable to the extent that the dispute is settled in favour of the supplier (including an admission by the person responsible for the administration of the debtor's insolvent estate) provided that:

(1) the Export Factor has complied with his obligations under paragraph (iv) a) of this Article;

(2) the Import Factor has been kept fully informed about the status of negotiations or proceedings at regular intervals; and

(3) the settlement provides for payment by the debtor to be

made within 30 days of the date of the settlement, if amicable, or the date of the coming into effect of the judgement in the case of a legal settlement.

(d) For the purpose of this Article, "legal settlement" means a dispute settled by way of a decision of a court or other tribunal of competent jurisdiction (which, for the avoidance of doubt, shall include arbitration) provided such legal proceedings have been formally commenced by proper service of legal process or demand for arbitration prior to the term set for an amicable settlement; and "amicable settlement" means any settlement which is not a legal settlement.

(v) The time limits referred to in paragraph (iv) c) above, for the Import Factor to accept again as approved a disputed receivable, are as follows:

(a) in the case of an amicable settlement, 180 days: and
(b) in the case of a legal settlement, 3 years; in each case after the receipt of the dispute notice in accordance with paragraph (ii) of this Article. If, however, during such periods, the debtor becomes officially insolvent or makes a general declaration or admission of his insolvency, the Import Factor shall remain at risk until the dispute has been settled.

(vi) In the case of a disputed receivable which the Import Factor has accepted again as approved in accordance with paragraph (iv) of this Article:

(a) if the receivable has been reassigned to the Export Factor the Import Factor shall have the right to an immediate assignment to him of all the Export Factor's or (as the case may be) the supplier's rights under the settlement;
(b) in every such case any payment under guarantee, which is to be made in accordance with Article 24, shall be made within 14 days of the date on which payment is to be made by the debtor according to the settlement provided that:

(1) any assignment required by the Import Factor under paragraph (vi) a) of this Article has been made effectively by the Export Factor within that period; and
(2) the end of that period of 14 days is later than the original due date for the payment under guarantee.

(vii) If the Export Factor does not comply with all his obligations under this Article the Import Factor shall have the right to reassign to the Export Factor the disputed receivable and the Export Factor shall promptly reimburse the Import Factor with the amount of the payment under guarantee; such payment shall include interest from date of payment under guarantee to date of reimbursement as calculated in accordance with paragraph (iii) (b) of Article 26.

(viii) If the dispute is solved in full in favour of the supplier, all related costs shall be the responsibility of the Import Factor. In all other cases the costs will be the responsibility of the Export Factor.

(N.B.: Paragraph (iv) (b) amended June 2004)

SECTION VII REPRESENTATIONS, WARRANTIES AND UNDERTAKINGS

Article 28 Representations, warranties and undertakings

(i) The Export Factor warrants and represents for himself and on behalf of his supplier:

  (a) that each receivable represents an actual and bona fide sale and shipment of goods or provision of service made in the regular course of business and in conformity with the description of the supplier's business and terms of payment;

  (b) that the debtor is liable for the payment of the amount stated in each invoice in accordance with the terms without defence or claim;

  (c) that the original invoice bears notice that the receivable to which it relates has been assigned and is payable only to the Import Factor as its owner or that such notice has been given otherwise in writing before the due date of the invoice, any such notice of assignment being in the form prescribed by the Import Factor.

  (d) that each one at the time of his assignment has the unconditional right to assign and transfer all rights and interest in and title to each receivable (including any interest and other costs relating to it which are recoverable from the debtor) free from claims of third parties;

  (e) that he is factoring all the receivables arising from sales as defined in Article 3 of any one supplier to any one debtor for which the Import Factor has given approval; and

  (f) that all such duties, forwarder's fees, storage and shipping charges and insurance and other expenses as are the responsibility of the supplier under the contract of sale or service has been fully discharged.

(ii) The Export Factor undertakes for himself and on behalf of his supplier:

    (a) that he will inform the Import Factor of any payment received by the supplier or the Export Factor concerning any assigned receivable; and

    (b) that as long as the Import Factor is on risk the Export Factor will inform the Import Factor in general or, if requested, in detail about any excluded transactions as defined in Article 3.

(iii) In addition to the provisions of Article 32, in the event of a breach of the warranty given in paragraph (i) e) or the undertaking given in paragraph (ii) b) of this Article the Import Factor shall be entitled to recover from the Export Factor

    (a) the commission and/or charges as agreed for that supplier on the receivables withheld, and

    (b) compensation for other damages, if any.

SECTION VIII MISCELLANEOUS

Article 29 Communication and electronic data interchange (EDI)

(i) Any written message as well as any document referred to in these Rules, which has an equivalent in the current EDI Standard can or, if so required by the Constitution and/or the Rules between the Members whenever either of them is applicable, must be replaced by the appropriate EDI-message.

(ii) The use of EDI is governed by the edifactoring.com Rules.

(iii) The originator of a communication shall assume full responsibility for the damages and losses, if any, caused to the receiver by any errors and/or omissions in such communication.

Article 30 Accounts and reports

(i) The Import Factor is responsible for keeping detailed and correct debtor ledgers and for keeping the Export Factor informed about the accounts showing on such ledgers.

(ii) The Export Factor shall be entitled to rely upon all information and reports submitted by the Import Factor provided that such reliance is reasonable and in good faith.

(iii) If for any valid reason the Import Factor or the Export Factor will not be able to make use of the EDI then the Import Factor shall account and report at least once a month to the Export Factor with respect to all transactions and each such monthly account and report shall be deemed approved and accepted by the Export Factor except to the extent that written exceptions are taken by the Export Factor within 14 days of his receipt of such account and report.

Article 31 Indemnification

(i) In rendering his services, the Import Factor shall have no responsibility whatsoever to the Export Factor's suppliers.

(ii) The Export Factor shall indemnify the Import Factor and hold him harmless against all suits, claims, losses or other demands which may be made or asserted against the Import Factor:

   (a) by any such supplier by reason of an action that the Import Factor may take or fail to take; and/or
   (b) by any debtor in relation to the goods and/or services, the invoices or the underlying contracts of such supplier;

   provided that in either case the Import Factor's performance in his action or failure to act is reasonable and in good faith.

(iii) The Import Factor shall indemnify the Export Factor against any losses, costs, interest or expenses suffered or incurred by the Export Factor by reason of any failure of the Import Factor to comply with his obligations under paragraph (i) of Article 13 or any breach of his warranty given in that paragraph. The burden of proof of any such loss, costs, interest or expense lies with the Export Factor.

(iv) Each of the Export Factor and the Import Factor shall reimburse the other for all losses, costs, damages, interest, and expenses (including legal fees) suffered or incurred by that other by reason of any of the matters for which the indemnities are given in paragraphs (ii) and (iii) of this Article.

Article 32 Breaches of provisions of these Rules

(i) If the Export Factor has substantially breached any provision of these Rules, the Import Factor shall not be required to make payment under guarantee to the extent that the breach has seriously affected the Import Factor to his detriment in his appraisal of the credit risk and/or his ability to collect any receivable. The burden of proof lies with the Import Factor. If the Import Factor has made payment under guarantee the Import Factor shall be entitled to reimbursement of the amount paid.

(ii) A substantial breach of paragraphs (i) a) and b) of Article 28 that results only from a dispute shall not be subject to the provisions of this Article and shall be covered by the provisions of paragraphs (i) to (viii) of Article 27.

(iii) A substantial breach must be asserted within 365 days after the due date of the invoice to which it relates.

(iv) The Export Factor shall promptly reimburse the Import Factor under this Article; such payment shall include interest from date of payment under guarantee to date of reimbursement as calculated in accordance with Article 26 (ii).

(v) The provisions of this Article are additional to and not in substitution for any other provisions of these Articles.

A DIAGRAMMATICAL COMPARISON OF FULL FACTORING WITH THE "TWO FACTOR" SYSTEM

(1) FULL FACTORING (Domestic)

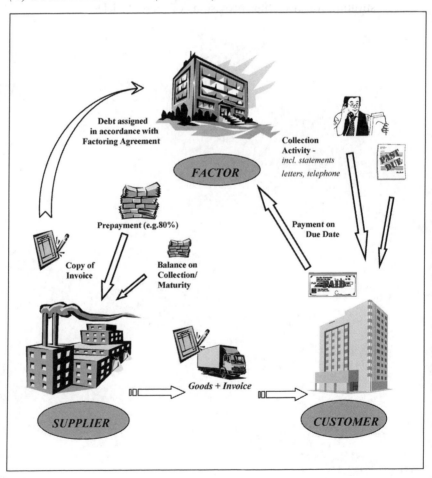

(2) THE "TWO FACTOR" SYSTEM (International)

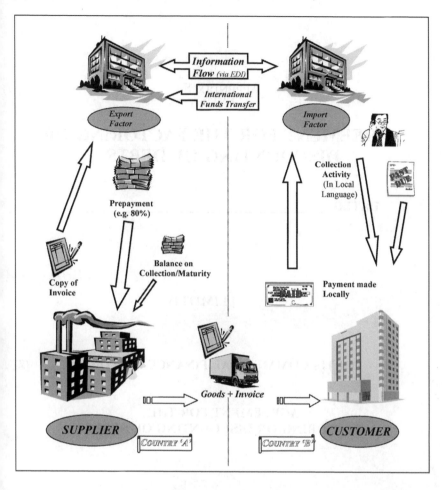

AGREEMENT FOR THE FACTORING OR DISCOUNTING OF DEBTS

DATED_____

[ ] LIMITED	(1)
TO	
FORTIS COMMERCIAL FINANCE LIMITED	(2)

**AGREEMENT FOR THE
FACTORING OR DISCOUNTING OF DEBTS**

FORTIS COMMERCIAL FINANCE LIMITED

AGREEMENT FOR THE FACTORING OR DISCOUNTING OF DEBTS

SCHEDULE OF PARTICULARS

These Particulars form part of an agreement for factoring or discounting of debts between you, the company whose name and address appears in section 1 below, and Fortis Commercial Finance Limited ("this Agreement"). You have chosen the following service:

- **Full Factoring with Recourse**
- **Full Factoring without Recourse**
- **Confidential Invoice Discounting with Recourse**
- **Confidential Invoice Discounting without Recourse**
- **Disclosed Invoice Discounting with Recourse**
- **Disclosed Invoice Discounting without Recourse**
- **Disclosed Delayed Dunning with Recourse**
- **Disclosed Delayed Dunning without Recourse**
- **Undisclosed Delayed Dunning with Recourse**
- **Undisclosed Delayed Dunning without Recourse**

The explanatory notes attached to (but not forming part of) this Agreement outline certain of these Particulars which apply to the service chosen by you.

**Section
number**

1.	**Your Name and Address**	
2.	**Registered Number** **Starting Date** (clause 2)	
3.	**States and Territories for Inclusion** (clause 5)	England and Wales Scotland *[etc. . . . .]*

4. **Debts within Credit Limits that are Unapproved** (clauses 9.2.5, 10.3.1 and 19.1.5)

[All]
[The first £500 of the amount owing by any one Debtor at any time]
[All Debts arising from the hiring of equipment]

5. **Prepayment Percentage** (definition of Prepayment)

%

6. **Maximum Funds in Use** (clause 10.5.3 and definition)

£

7. **Concentration Percentage** (clause 10.5.3.2)

%

8. **Discounting Charge Rate** (clause 13.4) %

[For Domestic Debts]: %
[For All Export Debts]: %
[For Export Debts in Members of the European Union]: %
[For Export Debts in name of state or territory]: %
and/or
[For Funds in Use up to £.......: %
For the next £........ of Funds in Use: .... %]
[etc]

9. **Administration Charge** (clause 14.1.1.)

[For Domestic Debts]: %
[For All Export Debts]: %
[For Export Debts in members of the European Union]: %
[For Export Debts in name of state or territory]: %

10. **Minimum Administration Charge** (clause 14.2 and definition of Shortfall)

£   per [month][year]

11. **Assignment Notices to Debtors**

[No notices until your agency is withdrawn]
(clauses 15.4 and 15.11)
[Notice to be given to Debtors for each debt when it becomes ... days overdue for payment]

		[Notice to be given in respect of all Debts upon the issue of each invoice]
12.	**Your Agency to Collect Debts**	*[no agency]* (clauses 15.8 to 15.10) *[you are appointed our agent] [in respect of Debts not more than [ ] days overdue]*
13.	**Nature of your Business** (clause 16.1)	
14.	**Currencies of Payment** (clause 16.1.1.)	United Kingdom *[etc …]*
15.	**Terms of Payment** (clause 16.1.1.)	(i) Payment Date: (ii) Maximum Settlement Discount:
16.	**Laws Governing Contracts of Sale** (clauses 16.1.2)	England and Wales
17.	Recourse Period (clauses 17.3 and 19.1.5 and definition)	.............*days*
18.	**Credit Periods** (definition of "Collection Date")	*[not applicable] [for every Export Debt a period of ...... Days starting on the date on which the Debt is due for payment]*
19.	**Electronic Exchange of Information**	*[Included] [Excluded]*
20.	**Security Documentation** (clause 10.5.1)	
21.	**Other Conditions Precedent** (clause 10.5.2)	
22.	**Additional Terms and Conditions**	

[22.1   No notice may be given by you under clause 4.1 for the termination of this agreement to expire earlier than…]

FORTIS COMMERCIAL FINANCE LIMITED

INDEX OF CLAUSES FOR AGREEMENT FOR THE FACTORING OR DISCOUNTING OF DEBTS

AGREEMENT FOR THE FACTORING OR DISCOUNTING OF DEBTS

1.   Parties

1.   This Agreement is made between Fortis Commercial Finance Limited (incorporated in England with the number 2713317) of Westcombe House, 2–4 Mount Ephraim, Tunbridge Wells, Kent, TN4 8AS, ("we" or "us") and the client ("you") named in section 1 of the particular terms attached to and forming part of this Agreement ("the Particulars").

2.   Date

2.   This Agreement is made on the date on which the party, last to sign it, does so.

3.   Definitions and Interpretation

3.1   You should refer to clause 27 for the meanings of technical expressions used in this Agreement; those are the expressions of which the initial letter is a capital. Clause 27 also contains a number of rules for the interpretation of this Agreement.

3.2   In this Agreement, except where otherwise stated, any reference to a clause is to a clause of this Agreement and any reference to a section is to a section of the Particulars.

4.   Period of this Agreement and its End

4.1   This Agreement will start on the date shown in section 2 and, unless it is ended by us under clause 21.1, it will continue until it is ended on the expiry of not less than three month's written notice to end it given by either you or us to the other.

4.2   Except as provided, the ending of this Agreement (including the ending of it under clause 21.1) will not affect the rights and obligations of you and us under this Agreement in relation to any transaction started before the end of this Agreement or any Debt in existence at that time and such rights and obligations will remain in full force and effect until duly satisfied.

4.3 All licences and authorities given to us by you in this Agreement are irrevocable and will continue after the end of this Agreement until all yourbligations have been fully discharged.

4.4 All the provisions of this Agreement will remain in effect in spite of any change of your name or your constitution.

5. Debts for Inclusion

The Debts included within the scope of this Agreement are all those, and only those, that arise from your Contracts of Sale under which the invoices are to be addressed to places in the states or territories listed in section 3. Any reference to Debt in this Agreement is to a Debt included in it.

6. Sale and Purchase of Debts

6.1 Immediately after the Starting Date (or as soon as the Goods have been Delivered if that is later) you will offer to sell to us every Debt in existence on that date by sending to us a schedule of all such Debts in a form acceptable to us.

6.2 We may accept or decline any Debt included in a schedule under clause 6.1. Our acceptance of any Debt will be evidenced by our crediting the Purchase Price of it to the Current Account.

6.3 You will sell to us and we shall purchase all Debts coming into existence during the period of this Agreement described in clause 4.1 so that those Debts will belong to us automatically as soon as they come into existence without the need for any other act of transfer.

6.4 All Debts purchased by us will be sold by you with full title guarantee.

7. Notification of Debts

7.1 At least once in each week you will notify us, in the way we require, of every Debt relating to Goods Delivered other than any Debt previously notified to us or offered to us under clause 6.1.

7.2 You will furnish us with such documents evidencing the Debts included in a Notification as we may require.

7.3 All Debts included in any one Notification are to be expressed in the same currency.

7.4 You will notify us separately of every Debt in respect of which you are unable to give us every warranty and undertaking included in this Agreement and on that separate Notification you will mark clearly the nature of the warranty or undertaking that you cannot give.

8. Ownership of Debts and Goods

8.1 If we ask you at any time to complete, sign and deliver to us a written assignment of any Debt and give written notice of that assignment to the Debtor then you will do so at your expense (including any applicable stamp duty) in the form that we require.

8.2 If, for any reason, the ownership of any Debt fails to be transferred to us then you will hold that Debt in trust for us.

8.3 You will hold in trust for us and keep separate from your own property any Goods in your possession at any time which are included in the Related Rights. You will mark all such Goods plainly with our name as owner and deal with any such Goods as we may require.

8.4 We shall have the right by oral or written notice to you to have transferred to us the ownership of any Goods (other than those referred to in clause 8.3) which are the subject of a Contract of Sale and of which the ownership has not passed to the Debtor. You will deal with those Goods as required by us.

9. Approved and Unapproved Debts and Eligible Debts

9.1 We may, without giving any reason, by written notice to you establish a Credit Limit and/or a Funding Limit in relation to any Debtor or increase any established Credit Limit or Funding Limit.

9.2 A Debt (but excluding any interest included in the Related Rights pertaining to that Debt) will rank as an Approved Debt at any time if:

    9.2.1 at that time, when added to the total of all other Debts owing by the same Debtor, it is within a Credit Limit relating to that Debtor; and

    9.2.2 it is not a Debt in respect of which you are at that time in breach of any representation, warranty or undertaking given by you in this Agreement; and

    9.2.3 it was not notified under clause 7.4; and

    9.2.4 it is not a Debt which the Debtor will be unable (or claims to be unable) to pay owing to the law or rules or regulations of any government (except those relating solely to the insolvency of the Debtor) or war or civil commotion or the circumstances in the territory in which the Debtor is situated; and

    9.2.5 it is not a Debt described in section 4.

For the purposes of this clause Debts will be deemed to fall into a Credit Limit in the order in which they are notified.

9.3 We may by oral or written notice to you reduce or cancel any established Credit Limit or Funding Limit to take effect immediately except in respect of any Approved Debt arising from Goods sold and Delivered before your receipt of that notice.

9.4   You undertake not to disclose to the Debtor or any other party the status of any Debt as Approved or Unapproved or whether or not Eligible or the amount of or absence of any Credit Limit or Funding Limit.

9.5   In any application by you to us for the establishment of a Credit Limit or Funding Limit you will supply to us the full correct name and address of the Debtor and any other information supporting the application that we may reasonably require.

9.6   You acknowledge that in establishing Credit Limits or Funding Limits we are not acting as a credit reference agency under the Consumer Credit Act 1974 and that we have no obligation to you in relation to any Credit Limit or Funding Limit except as specifically provided for in this Agreement.

10.   Purchase Price of Debts and our Payments to you

10.1   The Purchase Price payable by us for each Debt will be equivalent to the amount to be paid for it by the Debtor according to the Contract of Sale for that Debt less:

      10.1.1   any discount or other allowance taken or claimed by the Debtor; and

      10.1.2   the discount charge provided for in clause 13.4 so far as attributable to that Debt.

10.2   We shall credit the Purchase Price of every Debt to the Current Account upon Notification of the Debt. We may do so before making any deductions and debit any amount to be deducted as soon as it is known.

10.3   Except where any of the provisions of clauses 10.4, 10.5 or 21.2.2 apply you may draw against the credit balance on your Current Account and we shall pay to you:

      10.3.1   at your request a Prepayment in respect of any Eligible Debt at any time after Notification;

      10.3.2   the Purchase Price of any Debt (less any Prepayment made in respect of it) on its Collection Date.

    We may, if we see fit, pay to you a Prepayment in respect of any Debt even if you have not asked for it.

10.4   We may pay to you other amounts on account of the Purchase Price of Debts on terms (including an arrangement fee if we require it) to be agreed between you and us.

10.5   We shall not be obliged to make any Prepayment:

      10.5.1   before all the security documentation specified in section 20 has been completed to our satisfaction; or

10.5.2   while any other condition contained in section 21 remains unsatisfied; or

10.5.3   at any time if the effect of that payment would be that:

    10.5.3.1   the debit balance on the Funds in Use Statement would exceed the Maximum Funds in Use at that time; or

    10.5.3.2   the total of Prepayments made in respect of Outstanding Debts owing by any one Debtor would exceed the percentage shown in section 7 of the total amount of all Approved Debts Outstanding at the time of the payment.

10.6   Unless otherwise agreed all our payments to you in respect of the Purchase Prices will be as follows:

  10.6.1   in respect of Debts represented by invoices expressed in sterling, by BACS; and

  10.6.2   in respect of Debts represented by invoices expressed in any other currency, by telegraphic transfer.

Where the method of payment is to be other than BACS you will pay to us our standard charge for that method as made known to you from time to time.

11.   Purchase Price payable in a Currency other than that of the Invoice

11.1   If, at your request, we agree to pay the Purchase Price of a Debt in a currency other than that of its invoice then:

  11.1.1   we shall calculate the Purchase Price of that Debt by using the spot selling rate quoted in London by our Bankers on the Collection Date; and

  11.1.2   for the purpose of crediting its Purchase Price to the Current Account we may apply such rate as we may determine on the date of the Notification of the Debt and make any adjustment to that credit that may be required after the Collection Date.

11.2   You undertake to indemnify us against any additional loss and expense incurred by us in the collection or attempted collection of any such Debt and of the conversion of the currency of the amount received by us in payment of the Debt (including bank charges and commissions) and we may debit the Current Account for such loss or expense so incurred by us.

12.   Your Obligations to us and Group Companies

12.1   The amount of any of the monetary liabilities included in your Obligations or any liability of you to any Group Company of ours may be debited to the Current Account or applied in the discharge of any amount payable by us to you. For this purpose we may make a reasonable estimate of any of your Obligations the amount of which cannot be immediately ascertained.

12.2 At any time we may combine any two or more accounts held by us in your name and, if we so decide, we may combine any such account held by us with any such account held by any Group Company of ours.

12.3 Where (i) any monetary liability is in a currency other than that of the account to which it is to be debited or (ii) accounts held in different currencies are to be combined, then we may apply the middle spot rate of exchange quoted by our bankers in London at the time of the debit or combination.

12.4 You will pay to us upon our demand:

    12.4.1 any Prepayment made in respect of an Eligible Debt upon its ceasing to be Eligible;

    12.4.2 any debit balance owing to us on the Current Account at any time; and

    12.4.3 the equivalent of any amount by which a debit balance on the Funds in Use Statement (or if more than one a combination of them) at any time exceeds the Maximum Funds in Use at that time.

Such payments will be made by you in the currency of such of the Current Accounts as we require.

12.5 You undertake to indemnify us against all claims made against us by any Debtor (save any claim arising solely from our own default) and against all losses, costs, charges, interest and expenses (including legal costs and applicable taxes and duties) incurred by us at any time and arising from or in any way connected with any of the following:

    12.5.1 our entering into or enforcing, exercising or protecting our rights under this Agreement or any guarantee or indemnity or security given to us in respect of your Obligations;

    12.5.2 enforcing or attempting to enforce payment of any Unapproved Debt or settling or compromising any dispute with or claim by a Debtor or any other person in relation to any Debt;

    12.5.3 the securing by us of any release of any Debt from any trust charge or other encumbrance;

    12.5.4 any indemnity which we may be required to give to our bankers in connection with the collection on our behalf of any cheque or other instrument made payable to you;

    12.5.5 any agreement by us under clause 26 to provide you with the EDI Services (including any corruption of our data or systems by or through any Intermediary);

    12.5.6 any breach by you of any of the terms of this Agreement or any other of your Obligations;

12.5.7 any bank charges incurred by us for the collection of cheques from Debtors including the maintenance of any trust account in your name for our benefit for that purpose;

12.5.8 our dealing with cheques and other instruments of payment returned unpaid;

and we may debit to the Current Account the amount of any such losses, costs, charges, interest and expenses.

12.6 You will repay to us on our demand any amount paid to you by us in respect of any Unapproved Debt to the extent that payment by the Debtor or any guarantor of the Debt is subsequently recalled under the law of the country of the payer or by reason of any decision of a court or tribunal of competent authority in that country.

13. Current Accounts, Funds in Use Statements and Discounting Charge

13.1 We shall send to you once in every month or at such other intervals as may be agreed:

13.1.1 a statement of the Current Account and Funds in Use Statement in respect of each currency of your invoices; and

13.1.2 (except while you are our agent under clause 15.8) an analysis of the Outstanding Debts.

13.2 In the absence of any manifest error or any error in law:

13.2.1 every such account statement and analysis will be deemed to be correct and will be binding on you except for any error of which you advise us within seven days of its despatch;

13.2.2 you agree to be bound by a certificate signed by any of our directors or other officers or our auditors as to any of the balances on the Current Accounts and Funds in Use Statements and the total amount of the monetary liabilities included in your Obligations at any time.

13.3 We shall maintain a Funds in Use Statement in each currency of your invoices to which:

13.3.1 will be debited every payment made by us to you on the date on which it is available to you in cleared funds and every other amount charged to you or debited to the Current Account except in respect of credit notes or the exercise of Recourse;

13.3.2 will be credited every amount received by us in payment of or on account of payment any Debt on its Collection Date or from you on the date on which we receive it in cleared funds.

For the purpose of determining the date of the receipt of cleared funds by you or us you agree to accept the periods to be allowed for the clearance of cheques and other forms of remittance as advised by our Bankers and of which we shall notify you from time to time.

407

13.4 On the last day of each month you will pay to us or we may debit to the Current Account the total of the discounting charges for that month calculated by applying the rate shown in section 8 over the base rate of our Bankers for the relevant currency for the time being in force to the debit balance shown on the Funds in Use Statement at the end of each day.

13.5 Any change in the rate of the discounting charges arising from a change in the base rate of our Bankers will be effective from the start of the day of the announcement of that change. The discounting charges will continue to accrue after the end of this Agreement until all your Obligations have been fully discharged.

14. Administration Charges

14.1 You will pay to us (or we may in our discretion deduct from any payment to be made by us to you at any time):

14.1.1 an administration charge equal to the percentage shown in section 9 of the notified amount of each Debt (before deduction of any discount, credit note or other allowance) when the Debt is due to be notified; and

14.1.2 an arrangement fee for any variation of this Agreement requested by you or any services for you which we agree to provide outside the scope of this Agreement.

Every administration and other charge under this clause 14 which is calculated in a currency other than sterling will be converted into sterling at the selling rate for that currency notified to us by our Bankers on the date when the charge is due to be paid.

14.2 You will be liable to us for any administration charge Shortfall which:

14.2.1 where based on a monthly amount stated in section 10 will be payable by you at the end of each month; and

14.2.2 where based on an annual amount stated in section 10 will accrue monthly during any year with any requisite adjustment at the end of each subsequent month and will be so payable by you at the end of each month.

If the Shortfall is based on an annual amount and this Agreement is ended otherwise than on any anniversary of the Starting Date then the minimum amount for the purposes of this definition will be reduced by one twelfth for each complete month between the end of this Agreement and the next anniversary.

14.3 All our charges are quoted in this Agreement exclusive of applicable taxes or duties.

15. Sales Ledger Administration and Collection of Debts

15.1 We shall have the sole right to enforce payment of and collect any Debt so long as we are the owner of it or it is held by you in trust for us. We have the right to start, carry on, defend or compromise proceedings in respect of any Debt in such manner and upon such terms as we may choose and to use your name for those purposes if we think fit. However, nothing obliges us to take any such proceedings.

15.2 Whether or not you are our agent under clause 15.8 you will, at your expense, co-operate with us in any enforcement collection or proceedings in respect of any Debt including the production of such documents and the giving of such evidence as may be necessary for such enforcement or collection or proceedings.

15.3 Except where we appoint you as our agent under clause 15.8 you will not collect or attempt to collect any Debt.

15.4 Where assignment notices are required for the service chosen by you, you will ensure that:

    15.4.1 on the Business Day next following the Starting Date there is sent to every Debtor by whom any Debt is then owing a notice; and

    15.4.2 every invoice representing a Debt and issued after the Starting Date bears a prominent and legible notice;

in each case that the Debt has been purchased by and is payable only to us. Every notice shall be in a form specified by us.

15.5 You will deliver promptly upon its receipt to us or, if we so require, direct to our bank account (and meanwhile hold in trust for us) all the identical remittances received by you in or on account of payment of any Debt.

15.6 We may apply any payment or other benefit received from or credit granted to a Debtor in or on account of payment of any Approved Debt owing by that Debtor in priority to any Unapproved Debt in spite of any different allocation made by the Debtor.

15.7 You undertake to give immediate instructions to any banker or other person with whom you maintain an account to pay to us or direct to our bankers the proceeds of any credit transfer, relating to any Debt, which is received in that account. You will furnish our bankers with such instructions and/or indemnity as they may require in order that they may effect collection of any cheques made payable to you which are not transferable.

15.8 We may appoint you as our agent for the purposes of:

    15.8.1 maintaining and managing the accounts of Debtors; and

    15.8.2 sending statements and demands to Debtors and of enforcing payment of Debts and you will accept any such appointment.

15.9 If we appoint you as our agent under clause 15.8 you undertake:

    15.9.1 to act promptly and efficiently at your own expense in carrying out such tasks and to act in accordance with any directions which we may give to you from time to time;

15.9.2 to retain on our behalf all records and documents on or by which any Debts are recorded or evidenced until the full discharge of all your Obligations or any earlier delivery to us of such records;

15.9.3 to furnish us by such date in each month as we may direct such records, statements and accounts of transactions with Debtors and of Outstanding Debts made up to the end of the latest previous month as we may require; and

15.9.4 not to hold yourself out as our agent for any purpose other than the tasks mentioned above nor to hold yourself out as our agent for any purposes except while the agency remains in effect.

15.10 The appointment under clause 15.8 may be made by our notice to you in writing or by a note of the agency in section 12.

15.11 We may at any time end your appointment as our agent by written or oral notice to you and, upon the end of the agency, you will immediately send to every Debtor by whom any Debt is then owing or becomes owing the assignment notice described in clause 15.4.

15.12 Where it is stated in section 11 that notices are to be delayed until a specified period after the due date of each invoice then your agency under clause 15.8 will be automatically withdrawn in respect of any Debt which becomes overdue by that period and the provisions of clause 15.11 will then immediately apply to that Debt.

15.13 Where it is stated in section 12 that you are to be our agent in respect of Debts not overdue by more than the specified number of days then your agency under clause 15.8 will be automatically withdrawn in respect of any Debt as soon as it becomes overdue for payment to that extent.

15.14 For the protection and/or collection of any Debt we may at any time assign it to any factor or other finance company or collection agent.

16. Your Warranties and Undertakings in respect of Notified Debts

16. By notifying us of any Debt (except to the extent that clause 7.4 applies) you warrant or undertake (as applicable) in respect of that Debt that:

16.1 the Goods and the invoice for them have been Delivered and the Debt has arisen from a Contract of Sale entered into by you in the normal course of your business as described in section 13 and that the Contract of Sale:

16.1.1 provides for payment to be made in a currency of a state or territory shown in section 14 on terms not more liberal than those described in section 15;

16.1.2 is governed by the law of a state or territory shown in section 16;

16.1.3 is otherwise as approved by us in writing; and

you will not vary that Contract of Sale except with our written consent;

16.2 you have performed all your obligations to the Debtor and the Debtor is obliged to accept the Debt and the invoice for it as a legally binding obligation of the Debtor to pay the full amount as notified of the Debt;

16.3 the Debtor has no right to prohibit the assignment nor any right of set-off nor any other right by which we may be prevented from collecting the full amount of the Debt as notified except only the right to any settlement discount approved by us;

16.4 in the insolvency of the Debtor, the person having the duty to administer the estate will accept proof of debt for the amount as notified;

16.5 the Debt is free from all trusts, charges, liens and other encumbrances and no other person, including any of your suppliers, has any right or interest to or in the Debt or the Goods to which it relates;

16.6 you have no obligations to the Debtor other than under any Contract of Sale and you have no agreement or arrangement with the Debtor for retrospective discounts or otherwise whereby the amount of the Debt may be reduced except in accordance with the Contract of Sale;

16.7 the Debtor has an established place of business in the country to which the invoice is addressed and is not an Associate of yours;

16.8 the Debtor has complied with all formalities required by law or rules or regulations having the force of law necessary for the receipt and acceptance of the Goods and for payment to us on the due date in the currency in which the invoice is expressed according to the Contract of Sale; and

16.9 if the Goods are to be exported you have complied with all such formalities (if any) for the export of the Goods.

17. Other Undertakings by you

17. In addition to all other undertakings given by you in this Agreement **17.** you undertake:

17.1 to keep proper books and records of account and to make appropriate entries in them to show the sale to us of the Debts;

17.2 promptly to pay all taxes and carriage and freight charges and effect any insurance and to pay the premium and make any claim under it in every case in which you are liable to do so under the Contract of Sale;

17.3 to pay to us the amount of any Unapproved Debt which remains unpaid after the end of its Recourse Period so that your liability under this undertaking may be enforced against you as principal debtor without the need for us to make any prior demand on the Debtor by whom such Debt is payable;

17.4 without our prior written consent not to assign or create any charge over any of your rights or benefits under this Agreement nor to delegate any of your responsibilities under it;

17.5 not to enter into any agreement for the factoring or discounting or otherwise for the sale of any Debt except with us (and entry into any such agreement by any Associate of yours will be deemed to be a breach of this provision);

17.6 not to create any mortgage, charge or other encumbrance or any trust which affects or may affect any of your assets or rights or your undertaking;

17.7 if we require you to do so by written notice to you, to procure that any company which you control, or make your best endeavours to procure that any other Group Company of yours, enters into an agreement with us on terms and conditions similar to those of this Agreement;

17.8 for the purpose of procuring for our benefit a refund of any value added tax included in any Approved Debt which becomes bad or doubtful in any case in which the regulations of H M Customs and Excise for the recovery of such value added tax apply, to accept a transfer back to you of that Debt for the consideration of:

   17.8.1 your immediate payment to us of the amount of value added tax recoverable; and

   17.8.2 your payment to us of any recovery or dividend received by you in respect of that Debt and meanwhile to hold that recovery or dividend in trust for us; and

17.9 to comply with all procedures for the operation of this Agreement which we may make known to you from time to time.

18. Disagreements with Debtors, Credit Notes and Credit Balances:

18.1 You undertake that if, in spite of the warranties given by you in clause 16, a Debtor fails to accept its liability to pay to us the full amount of any Debt as notified (less only any discount for prompt payment in accordance with the Contract of Sale) on its due date then you will;

   18.1.1 immediately inform us of all the circumstances of the case; and

   18.1.2 use your best endeavours promptly to obtain the Debtor's acceptance of that liability; and

   18.1.3 promptly perform any obligations under the Contract of Sale giving rise to the Debt that have not been performed.

18.2 On or at any time after any of the events specified in clause 21.1 or at any other time if you fail to perform your obligations under clause

18.1 then we may, at your expense, settle or compromise any such dispute on such terms as we may think fit and/or to perform any such remaining obligations but shall not be bound to do so.

18.3 You will be bound by anything done or omitted to be done by us under clause 18.2 including any reduction in the Purchase Price of any Debt.

18.4 On the Starting Date you will furnish us with a copy of every credit note already then issued relating to any Debt then Outstanding. After that, on the Business Day next following the issue of any credit note by you, you will deliver to us a copy of that credit note. The amount of every credit note will be debited to the Current Account.

18.5 We may make payment in settlement of or on account of any credit balance appearing on a Debtor's account in our records at any time however it may have arisen.

19. Recourse:

19.1 We shall be entitled to exercise Recourse as follows:

19.1.1 in respect of any Debt included in a separate Notification under Clause 7.4, at any time after its Notification;

19.1.2 in respect of any Debt which is at any time the subject of a breach of any representation, warranty or undertaking given by you to us or which consists entirely of a deduction wrongly claimed or deducted by the Debtor, at any time after such breach or claim or deduction occurs;

19.1.3 in respect of any Unapproved Debt owing by a Debtor the subject of Insolvency Proceedings, at any time after the start of the Insolvency Proceedings;

19.1.4 in respect of any Debt which the Debtor claims to be unable to pay owing to rules or regulations of any Government or war or civil commotion or the circumstances in the territory in which the Debtor is situated, at any time after the event giving rise to the claim;

19.1.5 in respect of every other Unapproved Debt, at the end of the Recourse Period relating to that Debt.

19.2 We may exercise Recourse by written notice to you or by debiting the repurchase price to the Client Account. We shall remain the owner of every Debt in respect of which we shall exercise Recourse until the repurchase price has been fully discharged.

19.3 We shall account to you for any payment made to us in or on account of settlement of any Debt the ownership of which has been transferred back to you by reason of Recourse.

20. Disclosure of Information; Your Accounts and Records; our Relations with your Bankers and Auditors:

20.1   You warrant that you have told us about every fact or matter known to you or which you should have known and which might influence any decision of ours as to:

20.1.1   the entry into this Agreement or its continuation; or

20.1.2   the terms and conditions of this Agreement; or

20.1.3   the acceptance of any person as guarantor or indemnifier for any of your Obligations; or

20.1.4   the establishment, increase or reduction of the Maximum Funds in Use or any Credit Limit:
and in particular such facts or matters include:

20.1.5   any mortgage or charge or other encumbrance or trust affecting any of your assets or rights and your undertaking;

20.1.6   any change or proposed change in your constitution or management or the ownership or control of you or your business;

20.1.7   the name and address of any person who is an Associate of yours; and

20.1.8   any Insolvency Proceedings threatened or pending against you.

You undertake to disclose to us promptly any such fact or matter which arises during the course of this Agreement.

20.2   We shall be entitled at any time:

20.2.1   to inspect, to verify and/or at your expense to take copies of any of your records or documents on or by which any Debt is recorded or evidenced and/or to take possession of any such records or documents included in the Related Rights;

20.2.2   to inspect any records or documents relating to your financial position or the results of your operations.

For any of these purposes any of our officers or authorised agents may enter upon any premises at which you carry on business or at which any of your property is situated at any time during business hours on any Business Day.

20.3   You undertake to keep us informed at of the location of all your records and documents.

20.4   You will furnish us with a copy of your audited accounts for each year or other financial accounting period ending before the end of this Agreement within four months of the end of such year or period. You will prepare and furnish us with such management accounts of your business and at such times as we may from time to time prescribe.

20.5   You hereby authorise us:

20.5.1   to provide any of your bankers and auditors with such information in our possession relating to your affairs as any of them may require at any time; and

20.5.2 at any time to obtain from any of your bankers and auditors any information in their possession which we may then require regarding the state of your accounts or your financial affairs.

20.6 You warrant and undertake that you have given your existing bankers and your auditors, and will give to any banker and auditor whom you may in future appoint, the authority for them to give us any information relating to your affairs and that, if we so require, you will instruct your auditors to report direct to us at your expense on your financial position and the results of your operations.

21. Termination Events

21.1 On or at any time after the occurrence of any of the following events we shall have the right to bring this Agreement to an end immediately by notice to you:

21.1.1 any Insolvency Proceedings relating to you;

21.1.2 a resolution of your members for your winding up;

21.1.3 the seizure of the whole or any part of your income or assets under any execution, legal process or distress for rent or the making or the threat of any attachment on any Debt owing to you;

21.1.4 the occurrence of any of the events referred to in clauses 21.1.1, 21.1.2 or 21.1.3 in relation to any person who has given or may at any time give a guarantee or indemnity in respect of your Obligations or the death of that person or the end of any such guarantee or indemnity;

21.1.5 any breach or the ending of any covenant or undertaking given by any person in reliance on which we entered into or continued this Agreement;

21.1.6 the withdrawal or attempted withdrawal of any waiver or release or agreement as to priorities in our favour in respect of any security right over any of your assets;

21.1.7 the cessation of your business or your threat to cease business;

21.1.8 any adverse change in your financial position or your performance which we consider may increase the risk to us of the recovery of the Funds in Use;

21.1.9 any alteration in your ownership, control or constitution which we consider material;

21.1.10 the making of a statutory demand on you under the Act by any of your creditors or your failure to satisfy any judgment against you within seven days of its entry;

21.1.11 any borrowing by you becoming due for repayment before its stated maturity date owing to your breach of any of the conditions of that borrowing;

21.1.12 the absence of any Notification for a consecutive period of 28 days;

21.1.13 any breach of any of your Obligations (or of any obligation of you to a Group Company of us) considered by us to be material or not redressed by you within two Business Days of our request to you to do so.

21.2 At any time after any event listed in clause 21.1 (whether or not we bring this Agreement to an end) we shall be entitled to any one or more of the following:

21.2.1 Recourse in respect of all Debts then Outstanding (including all Approved Debts) but so that they will all continue to belong to us until the repurchase price of all of them has been fully discharged by you;

21.2.2 the withholding of all payments to you until the full discharge of all your Obligations;

21.2.3 a reduction in the Prepayment percentage shown in section 5 to such percentage as we may think fit;

21.2.4 on our demand the immediate repayment by you of all Prepayments previously made;

21.2.5 payment by you of the full cost and expense of any exercise of our rights under clause 20.2;

21.2.6 to appoint at your expense accountants or other professional experts to verify the Outstanding Debts and to obtain such information regarding your financial position as we may require;

21.2.7 as compensation for the additional expense of our collecting the Outstanding Debts, a service charge, additional to the administration charges under clause 14, equivalent to 7.5% of the notified amount of any Debt then Outstanding and of every Debt subsequently becoming Outstanding;

21.2.8 to require that no credit note be issued by you without our prior consent;

21.2.9 to change the status of any or all of the Approved Debts to Unapproved.

21.3 If you should see fit to issue any credit note at any time after we have exercised our rights under clause 21.2.8 you will promptly advise us of that credit note in such manner and with such documents (including the original of the credit note) as we may require. Upon our giving consent to the issue of any credit note of which the original is in our possession we shall despatch it (at your expense) to the Debtor.

21.4 Upon the occurrence of any Insolvency Proceedings in relation to you without any notice or other formality:

21.4.1 notice under clause 8.4 will be deemed to have been given to you to be effective on the day before such occurrence in respect of all Goods then ready for delivery and remaining in your possession; and

21.4.2 all accounts held by us in your name (other than any memorandum account) will be deemed to have been combined.

22. Data protection act 1998

22.1 We may disclose any details of this Agreement or any transaction under it or any entry on any account or any other information held by us in your name to:

22.1.1 any credit reference agency; or

22.1.2 any trade register for the purpose of credit decisions, fraud prevention or the tracing of Debtors; or

22.1.3 any of our Associates for any purpose (including training or marketing); or

22.1.4 any other person for the purpose of our business; or

22.1.5 any persons acting on our behalf.

22.2 You warrant and undertake in relation to any individual including:

22.2.1 a Debtor or a partner, shareholder, director or other officer of you or a Debtor;

22.2.2 a person who has or may give in our favour a guarantee or indemnity in respect of the Obligations or the obligations of a Debtor;

that:

22.2.3 you have strictly complied and will, until the end of this Agreement and the discharge of all your Obligations, strictly comply with the provisions of the Data Protection Act 1998 and the principles contained in the schedules to that Act; and

22.2.4 that you have told and will tell any such individual that you may at any time pass to us Data (as defined in that Act) which you hold in respect of him for the purposes of this Agreement.

23. Authority for us to act for you

23.1 As security for your Obligations you hereby appoint us and each of our directors and other officers jointly and each of us and them severally to be your attorney for any of the following purposes:

23.1.1 to sign deeds or documents;

23.1.2 to complete and endorse instruments;

23.1.3 to start or defend proceedings;

23.1.4 to do any other things;

as we may consider requisite for in order to:

23.1.5 collect or realise or perfect our ownership of any Debt; or

23.1.6 secure the performance of any of your Obligations or complete any Contract of Sale.

23.2 In addition you appoint as your attorney for the above purposes any person to whom we assign any Debt under clause 15.13.

24. Notices

24.1 Any written notice or demand which we have to or may give to or on you will be validly served or made:

24.1.1 if handed to any of your officers; or

24.1.2 if delivered or sent by first class prepaid post to your address stated in the Particulars or to any address at which you carry on business or to your registered office; or

24.1.3 if transmitted by facsimile or e-mail to any facsimile number or e-mail address (as the case may be) of you made known to us by you at any time.

Any such notice or demand, if served personally, will take effect on the date of its service and, if sent by post, shall take effect within two Business Days of the time of its posting and, if transmitted by facsimile or e-mail, will take effect on its transmission.

24.2 Any notice which you have to or may give to us shall be validly given if sent to us at our registered office by prepaid first class post and it will be effective on its receipt by us.

25. General provisions

25.1 If any act or event is to be done or is due to take place according to this Agreement on or within a period ending on a day which is not a Business Day the act or event shall be deemed to be done or to take place on or by the next Business Day.

25.2 If any provision of this Agreement is held to be invalid or unenforceable no other provision will be affected and all such other provisions will remain in full force and effect.

25.3 We shall be entitled to rely upon any act done or any letter or document signed or any communication sent to us by facsimile or by e-mail by any person purporting to act or sign or send on your behalf despite any defect in or absence of any authority of such person.

25.4 No person other than you or us will have any right under the Contracts (Rights of Third Parties) Act 1999 to enforce any term of this Agreement. This clause does not affect any rights or remedy of any person which exists or is available otherwise than under that Act.

25.5 Our rights under this Agreement will not be affected in any way by any grant by us of any time or indulgence to you or any other person nor by any delay or failure in our exercise of any right under this

Agreement or otherwise. Any waiver by us of any breach of your Obligations will not in any way serve as a waiver of any future or other breach.

25.6 The terms and conditions of this Agreement are the only terms and conditions agreed between you and us. All agreements, warranties, representation and other statement made by us or on our behalf by any means before the making of this Agreement are excluded. No variation of this Agreement will be effective unless that variation is made in writing and signed on your behalf by a director or your company secretary and on our behalf by an authorised signatory.

25.7 This Agreement shall be construed and take effect in accordance with English law and you hereby submit to the jurisdiction of the English courts without prejudice to our right to bring proceedings in the courts of any country in which you carry on business.

26. Exchange of information by electronic data transmission

26.1 Clauses 26.1 to 26.9 inclusive will apply only if either it is so indicated in section 19 or we and you have agreed in writing that it will apply.

26.2 We shall for the time being accept, on the terms and conditions contained in clauses 26.3 to 26.9 inclusive, the following interchange of information with you by electronic data transmission:

26.2.1 Notifications; and

26.2.2 access by you to information shown on any Business Day during normal working hours on our Accounts with you.

For these purposes we will licence you to use the Software but such licence is personal only to you and not transferable. The interchange of information is explained in our EDI Guide which will be revised from time to time and will be made available to you.

26.3 We shall make no additional charge for the EDI Services. However, you are solely responsible for all costs and any taxes or duties relating to your sending information to us and receiving it from us including telephone charges and charges made by any Intermediary.

26.4 You will obtain and maintain all equipment, software and communication services requisite for the proper functioning of the EDI Services and we shall have no responsibility for the reliability or proper functioning of such equipment, software or services or for the performance of any Intermediary.

26.5 You undertake:

26.5.1 to observe complete confidentiality in respect of any information received by you from us by the use of the EDI Services including information relating to matters other than the operation of this Agreement;

26.5.2 that you will at all times comply precisely with all requirements of law and of orders, rules and regulations having the

419

force of law for the time being in force in relation to any data held or received by you at any time;

26.5.3 to ensure that only your duly authorised officers or employees have access to any authorisation codes and passwords and that no unauthorised person has access to the EDI Services;

26.5.4 to ensure that each transmission by you correctly and clearly identifies:

26.5.4.1 the sender and the recipient; and

26.5.4.2 the approval of the information contained in the transmission by the sender;

by the agreed method of identifying their authenticity.

26.5.5 to ensure that your use of the EDI Services will not in any way corrupt our data processing systems or any of the data held by us whether by reason of any virus or otherwise;

26.5.6 to comply with all procedures specified by us for the use of the EDI Services including:

26.5.6.1 all instructions in the EDI Guide;

26.5.6.2 directions as to security of the Software; and

26.5.6.3 storage of data;

26.5.7 promptly to tell us about every fact or matter at any time known to you which constitutes or might lead to a breach of any of your obligations under this clause 26.

26.6 We shall have no responsibility whatsoever for any failure or delay in your obtaining access to any information from us or in your provision of information to us nor for any default of any Intermediary nor shall we be liable to you for loss costs or expense caused to you by any incorrect information received by either you or us by the use of the EDI Services except for any error arising solely from our own default.

26.7 You undertake that you will not at any time make any claim or take any proceedings against us in respect of any losses costs damages expenses or interest arising from:

26.7.1 the use of any equipment provided by us to you for electronic data transmission or processing; or

26.7.2 your reliance on any data transmitted to you (or purportedly to you) by us by the use of the EDI Services in spite of any absence of or defect in the authority of the person transmitting such data; or

26.7.3 any corruption of data held or to be held in your data processing system for any reason including the introduction of any virus into that system from any source.

26.8 The copyright and all other rights in the Software will at all times belong to us. You may not copy the Software without our prior written consent except only one copy for your own back-up purposes.

26.9 We may at any time by written or oral notice to you with immediate effect withdraw your right to use the EDI Services. Upon withdrawal of the EDI Services you will return to us immediately all copies of the EDI Guide, Software and other property of ours relating to the EDI Services then in your possession or under your control.]

27. Meanings of words and expressions

27.1 In this Agreement:
    27.1.1 the words **"we"** and **"us"** also refer to any successor or assignee of us;
    27.1.2 where the context allows the singular includes the plural and the plural includes the singular and any of the three genders includes either of the other two;
    27.1.3 the meanings of general words introduced by the word "other" are not limited by reference to any preceding word indicating a particular class of acts matters or things;
    27.1.4 where we have a right or option to do anything then the right or option is at our absolute discretion;
    27.1.5 the expressions **'including"**, **"includes"** and **"in particular"** do not limit or restrict any general words preceding any of them;
    27.1.6 where the meaning of any expression in or in relation to any place outside England and Wales is used and there is no exact equivalent to that expression in that place then the expression is to have the meaning of its closest equivalent in that place;
    27.1.7 the headings of clauses are for convenience only and do not limit or affect the extent or meaning of any clause;
    27.1.8 reference to any Act of Parliament includes such Act as amended or re-enacted from time to time and any order or regulation made under it;
    27.1.9 except where otherwise specified time limits described in days are in calendar days;
    27.1.10 the expression **"the United Kingdom"** includes the Channel Islands and the Isle of Man;
27.2 In this Agreement the following expressions have the meanings assigned to them below:
"the Act":
the Insolvency Act 1986;
"Approved":
in relation to any Debt, Approved in accordance with clause 9 and not subject to a change in status to Unapproved under clause 21.2.9;
"Associate":
any person whose relationship with you or us (as the case may be) is within the meaning of "associate" in section 435 of the Act or any of

your or our (as the case may be) directors or other officers or the spouse of any such person, director or officer;

"BACS":

Bankers' Automated Clearing Services;

"our Bankers"

Fortis Bank SA NV or such other bank as we may use from time to time:

"Business Day":

any day except any Saturday, Sunday or bank holiday;

"Collection Date":

in relation to any Debt, the date on which our Bankers receive for our account cleared funds in payment of it and in relation to any unpaid Approved Debt the earlier of:

   (i) the date on which we are informed of Insolvency Proceedings in relation to the Debtor by whom the Debt is payable; or

  (ii) the last day of the credit period stated in section 18.

"Contract of Sale":

a contract for the supply of goods or services or for hiring by you;

"Credit Limit":

a limit established, increased or reduced under clause 9 in relation to any Debtor for the purpose of determining which Debts owing by that Debtor may be Approved;

"Current Account":

the accounts maintained by us in your name and in the currencies in which we make payments to you for the purpose of recording transactions between you and us;

"Debt":

a debt (including any tax or duty payable) and any other obligation incurred by a Debtor under a Contract of Sale together with its Related Rights (and, where the context requires, a Debt means part of a Debt);

"Debtor":

any person who has incurred or may incur an obligation to you under a Contract of Sale;

"Delivered":

in the case of any goods or any invoice, despatched to the Debtor from a place in the United Kingdom and, in the case of services or hiring, completed (and the word "delivery" is to be construed accordingly);

"Domestic Debt"

a Debt which is not an Export Debt;

"EDI Services":

the availability for you to communicate with us by electronic means for the purposes described in clause 26;

"Eligible Debt"
any Debt which is eligible for a Prepayment being a Debt which either:
  (i) is Approved or would be Approved but for an entry in section 4; or
  (ii) is Outstanding and within a Funding Limit when aggregated to all other Outstanding debts then owing by the same Debtor and is not a Debt in respect of which we may exercise recourse under clause 19.1;

"Export Debt"
A Debt arising from any Contract of Sale under which the invoice is to be addressed to a place outside the United Kingdom (and where the name of a state or territory appears after this expression then it means that the Debt arises from a Contract of Sale under which the invoice is to be addressed to a place in that state or territory);

"Funding Limit"
a limit established, increased or reduced under clause 9 in relation to any Debtor for the purpose of determining which Debts owing by that Debtor may be Eligible;

"Funds in Use Statement":
the statement described in clause 13.1;

"Goods":
any goods or services or hiring the subject of a Contract of Sale;

"Group Company":
any company whose relation to you or us (as the case may be) is that of:
  (i) a parent undertaking;
  (ii) a subsidiary undertaking; or
  (iii) any subsidiary undertaking of that parent undertaking;
(in accordance with the meanings given to those expressions in section 258 of the Companies Act 1985) or any partnership or joint venture of which you or we (as the case may be) or any of the above is a member;

"Insolvency Proceedings":
  (i) the issue of a petition for winding up or bankruptcy; or
  (ii) an administration application under para.12 of Sch.B1 to the Act or the appointment of an administrator under para.14 or para.20 of the said Sch.B1; or
  (iii) a proposal for a voluntary arrangement under the Act; or
  (iv) the calling of any meeting of creditors; or
  (v) the appointment of a receiver in respect of any part or the whole of the undertaking or property of any firm or company;

"Intermediary":
any internet server or other concern through which you communicate with us by electronic means;

423

"Maximum Funds in Use":
the smaller of the amount shown in section 6 or an amount at any time equal to the percentage shown in section 5 of the total of all Approved Debts (or all those that would be Approved Debts but for an entry in section 4) which are Outstanding at that time;

"Notification":
  (i) a schedule of offer delivered to us by you in respect of an offer under clause 6.1; or
  (ii) a form prepared by you and delivered to us in accordance with clause 7.1 or clause 7.4;

and "notify" and "notified" in relation to a Debt will mean respectively include and included in a Notification;

"your Obligations":
all your monetary and other actual or contingent or prospective obligations incurred at any time to us whether arising under this Agreement or otherwise and whether arising in or by contract, tort, restitution or assignment;

"Outstanding":
in relation to any Debt, remaining unpaid and not reassigned to you and for this purpose a Debt is deemed to be paid on its Collection Date;

"Prepayment":
a payment by us to you on account of the Purchase Price of any Debt before its Collection Date up to the percentage specified in section 5 of the amount of the Debt as notified;

"Purchase Price":
the price payable by us for a Debt calculated as in clause 10.1;

"Recourse":
our right to require that you repurchase any Outstanding Debt at a repurchase price equivalent to the amount of that Debt as notified;

"Recourse Period":
in relation to any Debt, a period of the length specified in section 17 starting on the date when that Debt is due for payment in accordance with the Contract of Sale;

"Related Rights":
in respect of any Debt all of the following:
  (i) all your rights under the Contract of Sale other than your rights to any Goods;
  (ii) the benefit of all guarantees, indemnities, insurances and securities given to or held by you;
  (iii) all cheques, bills of exchange and other instruments held by or available to you;
  (iv) the right to possession of all ledgers, computer data records and documents on or by which any Debt is recorded or evidenced;
  (v) any Goods the subject of a Contract of Sale returned or rejected by the Debtor or repossessed by you;

(vi) our right to any other Goods under clause 8.4;

(vii) any interest to which you become entitled in relation to the Debt as a result of any law or any rule or regulation of government;

"Shortfall":

the amount by which the total of the administration charges under clause 14.1.1 in respect of Debts notified:

(i) in any year starting on the Starting Date or any anniversary of it; or

(ii) in any month starting during the period of this Agreement (as specified in clause 4.1);

is less than respectively the annual amount or the monthly amount shown in section 10;

"Software":

the software provided by us for your use in accordance with clause 26;

"Starting Date":

the date shown in section 2;

"Unapproved":

in relation to any Debt, not Approved;

"Writing":

any form of communication that is accessible so that it may be recorded in a permanent form and used at any time after it has been made and "written" is to be construed accordingly.

IN WITNESS WHEREOF this Agreement has been executed by you as a deed and signed on our behalf by an official duly authorised so to do as follows:

SIGNED and Delivered as a Deed on the   )

           day of   20)

by   **LIMITED** acting by:)

)

                  a director) ....

and   )   Director

             director/secretary) ....

                              #Director/Secretary

Signed for and on behalf of   )

FORTIS COMMERCIAL FINANCE   ....

LIMITED   )

acting by   )   Director

a Director and   )

                 a Director/its) ....

Secretary   ) #Director/Secretary

[# Delete as applicable]

EXPLANATORY NOTES:
[These notes do not form any part of the agreement between us]

Full Factoring with Recourse
This service does not provide protection against bad debts so that you must pay us back for any Debt that remains unpaid for any reason. You will need to give assignment notices in respect of all Debts to your customers and there is no agency for you to collect Debts on our behalf; we have the responsibility for managing the sales ledger and collecting the Debts. For the purposes of financing your business we will make Prepayments in respect of Eligible Debts.

Full Factoring without Recourse
This service provides protection against bad debts for Approved Debts except those referred to in section 4 of the Particulars. You will need to give assignment notices in respect of all Debts to your customers and there is no agency for you to collect Debts on our behalf. For the purposes of financing your business we will make Prepayments in respect of Approved Debts.

Confidential Invoice Discounting with Recourse
This service does not provide protection against bad debts so that you must pay us back for any Debt that remains unpaid for any reason. However, for the purposes of financing your business we will make Prepayments in respect of Eligible Debts.

You are not required to give assignment notices in respect of Debts to your customers until we tell you to do so. Until we withdraw your agency you will act as our agent for the collection of Debts and the management of the sales ledger.

Confidential Invoice Discounting without Recourse
This service provides protection against bad debts for Approved Debts except those referred to in section in section 4 of the Particulars. You are not required to give assignment notices in respect of Debts to your customers until we tell you to do so. Until we withdraw your agency you will act as our agent for the collection of Debts and the management of the sales ledger.

For the purposes of financing your business we will make Prepayments in respect of Eligible Debts.

Disclosed Invoice Discounting with Recourse
This service does not provide protection against bad debts so that you must pay us back for any Debt that remains unpaid for any reason. However, for the purposes of financing your business we will make Prepayments in respect of Eligible Debts.

You will need to give assignment notices in respect of all Debts to your customers; but, until we withdraw your agency, you will act as our agent for the collection of Debts and the management of the sales ledger.

426

Disclosed Invoice Discounting without Recourse

This service provides protection against bad debts for Approved Debts except those referred to in section in section 4 of the Particulars. For the purposes of financing your business we will make Prepayments in respect of Eligible Debts.

You will need to give assignment notices in respect of all Debts to your customers; but, until we withdraw your agency, you will act as our agent for the collection of Debts and the management of the sales ledger.

Disclosed Delayed Dunning with Recourse

This service does not provide protection against bad debts so that you must pay us back for any Debt that remains unpaid for any reason. However, for the purposes of financing your business we will make Prepayments in respect of Eligible Debts.

You will need to give assignment notices in respect of all Debts to your customers. However, until we withdraw your agency, you will act as our agent for the management of the sales ledger and the collection of those Debts which have not become seriously overdue for payment (see the period stated in section 11 of the Particulars). We ourselves will collect those seriously overdue Debts

Disclosed Delayed Dunning without Recourse

This service provides protection against bad debts for Approved Debts except those referred to in section in section 4 of the Particulars. For the purposes of financing your business we will make Prepayments in respect of Eligible Debts.

You will need to give assignment notices in respect of all Debts to your customers. However, until we withdraw your agency, you will act as our agent for the management of the sales ledger and the collection of those Debts which have not become seriously overdue for payment (see the period stated in section 11 of the Particulars). We ourselves will collect those seriously overdue Debts

Undisclosed Delayed Dunning with Recourse

This service does not provide protection against bad debts so that you must pay us back for any Debt that remains unpaid for any reason. However, for the purposes of financing your business we will make Prepayments in respect of Eligible Debts.

You are not required to give assignment notices in respect of Debts to your customers except in respect of any Debt that becomes seriously overdue for payment (see the period stated in section 11 of the Particulars) or until we tell you to do so.

Until we withdraw your agency, you will act as our agent for the collection of those Debts in respect of which no assignment notice has been given and the management of the sales ledger. We ourselves will collect those Debts in respect of which assignment notices have been given.

Undisclosed Delayed Dunning without Recourse

This service provides protection against bad debts for Approved Debts except those referred to in section 4 of the Particulars. For the purposes of financing your business we will make Prepayments in respect of Eligible Debts.

You are not required to give assignment notices in respect of Debts to your customers except in respect of any Debt that becomes seriously overdue for payment (see the period stated in section 11 of the Particulars) or until we tell you to do so.

Until we withdraw your agency, you will act as our agent for the collection of those Debts in respect of which no assignment notice has been given and the management of the sales ledger. We ourselves will collect those Debts in respect of which assignment notices have been given.

DEED OF WAIVER AND PRIORITIES

DATED_____

[NAME OF FACTOR]   **(1)**

[NAME OF BANK]   **(2)**

[NAME OF FACTOR'S CLIENT]   **(3)**

DEED OF WAIVER AND PRIORITIES

PAUL DAVIDSON TAYLOR
solicitors
chancery court, queen street,
horsham, west sussex, RH13 5AD
t: 01403 262333 f: 01403 262444
e: law@pdt.co.uk

APPENDIX 9

DEED OF WAIVER AND PRIORITIES

1. PARTIES

1.1 ....*[NAME OF FACTOR OR DISCOUNTER]* .... (a company registered in England and Wales with the number ....) of *[address of factor or discounter]* ....*]* ("the Factor").

1.2 ....*[NAME OF BANK]* ....(a company registered in England and Wales with the number ....) whose address for the purposes of this Deed is at .... *[address of bank's office dealing with these priorities]* .... ("the Bank").

1.3 .... *[NAME OF FACTOR'S CLIENT]* .... (a company registered in England and Wales with the number ....) of .... *[address of factor's client]* .... *]* ("the Client").

2. DATE

2. This Deed is deemed to be made on the date on which the party, last to execute it, does so.

3. DEFINITIONS AND INTERPRETATION:

In this Deed except where the context otherwise requires:

3.1 the expression **"the Agreement"** shall mean the agreement for the factoring or discounting of *Debts #[made between the Factor and the Client on .... 20......................] [made by the Client's acceptance on .... 20........................ of the Factor's letter of offer dated ....20........................] and any agreement made in replacement or variation of it or supplemental to it;

3.2 the expression **"*Debt"** and **"*Recourse"** shall have the meanings respectively assigned to them in the Agreement;

3.3 the expression **"*Related Rights"** shall have the meaning assigned to it in the Agreement but so that references to a "*Debt" and to a "*Contract of Sale" in or in connection with such definition shall include respectively reference to an Other Debt and to any contract giving rise to an Other Debt.

3.4 the expression **"Schedule B1"** shall mean Schedule B1 to the Act, the expression **"Administrator"** shall have the meaning assigned to it in paragraph 1(1) of Schedule B1 to the Act and the expression **"Receiver"** shall have the meaning assigned to it section 29(1)(a) of

430

the Act (not being an administrative receiver as defined in section 29(2) of the Act);

3.5   the following expressions shall have the meanings attributed to them below:

"the Act"

the Insolvency Act 1986 including that Act as amended or re-enacted from time to time and any order or regulation made under it;

"Bank's Security"

the debenture created by the Client, on .... 20........................, in favour of the Bank by which the Client charged in favour of the Bank all of the Client's property, assets, rights and undertaking both present and future.

"Chargeholders"

the Bank and the Factor together (and **"Chargeholder"** means either of them);

"the Client Account"

all amounts now or at any time hereafter payable by the Factor to the Client under the Agreement;

"Factor's Security"

the #[fixed and floating charge][debenture] created on .... 20............. in favour of the Factor by which the Client charged in favour of the Factor all of the Client's property, assets, rights and undertaking, both present and future, including all Specified *Debts and Other Debts and their proceeds and the Client's Account;

"Liabilities"

all obligations both monetary and otherwise now or at any time owing or incurred by the Client (whether solely or jointly with any other person), actual or contingent, present or future, liquidated or unliquidated and whether arising in or by contract, tort, restitution or assignment;

"Liabilities to the Bank"

the total amount of Liabilities to the Bank (including interest, charges and commission) secured by the Bank's Security;

"Liabilities to the Factor"

the total amount of Liabilities to the Factor secured by the Factor's Security, including discount and other charges, interest and any liability of the Client to the Factor in respect of *Recourse.

"Other Debt"

any amount of indebtedness now or at any time hereafter owing or becoming due to the Client on any account whatsoever and its proceeds (together with the Related Rights pertaining to it and their proceeds) other than any Specified *Debt and the Client Account;

"Securities"

the Bank's Security and the Factor's Security where reference is made to both of them (and the expression **"Security"** shall mean either of them);

"Specified Debt"

any *Debt (together with its proceeds) which has been purchased or purported to be purchased by the Factor (and not repurchased by and vesting in the Client) by virtue of the Agreement and of which the ownership fails to vest in the Factor for any reason;

3.6   reference to any Security shall in every case include any additional or substituted security held, or to be held, by the Bank or the Factor (as the case may be) affecting the undertaking or any of the property or rights of the Client whether or not created by the Client;

3.7   the singular shall include the plural and vice versa and any of the three genders shall include either of the other two;

3.8   references to clauses (except where otherwise specified) are to clauses of this Deed and the headings of clauses are for ease of reference only and shall not limit the meaning or extent of any clause;

3.9   the expressions "including" and "includes" do not limit or restrict any general words preceding either of them;

3.10   general words introduced by the word "other" shall not be given a restrictive meaning by reason of the fact that they are preceded by words indicating a particular class of acts, matters or things.

4. CONSENTS AND THE BANK'S WAIVER AND CONFIRMATION

4.1   Each of the Chargeholders hereby confirms that it has consented (so far as such consent is necessary) to the creation of the other's Security.

4.2   The Bank hereby confirms (notwithstanding any restriction, covenant or undertaking given or deemed to be given to it by the Client) that the Client was at liberty to enter into the Agreement at the time of its execution and that no such restriction, covenant or undertaking shall affect the operation of the Agreement.

4.3   The Bank agrees that all *Debts purchased or to be purchased by the Factor pursuant to the Agreement and any goods in respect of which the Factor shall have exercised its right of ownership, pursuant to the Agreement, shall be free from any lien, charge, assignment or other security held or to be held by the Bank or any trust in favour of the Bank whether created by its Security or otherwise.

4.4   Notwithstanding notice to the Factor by the Bank that the Bank's Security charges the Client Account, the Bank agrees that the Bank's Security and any assignment in its favour of the Client Account shall always be subject to any right of defence, debit, retention or set-off which the Factor may at any time have against the Client whether such right arose or shall arise before or after notice or any crystallisation of the Bank's Security or notice of any such assignment or the enforcement of any rights thereunder.

4.5 Nothing in this Deed or in the Factor's Security or in the Agreement shall prevent the Bank operating the bank accounts of the Client in the ordinary course of banking business including collecting cheques and other payment orders and accepting monies for the credit of the Client's bank account and allowing the Client to draw cheques and other payments and generally to withdraw funds from its bank accounts.

4.6 The Factor shall make no claim against the Bank in connection with any *Debt the proceeds of which are credited to any account of the Client with the Bank (otherwise than any account in the name of the Client designated as in trust for the Factor) unless:

4.6.1 before the Bank's receipt of such proceeds the Bank has received notice in writing from the Factor that a specified sum of money belongs or will belong to the Factor (such notice containing such information as the Bank may reasonably require to enable the Bank to identify such credit in the day to day operation of the relative account of the Client in accordance with the Bank's normal practice); or

4.6.2 the Bank has procured the payment to the Bank of a sum which to the actual knowledge of the Bank should have been paid to the Factor.

5. EXERCISE OF RIGHTS

5.1 Except as provided in clause 5.2 neither of the Chargeholders shall, without the prior written consent of the others, exercise its power of sale over any of the undertaking or property of the Client otherwise than through a Receiver of the Client or an Administrator appointed by the court or under paragraph 14 or paragraph 22 of Schedule B1.

5.2 Nothing of this Deed shall prevent the exercise by the Factor of its rights (whether pursuant to the Agreement or to the Factor's Security):

5.2.1 to collect in or realise any of the *Debts purchased or purported to be purchased pursuant to the Agreement or any goods of which the ownership shall have been transferred to the Factor under the Agreement; or

5.2.2 to apply all or any part of the Client Account in the discharge of all or any part of the Liabilities to the Factor.

5.3 If either of the Chargeholders shall at any time wish to appoint a Receiver or an Administrator then it shall consult the other with a view to agreeing upon a person suitable to be so appointed (and such consultation and agreement shall also precede any removal or application to the court to remove any agreed Receiver or Administrator and any appointment of a successor) but nothing in this clause shall prevent either of the Chargeholders appointing a Receiver or an Administrator when it is deemed by it to be urgent and immediately necessary to make such an appointment.

5.4 If either of the Chargeholders shall appoint a Receiver under its Security it shall immediately inform the other of such appointment and if. either of the Chargeholders shall appoint an Administrator under its Security then, unless that Chargeholder shall have given prior notice to the other in accordance with the provisions of paragraph 15 of Schedule B1, it shall immediately inform the other of such appointment

5.5 If either Chargeholder, seeking to enforce its security in accordance with clause 5.4, so requests in writing (and undertakes to pay the reasonable costs and expenses incurred in compliance with that request) then the other Chargeholder shall execute all such documents and do all such things as are available to it which may reasonably be required to facilitate the exercise of the powers of enforcement or realisation under clause 5.4 provided that the interests of that other Chargeholder are not thereby prejudice.

6. DISTRIBUTION OF PROCEEDS

6.1 All monies received by any Receiver appointed under either or both of the Securities shall be applied (subject to the claims of any secured and unsecured creditors having prior rights to such monies) for the following purposes in the following order:

6.1.1 in payment of all costs charges and expenses of and in relation to his appointment and the exercise of his powers and of any other expenses properly discharged by him;

6.1.2 in payment of his remuneration as agreed between him and the person who appointed him;

6.1.3 in payment of any costs relating to the realisation of any of the property charged by either or both of the Securities;

6.1.4 in or on account of the discharge of the Liabilities to the Chargeholders in accordance with the priorities for which provision has made in this Deed;

6.1.5 in payment of any surplus to the Client or any other party entitled thereto.

6.2 The distribution of all monies received by an Administrator appointed under either of the Securities shall be as provided in paragraphs 65 to 67 inclusive of Schedule B1 and where such an Administrator is to make a payment to a secured creditor it shall be made in accordance with the priorities for which provision is made in this Deed.

7. PRIORITIES

7.1   Subject to the provisions of clauses 6 and 7.4:

    7.1.1   all monies arising from the proceeds or the realisation of any of the Specified *Debts, Other Debts and the Client Account charged by the Securities shall be applied in or towards the satisfaction of the Liabilities to the Factor in priority to any of the Liabilities to the Bank without limitation: and

    7.1.2   subject to the provisions of clauses 4.2 and 4.3 all monies arising from the realisation of any of the property or undertaking of the Client charged by the Securities, other than any Specified *Debts, any Other Debts and the Client Account, shall be applied as follows:

        FIRST, in or towards the satisfaction of the Liabilities to the Bank to the extent of the sum of £........................ in addition to interest and other charges relating to that sum;

        SECOND, in satisfaction of the Liabilities to the Factor to the extent that they have not been satisfied under clause 7.1.1; and

        THIRD, in satisfaction of the Liabilities to the Bank to the extent that they have not been otherwise satisfied.

7.2   The priorities for which provision is made in this Deed shall not be affected by any fluctuation in the amount of any indebtedness of the Client to either of the Chargeholders or by the existence at any time of any credit or nil balance on any account of the Client with either of them.

7.3   Compliance by the Client with any covenant or undertaking in relation to any property of the Client contained in the Security of either the Bank or the Factor shall be deemed to be compliance of any similar covenant or undertaking in the Security of the other.

7.4   To the extent necessary to give effect to the provisions of clause 7.1 in any case in which it is provided in that clause that in relation to any property of the Client the Bank's or the Factor's Security (as the case may be) being a floating security shall have priority over the other's Security being a fixed security then the Bank or the Factor (as the case may be) shall be subrogated to all that other's rights to and interest in that property. However, nothing in this Deed shall cause any floating charge contained within either of the Securities to rank ahead of any fixed charge contained within either of the Securities.

8. EXCHANGE OF INFORMATION

8.   Whilst the provisions of this Deed remain in effect each of the Chargeholders shall have the right to the production of and copies of

any document relating to any security of the other affecting the property of the Client and the Bank shall have the right to the production of a copy of the Agreement and each of the Chargeholders may at any time disclose to the other any information regarding the Client, the state of its accounts or its affairs in such manner as the other may require and no action shall lie on the part of the Client in relation thereto.

9. FACILITIES AND PRIOR SECURITIES

9. Whilst the provisions of this Deed remain in effect

9.1 nothing contained in this Deed shall bind either of the Chargeholders to make any prepayment or to grant any credit or facilities to the Client; and

9.2 the Client shall not create any charge or other security having priority over either of Securities or the Agreement.

10. UNDERTAKING BY CLIENT

10. As a party to this Deed the Client acknowledges the agreement contained in this Deed as to priorities between the Chargeholders and undertakes to be bound by the provisions of it and not in any way to prejudice or affect the enforcement of such provisions nor to do anything or suffer anything to be done which shall be in breach of the terms of this Deed. However, the Client may not rely upon nor shall it be entitled to enforce any of the provisions of this Deed.

11. THIRD PARTY RIGHTS

11 A person who is not a party to this Deed shall have no rights under the Contracts (Rights of Third Parties) Act 1999 to enforce any term of this Deed. This clause does not affect any rights or remedy of any person which exists or is available otherwise than pursuant to that Act.

12. SECURITIES: CONTINUITY, CONFLICT AND INVALIDITY

12.1 The charges created by each of the Securities shall rank (where appropriate) as continuing securities for the repayment of the Liabilities to the Bank and the Liabilities to the Factor respectively.

12.2 If any of the provisions of this Deed conflict with any provisions of either or both of the Securities then the provisions of this Deed will prevail.

12.3 If either of the Securities shall be discharged or become invalid or ineffective in whole or in part then the Chargeholder, in whose favour that Security was created, shall have no right to any proceeds of any property, assets or rights over which that party has no effective security; but neither of the Chargeholders shall challenge the effectiveness of the Security of the other.

13. INTERPRETATION AND GENERAL PROVISIONS

13.1 This Deed may consist of any number of documents, each in identical form, all of which together shall be deemed to constitute one Deed.

13.2 This Deed shall be construed and take effect according to English law. If any provision of this Deed shall be held to be invalid or unenforceable no other provision hereof shall be affected and all such other provisions shall remain in full force and effect.

13.3 This Deed contains all the terms and conditions agreed between the Bank and the Factor for the regulation of the priorities relating to their respective Securities to the exclusion of any agreement, representation or other statement made by either of them by any means before the making of this Deed. No variation of it or any of its terms will be effective unless that variation is made in writing and executed as a Deed by all the parties to this Deed.

13.4 No purchaser dealing with either of the Chargeholders or any receiver shall be concerned in any way with the provisions of this agreement but shall assume that the respective one of the Chargeholders or such receiver as the case may be are acting in accordance with the provisions of this agreement.

13.5 Either of the Chargeholders may refrain from exercising or claiming any right under this Deed without in any way affecting that rights which shall remain in full force and effect unless that Chargeholder shall have specifically agreed in writing to its cancellation..

13.6 Neither of the Chargeholders shall assign or transfer its Security or any part of it unless the assignee or transferee shall have agreed to be bound by the provisions of this Deed and, if so required by either of the Chargeholders (including the assignor or the transferor), shall have executed such document as may be requisite to bind the assignee or transferee to the provisions of this Deed.

13.7 This Deed shall be construed and take effect according to English law and the parties hereby submits to the exclusive jurisdiction of the English Courts for the settlement of any disagreements arising out of the provisions of this Deed. If any provision of this Deed shall be held to be invalid or unenforceable no other provision of it shall be affected and all such other provisions shall remain in full force and effect.

IN WITNESS WHEREOF the Parties have executed this document as a Deed as follows:

BANK

SIGNED AND DELIVERED as a Deed)
on   by)
_____BANK PLC)

_____

acting by_____)
_____its duly appointed)
attorney in the presence of:)
)
                    (Signature of witness))
                        (Name of witness))
)
                    (Address of witness))
                (Occupation of witness))

FACTOR

SIGNED AND DELIVERED as a Deed   )
on   by)
[NAME OF FACTOR OR DISCOUNTER])
acting by _____)   Director
a Director and _____)
_____a Director/its)
Secretary   )   Director/Secretary

CLIENT

SIGNED AND DELIVERED as a Deed)
on   by)
[NAME OF CLIENT] _____)
acting by   )   Director
_____a Director and)
_____)
a Director/its Secretary   Director/Secretary

* "Debt" may be "Receivable" or "Book Debt"; and "Related Rights" may be "Associated Rights"

Delete as applicable

GLOSSARY OF TERMS

(* = Usage in the United States)

Account debtor. *Debtor.

Account receivable. *Debt *(q.v.)*.

Administration charge. An *ad valorem* charge made by the factor (often by deduction from the purchase price of debts) calculated on the amount of each debt purchased by the factor. The charge is made to compensate the factor for taking over certain administrative functions and/or the risk of bad debts.

Advance or advance payment. A prepayment *(q.v.)*.

Ageing. The analysis of outstanding debts by reference of their due dates.

Aged balance report. A schedule of outstanding debts analysed by reference to their due dates.

Agency factoring. Factoring disclosed to the debtors but with the sales accounting and collection functions retained by the client.

Ancillary rights. All rights under a contract of sale or service giving rise to a debt (including he right to returned goods) and all guarantees and insurance in relation to a debt.

Approved. In relation to a debt:

   (i) in the case of non-recourse factoring, not subject to recourse to the client by reason of the financial inability of the debtor to pay the debt; and/or

   (ii) in the case of most forms of factoring (except maturity), eligible for a prepayment on account of its purchase price.

Assignment notice. The written instruction to the debtor to pay the factor normally placed on the face of each invoice issued by the client other than in invoice discounting or undisclosed factoring.

Associate. A person connected with the client by reason of common control or relationship.

Associated rights. Ancillary rights *(q.v.)*.

Availability. The amount payable, at any one time, by the factor to the client for or on account of the purchase price of debts sold to the factor.

439

Back-to-back factoring. The provision of factoring services to a debtor in order to provide security for the approval of the debtor's indebtedness arising from the sales of another client.

Balance payment. Payment, of the purchase price of a debt purchased by the factor, on the due date for payment of the purchases price (the maturity date or collection date *(q.v.)*) after deducting any prepayment *(q.v.)* made in respect of that purchase price.

Batch. A bundle of copy invoices accompanying a notification *(q.v.)*.

Bulk factoring. Agency factoring *(q.v.)*.

Chain. An international association of correspondent factors.

Charge back. An amount payable by the client to the factor in respect of a debt the subject of recourse and debited to the client's account with the factor.

Client. A business with which the factor has entered into a factoring agreement.

Collection date. The date on which the factor has received payment (by way of cleared funds) for a debt.

Collection only. In relation to a factoring agreement, an arrangement whereby the factor is responsible to pay the purchase price only on the collection date with no prepayments.

Collection report. A periodic report by the factor to the client of payments received from debtors.

Commission. Administration charge *(q.v.)*.

Confidential factoring. Factoring (either with or without recourse), without notices of the assignments to the debtors, whereby the client administers the sales ledger and collects as agent for the factor. See also "invoice discounting", "non-notification factoring" and "undisclosed factoring."

Correspondent factor. A factor who is prepared to act as an import factor *(q.v.)* or an export factor *(q.v.)* under the two factor system *(q.v.)*.

Credit approval. The approval of a debt in non-recourse factoring whereby the credit risk *(q.v.)* in relation to that debt is accepted by the factor without recourse to the client.

Credit limit. A limit established by the factor in relation to a debtor within which outstanding debts are deemed to be approved.

Credit line. Credit limit *(q.v.)*.

Credit risk. The risk of the inability of the debtor to pay for a debt, purchased by a factor, solely by reason of financial inability to pay.

Current account. An account between the factor and the client for the recording of some or all of the transactions between them (according to the accounting system in use).

Customer. Debtor *(q.v.)*.

Cut-off clause. A clause in a contract of sale or service by which each invoice shall be deemed to arise from a separate contract.

Dated invoices. Invoices to which forward dating *(q.v.)* has been applied.

Debit back. Charge back *(q.v.)*.

Debt. All a debtor's obligations under a contract of sale or service.

Debtor. A person who is or may become indebted to a client under a contract or prospective contract for the sale of goods or the provision of services. *A business concern for which a financial facility is provided; *e.g.* a client.

Debts purchased accounts. An account maintained by the factor on which are recorded the value of all unmatured debts purchased by the factor. (This applies in a particular system of accounting referred to in Chapter 3).

Debt turn. The average period of credit taken by the debtors of a client.

Direct export factoring. The provision of factoring services to a client for his exports without the use by the factor of correspondent factors in the countries of the debtors.

Direct import factoring. The provision of factoring services by a factor in the country of the debtors to an exporter in another country without the intervention of a correspondent factor in that country.

Disapproved. In relation to a debt: unapproved *(q.v.)*.

Disclosed invoice discounting. Another term (possibly more apt) for agency factoring *(q.v.)*.

Discount/Discounting charge. The charge made by a factor (often as a deduction in calculating the purchase price of debts) for the provision of prepayments *(q.v.)*.

Discount tolerance letter. A letter from the client to the factor at the outset of factoring whereby the client agrees to the factor's allowing (at the client's expense) settlement discounts taken out of time up to agreed limits of time and amount.

Dispute. The failure of the debtor to accept the goods or services and the invoice the subject of a debt purchased by the factor for any reason whatsoever.

Dispute notice. A written notice from the factor to the client (or, in the two factor system *(q.v.)*, from the import factor the export factor) advising the latter of a dispute.

Domestic factoring. The factoring of debts arising from sales of a client to debtors in the same country.

Drop-in. A provision in non-recourse factoring whereby a debt (or a part of a debt) in excess of a credit limit may fall within it to the extent that an item within the limit is paid or credited.

Early payment. Prepayment *(q.v.)*.

Eligible debt. A debt in relation to which the factor has prescribed that the client may draw a prepayment on account of the purchase price.

Export factor. A factor (normally in the country of his client) providing factoring for exports and using the two factor system *(q.v.)*.

Facultative agreement. An agreement which provides for each debt to be offered by the client to the factor who may exercise his discretion as to whether or not to accept it.

Forward dating of invoices. A means by which the client allows an additional period of credit to the debtor; the client dates his invoice "as" a date later than that on which it is issued and the normal due date is calculated from such later date.

Full factoring (or full service factoring). A factoring arrangement whereby the factor takes on the administrative functions of the sales ledger and collection from debtors, relieves the client from bad debts and provides finance by way of prepayments.

Funds in use. The aggregate amount, at any one time, of prepayments and amounts charged to the client by the factor unrecovered by payments from the debtors.

Import factor. A correspondent factor (normally in the country of the debtors) who is prepared to take sub-assignment of debts owing by such debtor and consequently be responsible for collection and/or the credit risk.

Indirect payment. A payment made by a debtor to the client for a debt purchased by the factor contrary to a notice of the assignment of that debts.

Ineligible debt. A debt in relation to which the factor is not prepared to make a prepayment on account of the purchase price (for example, by reason of a breach of warranty by the client in relation to the debt or by reason of its being in excess of a limit prescribed by the factor in relation to the debtor).

Initial payment. Prepayment *(q.v.)*.

Interfactor agreement. An agreement between correspondent factors whereby they mutually agree to act as import and export factors in accordance with a code of practice.

Introductory letter. A letter sent to each of the debtors by a client at the start of factoring (on a disclosed basis) for the purpose of explaining the factoring arrangements and instructing the debtor to pay the factor for all supplies by the client until further notice.

Invoice discounting. Confidential factoring *(q.v.)* normally with recourse.

Maturity date. The due date for payment of the purchase price of a debt purchased by the factor after the deduction of any prepayment made in respect of that debt. It is normally the end of the maturity period *(q.v.)* in relation to each debt.

Maturity factoring. A factoring arrangement whereby payment of the purchase price of each debt is made on the maturity date *(q.v.)* often without any provision for prepayments. The term is sometimes used for an arrangement for payment of the whole of the purchase price of each debt on the collection date *(q.v.)* without any prepayments; in such a case the factoring is to relieve the client from administrative functions and bad debts.

Maturity period. The number of days after invoice date (or the end of the month in which the invoice is dated or the date of the receipt by the factor of copy invoices) fixed by reference to a historical average period of credit taken by debtors. The period is the basis for fixing a maturity date *(q.v.)*.

Minimum balance. Retention *(q.v.)*.

Non-notification factoring. Confidential factoring *(q.v.)*.

442

Non-recourse factoring. Full factoring *(q.v.)* or any variation by which the factor has no right of recourse in respect of approved debts unpaid by reason only of the financial inability of the debtor to pay.

Notification. A report by the client to the factor of the coming into existence of debts (already purchased by the factor pursuant to a whole turnover type of agreement *(q.v.)*) often by the submission of copy invoices. The expression is sometimes also used to denote notice to a debtor of the assignment of his indebtedness.

Old line factoring. *Full factoring *(q.v.)*; *i.e.* traditional factoring.

Open account credit. Credit not covered by a bill of exchange or promissory note.

Open item sales accounting. A system of accounting by which the balance owing is broken down into the individual invoices remaining outstanding and unallocated payments and credits.

Payment report. A periodic report from a factor to his client (or from an import factor to an export factor) of payments received from debtors since the last such report.

Permitted limit. Credit limit *(q.v.)*.

Prepayment. A payment, made by the factor to the client on receipt of a notification *(q.v.)* or schedule offer *(q.v.)*, on account of the purchase price of the debts included in the notification or offer.

Receivable. Debt *(q.v.)*.

Record Account. Another term for a debts purchased account *(q.v.)*.

Recourse. The right of the factor to be guaranteed the due payment of a purchased debt by the debtor or to have an unpaid debt repurchased by the client.

Refactoring charge. An additional administration charge *(q.v.)* made by some factors in respect of any debt, which is subject to recourse and remains unpaid after a specified period, in consideration for the factor's not exercising his right of recourse.

Related rights. Ancillary rights *(q.v.)*.

Retention. A minimum credit balance in favour of the client retained by the factor on the account (or a combination of accounts) of the client held by the factor. The retention is held to provide for the set-off of amounts payable to the factor by the client, particularly for the repurchase price of debts the subject of recourse.

Schedule of offer. A list of invoices constituting an offer (under a facultative type of agreement *(q.v.)*) to the factor by the client of the debts represented by the invoices.

Self billing. Arrangements by which the buyer raises invoices on the basis of orders placed and goods received.

Seller. Client *(q.v.)*.

Service charge. Administration charge *(q.v.)*.

Shipping limit. A limit of deliveries prescribed by the factor per specified period (often per month) for the purpose of determining which debts are approved for credit or eligible for prepayment *(q.v.)*.

Single factor system. A modification of the two factor system *(q.v.)* by which the correspondent factor becomes responsible for collection only when difficulties arise.

Supplier. Client *(q.v.)*.

Survey. An investigation by a factor as to the suitability of a prospective client.

Switch on. Take on *(q.v.)*.

Switch on letter. Introductory letter *(q.v.)*.

Take on (or take-over). The entering of the debts purchased by the factor and outstanding at the date of the commencement of a factoring agreement into the records of the factor and the start of the practical arrangements for factoring.

Take on (or take-over) debts. Debts purchased by the factor and outstanding at the start of factoring.

Two factor system. A system by which the client's factor sub-assigns export debts to correspondent factors in the countries of the debtors and by which the latter are responsible for collection and the credit risk in relation to such debts as are approved.

Unapproved. In relation to a debt: subject to recourse and (particularly in the case of any form of factoring with recourse in relation to *all* debts) not eligible for prepayment *(q.v.)*.

Undisclosed factoring. Confidential factoring *(q.v.)* normally as non-recourse factoring *(q.v.)*.

Waiver. A release of debts from a charge or other encumbrance.

Whole turnover agreement. An agreement which itself provides for the assignment to the factor of all existing and future debts (or all of a class of debts) of the client without any further act of transfer of the individual debts.

APPLICATION NOTE C—FACTORING OF DEBTS*

NB For ease of reading the parties to a factoring agreement are referred to in this Application Note as "seller" and "factor", notwithstanding that analysis of the transaction in accordance with this Application Note may result in the seller continuing to show the factored debts as an asset on its balance sheet.

Features

C1 Factoring of debts is a well established method of obtaining finance, sales ledger administration services, or protection from bad debts. The principal features of a factoring arrangement are as follows:

(a) Specified debts are transferred to the factor (usually by assignment). The transfer may be of complete debtor balances or of all invoices relating to named debtors (perhaps subject to restrictions on the amount that will be accepted from any one debtor).

(b) The factor offers a credit facility that permits the seller to draw up to a fixed percentage of the face value of the debts transferred. Normally these advances are repaid as and when the underlying debts are collected, often by paying the money that is collected into a specially nominated bank account for the benefit of the factor.

(c) The factor may also offer a credit protection facility (or insurance cover). This will limit or eliminate the extent to which the factor has recourse to the seller for debts that are in default.

(d) The factor may administer the sales ledger of the seller. Where such a service is provided, the factor becomes responsible for collecting money from debtors and pursuing those that are slow in paying. In such cases the fact that debts have been factored is likely

---

* An extract from FRS 5 published by the Accounting Standards Board, April 1994.

to be disclosed to the seller's customers; this may not be necessary in other circumstances.

C2 On the transfer of debts, the factoring charges levied on the seller will be set by the factor with reference to expected collections from the debtors and any credit protection services provided (sales ledger administration services are usually invoiced separately). These charges may be fixed at the outset or subject to adjustment at a later date to reflect actual collections; they may be payable immediately or on some future date.

Analysis

Overview of basic principles

C3 The purpose of the analysis below is to determine the appropriate accounting treatment in the seller's financial statements. There are three possible treatments:

    (a) to remove the factored debts from the balance sheet and show no liability in respect of any proceeds received from the factor ("derecognition");

    (b) to show the proceeds received from the factor deducted from the factored debts on the face of the balance sheet within a single asset caption (a "linked presentation"); or

    (c) to continue to show the factored debts as an asset, and show a corresponding liability within creditors in respect of the proceeds received from the factor (a "separate presentation").

C4 In order to determine the appropriate accounting treatment, it is necessary to answer two questions:

    (a) whether the seller has access to the benefits of the factored debts and exposure to the risks inherent in those benefits (referred to below as "benefits and risks"); and

    (b) whether the seller has a liability to repay amounts received from the factor.

Where the seller has transferred all significant benefits and all significant risks relating to the debts, and has no obligation to repay the factor, derecognition is appropriate; where the seller has retained significant benefits and risks relating to the debts but there is absolutely no doubt that its downside exposure to loss is limited, a linked presentation should be used; and in all other cases a separate presentation should be adopted.

446

Benefits and risks

C5 The main benefits and risks relating to debts are as follows:
Benefits: (i) the future cash flows from payment by the debtors.
Risks: (i) slow payment risk; and
(ii) credit risk (the risk of bad debts).

Analysis of benefits.

C6 At first glance it may appear that the factor has access to the cash flow from payments by debtors. This may be particularly so if the money that is collected is to be paid direct to the factor (or into a specially nominated bank account for its benefit). However, it may actually be the seller that benefits from payments by debtors, these payments merely representing the primary source from which the factor will be repaid. In particular, where the seller has an obligation to repay any sums received from the factor on or before a set date regardless of the level of collections from the underlying debts, it is clear that the seller has the benefit of payments by debtors, exposure to their inherent risks and a liability to the factor. Such an arrangement should be accounted for by using a separate presentation. Conversely, where the seller receives a single non-returnable cash payment from the factor and the only future payments to be made are by the seller passing to the factor all and any payments from debtors as and when paid, the seller will both have transferred the benefits and risks of the factored debts and have no obligation to repay amounts received from the factor. This latter arrangement would qualify for derecognition.

C7 Considering the benefits in isolation will not normally enable a clear decision to be made on the appropriate accounting treatment for a factoring. The cash flows may appear similar in both of the above arrangements— an initial cash inflow for the seller followed by a later cash outflow (or a sacrifice of a cash inflow that would otherwise occur). For this reason, the risks (both upside potential for gain and downside exposure to loss) are more significant than the benefits.

Slow payment risk: credit facility

C8 The first main risk associated with non-interest bearing debts is slow payment risk (including the upside potential from prompt payment by debtors). Where the finance cost charged by the factor is essentially a fixed sum determined at the time the transfer is made, the factor will bear the risk of slow payment; where it varies to reflect the speed of collection of the debts subsequently, the seller will bear that risk. Close attention to the arrangements and to their commercial effect in practice may be necessary to determine whether a variable finance cost falls upon the seller since it may take various forms, including a bonus for early settlement, or a retrospective adjustment to the purchase price.

Credit risk: credit protection facility

C9 Credit risk is the other main risk associated with trade debts. If there is no recourse to the seller for bad debts, the factor will bear this risk; if there is full recourse, the seller will bear it. Furthermore, as non-payment is merely the ultimate form of slow payment, where credit risk is retained by the seller, the latter will normally also bear at least some risk of slow payment. For example, where the arrangement takes the form of the seller repurchasing debts that remain outstanding after a given time, the seller bears the slow payment risk beyond this time as well as bearing the credit risk.

Administration arrangements and service-only factoring

C10 For the purpose of deciding upon the appropriate accounting treatment, the administration arrangements will not be directly significant (provided they are on an arm's length basis, and for a fee that is commensurate with the service provided). In a service-only factoring arrangement, where the factor administers the sales ledger but cash is received no earlier than if the debts had not been factored, the seller retains access to the benefits of the debts and exposure to their inherent risks. Thus such an arrangement should be accounted for by using a separate presentation.

Derecognition

C11 Derecognition (ie ceasing to recognise the factored debts in their entirety) is appropriate only where the seller retains no significant benefits and no significant risk relating to the factored debts.

C12 Whilst the commercial effect of any particular transaction should be assessed taking into account all its aspects and implications, the presence of all of the following indicates that the seller has not retained significant benefits and risks, and derecognition is appropriate:

    (a) the transaction takes place at an arm's length price for an outright sale;

    (b) the transaction is for a fixed amount of consideration and there is no recourse whatsoever, either implicit or explicit, to the seller for losses from either slow payment or non-payment. Normal warranties given in respect of the condition of the debts at the time of the transfer (eg a warranty that goods have been delivered or that the borrower's credit limit had not been breached at the time of granting him credit) would not breach this condition. However, warranties relating to the condition of the debts in the future or to their future performance (eg that debtors will not move into arrears in the future) would breach the condition. Other possible forms of recourse are set out in paragraph 83; and

(c)   the seller will not benefit or suffer in any way if the debts perform better or worse than expected. This will not be the case where the seller has a right to further sums from the factor which vary according to the future performance of the debts (ie according to whether or when the debtors pay). Such sums might take the form of deferred consideration, a retrospective adjustment to the purchase price, or rebates of certain charges; they include all forms of variable finance cost.

C13 Where any of the above three features is not present, this indicates that the seller has retained benefits and risks relating to the factor debts and, unless these are insignificant, either a separate presentation or a linked presentation should be adopted.

C14 Whether any benefit and risk retained are "significant" should be judged in relation to those benefits and risks that are likely to occur in practice, and not in relation to the total possible benefits and risks. For example, if for a portfolio of factored debts of 100, expected bad debts are 5 and there is recourse to the seller for credit losses of up to 10, significant risk will have been retained (as the seller would bear losses of up to twice those expected to occur). Accordingly, in this example, derecognition would not be appropriate and either a linked presentation or a separate presentation should be used. The terms of any roll-over provisions and their effect in practice require careful consideration since these may result in the seller continuing to bear significant risk where, at first sight, it appears that the arrangements do not have this effect. For example, the pricing of future transfers may be adjusted to reflect recent slow payment or bad debt experience and there may be a significant disincentive (eg a penalty) for the seller to cancel the arrangement. This may result in the seller continuing to bear significant risk, albeit disguised as revised charges for debts factored subsequently.

Linked presentation

C15 A linked presentation will be appropriate where, although the seller has retained significant benefits and risks relating to the factored debts, there is absolutely no doubt that its downside exposure to loss is limited to a fixed monetary amount. A linked presentation should be used only to the extent that there is both absolutely no doubt that the factor's claim extends solely to collections from the factored debts, and no provision for the seller to re-acquire the debts in the future. The conditions that need to be met in order for this to be the case are set out in paragraph 27 and explained in paragraphs 81–86. When interpreting these conditions in the context of a factoring arrangement the following points apply:

condition (a) (specified assets)—
    a linked presentation should not be used where the debts that have been factored cannot be separately identified.

condition (d) (that the factor agrees in writing there is no recourse and such agreement is noted in the financial statements)—
the inclusion of an appropriate statement in the factoring agreement will meet the first part of this condition.

C16 Where debts are factored on an ongoing basis, the arrangements for terminating the agreement must be carefully analysed in order to ensure that the conditions for a linked presentation are met. It will be necessary that, although the factor does not take on any new debts, it continues to bear losses on debts already factored and is not able to transfer them back to the seller. Where this is not the case, there remains the possibility that the factor will return debts that it suspects to be bad by terminating the arrangement. In such a case the seller's exposure to loss is not limited, and a separate presentation should be adopted.

Separate presentation

C17 Where the seller has retained significant benefits and risks relating to the debts and the conditions for a linked presentation are not met, a separate presentation should be adopted.

Required accounting

Derecognition

C18 Where the seller has retained no significant benefits and risks relating to the debts and has no obligation to repay amounts received from the factor, the debts should be removed from the balance sheet and no liability shown in respect of the proceeds received from the factor. A profit or loss should be recognised, calculated as the difference between the carrying amount of the debts and the proceeds received.

Linked presentation

C19 Where the conditions for a linked presentation are met, the proceeds received, to the extent they are non-returnable, should be shown deducted from the gross amount of the factored debts (after providing for bad debts, credit protection charges and any accrued interest) on the face of the balance sheet. An example is given in illustration 2 below. The interest element of the factor's charges should be recognised as it accrues and included in the profit and loss account with other interest charges. The notes to the financial statements should disclose: the main terms of the arrangement; the gross amount of factored debts outstanding at the balance sheet date; the factoring charges recognised in the period, analysed as appropriate (eg between interest and other charges); and the disclosures required by conditions (c) and (d) in paragraph 27.

Separate presentation

C20 Where neither derecognition nor a linked presentation is appropriate, a separate presentation should be adopted, ie a gross asset (equivalent in amount to the gross amount of the debts) should be shown on the balance sheet of the seller within assets, and a corresponding liability in respect of the proceeds received from the factor should be shown within liabilities. The interest element of the factor's charges should be recognised as it accrues and included in the profit and loss account with other interest charges. Other factoring costs should be similarly accrued and included in the profit and loss account within the appropriate caption. The notes to the financial statement should disclose the amount of factored debts outstanding at the balance sheet date.

Table

Indications that derecognition is appropriate (debts are not an asset of the seller	Indications that linked presentation is appropriate	Indications that a separate presentation is appropriate (debts are an asset of the seller)
Transfer is for a single, non-returnable fixed sum.	Some non-returnable proceeds received, but seller has rights to further sums from the factor (or vice versa) whose amount depends on whether or when debtors pay.	Finance cost varies with speed of collection of debts e.g.: —by adjustment to consideration for original transfer; or —subsequent transfers priced to recover costs of earlier transfers.
There is no recourse to the seller for losses.	There is either no recourse for losses, or such recourse has a fixed monetary ceiling.	There is full recourse to the seller for losses.
Factor is paid all amounts received from the factored debts (and no more). Seller has no rights to further sums from the factor.	Factor is paid only out of amounts collected from the factored debts, and seller has no right or obligation to repurchase debts.	Seller is required to repay amounts received from the factor on or before a set date, regardless of timing or amounts of collections from debtors.

451

Illustrations

Illustration 1—Factoring with recourse (separate presentation)

Company S enters into a factoring arrangement with F, with the following principal terms:

(a) S will transfer (by assignment) all its trade debts to F, subject only to credit approval by F and a limit placed on the proportion of the total that may be due from any one debtor;

(b) F administers S's sales ledger and handles all aspects of collection of the debts in return for an administration charge at an annual rate of 1 per cent, payable monthly, based upon the total debts factored at each month-end;

(c) S may draw up to 70 per cent of the gross amounts of debts factored and outstanding at any time, such drawings being debited in the books of F to a factoring account operated by F for S;

(d) weekly, S assigns and sends copy invoices to F as they are raised. F sends statements to debtors, following up all overdue invoices by telephone or letter;

(e) F credits collections from debtors to the factoring account, and debits the account monthly with interest calculated on the basis of the daily balances on the account using a rate of base rate plus 2 per cent. Thus this interest charge varies with the amount of finance drawn by S under the finance facility from F, the speed of payment of the debtors and base rate;

(f) any debts not recovered after 90 days are reassigned to S for an immediate cash payment, which is credited to the factoring account;

(g) F pays for all other debts, less any advances and interest charges made, 90 days after the date of their assignment to F, and debits the payment to the factoring account; and

(h) on termination of the agreement the balance on the factoring account is settled in cash.

The commercial effect of the above arrangements is that, although the debts have been legally transferred to F, the benefits and risks are retained by S. S continues to bear the slow payment risk as the interest charged by F varies with the speed of payment by the debtors; S continues to bear all of the credit risk as it must pay for any debts not recovered after 90 days, and it therefore has unlimited exposure to loss. In addition, S in effect has an

452

obligation to repay amounts received from F on or before a set date regardless of the levels of collections from the factored debts—either out of collections from debtors on the day they pay, or from its general resources after 90 days, whichever is the earlier. Thus a separate presentation should be adopted.

Illustration 2—Factoring without recourse (linked presentation)

S enters into an agreement with F with the following principal terms:

(a) S will transfer (by assignment) to F such trade debts as S shall determine, subject only to credit approval by F and a limit placed on the proportion of the total that may be due from any one debtor. F levies a charge of 0.15 per cent of turnover, payable monthly, for this facility;

(b) S continues to administer the sales ledger and handle all aspects of collection of the debts;

(c) S may draw up to 80 per cent of the gross amount of debts assigned at any time, such drawings being debited in the books of F to a factoring accounts operated by F for S;

(d) Weekly, S assigns and sends copy invoices to F as they are raised;

(e) S is required to bank the gross amounts of all payments received from debts assigned to F direct into an account in the name of F. Credit transfers made by debtors direct into S's own bank account must immediately be paid to F;

(f) F credits such collections from debtors to the factoring account, and debits the account monthly with interest calculated on the basis of the daily balances on the account using a rate of base rate plus 2.5 per cent. Thus this interest charge varies with the amount of finance drawn by S under the finance facility from F, the speed of payment of the debtors and base rate;

(g) F provides protection from bad debts. Any debts not recovered after 90 days are credited to the factoring account, and responsibility for their collection is passed to F. A charge of 1 per cent of the gross value of all debts factored is levied by F for this service and debited to the factoring account;

(h) F pays for the debts, less any advances, interest charges and credit protection charges, 90 days after the date of purchase, and debits the payment to the factoring account; and

(i) on either party giving 90 days' notice to the other, the arrangement will be terminated. In such an event, S will transfer no further debts to F, and the balance remaining on the factoring account at the end of the notice period will be settled in cash in the normal way.

The commercial effect of this arrangement is that, although the debts have been legally transferred to F, S continues to bear significant benefits and risks relating to them. S continues to bear slow payment risk as the interest charged by F varies with the speed of collections of the debts. Hence, the gross amount of the debts should continue to be shown on its balance sheet until the earlier of collection and transfer of all risks to F (ie 90 days). However, S's maximum downside loss is limited since any debts not recovered after 90 days are in effect paid for by F, which then assumes all slow payment and credit risk beyond this time. Thus, even for debts that prove to be bad, S receives some proceeds.* Hence, assuming the conditions given in paragraphs 26 and 27 are met, a linked presentation should be adopted. The amount deducted on the face of the balance sheet should be the lower of the proceeds received and the gross amount of the debts less all charges to the factor in respect of them. In the above example, for a debt of 100 this latter amount would be calculated as £100 less the credit protection fee of 1 and the maximum finance charge (calculated for 90 days at base rate plus 2.5 per cent). Assuming the proceeds received of 80 are lower than this, and accrued interest charges at the year-end are 2, the arrangement would be shown as follows:

Current assets

Stock		x
Debts factored without recourse:		
Gross debts (after providing for credit		
protection fee and accrued interest)	97	
less: non-returnable proceeds	(80)	
		17
Other debtors		x

In addition, the non-returnable proceeds of 80 would be included within cash and the profit and loss account would include both the credit protection expense of 1 and the actual interest charges of 2.

---

* For a debt of 100 that subsequently proves to be bad, the proceeds received would be 100, less the credit protection fee of 1, less an interest charge calculated for 90 days at base rate plus 2.5%.

UNITED NATIONS CONVENTION ON THE ASSIGNMENT OF RECEIVABLES IN INTERNATIONAL TRADE

PREAMBLE

The Contracting States,

Reaffirming their conviction that international trade on the basis of equality and mutual benefit is an important element in the promotion of friendly relations among States,

Considering that problems created by uncertainties as to the content and the choice of legal regime applicable to the assignment of receivables constitute an obstacle to international trade,

Desiring to establish principles and to adopt rules relating to the assignment of receivables that would create certainty and transparency and promote the modernization of the law relating to assignments of receivables, while protecting existing assignment practices and facilitating the development of new practices,

Desiring also to ensure adequate protection of the interests of debtors in assignments of receivables,

Being of the opinion that the adoption of uniform rules governing the assignment of receivables would promote the availability of capital and credit at more affordable rates and thus facilitate the development of international trade,

Have agreed as follows:

CHAPTER I
SCOPE OF APPLICATION

Article 1
Scope of application

1. This Convention applies to:

   (a) Assignments of international receivables and to international assignments of receivables as defined in this chapter, if, at the time of conclusion of the contract of assignment, the assignor is located in a Contracting State; and

(b) Subsequent assignments, provided that any prior assignment is governed by this Convention.

2. This Convention applies to subsequent assignments that satisfy the criteria set forth in paragraph 1 (a) of this article, even if it did not apply to any prior assignment of the same receivable.

3. This Convention does not affect the rights and obligations of the debtor unless, at the time of conclusion of the original contract, the debtor is located in a Contracting State or the law governing the original contract is the law of a Contracting State.

4. The provisions of chapter V apply to assignments of international receivables and to international assignments of receivables as defined in this chapter independently of paragraphs 1 to 3 of this article. However, those provisions do not apply if a State makes a declaration under article 39.

5. The provisions of the annex to this Convention apply as provided in article 42.

Article 2
Assignment of receivables

For the purposes of this Convention:

(a) "Assignment" means the transfer by agreement from one person ("assignor") to another person ("assignee") of all or part of or an undivided interest in the assignor's contractual right to payment of a monetary sum ("receivable") from a third person ("the debtor"). The creation of rights in receivables as security for indebtedness or other obligation is deemed to be a transfer;

(b) In the case of an assignment by the initial or any other assignee ("subsequent assignment"), the person who makes that assignment is the assignor and the person to whom that assignment is made is the assignee.

Article 3
Internationality

A receivable is international if, at the time of conclusion of the original contract, the assignor and the debtor are located in different States. An assignment is international if, at the time of conclusion of the contract of assignment, the assignor and the assignee are located in different States.

Article 4
Exclusions and other limitations

1. This Convention does not apply to assignments made:

(a) To an individual for his or her personal, family or household purposes;

(b) As part of the sale or change in the ownership or legal status of the business out of which the assigned receivables arose.

2. This Convention does not apply to assignments of receivables arising under or from:

(a) Transactions on a regulated exchange;

(b) Financial contracts governed by netting agreements, except a receivable owed on the termination of all outstanding transactions;

(c) Foreign exchange transactions;

(d) Inter-bank payment systems, inter-bank payment agreements or clearance and settlement systems relating to securities or other financial assets or instruments;

(e) The transfer of security rights in, sale, loan or holding of or agreement to repurchase securities or other financial assets or instruments held with an intermediary;

(f) Bank deposits;

(g) A letter of credit or independent guarantee.

3. Nothing in this Convention affects the rights and obligations of any person under the law governing negotiable instruments.
4. Nothing in this Convention affects the rights and obligations of the assignor and the debtor under special laws governing the protection of parties to transactions made for personal, family or household purposes.
5. Nothing in this Convention:

(a) Affects the application of the law of a State in which real property is situated to either:

(i) An interest in that real property to the extent that under that law the assignment of a receivable confers such an interest; or
(ii) The priority of a right in a receivable to the extent that under that law an interest in the real property confers such a right; or

(b) Makes lawful the acquisition of an interest in real property not permitted under the law of the State in which the real property is situated.

CHAPTER II
GENERAL PROVISIONS

Article 5
Definitions and rules of interpretation

For the purposes of this Convention:

(a) "Original contract" means the contract between the assignor and the debtor from which the assigned receivable arises;

(b) "Existing receivable" means a receivable that arises upon or before conclusion of the contract of assignment and "future receivable" means a receivable that arises after conclusion of the contract of assignment;

(c) "Writing" means any form of information that is accessible so as to be usable for subsequent reference. Where this Convention requires a writing to be signed, that requirement is met if, by generally accepted means or a procedure agreed to by the person whose signature is required, the writing identifies that person and indicates that person's approval of the information contained in the writing;

(d) "Notification of the assignment" means a communication in writing that reasonably identifies the assigned receivables and the assignee;

(e) "Insolvency administrator" means a person or body, including one appointed on an interim basis, authorized in an insolvency proceeding to administer the reorganization or liquidation of the assignor's assets or affairs;

(f) "Insolvency proceeding" means a collective judicial or administrative proceeding, including an interim proceeding, in which the assets and affairs of the assignor are subject to control or supervision by a court or other competent authority for the purpose of reorganization or liquidation;

(g) "Priority" means the right of a person in preference to the right of another person and, to the extent relevant for such purpose, includes the determination whether the right is a personal or a property right, whether or not it is a security right for indebtedness or other obligation and whether any requirements necessary to

458

render the right effective against a competing claimant have been satisfied;

(h) A person is located in the State in which it has its place of business. If the assignor or the assignee has a place of business in more than one State, the place of business is that place where the central administration of the assignor or the assignee is exercised. If the debtor has a place of business in more than one State, the place of business is that which has the closest relationship to the original contract. If a person does not have a place of business, reference is to be made to the habitual residence of that person;

(i) "Law" means the law in force in a State other than its rules of private international law;

(j) "Proceeds" means whatever is received in respect of an assigned receivable, whether in total or partial payment or other satisfaction of the receivable. The term includes whatever is received in respect of proceeds. The term does not include returned goods;

(k) "Financial contract" means any spot, forward, future, option or swap transaction involving interest rates, commodities, currencies, equities, bonds, indices or any other financial instrument, any repurchase or securities lending transaction, and any other transaction similar to any transaction referred to above entered into in financial markets and any combination of the transactions mentioned above;

(l) "Netting agreement" means an agreement between two or more parties that provides for one or more of the following:

    (i) The net settlement of payments due in the same currency on the same date whether by novation or otherwise;

    (ii) Upon the insolvency or other default by a party, the termination of all outstanding transactions at their replacement or fair market values, conversion of such sums into a single currency and netting into a single payment by one party to the other; or

    (iii) The set-off of amounts calculated as set forth in subparagraph (l) (ii) of this article under two or more netting agreements;

(m) "Competing claimant" means:

    (i) Another assignee of the same receivable from the same assignor, including a person who, by operation of law, claims a right in the assigned receivable as a result of its right in other property of the assignor, even if that receivable is not an international receivable and the assignment to that assignee is not an international assignment;

(ii) A creditor of the assignor; or

(iii) The insolvency administrator.

Article 6
Party autonomy

Subject to article 19, the assignor, the assignee and the debtor may derogate from or vary by agreement provisions of this Convention relating to their respective rights and obligations. Such an agreement does not affect the rights of any person who is not a party to the agreement.

Article 7
Principles of interpretation

1. In the interpretation of this Convention, regard is to be had to its object and purpose as set forth in the preamble, to its international character and to the need to promote uniformity in its application and the observance of good faith in international trade.

2. Questions concerning matters governed by this Convention that are not expressly settled in it are to be settled in conformity with the general principles on which it is based or, in the absence of such principles, in conformity with the law applicable by virtue of the rules of private international law.

CHAPTER III
EFFECTS OF ASSIGNMENT

Article 8
Effectiveness of assignments

1. An assignment is not ineffective as between the assignor and the assignee or as against the debtor or as against a competing claimant, and the right of an assignee may not be denied priority, on the ground that it is an assignment of more than one receivable, future receivables or parts of or undivided interests in receivables, provided that the receivables are described:

(a) Individually as receivables to which the assignment relates; or

(b) In any other manner, provided that they can, at the time of the assignment or, in the case of future receivables, at the time of conclusion of the original contract, be identified as receivables to which the assignment relates.

2. Unless otherwise agreed, an assignment of one or more future receivables is effective without a new act of transfer being required to assign each receivable.

3. Except as provided in paragraph 1 of this article, article 9 and article 10, paragraphs 2 and 3, this Convention does not affect any limitations on assignments arising from law.

Article 9
Contractual limitations on assignments

1. An assignment of a receivable is effective notwithstanding any agreement between the initial or any subsequent assignor and the debtor or any subsequent assignee limiting in any way the assignor's right to assign its receivables.

2. Nothing in this article affects any obligation or liability of the assignor for breach of such an agreement, but the other party to such agreement may not avoid the original contract or the assignment contract on the sole ground of that breach. A person who is not party to such an agreement is not liable on the sole ground that it had knowledge of the agreement.

3. This article applies only to assignments of receivables:

(a) Arising from an original contract that is a contract for the supply or lease of goods or services other than financial services, a construction contract or a contract for the sale or lease of real property;

(b) Arising from an original contract for the sale, lease or licence of industrial or other intellectual property or of proprietary information;

(c) Representing the payment obligation for a credit card transaction; or

(d) Owed to the assignor upon net settlement of payments due pursuant to a netting agreement involving more than two parties.

Article 10
Transfer of security rights

1. A personal or property right securing payment of the assigned receivable is transferred to the assignee without a new act of transfer. If such a right, under the law governing it, is transferable only with a new act of transfer, the assignor is obliged to transfer such right and any proceeds to the assignee.

2. A right securing payment of the assigned receivable is transferred under paragraph 1 of this article notwithstanding any agreement between the assignor and the debtor or other person granting that right, limiting in any way the assignor's right to assign the receivable or the right securing payment of the assigned receivable.

461

3. Nothing in this article affects any obligation or liability of the assignor for breach of any agreement under paragraph 2 of this article, but the other party to that agreement may not avoid the original contract or the assignment contract on the sole ground of that breach. A person who is not a party to such an agreement is not liable on the sole ground that it had knowledge of the agreement.

4. Paragraphs 2 and 3 of this article apply only to assignments of receivables:

    (a) Arising from an original contract that is a contract for the supply or lease of goods or services other than financial services, a construction contract or a contract for the sale or lease of real property;

    (b) Arising from an original contract for the sale, lease or licence of industrial or other intellectual property or of proprietary information;

    (c) Representing the payment obligation for a credit card transaction; or

    (d) Owed to the assignor upon net settlement of payments due pursuant to a netting agreement involving more than two parties.

5. The transfer of a possessory property right under paragraph 1 of this article does not affect any obligations of the assignor to the debtor or the person granting the property right with respect to the property transferred existing under the law governing that property right.

6. Paragraph 1 of this article does not affect any requirement under rules of law other than this Convention relating to the form or registration of the transfer of any rights securing payment of the assigned receivable.

CHAPTER IV
RIGHTS, OBLIGATIONS AND DEFENCES

SECTION I
ASSIGNOR AND ASSIGNEE

Article 11
Rights and obligations of the assignor and the assignee

1. The mutual rights and obligations of the assignor and the assignee arising from their agreement are determined by the terms and conditions set forth in that agreement, including any rules or general conditions referred to therein.

2. The assignor and the assignee are bound by any usage to which they

have agreed and, unless otherwise agreed, by any practices they have established between themselves.

3. In an international assignment, the assignor and the assignee are considered, unless otherwise agreed, implicitly to have made applicable to the assignment a usage that in international trade is widely known to, and regularly observed by, parties to the particular type of assignment or to the assignment of the particular category of receivables.

Article 12
Representations of the assignor

1. Unless otherwise agreed between the assignor and the assignee, the assignor represents at the time of conclusion of the contract of assignment that:

(a) The assignor has the right to assign the receivable;

(b) The assignor has not previously assigned the receivable to another assignee; and

(c) The debtor does not and will not have any defences or rights of set-off.

2. Unless otherwise agreed between the assignor and the assignee, the assignor does not represent that the debtor has, or will have, the ability to pay.

Article 13
Right to notify the debtor

1. Unless otherwise agreed between the assignor and the assignee, the assignor or the assignee or both may send the debtor notification of the assignment and a payment instruction, but after notification has been sent only the assignee may send such an instruction.

2. Notification of the assignment or a payment instruction sent in breach of any agreement referred to in paragraph 1 of this article is not ineffective for the purposes of article 17 by reason of such breach. However, nothing in this article affects any obligation or liability of the party in breach of such an agreement for any damages arising as a result of the breach.

Article 14
Right to payment

1. As between the assignor and the assignee, unless otherwise agreed and whether or not notification of the assignment has been sent:

(a) If payment in respect of the assigned receivable is made to the assignee, the assignee is entitled to retain the proceeds and goods returned in respect of the assigned receivable;

(b) If payment in respect of the assigned receivable is made to the assignor, the assignee is entitled to payment of the proceeds and also to goods returned to the assignor in respect of the assigned receivable; and

(c) If payment in respect of the assigned receivable is made to another person over whom the assignee has priority, the assignee is entitled to payment of the proceeds and also to goods returned to such person in respect of the assigned receivable.

2. The assignee may not retain more than the value of its right in the receivable.

SECTION II
DEBTOR

Article 15
Principle of debtor protection

1. Except as otherwise provided in this Convention, an assignment does not, without the consent of the debtor, affect the rights and obligations of the debtor, including the payment terms contained in the original contract.

2. A payment instruction may change the person, address or account to which the debtor is required to make payment, but may not change:

(a) The currency of payment specified in the original contract; or

(b) The State specified in the original contract in which payment is to be made to a State other than that in which the debtor is located.

Article 16
Notification of the debtor

1. Notification of the assignment or a payment instruction is effective when received by the debtor if it is in a language that is reasonably expected to inform the debtor about its contents. It is sufficient if notification of the assignment or a payment instruction is in the language of the original contract.

2. Notification of the assignment or a payment instruction may relate to receivables arising after notification.

3. Notification of a subsequent assignment constitutes notification of all prior assignments.

464

Article 17
Debtor's discharge by payment

1. Until the debtor receives notification of the assignment, the debtor is entitled to be discharged by paying in accordance with the original contract.

2. After the debtor receives notification of the assignment, subject to paragraphs 3 to 8 of this article, the debtor is discharged only by paying the assignee or, if otherwise instructed in the notification of the assignment or subsequently by the assignee in a writing received by the debtor, in accordance with such payment instruction.

3. If the debtor receives more than one payment instruction relating to a single assignment of the same receivable by the same assignor, the debtor is discharged by paying in accordance with the last payment instruction received from the assignee before payment.

4. If the debtor receives notification of more than one assignment of the same receivable made by the same assignor, the debtor is discharged by paying in accordance with the first notification received.

5. If the debtor receives notification of one or more subsequent assignments, the debtor is discharged by paying in accordance with the notification of the last of such subsequent assignments.

6. If the debtor receives notification of the assignment of a part of or an undivided interest in one or more receivables, the debtor is discharged by paying in accordance with the notification or in accordance with this article as if the debtor had not received the notification. If the debtor pays in accordance with the notification, the debtor is discharged only to the extent of the part or undivided interest paid.

7. If the debtor receives notification of the assignment from the assignee, the debtor is entitled to request the assignee to provide within a reasonable period of time adequate proof that the assignment from the initial assignor to the initial assignee and any intermediate assignment have been made and, unless the assignee does so, the debtor is discharged by paying in accordance with this article as if the notification from the assignee had not been received. Adequate proof of an assignment includes but is not limited to any writing emanating from the assignor and indicating that the assignment has taken place.

8. This article does not affect any other ground on which payment by the debtor to the person entitled to payment, to a competent judicial or other authority, or to a public deposit fund discharges the debtor.

Article 18
Defences and rights of set-off of the debtor

1. In a claim by the assignee against the debtor for payment of the assigned receivable, the debtor may raise against the assignee all defences and rights of set-off arising from the original contract, or any other contract

465

that was part of the same transaction, of which the debtor could avail itself as if the assignment had not been made and such claim were made by the assignor.

2. The debtor may raise against the assignee any other right of set-off, provided that it was available to the debtor at the time notification of the assignment was received by the debtor.

3. Notwithstanding paragraphs 1 and 2 of this article, defences and rights of set-off that the debtor may raise pursuant to article 9 or 10 against the assignor for breach of an agreement limiting in any way the assignor's right to make the assignment are not available to the debtor against the assignee.

Article 19
Agreement not to raise defences or rights of set-off

1. The debtor may agree with the assignor in a writing signed by the debtor not to raise against the assignee the defences and rights of set-off that it could raise pursuant to article 18. Such an agreement precludes the debtor from raising against the assignee those defences and rights of set-off.

2. The debtor may not waive defences:

(a) Arising from fraudulent acts on the part of the assignee; or

(b) Based on the debtor's incapacity.

3. Such an agreement may be modified only by an agreement in a writing signed by the debtor. The effect of such a modification as against the assignee is determined by article 20, paragraph 2.

Article 20
Modification of the original contract

1. An agreement concluded before notification of the assignment between the assignor and the debtor that affects the assignee's rights is effective as against the assignee, and the assignee acquires corresponding rights.

2. An agreement concluded after notification of the assignment between the assignor and the debtor that affects the assignee's rights is ineffective as against the assignee unless:

(a) The assignee consents to it; or

(b) The receivable is not fully earned by performance and either the modification is provided for in the original contract or, in the context of the original contract, a reasonable assignee would consent to the modification.

3. Paragraphs 1 and 2 of this article do not affect any right of the assignor or the assignee arising from breach of an agreement between them.

Article 21
Recovery of payments

Failure of the assignor to perform the original contract does not entitle the debtor to recover from the assignee a sum paid by the debtor to the assignor or the assignee.

Section III
Third Parties

Article 22
Law applicable to competing rights

With the exception of matters that are settled elsewhere in this Convention and subject to articles 23 and 24, the law of the State in which the assignor is located governs the priority of the right of an assignee in the assigned receivable over the right of a competing claimant.

Article 23
Public policy and mandatory rules

1. The application of a provision of the law of the State in which the assignor is located may be refused only if the application of that provision is manifestly contrary to the public policy of the forum State.

2. The rules of the law of either the forum State or any other State that are mandatory irrespective of the law otherwise applicable may not prevent the application of a provision of the law of the State in which the assignor is located.

3. Notwithstanding paragraph 2 of this article, in an insolvency proceeding commenced in a State other than the State in which the assignor is located, any preferential right that arises, by operation of law, under the law of the forum State and is given priority over the rights of an assignee in insolvency proceedings under the law of that State may be given priority notwithstanding article 22. A State may deposit at any time a declaration identifying any such preferential right.

Article 24
Special rules on proceeds

1. If proceeds are received by the assignee, the assignee is entitled to retain those proceeds to the extent that the assignee's right in the assigned receivable had priority over the right of a competing claimant in the assigned receivable.

467

2. If proceeds are received by the assignor, the right of the assignee in those proceeds has priority over the right of a competing claimant in those proceeds to the same extent as the assignee's right had priority over the right in the assigned receivable of that claimant if:

(a) The assignor has received the proceeds under instructions from the assignee to hold the proceeds for the benefit of the assignee; and

(b) The proceeds are held by the assignor for the benefit of the assignee separately and are reasonably identifiable from the assets of the assignor, such as in the case of a separate deposit or securities account containing only proceeds consisting of cash or securities.

3. Nothing in paragraph 2 of this article affects the priority of a person having against the proceeds a right of set-off or a right created by agreement and not derived from a right in the receivable.

Article 25
Subordination

An assignee entitled to priority may at any time subordinate its priority unilaterally or by agreement in favour of any existing or future assignees.

CHAPTER V
AUTONOMOUS CONFLICT-OF-LAWS RULES

Article 26
Application of chapter V

The provisions of this chapter apply to matters that are:

(a) Within the scope of this Convention as provided in article 1, paragraph 4; and

(b) Otherwise within the scope of this Convention but not settled elsewhere in it.

Article 27
Form of a contract of assignment

1. A contract of assignment concluded between persons who are located in the same State is formally valid as between them if it satisfies the requirements of either the law which governs it or the law of the State in which it is concluded.

2. A contract of assignment concluded between persons who are located

in different States is formally valid as between them if it satisfies the requirements of either the law which governs it or the law of one of those States.

Article 28
Law applicable to the mutual rights and obligations of the assignor and the assignee

1. The mutual rights and obligations of the assignor and the assignee arising from their agreement are governed by the law chosen by them.
2. In the absence of a choice of law by the assignor and the assignee, their mutual rights and obligations arising from their agreement are governed by the law of the State with which the contract of assignment is most closely connected.

Article 29
Law applicable to the rights and obligations of the assignee and the debtor

The law governing the original contract determines the effectiveness of contractual limitations on assignment as between the assignee and the debtor, the relationship between the assignee and the debtor, the conditions under which the assignment can be invoked against the debtor and whether the debtor's obligations have been discharged.

Article 30
Law applicable to priority

1. The law of the State in which the assignor is located governs the priority of the right of an assignee in the assigned receivable over the right of a competing claimant.
2. The rules of the law of either the forum State or any other State that are mandatory irrespective of the law otherwise applicable may not prevent the application of a provision of the law of the State in which the assignor is located.
3. Notwithstanding paragraph 2 of this article, in an insolvency proceeding commenced in a State other than the State in which the assignor is located, any preferential right that arises, by operation of law, under the law of the forum State and is given priority over the rights of an assignee in insolvency proceedings under the law of that State may be given priority notwithstanding paragraph 1 of this article.

Article 31
Mandatory rules

1. Nothing in articles 27 to 29 restricts the application of the rules of the law of the forum State in a situation where they are mandatory irrespective of the law otherwise applicable.

2. Nothing in articles 27 to 29 restricts the application of the mandatory rules of the law of another State with which the matters settled in those articles have a close connection if and insofar as, under the law of that other State, those rules must be applied irrespective of the law otherwise applicable.

Article 32
Public policy

With regard to matters settled in this chapter, the application of a provision of the law specified in this chapter may be refused only if the application of that provision is manifestly contrary to the public policy of the forum State.

CHAPTER VI
FINAL PROVISIONS

Article 33
Depositary

The Secretary-General of the United Nations is the depositary of this Convention.

Article 34
Signature, ratification, acceptance, approval, accession

1. This Convention is open for signature by all States at the Headquarters of the United Nations in New York until 31 December 2003.

2. This Convention is subject to ratification, acceptance or approval by the signatory States.

3. This Convention is open to accession by all States that are not signatory States as from the date it is open for signature.

4. Instruments of ratification, acceptance, approval and accession are to be deposited with the Secretary-General of the United Nations.

Article 35
Application to territorial units

1. If a State has two or more territorial units in which different systems of law are applicable in relation to the matters dealt with in this Convention, it

may at any time declare that this Convention is to extend to all its territorial units or only one or more of them, and may at any time substitute another declaration for its earlier declaration.

2. Such declarations are to state expressly the territorial units to which this Convention extends.

3. If, by virtue of a declaration under this article, this Convention does not extend to all territorial units of a State and the assignor or the debtor is located in a territorial unit to which this Convention does not extend, this location is considered not to be in a Contracting State.

4. If, by virtue of a declaration under this article, this Convention does not extend to all territorial units of a State and the law governing the original contract is the law in force in a territorial unit to which this Convention does not extend, the law governing the original contract is considered not to be the law of a Contracting State.

5. If a State makes no declaration under paragraph 1 of this article, the Convention is to extend to all territorial units of that State.

Article 36
Location in a territorial unit

If a person is located in a State which has two or more territorial units, that person is located in the territorial unit in which it has its place of business. If the assignor or the assignee has a place of business in more than one territorial unit, the place of business is that place where the central administration of the assignor or the assignee is exercised. If the debtor has a place of business in more than one territorial unit, the place of business is that which has the closest relationship to the original contract. If a person does not have a place of business, reference is to be made to the habitual residence of that person. A State with two or more territorial units may specify by declaration at any time other rules for determining the location of a person within that State.

Article 37
Applicable law in territorial units

Any reference in this Convention to the law of a State means, in the case of a State which has two or more territorial units, the law in force in the territorial unit. Such a State may specify by declaration at any time other rules for determining the applicable law, including rules that render applicable the law of another territorial unit of that State.

Article 38
Conflicts with other international agreements

1. This Convention does not prevail over any international agreement that has already been or may be entered into and that specifically governs a transaction otherwise governed by this Convention.

2. Notwithstanding paragraph 1 of this article, this Convention prevails over the Unidroit Convention on International Factoring ("the Ottawa Convention"). To the extent that this Convention does not apply to the rights and obligations of a debtor, it does not preclude the application of the Ottawa Convention with respect to the rights and obligations of that debtor.

Article 39
Declaration on application of chapter V

A State may declare at any time that it will not be bound by chapter V.

Article 40
Limitations relating to Governments and other public entities

A State may declare at any time that it will not be bound or the extent to which it will not be bound by articles 9 and 10 if the debtor or any person granting a personal or property right securing payment of the assigned receivable is located in that State at the time of conclusion of the original contract and is a Government, central or local, any subdivision thereof, or an entity constituted for a public purpose. If a State has made such a declaration, articles 9 and 10 do not affect the rights and obligations of that debtor or person. A State may list in a declaration the types of entity that are the subject of a declaration.

Article 41
Other exclusions

1. A State may declare at any time that it will not apply this Convention to specific types of assignment or to the assignment of specific categories of receivables clearly described in a declaration.

2. After a declaration under paragraph 1 of this article takes effect:

(a) This Convention does not apply to such types of assignment or to the assignment of such categories of receivables if the assignor is located at the time of conclusion of the contract of assignment in such a State; and

(b) The provisions of this Convention that affect the rights and obligations of the debtor do not apply if, at the time of conclusion of the original contract, the debtor is located in such a State or the law governing the original contract is the law of such a State.

3. This article does not apply to assignments of receivables listed in article 9, paragraph 3.

Article 42
Application of the annex

1. A State may at any time declare that it will be bound by:

(a)   The priority rules set forth in section I of the annex and will participate in the international registration system established pursuant to section II of the annex;

(b)   The priority rules set forth in section I of the annex and will effectuate such rules by use of a registration system that fulfils the purposes of such rules, in which case, for the purposes of section I of the annex, registration pursuant to such a system has the same effect as registration pursuant to section II of the annex;

(c)   The priority rules set forth in section III of the annex;

(d)   The priority rules set forth in section IV of the annex; or

(e)   The priority rules set forth in articles 7 and 9 of the annex.

2. For the purposes of article 22:

(a)   The law of a State that has made a declaration pursuant to paragraph 1 (a) or (b) of this article is the set of rules set forth in section I of the annex, as affected by any declaration made pursuant to paragraph 5 of this article;

(b)   The law of a State that has made a declaration pursuant to paragraph 1 (c) of this article is the set of rules set forth in section III of the annex, as affected by any declaration made pursuant to paragraph 5 of this article;

(c)   The law of a State that has made a declaration pursuant to paragraph 1 (d) of this article is the set of rules set forth in section IV of the annex, as affected by any declaration made pursuant to paragraph 5 of this article; and

(d)   The law of a State that has made a declaration pursuant to paragraph 1 (e) of this article is the set of rules set forth in articles 7 and 9 of the annex, as affected by any declaration made pursuant to paragraph 5 of this article.

3. A State that has made a declaration pursuant to paragraph 1 of this article may establish rules pursuant to which contracts of assignment concluded before the declaration takes effect become subject to those rules within a reasonable time.

4. A State that has not made a declaration pursuant to paragraph 1 of this article may, in accordance with priority rules in force in that State, utilize the registration system established pursuant to section II of the annex.

5. At the time a State makes a declaration pursuant to paragraph 1 of this article or thereafter, it may declare that:

(a) It will not apply the priority rules chosen under paragraph 1 of this article to certain types of assignment or to the assignment of certain categories of receivables; or

(b) It will apply those priority rules with modifications specified in that declaration.

6. At the request of Contracting or Signatory States to this Convention comprising not less than one third of the Contracting and Signatory States, the depositary shall convene a conference of the Contracting and Signatory States to designate the supervising authority and the first registrar and to prepare or revise the regulations referred to in section II of the annex.

Article 43
Effect of declaration

1. Declarations made under articles 35, paragraph 1, 36, 37 or 39 to 42 at the time of signature are subject to confirmation upon ratification, acceptance or approval.

2. Declarations and confirmations of declarations are to be in writing and to be formally notified to the depositary.

3. A declaration takes effect simultaneously with the entry into force of this Convention in respect of the State concerned. However, a declaration of which the depositary receives formal notification after such entry into force takes effect on the first day of the month following the expiration of six months after the date of its receipt by the depositary.

4. A State that makes a declaration under articles 35, paragraph 1, 36, 37 or 39 to 42 may withdraw it at any time by a formal notification in writing addressed to the depositary. Such withdrawal takes effect on the first day of the month following the expiration of six months after the date of the receipt of the notification by the depositary.

5. In the case of a declaration under articles 35, paragraph 1, 36, 37 or 39 to 42 that takes effect after the entry into force of this Convention in respect of the State concerned or in the case of a withdrawal of any such declaration, the effect of which in either case is to cause a rule in this Convention, including any annex, to become applicable:

(a) Except as provided in paragraph 5 (b) of this article, that rule is applicable only to assignments for which the contract of assignment is concluded on or after the date when the declaration or withdrawal takes effect in respect of the Contracting State referred to in article 1, paragraph 1 (a);

(b) A rule that deals with the rights and obligations of the debtor applies only in respect of original contracts concluded on or after the date when the declaration or withdrawal takes effect in respect of the Contracting State referred to in article 1, paragraph 3.

6. In the case of a declaration under articles 35, paragraph 1, 36, 37 or 39 to 42 that takes effect after the entry into force of this Convention in respect of the State concerned or in the case of a withdrawal of any such declaration, the effect of which in either case is to cause a rule in this Convention, including any annex, to become inapplicable:

(a) Except as provided in paragraph 6 (b) of this article, that rule is inapplicable to assignments for which the contract of assignment is concluded on or after the date when the declaration or withdrawal takes effect in respect of the Contracting State referred to in article 1, paragraph 1 (a);

(b) A rule that deals with the rights and obligations of the debtor is inapplicable in respect of original contracts concluded on or after the date when the declaration or withdrawal takes effect in respect of the Contracting State referred to in article 1, paragraph 3.

7. If a rule rendered applicable or inapplicable as a result of a declaration or withdrawal referred to in paragraph 5 or 6 of this article is relevant to the determination of priority with respect to a receivable for which the contract of assignment is concluded before such declaration or withdrawal takes effect or with respect to its proceeds, the right of the assignee has priority over the right of a competing claimant to the extent that, under the law that would determine priority before such declaration or withdrawal takes effect, the right of the assignee would have priority.

Article 44
Reservations

No reservations are permitted except those expressly authorized in this Convention.

Article 45
Entry into force

1. This Convention enters into force on the first day of the month following the expiration of six months from the date of deposit of the fifth instrument of ratification, acceptance, approval or accession with the depositary.

2. For each State that becomes a Contracting State to this Convention after the date of deposit of the fifth instrument of ratification, acceptance, approval or accession, this Convention enters into force on the first day of the month following the expiration of six months after the date of deposit of the appropriate instrument on behalf of that State.

3. This Convention applies only to assignments if the contract of assignment is concluded on or after the date when this Convention enters into force in respect of the Contracting State referred to in article 1, paragraph 1 (a), provided that the provisions of this Convention that deal with the rights and obligations of the debtor apply only to assignments of receivables arising from original contracts concluded on or after the date when this Convention enters into force in respect of the Contracting State referred to in article 1, paragraph 3.

4. If a receivable is assigned pursuant to a contract of assignment concluded before the date when this Convention enters into force in respect of the Contracting State referred to in article 1, paragraph 1 (a), the right of the assignee has priority over the right of a competing claimant with respect to the receivable to the extent that, under the law that would determine priority in the absence of this Convention, the right of the assignee would have priority.

Article 46
Denunciation

1. A Contracting State may denounce this Convention at any time by written notification addressed to the depositary.

2. The denunciation takes effect on the first day of the month following the expiration of one year after the notification is received by the depositary. Where a longer period is specified in the notification, the denunciation takes effect upon the expiration of such longer period after the notification is received by the depositary.

3. This Convention remains applicable to assignments if the contract of assignment is concluded before the date when the denunciation takes effect in respect of the Contracting State referred to in article 1, paragraph 1 (a), provided that the provisions of this Convention that deal with the rights and obligations of the debtor remain applicable only to assignments of receivables arising from original contracts concluded before the date when the denunciation takes effect in respect of the Contracting State referred to in article 1, paragraph 3.

4. If a receivable is assigned pursuant to a contract of assignment concluded before the date when the denunciation takes effect in respect of the Contracting State referred to in article 1, paragraph 1 (a), the right of the assignee has priority over the right of a competing claimant with respect to the receivable to the extent that, under the law that would determine priority under this Convention, the right of the assignee would have priority.

Article 47
Revision and amendment

1. At the request of not less than one third of the Contracting States to this Convention, the depositary shall convene a conference of the Contracting States to revise or amend it.
2. Any instrument of ratification, acceptance, approval or accession deposited after the entry into force of an amendment to this Convention is deemed to apply to the Convention as amended.

ANNEX TO THE CONVENTION

SECTION I
PRIORITY RULES BASED ON REGISTRATION

Article 1
Priority among several assignees

As between assignees of the same receivable from the same assignor, the priority of the right of an assignee in the assigned receivable is determined by the order in which data about the assignment are registered under section II of this annex, regardless of the time of transfer of the receivable. If no such data are registered, priority is determined by the order of conclusion of the respective contracts of assignment.

Article 2
Priority between the assignee and the insolvency administrator or creditors of the assignor

The right of an assignee in an assigned receivable has priority over the right of an insolvency administrator and creditors who obtain a right in the assigned receivable by attachment, judicial act or similar act of a competent authority that gives rise to such right, if the receivable was assigned, and data about the assignment were registered under section II of this annex, before the commencement of such insolvency proceeding, attachment, judicial act or similar act.

SECTION II
REGISTRATION

Article 3
Establishment of a registration system

A registration system will be established for the registration of data about assignments, even if the relevant assignment or receivable is not international, pursuant to the regulations to be promulgated by the registrar and the supervising authority. Regulations promulgated by the registrar and the supervising authority under this annex shall be consistent with this annex. The regulations will prescribe in detail the manner in which the registration system will operate, as well as the procedure for resolving disputes relating to that operation.

Article 4
Registration

1. Any person may register data with regard to an assignment at the registry in accordance with this annex and the regulations. As provided in the regulations, the data registered shall be the identification of the assignor and the assignee and a brief description of the assigned receivables.

2. A single registration may cover one or more assignments by the assignor to the assignee of one or more existing or future receivables, irrespective of whether the receivables exist at the time of registration.

3. A registration may be made in advance of the assignment to which it relates. The regulations will establish the procedure for the cancellation of a registration in the event that the assignment is not made.

4. Registration or its amendment is effective from the time when the data set forth in paragraph 1 of this article are available to searchers. The registering party may specify, from options set forth in the regulations, a period of effectiveness for the registration. In the absence of such a specification, a registration is effective for a period of five years.

5. Regulations will specify the manner in which registration may be renewed, amended or cancelled and regulate such other matters as are necessary for the operation of the registration system.

6. Any defect, irregularity, omission or error with regard to the identification of the assignor that would result in data registered not being found upon a search based on a proper identification of the assignor renders the registration ineffective.

Article 5
Registry searches

1. Any person may search the records of the registry according to identification of the assignor, as set forth in the regulations, and obtain a search result in writing.

2. A search result in writing that purports to be issued by the registry is admissible as evidence and is, in the absence of evidence to the contrary, proof of the registration of the data to which the search relates, including the date and hour of registration.

Section III
Priority Rules Based on the Time of the Contract of Assignment

Article 6
Priority among several assignees

As between assignees of the same receivable from the same assignor, the priority of the right of an assignee in the assigned receivable is determined by the order of conclusion of the respective contracts of assignment.

Article 7
Priority between the assignee and the insolvency administrator or creditors of the assignor

The right of an assignee in an assigned receivable has priority over the right of an insolvency administrator and creditors who obtain a right in the assigned receivable by attachment, judicial act or similar act of a competent authority that gives rise to such right, if the receivable was assigned before the commencement of such insolvency proceeding, attachment, judicial act or similar act.

Article 8
Proof of time of contract of assignment

The time of conclusion of a contract of assignment in respect of articles 6 and 7 of this annex may be proved by any means, including witnesses.

Section IV
Priority Rules Based on the Time of Notification of Assignment

Article 9
Priority among several assignees

As between assignees of the same receivable from the same assignor, the priority of the right of an assignee in the assigned receivable is determined by the order in which notification of the respective assignments is received by the debtor. However, an assignee may not obtain priority over a prior assignment of which the assignee had knowledge at the time of conclusion of the contract of assignment to that assignee by notifying the debtor.

Article 10
Priority between the assignee and the insolvency administrator or creditors of the assignor

The right of an assignee in an assigned receivable has priority over the right of an insolvency administrator and creditors who obtain a right in the assigned receivable by attachment, judicial act or similar act of a competent authority that gives rise to such right, if the receivable was assigned and notification was received by the debtor before the commencement of such insolvency proceeding, attachment, judicial act or similar act.

DONE at New York, this 12th day of December two thousand one, in a single original, of which the Arabic, Chinese, English, French, Russian and Spanish texts are equally authentic.

IN WITNESS WHEREOF the undersigned plenipotentiaries, being duly authorized by their respective Governments, have signed the present Convention.

Index

Account
  see also **Accounting conventions**
  accounting methods
    maintaining two accounts, 3–53
    payment on collection date,
      3–41—3–45
    payment on maturity date, 3–46—3–52
  client account
    see **Client account**
  current account
    see **Current account**
Accounting conventions
  Accounting Standards Board, 5–18
  financial reporting
    assets, 5–18
    balance sheet entries, 5–17, 5–18
    derecognition, 5–19
    linked presentation, 5–18, 5–19
    separate presentation, 5–18, 5–19
    standards, 5–18—5–19
  non-recourse factoring, 5–17
  recourse factoring, 5–17
    and see **Recourse factoring**
  significant interests
    assets, 5–18
    debts, 5–18
Administration
  see also **Administration procedure**
  administration orders
    administrative receivers, and, 11–39
    application, for, 11–40, 11–48
    company rescue, 11–41
    partnerships, and, 11–71
    purposes, of, 11–41, 11–43
    statutory provisions, 11–38
  administrator
    appointment, of, 11–38, 11–43,
      11–44, 11–46, 11–48, 11–52
    continuation of factoring, 11–52
    distribution, by, 11–47
    proposals, from, 11–46
    status, of, 11–45
  compulsory liquidation, 11–54
    and see **Compulsory liquidation**

Administration—*cont.*
  debts
    existing contracts, under, 11–50
    factor's rights, 11–49, 11–50
    facultative agreement, 11–49
    whole turnover agreements, 11–49,
      11–50
  effects, of, 11–48, 11–49
  factoring agreement, and, 11–52,
    11–53, 11–56, 11–57
    and see **Factoring agreement**
  factor's rights
    combination of accounts, 11–51
    current accounts, 11–51
    debts, 11–49, 11–50
    enforcement rights, 11–51
    factoring agreement, under, 11–51
    partnerships, and, 11–72
    power of attorney, 11–51
    set-off rights, 11–51
    withholding payments, 11–51
  statutory provisions, 1–53
  voluntary liquidation, 11–55
    and see **Voluntary liquidation**
  winding-up
    see **Winding-up**
Administration procedure
  Crown preference, 11–03—11–05
  debenture holders, 11–02
  Enterprise Act (2002), 11–02
  out-of-court, 11–02, 11–07, 11–40,
    11–42, 11–44
  purchase of debts, and, 1–09
  qualifying floating charge, 11–02,
    11–42, 11–44
  top slicing, 11–05
Administrative receivers
  administration orders, and, 11–39
    see also **Administration**
  appointment, 4–50, 11–02,
    11–07—11–10, 11–44, 12–14
  continuation of factoring
    claims settlement, 11–34
    dispute resolution, 11–34

493

499

UNIDROIT (International Institute for the Unification of Private Law)—cont.
Convention
adoption, of, 12–26
application, 12–29
countervailing rights, 12–31
debtor's rights, 12–32
defective performance, 12–32
factoring, under, 12–28
prohibition of assignment, 12–33
ratification, 12–27
scope, 12–34
substantive rules, 12–30
validity of assignments, 12–30
cross-border transactions, 12–24
domestic transactions, 12–24
establishment, of, 12–24
factoring
assignment of debt, 12–28
characteristics, 12–28
definition, 12–28
factoring rules, 12–24
functions, 12–28
notice requirements, 12–28
freedom of contract, 12–24
legal diversity, and, 12–25
purposes, of, 12–24
United Kingdom
credit information, 1–41
credit insurance, 1–24, 1–39
and see **Credit insurance**
discounting trade debts
bills of exchange, and, 1–19, 1–20
discounter's rights, 1–20
lack of security, 1–20, 1–21
liquidators, and, 1–20
procedure, 1–18
factoring
administrative service, 1–39, 1–41
agency factoring, 1–41
bad debts, against, 1–39, 1–41
clearing banks, and, 1–40, 1–41
export factoring, 1–42
floating charges, and, 1–16
invoice discounting, 1–41
misuse, 1–39

United Kingdom—cont.
factoring—cont.
non-recourse factoring, 1–39
undisclosed basis, 1–39, 1–40
and see **Factoring**
origins of factoring
copy invoices, 1–16, 1–18
discounting trade debts, 1–17
European banking, 1–10
invoice discounting, 1–17
mercantile agents, 1–10
provision of finance, 1–39, 1–40
United Nations Commission on International Trade Law (UNCITRAL)
see **UNCITRAL**
United States of America
accounts receivable financing, 1–15, 1–23, 1–26
assignments
future debts, 1–15
registration, 1–15
competition, effect of, 1–26, 1–27
credit information, 1–24, 1–25
factoring
definition, 1–02
lien over goods, 1–12
mercantile agents, 1–11, 2–03
origins, 1–11—1–15
prescriptive rights, 1–12
services provided, 1–13
and see **Factoring**
factoring of debts
assignment, 1–14, 1–15
development, 1–14—1–15, 1–23
origins, 1–13
Uniform Commercial Code, 1–15, 1–23
invoice discounting
disclosed basis, 1–23
undisclosed basis, 1–23
without recourse, 1–24
and see **Invoice discounting**

Value Added Tax (VAT)
agency factoring, 10–54
and see **Agency factoring**
bad debt refunds, 10–55, 10–56
cash accounting scheme, 10–57